STANDARD LOAN
Renew Books on PHONE-it: 01443 654456
Help Desk: 01443 482625
Media Services Reception: 01443 482610
Books are to be returned on or before the last date below

Treforest Learning Resources Centre
University of Glamorgan

Microsoft

MCSE

Exam
70-220

Designing Microsoft® Windows® 2000 Network Security

Training Kit

IT Professional

Learning Resources
Centre

13072994

PUBLISHED BY
Microsoft Press
A Division of Microsoft Corporation
One Microsoft Way
Redmond, Washington 98052-6399

Library of Congress Cataloging-in-Publication Data
MCSE Training Kit—Designing Microsoft Windows 2000 Network Security / Microsoft Corporation.
  p. cm.
 Includes index.
 ISBN 0-7356-1134-3
  1. Computer networks--Security measures. 2. Microsoft Windows NT. I. Microsoft
Corporation.
 TK5105.59 .M485 2001
 005.8--dc21   00-053301

Printed and bound in the United States of America.

5 6 7 8 9 QWT 6 5 4

Distributed in Canada by H.B. Fenn and Company Ltd.

A CIP catalogue record for this book is available from the British Library.

Microsoft Press books are available through booksellers and distributors worldwide. For further information about international editions, contact your local Microsoft Corporation office or contact Microsoft Press International directly at fax (425) 936-7329. Visit our Web site at mspress.microsoft.com. Send comments to *tkinput@microsoft.com*.

For Microsoft Press
Acquisitions Editor: Thomas Pohlmann
Project Editor: Julie Miller

For nSight, Inc.
Project Manager: Susan H. McClung
Copy Editor: Joseph Gustaitis
Desktop Publisher: Joanna Zito
Technical Editor: John M. Panzarella
Indexer: James Minkin

Author: Brian Komar

Part No. X08-00399

Contents

About This Book

Welcome to the *MCSE Training Kit—Designing Microsoft Windows 2000 Network Security*. This kit prepares you to analyze an organization's business and technical requirements and design security for a Windows 2000 network. You will learn how to design security for all aspects of Windows 2000, from authentication strategies to Demilitarized Zones to protecting Internet-accessible resources.

This course supports the Microsoft Certified Systems Engineer program.

Note For more information on becoming a Microsoft Certified Systems Engineer, see the section of this chapter entitled "The Microsoft Certified Professional Program."

Most of the chapters in this book are divided into lessons, activities, labs, and reviews. Lessons include discussions of the key design objectives and then provide evaluations of possible decisions to be made within each design objective, and each lesson ends with a lesson summary. The activities and labs are designed to allow you to practice or demonstrate your understanding of the design objectives discussed within a chapter. Each chapter ends with a set of review questions to test your knowledge of the chapter material. Within each chapter a common scenario will be used to illustrate the design decisions you face when designing Windows 2000 security.

Intended Audience

This book's target reader is the information technology (IT) professional involved in network security design (network architect, senior support professional, or consultant) who has a minimum of one year of experience implementing, administering, and configuring network operating systems, including Novell NetWare, UNIX, or Macintosh networks. The network designer has gained his or her experience in environments that have the following characteristics:

- Supported users range from 100 to more than 25,000.

- Physical locations range from 5 to more than 150.

- Typical network services and applications include file and print, database, messaging, firewalls, dial-in server, desktop management, and Web hosting.

- Connectivity needs include connecting individual offices and users at remote locations to the corporate network and connecting corporate networks to the Internet.

This book was developed for IT professionals who need to design, plan, implement, and support Microsoft Windows 2000 security or who plan to take the related Microsoft Certified Professional Exam 70-220, *Designing Security for a Microsoft Windows 2000 Network*.

Prerequisites

This course requires that students meet the following prerequisites:

- A working knowledge of current networking technology

- A minimum of one year of experience implementing, administering, and configuring network operating systems

- Successful completion of the following core exams for the Microsoft Windows 2000 MCSE track is recommended: Exam 70-210: *Installing, Configuring, and Administering Microsoft Windows 2000 Professional*; Exam 70-215: *Installing, Configuring, and Administering Microsoft Windows 2000 Server*; Exam 70-216: *Implementing and Administering a Microsoft Windows 2000 Network Infrastructure*; Exam 70-217: *Implementing and Administering a Microsoft Windows 2000 Directory Services Infrastructure*; or Exam 70-240: *Microsoft Windows 2000 Accelerated Exam for MCPs Certified on Microsoft Windows NT 4.0.*

Reference Materials

You might find the following reference materials useful:

- Microsoft Corporation. *Microsoft Windows 2000 Server Resource Kit.* Redmond, Wash.: Microsoft Press, 2000.

- Microsoft Corporation. *MCSE Training Kit—Microsoft Windows 2000 Active Directory Services.* Redmond, Wash.: Microsoft Press, 2000.

- Stallings, William. *Cryptography and Network Security.* Upper Saddle River, N.J.: Prentice Hall, 1999.

- Windows 2000 white papers and case studies, available online at *www.microsoft.com/windows2000/library/.*

About the Supplemental Course Materials CD-ROM

The Supplemental Course Materials compact disc contains a variety of informational aids that may be used throughout this book, including Windows 2000 white papers and an online version of this book (including a glossary, which does not appear in the printed book). You can use these files directly from the CD-ROM or copy them onto your hard drive. For more information regarding the contents of this CD-ROM, see the section of this introduction entitled "Getting Started."

The materials on the CD-ROM supplement some of the key concepts covered in the book. You should view these materials when suggested, and then use them as a review tool while you work through the training. An online version of this book is also available on the CD-ROM with a variety of viewing options available. For information about using the online book, see the section of this introduction entitled "About the Online Book."

The other CD-ROM included with this book contains an evaluation edition of Windows 2000 Advanced Server. Although you won't need this software to perform any of the activities and labs in this book, it is helpful to have a system with which to practice, and you may find it useful for evaluating Windows 2000 solutions.

Features of This Book

Each chapter opens with a "Before You Begin" section, which prepares you for completing the chapter. Then the text presents a scenario involving fictitious companies, which is used to illustrate the design decisions you will face when designing Windows 2000 security.

The chapters are then divided into lessons. Most of the chapters contain activities and labs that give you an opportunity to use and explore the design skills presented.

The "Review" section at the end of the chapter allows you to test what you have learned in the chapter's lessons.

The appendix, "Answers," contains all of the answers to the questions asked in each chapter.

Notes

Several types of Notes appear throughout the lessons.

- Notes marked **Tip** contain explanations of possible results or alternative methods.
- Notes marked **Important** contain information that is essential to completing a task.
- Notes marked **Note** contain supplemental information.
- Notes marked **Caution** contain warnings about possible loss of data.

Conventions

The following conventions are used throughout this book:

Notational Conventions

- Characters or commands that you type appear in **bold** type.
- *Italic* in syntax statements indicates placeholders for variable information. *Italic* is also used for book titles.
- Names of files and folders appear in Title Caps, except when you are to type them directly. Unless otherwise indicated, you can use all lowercase letters when you type a file name in a dialog box or at a command prompt.
- File name extensions appear in all lowercase.
- Acronyms appear in all uppercase.
- `Monospace` type represents code samples, examples of screen text, or entries that you might type at a command prompt or in initialization files.

- Icons represent specific sections in the book as follows:

Icon	Represents
	Supplemental course materials. This material includes Windows 2000 white papers and Knowledge Base articles. You will find these files on the book's Supplemental Course Materials CD-ROM.
	An activity or lab. You should perform the activity or lab to give yourself an opportunity to use the design skills being presented in the lesson. You will find the answers to the activity and lab exercise questions in the appendix, "Answers."
	Chapter review questions. These questions at the end of each chapter allow you to test what you have learned in the lessons. You will find the answers to the review questions in the appendix, "Answers."

Fictitious Name Conventions

The content of this training kit requires the use of fictitious company and domain names in fictitious scenarios. This training kit makes every effort to avoid using domain names that represent live Web sites. To accomplish this, each domain name illustrated in the book for fictitious companies uses the nonexistent top-level domain .tld, rather than the standards of .com or .net. In reality, domain names should represent an organization's identity.

Chapter and Appendix Overview

This self-paced training course combines notes, hands-on activities and labs, and review questions to teach you how to design security for a Windows 2000 network. It's designed to be completed from beginning to end, but you can choose a customized track and complete only the sections that interest you. (See the next section, "Finding the Best Starting Point for You," for more information.)

The book is divided into the following chapters:

- The "About This Book" section contains a self-paced training overview and introduces the components of this training. Read this section thoroughly to get the greatest educational value from this self-paced training and to plan which lessons you will complete.

- Chapter 1, "Introduction to Microsoft Windows 2000 Security," introduces the concept of planning security for a Windows 2000 network by looking at Windows 2000 security services design. The chapter also looks at business and technical requirements that affect your security design.

- Chapter 2, "Designing Active Directory for Security," introduces the decisions you face when designing Active Directory directory services. The decisions that you must make include determining the number of forests, domains, and organizational units to deploy based on security requirements.

- Chapter 3, "Designing Authentication for a Microsoft Windows 2000 Network," examines the authentication protocols that are used in a Windows 2000 network. The chapter also discusses issues you face when down-level clients are deployed on the network and how to place Windows 2000 servers to optimize the authentication process.

- Chapter 4, "Planning a Microsoft Windows 2000 Administrative Structure," discusses the membership design of Windows 2000 administrative groups. The chapter also helps you to secure administrative access of the network by using secondary logon or by restricting administration to specific workstations.

- Chapter 5, "Designing Group Security," shows you how to design group membership for security. The chapter discusses methodologies that are used to define group memberships and strategies that are used to secure user rights assignments.

- Chapter 6, "Securing File Resources," discusses the security planning for stored data on the network. You secure data by designing share permissions and NT file system (NTFS) permissions to restrict access to only authorized data. In high security scenarios you may also need to use the Encrypting File System (EFS) to provide encryption of the stored data.

- Chapter 7, "Designing Group Policy," explores the design issues related to Group Policy deployment. The issues include planning for inheritance and troubleshooting Group Policy application problems.

- Chapter 8, "Securing Microsoft Windows 2000–Based Computers," shows how you can use security templates and deploy them to standardize security configuration of Windows 2000–based computers.

- Chapter 9, "Designing Microsoft Windows 2000 Services Security," discusses the security issues that you must address when Domain Name System (DNS), Dynamic Host Configuration Protocol (DHCP), Remote Installation Services (RIS), Simple Network Management Protocol (SNMP), or Terminal Services are deployed on your network. Each service has specific security issues that must be addressed by your security design.

- Chapter 10, "Planning a Public Key Infrastructure," discusses the planning issues an organization faces when it deploys a Public Key Infrastructure. The topics include designing Certification Authority hierarchies and securing the certificate acquisition process.

- Chapter 11, "Securing Data at the Application Layer," explores the security required to secure transmitted data by using application layer protocols.

- Chapter 12, "Securing Data with Internet Protocol Security (IPSec)," explores the security design required to protect transmitted data by using IPSec. The topics include designing IPSec security associations and common IPSec deployment strategies.

- Chapter 13, "Securing Access for Remote Users and Networks," looks at the security required to allow remote users and offices to connect to the corporate network. The security design must ensure that allowing remote access to the network does not compromise network security.

- Chapter 14, "Securing an Extranet," discusses the security issues you face when data is exposed to a public network such as the Internet. The security design must allow access to resources in the publicly accessible Extranet without compromising the private network's security.

- Chapter 15, "Securing Internet Access," discusses the security issues that you face when private network users require access to a public network such as the Internet. The security design must ensure that the users don't compromise the private network's security when they access the Internet.

- Chapter 16, "Securing Access in a Heterogeneous Network Environment," examines the security issues that you need to address when non-Microsoft, or heterogeneous, clients require access to resources in a Windows 2000 network. The design must include provisions for authentication and authorization to ensure that security is maintained.

- Chapter 17, "Designing a Security Plan," concludes the book by looking at the issues you face when designing a security plan for a project. A security plan must reflect an organization's security policy to ensure that the organization's security goals are met.

- The appendix, "Answers," lists the answers to the questions from the book showing the page number where the questions for that section begin and the suggested answers.

- The glossary lists and defines the terms associated with your study of Windows 2000 security. Although it is not in the printed version of the book, the glossary is included in the online book on the Supplemental Course Materials CD-ROM.

Finding the Best Starting Point for You

Because this book is self-paced, you can skip some lessons and revisit them later. Use the following table to find the best starting point for you:

If You	Follow This Learning Path
Are preparing to take the Microsoft Certified Professional exam 70-220, *Designing Security for a Microsoft Windows 2000 Network*	Read the "Getting Started" section. Then work through Chapters 1 through 17 in order.
Want to review information about specific topics from the exam	Use the "Where to Find Specific Skills in This Book" section that follows this table.

Note Exam skills are subject to change without prior notice and at the sole discretion of Microsoft.

Where to Find Specific Skills in This Book

The following table provides a list of the skills measured on certification exam 70-220, *Designing Security for a Microsoft Windows 2000 Network*. The table lists the skill and where in this book you will find the lesson relating to that skill.

Analyzing Business Requirements

Skill Being Measured	Location in Book
Analyze the existing and planned business models.	
▪ Analyze the company model and the geographical scope. Models include regional, national, international, subsidiary, and branch offices.	Chapter 2: Lesson 2
▪ Analyze company processes. Processes include information flow, communication flow, service and product life cycles, and decision-making.	Chapter 1: Lesson 2 Chapter 1: Lesson 3
Analyze the existing and planned organizational structures. Considerations include management model; organization; vendor, partner, and company customer relationships; and acquisition plans.	Chapter 1: Lesson 2
Analyze factors that influence company strategies.	
▪ Identify company priorities.	Chapter 1: Lesson 2
▪ Identify the projected growth and growth strategy.	Chapter 1: Lesson 2
▪ Identify relevant laws and regulations.	Chapter 12: Lesson 1
▪ Identify the company's tolerance for risk.	Chapter 1: Lesson 2
▪ Identify the total cost of operations.	Chapter 1: Lesson 2

Analyze business and security requirements for the end user.	Chapter 1: Lesson 2 Chapter 2: Lesson 2 Chapter 5: Lesson 1 and Lesson 2
Analyze the structure of IT management. Considerations include type of administration, such as centralized or decentralized; funding model; outsourcing; decision-making process; and change-management process.	Chapter 4: Lesson 1
Analyze the current physical model and information security model.	Chapter 2: Lesson 2 and Lesson 3
▪ Analyze internal and external security risks.	Chapter 1: Lesson 2

Analyzing Technical Requirements

Skill Being Measured	**Location in Book**
Evaluate the company's existing and planned technical environment.	
▪ Analyze company size and user and resource distribution.	Chapter 2: Lesson 2 and Lesson 3
▪ Assess the available connectivity between the geographic location of work sites and remote sites.	Chapter 13: Lesson 3
▪ Assess the net available bandwidth.	Chapter 2: Lesson 3
▪ Analyze performance requirements.	Chapter 1: Lesson 3
▪ Analyze the method of accessing data and systems.	Chapter 5: Lesson 1 Chapter 6: Lesson 1
▪ Analyze network roles and responsibilities. Roles include administrative, user, service, resource ownership, and application.	Chapter 2: Lesson 2 and Lesson 3 Chapter 4: Lesson 1 and Lesson 2
Analyze the impact of the security design on the existing and planned technical environment.	
▪ Assess existing systems and applications.	Chapter 1: Lesson 3 Chapter 2: Lesson 3
▪ Identify existing and planned upgrades and rollouts.	Chapter 1: Lesson 2 and Lesson 3 Chapter 8: Lesson 1 and Lesson 3
▪ Analyze technical support structure.	Chapter 4: Lesson 1 and Lesson 2
▪ Analyze existing and planned network and systems management.	Chapter 4: Lesson 1 and Lesson 2 Chapter 9: Lesson 4

Analyzing Security Requirements

Skill Being Measured	Location in Book
Design a security baseline for a Windows 2000 network that includes domain controllers, operations masters, application servers, file and print servers, RAS servers, desktop computers, portable computers, and kiosks.	Chapter 8: Lesson 1
Identify the required level of security for each resource. Resources include printers, files, shares, Internet access, and dial-in access.	Chapter 6: Lesson 1, Lesson 2, and Lesson 3 Chapter 13: Lesson 2 Chapter 15: Lesson 2 and Lesson 3

Designing a Windows 2000 Security Solution

Skill Being Measured	Location in Book
Design an audit policy.	Chapter 2: Lesson 4
Design a delegation of authority strategy.	Chapter 2: Lesson 3 Chapter 4: Lesson 1
Design the placement and inheritance of security policies for sites, domains, and organizational units.	Chapter 7: Lesson 1 and Lesson 2 Chapter 8: Lesson 3
Design an Encrypting File System strategy.	Chapter 6: Lesson 3
Design an authentication strategy.	
■ Select authentication methods. Methods include certificate-based authentication, Kerberos authentication, clear-text passwords, digest authentication, smart cards, NTLM, RADIUS, and SSL.	Chapter 3: Lesson 1, Lesson 2, Lesson 3, and Lesson 4 Chapter 10: Lesson 3 Chapter 13: Lesson 5
■ Design an authentication strategy for integration with other systems.	Chapter 3: Lesson 2 Chapter 10: Lesson 3 Chapter 16: Lesson 2
Design a security group strategy.	Chapter 4: Lesson 1 Chapter 5: Lesson 1
Design a Public Key Infrastructure.	
■ Design Certificate Authority (CA) hierarchies.	Chapter 10: Lesson 1
■ Identify certificate server roles.	Chapter 10: Lesson 1 and Lesson 2
■ Manage certificates.	Chapter 10: Lesson 2
■ Integrate with third-party CAs.	Chapter 10: Lesson 1
■ Map certificates.	Chapter 10: Lesson 3

Design Windows 2000 network services security.

- Design Windows 2000 DNS security.   Chapter 9: Lesson 1
- Design Windows 2000 Remote Installation Services   Chapter 9: Lesson 3
  (RIS) security.
- Design Windows 2000 SNMP security.   Chapter 9: Lesson 4
- Design Windows 2000 Terminal Services security.   Chapter 9: Lesson 5

Designing a Security Solution for Access Between Networks

Skill Being Measured	Location in Book
Provide secure access to public networks from a private network.	Chapter 15: Lesson 1, Lesson 2, Lesson 3, and Lesson 4
Provide external users with secure access to private network resources.	Chapter 14: Lesson 1, Lesson 2, and Lesson 3
Provide secure access between private networks.	
• Provide secure access within a LAN.	Chapter 11: Lesson 1 and Lesson 2 Chapter 12: Lesson 1 and Lesson 2
• Provide secure access within a WAN.	Chapter 12: Lesson 1 and Lesson 2 Chapter 13: Lesson 3
• Provide secure access across a public network.	Chapter 12: Lesson 1 and Lesson 2 Chapter 13: Lesson 3
Design Windows 2000 security for remote access users.	Chapter 13: Lesson 1, Lesson 2, Lesson 4, and Lesson 5

Designing Security for Communication Channels

Skill Being Measured	Location in Book
Design an SMB-signing solution.	Chapter 11: Lesson 1
Design an IPSec solution.	Chapter 12: Lesson 1 and Lesson 2
• Design an IPSec encryption scheme.	Chapter 12: Lesson 1
• Design an IPSec management strategy.	Chapter 12: Lesson 2
• Design negotiation policies.	Chapter 12: Lesson 1
• Design security policies.	Chapter 12: Lesson 1 and Lesson 2

▪ Design IP filters.	Chapter 12: Lesson 1
▪ Define security levels.	Chapter 12: Lesson 1

Getting Started

This self-paced training course contains activities and labs to help you learn how to design Windows 2000 network security. To improve your understanding of Windows 2000 security, it's recommended to deploy security using Windows 2000 Advanced Server; however, the software isn't needed to perform any of the activities or labs in this course.

Hardware Requirements

To successfully run the evaluation edition of Windows 2000 Advanced Server, all hardware should be on the Microsoft Windows 2000 Hardware Compatibility List (HCL). You can download the latest version of the HCL from the Hardware Compatibility List Web page at *www.microsoft.com/hwtest/hcl/*. Each computer must have the following minimum configuration:

- 32-bit 166 MHz Pentium processor
- 64 MB memory for networking with one to five client computers; 128 MB minimum is recommended for most network environments
- 2 GB free hard drive space
- 12X or faster CD-ROM drive
- SVGA monitor capable of 800×600 resolution (1024×768 recommended)
- High-density 3.5-inch disk drive, unless your CD-ROM is bootable and supports starting the setup program from a CD-ROM
- Microsoft Mouse or compatible pointing device

Software Requirements

A copy of the 120-day evaluation edition of Windows 2000 Advanced Server isn't required to do the activities and labs in this course.

Caution The 120-day Evaluation Edition of Windows 2000 Advanced Server provided with this training kit is not the full retail product and is provided only for training purposes. Microsoft Technical Support doesn't support this evaluation edition. For additional support information regarding this book and the CD-ROMs (including answers to commonly asked questions about installation and use), visit the Microsoft Press Technical Support Web site at *mspress.microsoft.com /support*. You can also e-mail TKINPUT@MICROSOFT.COM, or send a letter to Microsoft Press, Attn: Microsoft Press Technical Support, One Microsoft Way, Redmond, WA 98052-6399.

Setup Instructions

The following information is a checklist of the tasks that you need to perform to prepare your computer to install the evaluation software. If you don't have experience installing Windows 2000 or another network operating system, you may need help from an experienced network administrator. As you complete a task, mark it off in the check box. Step-by-step instructions for each task follow.

- Create Windows 2000 Advanced Server setup disks
- Run the Windows 2000 Advanced Server Pre-Copy and Text Mode Setup Routine
- Run the GUI mode and gathering information phase of Windows 2000 Advanced Server Setup
- Complete the Installing Windows Networking Components phase of Windows 2000 Advanced Server Setup
- Complete the hardware installation phase of Windows 2000 Advanced Server Setup

Note The installation information provided will help you prepare a computer to install the evaluation software. It's not intended to teach you installation.

Installing Windows 2000 Advanced Server

You should install Windows 2000 Advanced Server on a computer with no formatted partitions. During installation, you can use the Windows 2000 Advanced Server Setup program to create a partition on your hard drive, on which you install Windows 2000 Advanced Server as a stand-alone server in a workgroup.

▶ **To create Windows 2000 Advanced Server Setup disks**

Complete this procedure on a computer running MS-DOS or any version of Windows with access to the Bootdisk directory on the Windows 2000 Advanced Server installation CD-ROM. If your computer is configured with a bootable CD-ROM drive, you can install Windows 2000 without using the Setup disks. To complete this procedure as outlined, bootable CD-ROM support must be disabled in the basic input/output system (BIOS).

Important This procedure requires four formatted 1.44-MB disks. If you use disks that contain data, the data will be overwritten without warning.

1. Label the four blank, formatted 1.44-MB disks as follows:
   - Windows 2000 Advanced Server Setup Disk #1
   - Windows 2000 Advanced Server Setup Disk #2
   - Windows 2000 Advanced Server Setup Disk #3
   - Windows 2000 Advanced Server Setup Disk #4

2. Insert the Microsoft Windows 2000 Advanced Server CD-ROM into the CD-ROM drive.

3. If the Windows 2000 CD-ROM dialog box appears prompting you to install or upgrade to Windows 2000, click No.

4. Open a command prompt.

5. At the command prompt, change to your CD-ROM drive. For example, if your CD-ROM drive name is E, type **e:** and press Enter.

6. At the command prompt, change to the Bootdisk directory by typing **cd bootdisk** and pressing Enter.

7. If you are creating the setup boot disks from a computer running MS-DOS or a Windows 16-bit operating system, type **makeboot a:** (where A is the name of your floppy disk drive) and press Enter. If you are creating the setup boot disks from a computer running Windows NT or Windows 2000, type **makebt32 a:** (where A is the name of your floppy disk drive), then press Enter. Windows 2000 displays a message indicating that this program creates the four setup disks for installing Windows 2000. It also indicates that four blank, formatted, high-density floppy disks are required.

8. Press any key to continue. Windows 2000 displays a message prompting you to insert the disk that will become the Windows 2000 Setup Boot Disk.

9. Insert the blank formatted disk labeled Windows 2000 Advanced Server Setup Disk #1 into the floppy disk drive and press any key to continue. After Windows 2000 creates the disk image, it displays a message prompting you to insert the disk labeled Windows 2000 Setup Disk #2.

10. Remove Disk #1, insert the blank formatted disk labeled Windows 2000 Advanced Server Setup Disk #2 into the floppy disk drive, and press any key to continue. After Windows 2000 creates the disk image, it displays a message prompting you to insert the disk labeled Windows 2000 Setup Disk #3.

11. Remove Disk #2, insert the blank formatted disk labeled Windows 2000 Advanced Server Setup Disk #3 into the floppy disk drive, and press any key to continue. After Windows 2000 creates the disk image, it displays a message prompting you to insert the disk labeled Windows 2000 Setup Disk #4.

12. Remove Disk #3, insert the blank formatted disk labeled Windows 2000 Advanced Server Setup Disk #4 into the floppy disk drive, and press any key to continue. After Windows 2000 creates the disk image, it displays a message indicating that the imaging process is done.

13. At the command prompt, type **exit** and then press Enter.

14. Remove the disk from the floppy disk drive and the CD-ROM from the CD-ROM drive.

▶ **Running the Windows 2000 Advanced Server pre-copy and text mode setup routine**

It's assumed for this procedure that your computer has no operating system installed, the disk is not partitioned, and bootable CD-ROM support, if available, is disabled.

1. Insert the disk labeled Windows 2000 Advanced Server Setup Disk #1 into the floppy disk drive, insert the Windows 2000 Advanced Server CD-ROM into the CD-ROM drive, and restart your computer.

   After the computer starts, Windows 2000 Setup displays a brief message that your system configuration is being checked, and then the Windows 2000 Setup screen appears. Notice that the gray bar at the bottom of the screen indicates that the computer is being inspected and that the Windows 2000 Executive is loading, which is a minimal version of the Windows 2000 kernel.

2. When prompted, insert Setup Disk #2 into the floppy disk drive and press Enter.

   Notice that Setup indicates that it is loading the hardware abstraction layer (HAL), fonts, local specific data, bus drivers, and other software components to support your computer's motherboard, bus, and other hardware. Setup also loads the Windows 2000 Setup program files.

3. When prompted, insert Setup Disk #3 into the floppy disk drive and press Enter.

   Notice that Setup indicates that it is loading disk drive controller drivers. After the drive controllers load, the setup program initializes drivers appropriate to support access to your disk drives. Setup might pause several times during this process.

4. When prompted, insert Setup Disk #4 into the floppy disk drive and press Enter.

   Setup loads peripheral support drivers, like the floppy disk driver and file systems, and then it initializes the Windows 2000 Executive and loads the rest of the Windows 2000 Setup program. If you're installing the evaluation version of Windows 2000, a Setup notification screen appears, informing you that you are about to install an evaluation version of Windows 2000.

5. Read the Setup Notification message and press Enter to continue.

   Setup displays the Welcome To Setup screen. Notice that, in addition to the initial installation of Windows 2000, you can use Windows 2000 Setup to repair or recover a damaged Windows 2000 installation.

6. Read the Welcome To Setup message and press Enter to begin the installation phase of Windows 2000 Setup. Setup displays the License Agreement screen.

7. Read the license agreement, pressing Page Down to scroll down to the bottom of the screen.

8. Select I Accept The Agreement by pressing F8.

   Setup displays the Windows 2000 Server Setup screen, prompting you to select an area of free space or an existing partition on which to install

Windows 2000. This stage of setup provides a way for you to create and delete partitions on your hard drive.

If your computer does not contain any disk partitions (as required for this exercise), you will notice that the hard drive listed on the screen contains an existing unformatted partition.

9. Make sure that the Unpartitioned space partition is highlighted and then type **c**. Setup displays the Windows 2000 Setup screen, confirming that you've chosen to create a new partition in the unpartitioned space and informing you of the minimum and maximum sizes of the partition you might create.

10. Specify the size of the partition you want to create (at least 2048 MB) and press Enter to continue. Setup displays the Windows 2000 Setup screen, showing the new partition as C: New (Unformatted).

Note   Although you can create additional partitions from the remaining unpartitioned space during setup, it's recommended that you perform additional partitioning tasks after you install Windows 2000. To partition hard drives after installation, use the Disk Management console.

11. Make sure the new partition is highlighted and press Enter. You are prompted to select a file system for the partition.

12. Use the arrow keys to select Format The Partition Using The NTFS File System and press Enter.

The Setup program formats the partition with NTFS. After it formats the partition, Setup examines the hard drive for physical errors that might cause Setup to fail and then copies files to the hard drive. This process takes several minutes.

Eventually, Setup displays the Windows 2000 Advanced Server Setup screen. A red status bar counts down for 15 seconds before Setup restarts the computer.

13. Remove the Setup disk from the floppy disk drive.

Important   If your computer supports booting from the CD-ROM drive and this feature wasn't disabled in the BIOS, the computer could boot from the Windows 2000 Advanced Server installation CD-ROM after Windows 2000 Setup restarts. This will cause Setup to start again from the beginning. If this happens, remove the CD-ROM and then restart the computer.

14. Setup copies additional files and then restarts your machine and loads the Windows 2000 Setup Wizard.

▶ **Running the GUI Mode and Gathering Information phase of Windows 2000 Advanced Server Setup**

This procedure begins the graphical portion of Setup on your computer.

1. On the Welcome To The Windows 2000 Setup Wizard page, click Next to begin gathering information about your computer.

   Setup configures NTFS folder and file permissions for the operating system files, detects the hardware devices in the computer, and then installs and configures device drivers to support the detected hardware. This process takes several minutes.

2. On the Regional Settings page, make sure that the system locale, user locale, and keyboard layout are correct for your language and location, and then click Next.

   Note You can modify regional settings after you install Windows 2000 by using Regional Options in Control Panel.

   Setup displays the Personalize Your Software page, prompting you for your name and organization name. Setup uses your organization name to generate the default computer name. Many applications that you install later will use this information for product registration and document identification.

3. In the Name field, type your name; in the Organization field, type the name of an organization; then click Next.

   Note If the Your Product Key screen appears, enter the product key, which is located on the sticker attached to the Windows 2000 Advanced Server, Evaluation Edition, CD sleeve bound into the back of this book.

   Setup displays the Licensing Modes page, prompting you to select a licensing mode. By default, the Per Server licensing mode is selected. Setup prompts you to enter the number of licenses you've purchased for this server.

4. Select the Per Server Number of concurrent connections button, type **5** for the number of concurrent connections, then click Next.

   Important Per Server Number of concurrent connections and five concurrent connections are suggested values to use to complete your self-study. You should use a legal number of concurrent connections based on the actual licenses that you own. You can also choose to use Per Seat instead of Per Server.

   Setup displays the Computer Name And Administrator Password page. Notice that Setup uses your organization name to generate a suggested name for the computer.

5. In the Computer Name field, type **server1**. Windows 2000 displays the computer name in all capital letters regardless of how it's entered.

Caution   If your computer is on a network, check with the network administrator before assigning a name to your computer.

6. In the Administrator Password field and the Confirm Password field, type **password** (all lowercase) and click Next. Passwords are case-sensitive, so make sure you type **password** in all lowercase letters.

   For the labs in this self-paced training kit, you will use "password" for the Administrator account. In a production environment you should always use a complex password for the Administrator account (one that others cannot easily guess). Microsoft recommends mixing uppercase and lowercase letters, numbers, and symbols (for example, Lp6*g9).

   Setup displays the Windows 2000 Components page, indicating which Windows 2000 system components Setup will install.

7. On the Windows 2000 Components page, click Next.

   You can install additional components after you install Windows 2000 by using Add/Remove Programs in Control Panel. Make sure to install only the components selected by default during setup. Later in your training, you will be installing additional components.

   If a modem is detected in the computer during setup, Setup displays the Modem Dialing Information page.

8. If the Modem Dialing Information page appears, enter the correct area code and click Next. The Date And Time Settings page appears.

Important   Windows 2000 services perform many tasks whose successful completion depends on the computer's time and date settings. Be sure to select the correct time zone for your location to avoid problems in later labs.

9. Enter the correct Date And Time and Time Zone settings, then click Next. The Network Settings page appears and Setup installs networking components.

▶ **Completing the Installing Windows Networking Components phase of Windows 2000 Advanced Server Setup**

Networking is an integral part of Windows 2000 Advanced Server. Many selections and configurations are available. In this procedure you configure basic networking. In a later exercise you will install additional network components.

1. On the Networking Settings page, make sure that Typical Settings is selected, then click Next to begin installing Windows networking components.

   This setting installs networking components that are used to gain access to and share resources on a network and configures Transmission Control Protocol/Internet Protocol (TCP/IP) to automatically obtain an IP address from a DHCP server on the network. Setup displays the Workgroup or Computer Domain page, prompting you to join either a workgroup or a domain.

2. On the Workgroup or Computer Domain page, make sure that the button No, This Computer Is Not On A Network Or This Computer Is On A Network Without A Domain is selected, and that the workgroup name is WORKGROUP, and then click Next.

   Setup displays the Installing Components page, displaying the status as Setup installs and configures the remaining operating system components according to the options you specified. This will take several minutes.

   Setup then displays the Performing Final Tasks page, which shows the status as Setup finishes copying files, making and saving configuration changes, and deleting temporary files. Computers that don't exceed the minimum hardware requirements might take 30 minutes or more to complete this phase of installation. Setup then displays the Completing The Windows 2000 Setup Wizard page.

3. Remove the Windows 2000 Advanced Server CD-ROM from the CD-ROM drive, and then click Finish. Windows 2000 restarts and runs the newly installed version of Windows 2000 Advanced Server.

▶ **Completing the Hardware Installation phase of Windows 2000 Advanced Server Setup**

During this final phase of installation, any Plug and Play hardware not detected in the previous phases of Setup will be detected.

1. At the completion of the startup phase, log on by pressing Ctrl+Alt+Delete.

2. In the Enter Password dialog box, type **administrator** in the User Name field and type **password** in the Password field.

3. Click OK. If Windows 2000 detects hardware that wasn't detected during Setup, the Found New Hardware Wizard screen appears, indicating that Windows 2000 is installing the appropriate drivers.

4. If the Found New Hardware Wizard screen appears, verify that the Restart The Computer When I Click Finish check box is cleared and click Finish to complete the Found New Hardware Wizard.

   Windows 2000 displays the Windows 2000 Configure Your Server dialog box. From this dialog box, you can configure a variety of advanced options and services.

5. Select I Will Configure This Server Later, and then click Next.

6. From the next screen that appears, clear the Show This Screen At Startup check box.

7. Close the Configure Your Server screen.

You have now completed the Windows 2000 Advanced Server installation and are logged on as Administrator.

Note   To properly shut down Windows 2000 Advanced Server, click Start, choose Shut Down, then follow the directions that appear.

Caution   If your computers are part of a larger network, you *must* verify with your network administrator that the computer names, domain name, and other information used in setting up Windows 2000 Advanced Server as described in this section don't conflict with network operations. If they do conflict, ask your network administrator to provide alternative values.

About The Online Book

The CD-ROM also includes an online version of the book that you can view onscreen using Microsoft Internet Explorer 4.01 or later. As mentioned above, the online version of the book contains the glossary.

▶   **To use the online version of this book**

1. Insert the Supplemental Course Materials CD-ROM into your CD-ROM drive.

2. Select Run from the Start menu on your desktop, and type **D:\Ebook\Setup.exe** (where D is the name of your CD-ROM disk drive). This will install an icon to for the online book to your Start menu.

3. Click OK to exit the Installation Wizard.

Note   You must have the Supplemental Course Materials CD-ROM inserted in your CD-ROM drive to run the online book.

Sample Readiness Review Questions

With this Training Kit, Microsoft provides 180 days of unlimited access to 25 practice test questions for the exam 70-220. The exam preparation questions are a subset of practice test questions offered in the *MCSE Readiness Review—Exam 70-220: Designing Microsoft Windows 2000 Network Security* (ISBN 0-7356-1365-6) book developed by Microsoft and MeasureUp, a Microsoft Certified Practice Test Provider.

To use these questions, create a free user account at *mspress.measureup.com/* and register with the key provided on the sticker attached to the Supplemental Course Materials CD-ROM sleeve near the back of this book. If you encounter any problems accessing the questions, please call MeasureUp's customer service at (678) 356-5050.

The Microsoft Certified Professional Program

The Microsoft Certified Professional (MCP) program provides the best method to prove your command of current Microsoft products and technologies. Microsoft, an industry leader in certification, is on the forefront of testing methodology. Our exams and corresponding certifications are developed to validate your mastery of critical competencies as you design and develop, or implement and support, solutions with Microsoft products and technologies. Computer professionals who become Microsoft certified are recognized as experts and are sought after industry-wide.

The Microsoft Certified Professional program offers eight certifications, based on specific areas of technical expertise.

- **Microsoft Certified Professional (MCP).** Demonstrated in-depth knowledge of at least one Microsoft operating system. Candidates may pass additional Microsoft certification exams to further qualify their skills with Microsoft BackOffice products, development tools, or desktop programs.

- **Microsoft Certified Systems Engineer (MCSE).** Qualified to effectively plan, implement, maintain, and support information systems in a wide range of computing environments with Windows NT Server and the BackOffice integrated family of server software.

- **Microsoft Certified Database Administrator (MCDBA).** Individuals who derive physical database designs, develop logical data models, create physical databases, create data services by using Transact-SQL, manage and maintain databases, configure and manage security, monitor and optimize databases, and install and configure Microsoft SQL Server.

- **Microsoft Certified Solution Developer (MCSD).** Qualified to design and develop custom business solutions with Microsoft development tools, technologies, and platforms, including Microsoft Office and BackOffice.

- **Microsoft Certified Trainer (MCT).** Instructionally and technically qualified to deliver Microsoft Official Curriculum through a Microsoft Certified Technical Education Center (CTEC).

Microsoft Certification Benefits

Microsoft certification, one of the most comprehensive certification programs available for assessing and maintaining software-related skills, is a valuable measure of an individual's knowledge and expertise. Microsoft certification is awarded to individuals who have successfully demonstrated their ability to perform specific tasks and implement solutions with Microsoft products. Not only does this provide an objective measure for employers to consider; it also provides guidance for what an individual should know to be proficient. And as with any skills-assessment and benchmarking measure, certification brings a variety of benefits: to the individual, and to employers and organizations.

Microsoft Certification Benefits for Individuals

Microsoft Certified Professionals receive the following benefits (effective January 1, 2001):

- Industry recognition of your knowledge and proficiency with Microsoft products and technologies.

- A Microsoft Developer Network subscription. MCPs receive rebates or discounts on a one-year subscription to the Microsoft Developer Network (*http:// msdn.microsoft.com/subscriptions/*) during the first year of certification. (Fulfillment details will vary, depending on your location; please see your Welcome Kit.) The rebate or discount amount is U.S. $50 for MSDN Library.

- Access to technical and product information direct from Microsoft through a secured area of the MCP Web site (go to *www.microsoft.com/ trainingandservices/default.asp*, then expand the Certification node from the tree directory in the left margin, and then select the "For MCPs Only" option).

- Access to exclusive discounts on products and services from selected companies. Individuals who are currently certified can learn more about exclusive discounts by visiting the MCP secured site (go to *www.microsoft.com/ trainingandservices/default.asp*, then expand the Certification node from the tree directory in the left margin, and then select the "For MCPs Only" option) and selecting "Other Benefits."

- MCP logo, certificate, transcript, wallet card, and lapel pin to identify you as a Microsoft Certified Professional (MCP) to colleagues and clients. Electronic files of logos and transcript may be downloaded from the MCP secured web site (go to *www.microsoft.com/trainingandservices/default.asp*, then expand the Certification node from the tree directory in the left margin, and then select the "For MCPs Only" option) upon certification.

- Invitations to Microsoft conferences, technical training sessions, and special events.

- Free access to *Microsoft Certified Professional Magazine Online,* a career and professional development magazine. Secured content on the *Microsoft Certified Professional Magazine Online* Web site includes the current issue (available only to MCPs), additional online-only content and columns, an MCP-only database, and regular chats with Microsoft and other technical experts.

An additional benefit is received by Microsoft Certified System Engineers (MCSEs):

- A 50 percent rebate or discount off the estimated retail price of a one-year subscription to *TechNet* or *TechNet Plus* during the first year of certification. (Fulfillment details will vary, depending on your location. Please see your Welcome Kit.) In addition, about 95 percent of the CD-ROM content is available free online at the *TechNet* Web site (*www.microsoft.com/technet/*).

Microsoft Certification Benefits for Employers and Organizations

Through certification, computer professionals can maximize the return on investment in Microsoft technology. Research shows that Microsoft certification provides organizations with

- Excellent return on training and certification investments by providing a standard method of determining training needs and measuring results.
- Increased customer satisfaction and decreased support costs through improved service, increased productivity, and greater technical self-sufficiency.
- A reliable benchmark for hiring, promoting, and career planning.
- Recognition and rewards for productive employees by validating their expertise.
- Retraining options for existing employees so they can work effectively with new technologies.
- Assurance of quality when outsourcing computer services.

To learn more about how certification can help your company, see the backgrounders, white papers, and case studies available at *www.microsoft.com/ mcp/mktg/bus_bene.htm*:

- Financial Benefits to Supporters of Microsoft Professional Certification, IDC white paper (1998wpidc.doc 1,608K)
- Prudential Case Study (Prudentl.exe 70K self-extracting file)
- The Microsoft Certified Professional Program Corporate Backgrounder (Mcpback.exe 50K)
- A white paper (Mcsdwp.doc 158K) that evaluates the Microsoft Certified Solution Developer certification
- A white paper (Mcsestud.doc 161K) that evaluates the Microsoft Certified Systems Engineer certification
- Jackson Hole High School Case Study (Jhhs.doc 180K)
- Lyondel Case Study (Lyondel.doc 21K)
- Stellcom Case Study (Stellcom.doc 132K)

Requirements for Becoming a Microsoft Certified Professional

The certification requirements differ for each certification and are specific to the products and job functions addressed by the certification.

To become a Microsoft Certified Professional, you must pass rigorous certification exams that provide a valid and reliable measure of technical proficiency and expertise. These exams are designed to test your expertise and ability to perform a role or task with a product, and are developed with the input of professionals in the industry. Questions in the exams reflect how Microsoft products are used in actual organizations, giving them "real-world" relevance.

Microsoft Certified Product Specialists are required to pass one operating system exam. Candidates may pass additional Microsoft certification exams to further qualify their skills with BackOffice products, development tools, or desktop applications.

Microsoft Certified Systems Engineers are required to pass a series of core Windows operating system and networking exams and BackOffice technology elective exams.

Microsoft Certified Database Administrators are required to pass three core exams and one elective exam that provide a valid and reliable measure of technical proficiency and expertise.

Microsoft Certified Solution Developers are required to pass two core Windows operating system technology exams and two BackOffice technology elective exams.

Microsoft Certified Trainers are required to meet instructional and technical requirements specific to each Microsoft Official Curriculum course they are certified to deliver. In the United States and Canada, call Microsoft at (800) 636-7544 for more information on becoming a Microsoft Certified Trainer or visit *www.microsoft.com/train_cert/mct/*. Outside the United States and Canada, contact your local Microsoft subsidiary.

Technical Training for Computer Professionals

Technical training is available in a variety of ways, with instructor-led classes, online instruction, or self-paced training available at thousands of locations worldwide.

Self-Paced Training

For motivated learners who are ready for the challenge, self-paced instruction is the most flexible, cost-effective way to increase your knowledge and skills.

A full line of self-paced print and computer-based training materials is available direct from the source—Microsoft Press. Microsoft Official Curriculum courseware kits from Microsoft Press designed for advanced computer system professionals are available from Microsoft Press and the Microsoft Developer Division. Self-paced training kits from Microsoft Press feature print-based instructional materials, along with CD-ROM–based product software, multimedia presentations, lab exercises, and practice files. The Mastering Series provides in-depth, interactive training on CD-ROM for experienced developers. They're both great ways to prepare for Microsoft Certified Professional (MCP) exams.

Online Training

For a more flexible alternative to instructor-led classes, turn to online instruction. It's as near as the Internet and it's ready whenever you are. Learn at your own pace and on your own schedule in a virtual classroom, often with easy access to an online instructor. Without ever leaving your desk, you can gain the expertise you need. Online instruction covers a variety of Microsoft products and technologies. It includes options ranging from Microsoft Official Curriculum to choices available nowhere else. It's training on demand, with access to learning resources 24 hours a day. Online training is available through Microsoft Certified Technical Education Centers.

Microsoft Certified Technical Education Centers

Microsoft Certified Technical Education Centers (CTECs) are the best source for instructor-led training that can help you prepare to become a Microsoft Certified Professional. The Microsoft CTEC program is a worldwide network of qualified technical training organizations that provide authorized delivery of Microsoft Official Curriculum courses by Microsoft Certified Trainers to computer professionals.

For a listing of CTEC locations in the United States and Canada, visit *www.microsoft.com/CTEC/default.htm.*

Technical Support

Every effort has been made to ensure the accuracy of this book and the contents of the companion disc. If you have comments, questions, or ideas regarding this book or the companion disc, please send them to Microsoft Press using either of the following methods:

E-mail

TKINPUT@MICROSOFT.COM

Postal Mail

Microsoft Press
Attn: *MCSE Training Kit—Designing Microsoft Windows 2000
    Network Security* Editor
One Microsoft Way
Redmond, WA 98052-6399

Microsoft Press provides corrections for books through the World Wide Web at the following address:

mspress.microsoft.com/support/

Please note that product support isn't offered through the above mail addresses. For further information regarding Microsoft software support options, please connect to *www.microsoft.com/support/* or call Microsoft Support Network Sales at (800) 936-3500.

Evaluation Edition Software Support

The Evaluation Edition of Microsoft Windows 2000 Advanced Server included with this book is unsupported by both Microsoft and Microsoft Press, and shouldn't be used on a primary work computer. For online support information relating to the full version of Microsoft Windows 2000 Advanced Server that might also apply to the Evaluation Edition, you can connect to

support.microsoft.com/

For information about ordering the full version of any Microsoft software, please call Microsoft Sales at (800) 426-9400 or visit *www.microsoft.com/.* Information about any issues relating to the use of this evaluation edition with this training kit is posted to the Support section of the Microsoft Press Web site (*mspress.microsoft.com/support/*).

CHAPTER 1

Introduction to Microsoft Windows 2000 Security

About This Chapter

This chapter will introduce you to planning security for a Microsoft Windows 2000 network. It will look first at the security services design within the Windows 2000 architecture and then examine business and technical requirements that will affect your security design.

Before You Begin

To complete this chapter, you must read the chapter scenario. This scenario is used throughout the chapter to apply the design decisions discussed in each lesson.

Chapter Scenario: Lucerne Publishing

Lucerne Publishing is an organization that's considering migrating to Windows 2000 for their networking services. The firm has hired you to see to it that all the planning for the Windows 2000 network ensures that the proposed network design will achieve the desired network security.

Current Network

The Lucerne Publishing network is spread worldwide, with major offices in Tokyo, Denver, Caracas, Casablanca, Moscow, and Brisbane. The head office is in Tokyo and the offices are linked with dedicated Wide Area Network (WAN) links, as shown in Figure 1.1.

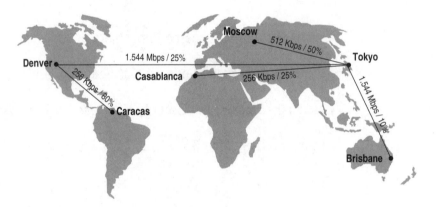

Figure 1.1   The Lucerne Publishing network

As shown in Figure 1.1, the offices are connected with WAN links that range from 256 kilobits per second (Kbps) to 1.544 megabits per second (Mbps). The only link that currently has high utilization is the one between Denver and Caracas, which has an 80 percent utilization rate.

Sales force personnel who have visited the Caracas office on sales trips have commented that logon performance is very sluggish when they connect there.

Account Management

Lucerne Publishing's Information Technology (IT) department is in Tokyo. The Tokyo IT department creates all user accounts for all offices. Every other office has its own IT department that's in charge of managing servers. To assist with common problems, an international help desk has been created. All help desk personnel must be able to reset passwords on existing accounts and view all account properties to determine if there's any misconfiguration of the accounts. If there are any issues with an account's configuration, the help desk personnel send a request to the IT department to have the account modified.

Expansion Plans

Lucerne Publishing wants to expand into uncharted territories. This includes an initiative to sell books in Cuba, which will require the establishment of a branch office in Havana to ensure that the ordering system can be accessed.

In addition to expanding into Cuba, Lucerne Publishing sees a need to create distribution offices throughout Europe and North America, their primary markets. Lucerne Publishing has found that the maximum time between a customer placing an order and the books being delivered is now two weeks—up from an average of one week just two years ago. Management attributes the increased delays to increased production and orders.

Online Ordering

To increase sales, Lucerne Publishing has established a Web site that was initially set up by an Internet Service Provider (ISP) with a Microsoft Access database storing all order information. The Web site's clients are allowed to establish an account that they can use for ordering books.

Lucerne Publishing wants to start managing the Web site itself instead of continuing to outsource the management duties to the ISP. Although the current Web administrator has never managed an e-commerce site, the Web administrator believes that three weeks of training will be enough to acquire the necessary skills.

Security Issues

The Web site was recently hacked, and the attack resulted in customer information being compromised. The attacker obtained phone, e-mail, and credit card information from the Access database. Lucerne Publishing wants the new network's design to lessen the chance of such a hacker attack.

Lesson 1: Microsoft Windows 2000 Security Services Overview

This lesson will look at how security is integrated into the Windows 2000 architecture. Knowing how security integrates into the Windows 2000 architecture will assist you in designing security for your Windows 2000 network.

After this lesson, you will be able to

- Discuss how security services are integrated into the Windows 2000 architecture

Estimated lesson time: 45 minutes

The Windows 2000 operating system provides two processor access modes to ensure that applications are unable to directly access hardware and system code. Applications generally run in what is known as *user mode* and operating system functions run in *kernel mode.*

The separation of the Windows 2000 architecture into user mode and kernel mode ensures that a runaway user process is unable to corrupt lower-level system drivers that are located in kernel mode. All access to kernel mode is protected. When a user application needs to make a request to system services located in kernel mode, the request must be made through an application programming interface (API). The API will then forward any necessary requests to the required services in kernel mode.

Security in Windows 2000 is split between user mode and kernel mode. In user mode the security subsystem is the actual subsystem where Active Directory directory service runs. In kernel mode the security reference monitor enforces the security rules of the security subsystem. The actual enforcement of security takes place in kernel mode, where user intervention can't occur (see Figure 1.2).

The integration of Active Directory within the security subsystem ensures that distributed security can exist in a Windows 2000 network. Because Active Directory is located in the security subsystem, you can protect all access by a combination of three elements:

- Authentication
- The security principal proving identity and authorization
- The validation that the security principal has the necessary permissions to perform the task

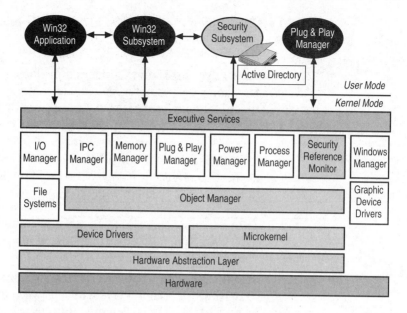

Figure 1.2   Security within the Windows 2000 architecture

The security subsystem performs the authorization by passing the request to the security reference monitor in kernel mode in order to compare the request to the *discretionary access control list* (DACL) of the object that's being connected to. The DACL contains *access control entries* (ACEs) that define the permissions assigned to security principals for the object. Each ACE defines a security principal and the permissions that are assigned to that security principal for the object.

Security Subsystem Components

The security subsystem runs within the security context of the local security authority (LSA) process. This process is split between user mode and kernel mode. The components within the local security authority process include:

- **Netlogon service (Netlogon.dll).** The Netlogon service maintains a computer's secure channel to a domain controller in its domain. The Netlogon service passes credentials to the domain controller through a secure channel and returns an access token populated with security identifiers and user rights for the security principal.

Note   In mixed mode, the Netlogon service is responsible for the replication of Active Directory data to any Windows NT backup domain controllers that exist in the domain. (Unless otherwise noted, "Windows NT" refers to versions 3.51 and 4.0.)

- **NTLM authentication protocol (Msv1_0.dll).** NTLM is used to authenticate clients that are unable to use Kerberos authentication. This includes Windows 95, Windows 98, and Windows NT computers.

- **Secure Sockets Layer (SSL) authentication protocol (Schannel.dll).** SSL provides encryption services to transported data at the application layer. All data that's passed through the encrypted channel is protected against inspection on the network. To use SSL, the application must be coded to recognize and implement SSL.

- **Kerberos v5 authentication protocol (Kerberos.dll).** Kerberos v5 is the default authentication protocol used by Windows 2000. Kerberos authentication is based on the use of ticket-granting tickets (TGTs) and service tickets.

Note You'll find a more detailed discussion of the Kerberos v5 protocol in Chapter 3, "Designing Authentication for a Microsoft Windows 2000 Network."

- **Kerberos Key Distribution Center (KDC) service (Kdcsvc.dll).** The KDC service is responsible for issuing TGTs to clients when they initially authenticate with the network. A TGT is then used for subsequent requests to acquire service tickets to provide authentication of the requesting client.

- **LSA server service (Lsasrv.dll).** The LSA server service enforces all defined security policies within Active Directory.

- **Security Accounts Manager (SAM) (Samsrv.dll).** The SAM is used on non-domain controllers for the storage of local security accounts. The SAM also enforces all locally stored policies.

- **Directory Service module (ntdsa.dll).** The Directory Service module supports replication between Windows 2000 domain controllers, all Lightweight Directory Access Protocol (LDAP) access to Active Directory and management of naming contexts stored in Active Directory. The naming contexts include the domain naming context, the configuration naming context, and the schema naming context.

- **Multiple Authentication Provider (Secur32.dll).** This Security Support Provider (SSP) supports all security packages available on the system. The security packages include the Kerberos, Windows NT LAN Manager (NTLM), Secure channel, and Distributed Password Authentication (DPA) packages.

LSA Functionality

The LSA maintains all local security information for a Windows 2000–based computer. The LSA provides the following functionality:

- It allows users to authenticate interactively with the Windows 2000–based computer.

- It generates an access token for the security principal during the authentication process. The access token contains the security identifiers (SIDs) for the user account and all groups that contain the user account as a member.

Note If the user account or group account was previously a member of a different domain, the sIDHistory attribute is also included in the user's access token. This allows the user to access any resources that contain the previous SID in the object's DACL.

- It manages local security policy. This includes all security policies that have been defined for the local computer. These settings may be overridden if any Group Policies are defined at the site, domain, or organizational unit (OU) level in Active Directory.

- It manages audit policy and settings. This includes writing the alert to the correct event log when an audit alert is generated by the security reference monitor in kernel mode.

- It builds a list of trusted domains that are provided to populate the Log On To drop-down list in the Windows 2000 authentication dialog box.

- It determines which users have been assigned privileges.

- It reads the system access control lists (SACL) for each object to determine what security auditing has been defined for the object.

- It determines what user rights have been assigned to a security principal and ensures that a security principal can't perform tasks they don't have the necessary rights for.

- It manages memory quotes for the usage of both paged and nonpaged memory usage.

Windows 2000 Security Protocols

Windows 2000 allows multiple network security protocols to provide authentication services. This ensures the maximum compatibility for network clients. These clients can include Microsoft clients from previous operating systems as well as foreign clients, such as UNIX clients. Supporting multiple security protocols ensures maximum secure access to a Windows 2000 network. You aren't forced to use a specific security protocol.

Windows 2000 supports four different security protocols, as shown in Figure 1.3.

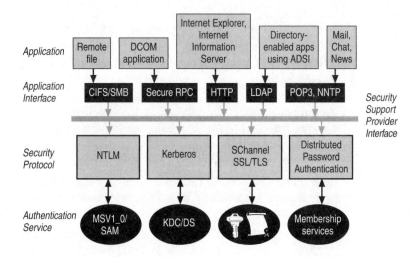

Figure 1.3   Windows 2000 supports multiple security protocols

- **Windows NT LAN Manager (NTLM).** Used by Windows NT, Windows 95, and Windows 98 clients with the Directory Services client installed. NTLM is used for pass-through network authentication, local account authentication for Windows 2000 Professional and Windows 2000 member servers, and access to previous Microsoft operating systems. The NTLM security provider uses the MSV1_0 authentication service and the Netlogon service to provide client authentication and authorization.

- **Kerberos v5.** The default security protocol for Windows 2000–based computers. Kerberos provides mutual authentication of client and server, better performance, and support for delegation. The Kerberos security provider uses the Key Distribution Center (KDC) service on a domain controller and Active Directory for obtaining TGTs and service tickets.

- **Distributed Password Authentication (DPA).** A shared secret authentication protocol used by Internet membership organizations such as MSN. DPA is part of Microsoft Commercial Internet System (MCIS) services and allows you to use a single account and password to connect to all Internet sites that are a member of the same Internet membership organization. DPA uses the MCIS security services (known as the membership service) for membership authentication and server-specific access information.

- **Secure channel (SChannel) services.** Provide the ability to authenticate using public key–based protocols such as SSL and Transport Layer Security (TLS). If you use a public key infrastructure (PKI), these protocols can provide authentication of both client and servers in a distributed network. Within Windows 2000, you can deploy a public key infrastructure using Certificate Services to establish Certification Authorities (CAs). These CAs are responsible for issuing digital certificates that will be used for authentication.

The Security Support Provider Interface (SSPI)

The Security Support Provider Interface (SSPI) prevents applications from determining what Windows 2000 security protocols are used to authenticate the security principal. The SSPI communicates with a Win32 API based on the Generic Security Service Application Program Interface (GSSAPI) and provides similar interface abstraction for security context management.

Note   The GSSAPI is defined in Request for Comment (RFC) 1508, "Generic Security Services Application Program Interface." All definitions of standard Transmission Control Protocol/Internet Protocol (TCP/IP)–based protocols and services are defined in RFCs. You can find RFCs by going to *www.rfc-editor.org/rfc.html* and searching for the RFC number.

When the security protocol has been concealed, applications don't have to be coded to specifically support each of the network security protocols. The application only needs to call SSPI routines directly or use connection management protocols provided by Remote Procedure Calls (RPCs) or Distributed Component Object Model (DCOM) processes to authenticate.

Lesson Summary

This lesson examined the Windows 2000 security services model. It provided an overview of the Windows 2000 security subsystem components, the functionality of the LSA, Windows 2000 security protocols, and the SSPI.

You don't have to understand how security is implemented in Windows 2000 in order to design security. But it's useful to know how the security functions interact with the Windows 2000 operating system. Knowing the Windows 2000 security services helps you design Windows 2000 security solutions.

Lesson 2: Determining Security Business Requirements

Your security design must take into account all of your organization's business requirements, because these will serve as the criteria that your security design must meet. When designing security for your network, you must ensure that you gather and understand all business requirements.

After this lesson, you will be able to

- Determine how to design security for your organization to meet business objectives

Estimated lesson time: 45 minutes

Determining Business Requirements

Your network's security design will be based on meeting your organization's business requirements, which will range from identifying company priorities to recognizing your organization's risk level.

You must analyze the following business factors when you design your organization's Windows 2000 security:

- **The business model.** The security that's deployed in an organization can be greatly affected by the business model implemented for the organization. An organization with branches around the world may have different business requirements for security than a company with a single office at a single location. You have to know how decisions are made within the company. A centralized decision process will generally lead to a centralized security plan.

- **The business processes.** Security must not hamper day-to-day business within an organization. You need to know how business processes flow. If many people work on a project, you have to know exactly what part they play in the project and what actions they take in the business process. This knowledge will assist you in defining permissions for resources and with group strategies in Active Directory. If the business process has managers, you have to know what rights they require for management. This information will help you define the way you delegate administration structure.

- **The projected growth.** You must develop a security plan that can change and grow with the organization. You don't want to deploy a security plan with a short life span. Be aware of the relationships that the organization has with partners and whether there are any mergers or acquisitions planned in the foreseeable future. The security plan that you deploy must be extensible to handle growth over the next few years.

- **The management strategy.** Does the organization use a centralized or decentralized management strategy? This isn't always an easy question to answer. In many cases the management strategy will be a mix of centralized and decentralized administrative practices. For example, an IT department may centrally manage the creation of all user and group accounts. This is accomplished by restricting this practice to a central team of account administrators. Yet the same organization may delegate administration of servers to each branch office in order to allow local administration where the servers exist on the network. Always ask who manages a resource.

- **The current security policy.** Many organizations will have a predefined security policy. A security policy defines the organization's aversion to risk. This means that the organization clearly states what it considers the minimum acceptable levels of security within their organization. Each facet of the network that you secure may have its own security policy. For example, because certain Internet protocols may have potential security weaknesses, the organization may restrict them from being used on the corporate network.

- **The tolerance of risk.** Organizations can differ on what they consider risky. Some organizations might consider passwords with fewer than 10 characters a security risk, while other organizations may consider 6 characters to be sufficient. Determining an organization's risk tolerance will help you design a security solution that reduces the organization's perceived risks.

Note Remember that risk is best defined by the costs faced if the risk occurs multiplied by the probability that the risk will actually take place. In other words, Risk = Cost × Probability. Converting risk into a numeric formula will help you prioritize risks as you develop a security solution.

- **The laws and regulations that affect the organization.** An organization must abide by the laws and regulations of the jurisdictions where it performs business. Some countries require network management to take place within that country. This rule affects your security design because it requires decentralized management of security within that country. Know the laws and regulations that may affect your security design. For example, if you wish to use strong encryption in your security solution (for example, using 3DES encryption with IPSec), you should be aware that it is forbidden to export strong encryption to countries on the U.S. embargo list. Not only are you affected by U.S. export rules, you are also affected by the import laws of all the countries you do business in. If the country doesn't allow the importing of strong encryption, you need to configure alternate encryption strength for transmissions within that country.

Note For more information on export rules, go to *www.microsoft.com* and search for "Exporting Microsoft Products."

- **The organization's financial status.** Because a security solution is going to have a dollar value associated with it, you must always determine its projected cost. In the event that the best solution to a problem is financially impossible, you must develop alternate solutions that meet business requirements.

- **The employees' skills.** A security solution might involve several new technologies that an organization's employees don't have expertise in. You must identify these shortfalls and determine whether the staff must learn these technologies or whether the organization should use outsourcing to bring in expert consultants. Either method will cost money.

Making the Decision

You can use Table 1.1 to identify business factors that will affect an organization's security strategies and the actions that you need to include in your security planning in order to address those business factors.

Table 1.1   Identifying the Ways Business Factors Affect Security Design

If the Organization	Include the Following in Your Security Plan
Uses a centralized administration model	■ Management of administrative group membership ■ Minimize the number of domains
Uses a decentralized administration model	■ Determine which users will require administrative abilities on the network ■ Determine exactly what rights and permissions the users will require ■ Determine whether the administration can be limited to specific classes of objects or to specific attributes of an object ■ Determine if delegation of administration will meet the organization's needs
Implements business processes	■ Identify the flow of all information involved in the business process ■ Determine which users require access to the services involved in the business process ■ Determine the level of access that each participant will require
Projects growth in the near future	■ Determine the future number of users and computers that will be a part of the network ■ Determine the geographic spread of the organization ■ Include the expected growth of your company in the security plan so that the plan doesn't need to be modified
Shows an aversion to risk	■ Determine exactly what the organization considers to be risky ■ Ensure that the security plan mitigates the risks and includes actions to take if the risks occur
Performs business in many countries	■ Determine if any of the participating country's laws will affect security implementation decisions ■ Identify all import and export laws that could affect your security design
Is constrained by costs	■ Ensure that the security plan fits within the organization's budget ■ Report all forecasted costs early in the design process so that if costs are too high, the design can be modified early
Does not have the required skill sets	■ Determine which skill sets are lacking in the organization ■ Determine whether it is more effective to bring in third-party skills or implement staff training

Applying the Decision

Lucerne Publishing must meet the following business requirements in its Windows 2000 security design:

- **Centralized administration of user accounts.** Lucerne Publishing uses a centralized management style for user accounts. The user accounts are all created and modified at the head office in Tokyo. To meet this business requirement, the number of domains in the forest must be minimized and membership in the Domain Admins, Enterprise Admins, Administrators, and Account Operators groups must be carefully monitored to ensure that only approved IT staff are members.

- **Decentralized administration of servers.** Lucerne Publishing uses a decentralized management methodology for its servers. At each office the local servers are managed by the local IT staff. The nearness of the IT support staff allows for quicker recovery times in the event of a server failure. Lucerne Publishing should ensure that IT support staff are members of the Server Operators group in the domains where the servers are located.

- **Decentralized administration of user passwords.** The help desk staff must have the ability to reset all user passwords. If you use delegation of administration, you can delegate the right to reset passwords to a local group that contains all help desk user accounts. This will ensure that the help desk personnel can perform necessary tasks but not grant excess privileges.

- **Match the business process.** Granting help desk operators only the ability to reset passwords ensures that the help desk personnel must contact the Tokyo IT department for any other necessary changes to user accounts.

- **Plans for growth.** Windows 2000 Active Directory can support much larger domains than Windows NT 4.0 could. The expansion plans for Lucerne Publishing will affect the physical design of the network because additional sites must be defined for each of the distribution centers. The only planned expansion that could affect the Active Directory design is the plan to expand into Cuba. Due to current embargoes on Cuba, there may be a requirement for a separate domain to be established for the Havana office.

- **Issues concerning the Havana office.** Cuba is currently on the list of U.S. embargoed countries, which will affect the security design for Lucerne Publishing because strong encryption products can't be exported to Cuba. This will also affect the design of the online ordering application because 128-bit encryption wouldn't be allowed for access from Cuba.

- **Meets current risk aversion.** Because Lucerne Publishing's Web site was recently hacked, the security design for the Web site must take into account how it happened. The design must address the weaknesses exposed during the previous attack to ensure that the same methods can't be used again.

- **Skill set shortages.** The current Web administrator doesn't have the required skill set needed to set up the online ordering Web site. Just sending the Web administrator for three weeks of training won't be sufficient. This is especially true since there is a business requirement to reduce the risk of the ordering Web site being hacked. Consultants must be brought in to design the ordering Web site. Alternatively, the actual creation of the Web site and all necessary security mechanisms could be outsourced.

Lesson Summary

A security plan must meet all of an organization's business requirements. These business requirements will serve as criteria for your security design. When you begin to design your security plan, make sure that you collect all the business requirements so that your plan will meet them. Doing this will also prevent changes to the security plan during the deployment stage.

Lesson 3: Designing Security to Meet Technical Requirements

Not only must a security plan meet *business* requirements, but it also must meet any *technical* requirements that an organization defines.

After this lesson, you will be able to

■ Identify technical requirements that will affect your security design

Estimated lesson time: 30 minutes

Determining Technical Requirements

Technical requirements serve as constraints in your security plan. When you develop your security plan, you must make sure that your solution meets all the technical requirements.

Technical requirements that can affect your security plan include

■ **Total size and distribution of resources.** The size and distribution of users and computers will determine how security must be defined for an organization. The distribution will help you to define Active Directory sites, domains, and OUs based on your organization's security requirements.

■ **Performance considerations.** Implementing encryption technologies in a network will result in performance costs. Before defining a security plan, an organization must define what is acceptable performance for common tasks that will be performed on the network. For example, an organization might define that for a database application, queries that return fewer than 100 records in the solution set must be returned within 2 seconds of the query being submitted. The security design must ensure that any security solutions to protect the database application, such as using Internet Protocol Security (IPSec) to protect the submitted query and the returned dataset, still fall within acceptable performance requirements.

■ **Wide Area Network links.** Your security plan must evaluate how remote offices are connected to the corporate office. You must determine whether dedicated network links exist or whether to use virtual networking by using tunneling protocols such as Point to Point Tunneling Protocol (PPTP) or Layer 2 Tunneling Protocol (L2TP) with IPSec. Your security plan must determine what level of encryption is required for WAN links. It also must determine whether the tunneling protocol (if selected) is supported by any third-party products in use, such as a Cisco router.

- **Wide Area Network usage.** Your network security design may include branch offices or remote offices that are connected to the corporate head office with WAN links. If links exist, your network security plan must consider their current utilization. Don't fall into the trap of simply identifying the speed of the WAN links. For example, you may have a 512 Kbps fractional-T1 link to a branch office and a 128 K ISDN link to another office. At first glance, you might assume that there is more available bandwidth to the first branch office. Only after analyzing current usage can you verify this assumption.

- **How data is accessed.** Your network security plan must identify how data is accessed on the network. This must include which protocols, applications, users, and computers are used to access the data. By identifying these components of data access, you can define your security plan to overcome any existing security weaknesses and ensure that security is maintained as data is accessed.

- **Administrative structure.** Identifying who runs the network and where administration takes place will help you design a Windows 2000 network that meets your needs. Determining the administrative structure will lead you to the best Active Directory structure for an organization and administrative group memberships. The administrative structure will also help you design your delegation of administration strategy for managing objects in Active Directory and network resources.

- **Current application base.** Windows 2000 introduces a stronger base security for computers. This stronger base security isn't always compatible with older versions of applications. If you identify any applications that may not work in a Windows 2000 network, your security plan can include any necessary upgrades or updates that must be applied to the applications before the migration can take place. The security plan must contain all required testing and proposed solutions for the migration to a Windows 2000–compatible version of the application.

Making the Decision

To plan for technical requirements, first you have to gather the technical requirements that affect your organization. Once you define these requirements, you'll have the performance guidelines that you need to meet. Remember that the implementation of security within a network does have a cost. Most often this cost is a loss of productivity or performance. The organization must always determine what is an acceptable cost before implementing the security design.

When planning for technical requirements, you should consider the points laid out in Table 1.2.

Table 1.2   Applying Technical Requirements to Your Security Design

If the Organization	Determine the Following for Your Security Plan
Is spread across many physical sites	■ Whether logon performance requirements will be the same for central and branch offices. ■ Determine all physical sites for defining your Active Directory sites. ■ Determine placement of network services to meet performance requirements.
Has performance requirements	■ Develop physically measurable numbers for performance. For example, a logon attempt must take place within a 5-second window. ■ Test performance using a network that emulates the production environment. This must include all additional services that are running in the production network. Time trials performed in a network that don't mirror the production network aren't useful.
Has existing WAN links	■ Determine what applications currently use the WAN links. ■ Identify each application's current bandwidth usage. ■ Determine if the introduction of Active Directory replication and WAN usage can be handled using the currently available bandwidth.
Has a current administrative structure in place	■ Design Active Directory to mirror the current administrative structure. If the organization uses centralized management, restrict access to the Domain Admins group. If it's decentralized, design an OU structure that supports delegation of administration.
Has a current application base	■ Test all applications to determine compatibility of the applications in a Windows 2000 environment. Identify whether the applications are supported, require an update, or will prevent an upgrade to Windows 2000.

Applying the Decision

Lucerne Publishing's security design must meet the following technical requirements:

■ **Logon performance.** The Caracas site is connected to the corporate network by a 256K WAN link that's currently 80 percent utilized. Remote sales force personnel are complaining about authentication speed when they connect over the WAN. Logon performance gains can only be increased by locating DNS services, a domain controller, and a global catalog server at the Caracas site to prevent transmission of data to the Denver office. This will increase the amount of replication traffic on the link. The WAN link must be monitored to determine if additional bandwidth ultimately will be required.

- **Site definitions.** To ensure that only local network services satisfy network requests, Lucerne Publishing must define Active Directory sites that map to their physical network topology. They must define a site for each physical location of the network and map the subnet address for that location to the site name. This will ensure that clients can find a local network service instead of sending requests across the WAN. Table 1.3 shows one potential site configuration.

Table 1.3   Proposed Site Configuration for Lucerne Publishing

Site Name	Location	Subnet IP Address
Tokyo	Tokyo, Japan	172.16.0.0/22
Denver	Denver, Colorado	172.16.4.0/22
Moscow	Moscow, Russia	172.16.8.0/22
Brisbane	Brisbane, Australia	172.16.12.0/22
Casablanca	Casablanca, Morocco	172.16.16.0/22
Caracas	Caracas, Venezuela	172.16.20.0/22

- **Server placement.** To ensure that authentication takes place locally, each site should have at least one DNS server, one domain controller for each domain that users and computers will require for authentication, and one global catalog server. For redundancy, it would be wise to include two of each category in the event of failure.

- **Other performance requirements.** The planned expansion of Lucerne Publishing to include multiple distribution centers in Europe and North America will require the establishment of additional WAN links and site definitions. These distribution centers will require that local domain controllers and global catalog servers also be established to ensure local authentication.

- **Current administrative structure.** The Active Directory design for Lucerne Publishing must ensure that it reflects the current administrative structures. The Active Directory design that you select must allow for centralized user account management and decentralized server management. Lucerne Publishing must manage membership of the Domain Admins, Enterprise Admins, Administrators, and Account Operators groups to ensure centralized management of all user accounts. Likewise, membership in the Server Operators groups will allow decentralized management of servers.

Lesson Summary

As with business requirements, you need to determine all technical requirements that will affect the design of your security plan. Technical requirements will give you measurable criteria that your security plan must meet.

When you gather technical requirements, make sure that each one is measurable so that you can test the security plan to ensure that it meets those requirements. Also make sure that testing takes place in a lab environment that emulates the production network. The lab environment must match current network usage so that the result that you get will reflect actual performance results when they're deployed in the production network.

Review

Answering the following questions will reinforce key information presented in this chapter. If you are unable to answer a question, review the appropriate lesson and then try the question again. Answers to the questions can be found in the appendix.

1. Windows 2000 Security Services provides support for multiple security protocols. How does this help with the deployment of security in a heterogeneous network?

2. A UNIX client is installed on your organization's network. What security protocols can you use to authenticate the UNIX client when the UNIX client authenticates with Active Directory?

3. A company implements its administrative model using a decentralized account management strategy. How will this decentralized strategy affect your Active Directory design?

4. An organization has offices around the world. In what way could this affect the security design of the Windows 2000 network?

5. You've been hired to create a security plan for a large corporation. When you determine technical requirements for the security plan, what guidelines do you need to follow?

6. You've gathered the technical requirements for your security design and have created a lab environment to test the security design. How should you configure the lab environment to ensure that the technical requirements are met?

CHAPTER 2

Designing Active Directory for Security

About This Chapter

This chapter prepares you to design your Active Directory directory service structure. It includes an overview of the decisions that you face when designing the Active Directory, and it also looks at the factors involved in determining the number of forests, domains, and organizational units to deploy in your network environment. The chapter concludes with a discussion of auditing in a Microsoft Windows 2000 network.

Active Directory provides the foundation for your organization's security. You must design an Active Directory structure that will meet your administrative needs and support your organization's business directives. If you make the wrong choices as you design your Active Directory, you might end up having to redeploy all existing systems and reconfigure all security mechanisms.

The choices that you face in your Active Directory design include

- Determining the number of forests required for an organization
- Determining the number of domains required within a forest
- Determining the organizational unit (OU) structure required within a domain
- Designing an audit strategy to ensure that security is maintained within your organization

Before You Begin

To complete this chapter, you must read the chapter scenario. This scenario is used throughout the chapter to apply the design decisions discussed in each lesson.

Chapter Scenario: Wide World Importers

This chapter will examine the decisions you have to make for an imaginary company called Wide World Importers. Wide World Importers is a North American corporation with distribution centers and service centers across the continent.

The Existing Network

Distribution centers are located in Washington, D.C., Vancouver, Toronto, Portland, Dallas, and Mexico City. Regional offices are located at each distribution center and each center has roughly 500 users. At the corporate head office in Washington, 2000 user accounts need to be created.

There are many service centers across Canada, the United States, and Mexico. At each one, there are 10 or fewer computers that must be connected back to the nearest distribution center for ordering purposes. The service centers don't have local Information Technology (IT) staff.

All the distribution centers are linked to the corporate head office with T3 connections. Each service center is connected to the nearest distribution center using Fractional T1 lines with 256 K of available bandwidth.

User Account Management

The IT department of Wide World Importers wants to maintain control of the creation of user accounts from the head office in Washington. But it will allow local administrators at each distribution center to manage existing user accounts.

Due to the nature of its work, the Engineering department wants to implement more rigorous password requirements than the rest of the company. While the rest of the organization wants six characters as the minimum password length, the Engineering department requires eight characters. The head of the Engineering IT department, Kim Abercrombie, will manage the Engineering accounts.

Application Support

Wide World Importers has standardized on the Microsoft suite of applications for both the desktop and the server platform. With the rollout of Windows 2000, Wide World Importers wants to deploy Microsoft Exchange 2000 Server for e-mail and Microsoft Office 2000 as the corporate desktop standard application suite.

Wide World Importers uses the Office 2000 suite of applications. Office 2000 must be available to all users in the organization so that all employees can use the applications. In addition, the accounting department employees need to have the custom accounting software available. The custom accounting software implements Microsoft Installer (MSI) packages for the deployment of software.

Client Desktops

All client desktops at the distribution centers need to be upgraded so that Windows 2000 Professional can become the corporate desktop standard. The plan is to eventually upgrade the client desktops at the service centers to Windows 2000 in the next two calendar years, but at first several service centers will use Windows 95, Windows 98, or Windows NT 4.0 Workstation in addition to Windows 2000 Professional.

Security Templates

To ensure that all desktop and server software is configured with the required security settings, Wide World Importers wants to deploy standardized security settings using Windows 2000 Group Policy. All workstations will be configured with the Basic Workstation template (Basicwk.inf). Servers (non-domain controllers) will be configured with the Basicsv.inf, and domain controllers (DCs) will be configured with the Basicdc.inf template.

Windows 2000 Security Goals

Wide World Importers is planning to migrate to Windows 2000 and wants to ensure that security is maintained throughout its entire network. The company wants to maintain the simplest Active Directory design that will meet its business requirements.

Lesson 1: Designing Your Forest Structure

One of the most important decisions that you need to make when designing Active Directory for your organization is whether to implement a single forest or multiple forests. This decision has a major effect on how the administration of your Active Directory is performed and whether you have to duplicate any effort to ensure that consistent security is deployed across the enterprise network.

After this lesson, you will be able to

- Determine the number of forests required for your organization based on security and business requirements

Estimated lesson time: 30 minutes

Active Directory Design Basics

Anyone who designs an Active Directory for an organization needs to know common terms used in Active Directory design. These common terms and concepts include

- **Forest.** A forest is a collection of domains that share a common schema, configuration, and global catalog. All domains in a forest are connected using transitive trust relationships.

- **Domain Tree.** A domain tree is a collection of domains that share a contiguous name space. For example, Figure 2.1 shows a forest with three domain trees.

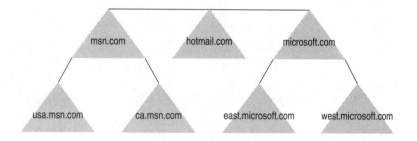

Figure 2.1   A forest with three domain trees

The microsoft.com tree includes the microsoft.com, east.microsoft.com, and west.microsoft.com domains. Each of the three domains contains microsoft.com as part of the domain name. The msn.com tree includes the msn.com domain, the usa.msn.com domain, and the ca.msn.com domain. Finally, there's the hotmail.com domain.

- **Domain.** A domain represents a unit of replication within Active Directory. You can break up your forest for replication and account policy purposes by creating multiple domains within a forest.

- **Organizational Unit (OU).** An OU is a container that's used to organize security principals for the purpose of deploying Group Policy and delegating administrative authority. OUs can exist within domains or other OUs.

Note   An OU that exists within another OU is commonly referred to as a child OU. The OU that contains the child OU is referred to as a parent OU.

- **Sites.** Sites are used within Active Directory to represent the physical network that exists for an organization. A site is defined as a section of the network with high network speeds. For example, if you had an office with two locations, one in Seattle and the other in San Francisco, you should define two sites based on the geographical location. Sites are used within Active Directory to find network services that are in the same network location as the client attempting to connect to the network service.

Deploying a Single Forest

The most common configuration for deploying an Active Directory in an organization is a single forest. The main reason to deploy a single forest is that it will share common information across each of its component domains. The information that is shared includes

- **Schema.** A schema defines all classes and attributes that can be used within the forest. The write-enabled copy of the schema is maintained on the schema operations master. By default, the first DC installed on the forest is designated as the schema operations master.

- **Configuration.** The configuration naming context maintains a listing of all domains and sites within a forest, thus ensuring that no duplicate names are created.

- **Global catalog.** The global catalog maintains a partial set of attributes for all objects that exist within a forest.

The domains within a forest are joined together by Kerberos v5 transitive trust relationships. These differ from Windows NT 4.0 trust relationships in that if a domain trusts another domain, it also trusts all other domains trusted by that domain. For example, in Figure 2.2 a user in the asia.microsoft.com domain can access resources in the namerica.microsoft.com domain, even though an explicit trust relationship isn't defined between the two domains. Due to the transitive nature of Kerberos v5 trusts, the transitive trust relationships between namerica.microsoft.com and microsoft.com and between asia.microsoft.com and microsoft.com provide access as required.

It's always recommended to begin your Active Directory design with the intention of deploying a single forest. You should change your Active Directory design to include multiple forests only if your business circumstances require them.

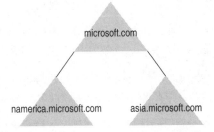

Figure 2.2   Default transitive trust relationships

Note   The only exception to this is when you are testing schema modification changes. Because any change made to the schema is permanent and can't be deleted in Windows 2000, you should maintain a DC in a separate forest to test all schema modifications before deploying them in a production environment.

Making the Decision

Consider implementing a single forest for your enterprise if your organization meets the following criteria:

- The same software is used across the organization. If the software is Active Directory–aware, the installation of the software might make changes to the schema. If the same software is used across the organization, the chance of objection to a schema modification is lessened.

- You want to minimize forest-wide configuration. Maintaining a single forest reduces the number of administration tasks that globally affect a forest. For example, if an Active Directory–integrated application such as Exchange Server is deployed for an organization, the schema modifications have to be applied only once for the entire organization, not once for each forest.

- You want to manage forest-wide administrative groups with minimal complications. Several enterprise administrative groups, including the Enterprise Admins and Schema Admins groups, are located in the forest root domain. If multiple forests are maintained, multiple sets of these groups also must be maintained to ensure forest security.

- You want to be able to carry out single, enterprise-wide searches. You can query the global catalog server to perform a forest-wide search for an object only within a single forest. If there are multiple forests, you have to implement additional software or multiple searches to do an enterprise search in a single command.

- You want to reduce management of trust relationships. Within a forest all domains are connected using transitive trust relationships. This allows a security principal in any domain in the forest to access any resource in the forest, subject to the security defined for the resource. You don't have to manually define trust relationships between domains in a single-forest deployment.

Note Sometimes you might want to define shortcut or cross-link trust relationships within a forest. These shortcut trusts will speed authentication when a resource is accessed in a domain other than where the security principal accessing the account resides.

Applying the Decision

The description of Wide World Importers hasn't included any business case that would require the deployment of multiple forests. Even though Wide World Importers has distribution and service centers spread across national boundaries, this isn't a sound business reason for creating separate forests.

With a standardized set of applications and the need to centrally manage user account creation from the head office, these circumstances lead you to decide on a single forest for the Wide World Importers network.

Deploying Multiple Forests

There are limited scenarios in which you have to implement multiple forests. These scenarios generally involve decentralized organizations that perform much of their network operations within each individual sector. Another common scenario is an Internet Service Provider (ISP) that doesn't want to have a common directory for all their clients. It's preferable in this case to create separate forests for each client to prevent clients from browsing the directory of another client of the ISP.

You face some additional difficulties when you deploy multiple forests, so don't make this decision hastily. These disadvantages range from actual monetary costs to a loss of functionality or flexibility in your network design. Possible problems include:

- **A more complicated and expensive domain structure.** Every forest must have at least one domain. Within each domain there must be at least one domain controller. To ensure redundancy in the case of server failure, at least two DCs will be needed. Creating additional forests can lead to additional hardware costs for domain DCs.

- **Additional management costs for forest-wide components such as the schema and configuration naming contexts.** Even if the two forests have identical schemas, the work effort is doubled if additional attributes or classes are added to the schema. The schema modifications must now be performed in two separate processes (one for each forest). In addition, group memberships in groups such as schema administrators and enterprise administrators must be managed in two separate forests.

- **Additional management costs for trust relationships.** If you deploy multiple forests, you have to establish explicit one-way trust relationships between domains in the forests where resources must be accessed. Users from one forest can't access resources in another forest without these relationships. In addition, you can't create trust relationships between forests, only between domains. If the users in one forest are spread among multiple domains, individual explicit trust relationships must be established between each domain and the domain in the other forest (see Figure 2.3).

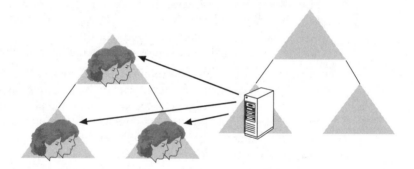

Figure 2.3   Establishing trust relationships between multiple forests

- **Limited use of universal principal names.** User principal names are normally resolved by querying the global catalog to determine the account that's associated with the user principal name. If multiple forests exist, only default user principal names can be used if users are going to authenticate by using user principal names. If the default user principal name is used, the user has to log on using the user principal name of *account@DNSDomainName*. For example, if the user account neilsmith existed in the north.nwtraders.tld domain, users would have to authenticate using the default user principal name neilsmith@north.nwtraders.tld. Even if alternative user principal name suffixes were defined for the account, like neilsmith@microsoft.com, these wouldn't be accessible, because the global catalogs aren't shared between forests.

- **Limiting smart cards to using default user principal names.** If a cross-forest logon process must take place, the user principal name associated with a smart card must be based on the default user principal name, not on an alternative user principal name. Again, this is because forests don't share a global catalog service.

In conclusion, the decision to implement multiple forests most affects the users within your network. Only in a single-forest environment does the global catalog contain a partial replica of all objects in the organization. Deploying multiple forests can result in loss of functionality for the users within an organization.

Making the Decision

That said, there are several cases where an organization might want to deploy multiple forests. When the following situations exist within your organization, you can consider implementing multiple forests instead of a single forest:

- **Short-lived joint ventures.** In cases were organizations are paired together for short-term projects, it's often unnecessary to merge the two organizations into a single forest. Other than work performed on the joint project, the organizations will remain autonomous during and after the joint venture.

- **Mergers between two companies running separate Active Directories.** Initially, you can achieve coexistence by maintaining separate Active Directory forests. If the merger is to be permanent, the next task is to merge the two forests into a single forest using directory migration tools such as the Active Directory Migration Tool (ADMT) from Microsoft. These tools allow you to migrate security principals between forests and to reapply security to resources once the resources are merged into a single forest.

- **Disagreement on change policies.** A forest shares a common schema and configuration. Any modifications to the schema or configuration affect all domains in the forest. If the participants in a forest can't agree on a business process for schema change or on membership of enterprise-level groups such as the Enterprise Admins or Schema Admins groups, the organization should consider separate forests.

- **Differing schema requirements.** A forest shares a single schema. If two divisions within a forest can't agree to schema modifications required by Active Directory–aware applications, you need separate forests. You can't limit schema modifications to a single domain within a forest.

Caution   Any modifications to the schema are permanent. You can never remove any classes or attributes that are added to the schema. They can only be marked as defunct.

- **Distrust among administrators.** Within a forest the Enterprise Admins group is assigned privileges that allow the group to manage all domains within a forest. Some departments within an organization don't trust other departments' administrators to have administrative rights within their domain. You can prevent this by changing the default group memberships to remove the Enterprise Admins group from the Administrators group in each domain.

- **Scope of transitive trust relationships.** In many Windows NT 4.0 deployments trust relationships were established to allow a master domain's users to access resources in a resource domain. The trust relationships were established in a single direction to prevent users in the resource domain from accessing resources in the master domain. Within a forest, users in a domain can access resources in all other domains in the forest due to the transitive trust relationships that exist between domains in a forest. If you want to restrict the ability to grant access to resources using trust relationships, you must establish separate forests.

Note   Trust relationships must be established between domains in the two forests. You can't simply establish a trust relationship between forests.

- **Limited replication of the global catalog.** All objects in the forest will have a partial set of attributes replicated to the global catalog. If several objects are added to a domain or deleted from it, this affects all domains in terms of replication of the global catalog. In addition, if you configure additional attributes to be replicated to the global catalog, this will result in the entire global catalog being replicated to all global catalog servers in the forest.

- **If user accounts need to be prevented from appearing in the global catalog.** In highly secure environments it may be necessary to prevent users from knowing the existence of specific user accounts in the organization. For example, within a government office, there may be "undercover agents." These agents aren't known to be government employees. Therefore, you wouldn't want their user information to appear in the global catalog. If you put these user objects in a separate forest, you can prevent their user accounts from appearing in the global catalog. Another scenario would be the case of an ISP that wants to prevent accounts from one client from being viewed by another company's clients.

Applying the Decision

Because you have decided to deploy a single forest for Wide World Importers, this section examines scenarios that would make Wide World Importers consider deploying additional forests due to altered circumstances.

If Wide World Importers merged with another company through either a takeover or acquisition, the other organization might already have a Windows 2000 Active Directory. For the initial merger period, you can maintain separate forests to allow connectivity between the two forests.

The existence of separate forests requires more management for the corporate network. Explicit trust relationships must be defined between domains where resource access must take place. In addition, if the long-term goal is to merge the two organizations into a single forest, you have to analyze details such as the schema modifications that might have occurred to ensure a smooth transition to a single forest.

Lesson Summary

You must consider the decision to implement more than one forest in an organization carefully. Most often the advantages of a single forest far outweigh the factors that would lead you to implement multiple forests on anything other than a temporary basis.

Lesson 2: Designing Your Domain Structure

Once you've decided to create either a single forest or multiple forests for an organization, the next step is to determine how many domains the organization needs. As with forests, the goal is to start with a simple model, such as a single domain, and then determine if you need multiple domains.

After this lesson, you will be able to

- Design a domain structure for your organization based on security and business requirements

Estimated lesson time: 45 minutes

Deploying a Single Domain

A single-domain forest is commonly implemented in organizations that maintain centralized control of user and computer accounts. By maintaining only a single domain, membership in the Administrators group is easily monitored to ensure that no users are granted excess privileges on the network.

Making the Decision

When simplicity within the forest is the goal, a single domain is the best decision for an Active Directory design. Choosing to implement a single domain will have the following effects on your Active Directory:

- It reduces management of the forest. When only a single domain exists in the forest, the domain's administrators are ultimately the forest's administrators as well. This arrangement ensures that there is no differentiation between the enterprise administrators and the domain administrators. Instead of creating domains to perform administrative tasks, designers commonly use OUs to delegate administrative tasks to specific individuals in the domain.

- It reduces the number of required DCs. Every domain that you create requires separate DCs. By deploying a single domain, you reduce the total number of DCs. If your forest has multiple sites, you only have to place DCs from a single domain at each site for authentication purposes. You don't have to place DCs from multiple domains at a single site.

- It reduces the dependency on global catalog servers for authentication. When authenticating in a native mode domain, the authenticating DC connects to a global catalog server to determine universal group membership for the authenticating security principal. This isn't required in a single-domain environment because the authenticating DC knows about all objects in the forest.

Note The authenticating DC knows that only a single domain exists in the forest by querying the CN=configuration, DC=*forestrootdomain* naming context (where *forestrootdomain* is a variable representing the name of the domain in question) to determine which domains exist in the forest.

- It provides an easier migration path to multiple domains. If you deploy a single domain, it's easy to migrate the forest to a multiple-domain environment. It's harder to reduce the number of domains in an existing forest because this requires the migration of user accounts between domains in the forest to "empty" the domain that's to be removed from the forest.

Applying the Decision

Wide World Importers can start initially with a single domain for its organization, but as we will see, its business objectives require the implementation of multiple domains. Because it's easy to migrate from a single domain to multiple domains, there aren't additional costs involved with initially deploying a single domain for the Wide World Importers network.

Deploying Multiple Domains

In Windows 2000, there are several technical reasons that will influence your Active Directory design to implement multiple domains. One of the key reasons to implement multiple domains is a requirement for differing account policies. Account policies can only be applied at a domain level. There's no way to implement varying account policies within a single domain. If varying account policies are defined, this requires that multiple domains exist within the forest.

Understanding Account Policies

Account policies include the following three categories of configuration:

- **Password Policy.** Defines the characteristics of passwords that may be used to authenticate to the domain.
- **Account Lockout Policy.** Defines which actions must be taken when a specified amount of failed logon attempts occur in a short period of time.
- **Kerberos Policy.** Defines maximum ticket lifetimes for Kerberos authentication and tolerances for clock synchronization between client computers and servers.

Tip When implementing account policy, be sure to set it at the domain level so that the domain settings are configured. Account policy configured at the OU level only affects the local account databases of any computers in that OU. It won't affect any users authenticating with the domain when using that computer.

The account policies you set must be carefully balanced. You don't want to make the settings too restrictive because this can lead to increased help desk calls from users whose accounts have been locked out. Likewise, you don't want to have too few restrictions that result in users implementing blank passwords.

In addition, specifying restrictive password policy can actually reduce the security of the network. For example, if you require passwords to be longer than seven characters, most users have difficulty remembering them. They might write their passwords down and leave them where an intruder can easily find them.

Password Policy

Password policy defines the characteristics of allowed passwords for user accounts in a domain. As with all account policies, if different areas within an organization can't agree on a common password policy, multiple domains must be defined or consensus must be reached on a standard set of password policies. The following settings can be defined for password policy:

- **Enforce Password History.** Allows you to configure how many previous passwords are maintained to prevent users from reusing the same password when they're required to change their password. The policy can have a value between 0 and 24 passwords being remembered.

- **Maximum Password Age.** Defines how frequently a password must be changed. When the age defined in this policy is reached, users are required to change their existing password to a new password. The value of this policy can be set from zero (defined as password will not expire) to 999 days.

- **Minimum Password Age.** Defines how long a newly changed password must exist before the user can change it. By setting this value, you can prevent users from getting around the Enforce Password History policy by repeatedly performing "quick switches" of their password.

- **Minimum Password Length.** Defines the minimum character length for a user's password. If the user enters a password that's less than the minimum length, the password will be rejected.

- **Passwords Must Meet Complexity Requirements.** Controls the format of passwords entered by the user. Passwords must meet three of the following four requirements:

  - UPPER CASE
  - lower case
  - 1234567890 (numeric)
  - !@#$%^&*() (symbols)

In addition, passwords can't contain the user's account name.

Note   The requirement of complex passwords helps protect against dictionary attacks against the passwords stored in Active Directory. A dictionary attack encrypts all the words found in a dictionary file provided by an attacker. The encryption is performed using the same algorithm used to encrypt passwords within Active Directory. A hacker may determine the password by comparing the data found in Active Directory with the encrypted results from the dictionary file.

■ **Store Password Using Reversible Encryption For All Users In The Domain.** Stores the password in a reversible encryption format for all users. The password is saved in this format only after the user has changed the password for the first time after this policy is set. Reversible encryption is used by the Internet Information Server when configured to use digest authentication and by dial-in users using Challenge Handshake Authentication Protocol (CHAP).

Account Lockout Policy

Account lockout policy defines how Active Directory deals with an account when a preconfigured threshold for incorrect logon attempts is surpassed. The following list outlines the policies that can be defined:

■ **Account Lockout Duration.** Defines the time that an account is locked out once the account lockout threshold is exceeded. The policy can be defined to be a value between 0 and 99,999 minutes. If defined to be 0, this indicates that the account is locked out until an administrator manually resets it.

■ **Account Lockout Threshold.** Defines how many incorrect logon attempts are allowed before an account is locked out. This policy can be set to a value between 0 and 999 logon attempts.

■ **Reset Account Lockout Counter After.** Defines how frequently the account lockout counter is reset to zero. For example, if this policy is defined as 30 minutes, the account lockout counter will be reset to a value of zero after a period of 30 minutes has passed since the last failed logon attempt.

You must define the account lockout policy to fit the help desk service implemented at your organization. If you have a help desk that's always available (24 hours a day, seven days a week), then specify to lock out an account until an administrator manually resets it. You must also be careful to reset the account lockout counter after a short period of time to ensure that unsuccessful logon attempts over a long period of time don't result in an account being locked out.

Kerberos Policy

The Kerberos policy defines settings for the Kerberos v5 authentication protocol. These settings apply to all computers and users in the domain where the policy is defined. The Kerberos policy settings available in account policy include

- **Enforce User Logon Restrictions.** Specifies that Kerberos will verify that the account hasn't been locked out each time that a Kerberos service ticket is requested. This prevents a locked out account from acquiring any additional service tickets after an administrator locks out the account.

- **Maximum Lifetime For Service Ticket.** Defines how long a service ticket can be stored in the service ticket cache. Once the maximum lifetime is reached, the service must discard the service ticket and acquire a new service ticket or renew the existing service ticket.

- **Maximum Lifetime For User Ticket.** Defines the maximum lifetime for a Kerberos ticket issued to a user account. Once the maximum lifetime is reached, the ticket is discarded from the user's Kerberos ticket cache.

- **Maximum Lifetime For User Ticket Renewal.** Defines the maximum amount of time during which a ticket may be renewed. Once this period expires, a new ticket must be acquired from the Key Distribution Center (KDC).

- **Maximum Tolerance For Computer Clock Synchronization.** Defines how much a client computer's clock can be out of sync with a server's computer clock. The Kerberos protocol uses a time stamp to prevent replay attacks of a Kerberos authentication stream. If the clocks are out of sync by a period greater than this policy setting, the authentication attempt will fail.

Kerberos settings must be the same for an entire domain. If you require different Kerberos settings, you have identified the need for multiple domains. When you configure Kerberos settings, the main settings you should consider modifying (in regards to security) are the enforce user logon restrictions and maximum tolerance for computer clock synchronization settings. These settings will ensure that a disabled account will be immediately prevented from accessing further resources on the network. The clock synchronization setting will ensure that replay attacks are prevented on the network.

Making the Decision

You must decide to implement multiple domains if any of the following scenarios exist in your organization:

- **Differing account policies.** If departments can't agree on account policy settings such as minimum password length, account lockout duration, or Kerberos ticket lifetime settings, you need to create multiple domains. All account policy settings are applied at the domain level. Any requirements for differing account policy settings will require the establishment of separate domains.

Note   You can define account policy at the OU level in Group Policy. This won't affect domain account policies, but it will affect local account database policies. This means that you can specify different account policy settings for users who authenticate using the local security account management database of their computer instead of those that are set for domain authentication.

- **Replication issues.** For offices that have smaller branch offices connected by slow wide area network (WAN) links, the traffic associated with replication can lead to saturation of the WAN link. By configuring a separate domain at the branch office, you limit replication to the schema, configuration, and global catalog.

Note   The separate domain can be implemented as a child domain of the current domain or as a domain in a separate tree within the forest.

- **International considerations.** Some countries require management of the network to take place within the country where the network is located. If these restrictions are in place, you must establish a separate domain at the remote site to ensure that all network management occurs within the country where the network exists.

- **Political reasons.** In many organizations, departments don't cooperate and may wish to maintain their autonomy by managing separate domains within a forest. Although this isn't a business reason for creating separate domains, it's a common scenario that needs to be addressed. In some scenarios a business case can be built to use OUs and delegation of administration instead of creating separate domains.

- **The need to put enterprise administration accounts into a separate domain.** Within a forest, enterprise-level administration groups exist in the forest root domain. These accounts include the Schema Admins and Enterprise Admins groups. By creating an empty forest root domain, you will restrict who can manage these accounts.

Warning   All members of the Domain Admins group in the forest root have the ability to change membership in the Enterprise Admins and Schema Admins groups. Membership in all three groups should be carefully monitored to ensure that group memberships aren't changed without authorization.

Applying the Decision

In its initial requirements, Wide World Importers said it needed separate account policies to be defined for the Engineering department. Because account policies are defined at the domain level, you need multiple domains for the Wide World Importers network architecture.

Based on account policies, the Wide World Importers network requires at least two domains: one to contain all members of the Engineering department and the other to contain the remaining users.

Having offices in both the United States and Canada doesn't necessarily require a company to have separate domains for each one. Likewise, the WAN links between the offices are sufficient for replication of a single domain, subject to the current utilization of the WAN links.

Wide World Importers could deploy either a two-domain forest or a three-domain forest, depending on its security needs for restricting membership in the Enterprise Admins, Schema Admins, and forest root Domain Admins groups. Figure 2.4 shows the proposed domain tree layouts depending on whether or not Wide World Importers implements an empty forest root.

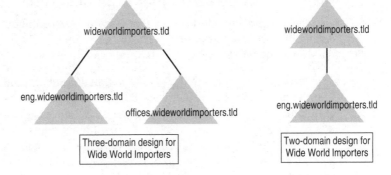

Figure 2.4   The potential domain models for Wide World Importers

Lesson Summary

Design the number of domains needed within an Active Directory forest by analyzing the organization's business requirements. Base your determination of whether you need multiple domains on the circumstances that make multiple domains necessary.

Be aware that differing account policies—password policy, account lockout policy, or Kerberos policy—will require the deployment of multiple domains in your organization's forest.

Lesson 3: Designing an OU Structure

Within every domain in your forest you must create an OU structure. This OU structure must provide the framework for delegating administration to portions of your Active Directory. It also must provide the necessary structure to allow Group Policy deployment.

After this lesson, you will be able to

- Design an OU structure that meets both delegation of administration and group policy deployment needs for your organization

Estimated lesson time: 45 minutes

Planning for Delegation of Administration

One of the more common Active Directory designs is based on the capability of delegating administration to specific organizational units, to specific objects within an OU, or to specific attributes of an object.

The ability to delegate administration is a major enhancement to Windows 2000. In previous versions of Windows NT, you had to delegate administration by creating a resource domain, selecting those users you wished to delegate administrative responsibilities to, and making them administrators of the resource domain. This often led to the assigning of excessive user rights to these resource domain administrators and the creation of excess resource domains to allow for delegated administration.

Delegating Control to an Organizational Unit

In Windows 2000, you can delegate administration to a specific OU by using the Delegation of Control Wizard.

The Delegation of Control Wizard allows you to delegate management of Active Directory objects to a user or security group that isn't explicitly a member of the Administrators local group. You access the Delegation of Control Wizard by right-clicking a container in Active Directory Users And Computers and selecting Delegate Control, as shown in Figure 2.5.

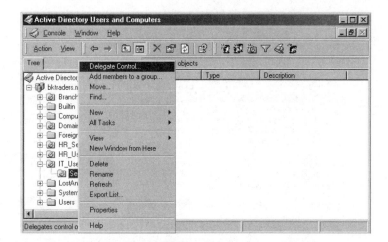

Figure 2.5   Accessing the Delegation of Control Wizard

The Delegation of Control Wizard allows you to set the following default options:

- **Users Or Groups.** You can select which users or groups will be delegated administrative control over the container you're delegating control to.

- **Tasks To Delegate.** You can select from a list of common tasks that include management of user accounts, resetting passwords, reading user information, managing groups, modifying membership of groups, and managing Group Policy links. Or you can select to create custom tasks for delegation.

- **Custom Tasks.** If you select custom tasks for delegation, you can choose to delegate full control of all objects in the folder or specifically reference the object classes that the user or security group can manage.

- **Custom Permissions.** If custom tasks are selected, you can then define the permissions that will be delegated to the user or security group selected.

As an alternative, you can manually delegate permissions from the Advanced option on any Active Directory container's Security tab.

Tip   The Security tab is available only when Advanced Features are enabled in Active Directory Users And Computers.

In the Permission Entry dialog box, shown in Figure 2.6, you can then configure custom permissions for the container. You can apply the custom permissions to the container and to all child objects, to just the container, or only to specific objects that exist in the container.

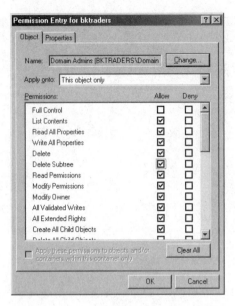

Figure 2.6   Assigning custom permissions for delegation of control

Making the Decision

When it actually comes time to create your delegation of administration design, you must ensure that only the minimum rights are delegated to the selected security principals.

You can test your design by delegating the desired permissions to an empty security group. You can then create a new user account that's only a member of the newly created security group. When logged on as the newly created user, be sure to attempt not only the tasks that you want the delegated administrator to perform, but also tasks that you don't want the delegated administrator to perform. This ensures that only the correct permissions are delegated.

To ensure that only approved management functions take place, it's recommended that you configure the audit policy to audit success and failures for account management. Because the OUs are stored on DCs, you should configure these audit settings on the Default Domain Controllers policy (assuming that all DCs remain in the OU). The audit policy is applied to the computers located within the OU where the Group Policy object is applied.

Note   For more information on configuring auditing, see "Lesson 4: Designing an Audit Strategy," later in this chapter.

Delegation of administration requires you to give careful thought to which rights to delegate to specific users or groups. With Windows 2000 you don't have to assign rights based on all encompassing groups, such as Account Operators or Server Operators. Your delegation of administration design must include

■ **Which users should have administration privileges delegated to them.** Be sure to select only the users that require delegated user rights for delegation. The best strategy is to create a separate security group and delegate the permissions directly to that group rather than to assign the permissions directly to a user. That way, if the role of a user changes, you have to change only the membership of the security group, not the delegated permissions on the OU.

■ **Where to delegate administration in the OU hierarchy.** It's often best to delegate control higher in the OU hierarchy. This reduces the number of places in which delegation must take place. For example, if the security group Marketing Admins requires the ability to manage users in the Marketing OU, the USA OU, and the Canada OU, as shown in Figure 2.7, it's more efficient to delegate administration of user accounts to the Marketing Admins group at the Marketing OU, rather than individually at each of the three OUs.

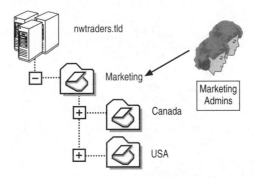

Figure 2.7   Delegate administrative control higher in the OU hierarchy

■ **Which types of objects should be delegated for administration.** Delegated administration is often only required for a specific class of objects. Rather than delegating full control of all classes of objects, limit delegation to the classes of objects that the delegated user will manage. For example, if the delegation is simply to manage the membership of group accounts, don't delegate administrative privileges for user accounts to that user or group.

■ **The minimum set of rights that are required.** Although the Delegation of Control Wizard allows delegation to administration based on an entire object, the best solution often is to provide administration rights to only a subset of attributes for an object. For example, the Helpdesk security group may require only the ability to reset a user's password. By delegating only the ability to reset the password for user accounts to the Helpdesk group, you ensure that excess privileges aren't delegated on the network.

Combining these four factors will lead you to an OU structure that supports your delegation requirements.

Applying the Decision

Wide World Importers wants to create an OU structure for the Engineering domain that will allow each distribution center's Engineering department to nominate an engineer to manage the user accounts. The nominated manager will also be responsible for maintaining group memberships of the Engineering user accounts for her distribution center.

At the head office in Washington, the head of the IT department for engineers, Kim Abercrombie, is required to manage all Engineering accounts within the domain. This will allow her to disable accounts when necessary without having to contact an IT administrator at each distribution center.

Based on these criteria, you could create the OU structure shown in Figure 2.8 for the Engineering department within the engineering.wideworldimporters.tld domain.

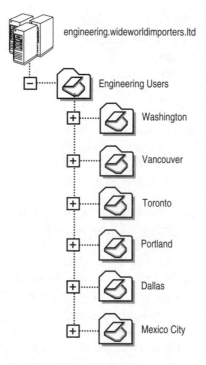

Figure 2.8   Proposed OU structure for the Engineering department

This OU facilitates the delegation of authority that the Engineering department needs. For the Engineering Users OU, a domain local group can be given the ability to manage all user accounts. The head of the IT department for engineers can be made a member of this group in order to manage the users. Because delegation of authority is inherited by default, the head of the Engineering IT department will be able to manage all user accounts in the Engineering department.

Likewise, you can delegate user account administration to separate domain local groups for each distribution center OU. You can make the nominated engineers at the distribution centers members of the domain local group so that they are limited to managing user accounts from their own distribution center.

This design is based on an OU structure that facilitates delegation of administration.

Planning for Group Policy Deployment

Another factor that affects your organizational unit design is planning for the deployment of Group Policy. Group Policy can be applied to local computers, sites, domains, and OUs, as shown in Figure 2.9.

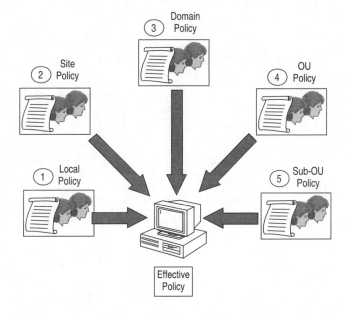

Figure 2.9 Applying Group Policy in a specific order to arrive at the effective policy

Group Policy is always processed in a specific order:

1. If local policy is defined at the Windows 2000 computer, that local policy is applied.
2. If any site policies are defined, they're applied to the object.
3. If any domain policies are defined, they're applied to the object.
4. If any top level OU policies are defined, they're applied to the object.
5. If any child OU policies exist, they're applied until the OU where the object exists is located.

You can configure Group Policy settings for both users and computers. When you design your OU structure, you may arrive at an OU structure that ultimately puts computers and users in separate OUs.

By default, Group Policy is inherited. If a policy is defined at the domain level, all OUs under that domain will have the Group Policy setting applied, unless the Group Policy setting is defined in an OU closer to the user that overrides the previous setting. Likewise, a Group Policy setting defined at a parent OU will be inherited by child OUs in the OU hierarchy, as shown in Figure 2.10.

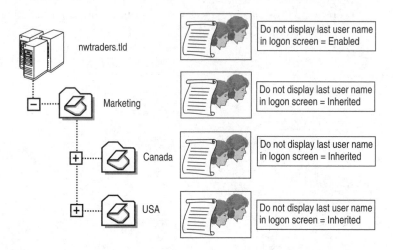

Figure 2.10   Group Policies inherited by child OUs by default

If you defined the security option as not displaying the last user name in the logon screen at the nwtraders.tld domain, Group Policy inheritance would assure that this setting is inherited by all computers within the Marketing, Canada, and USA OUs. The only case where they wouldn't be inherited is if the Do Not Display Last User Name In Logon Screen policy was disabled at one of the OUs closer to the user account.

Tip   While Group Policy settings are inherited *within* a domain, they aren't inherited *between* domains. If a Group Policy is defined at the forest root domain, it isn't inherited by child domains created below the forest root. A domain can inherit only site Group Policy settings.

In some cases it may be desirable to prevent the default inheritance of Group Policy. In Figure 2.9, we saw that all of the OUs in the nwtraders.tld domain inherited the Group Policy "Do Not Display Last User Name In Logon Screen." It's possible to block the inheritance of a Group Policy from a parent container by configuring the Block Policy Inheritance option within the Group Policy Properties page tab, as shown in Figure 2.11.

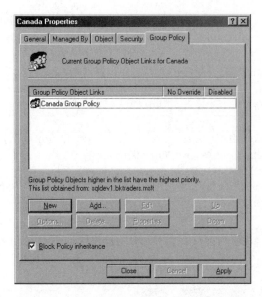

Figure 2.11   Configuring block policy inheritance at the OU level

Blocking inheritance will prevent Group Policy settings defined in parent containers from being applied at child containers. For example, if the Canada OU blocked policy inheritance, the Do Not Display Last User Name In Logon Screen policy wouldn't be enabled for any computers in the Canada OU.

Some administrators may not appreciate these settings being blocked at lower-level OUs. This is especially true for policy settings applied at the domain level that are intended to affect all computers in the domain. In this case it's possible for a higher-level policy to prevent lower-level Group Policy objects from overriding the policies defined at higher levels of the Active Directory structure by enabling the No Override option, as shown in Figure 2.12.

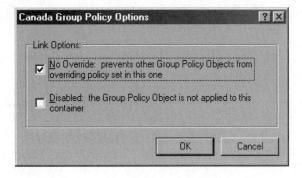

Figure 2.12   The No Override option prevents lower-level OUs from blocking
inheritance

If both the No Override and Block Policy Inheritance settings are selected, the No Override option takes precedence.

Tip   Always try to design your OU structure so that blocking policy inheritance isn't required. The use of blocking policy inheritance makes it very difficult for administrators to troubleshoot Group Policy application errors.

The final option that you can use to further configure which Group Policy is applied to objects within a container is to apply filtering to Group Policy. Filtering allows you to limit the application of a Group Policy to specific Windows 2000 security groups. You do this in the Security tab of the Group Policy object, as shown in Figure 2.13.

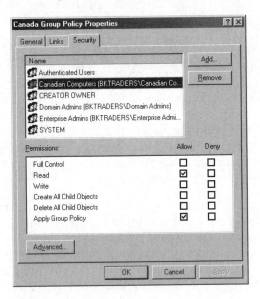

Figure 2.13   You can filter Group Policy so that the policy is only applied to specific security groups

To apply the Group Policy, you must assign the security group two specific permissions: Read and Apply Group Policy. The Read permission allows the members of the security group to read the properties and settings of the Group Policy object, and the Apply Group Policy permission indicates that those properties and settings will be applied to the security group.

Tip   When you're troubleshooting Group Policy application problems, you can use the *Microsoft Windows 2000 Server Resource Kit* tool Gpresult.exe to determine exactly which Group Policies are being applied to a specific computer and user account. This will limit the troubleshooting to the Group Policies that were actually applied to the user or computer object.

Making the Decision

Your OU design should meet the following Group Policy requirements to assist in troubleshooting Group Policy application problems:

- Create an OU structure that doesn't require blocking inheritance. When Group Policy inheritance is blocked, the default application model for Group Policy doesn't take place. This makes it difficult to troubleshoot Group Policy applications and may require tools such as Gpresult.exe from the *Microsoft Windows 2000 Server Resource Kit* for resolution.

- Limit the use of Site Group Policies in a multiple-domain environment. Site Group Policies are stored in the domain where the Site Group Policy was defined. This can result in a user or computer having to contact a remote DC to load the Site Group Policy, and this can cause slower authentication to the network.

- Limit the number of levels where Group Policy is applied in order to increase logon performance. The number of OU levels doesn't affect logon performance; rather, it's the number of OUs where Group Policy is applied. If too many Group Policy objects are defined, the time to authenticate with the network can be lengthy as each Group Policy is downloaded to the computer.

- Apply only the necessary settings. When you design your Group Policy objects, you should prevent user settings from being applied if the Group Policy object is only supposed to apply computer settings. Applying both computer and user settings when only computer settings are required increases processing time and prevents extraneous information from accidentally being added to the Group Policy.

Applying the Decision

Two requirements make it necessary for you to configure Group Policy: the deployment of software for users and the deployment of consistent security configuration for all computers.

To facilitate the deployment of the security templates, you need to create an OU structure that groups the computers into OUs based on security templates. You will create separate OUs for each security template that must be applied as shown in Figure 2.14.

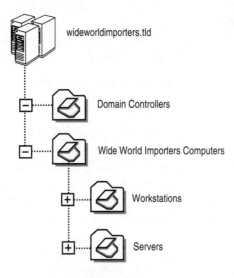

Figure 2.14   Proposed OU Structure for the deployment of security templates

Domain controllers will be located in the Domain Controllers OU. A separate OU for all other computers named Wide World Importers Computers will contain two sub-OUs: Workstations and Servers. This configuration will allow the deployment of the three security templates with the least amount of configuration. The Basicdc.inf template would be deployed at the Domain Controllers OU. The Basicwk.inf would be deployed at the Workstations OU. Finally, the Basicsv.inf template would be deployed at the Servers OU.

To facilitate the deployment of applications, you must define only a single OU. In Figure 2.15, this OU is located directly below the domain, but in reality it can be anywhere within the OU structure.

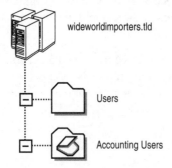

Figure 2.15   Proposed OU Structure for the deployment of applications

The Accounting Users OU would contain all of the Accounting department user accounts. For this OU you can define a Group Policy object that assigns the Accounting software to all user accounts within the OU.

For the distribution of Office 2000, you can deploy this at the domain Group Policy object. This will ensure that all users in the domain will have the software assigned to their user accounts.

Note   A Group Policy object cannot be defined for the Users container because the Users container is not an OU. Group Policy objects can be defined for domains, sites, and OUs, but not for container objects.

Lesson Summary

Designing an OU structure takes a long time. The design must allow for both delegation of administration and deployment of Group Policy. Be aware that the process is lengthy and that you must test it before deploying it.

Lesson 4: Designing an Audit Strategy

A major part of securing a Windows 2000 network is determining who accessed specific resources or who performed specific actions on the network. Auditing lets an administrator track these events in the Security Log of the Windows 2000 Event Viewer.

After this lesson, you will be able to

- Design an audit strategy that will allow inspection of critical events for Windows 2000–based computers in your organization

Estimated lesson time: 30 minutes

Configuring Audit Settings

Within Windows 2000 you can configure several auditing settings. In some cases all you have to do is configure the audit settings within the audit policy shown in Figure 2.16. In other cases, such as object access or directory service access, you have to also indicate which individual objects will be included in the audit.

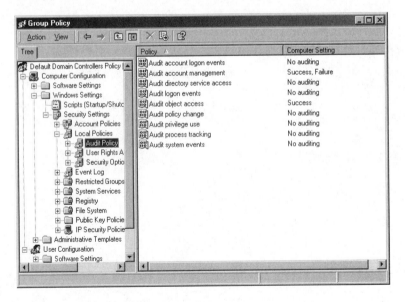

Figure 2.16   Configuring audit settings

The audit policies that can be defined for a domain include

- **Audit Account Logon Events.** Occurs any time a user logs on to a computer. If the user logs on to the local computer, the event is recorded in the computer's audit log. If the user logs on to a domain, the authenticating domain controller records the account logon event.

- **Audit Account Management.** Occurs whenever a user creates, changes, or deletes a user account or group. It also occurs when a user account is re-named, disabled, or enabled, or a password is set or changed.

- **Audit Directory Service Access.** Occurs whenever a user gains access to an Active Directory object. To log this type of access, you must configure specific Active Directory objects for auditing.

- **Audit Logon Events.** Recorded any time a user authenticates with the local computer or with Active Directory. This includes physically logging on at a computer or establishing a network connection to the computer.

- **Audit Object Access.** Logged any time a user gains access to a file, folder, or printer. The administrator must configure specific files, folders, or printers for auditing.

- **Audit Policy Change.** Occurs any time local policies are changed in Group Policy. This includes user rights, audit policy, or security options.

- **Audit Privilege Use.** Occurs any time a user exercises a user right, such as changing the system time, or any time an administrator takes ownership of a file.

- **Audit Process Tracking.** Occurs any time an application performs an action. This setting is used to determine which files and registry keys an application requires access to when operating.

- **Audit System Events.** Occurs any time a server is restarted or shut down. It also occurs any time the security log is reset on the computer.

Making the Decision

By defining audit settings within Active Directory by using Group Policy, you can ensure that the desired settings are maintained forest-wide. This ensures that users are unable to change their audit settings locally in an attempt to keep from viewing the security log.

When you define your audit strategy, you must consider the following design points:

- Determine where to apply the audit settings. As with all Group Policy, you can define audit settings locally, at the site level, at the domain level, or at individual OUs. As with all Group Policy, the audit policies will be applied in the following order:

  1. If audit policy is defined at the local computer, these audit settings will be applied first to the local computer.

  2. If audit policy is defined at the site level, these audit settings are applied.

  3. If audit policy is defined at the domain, these audit settings are applied.

  4. If audit policy is defined at the first level of OUs, these audit settings are applied.

5. Any audit policies defined at any of the child OUs will be applied until the audit policy defined at the actual OU where the computer object is located will be applied.

- Define DC auditing settings in the Domain Controllers OU. By default, all DCs are located in the Domain Controllers OU. By defining auditing settings to the Domain Controllers OU, you ensure that consistent auditing is performed across all DCs in a domain.

- Collect computers with similar audit requirements into common OUs. By grouping computer accounts into common OUs, you can apply the required audit policy settings at the OU level.

- Do not audit all events. The more auditing that you configure, the more audit events will fill the event log with unnecessary data. It's essential that you select only the events that are important to your auditing needs.

Note   The configuration of auditing also includes increasing the default size of the security log from 512 K. When auditing is enabled, you can be sure that you will require more space than the default size. The actual size must be set based on the amount of data that will be included in the auditing configuration. These settings can be configured for DCs in the Default Domain Controllers Policy in the Computer Configuration\Windows Settings\Security Settings\Event Log \Settings for Event Logs.

- Determine the appropriate mix of failure and success audits to meet your security requirements. Include failure audits in your audit strategy to detect intrusion attempts before they are successful, catch intruders before they cause damage to the network, and detect internal users attempting tasks that they're not authorized to perform. Include success audits to determine whether an attacker is successful in an intrusion attempt and to determine if excess privileges are assigned to a security principal.

- Define your audit strategy to match the organization's risk level. The lower the risk level that the organization is comfortable with, the more events you include in the audit strategy. For example, a lower-security network might audit only failed logon attempts, while a higher-security network might choose to audit both successful and failed logon attempts.

Applying the Decision

Because the current network deployment at Wide World Importers is concerned only with internal network auditing, you can put less emphasis on auditing for external attacks and more emphasis on maintaining security.

As mentioned earlier, you generally use failure auditing to determine if attacks are attempted and success auditing to reveal when actual intrusions or security breakdowns have taken place.

As a starting point for auditing, Table 2.1 outlines a common auditing structure that organizations use to ensure that the security log contains any attempts at intrusion:

Table 2.1   A Proposed Auditing Structure for Wide World Importers

Policy	Success	Failure
Audit account management	X	X
Audit account logon events		X
Audit directory service access		
Audit logon events		
Audit object access	X	X
Audit policy changes	X	X
Audit privilege use		
Audit process tracking		
Audit system events	X	X

These auditing settings provide the following information in the security log:

- All account management tasks are audited. This allows the network administrator to determine when user accounts were created, modified, or deleted and who performed the task.

- Auditing account logon event failures helps determine if failed logon attempts are occurring. This identifies any attempted break-in attempts by logging all failed logons. If you raise the security requirements, you could also include success events to determine if a break-in attempt is successful.

- Assuming that there are files that Wide World Importers might want to audit for usage, you must enable both success and failure auditing for object access. This allows you to determine who is accessing a file or folder object. This setting also requires that the file or folder is stored on an NT file system (NTFS) volume and that auditing is enabled on the Advanced tab for the object.

- Auditing success and failure events for policy changes ensures that any changes to the audit policy will be recorded in the audit logs.

- Auditing success and failure for system events detects any attempts to restart the server. The events record who attempted to restart the server and when the restart event took place.

Lesson Summary

You must define an audit strategy for your organization. Your decision on what audit settings to deploy balances the information that you require from auditing and the effect on performance and resource usage that the auditing requires.

Activity: Designing an Audit Strategy

Trey Research must determine the best auditing strategy to use for its Windows 2000 network. Your solution must identify the computers, events, and objects that you want to audit.

The network administrator at Trey Research has provided the following objectives for auditing. The Trey Research administrator must be able to determine the following information from the security log:

- Identify any attempts to break into the network
- Identify when an attempt is made to create new user accounts and which account attempted to create the new user account
- Identify all access attempts to documents stored at \\server\budget
- Identify if anyone attempts to change the current audit settings for the domain
- Identify if the DCs have been restarted and whether a user caused the restart of the server

To meet these auditing requirements, you must analyze each of the requirements and determine what audit policy must be defined and whether to audit successes or failures or both.

Answer the following questions about this situation. The answers to these questions can be found in the appendix.

1. Complete the following table to meet the audit requirements:

Policy	Success	Failure
Audit account logon events		
Audit account management		
Audit directory service access		
Audit logon events		
Audit object access		
Audit policy changes		
Audit privilege use		
Audit process tracking		
Audit system events		

2. What additional configuration is required to meet the desired audit settings?

3. Assuming that DCs are located in the default location in Active Directory, where should you apply this audit policy?

Lab 2-1: Designing Active Directory for Security

Lab Objectives

This lab prepares you to develop an Active Directory design to meet security requirements by meeting the following objectives:

- Determine the number of forests required based on security requirements
- Determine the number of domains required based on security requirements
- Design an OU structure for delegation of administration
- Design an OU structure for Group Policy deployment

About This Lab

This lab will help you test your ability to design an Active Directory for an organization named Contoso Ltd. The lab is based on the material learned in this chapter.

Before You Begin

Make sure that you've completed reading the chapter material before starting the lab. Pay close attention to the sections where the design decisions were applied throughout the chapter for information on building your administrative structure.

Scenario: Contoso Ltd.

Contoso Ltd. is an international magazine sales company with major offices in Great Britain, the United States, and Peru. The corporate office is located in London, with the North American central office in Seattle and the South American office in Lima.

Contoso is migrating to a Windows 2000 network and you're acting as a consultant assisting them with their Windows 2000 network design. Contoso currently has no organization-wide network and wants to establish one that will increase security and lower total cost of ownership.

Existing Network

The Contoso network is laid out as shown in Figure 2.17.

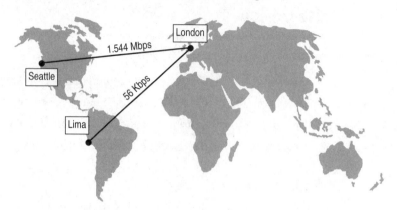

Figure 2.17   The Contoso Wide Area Network

The WAN link between London and Seattle is a dedicated T1 link, and the link between London and Lima is a 56 K link. The link between London and Lima is currently 90 percent utilized. There is concern about minimizing the replication traffic between Lima and London without increasing the bandwidth of the network link.

There are currently 20,000 users at the London office, 5000 users at the Seattle office, and 500 users at the Lima office.

Design Considerations

In order to save costs associated with DCs, Contoso would like to create a Windows 2000 network that minimizes the number of required forests and domains. In addition, the network design must meet the following business requirements:

- Replication traffic on the WAN link to Lima must be minimized.

- The Seattle office wants to use a minimum password length of eight characters, while the rest of the organization wants a minimum password length of six characters.

- The IT staff at each of the three locations is concerned about the management of the forest-wide administration groups. The Active Directory design should limit the number of users who can modify membership in the Enterprise Admins and Schema Admins groups.

- Contoso wants to ensure that standard applications are deployed on both clients and servers.

Group Policy Requirements

You use Group Policy to deploy consistent security configuration to all Windows 2000 desktop computers. The following categories of computer have been defined for the organization:

- Desktops
- Portables
- File servers
- Domain controllers
- Web servers

Each category has its own unique security template that will be deployed using Group Policy in Active Directory.

Administration Requirements

Contoso wishes to delegate some of the administrative functions within a domain to various teams within its organization. This includes the following delegation requirements:

- The help desk must be able to reset all passwords within the domain so the staff can assist users who have logon problems because of expired or forgotten passwords.
- The Human Resources department must be able to change all management, address, and phone-related information for all user objects.
- The Marketing, Sales, Accounting, and Finance departments want to manage their employees' user accounts.

Exercise 1: Determining the Number of Forests

This lab exercise will have you determine the number of forests that Contoso needs for their Windows 2000 network. You must base your decision on technical reasons for creating a separate forest. The answers to these questions can be found in the appendix.

1. Are there any business factors that may lead you to implementing more than one forest?

2. What effect would multiple forests have on your Active Directory design?

3. How many forests are required for the Contoso Windows 2000 network?

4. Are there any circumstances that may cause Contoso to require more than one forest in the future?

Exercise 2: Determining the Number of Domains

This lab exercise will have you determine the number of domains required for the Contoso Windows 2000 network based on the provided business requirements. The answers to these questions can be found in the appendix.

1. Which business factors will require Contoso to deploy multiple domains?

2. Draw an Active Directory domain design for Contoso.

3. If the link between London and Lima were upgraded to a 512 Kbps fractional-T1, how would this affect the Active Directory design?

Exercise 3: Designing an OU Structure

This exercise will have you design an OU structure for delegation of administration. Your design must be based on the information presented in the scenario at the beginning of the lab. The answers to these questions can be found in the appendix.

Designing an OU Structure for Administration

1. In the space below, draw an OU structure for the Seattle domain for all user accounts. The OU structure must allow for delegation of administration as outlined in the opening scenario.

2. Based on your OU structure, complete the following table of delegation assignments.

Domain/OU	Administrators	Permissions
■		
■		
■		
■		
■		
■		

Designing an OU Structure for Group Policy Deployment

The following exercise requires you to design an OU structure that will ensure that the security templates described at the beginning of the lab are deployed to the correct computers in the London domain. For this exercise, assume that you can move Windows 2000 computer accounts from their default location in Active Directory if this will facilitate your OU structure design. The answers to these questions can be found in the appendix.

1. Draw an OU structure for the deployment of the following security templates in the space provided below: Desktops, Portables, File Servers, Domain Controllers, and Web Servers.

2. Complete the following table to determine where in the OU structure you should apply the security templates by using Group Policy to ensure consistent security settings.

OU	Apply the Security Template
■	Desktops
■	Portables
■	File Servers
■	Domain Controllers
■	Web Servers

Review

Answering the following questions will reinforce key information presented in this chapter. If you are unable to answer a question, review the appropriate lesson and then try the question again. Answers to the questions can be found in the appendix.

1. A client has approached you to assist with the Windows 2000 Active Directory design. What are the design factors that would cause a company to create multiple forests within a single organization?

2. You're responsible for defining the domain structure for your Active Directory forest. Why do some organizations consider implementing an empty forest root domain as part of the forest structure?

3. You're attempting to troubleshoot a Group Policy application problem. Group Policy doesn't appear to be following the default application rules. What are some possible reasons that Group Policy isn't working as expected? What tools can you use to troubleshoot the problem?

4. Should your OU design be based on administrative delegation or Group Policy deployment considerations?

5. A company has approached you to design an audit policy for their organization. What risks are involved in simply enabling all auditing options?

C H A P T E R   3

Designing Authentication for a Microsoft Windows 2000 Network

About This Chapter

All access to Microsoft Windows 2000 resources is based on the credentials that users provide when they authenticate with the network. This chapter will examine the authentication protocols that are used in Windows 2000, the ways to authenticate down-level clients, and the optimum placement of domain controllers (DCs) to facilitate the authentication process.

Before You Begin

To complete this chapter, you must read the chapter scenario. This scenario is used throughout the chapter to apply the design decisions discussed in each lesson.

Chapter Scenario: Market Florist

Market Florist is an Internet-based floral delivery company that allows customers to purchase floral arrangements over the Internet and have them delivered anywhere in North America. You have been called in as a security consultant to design an authentication strategy for the Market Florist internal network that will ensure that user credentials are protected during the authentication process.

The Existing Network

Market Florist's head office is in Seattle, the Canadian office is in Winnipeg, and the Mexican office is in Monterrey. Market Florist's marketing department is in San Francisco.

Figure 3.1 shows the network links among Market Florist's four offices.

Figure 3.1   The Market Florist Wide Area Network

Market Florist Active Directory Design

Market Florist's Active Directory directory service design is comprised of three separate domains: marketflorist.tld, ca.marketflorist.tld, and mx.marketflorist.tld. The Seattle and San Francisco sites authenticate in the marketflorist.tld domain and the Winnipeg and Monterrey sites authenticate with their country's subdomain, as shown in Figure 3.2.

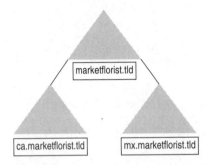

Figure 3.2   The Market Florist Active Directory structure

Market Florist Server Configuration

Market Florist has Windows 2000 servers distributed across its network as shown in Table 3.1.

Table 3.1   Windows 2000 Servers in the Market Florist Network

Location	Windows 2000 Servers
Seattle	■ Three Windows 2000 DCs for the marketflorist.tld domain. ■ Two of the DCs are configured as Active Directory–integrated Windows 2000 DNS servers hosting the marketflorist.tld DNS zone. ■ Two of the Windows 2000 DCs are configured as global catalog servers. ■ One Windows 2000 member server configured as a WINS server.
San Francisco	■ Two Windows 2000 DCs for marketflorist.tld. ■ One of the Windows 2000 DCs is configured as a global catalog server.
Winnipeg	■ Three Windows 2000 DCs for the ca.marketflorist.tld domain. ■ One of the DCS is configured as an Active Directory–integrated Windows 2000 DNS servers hosting the ca.marketflorist.tld zone.
Monterrey	■ Two Windows 2000 DCs for the mx.marketflorist.tld domain. ■ One of the DCS is configured as an Active Directory–integrated Windows 2000 DNS server hosting the mx.marketflorist.tld zone.

Market Florist Client Computers

The Market Florist network uses a mix of Microsoft Windows 95, Windows NT 4.0 workstation, and Windows 2000 Professional client computers. All client computers were updated to the latest service pack version before January 1, 2000, to ensure that the Market Florist network was Year 2000 compliant.

Table 3.2 shows how the client computers are distributed across the network.

Table 3.2   Market Florist Client Computer Distribution

Location	Client Computers
Seattle	▪ 700 Windows 2000 Professional clients
San Francisco	▪ 200 Windows 95 clients ▪ 300 Windows NT 4.0 workstations ▪ 100 Windows 2000 Professional clients
Winnipeg	▪ 200 Windows NT 4.0 clients ▪ 300 Windows 2000 Professional clients
Monterrey	▪ 300 Windows 95 clients ▪ 100 Windows 2000 Professional clients

Lesson 1: Designing Authentication in a Microsoft Windows 2000 Network

Authentication allows network administrators to determine who is accessing the network and to design restrictions so that each authenticated user can access only desired areas of the network. If you don't have a good authentication design, trusted users might be unable to access the network at all times.

After this lesson, you will be able to

- Determine business and technical requirements that will affect your authentication design for a Windows 2000 network

Estimated lesson time: 20 minutes

Determining Business and Technical Requirements

When designing authentication for your Windows 2000 network, you must meet certain business and technical requirements. These requirements define how you can make sure that authentication mechanisms are secured within a Windows 2000 network. The business requirements include these areas:

- Many organizations require that all projects should ultimately reduce the company's total cost of ownership. You can do this by using Group Policy to enforce standardized security configurations. In a Windows NT 4.0 network, you had to edit the registry manually to apply many advanced security settings. This required an administrator either to connect to each computer in the domain or to configure each computer in the domain manually. With Group Policy, Windows 2000 can ensure that common registry modifications are enforced centrally using Active Directory.

- Identify security risks in the network. In a Windows NT network, many client computers were unable to use more secure methods of authentication. (Unless otherwise noted, "Windows NT" refers to versions 3.51 and 4.0.) For example, Windows 95 and Windows 98 clients used LAN Manager (LM) authentication. LM authentication gives attackers an easy way to crack passwords. LM passwords are easily solved because they can be attacked in seven character sections. With the installation of the Directory Services Client in a Windows 2000 network, Windows 95 and Windows 98 clients use the NTLMv2 authentication protocol, which gives higher authentication security and reduces the risk of password cracking.

In addition to business requirements, technical requirements also play a part in the design of your network's authentication strategy. These technical requirements might include the following:

- Network authentication must be available even if WAN links are not. By deploying Domain Name System (DNS) servers, DCs, and global catalog servers at each remote site, you ensure that each site has the services needed to provide local authentication. While only Windows 2000 clients are site-aware by default, installing the Directory Services Client software on Windows 95, Windows 98, and Windows NT 4.0 clients makes these down-level client systems site-aware.

- Network authentication must occur quickly. When authentication takes place over WAN links, authentication performance suffers. By ensuring that all clients are site-aware, you ensure that the clients will attempt to find network services on their local segment of the network. This solution requires you to deploy the Directory Services Client software to all down-level clients and to deploy Active Directory sites correctly.

- DCs must not be overloaded with authentication requests. Microsoft provides a tool known as the Active Directory Sizer (ADSizer), which helps you plan the optimal number of DCs that you require for your network. This includes determining the ideal number of DCs and the processor and memory requirements for each one.

Note You can get the ADSizer tool by going to *www.microsoft.com* and searching for "ADSizer tool."

Lesson Summary

You must design authentication for your network to meet all business and technical objectives defined by your organization. These objectives will provide the framework for your design. If you don't meet all objectives, it's quite possible that you will face a redesign in the near future. Ensure that you have collected all business and technical objectives before completing your authentication design.

Lesson 2: Designing Kerberos Authentication

Windows 2000 is designed to use Kerberos v5 as the default authentication protocol. Kerberos v5 provides more flexibility in authentication than the NTLM authentication protocol did.

After this lesson, you will be able to

- Design a network to support Kerberos authentication for Windows 2000–based clients

Estimated lesson time: 45 minutes

Reviewing Kerberos Components

This lesson examines in detail how Kerberos authentication is used as the default authentication mechanism for Windows 2000–based computers. Before we start looking into design considerations of how Kerberos authentication works and how you can optimize and secure Kerberos authentication, let's look at the core components of Kerberos authentication. The components of the Kerberos v5 protocol include

- **Key distribution center (KDC).** A network service that supplies both ticket-granting tickets (TGTs) and service tickets to users and computers on the network. The KDC manages the exchange of shared secrets between a user and a server when they authenticate with each other. The KDC contains two services: the Authentication Service and the Ticket Granting Service. The Authentication Service provides the initial authentication of the user on the network and provides the user with a TGT. Whenever users request access to a network service, they supply their TGT to the Ticket Granting Service. The Ticket Granting Service then provides the user with a service ticket for authentication with the target network service. In a Windows 2000 network, the KDC service is run at all Windows 2000 DCs.

Note In some cases, a computer account must also request a TGT. Because a computer is also a security principal in a Windows 2000 network, the process proceeds in the same manner as user authentication, except that a computer account is being authenticated.

- **TGT.** Provided to users the first time they authenticate with the KDC. The TGT is a service ticket for the KDC. Whenever the user needs to request a service ticket for a network service, she presents the TGT to the KDC to validate that she has already authenticated with the network.

Note For additional security, Windows 2000 by default always verifies that the user account is still active every time a TGT is presented to the KDC. In other words, the KDC verifies that the account hasn't been disabled. If the account has been disabled, the KDC won't issue any further service tickets to the user.

- **Service ticket.** The user provides a service ticket whenever he connects to a service on the network. The user acquires the service ticket by presenting the TGT to the KDC and requesting a service ticket for the target network service. The service ticket contains the target server's copy of a session key and also contains information about the user who's connecting. This information is used to verify that the user is *authorized* to access the desired network service by comparing the authentication information—namely, the user's Security Identifier (SID) and their group SIDs—against the Discretionary Access Control List (DACL) for the object that the user is seeking access to. The service ticket is encrypted using the key that's shared between the KDC and the target server. This ensures that the target server is authenticated because only the target server can decrypt the session key.

- **Referral ticket.** Issued anytime a user attempts to connect to a target server that's a member of a different domain. The referral ticket is actually a TGT to the domain where the resource is located that's encrypted using the interdomain key between the initial domain and the target domain.

These four components allow Kerberos authentication to take place between Windows 2000 clients and Windows 2000 DCs.

Designing Kerberos Authentication

Kerberos provides the following advantages over the NTLM protocol:

- **Mutual authentication.** For all Kerberos transactions, both the user and the server are authenticated. This prevents identity spoofing of both the user and the server and ensures that only the desired communications take place. For example, if a client computer is connecting to a server and is protecting the data transmission using IPSec, Kerberos can be used to authenticate both ends of the data transmission.

- **Single sign-on.** Within a forest, a user who authenticates to the network using Kerberos v5 authentication won't have to provide any other credentials when accessing any resources in the forest.

- **Ticket caching.** After acquiring a service ticket from the KDC, the user then caches the service ticket in the client's personal ticket cache. This reduces the number of times that a user must contact DCs for authentication. For the lifetime of the service ticket, the user can simply present the ticket anytime he or she is required to authenticate with the server. The user needs to contact a DC to acquire another service ticket only when the ticket expires.

Tip   You can view your ticket cache at any time by using *Microsoft Windows 2000 Server Resource Kit* utilities. Klist.exe provides a text-based listing of your currently cached TGTs and STs. The Kerbtray.exe utility provides a graphical viewing of the currently cached tickets. The Kerbtray.exe utility loads an easily accessible icon in the system tray.

- **Delegation.** Kerberos lets services impersonate connecting users when the service connects to services located on other servers. For example, if a user is connecting to an application server using his network credentials, that application server can then query a database under the security context of the connecting user.

- **Standards-based protocol.** Kerberos is an industry standard authentication protocol. The Windows 2000 implementation of Kerberos v5 is compliant with Request for Comment (RFC) 1510 and RFC 1964.

Note   Kerberos v5 is defined in RFC 1510. You can obtain a copy of this RFC by going to *www.ietf.org/rfc* and searching for "RFC 1510."

- **Interoperability.** You can use Kerberos authentication to provide interoperable authentication between Windows 2000 domains and Kerberos realms in a UNIX environment. This allows ease of access to resources using a secure authentication protocol.

Understanding the Kerberos Message Exchanges

Three different message exchanges are used within Kerberos. All Kerberos authentication transactions will be composed from these three message exchanges.

The Kerberos message exchanges are

- **Authentication Service Exchange.** Used by the KDC to provide a user with a logon session key and a TGT for future service ticket requests. The Authentication Service Exchange is comprised of a Kerberos Authentication Service Request (KRB_AS_REQ) sent from the user to the KDC and a Kerberos Authentication Service Reply (KRB_AS_REP) returned by the KDC to the user.

- **Ticket Granting Service Exchange.** Used by the KDC to distribute service session keys and service tickets. The service ticket that's returned is encrypted using the master key shared by the KDC and the target server so that only the target server can decrypt the service ticket. A Ticket Granting Service Exchange is comprised of a Kerberos Ticket-Granting Service Request (KRB_TGS_REQ) sent from the user to the KDC and a Kerberos Ticket-Granting Service Reply (KRB_TGS_REP) returned by the KDC to the user.

- **Client/Server Authentication Exchange.** A user uses this message exchange when presenting a service ticket to a target service on the network. The message exchange is comprised of a Kerberos Application Request (KRB_AP_REQ) sent from the user to the server and a Kerberos Application Response (KRB_AP_REP) returned by the target server to the user.

Note   In the case of a failed authentication, all three message exchanges would replace the response sent from the KDC or the target server to the client with a Kerberos Error message (KRB_ERROR) that explains why the authentication attempt failed.

Analyzing Kerberos Authentication

Kerberos authentication is used in a Windows 2000 network in many circumstances. The following sections outline the transactions that occur as Kerberos authentication takes place.

Initial Authentication with the Network

The Authentication Service Exchange is used when a user initially logs on to the network. This exchange provides the user with a logon session key and a TGT that will be used to acquire service tickets during the session. The process involves a message sent from the client computer to the server (KRB_AS_REQ) and a response sent from the server to the client (KRB_AS_REP). The information contained within the KRB_AS_REP is encrypted with the user's long-term key so that only the user can decrypt the session key and the TGT within the response message. Each user shares a long-term key with the KDC. The long-term key is derived from the account's password.

The Importance of Time in Kerberos Transactions

In Windows 2000 the current time of the client is included in any client requests sent to a target server or to the KDC. The time is compared with the target server's current time. By default, if the difference between the two times is greater than 5 minutes, the connection attempt is considered invalid. In this instance, the connection attempt is considered to be a replay attack.

To ensure that all computers in a forest have synchronized clocks, Windows 2000 uses the Windows Time Synchronization Service (W32time.exe) that's based on the Simple Network Time Protocol (SNTP).

The following processes occur in order to ensure time synchronization:

1. The Primary Domain Controller (PDC) emulator in the forest root domain is considered the authoritative time source for the entire forest. The PDC emulator should synchronize its clock to an Internet Network Time Protocol (NTP) time source using the following command:

   ```
   net time /setsntp:<NTP host name>
   ```

2. For every other domain in the forest, the PDC emulator in that domain contacts the PDC emulator in the parent domain for clock synchronization. If the domain is parallel to the forest root domain (a separate tree in the forest), the PDC emulator contacts the PDC emulator in the forest root domain for time synchronization.

3. Within each domain, all DCs synchronize their clocks with the PDC emulator of their domain.

All client computers in the domain synchronize their clocks with the authenticating DC. If the authenticating DC's clock is ahead of the local time or the time difference between the two clocks is more than 2 minutes, the time is immediately reset to match the DC's clock. If the authenticating DC's clock is behind the current time, the computer's clock is recalibrated over the next 20 minutes until the times match.

The Kerberos authentication exchange, shown in Figure 3.3, proceeds as follows:

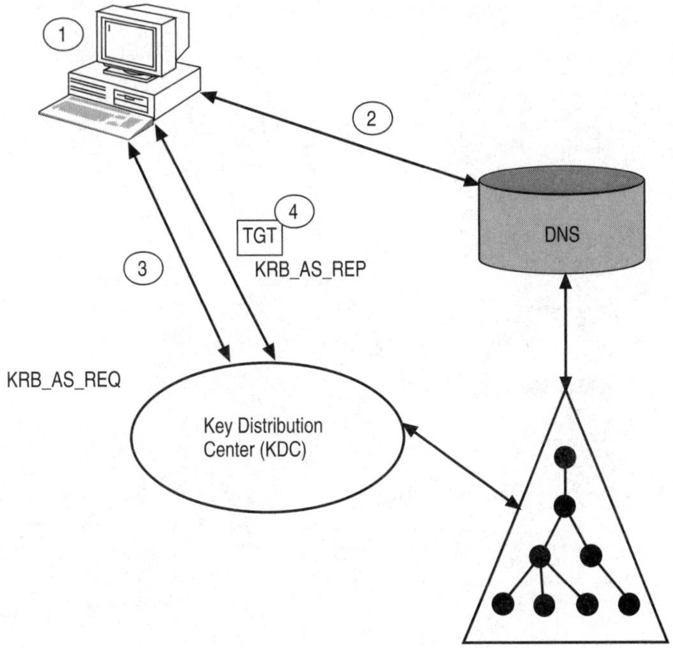

Figure 3.3 The Kerberos authentication exchange

1. The user presses CTRL+ALT+DEL to display the Windows 2000 Login dialog box. Within the dialog box, the user enters his login name, password, and the domain he wants to authenticate to.

2. The client computer queries the DNS server to find a _Kerberos service locator (SRV) resource record based on the client's domain and site. The returned SRV resource record is for a KDC that's at the client's local site for the domain the user wants to log on to.

3. The user sends a Kerberos Authentication Service Request (KRB_AS_REQ) to the DC indicated in the returned SRV resource record. The user's account information and the current computer time are encoded using the long-term key shared between the user's account and the KDC. As mentioned earlier, this long-term key is based on the user's password.

4. The authentication service at the KDC authenticates the user, generates a TGT for the user, and then sends back the TGT to the user in a Kerberos Authentication Service Response (KRB_AS_REP) message.

This provides the user with the proper TGT. If the user is using a Windows 2000–based computer, he must now acquire a service ticket for that computer, as shown in Figure 3.4.

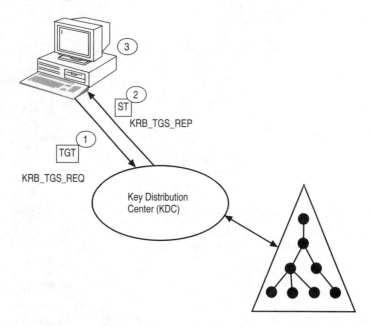

Figure 3.4   Acquiring a service ticket for the computer that the user logs on to

The following steps explain how to acquire the service ticket for the computer:

1. The user sends a Ticket Granting Service Exchange Request (KRB_TGS_REQ) to the KDC to acquire a service ticket for his computer. The KRB_TGS_REQ contains an authenticator and the TGT that was issued to the user.

2. The Ticket Granting Service of the KDC checks the TGT and the authenticator. If both are valid, the Ticket Granting Service generates a service ticket and sends it back to the user using a Ticket Granting Service Response (KRB_TGS_REP).

3. At the client computer, the service ticket is presented to the Local Security Authority, which will create an access token for the user. From then on, any process acting on behalf of the user can access the local machine's resources.

Network Authentication

Having initially authenticated with the network, the user has to authenticate with other computers as he accesses resources on those other computers. Each and every time that the user connects to a resource or service on a remote computer, he has to perform a network authentication as shown in Figure 3.5.

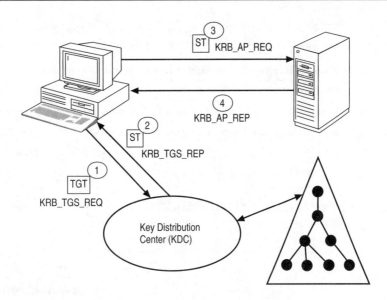

Figure 3.5   Network authentication

The following steps outline the authentication sequence that takes place when a user connects to a remote resource on the network:

1. The user sends a Ticket Granting Service Request (KRB_TGS_REQ) to the KDC to acquire a service ticket for the target computer. The KRB_TGS_REQ includes the TGT and an authenticator.

2. The Ticket Granting Service of the KDC checks the authenticator and the TGT, generates a new service ticket, and sends it back to the user using a Kerberos Ticket Granting Service Response (KRB_TGS_REP). The service ticket is encrypted using the long-term key between the KDC and the target service.

3. The user sends the service ticket and an authenticator to the target server using a Kerberos Application Request (KRB_AP_REQ).

4. The target server verifies the ticket with the authenticator, decrypts the session key using the master key that's shared with the KDC, and sends back an authenticator to the user in a Kerberos Application Response (KRB_AP_REP). This authenticator provides mutual authentication of the user and server.

Smart Card Authentication

Windows 2000 supports the use of smart card authentication by using PKINIT extensions for Kerberos. This allows public/private keys to be used to authenticate the user when he logs on to the network in place of the standard Kerberos Authentication Service Request and Response. KRB_AS_REQ and KRB_AS_REP are replaced with the PA_PK_AS_REQ and PA_PK_AS_REP messages.

Table 3.3 shows how the Kerberos Authentication Service uses the client's public key and private key when smart cards are used for logon.

Table 3.3   Private and Public Key Usage for Smart Card Logon

Process	Key Used
Client-side encryption of the preauthentication data	Private key
KDC-side decryption of the preauthentication data	Public key
KDC-side encryption of session key	Public key
Client-side decryption of session key	Private key

When the smart card is inserted into the computer, the process shown in Figure 3.6 takes place:

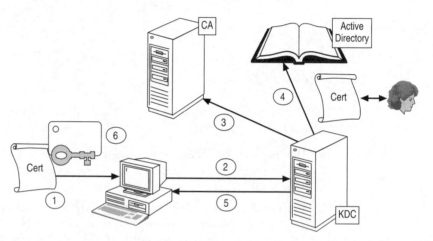

Figure 3.6   Smart card authentication

1. The user starts the logon process by introducing a smart card and by authenticating to the card using the user PIN code. The smart card contains the user's public key credentials, private/public key pair, and certificate.

2. A modified Kerberos Authentication Service Request (PA_PK_AS_REQ) message is sent to the KDC. This request contains the user principal name and time stamp and a copy of the user's certificate. The user principal name and time stamp are signed by the user's private key.

3. The KDC validates the request by verifying the user's certificate and the digital signature with the Certification Authority (CA) that issued the certificate.

4. The KDC queries Active Directory to determine the mapping between the certificate included in the PA_PK_AS_REQ and a Windows 2000 SID. When the mapping is determined, the KDC will issue a TGT for the corresponding SID.

5. The KDC sends the TGT back to the user in a modified Kerberos Authentication Service Response (PA_PK_AS_REP). Within the response, the session key is encrypted with the user's public key. This ensures that only the correct user can decrypt the session key.

6. The user retrieves the session key by decrypting the session key with the private key located on the smart card.

Multiple Domain Authentication

Your forest often needs to have more than one domain. If it does, authentication will be accomplished by using TGTs, referral tickets (TGTs for other domains), and service tickets. Figure 3.7 shows the typical process that occurs when a user accesses a resource in another domain.

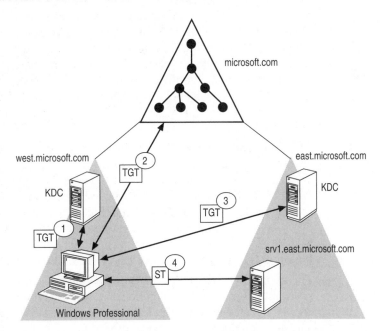

Figure 3.7   Authentication in a multiple-domain environment

The following process would take place if a user in the west.microsoft.com domain attempted to access a network share on the computer named srv1.east.microsoft.com:

1. The user sends a Ticket Granting Service Request (KRB_TGS_REQ) to the KDC in his domain to acquire a service ticket for the srv1.east.microsoft.com computer. Because the target computer is in a different domain, the KDC that receives the request looks at the trust relationships that exist for the domain. Because no explicit trust relationship exists between the west.microsoft.com

domain and the east.microsoft.com domain, only the default transitive trusts of a Windows 2000 forest, the KDC issues a TGT referral ticket to the microsoft.com domain in the KRB_TGS_REP packet that's sent back to the client. The TGT is encrypted using the interdomain key between the west.microsoft.com domain and the microsoft.com domains.

Tip   If users in the west.microsoft.com domain frequently access resources in the east.microsoft.com domain, you could shorten the length of this process transaction by creating a shortcut trust, or cross-link trust, between the west.microsoft.com and east.microsoft.com domains. If you did this, the TGT issued at this stage would be for the east.microsoft.com domain.

---

2. The user sends a KRB_TGS_REQ message to a KDC located in the microsoft.com domain to acquire a service ticket for the srv1.east .microsoft.com computer. Because the target computer is in a different do-main, the KDC that receives the request looks at the explicit trust relation-ships that exist for the domain. The KDC in the microsoft.com domain issues a TGT referral ticket to the east.microsoft.com domain in the KRB_TGS_REP packet that's sent back to the client. The TGT is encrypted using the interdomain key between the microsoft.com domain and the east.microsoft.com domains.

3. The user sends a KRB_TGS_REQ message to a KDC located in the east.microsoft.com domain to acquire a service ticket for the srv1.east.microsoft.com computer. Because the target computer is in this domain, the KDC that receives the request verifies the TGT and the authentica-tor provided in the KRB_TGS_REQ. If it's valid, the KDC issues a KRB_TGS_REP that contains a service ticket to connect to the SRV1.east.microsoft.com computer. The service ticket is encrypted using the long-term key shared by the KDC and the srv1.east.microsoft.com computer.

4. The user sends a KRB_AP_REQ containing the service ticket to the srv1.east.microsoft.com computer. The srv1.east.microsoft.com validates the service ticket, and if it's valid, it responds with a KRB_AP_REP message. The user can now access the resource.

Delegation

In client/server environments you might sometimes deploy multitiered client/ server applications (commonly referred to as *n*-tiered applications). In these sce-narios, the first server that the user connects to must often impersonate that user when that server connects to additional servers in order to ensure that the entire process is run in the connecting user's security context. Kerberos provides the functionality for this procedure through the process of delegation.

Delegation can take place only when the following criteria are met:

- The computers that are hosting the client process, the service process, and processes for any back-end services must all be running Windows 2000 in a Windows 2000 domain.
- The client's user account must be enabled for delegation.

Note To enable a user account for delegation, edit the properties of the user account in Active Directory Users And Computers. On the Account tab you can select the Account Is Trusted For Delegation check box under Account Options and ensure that the Account Is Sensitive And Cannot Be Delegated option is cleared.

- The service's account must be enabled for delegation.

Note If the service account is running under the local system account, the computer account itself must be trusted for delegation. To enable this, open the properties of the computer account in Active Directory Users And Computers. In the General tab select the Trust Computer For Delegation check box.

When the account is designated as trusted for delegation, this enables the forwardable flag on the service ticket. This flag allows services to request service tickets on behalf of the client and run processes in the security context of the client.

Figure 3.8 shows the authentication process that occurs when delegation takes place in a client/server system where two servers are involved (Server1 and Server2):

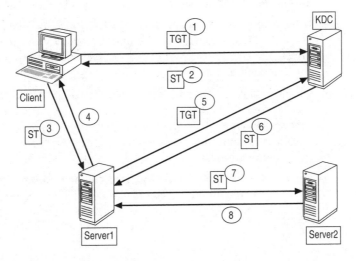

Figure 3.8 Kerberos authentication when delegation takes place

1. The user sends a KRB_TGS_REQ message to the KDC requesting a service ticket for Server1.

2. The KDC sends the service ticket in a KRB_TGS_REP message back to the user.

3. The user sends the service ticket to Server1 in a KRB_AP_REQ message.

4. Server1 responds to the authentication request with a KRB_AP_REP message.

5. Server1 sends a KRB_TGS_REQ message, impersonating the user, to the KDC for a service ticket to access Server2 in the security context of the user.

6. The KDC sends a KRB_TGS_REP message containing the service ticket that allows the user to access Server2.

7. Server1 sends the service ticket to Server2 in a KRB_AP_REQ message.

8. Server2 responds to the authentication request with a KRB_AP_REP message validating the authentication. Server1 now has access to services on Server2 at the security level of the original user.

Making the Decision

When you design your network for Kerberos Authentication support, you must consider the following points:

- Kerberos authentication relies on Windows 2000 DCs being available on the network. Each site defined in Active Directory should have at least one domain controller available to ensure that authentication can take place.

- DNS services must be available to find Windows 2000 DCs for Kerberos authentication services. When a Windows 2000 client computer attempts to connect to a KDC, it queries DNS for a _Kerberos SRV resource record. If DNS services are unavailable, the client won't be able to find a KDC for authentication.

- If the Windows 2000 domain is in native mode and the forest has multiple domains, the authenticating DC must contact a global catalog server to enumerate universal group membership. A global catalog server should be located at each remote site.

- Global catalog server SRV resource records are stored in the _msdcs.*forestrootdomain* zone, where *forestrootdomain* is a variable representing the name of the domain in question. This zone should be delegated to DNS servers at remote sites to ensure that global catalog servers can be found by authenticating DCs.

- Only Windows 2000 clients and UNIX clients can use Kerberos authentication. Even with the Directory Services Client loaded, Windows 95, Windows 98, and Windows NT clients can't authenticate using Kerberos.

- Smart card logon requires that Kerberos be used for authentication. If Kerberos services are unavailable, the smart card logon attempt fails.

- Kerberos settings are part of the domain account policy. Within the Kerberos settings is the option to enforce logon restrictions. This setting should always be applied to ensure that disabled user accounts can no longer acquire service tickets. These Kerberos settings can be edited in the Default Domain Policy for the domain as shown in Figure 3.9.

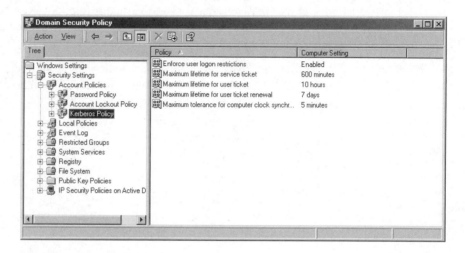

Figure 3.9   Setting the Kerberos policy for a domain

Applying the Decision

Only the Windows 2000 clients in the Market Florist network can authenticate using Kerberos v5. (Remember that Windows 95 and Windows NT clients can't use Kerberos for authentication.) To ensure that Kerberos authentication is optimized for all four sites, you must include the following components in the authentication design for Market Florist:

- Each of the domains has sufficient DCs at each of the four sites.

- The San Francisco site doesn't have a dedicated DNS server. If the WAN link to Seattle is unavailable, the clients will be unable to access a DNS server to find SRV resource records for Kerberos authentication. This can result in cached credentials being used for authentication.

- The DNS servers in Winnipeg and Monterrey don't have a secondary zone for the _msdcs.marketflorist.tld domain. If the WAN link to either of these sites is down, this can render the authenticating DCs unable to find a global catalog server for universal group enumeration. You should configure this zone as a secondary zone on the DNS servers in Winnipeg and Monterrey.

- The Winnipeg and Monterrey sites don't have a local global catalog server. You should configure at least one DC at each site as a global catalog server to ensure that all global catalog access isn't over the WAN links as currently configured.

Lesson Summary

Because Windows 2000 uses Kerberos as the default authentication protocol, you must ensure that your network infrastructure supports Kerberos authentication. This includes ensuring that essential network services, such as DNS, DCs, and global catalog servers are available in the event of a WAN link failure.

Also make sure that you understand how the Kerberos authentication process works for different scenarios. Knowing the process will help you troubleshoot authentication problems when they occur.

Lesson 3: NTLM Authentication

Only Windows 2000 clients and UNIX clients can use Kerberos authentication in a Windows 2000 domain. To provide access to Windows NT 4.0 clients and Windows 95 and Windows 98 clients running the Directory Service client, Windows 2000 continues to support the use of the Windows NT LAN Manager (NTLM) authentication protocol.

After this lesson, you will be able to

- Design NTLM authentication for Windows 2000–based clients and down-level clients in a Windows 2000 network

Estimated lesson time: 30 minutes

Designing NTLM Authentication

In addition to providing NTLM authentication for down-level clients, NTLM is also used to authenticate logons to Windows 2000 computers that aren't participating in a domain or when authentication against the local account database of a member server or Windows 2000 Professional computer takes place.

In the last few years, security weaknesses were found with the NTLM protocol. Password crackers were developed that were able to decrypt NTLM-protected authentication. To counteract this, NTLM version 2 was developed for Windows NT 4.0 Service Pack 4. NTLMv2 introduces additional security features, including

- **Unique session keys per connection.** Each time a new connection is established, a unique session key is generated for that session. This way a captured session key will serve no useful purpose after the connection is completed.

- **Session keys protected with a key exchange.** The session key can't be intercepted and used unless the key pair used to protect the session key is obtained.

- **Unique keys generated for the encryption and integrity of session data.** The key that's used for the encryption of data from the client to the server will be different from the one that's used for the encryption of data from the server to the client.

Figure 3.10 shows how NTLMv2 authentication takes place.

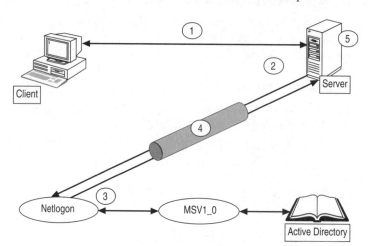

Figure 3.10   NTLM authentication

In this environment the client is connecting to a server. Active Directory uses the MSV1_0 sub-authentication filter to perform the authentication.

1. The NTLM challenge response is sent from the client computer to the server that the client is connecting to.

2. The application server uses the local security authority (LSA) to log on to the domain using the Netlogon service.

3. The Netlogon service queries Active Directory using the MSV1_0 sub-authentication filter to validate the user.

4. If the user is validated, the Netlogon service returns the user and group SIDs from the authenticating DC back to the server.

5. For the logon process, NTLMv2 introduces a secure channel to protect the authentication process.

Making the Decision

Because Kerberos authentication is available only to Windows 2000 client computers, your network design must ensure that the next strongest form of authentication is available to non–Windows 2000 client computers and Windows 2000 client computers.

Clients use NTLMv2 authentication in the circumstances shown in Table 3.4.

Table 3.4   Determining when NTLMv2 Authentication is Used

Client	Use NTLMv2 when
Windows 2000	■ Authenticating to the local SAM database of a stand-alone Windows 2000–based computer ■ Authenticating with a Windows NT 4.0 computer with SP4 or higher installed
Windows NT 4.0	■ Authenticating with Windows 2000 and Windows NT 4.0 servers and the client has Service Pack 4 or higher applied ■ Authenticating with Windows 2000 and Windows NT 4.0 servers and the client has the Directory Services Client installed
Windows 95/Windows 98	■ Authenticating with Windows 2000 and Windows NT 4.0 servers and the client has the Directory Services Client installed

Applying the Decision

The Market Florist network has a combination of Windows NT 4.0 Workstation and Windows 95 clients that are unable to use Kerberos when authenticating with the network.

Based on the scenario, Market Florist must include the deployment of the Directory Services Client only to the Windows 95 clients to ensure that all non–Windows 2000 clients on the network use NTLMv2 authentication. The Windows NT 4.0 Workstation clients won't require the Directory Service Client software to enable NTLMv2 authentication because the clients had the latest service pack applied for Year 2000 compliance. This doesn't mean that there isn't a business case to distribute the Directory Service Client software to Windows NT 4.0 workstations. It only means that the Windows NT 4.0 clients don't require the Directory Service Client software to ensure that NTLMv2 is used for authentication.

Lesson Summary

NTLM authentication is still used in a Windows 2000 network. Be sure that you know when NTLM authentication is used and plan the deployment of the Directory Services Client software to ensure that Windows 95, Windows 98, and Windows NT 4.0 clients can use the added security of NTLMv2 authentication. When Kerberos can't be used, NTLMv2 provides strong authentication security.

Lesson 4: Authenticating Down-Level Clients

Because down-level clients don't support Kerberos authentication, you need to do some planning to allow these clients to authenticate with Active Directory without compromising security on the network.

After this lesson, you will be able to

- Design secure authentication for down-level clients by deploying the Microsoft Directory Services Client

Estimated lesson time: 30 minutes

Analyzing Standard Authentication

Without service packs or additional software, Windows NT 4.0, Windows 95, and Windows 98 clients introduce security weaknesses for authentication on a Windows 2000 network.

Windows NT 4.0 clients without service packs will use the NTLM authentication protocol. Password crackers recently have found ways to decrypt the authentication information that's exchanged between a DC and an authenticating client if it's only protected using NTLM. As mentioned earlier, NTLMv2, introduced in Windows NT 4.0 Service Pack 4, provides stronger authentication protection by using NTLMv2 for authentication.

With Windows 95 and Windows 98 clients the problems are even more evident. By default, these clients use LAN Manager (LM) authentication protocol which is the weakest of the authentication protocols in a Windows 2000 environment. As discussed in Lesson 1, the continued use of LM authentication can lead to the decryption of sensitive account passwords if they're maintained in LM format within Active Directory.

The Microsoft Directory Service Client (DSClient) has been developed to counteract these weaknesses. The DSClient software allows Windows NT 4.0, Windows 95, and Windows 98 clients to use NTLMv2 for authentication in the Windows 2000 network. The following section outlines some of the features of the DSClient software.

Note   The DSClient software for Windows 95 and Windows 98 is included on the Windows 2000 CD in the \clients\win9x folder. The Windows NT 4.0 DSClient software will be shipped with Windows NT 4.0 Service Pack 7.

Analyzing the Directory Services Client

The Directory Services Client provides additional functionality to down-level clients so that they can operate securely and efficiently in a Windows 2000 network environment. When it's installed, the DSClient software adds the following functionality to a client:

- **NTLMv2 authentication protocol.** Windows 95, Windows 98, and Windows NT 4.0 clients will use NTLMv2, rather than weaker forms of authentication, when authenticating with Active Directory.

- **Site awareness.** The DSClient software allows the client to query DNS to find a DC in the same site.

- **Search for objects in Active Directory.** The DSClient software allows clients to search Active Directory for printers and users from the Start|Search menu.

- **Reduces dependency on the PDC.** Rather than having to connect to the PDC of the domain for password changes, the DSClient software allows down-level clients to connect to any DC in the domain for password changes.

- **Active Directory Services Interface (ADSI).** The DSClient software provides a common programming API for Active Directory programmers. This allows scripting to take place at the client that writes changes to Active Directory.

- **Distributed Files System (DFS) fault tolerance client.** The DSClient software allows clients to access and find Windows 2000 DFS file shares in Active Directory.

- **Active Directory Windows Address Book (WAB) property pages.** The DSClient software allows users to change attributes of their user object using the Start|Search|For People menu option. This is, of course, subject to the security settings on their user object.

It's also important to note that there are some features that the DSClient software doesn't provide. These features require you to upgrade to Windows 2000 as the client operating system:

- **Kerberos support.** The DSClient software doesn't provide Kerberos support to Windows 95, Windows 98, and Windows NT 4.0 clients. They can use only NTLMv2 to strengthen authentication security.

- **Group Policy/Intellimirror support.** Even with the DSClient software loaded, a Windows 95, Windows 98, or Windows NT 4.0 client won't participate in Group Policy or Intellimirror. To deliver similar functionality, system policy must be maintained in the Active Directory environment.

Note   By default, Windows 95 and Windows 98 clients will connect to the PDC unless the Load Balancing option is enabled in system policy. This is enabled in Default Computer|Network|System Policies Update|Remote Update And Setting The Load Balancing option. This will allow the Windows 95 or Windows 98 client to load system policy from the authenticating DC.

- **IPSec/L2TP support.** Windows 95, Windows 98, and Windows NT 4.0 clients only support PPTP for VPN connections. There's no support for L2TP/IPSec connections.

- **Server Principal Name (SPN)/mutual authentication.** The DSClient doesn't provide SPNs or mutual authentication to Windows 95, Windows 98, and Windows NT clients.

- **Dynamic DNS support.** The DSClient software doesn't allow Windows 95, Windows 98, or Windows NT clients to update their own DNS resource records using dynamic update. For Windows 95, Windows 98, and Windows NT clients, the Dynamic Host Configuration Protocol (DHCP) server must be configured to update the DNS resource records on behalf of the client computers.

- **User Principal Name (UPN) authentication.** The DSClient software doesn't allow users to authenticate using their UPN (user@domain.com). This functionality is only available in Windows 2000 clients.

Once you've distributed the DSClient software to your down-level client com puters, you can restrict which protocols can be used to authenticate with a Windows 2000 computer. You do this by adjusting registry value HKLM\System\CurrentControlSet\Control\LSA\LMCompatibilityLevel at all Windows 2000–based computers in the domain, and setting one of the following six values for the REG-DWORD value:

- **0 (send LM & NTLM responses).** Offers the most interoperability. Any previous down-level clients that use either LM or NTLM for authentication can authenticate with the server.

- **1 (Send LM & NTLM–use NTLMv2 session security if negotiated).** Offers more security when the DSClient software is deployed. If the client computers support NTLMv2, this setting allows the use of NTLMv2 to be negotiated. It's best to use this setting during the deployment of the DSClient software. Clients that have the DSClient software installed use NTLMv2, but the setting won't prevent the authentication of clients who haven't installed the software yet.

- **2 (Send NTLM response only).** More useful in Windows NT networks where you want to restrict the use of Windows 95 and Windows 98 clients. This setting prevents the connection of all down-level clients if the DSClient software were deployed to all Windows 95, Windows 98, and Windows NT clients.

- **3 (Send NTLMv2 response only).** Configures the Windows 2000 computer to respond with NTLMv2 authentication for down-level authentication requests. You should use this only if all down-level clients have the DSClient software installed, because it will prevent those clients from authenticating with the network.

- **4 (Send NTLMv2 response only\refuse LM).** Configures the Windows 2000 computer to respond with only NTLMv2 authentication for down-level authentication requests. If LM authentication requests are sent to the Windows 2000 computer, they're rejected and no NTLMv2 response is sent. This will restrict access to only Windows 2000 computers, and Windows NT, Windows 95 and Windows 98 clients using the DSClient software.

Note Windows NT 4.0 with Service Pack 4.0 or later will also support NTLMv2 authentication.

- **5 (Send NTLMv2 response only\refuse LM & NTLM).** Ensures that only NTLMv2 responses are sent and that authentication requests that don't use NTLMv2 will be rejected. This prevents Windows NT 4.0 clients that don't have Service Pack 4 or greater from connecting to the server. In this scenario, only Windows 2000, Windows NT 4.0 clients with either SP4 or later, or Windows NT 4.0, Windows 95, and Windows 98 clients with the DSClient software will be able to connect to the Windows 2000 computers.

You can deploy the LMCompatibilityLevel setting using Windows 2000 Group Policy. You do this by editing Group Policy at the container where the Windows 2000 computer accounts reside with the following Group Policy setting:

```
Group Policy Container\Computer Configuration\Windows
Settings\Security Settings\Local Policies\Security Options\LAN Manager
Authentication Level.
```

This Group Policy setting will ensure that consistent application of the LMCompatibilityLevel setting takes place. For DCs, be sure to apply this at the Domain Controllers OU. For all other Windows 2000 computers, you can simply apply this Group Policy setting at the domain level.

Note For details on configuring Windows 95 and Windows 98 clients to use NTLMv2 authentication, see *Q239869—How to Enable NTLM 2 Authentication for Windows 95-98 Clients* on the Supplemental Course Materials CD-ROM (\chapt03\Q239869.mht).

Making the Decision

When Windows 95, Windows 98, and Windows NT 4.0 clients exist on the network, the default authentication mechanisms for the clients don't use the strongest available form of authentication. To increase the authentication level, you must include the following steps in your design process for authentication:

- Distribute the DSClient software to all clients. All Windows 95, Windows 98, and Windows NT 4.0 clients should have the DSClient software installed. Not only does it allow the use of NTLMv2 for authentication, but also the DSClient software makes clients site-aware and less dependent on the Primary Domain Controller (PDC).

- Ensure that all Windows NT 4.0 clients have the latest service pack installed. NTLMv2 functionality was introduced in Windows NT 4.0 Service Pack 4.

- Develop a plan for the distribution of the DSClient software and any registry updates that must be performed for client computers.

- Once all clients have been upgraded to use the DSClient software, set the LMCompatibilityLevel at the servers to require NTLMv2 authentication.

- Replace or upgrade all older client computers from the network if they can't support NTLMv2 authentication.

Applying the Decision

Each of Market Florist's four office locations has down-level clients. Based on the current network configuration, these down-level clients by default use less secure authentication mechanisms.

In the authentication security plan, Market Florist must include the following steps:

- Market Florist must ensure that a plan is created for the distribution of the DSClient software to all Windows 95 and Windows NT 4.0 client computers. The DSClient software will increase the performance and strength of down-level client authentication by allowing local password changes and use of NTLMv2 for authentication.

- Market Florist must ensure that all necessary registry settings are deployed to Windows NT 4.0 and Windows 95 clients to ensure that the client computers will use NTLMv2 rather than LM or NTLM authentication.

- You must configure Group Policy *after the DSClient software is fully deployed* to allow only NTLMv2 authentication to be used. You must not configure this setting until all down-level clients have the DSClient software and necessary registry settings, or the down-level clients will lose access to all network data. The setting that you must apply is Group Policy Container \Computer Configuration\Windows Settings\Security Settings\Local Policies \Security Options\LAN Manager Authentication Level. This must be applied at each OU where Windows 2000 computers exist.

- DNS services must be configured locally at each site to ensure that down-level clients using the DSClient software can locate local DCs and global catalog servers in the event that the WAN link is down and DNS services can't be contacted.

Lesson Summary

Down-level clients can potentially introduce security weaknesses to the network if you don't create the proper design. Plan the deployment of the Directory Services Client so that Windows 95 and Windows 98 can utilize NTLMv2 authentication. The deployment of the Directory Services Client will also change your infrastructure requirements as it removes the dependency of down-level clients on the PDC emulator in a domain.

Your network design must include server placement strategies. A down-level client must be able to access the necessary services in the event of a WAN link failure to access the network. Careful planning can reduce down time in the event of a WAN failure.

Lesson 5: Planning Server Placement for Authentication

DCs perform Windows 2000 authentication. A key part of your security design is ensuring that Windows 2000 DCs are readily available to clients when they require DC services. This lesson looks at server placement issues that affect authentication.

After this lesson, you will be able to

- Design the optimal placement of Windows 2000 servers for authentication performance and reliability

Estimated lesson time: 45 minutes

Determining Server Placement for Authentication

When you're planning server placement for authentication services, the only servers to consider are those that play a part in the authentication process. These include

- DNS servers
- DCs
- Global catalog servers
- The PDC emulator

Planning DNS Server Placement

DNS servers act as the locator service in a Windows 2000 network. To ensure that DNS services are available on all portions of the network, you must use a DNS server that contains zone information for all domains located at each remote site. In other words, you want to make sure that each site has a locally accessible DNS server. This ensures that if the network link goes down, DNS services are still available. Of course, the DNS server must also be hosting the zone data for the domains located at that site.

In addition, you must ensure that the _msdcs.*forestrootdomain* zone is also available at all remote sites because the following information is stored within this zone:

- **All global catalog servers in the forest.** DNS doesn't store the global catalog server SRV resource records based on domains. They're all stored in the forest root domain. Site location is more relevant for global catalog servers.
- **The Globally Unique Identifier (GUID) representation of each domain.**
  In future versions of Windows 2000, it will be possible to rename domains. If the domain name is renamed, the GUID host record can be referenced to find the renamed domain.

- **The GUID representation of each DC.** DCs find replication partners based on the DC's GUID, not on the DC's DNS fully qualified domain name.

If the DNS service can't be contacted, the Windows 2000–based client computers won't be able to find the nearest KDC for authentication. The user at the Windows 2000–based computer will use cached credentials if he has successfully authenticated before. Otherwise, the logon attempt will fail.

Warning   If there are clients on the network that aren't Windows 2000–based, or if there are down-level clients with the DSClient software installed, you probably need to deploy WINS for NetBIOS name resolution. Make sure that a locally accessible WINS server is at each remote site and that WINS replication is correctly configured so that clients can authenticate with remote DCs if necessary.

Making the Decision

When designing your Windows 2000 network for authentication, you must configure the DNS service to provide the following:

- A DNS server should be located at each remote site to ensure DNS lookup capabilities to all clients if the WAN link to a central site is down.

- Each domain must have at least two DNS servers to provide fault tolerance in the event of server or WAN link failure.

- The DNS service at each site must contain zone information for all domains that must be accessed at that site. If clients can authenticate with two different domains at a site, DNS services should have replicas of the zones for those two domains hosted at a local DNS server.

- All global catalog resource records are stored in the forest root domain. Each DNS server in a forest should have a replica of the _msdcs.*forestrootdomain* zone to ensure that the local DNS server can resolve global catalog (_gc) resource records.

Applying the Decision

Market Florist's current network design doesn't have sufficient DNS coverage should WAN links be unavailable. To prevent the loss of DNS access in the event of a WAN link failure, you should add the following components to the Market Florist network, as shown in Figure 3.11.

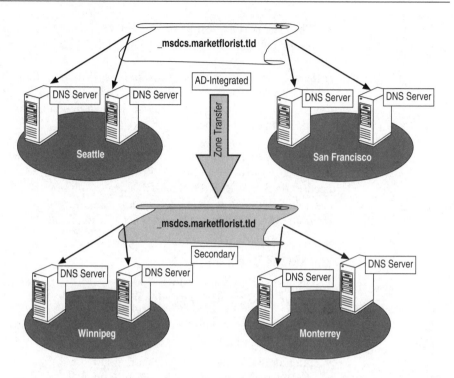

Figure 3.11   The recommended DNS configuration for Market Florist

- The DNS servers at the Seattle site should configure the _msdcs.marketflorist.tld domain as a separate Active Directory–integrated zone to allow the zone to be replicated to child domains for the purpose of locating global catalog servers.

- A DC at the San Francisco site should be configured as a DNS server. By using Active Directory–integrated zones, the DNS server would have a full replica of the forest root domain. For fault tolerance, the second DC can also be configured as a DNS server.

- A second DC in the ca.marketflorist.tld domain should be configured as a DNS server to provide fault tolerance of the ca.marketflorist.tld domain.

- The two DNS servers at the Winnipeg site should be configured as secondaries of the _msdcs.marketflorist.tld domain.

- The second DC in the mx.marketflorist.tld domain should be configured as a DNS server to provide fault tolerance of the mx.marketflorist.tld domain.

- The two DNS servers at the Monterrey site should be configured as secondaries of the _msdcs.marketflorist.tld domain.

- All Windows 95, Windows NT, and Windows 2000 clients should be configured to use two DNS servers at their site as their primary and secondary DNS services. This can be either configured locally at each client computer or by using DHCP to assign the correct DNS IP addresses based on IP address scope.

Planning DC Placement

DCs host the KDC service for Windows 2000. When a user authenticates with the network, she attempts to authenticate with a local DC. If a local DC is unavailable, the site link costs are checked to determine which is the closest site to the current site, based on the lowest cost.

Making the Decision

To ensure that clients authenticate locally, place at least two DCs at each remote site. If there are no client computers or users at a remote site for a specific domain, there's no reason to deploy a DC for that domain at that remote site. Remember that if the WAN link goes down, users are restricted to logging on to the network with cached credentials. This can result in users accessing the network with group memberships that have changed since the last successful logon attempt.

Applying the Decision

Each of Market Florist's four sites has at least two DCs. Their presence ensures that all authentications for the local domain won't occur over the WAN. By installing the DSClient software to all Windows 95 and Windows NT 4.0 clients, Market Florist also ensures that all password changes can be made to local DCs, rather than to the PDC emulator for the domain.

Planning Global Catalog Server Placement

Global catalog servers are contacted during the following authentication scenarios:

- When the domain is in native mode, the authenticating DC contacts a global catalog server to determine if the authenticating user is a member of any universal groups. If a global catalog server can't be contacted, the user must be authenticated with cached credentials. The reason is that there might be explicit deny permission assignments for universal groups that the user is a member of.

Note   In two cases a global catalog server isn't required for authentication purposes. The first is when the forest has only a single domain. Because there's only a single domain, all universal group memberships can be determined by querying the domain itself. The second is when a domain is in mixed mode. Universal security groups don't exist in a mixed mode domain, so there's no need to enumerate universal security groups.

- When a user logs on at a Windows 2000–based computer using a User Principal Name (UPN), the global catalog is referenced to determine the account that's associated with the UPN. If a global catalog server is unavailable, the user will fail the authentication.

Making the Decision

To ensure that global catalog servers are available for authentication purposes, consider the following when placing global catalog servers:

- Locate at least one global catalog server at each site. This ensures that clients will be able to contact a local global catalog server if the WAN link is unavailable. There's no additional WAN replication cost if additional global catalog servers are placed at the remote site. At each site one global catalog server will be nominated as the bridgehead server for global catalog replication. There won't be extra intersite replication related to the global catalog server.

Note   To configure a DC as a global catalog server you must use the Active Directory Sites And Services console. By editing the properties for the NTDS Settings for a DC, you can enable the Global Catalog check box.

- Ensure that the _msdcs.*forestrootdomain* DNS domain is available at all remote sites on a local DNS server. This ensures that the SRV resource records associated with global catalog servers are available when the WAN link isn't. You can implement the _msdcs.*forestrootdomain* DNS domain as an Active Directory–integrated zone in the forest root domain and as a secondary DNS zone in all other domains in the forest.
- Even in a single-domain environment, you must designate global catalog servers. Any LDAP queries against the entire forest will be sent to a global catalog server listening on TCP port 3268. TCP port 3268 is only available on a DC when it's configured as a global catalog server.

Applying the Decision

Market Florist's current network design has no local global catalog servers at the Winnipeg and Monterrey sites. At least one DC at each of the sites should be configured as a global catalog server to ensure that global catalog access isn't taking place over the WAN. If the WAN link became unavailable, all Windows 2000 clients would be authenticated using cached credentials.

In addition, the local DNS servers at each site should have a replica of the _msdcs.marketflorist.tld domain to ensure that authenticating clients can find a local global catalog server.

Planning PDC Emulator Placement

Windows NT 4.0, Windows 95, and Windows 98 clients connect to the PDC emulator for password changes, and Windows 95 and Windows 98 clients will connect to the PDC emulator for system policy application by default. If the DSClient software isn't installed on all Windows 95, Windows 98, and Windows NT client workstations, these clients will continue to depend on the PDC emulator for domain browse master functions, password changes, and system policy application.

Making the Decision

To reduce the dependency on the PDC emulator, you can take the following actions:

- Install the DSClient software so that Windows NT 4.0, Windows 95, and Windows 98 clients aren't as dependent on the PDC emulator for password changes. With the DSClient software loaded, down-level clients can change their passwords at any available DC.

- Ensure that system policy is configured to load balance the application of Group Policy as discussed earlier in this chapter. This ensures that system policy is applied from the authenticating DC, not the PDC emulator.

- Upgrade all Windows NT 4.0 BDCs to Windows 2000 DCs as soon as possible. Windows 2000 DCs use multimaster replication instead of depending on the PDC emulator for all Active Directory database changes.

- If the DSClient software isn't deployed, ensure that the PDC emulator is on a central portion of the network that's easily accessible from all remote sites.

Applying the Decision

The Market Florist network must ensure the quick deployment of the DSClient software to the client computers. The main location of the network that will benefit from the application of the DSClient software is the San Francisco site. This is because the PDC Emulator for the marketflorist.tld domain is located at the Seattle site and all Windows 95 and Windows NT 4.0 clients will perform password changes across the WAN link to Seattle without the DSClient software installed.

This isn't as much of an issue at the Monterrey and Winnipeg locations, because the PDC emulator for those domains will be located on the local network.

Lesson Summary

Server placement is the key design point for authentication services in a Windows 2000 network. Your design must include the placement of DNS servers, domain controllers, global catalog servers, and the PDC emulator to ensure that authentication requests are handled in a timely manner. If the services can't be contacted, it can result in logons with cached credentials and, in the worst case, failed logons.

Make sure that your network design includes the necessary services at each large site on the network. There will be cases where a site is too small to require localized network services, but make sure that your business and technical objectives allow for the risk of WAN-based authentication.

Activity: Analyzing Authentication Network Infrastructure

You're a consultant asked to troubleshoot authentication problems for your company. The organization is comprised of a central corporate office and a branch office that's connected to the remote office with a 128 K WAN link.

At the remote office, users are intermittently logged on using cached credentials even though a DC has been located at the remote site to authenticate users. The structure of the network is shown in Figure 3.12.

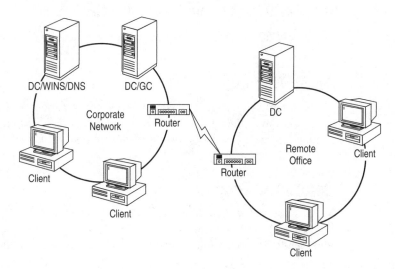

Figure 3.12   The network layout

Answer the following questions about this situation. The answers can be found in the appendix.

1. What would cause a user to be logged on using cached credentials?

2. Since cached credentials are used intermittently at logon for remote clients, how many domains must exist in the network?

3. What services must be added at the remote network to ensure that Windows 2000 clients can log on to the network?

4. Will down-level clients have problems at logon at the remote office?

Lab 3-1: Designing Authentication for the Network

Lab Objectives

This lab prepares you to design authentication for a Windows 2000 network by meeting the following objectives:

- Ensure availability of Kerberos authentication mechanisms in a Windows 2000 network
- Ensure secure authentication for down-level clients
- Determine placement of network services to optimize authentication in a Windows 2000 Network

About This Lab

This lab looks at designing authentication for a Windows 2000 network that contains Windows 2000, Windows NT, Windows 98, and Windows for Workgroups clients. The network is comprised of multiple sites that are connected using dedicated WAN links.

Before You Begin

Make sure you've completed reading the chapter material before starting the lab. For hints on how to design authentication security, pay close attention to the sections where the design decisions were applied throughout the chapter.

Scenario: Contoso Ltd.

Contoso Ltd., an international magazine sales company, wants to ensure that the highest form of security is used for authentication on its corporate network. You have been asked to design the Windows 2000 network to ensure that security is maintained during the authentication process.

Existing Network Configuration

The network is configured into three native-mode domains, as shown in Figure 3.13.

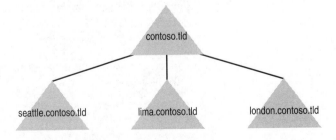

Figure 3.13   The Contoso Ltd. domain structure

Contoso uses a centralized management approach for Windows 2000 operation masters. The PDC emulator role for each domain is maintained on a domain controller at the London location. This ensures that the forest-wide administrators in London have ready access to the operation masters.

In addition to the corporate offices in London, Seattle, and Lima, there's an East Coast office in Tampa. The Tampa office users authenticate with the seattle.contoso.tld domain. The WAN links between the offices are configured as shown in Figure 3.14.

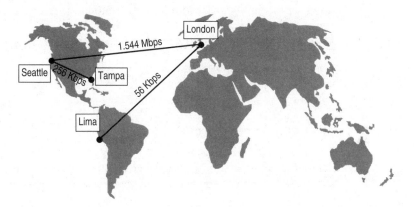

Figure 3.14   WAN links for the Contoso Ltd. office

Existing Network Server Placement

The network currently has network servers deployed as shown in the table below.

Location	Network Servers
Seattle	■ Three DCs for the seattle.contoso.tld are located at the Seattle office. ■ One of the DCs is configured as a global catalog server for the Seattle site.
Tampa	■ There are no DCs at the Tampa office.
London	■ Two DCs for the contoso.tld, seattle.contoso.tld, lima.contoso.tld, and london.contoso.tld domains are at the London location. ■ The PDC emulator for all four domains are at this location. ■ Two DCs are configured as global catalog servers for the London site. ■ Two DCs in the contoso.tld domain are configured as DNS servers. The DNS servers are authoritative for the contoso.tld domain and all subdomains.
Lima	■ Two DCs for the lima.contoso.tld are located at the Lima office.

Client Computer Details

Within Contoso, each office has a mix of Windows 2000, Windows NT 4.0, and Windows 98 client computers. The Lima office also has 10 Windows for Workgroups 3.11 client computers deployed. Each office has fewer than 1000 users. The Windows NT 4.0 Workstation computers have Windows NT 4.0 Service Pack 3 applied, and the Windows 98 clients don't have any service packs applied.

In all cases, both the computer and user accounts are located in the domain defined for the site in order to reduce authentication over WAN links.

Exercise 1: Designing Windows 2000 Client Authentication

This exercise will look at the design of Windows 2000 client authentication. Each of the Contoso network's four sites has Windows 2000 client computers that will require secure access to the corporate network.

Analyzing Server Placement

To ensure that authentication can take place for Windows 2000 clients, you must determine whether servers are placed on the network so that authentication can take place as desired. The answers to these questions can be found in the appendix.

1. Are there any issues for Windows 2000 computers having the PDC emulators for each domain located at the London office?

2. Are DCs placed correctly on the network to ensure local authentication at each remote office?

3. Are global catalog servers placed correctly on the network to ensure that cached credentials aren't used at authentication?

4. When the WAN link between the remote offices and the London office is unavailable, users can't locate resources on the network. What can you do to optimize network locator services for the Contoso network based on the current DNS design?

Analyzing Default Trust Relationships

The Contoso forest currently has four domains: contoso.tld, seattle.contoso.tld, lima.contoso.tld, and london.contoso.tld. This section looks at optimizing the trust relationships between the domains. The answers to these questions can be found in the appendix.

1. Based on the current domain structure, what default trust relationships are established for the contoso.tld forest?

2. If users in the seattle.contoso.tld domain frequently access resources in the London.contoso.tld domain, what can you do to optimize the Kerberos authentication process?

Exercise 2: Designing Down-Level Client Authentication

This exercise looks at the design issues that Contoso will face with the Windows 98, Windows NT 4.0, and Windows for Workgroups clients. The answers to these questions can be found in the appendix.

1. Based on the current client computer distribution, are there any security risks? Detail all security risks for authentication.

2. What do you need to do to reduce the security risk for authentication?

3. How does the deployment of the DSClient software improve performance?

4. Once you've deployed the DSClient software to all Windows 98 and Windows NT 4.0 clients, what changes must be made at the DCs?

Review

Answering the following questions will reinforce key information presented in this chapter. If you are unable to answer a question, review the appropriate lesson and then try the question again. Answers to the questions can be found in the appendix.

1. As network administrator, you've received many calls that authentication is failing on the network for several clients. On inspection, you find that the system log displays a 5502 error message saying that the time difference with the primary DC name exceeds the maximum allowed number of seconds. What action must you take?

2. How does the Kerberos Authentication Service Exchange differ from the Kerberos Ticket Granting Exchange?

3. You've decided to implement strong authentication on the network by using smart card logons. Are there any restrictions with smart card logons that will affect your design decision?

4. You've developed a three-tiered client server application. The application depends on running stored procedures at the security context of the user running the application. How does Kerberos provide this support to your application?

5. Your network has several Windows 98 computers deployed. You want to migrate these client computers to Windows 2000 by the end of the year. What interim step can you take to increase logon security and performance for the Windows 98 computers?

6. You've noticed that users at a remote site are continually logging on with cached credentials. New group memberships that have been created aren't taking effect. What could be causing this?

C H A P T E R   4

Planning a Microsoft Windows 2000 Administrative Structure

About This Chapter

The network users whom you designate as administrators will have additional privileges on the network. You must make sure that your security design determines which users need to be members of the administrative groups. Your security plan must include a process for verifying that only authorized users are members of the administrative groups. It must also provide steps to remove unauthorized accounts from the administrative groups.

Before You Begin

To complete this chapter, you must read the chapter scenario. This scenario is used throughout the chapter to apply the design decisions discussed in each lesson.

Chapter Scenario: Hanson Brothers

Hanson Brothers is a hockey equipment manufacturing company with a head office in Warroad, Minnesota. Hanson Brothers uses Microsoft Windows 2000 as its network operating system and currently uses a centralized administration model for user accounts. With its upcoming expansion to Boise, Idaho, and Calgary, Alberta, the company plans to decentralize the administration of user accounts.

To assist in the decentralization of management tasks in the network, you've been hired to assist the Hanson Brothers' Information Technology (IT) staff in designing their Active Directory directory service to support the required delegation of administration. You must also ensure that administration of the network doesn't weaken network security.

The Existing Network

All of Hanson Brothers' network operations are currently managed out of the head office in Warroad, but with the expansion to Boise and Calgary, the company plans to delegate account administration to these offices.

Figure 4.1 shows the network links that exist among Hanson Brothers' three offices.

Figure 4.1   The Hanson Brothers Wide Area Network

Both the Calgary and the Boise offices are connected to the Warroad office with T1 connections. The connections are currently experiencing 5 percent utilization of available network bandwidth.

Hanson Brothers' Active Directory Design

Hanson Brothers initially implemented Active Directory using a single domain (hansonbrothers.tld). The IT department wants to maintain a single domain for the entire organization in order to reduce the management requirements that would be involved if the organization implemented multiple domains.

All user accounts, computer accounts, and domain controllers (DCs) are currently stored in the default locations in Active Directory. Hanson Brothers realizes that to properly implement its planned single-domain model to allow for delegation of administration, they must create an organizational unit (OU) structure that will facilitate such delegation.

Hanson Brothers' Administrative Needs

In your meetings with the IT staff, you've determined the following requirements for administration of the network:

- Membership in administrative groups that can affect the domain and forest must be monitored regularly to ensure that no unauthorized membership exists. Specifically, the monitoring must include the following groups:
  - Domain Admins
  - Enterprise Admins
  - Schema Admins
  - Administrators
- Hanson Brothers maintains a help desk around the clock. The help desk personnel must be able to reset passwords and unlock any locked-out user accounts.
- Hanson Brothers uses a Human Resources program that stores its data in Active Directory. The members of the Human Resources department must be able to modify Human Resources–specific attributes of all users in the organization.
- Local administrators in Boise and Calgary must be able to manage all user and computer accounts at their location. To ensure maximum security, the administrators must be able to manage accounts only at their local offices, and not at any of the other two offices.
- At the Boise office, one of the network administrators uses a UNIX Scalable Processor Architecture (SPARC) workstation as that person's primary desktop. This administrator wishes to perform network management functions from the UNIX workstation.

The Central Administration Team

A central IT team at the Warroad office designed Hanson Brothers' corporate network. The group split network administration tasks among themselves and defined the following roles and tasks, shown in Table 4.1.

Table 4.1   Administrative Roles for Hanson Brothers Central IT Team

IT Team Member	Roles
Stephanie Conroy	Backups and Group Policy management
Derek Graham	Domain Name System (DNS) and Dynamic Host Configuration Protocol (DHCP) management
Steve Masters	Management of all user accounts except administrative accounts
Kim Hightower	Restoration of network backups
Yvonne Schleger	Schema design
Eric Miller	Backup and restore management, share management, manage services

Hanson Brothers' Current Issues

It's believed that some network administrators are using their administrative accounts for day-to-day activities on the network. A few months ago, an account's password was changed from an administrator's console when the administrator forgot to lock the computer during the lunch hour. Due to the security issues, you must include the following items in your administrative security design:

- Administrators must have two accounts for working on the network. One would be used for administrative tasks and the second would be used for day-to-day activities.

- Accounts with a forest-wide scope must be restricted to specific workstations.

- It should be easy to determine whether an account on the network is an administrative account or a day-to-day user account.

Lesson 1: Planning Administrative Group Membership

When designing security for your network, you must consider the membership requirements for Windows 2000 administrative groups. Administrators are able to perform tasks that could change your network's security design. You must carefully consider the criteria for membership in these groups (and their component groups) to ensure that security can't be weakened on the network.

After this lesson, you will be able to

- Plan membership within Windows 2000 administrative groups and identify when to create custom administrative groups

Estimated lesson time: 30 minutes

Designing Default Administrative Group Membership

Windows 2000 contains several predefined administrative groups. When designing security for your Windows 2000 network, you must determine appropriate membership in each group. By understanding the capabilities of each group and assigning the correct memberships, you can ensure that users aren't assigned excess privileges on the Windows 2000 network.

The Default Windows 2000 Administrative Groups

Several default groups exist within Active Directory and are assigned rights on the network. Understanding the rights each group is assigned can assist you in determining the appropriate administrative group memberships within your Active Directory.

Table 4.2 identifies the default administrative groups that exist in a Windows 2000 network.

Table 4.2   The Default Windows 2000 Administrative Groups

Group Name	Group Type	Purpose
Enterprise Admins	Universal	Exists only within the forest root domain. Has forest-wide administrative scope. Members of this group are allowed to modify Enterprise-wide configuration. Membership must be monitored at all times.
Schema Admins	Universal	Exists only within the forest root domain. Members can make changes to the forest schema, including the modification of existing attributes and classes or the addition of new attributes or classes.

Table 4.2   The Default Windows 2000 Administrative Groups   *(continued)*

Group Name	Group Type	Purpose
Domain Admins	Global	A member of the Administrators group within each domain of the forest. When a member server or workstation joins the domain, the Domain Admins group is added as a member of the local Administrators group. Members can administer the domain in which they are defined. Additionally, members of the Domain Admins group in the forest root domain are permitted to modify membership of the Enterprise Admins or Schema Admins groups as they exist in the forest root domain.
Group Policy Creator Owners	Global	Members are allowed to create new Group Policy objects in Active Directory.
Administrators	Domain Local	Members are allowed to fully manage the domain in which the group exists, including management of services and accounts within Active Directory.
Power Users	Local Group	Exists only on nondomain controllers. Members are allowed to manage users and groups in the local SAM database, modify or delete accounts that they created, and manage membership in the Users, Guests, and Power Users groups. Power Users also can install most applications; create, manage, and delete local printers; and create and delete file shares.
Account Operators	Domain Local	Members of this group can create, modify, or delete accounts for users, groups, and computers in any container within the domain where the Account Operators group exists. The only exceptions are the Builtin container and the Domain Controllers OU. The only groups that Account Operators are prohibited from managing are the Administrators and Domain Admins groups. In the forest root domain, members can't modify the properties of the Enterprise Admins or Schema Admins groups.
Server Operators	Domain Local	Members are allowed to log on locally at a server, manage network shares, stop and start services, back up and restore data, format hard disk drives, and shut down the computer.

Group Name	Group Type	Purpose
Print Operators	Domain Local	Members can manage printers and printer queues, including managing print jobs that weren't submitted by the member.
Backup Operators	Local	Members are allowed to back up and restore all files on the computer. Members aren't subject to permissions on files when performing the backup. Members also can log on locally and shut down the computer.
Replicators	Domain Local	In Windows NT domains, it's a built-in group used by the File Replication service on DCs.
DHCP Administrators	Domain Local	Members can administer DHCP services within the domain where the group exists. This group is created automatically when the DHCP service is installed.
DNS Admins	Domain Local	Members can administer DNS services in the domain where the group is defined. This group has members in any domain where the DNS service is installed.
WINS Admins	Domain Local	Members can administer the Windows Internet Naming Service (WINS) service within the domain where the group is defined. This group is *not* created automatically when the WINS service is installed in a domain.
DNSUpdate Proxy	Global	Members can create DNS resource records without taking ownership of the DNS resource records. Generally, DHCP servers are made members of this group to ensure that a client workstation using Windows 95, Windows 98, or Windows NT can take ownership of the resource record after the computers are upgraded to Windows 2000.
Pre–Windows 2000 Compatible Access	Domain Local	Members can query Active Directory using a NULL session. During the DCPROMO process, which installs and configures Active Directory to promote a server to a DC, if the option to enable pre–Windows 2000 compatible access for remote access is enabled, the Everyone group is added as a member to this group.

Note   Unless otherwise noted, Windows NT refers to versions 3.51 and 4.0.

Assessing Administrative Group Membership Design

Poor administrative group design can hurt your network security. If you don't control administrative group membership, your network security can be severely compromised.

In a Windows 2000 network you can use two common strategies to control the membership of Windows 2000 administrative groups. The two methods are

- Periodically audit the membership of administrative group membership
- Implement restricted groups in Group Policy to control membership in administrative groups

Auditing Group Membership

You can use Windows 2000 auditing and periodic manual audits to ensure that group membership is as it should be in your Windows 2000 network. Your network must determine which groups must be periodically audited.

The audit must ensure that both users directly configured as members of the administrative group and the membership of any composite groups are verified against documented membership. You can do this either by performing regularly scheduled manual inspection of the administrative groups or by using third-party products that report group memberships to precustomized reports.

Using Third-Party Tools to Determine Group Membership

You can use several alternatives to report on group memberships in a Windows 2000 network. Common methods used in the industry include the following:

- **SomarSoft's Dumpevt.** The Dumpevt utility (formerly known as DumpACL) is commonly used to report on the configured discretionary access control lists (DACLs) that are defined for file and share resources. In addition, this software reports on group memberships for all groups within Active Directory. You can download this utility for free at *www.somarsoft.com/*.

- **Windows Scripting Host.** You can use the Windows Scripting Host (WSH) to generate scripts that report on group membership. Many example scripts are available at *cwashington.netreach.net/*.

Whatever method you choose, ensuring that the reports are run at regular intervals and are examined to verify that no anomalies exist in the administrative group memberships will prevent excess rights from being applied to unauthorized user accounts.

You must determine which group meets your needs. Consider that the Account Operators and Server Operators are assigned only a subset of the privileges of the Administrators group. If a user is only required to perform user and group management, then assign her membership only in Account Operators.

Using Restricted Groups to Maintain Group Memberships

If you want to limit membership within a specific group, you can use the Restricted Groups option within Group Policy to predefine membership within the groups. This Group Policy ensures that membership matches the defined membership. If members are added or deleted, the Group Policy will ensure that the desired membership is reestablished.

You can apply Restricted Groups policy at the site, domain, or OU level. When applied, the Restricted Groups policy setting provides two forms of protection for a defined group, as shown in Figure 4.2.

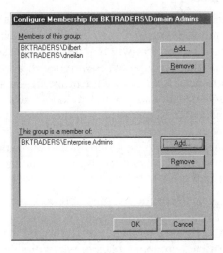

Figure 4.2   Defining both the membership within the group and the groups that the group can be a member of for a restricted group

- It protects membership in the group. Within restricted groups, you can define which accounts can be members of the group. If the membership is changed, the next time that Group Policy is applied it will modify the membership to match the membership defined in the policy.

Note   Group Policy will be automatically applied to DCs every 5 minutes. Windows 2000 Professional workstations and Windows 2000 member servers that are members of the domain will apply the computer policies every 90 minutes by default. You can force the application of the security policy by running the following command from the command prompt at the target workstation: **SECEDIT/ REFRESHPOLICY MACHINE_POLICY/ENFORCE.**

- It limits groups that the restricted group can be a member of. In addition to protecting the membership within the restricted group, you can also configure what groups the restricted group can be a member of. This prevents security from being modified by adding the restricted group to an administrative group that isn't desired.

Making the Decision

When making your decision on administrative group design, you must do the following:

- Determine exactly who must be a member of each administrative group. By predetermining group membership and documenting the proposed membership, you can use this documentation to periodically audit the group membership. By having the membership documented, you can ensure that membership hasn't been modified.

- Don't grant membership to a group that provides excess privileges. When making your administrative group membership decisions, always determine exactly what rights the member will require. Don't make the user account a member of a group that provides excess privileges. For example, if you wish the user account to be able to modify the properties of all nonadministrative groups, either use delegation of administration to OUs where the user accounts exist or make the user a member of the Account Operators group. Don't make the user a member of the Administrators or Domain Admins security groups. Membership in these groups would allow the user to perform the desired tasks but would also grant the user rights on the network that are beyond the desired rights.

- Use restricted groups to ensure that only approved membership is maintained. Restricted groups ensure that membership is maintained to match your desired memberships. Be sure to document all desired memberships and to require that the restricted group membership definition be modified if the desired membership changes.

- Ensure that membership is audited for these groups. You should periodically audit all administrative group membership, either manually or with automated reporting utilities. Whatever method you select, the audit should occur at regularly scheduled intervals.

- Watch membership in the forest root domain's Domain Admins group. Within a forest, the Domain Admins group in the forest root domain is able to modify the membership of the Enterprise Admins and Schema Admins groups. Due to the forest-wide implications, you must carefully monitor membership in these groups to ensure that only authorized memberships exist.

Applying the Decision

The decisions that Hanson Brothers faces include determining membership in the administrative groups for the Central IT team and ensuring that membership is guarded and audited for enterprise-level administrative groups.

Based on the role definitions provided in the chapter scenario, you must define the administrative group membership for Hanson Brothers, shown in Table 4.3.

Table 4.3   Administrative Group Memberships for Hanson Brothers

Group	Membership
Enterprise Admins	Only the default administration account. The account must be restricted further to be used at only specific locations on the network.
DNSAdmins	Derek Graham
DHCP Administrators	Derek Graham
Account Operators	Steve Masters
Schema Admins	Yvonne Schleger
Server Operators	Eric Miller
Group Policy Creator Owners	Stephanie Conroy

Note that in the table no members are assigned to the Backup Operators group. This is because Hanson Brothers requires that the Backup and Restore privileges be divided between Stephanie Conroy and Kim Hightower. Membership in the Backup Operators group would be an excess assignment of user rights.

The other requirement you must manage is the membership of the Domain Admins, Enterprise Admins, Schema Admins, and Administrators groups. You can manage these groups by

- Defining restricted groups in Group Policy
- Auditing success and failure events for account management
- Auditing membership in these groups at regular intervals

For restricted groups, you can set the properties for Hanson Brothers as shown in Table 4.4 to ensure that group membership isn't changed from the desired membership. To ensure that the group memberships are maintained on the domain, the Restricted Groups policy must be deployed at the Domain Controllers OU for Hanson Brothers.

Table 4.4   Restricted Group Definitions for Hanson Brothers

Group	Members	Member of
Domain Admins	▪ Administrator	▪ Administrators ▪ Enterprise Admins
Enterprise Admins	▪ Administrator	None
Schema Admins	▪ Administrator ▪ Yvonne Schleger	None
Administrators	▪ Domain Admins ▪ Enterprise Admins ▪ Administrators	None

Designing Custom Administrative Groups

Sometimes you will require a group to have only a subset of the rights that an administrative group is assigned. For example, your security policy may require that the backup and restore privileges are separated. In Windows 2000 the Backup Operators group provides both privileges.

By creating two custom groups and assigning one group the right to back up files and the other group to restore files, as illustrated in Figure 4.3, you can reduce the risk associated with a single user account having the rights to back up and restore files from the network.

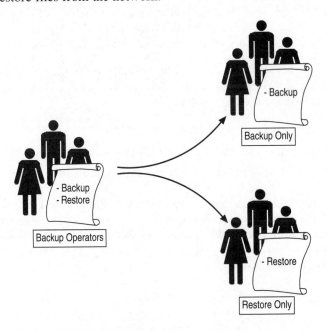

Figure 4.3   Splitting backup rights between a custom Backup and custom Restore group

Note   The main concern that network administrators have with the mixing of the rights to back up and restore files is that an account with the right to back up files can back up all files on the network. This includes files that the account may not have access to on the network.

Determining When to Create Custom Groups

The key to creating custom administrative groups is to determine exactly which rights a specific account requires. One group that has a large number of rights on a network is the Enterprise Admins universal group in the forest root domain. An organization will often create custom groups to delegate only specific rights to an account, rather than make the account a member of the Enterprise Admins group and provide the account with excess privileges.

To carry this example further, membership in the Enterprise Admins group is required to perform the following security tasks in a Windows 2000 forest:

- Create new domains and new DCs in the forest. Whenever a new domain or DC is added to an existing forest, a member of the Enterprise Admins group (or at least their credentials) must normally be provided to execute the Dcpromo process. By using Ntdsutil to create the necessary cross-reference and server objects in Active Directory in advance, a member of the Enterprise Admins group can allow users who aren't members to perform the actual Dcpromo process.

Note   The Enterprise Admins must create the domains and servers in advance by using the domain management set of commands in Ntdsutil. Within this menu, they can create the domain cross-reference object by using the following command: **PRECREATE %1 %2**, where %1 is the name of the domain to create and %2 is the name of the DC that will be added to the domain.

- Authorize Remote Installation Services (RIS) and DHCP servers in Active Directory. To authorize a RIS server in Active Directory, you must log on with an account that's a member of the Enterprise Admins group in the forest where you want the RIS server to be authorized. By default, members of the Enterprise Admins group are the only users who can authorize DHCP/RIS servers. Before a RIS server can accept requests, you must authorize it to run. To authorize a RIS server in Active Directory, you must log on with an account that's a member of the Enterprise Admins group in the forest where you want the RIS server to be authorized. By default, members of the Enterprise Admins group are the only users who can authorize DHCP/RIS servers by default. This right can be delegated in Active Directory.

- Install Enterprise Certification Authorities. Only members of the Enterprise Administrators group are allowed to create Enterprise Certification Authorities. This is because the creation of an Enterprise CA requires that the account performing the installation be able to create objects in the CN=Public Key Services, CN=Service, CN=Configuration subtree. This right can't be delegated to other users or groups in Active Directory.

- Manage sites and subnets. By default, only Enterprise Administrators are allowed to create new site or subnet objects to design replication for your Windows 2000 network. This right can be delegated by delegating the right to create new objects in the CN=Sites, CN=Configuration subtree.

Making the Decision

You should base your decision on whether to create custom security groups for the purpose of administration in your Active Directory on the following guidelines:

- Determine that an existing administrative security group doesn't meet your security requirements. This can be one of two scenarios. Either the existing security groups don't offer sufficient rights for the tasks that are required or the existing groups offer excess rights. The assignment of excess rights is considered a weakness in security.

- Determine which rights are required by the custom administrative groups. By testing and iteration, you must determine what areas of Active Directory, the NT file system (NTFS), and possibly the registry keys that the custom administrative group will require elevated privileges to access. By determining these rights, you ensure that excess privileges aren't assigned.

- Determine if the necessary administrative rights can be delegated. If administrative delegation is supported, you can develop your OU design to facilitate delegation of administration either to all objects, only specific objects, or only for specific attributes.

- Determine which objects are accessed by the permissions. This will help you to set the DACL on these objects to permit the newly created group to access the object with the necessary permissions.

- Create a domain local group that will be assigned the determined permissions and rights. By creating a group that will be assigned the desired rights and permissions, you can test the designed permissions and rights by creating a user account that's a member only of the newly created domain local group. This way, other group memberships don't affect the testing of rights and permission assignments.

Applying the Decision

Hanson Brothers must create custom administration groups to meet the following requirements outlined in this chapter's case scenario:

- **Help desk personnel.** You must create a custom domain local group that contains all the staff that work at the help desk. This custom group can then be given the ability to reset passwords and clear the account lockout attribute for all user accounts. You do this by performing the delegation at the hansonbrothers.tld domain.

- **Human Resources.** You must also create a custom domain local group for members of the Human Resources department. At the hansonbrothers.tld domain, this group must be given the ability to modify all Human Resources–related attributes, such as address and home phone number.

- **BoiseAdmins and CalgaryAdmins.** You must create a custom domain local group for administrators at each office, and then give these custom groups the ability to manage both user and computer objects, as shown in Figure 4.4.

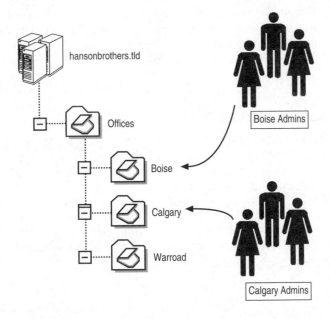

Figure 4.4   OU structure necessary to delegate administration to the remote offices

- **BackupsAdmins.** This domain local group would be assigned the user right to Backup Files And Directories, as illustrated in Figure 4.5. If Stephanie Conroy is required to back up only Domain Controllers, then this user right must be applied at the Domain Controllers OU. If the requirement is to back up all Windows 2000–based computers, then this user right must be assigned at both the Domain Controllers OU in the Default Domain Controller Group Policy object and at the Domain in the Default Domain Group Policy object.

Figure 4.5 Assigning a Custom Local group the Backup Files And Directories right

- **RestoreAdmins.** This domain local group would be assigned the user right to Restore Files And Directories. Assuming that Kim Hightower would have to restore backup data to any Windows 2000–based computer in the network, this user right must be assigned at both the Domain and the Domain Controllers OU.

Lesson Summary

When designing the administrative group structure for your forest, you must make sure that membership is designed not to grant excess rights on the network. You do this by only assigning security principals to an administrative group that provides the required rights on the network. Don't just add the security principal to the Administrator or Domain Admins group because it "works."

By using the restricted groups in Group Policy and performing regular audits of administrative groups, you can verify that only authorized users are members of administrative groups.

Lesson 2: Securing Administrative Access to the Network

Once you've designed the groups that will be allowed to perform administrative tasks on your network, the next phase of your security plan is to design how these administrative accounts may be used on the network. This includes planning restrictions on the use of administrative accounts and planning methods that can be used to allow administrative access.

After this lesson, you will be able to

- Plan methods for administrators to access the network and securely perform administrative tasks

Estimated lesson time: 30 minutes

Designing Secure Administrative Access

You can use several methods to secure how administrators can access the network. These include

- **Requiring smart card logon.** You can use smart cards to restrict logon to a specific management location. Only management stations will have the necessary smart card reader. You can lock the smart card in a safe that requires two people to open it to access the smart card or to access the PIN for the smart card for unlocking the private key on the card. You can also restrict logon to require a smart card for authentication in the user account's properties.

- **Restricting which workstation administrators can log on to.** This option requires that NetBIOS is supported on the network, but it can restrict logon to specific management stations using NetBIOS. If logon is attempted from a different location, the logon attempt will fail. These workstations can be located in a restricted part of the office.

- **Configuring logon hours.** You can restrict an administration account to usage only at specific hours. You can do this when policy requires that specific administrative tasks must take place at specific times. For example, the addition of new domains in the forest must take place after business hours so it won't affect bandwidth due to initial replication to the new domain.

- **Renaming the default administrator account.** While not the utmost in security, this prevents an attacker from guessing that the administrator account is named Administrator. This ensures that if an attacker is attempting to compromise the administrator account, they must determine the account name before attempting to guess the password.

- **Enforcing strong passwords.** Make sure that the administrator accounts use complex passwords. You could enforce this through domain account policy, but that would affect all users of the network. In general, administrator accounts should use a more restrictive password policy than typical user accounts. One organization uses a password for the admin account that's more than 30 characters long, uses a mix of uppercase, lowercase, and symbols, and is changed every 30 days.

Making the Decision

In a high-security network, you can use the decision matrix shown in Table 4.5 to restrict administrative access to the network.

Table 4.5   Restricting Administrative Access

To	Do the Following
Restrict administrative access to specific workstations	■ Implement workstation restrictions so that only specific workstations can be used by administrative accounts. ■ Implement smart card authentication for administrative accounts and install smart card readers only at desired workstations.
Protect administrative passwords	■ Manually implement complex passwords for the administrator account that exceed the domain account policy. ■ Implement smart card logon that doesn't expose the password of the administrator account.
Protect the administrator account from being compromised	■ Rename the administrator account. Don't use easily guessed accounts. ■ Don't leave the administrator account logged on at a workstation. ■ Require smart card logon for the administrator account and store the smart card in a restricted location, such as a safe. ■ Don't make day-to-day accounts administrators of the network. Require that each administrator have a day-to-day account for normal network access.

Applying the Decision

Hanson Brothers can take several actions to secure administrative access to their network. These include

- **Renaming the Administrator account.** A common attack that's performed against networks is to use default accounts that ship with the operating system. For example, the Administrator account has the most rights in a Windows 2000 network. By renaming the Administrator account, you can reduce the chance that the Administrator account will be used to attack the network.

Maintaining an Alternative Administrator Account

In some networks, after the Administrator account is renamed, a network administrator will create a new account named Administrator. But instead of having administrative rights on the network, this account is only a member of the Domain Guest group. By mixing the creation of a nonadministrative Administrator account with a strategy of auditing account logon failures and successes, you can determine if someone is attempting to use the Administrator account.

- **Creating dedicated administrative accounts.** Rather than assigning the day-to-day user accounts for the six administrators into the administrative groups on the network, you can create dedicated administrative accounts that are used to perform administrative tasks. To ensure that these accounts are recognizable on the network, you could create the accounts using a common prefix, such as "a_". For example, you could create two accounts for Steve Master: smaster for day-to-day activities and a_smaster for administrative tasks.

- **Protecting administrative accounts.** If additional administrative accounts are added to the Domain Admins, Administrators, or Enterprise Admins groups, further restriction can be made to limit use of these accounts to specific workstations. Restrictions can include restricting the account to specific administrative workstations or requiring a smart card for logon, as shown in Figure 4.6.

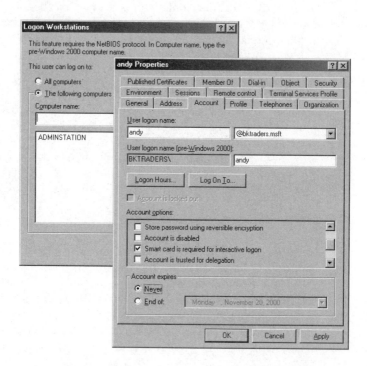

Figure 4.6   Restricting administrators to a specific computer by workstation restrictions or by requiring smart card logon

Note   The default Administrator account can't be restricted to specific workstations or required to use a smart card for logon. To protect this account, a complex password must be implemented along with additional security processes, such as storage of the password in a location like a central safe in the IT department.

Designing Secondary Access

Windows 2000 allows administrative tasks to be launched at a higher security level than the current user's account. This is done by providing alternate credentials to the RunAs service when launching the administrative tasks.

Understanding the RunAs Service

The RunAs service allows you to launch processes under a different security context. While the user remains logged on using her normal day-to-day account, the process that she launches using the RunAs service runs under the security context of the provided user account. Typically, this account is one with the required administrative privileges on the network.

You can use several methods to launch a process by using the RunAs service. These include

- **Holding the Sʜɪꜰᴛ key while right-clicking a shortcut.** This enables the RunAs option on the pop-up menu. The user can then provide alternative credentials for running the application, as shown in Figure 4.7.

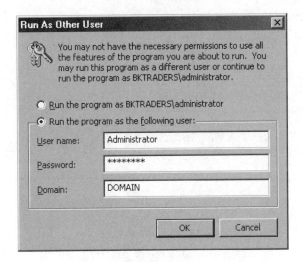

Figure 4.7   Providing alternative credentials when running an application

- **Using the RUNAS command at a command prompt.** The RUNAS command allows you to provide both the alternative credentials and the application that you wish to run using the alternative credentials. The syntax of the command is as follows:

```
RUNAS /user:UserName program
```

For example, if you wished to launch Active Directory Users And Computers under the security context of administrator of the domain nwtraders.tld, you would use the following command:

```
RUNAS /user:administrator@nwtraders.tld "mmc
c:\winnt\system32\dsa.msc"
```

The RunAs service would then prompt you for the administrator@nwtraders.tld account password before launching the Active Directory Users And Computers console.

- **Creating administrative scripts.** You can create administrative scripts that launch administrative processes at a higher security context. To further secure these scripts, you can protect access to them by configuring the DACLs on the scripts to allow only approved users to access the scripts.

- **Changing a shortcut's properties.** Within the property pages of a shortcut, you can configure the shortcut to Run As A Different User, as shown in Figure 4.8. This action brings up the Run As Another User dialog box and allows you to provide alternative credentials.

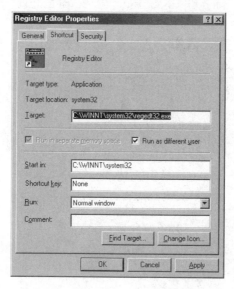

Figure 4.8   Configuring a shortcut to use alternative credentials

To distinguish administrator accounts from everyday accounts, you can require all administrator accounts to use a prefix such as a_. For example, if my day-to-day account is johndoe, then my matching administrative account would be a_johndoe. This allows for auditing to determine which administrator performed the task.

Note   If tasks are launched using the RunAs service, you can determine which security context an application is running in by using the *Microsoft Windows 2000 Resource Kit* utility Pulist.exe. This displays a list of current running processes and the user account used to launch each process. Alternatively, if Terminal Service is loaded, you can configure the Task Manager to display the username column to show the security context of each running process.

Making the Decision

If you plan to implement the RunAs service to allow processes to be run under alternative security credentials, you must include the following considerations in your security design:

- The RunAs service doesn't provide facilities for smart card logon. The account used to authenticate with the RunAs service can't require smart card logon because the RunAs interface doesn't provide support for the insert of a smart card. All credentials must be manually typed into the interface.

- There is more than one way to launch the RunAs service. The RunAs service can be launched either from the command prompt, a shortcut's properties, or by right-clicking a shortcut and selecting RunAs from the pop-up menu. You and all other administrators must determine the method that works best. Remember that whatever method you choose, the final result is the same.

- Use a standard prefix for administrative accounts. If you use a standard prefix for administrative accounts, the administrative accounts can be recognized when they're used on the network simply by inspecting the user's logon name.

- Create a policy for the usage of administrative accounts on the network. Ensure that administrative accounts aren't used for day-to-day activities and are restricted to performing administrative tasks.

Applying the Decision

Hanson Brothers could define a policy requiring all users with administrative accounts on the network to use the RunAs service to launch administrative tasks rather than logging on directly to the network. Because the process then runs in the security context of the administrative task, the task can be performed without having to log off the network and then log on using the administrative account.

The only scenario where this wouldn't work would be any administrative accounts that are defined to require smart card logon. If an account is defined to require smart card logon, it can't be used for the RunAs service. This is because the interface for the RunAs service doesn't support the use of smart cards.

Designing Telnet Administration

Some tasks can be performed from a command prompt. To allow remote administration using these command line tools, you can use the Telnet Service that ships with Windows 2000. You can use the Telnet Service only to run text-based utilities such as scripts and batch files. If the utility requires a graphical interface, you must deploy alternative methods, such as RunAs or Terminal Services.

Your security plan must take into account that Telnet uses clear text for the transmission of authentication and screen data by default. In Windows 2000 you can protect authentication credentials by configuring the Telnet Service to use NTLM authentication. This protects the password used to access the Telnet service but restricts access to the Telnet Service and prevents UNIX clients from accessing the service.

To protect all data in the Telnet sessions, you must configure IPSec to encrypt all data transmitted between the client workstation running the Telnet client and the Telnet Service. You do this by creating an IPSec filter that requires encryption for all connections to TCP port 23 on the Telnet Server. By using IPSec Encapsulating Security Payloads (ESP), you can encrypt all data transmitted between the client and the server. This doesn't require a modified Telnet client.

Making the Decision

You can't use Telnet administration in all circumstances. Remember that Telnet assumes that text-based administration is taking place. When you design administrative access by using Telnet, use the following considerations when you make your security plan:

- All management commands can be performed from a text-based utility. This includes script files, batch files, and management utilities such as Netsh.exe and Netdiag.exe.

- You can use NTLM authentication to protect the authentication credentials when transmitted to the Telnet Services. NTLM can only be used by clients that support the NTLM protocol for authentication. This can exclude UNIX clients from using Telnet.

Note   You can configure Telnet authentication methods by using Telnet Server Administration from Administrative Tools. Within the tool you can configure the Telnet server to use either clear-text authentication, NTLM authentication, or to first attempt NTLM authentication but fall back to clear text if required.

- Use IPSec to encrypt all data transmitted between the client and server to prevent inspection of the data as it's transmitted. Remember that the use of NTLM only protects the credentials provided during authentication. All other information entered into the Telnet session is passed in clear text across the network.

Applying the Decision

Hanson Brothers can use Telnet for network administration only in specific cases. As discussed, Telnet can be used only for text-based utilities. The *Microsoft Windows 2000 Server Resource Kit* does provide several utilities that you can use to manage Windows 2000 services from the command line. These include Netsh and Dnscmd.

For Hanson Brothers, the Telnet service must not be configured to use NTLM for authentication. This is because there's an administrator who uses a UNIX SPARC workstation, which won't support NTLM authentication. If additional security were required for administration from this station, IPSec would be required to encrypt all Telnet transmissions to and from the Telnet server where the administration takes place.

Designing Terminal Services Administration

You can install Terminal Services on a Windows 2000 Server to allow administration of a computer from a remote location. The Terminal Services session provides a virtual desktop that's running within the memory space of the server hosting the Terminal Services session.

The advantage of Terminal Services over other methods of remote administration is that the client computer doesn't have to be running the Windows 2000 operating system. Windows 95, Windows 98, and Windows NT clients can all be used to run the Terminal Services Client. In addition, Microsoft released the Terminal Services Advanced Client around the same time as the Windows 2000 Service Pack 1. This ActiveX control allows clients running Microsoft Internet Explorer to connect to a terminal server without loading any client software locally.

Note   You can download the Terminal Services Advanced Client by going to *www.microsoft.com* and searching for "Terminal Services Advanced Client."

Assessing Terminal Services Administration

You can install Terminal Services in one of two modes. Application mode allows multiple connections by regular user accounts (as long as they've been granted Terminal Service access in Active Directory Users And Computers). For remote administration, it's preferable to configure Terminal Services to run in Remote Administration mode.

Remote Administration mode has two key benefits when you're designing secure administration of the network. First, it's limited to only two concurrent connections. Second, by default, only members of the Administrators group are allowed to connect to the terminal server. This ensures that only administrators of the network can utilize the terminal server.

If the terminal server must run in Application mode, you can configure additional security by applying the Notssid.inf security template, which removes the Terminal Services ID (TSInternetUser) from all DACLs. This user is normally used to ensure that all Terminal Services users can access particular resources. Rather than having a common SID that allows all Terminal Services users access to resources, access is instead based on the individual user accounts of the Terminal

Services users. This ensures that security is based only on the individual user accounts and not on the state of the user.

Making the Decision

When designing network administration by using Terminal Services, you can use Table 4.6 to finalize your security design for Terminal Service access.

Table 4.6   Securing Terminal Server Access

To	Do the following
Limit what utilities can be that run by a Terminal Services client	• Create a custom desktop and Start menu profile will be used by the Terminal Service client.
Restrict access to Terminal Services to only administrative personnel	• Configure Terminal Services to use Remote Administration mode. This restricts access to only the members of the Administrators group.
Secure transmission of data between the Terminal Services client and the terminal server	• Configure the encryption level for the Terminal Services session to be medium or high security. Both medium and high security ensure that data is encrypted in both directions between the client and the server. High security utilizes 128-bit encryption, while medium encryption uses either 40-bit or 56-bit encryption, depending on the client.
Determine Terminal Service access based on individual user permissions	• Apply the Notssid.inf security configuration template to the terminal server.
Prevent excess rights to DCs	• Don't install Terminal Services on a DC. This requires the Terminal Service users to have the Logon Locally right, which means that they can log on locally at all DCs.
Allow access to Terminal Services from the widest range of platforms	• Install the Terminal Services Advanced Client on a Web server to allow all Internet Explorer clients to connect to the terminal server by downloading the ActiveX control that allows access to the terminal server.

Applying the Decision

For Hanson Brothers, Terminal Services could be restricted to administrators of the network by configuring Terminal Service to use Remote Administration mode. This, by default, restricts Terminal Services to only members of the Administrators domain local group.

The other advantage of Terminal Services is that the new Terminal Services Advanced Client could be deployed. This would allow clients running other operating systems (but using Internet Explorer) to perform administrative tasks on the Windows 2000 domain from the alternative client operating system computer.

This would be another alternative to providing administrative capabilities to the administrator using a UNIX SPARC workstation.

Note The only accounts that couldn't be used in the Terminal Services client would be administrative accounts that are required to use smart cards for authentication. Smart card authentication isn't supported for Terminal Services.

Lesson Summary

The task of designing network administration involves not only deciding who will be an administrator of the network, but also restricting where administration can take place on the network.

Depending on the methods that you allow for network administration, you can restrict administration tasks to specific utilities, such as Terminal Services or Telnet Services.

Activity: Administering the Network

Your organization has decided to develop guidelines for remote administration of the network. In an earlier review you found that most administrators had taken the steps to make their day-to-day accounts members of the Administrators or Domain Admins groups to give them administrative permissions on the network.

Your goal is to match the potential remote administrative methods to the tasks that are presented to you by circling the best remote administration method. Also, in the space provided, furnish an analysis of why you made your decision. Answers to these questions can be found in the appendix.

Tasks	Remote Administration Method
Create a new user account by using Active Directory Users And Computers	a. RUNAS command b. Telnet Service c. Terminal Services d. Can't use Remote Administration in this scenario
What factors affected your decision?	
Recover an encrypted file using the domain's EFS Recovery account	a. RUNAS command b. Telnet Service c. Terminal Services d. Can't use Remote Administration in this scenario
What factors affected your decision?	
Run a batch file command that requires administrative access to the network	a. RUNAS command b. Telnet Service c. Terminal Services d. Can't use Remote Administration in this scenario
What factors affected your decision?	

Tasks	Remote Administration Method
Manage a Certification Authority from a Windows 95 or Windows 98 computer	a. RUNAS command b. Telnet Service c. Terminal Services d. Can't use Remote Administration in this scenario

What factors affected your decision?

Run an administrative process by using an account that requires a smart card for authentication	a. RUNAS command b. Telnet Service c. Terminal Services d. Can't use Remote Administration in this scenario

What factors affected your decision?

Verify whether a user account is locked out without interrupting an application that's running an hour-long process	a. RUNAS command b. Telnet Service c. Terminal Services d. Can't use Remote Administration in this scenario

What factors affected your decision?

Lab 4-1: Designing Administration for a Microsoft Windows 2000 Network

Lab Objectives

This lab prepares you to design administration of a Windows 2000 network by meeting the following objectives:

- Designing the membership of the default administrative groups in Windows 2000
- Planning a method to ensure that administrative group membership isn't modified by adding unauthorized security principals to the groups
- Designing remote administration methods for managing the network

About This Lab

This lab looks at designing administration of a Windows 2000 network. It will look at designing the membership of the default administrative groups, identifying when to create custom administrative groups, and designing remote administration of the network.

Before You Begin

Make sure that you've completed reading the chapter material before starting the lab. Pay close attention to the sections where the design decisions were applied throughout the chapter for information on building your administrative structure.

Scenario: Contoso Ltd.

Contoso Ltd., an international magazine sales company, wants to design the administration of its network. When the proposal was originally distributed to the IT department, all the IT department members asked for their accounts to have administrative capabilities on the network. You've been hired to assist in determining group membership design for Contoso to ensure that members of the IT department aren't granted excess rights on the network.

Domain Structure

Contoso's Active Directory design is comprised of four domains: contoso.tld, seattle.contoso.tld, lima.contoso.tld, and london.contoso.tld as shown in Figure 4.9.

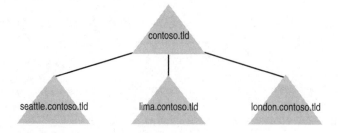

Figure 4.9   The Contoso Ltd. domain structure

The following table outlines the administrative tasks that are assigned to the members of the Contoso IT department.

IT Staff Member	Tasks
Peter Connelly	Backup and restore for all four domains
Scott Gode	Management of all DNS Servers
Kate Dresen	Management of the schema
Elizabeth Boyle	Creation and management of all user and computer accounts in the Lima domain
Suzan Fine	Creation and management of all user and computer accounts in the Seattle domain
Thom McCann	Creation and management of all user and computer accounts in the London domain
Jörg Frey	Group Policy design for all domains
Lisa Garmaise	Manage membership of forest-wide administration accounts

Concerns with Group Memberships

Contoso wants to monitor and restrict who can modify the memberships of the following groups in Active Directory:

- Enterprise Admins
- Schema Admins
- Domain Admins
- Administrators

Administration Requirements

For the development of their administration plan, Contoso has collected the following administration requirements:

- Enterprise Admin accounts must be restricted to logging on at the DCs located in the computer room in London. The names of the two DCs are LONDONDC1 and LONDONDC2.

- Schema administration must be performed at the schema operations master. The schema operations master is named SCHEMADC and is also located in the computer room in London.

- Each member of the administration team must have two accounts: one for administrative duties and one for day-to-day tasks. The account name must help differentiate between the two accounts.

- The administrators responsible for maintaining user and computer accounts for the london.contoso.tld, lima.contoso.tld, and seattle.contoso.tld domains must be able to perform administration of the domains while remaining logged on with their day-to-day user accounts.

- Elizabeth, the administrator at the Lima office, has only a Windows 98 client computer. The administration plan must allow Elizabeth to manage user and computer accounts for the Lima domain.

- An administrator in the Seattle office uses a UNIX workstation as the primary desktop. This administrator must be able to run various administrative scripts without having to move to another computer.

Exercise 1: Designing Preexisting Administration Groups

This exercise will look at designing the membership of the default administration groups in an Active Directory forest. The exercise will also look at methods that you can use to guard the membership of administrative groups. Answers to these questions can be found in the appendix.

Analyzing Administrative Group Membership

A key to managing administrative groups is initially designing proper membership in the administrative groups to prevent excess privileges from being granted to administrators of the network.

1. For all of the administrators mentioned for Contoso, what must you do to separate their administrative tasks from day-to day tasks?

2. What group memberships does Peter Connelly require?

3. What group memberships does Scott Gode require? How can the DNS design affect the group memberships?

4. What group memberships does Kate Dresen require?

5. Are there any issues with this group membership requirement if Kate's accounts are located in the Seattle domain?

6. Complete the following table to define administrative group memberships for Elizabeth Boyle, Suzan Fine, and Thom McCann:

User	Group Membership
Elizabeth Boyle	
Suzan Fine	
Thom McCann	

7. Rather than using administrative group memberships, what alternative method could have been used to provide the necessary rights to Elizabeth, Suzan, and Thom?

8. What administrative group memberships does Jörg Frey require?

9. What is the minimum group membership required for Lisa Garmaise to manage forest-wide administration accounts?

Protecting Administrative Group Membership

Once you've defined administrative group memberships, the next stage is developing a plan to make sure that only desired memberships are maintained for all administrative groups in the forest. Answers to these questions can be found in the appendix.

1. Assuming that you will use restricted groups to enforce memberships in administrative groups, where must the Restricted Groups policy be set to have the desired protection of the administrative groups?

2. Is it possible to change the membership of a group when a Restricted Groups policy is applied? Provide details.

3. What can you do to track who changes membership of a protected administrative group?

4. Complete the following table of restricted group configuration for the required administrative groups:

Group	Members	Member of
Enterprise Admins		
Schema Admins		
Contoso\Domain Admins		
Lima\Domain Admins		
London\Domain Admins		
Seattle\Domain Admins		
Contoso\Administrators		
Lima\Administrators		
London\Administrators		
Seattle\Administrators		

5. In addition to using restricted groups, what other methods should Contoso consider to protect administrative group membership?

Exercise 2: Designing Administrative Access

In higher security networks administrative design also incorporates the implementation of additional restrictions on the usage of administrative accounts. This exercise will look at the design of restrictions for the use of administrative accounts on the Contoso network. Answers to these questions can be found in the appendix.

1. How would you meet the requirement for each administrator to have two accounts?

2. Can you restrict the default Administrator account that's a member of the Enterprise Admins group in the forest root domain as defined in the requirements?

3. What can you do as an alternative to restricting an Enterprise Admin?

4. How would the creation of a new Enterprise Admins account affect your restricted groups design?

5. What methods could Suzan and Thom use to manage their respective domains without having to log off their day-to day accounts?

6. What method of administration can Elizabeth use to manage user accounts in the Lima domain?

7. What method could the Seattle administrator who uses a UNIX workstation use to run administrative scripts? What additional security considerations must be examined?

Review

Answering the following questions will reinforce key information presented in this chapter. If you are unable to answer a question, review the appropriate lesson and then try the question again. Answers to the questions can be found in the appendix.

1. What risk do you run by making every administrator a member of the Administrators group in a Windows 2000 domain?

2. Does the implementation of restricted groups assure that additional users can never be added to a restricted group without modifying the definition of the group?

3. If you decide to make help desk personnel members of the Account Operators group so that they can reset passwords for an organization, what issues does that raise?

4. What issues are faced for remote administration if an account requires the use of a smart card for logon?

5. When features such as Terminal Services or the RunAs service are used, it's possible for several different credentials to be active at the workstation. What methods can you use to determine what security context a process is running under?

6. An administrator of the network prefers working at a UNIX workstation. While that person knows that he could perform all administrative tasks from a Windows 2000 workstation, what types of tasks is the administrator limited to at the UNIX workstation using Telnet to administer the network? What are the security risks?

CHAPTER 5

Designing Group Security

About This Chapter

Microsoft Windows 2000 enables administrators to create highly customized security groups and user rights. Administrators can control user accounts by granting users and groups access to resources on a network. Your goal is to carefully define these rights so that user accounts are granted the intended level of access and the security of your network is maintained.

Before You Begin

To complete this chapter, you must read the chapter scenario. This scenario is used throughout the chapter to apply the design decisions discussed in each lesson.

Chapter Scenario: Hanson Brothers

Hanson Brothers is a hockey equipment manufacturing company with a head office in Warroad, Minnesota, and distribution offices in Calgary, Alberta, and Boise, Idaho. You've been hired to help Hanson Brothers develop a methodology for designing Windows 2000 security groups.

The Microsoft Exchange 2000 Server Deployment

Hanson Brothers wishes to deploy Exchange Server to provide e-mail services between the Warroad, Calgary, and Boise offices. The Exchange Server deployment will include installation of Exchange Server at each office.

Last month Hanson Brothers bought out a former competitor in Hull, Quebec. As a result of the acquisition, Hanson Brothers has moved from a single domain model to a forest with two domains in it, as shown in Figure 5.1.

Figure 5.1   The modified Hanson Brothers Active Directory directory
service structure

Now the security methodology you develop must include the ability to deploy Exchange Server in a multiple-domain environment.

Deployment of Microsoft Outlook 2000

Microsoft Outlook 2000 must be installed on all the desktop computers of users who have been designated for the Exchange project. Not all users will be included during the initial rollout of Exchange Server, and Hanson Brothers wants to use Windows 2000 security groups to ensure that only authorized users can install or configure the Outlook 2000 client software.

To assist with the deployment, a central share called Software has been created on the server at the Warroad office. You must design custom groups to ensure that only approved employees will be able to install the Outlook 2000 software. In addition, members of the Exchange deployment team will need to be able to modify the configuration files within the share.

User Rights Requirements

Exchange Server requires the creation of a service account. The service account must have the following user rights assigned in any domain where Exchange Server is deployed:

- Act as part of the operating system
- Restore files and directories
- Log on as a service

Lesson 1: Designing Microsoft Windows 2000 Security Groups

When designing your network's security, consider how you must deploy groups to assist in providing access to network resources. Your choice of security group type and scope will determine your network's security and manageability levels.

After this lesson, you will be able to

- Determine the best strategies for creating custom groups in Windows 2000 to provide secure access to Windows 2000 resources

Estimated lesson time: 30 minutes

Windows 2000 Groups

In a Windows 2000 network, access to network resources is authorized through the inspection of the user Security Identifier (SID) and any group SIDs for the user account. To allow auditing of security access and to simplify the administration of network resources, use groups when you design security assignments.

When you create a custom group, you must define the group type and the group scope for the custom group, as shown in Figure 5.2.

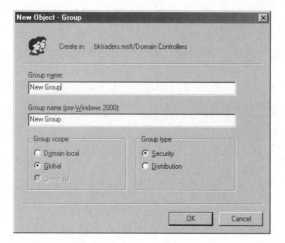

Figure 5.2   Configuring the group scope and group type for a new group

Note   While it's critical to select the proper group scope and group type for a newly created group, you may change these properties once a group has been created. Of course, this is subject to the rules of membership for the group scope.

Windows 2000 Group Types

You can define two different types of Windows 2000 groups: *security groups* and *distribution groups*. Use security groups for entries in discretionary access control lists (DACLs) and system access control lists (SACLs) to define security and auditing settings for an object. Membership in a security group provides the equivalent rights and permissions assigned to that group. Use distribution groups for such applications as e-mail distribution lists. When an access token is built for a user, security group SIDs are included in the access token but distribution group memberships are ignored. If a group's purpose is to define security for a resources, always make sure that you define the group type to be security.

Do Distribution Groups Have SIDs?

Yes. Even though you can't assign a distribution group permissions to an object, you can still convert the distribution group into a security group in Active Directory Users And Computers. Because you can convert group types, SIDs are automatically assigned to newly created distribution groups in case they are converted to security groups.

You can identify the SID of a distribution group by using the Active Directory Administration Tool (Ldp.exe) that's included with the Windows 2000 Support Tools. This tool allows you to bind to Active Directory and query objects in Active Directory by issuing Lightweight Directory Access Protocol (LDAP) commands. Figure 5.3 shows the details of the Distribution Group named OfficeMail.

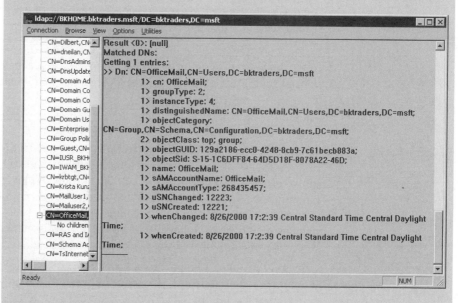

Figure 5.3 Distribution groups with SIDs

Note that the OfficeMail distribution group has been assigned the SID S-15-1C6DFF84-64D5D18F-8078A22-46D.

Windows 2000 Group Scopes

Once you've selected the group type, you must set the scope for the group. The scope defines where the group can be used, where the membership of the group is maintained, and how the group can be used.

Note By implementing native mode in a Windows 2000 domain, you increase your options for setting security group scopes. Mixed-mode domains may contain Windows NT backup domain controllers (BDCs) that limit the types of groups you can create because they don't recognize the newer Windows 2000 scopes (domain local and universal groups) and don't recognize new functionality, such as nesting global groups within other global groups. (Unless otherwise noted, "Windows NT" refers to versions 3.51 and 4.0.)

When Windows 2000 Active Directory is configured to run in native mode, you can select four group scopes for a Windows 2000 group. These are

- **Domain local groups.** Use domain local groups to grant permissions to resources. You can use a domain local group on any computer that's a member of the domain in native mode. The advantage of using domain local groups for permission assignments is that a domain local group may contain groups from other domains in its membership. This allows you to simply add new groups to the existing domain local group instead of modifying the DACL to provide additional users or groups access to the resource. Membership of domain local groups is maintained in the domain where the domain local group exists.

Note In a mixed-mode environment, domain local groups can only be used on domain controllers (DCs), much like local groups in a Windows NT environment.

- **Global groups.** Use global groups to combine users (and other global groups) who have similar business requirements. For example, it's common to create global groups for each department or project team within an organization. Instead of assigning permissions directly to a global group, make the global group a member of a domain local group so that members of that global group inherit the permissions assigned to the domain local group. Global groups may only contain user accounts and global groups from the same domain as members. Membership of global groups is maintained in the domain where the domain local group exists.

- **Universal groups.** Use universal groups to collect similar groups that exist in multiple domains. The key difference between universal groups and other security groups is that memberships are stored both in the domain where the universal group exists and in the global catalog. If the membership is stored in the global catalog, membership can be verified without contacting a DC where the universal group is defined. Storing membership in the global catalog may also be a disadvantage because any change to universal group membership will result in modification and replication of the global catalog. Instead of assigning permissions directly to a universal group, make the universal groups members of domain local groups and assign the necessary permissions to the domain local group.

Tip   To reduce the replication traffic associated with changes in universal group membership, assign global groups as members of the universal group instead of as user accounts. This way, you can modify the membership within the composite global groups without adding or removing global groups from within the universal group.

- **Computer local groups.** Windows 2000–based computers that aren't DCs maintain their own user accounts database. Within these databases, you can create computer local groups to define permissions for resources stored at that computer. Computer local groups aren't shared between computers; you must define them at each computer where they must exist.

Assessing Group Usage

When designing your network's security, consider how you will assign permissions to resources. This process includes the creation of custom groups to provide the permissions to protect these resources.

To create the necessary groups, you must understand the way you can set group memberships. Table 5.1 outlines the memberships that are allowed within groups.

Table 5.1   Group Membership in a Windows 2000 Domain

Group Scope	Mixed Mode Membership	Native Mode Membership
Domain Local	<ul><li>User accounts from any domain</li><li>Global groups from any domain</li></ul>	<ul><li>User accounts from any domain</li><li>Global groups from any domain</li><li>Universal groups from any domain</li><li>Domain local groups from the same domain</li></ul>
Global	<ul><li>User accounts from the same domain</li></ul>	<ul><li>User accounts from the same domain</li><li>Global groups from the same domain</li></ul>
Universal	<ul><li>N/A</li></ul>	<ul><li>User accounts from any domain</li><li>Global groups from any domain</li><li>Universal groups from any domain</li></ul>
Computer Local	<ul><li>Local user accounts</li><li>Domain user accounts from any domain</li><li>Global groups from any domain</li></ul>	<ul><li>User accounts from any domain</li><li>Global groups from any domain</li></ul>

The next step is to design a methodology of using groups to provide access to resources on the network. As Table 5.1 shows, it's possible to place user accounts into each of the four group types. While it's possible, however, it's often not desirable because doing so can lead to difficulties in determining the correct group membership.

One of the more common strategies, known as A-G-DL-P, is shown in Figure 5.4.

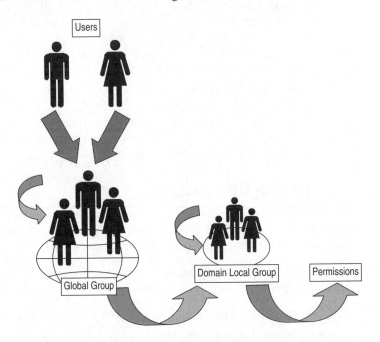

Figure 5.4   Assigning permissions by using A-G-DL-P

In this strategy you place accounts only into global groups to simplify administration. In native mode, global groups may also have other global groups as members. You then make these global groups members of a domain local group, which may be a member of additional domain local groups. You assign permissions to the domain local group. The permissions assigned affect all members of the domain local group.

Tip   You most often use A-G-DL-P in a forest that has a single domain. You don't need to use universal groups if the forest has only a single domain.

The A-G-DL-P strategy simplifies the troubleshooting of permissions because you only have to inspect domain local groups. Within any listing of Access Control Entries (ACEs), there should only be domain local groups.

Another strategy you can use in a Windows 2000 native domain is to integrate universal groups into the assignment of permissions, as shown in Figure 5.5.

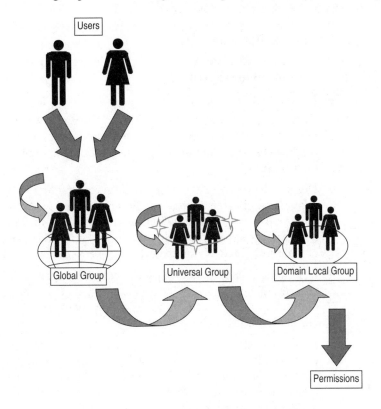

Figure 5.5   Assigning permissions by using A-G-U-DL-P

As in the previous strategy, you assign users only to global groups, which can be made members of other global groups. The difference with this methodology is that you can collect global groups from multiple domains into a single universal group. You then add the universal group as a member of a domain local group. Finally, you assign the domain local group permissions to the object to which it requires access.

The key to this strategy is to have only global groups and other universal groups as the membership of a universal group. By not placing user accounts directly into the universal group, you can minimize changes to group membership of the universal group and subsequent changes to the global catalog. By reducing the changes in membership of the universal group, you then reduce replication traffic related to global catalog replication.

You must determine the appropriate methodology for protecting each resource. When a resource requires multiple levels of access, the result is the creation or usage of multiple groups.

Making the Decision

When you design custom groups to provide access to Windows 2000 resources, consider the following criteria:

- Determine if an existing group meets your requirements. Over time, several custom groups will be created within your Windows 2000 forest. You should always determine if you can use an existing group to secure the new resource on the network, rather than creating a group that duplicates functionality on the network.

- Define what purpose the group will serve. Defining the purpose of the group helps determine the appropriate group type and group scope. For example, if the group will be used to assign permissions to a resource, the group must be a security group and not a distribution group. If the group must cross domain boundaries, you can't set the group scope to domain local.

- Determine if additional groups are required. If you're using A-G-DL-P or A-G-U-DL-P, you probably have to create more than one group. Determine all required groups so that you're optimizing network traffic and following your permission assignment strategy.

- Don't assign excess permissions. Never assign permissions that would allow users to intentionally or accidentally perform an undesirable task. For example, if the members of the domain local group require only the ability to read a document, don't provide them with permissions that could allow them to delete or modify it.

Note   For additional information on assigning permissions to file resources, see Chapter 6, "Securing File Resources."

- Document the new groups. Be sure to document the group's name, the initial group membership, memberships of the new group in other groups, and what purpose the group serves. By including the purpose of the group, you may avoid the creation of groups that duplicate the functionality of existing groups.

Applying the Decision

Based on the scenario, Hanson Brothers needs to make the following decisions for the deployment of Exchange Server and the creation of custom security groups:

- Determine existing groups. Hanson Brothers requires custom groups to be created for the deployment of the Outlook 2000 client software. No default group has the necessary access permissions required for the distribution share, "Outlook 2000," on the software server, so you must deploy custom security groups.

- Determine the number of groups using A-G-DL-P. If Hanson Brothers uses A-G-DL-P to create security groups, you must create the groups shown in Table 5.2 to meet the requirements for the deployment of the Outlook 2000 software.

Table 5.2   Groups Required to Deploy Outlook 2000 Using A-G-DL-P

Group Name	Group Scope	Membership
Corporate\OutlookUsers	Global Group	All users who require the Outlook 2000 software at the Warroad, Calgary, or Boise offices
Quebec\OutlookUsers	Global Group	All users who require the Outlook 2000 software at the Hull office
Corporate\OutlookAdmins	Global Group	All Outlook administrators who need to configure the Outlook 2000 client software
Corporate\OutlookRead	Domain Local Group	Corporate\OutlookUsers Quebec\OutlookUsers
Corporate\OutlookWrite	Domain Local Group	Corporate\OutlookAdmins

- Determine the number of groups using A-G-U-DL-P. If Hanson Brothers uses A-G-U-DL-P to create security groups, you must create the groups shown in Table 5.3 to meet the requirements for the deployment of the Outlook 2000 software.

Table 5.3   Groups Required to Deploy Outlook 2000 Using A-G-U-DL-P

Group Name	Group Scope	Membership
Corporate\OutlookUsers	Global Group	All users who require the Outlook 2000 software at the Warroad, Calgary, or Boise offices
Quebec\OutlookUsers	Global Group	All users who require the Outlook 2000 software at the Hull office
Corporate\Outlook	Universal Group	Corporate\OutlookUsers Quebec\OutlookUsers
Corporate\OutlookAdmins	Global Group	All Outlook administrators who need to configure the Outlook 2000 client software
Corporate\OutlookRead	Domain Local Group	Corporate\Outlook
Corporate\OutlookWrite	Domain Local Group	Corporate\OutlookAdmins

- Choose a methodology. Either methodology will work for the deployment of the Outlook 2000 software for Hanson Brothers. The best decision may depend on the company's growth. If they don't expect much more growth, A-G-DL-P will meet their security needs and won't require additional security groups to be created. A-G-DL-U-P is more beneficial if you can foresee the use of the Outlook universal group for additional security assignments. Rather than having to add the OutlookUsers global groups from each domain to a Domain Local group, you can simply add the single universal group, Outlook, to the Domain Local group.

- Document the newly created groups. After you've created all the groups, you must document why the group was created, the initial membership of the group, and any permissions assigned directly to the groups.

Lesson Summary

To design Windows 2000 security group memberships, you must know how security groups can interact with each other. When designing security group memberships, determine the methodology that your organization will use for assigning permissions to resources. Typically, the decision comes down to A-G-DL-P or A-G-U-DL-P. You'll make that decision based on the number of domains in your organization, whether the domains are in native mode, and the amount of replication traffic related to universal group membership changes.

Activity: Reviewing Group Memberships

You've been called in as a consultant to review security group design proposals for a technology firm. Several sources have submitted the proposals, and the firm fears that some of the proposals are technically incorrect. The proposals all pertain to providing access to a shared folder named Technologies. The folder is stored on a member server named Development that's a member server in the east.technology.tld domain. The shared folder must be accessible to user accounts in both the west.technology.tld and technology.tld domains, as shown in Figure 5.6.

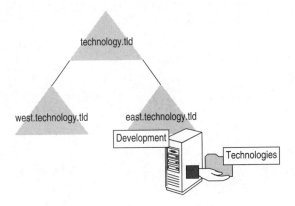

Figure 5.6   The technology.tld domain structure

Only members of the marketing, sales, and management teams must have access to the technologies share. No other users should have access.

Due to some legacy applications running on Windows NT 4.0 BDCs, all domains in the Windows 2000 forest are currently running in mixed mode.

Proposal 1

To provide access to the \\Development\Technologies share, you must define the following groups:

- **Marketing.** A global group defined in each domain that will contain marketing users for that domain.

- **Sales.** A global group defined in each domain that will contain Sales department users for that domain.

- **Management.** A global group defined in each domain that will contain management staff for that domain.

- **TechUsers.** A global group defined in each domain that will contain the Marketing, Sales, and Management global groups.

- **TechAccess.** A domain local group defined in the east.technologies.tld domain. This group will contain the TechUsers groups from each of the three domains.

Proposal 2

To provide access to the \\Development\Technologies share, you must define the following groups:

- **Marketing.** A global group defined in each domain that will contain marketing users for that domain.

- **Sales.** A global group defined in each domain that will contain Sales department users for that domain.

- **Management.** A global group defined in each domain that will contain management staff for that domain.

- **TechAccess.** A computer local group defined in the east.technologies.tld domain. This group will contain the Marketing, Sales, and Management global groups from each of the three domains.

Proposal 3

To provide access to the \\Development\Technologies share, you must define the following groups:

- **Marketing.** A global group defined in each domain that will contain marketing users for that domain.

- **Sales.** A global group defined in each domain that will contain Sales department users for that domain.

- **Management.** A global group defined in each domain that will contain management staff for that domain.

- **TechUsers.** A universal group defined in the east.technologies.tld domain that will contain the Marketing, Sales, and Management global groups.

- **TechAccess.** A computer local group defined in the east.technologies.tld domain. This group will contain the TechUsers groups from each of the three domains.

Proposal 4

To provide access to the \\Development\Technologies share, you must define the following groups:

- **Marketing.** A global group defined in each domain that will contain marketing users for that domain.

- **Sales.** A global group defined in each domain that will contain Sales department users for that domain.

- **Management.** A global group defined in each domain that will contain management staff for that domain.
- **TechAccess.** A domain local group defined in the east.technologies.tld domain. This group will contain the Marketing, Sales, and Management global groups from each of the three domains.

Questions

Answer the following questions about this situation. Answers can be found in the appendix.

1. Will the first proposal work in technology.tld's environment? If your answer is no, what's wrong with the proposal?

2. Will the second proposal work in technology.tld's environment? If your answer is no, what's wrong with the proposal?

3. Will the third proposal work in technology.tld's environment? If your answer is no, what's wrong with the proposal?

4. Will the fourth proposal work in technology.tld's environment? If your answer is no, what's wrong with the proposal?

Lesson 2: Designing User Rights

Windows 2000 allows administrators to define precisely what users can and can't do. By defining user rights, administrators authorize users to perform specific actions. Although you can apply these rights to user accounts, you're better off administering them on group accounts so that users will inherit the rights associated with that group.

After this lesson, you will be able to

- Determine how to design user rights for your Active Directory

Estimated lesson time: 30 minutes

Defining User Rights with Group Policy

User rights define who can log on to a computer, the methods that can be used to log on to a computer, and the privileges that have been assigned to a user or group on that computer. Although user rights can be applied locally at a computer, in a Windows 2000 network it's preferable to define user rights by using Group Policy. Using Group Policy to apply user rights ensures consistent application of user rights and ensures that local changes won't be able to override settings applied at a site, domain, or organizational unit (OU).

Note Within a Group Policy Object, user rights are defined in the following location: Computer Configuration\Windows Settings\Security Settings \Local Policies\User Rights Assignments. As with all Group Policy settings, the Group Policy Object defined closest to the computer object in Active Directory will take precedence in the case of conflicting settings. The only exception is Account Policy settings within Group Policy. Account Policy settings are always applied from the Default Domain Policy.

User Rights Within Windows 2000

The following user rights can be defined within local policy or applied through Windows 2000 Group Policy, as shown in Figure 5.7.

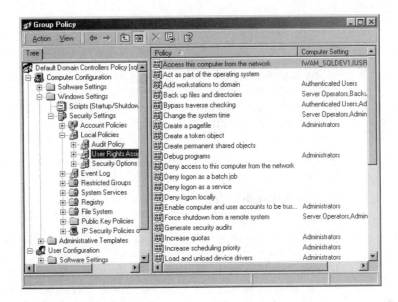

Figure 5.7 Defining user rights in local policies of Group Policy

You can define several user rights. You have to base your choice on knowing which privileges a user right provides to any security principals (users or security groups) assigned the user right. You can assign the following user rights:

- **Access This Computer From Network.** This user right allows a security principal to access the computer from the network. Default membership in this group includes Administrators, Everyone, and Power Users.

- **Act As Part Of The Operating System.** You commonly assign this user right to service accounts that must authenticate as a user and access resources where they must authenticate as a user. Because this right provides elevated privileges to a security principal, use it sparingly.

- **Add Workstations To A Domain.** This user right allows a security principal to add a computer to a specific domain. You must assign this right at the Domain Controllers OU to affect the domain. A security principal assigned this permission may add only up to 10 computers within the domain.

Note Alternatively, you can delegate a security principal the Create Computer Objects permission in Active Directory. This permission allows a security principal to create an unlimited number of computers within the domain or OU where the permission is delegated.

- **Backup Files And Directories.** This user right allows a security principal to access files using the NTFS backup application programming interface (API) even if NTFS permissions don't normally allow the security principal access.

- **Bypass Traverse Checking.** This user right allows security principals to navigate through folders where they don't have explicit or implicit permissions when navigating to a folder or object where they do have permissions. The security principal can't list the contents of the folder but can only traverse the folder. This applies to both the NTFS file system and the registry.

- **Change The System Time.** This user right allows a security principal to modify the time of the computer's internal clock.

- **Create Pagefile.** This user right allows a security principal to create a new pagefile on any computer volume or to modify the size of an existing pagefile.

- **Create A Token Object.** This user right allows a security principal associated with a process to create an access token through an API.

- **Create Permanent Shared Objects.** This user right allows a security principal associated with a process to create a directory object in the Windows 2000 object manager. This task is commonly performed by components that run in kernel mode. This right is necessary only if the object doesn't run in kernel mode.

- **Debug Programs.** This user right allows a security principal to debug any process using a kernel or application debugger.

- **Deny Access To This Computer From The Network.** This user right prevents a security principal from connecting to the computer where the user right is applied from the network.

- **Deny Logon As A Batch Job.** This user right prevents a security principal from authenticating with the computer where the user right is applied through a batch-queue process.

- **Deny Logon As A Service.** This user right prevents a security principal's credentials from being used by a service for authentication.

- **Deny Logon Locally.** This user right prevents a security principal from logging on at the console of the computer with this user right applied.

- **Enable Computer And User Accounts To Be Trusted For Delegation.** This user right allows a security principal to change the Trusted For Delegation setting on a user or computer object within Active Directory. In addition to this user right, the security principal must also have write access to the object's account control flags. Setting the Trusted For Delegation setting lets a computer or process hosting an application authenticate to a back-end service by using the credentials of the user running the application.

- **Force Shutdown From A Remote System.** This user right allows a security principal to shut down a computer remotely by using tools such as Shutdown.exe from the *Microsoft Windows 2000 Server Resource Kit.*

- **Generate Security Audits.** This user right ensures that a security principal associated with a process generates entries in the security log.

- **Increase Quotas.** This user right allows a process associated with a security principal to increase the processor quota assigned to other processes. To do this, the initial process must have write access to the second process.

- **Increase Scheduling Priority.** This user right allows a security principal to increase the execution priority of another process programmatically or by using Task Manager.

- **Load And Unload Device Drivers.** This user right allows a security principal to install and uninstall Plug and Play device drivers. Only administrators can install or uninstall non-Plug and Play device drivers.

- **Lock Pages In Memory.** This user right allows a security principal associated with a process to prevent memory used by the process from being swapped from physical memory to the paging file. In Windows 2000 this privilege is obsolete and isn't set by default.

- **Log On As A Batch Job.** This user right allows a security principal to log on by using a batch-queue process.

- **Log On As A Service.** This user right allows a security principal's credentials to be used by a service for authentication.

- **Log On Locally.** This user right allows a security principal to log on at the local console (the keyboard) of the computer where this user right applied.

- **Manage Auditing And Security Log.** This user right allows a security principal to modify the SACL for individual objects. The SACL specifies auditing options for the object.

Note Just modifying the SACL doesn't enable auditing for object access. In addition, the audit policy for the computer must enable either Success or Failure auditing for object access.

- **Modify Firmware Environment Values.** This user right allows a security principal to modify system environment variables. The modification can take place manually by using the System program in Control Panel or through an API call.

- **Profile Single Process.** This user right allows a security principal to run performance-monitoring utilities such as the Performance Logs and Alerts MMC console to monitor nonsystem processes.

- **Profile System Performance.** This user right allows a security principal to run performance-monitoring utilities such as the Performance Logs and Alerts MMC console to monitor system processes.

- **Remove Computer From A Docking Station.** This user right allows a security principal to undock a portable computer from a docking station.

- **Replace A Process Level Token.** This user right allows a security principal associated with a process to replace the access token for a child process that's spawned by the initial process.

- **Restore Files And Directories.** This user right allows a security principal to restore backed-up files and directories to the file system even if the security principal doesn't have permissions to the affected directories. This user right also allows the security principal to change the owner of the object.

- **Shut Down The System.** This user right allows a security principal to shut down the local computer.

- **Synchronize Directory Service Data.** This user right allows a security principal associated with a process to provide directory synchronization services. This user right is only applied at DCs where the Active Directory is maintained.

- **Take Ownership Of Files Or Other Objects.** This user right allows a security principal to take ownership of any securable object in the system. Objects that this affects include Active Directory objects, files, folders, printers, registry keys, processes, and threads.

Assessing Where to Apply User Rights

You can define user rights in local computer policy or at Group Policy defined at the site, domain, or OU. Group Policy settings always take precedence over local computer policy. Therefore, for a centrally administered network, it's always preferable to define user rights by using Group Policy.

When you decide where to apply user rights, it's important for you to group computers that require like assignments into the same container. Consider the following strategy:

- Maintain the default of storing DCs within the Domain Controllers OU and apply user rights for DCs in the Default Domain Controllers Policy. This action ensures that user rights are consistent across all DCs.

- Collect all Windows 2000 member servers into a common OU structure. If user rights are consistent among member servers, apply the user rights Group Policy at the parent OU. If specific user rights assignments are required, based on the type of information stored at the member server, apply the user rights Group Policy settings at the individual OUs, as shown in Figure 5.8.

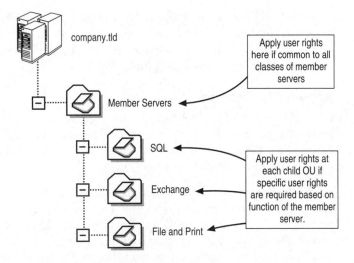

Figure 5.8 Determining where to apply user rights

- Assuming that the same user rights must be assigned to all computers uniformly, apply the user rights settings at the domain to affect all computers running Windows 2000 Professional in the domain. Unless different user rights settings are defined at the OU level, the domain level settings will be applied uniformly to all Windows 2000–based computer accounts in the domain.

Making the Decision

When you determine the user rights definitions for your organization, you must make the following decisions:

- Determine what user rights to grant to a security principal. It's best to assign user rights to a group rather than to an individual user account. Assigning the user right to a group ensures that if you need to change who requires the user right, you only have to modify the group's membership, not the user right assignment.

- Determine where to apply user rights. You can apply user rights to the local computer policy or by using Group Policy at the site, domain, or OU level. For DCs, you should always apply user rights at the Domain Controllers OU. This ensures consistent application of user rights at all DCs within a domain.

- Determine whether to apply user permissions or user rights. The key to this decision is to realize that user rights always take precedence over permissions on objects. For example, you could assign permissions to a user for a directory structure so that the user can read each file in the directory structure. This action is sufficient to allow the user to back up all folders and files that the user has permissions to. However, if the folder structure contains any files to which the user doesn't have access, the user would be unable to back up these files. If the user were assigned the permission Backup Files And Directories, it wouldn't matter what permissions existed on the files and folders for the purpose of backup. The user right would take precedence over the permissions assigned at the file and folder level.

Applying the Decision

For the deployment of Exchange Server, the Exchange service account must be assigned the required user rights in each domain where an Exchange Server will be installed. Because Hanson Brothers has two domains, the assignment of user rights must be duplicated in each of them.

Normally, the assignment of user rights should be applied to a domain local group rather than to an individual user account. Because the Exchange service account is often dedicated solely to the purpose of Exchange Server, however, it's permissible to consider assigning user rights directly to the user account. When you design the user rights assignments for the Exchange service account, you must make the following decisions:

- Determine a name for the service account. You must name the Exchange service account so that the name doesn't reveal the service account's purpose. For example, using an account name such as Exchange, Service, or Exservice wouldn't be appropriate for a secure network. Selecting a fictitious name for the service account, such as Amy Jones (Ajones), often provides the best security.

Warning   You should name all service accounts and administrative accounts so that the name doesn't reveal the user account's security level. Revealing the purpose through the name can introduce security weaknesses to the network.

- Determine which user rights to assign to the service account. As mentioned in the scenario's requirements, the Exchange service account requires three user rights to be assigned directly to the Exchange service account. These user rights are: Act As Part Of The Operating System, Log On As A Service, and Restore Files And Directories.
- Determine where to assign the user rights. If the Exchange servers are installed as member servers in the domain, you should create a separate organizational unit (OU) in both the Corporate and Quebec domains to contain the Exchange servers. At the OU you must define a Group Policy that assigns the three user rights to the Exchange service account. If the Exchange servers are installed as DCs, then Group Policy would be defined at the Domain Controllers OU. Whatever type of Windows 2000–based computer is used for Exchange Server, the user rights assignments must be performed in both the Corporate and Quebec domains.

Lesson Summary

User rights take precedence over any explicit permissions assigned to objects in a Windows 2000 domain, Your security design must ensure that excess rights are not assigned to security principals in your domain.

Ensure that your security plan evaluates what user rights must be assigned to a security principal to accomplish specific tasks. In addition, the design must determine the correct location to apply the user rights. Typically, user rights are always applied at the highest level in Active Directory as possible. This ensures that uniform user rights are applied to all Windows 2000–based computers in the domain.

Lab 5-1: Designing Security Groups and User Rights

Lab Objectives

This lab prepares you to design security groups and user rights assignments by meeting the following objectives:

- Determine the correct group type and group scope for a required group
- Determine a methodology to use for group creation
- Determine where to apply user rights in Active Directory for a given scenario

About This Lab

This lab looks at the design of security groups for an *n*-tiered client server deployment for Contoso Ltd. (where *n* represents the number of levels). The client/server deployment will involve clients and servers spread among Contoso's four domains.

Before You Begin

Make sure that you've completed reading the chapter material before starting the lab. For information on designing your administrative structure, pay close attention to the sections where the design decisions were applied throughout the chapter.

Scenario: Contoso Ltd.

Contoso Ltd., an international magazine sales company, wants to develop a methodology for creating security groups and deploying user rights in their organization. You've been asked to assist with designing the necessary user rights and security groups for the deployment of a new Human Resources application.

The Human Resources Application

The new Human Resources (HR) application is an Active Directory–integrated application that uses an *n*-tiered client/server model for the storage of Human Resources–related information.

The Human Resources application must be able to categorize its users into one of four categories. Each location has users who could be placed into one of four categories of application users. A user must be placed into only one of the available categories. The four categories of user access for the Human Resources application are defined in the following table:

Category	Access Level
Application Managers	Must have full control of all areas of the application to manage and configure the application.
HR Manager	Must be able to grant access to the Human Resources application and determine the level of access to the application. Can assign any level of access except Application Manager.
HR Department	Able to modify content in Human Resources–related documents and databases.
Employee	Able to view all Human Resources public documents, including job postings, weekly bulletins, and United Way campaign information.

Being an *n*-tiered application, the application takes advantage of the Windows 2000 capability to use Kerberos delegation. This allows the Human Resources application service account to process queries at the security level of the user running the application, rather than at the system account's permissions level.

To allow impersonation, the Human Resources application service account must be able to log on as a service and act as part of the operating system. This service account is used on all servers involved in the Human Resources application deployment. It isn't used at the client computers running the front-end application.

Deployment of the Human Resources Application Servers

The application servers that support the Human Resources application are spread among the Seattle, Lima, and London offices, as shown in Figure 5.9.

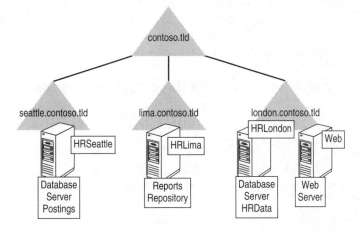

Figure 5.9   Application server distribution for the Human Resources application

In Seattle all job postings are stored on the server called HRSeattle. When a query on job postings is made, the request is redirected to the HRSeattle server without the knowledge of the user running the Human Resources application.

In Lima a server has been configured that stores common Human Resources reports. The reports are physically located on the HRLima server, but this is accessible from the Web server in London through a virtual directory running available in Internet Information Services (IIS). The company is concerned about access times for the Human Resources reports because of to the slow 56 K WAN link between London and Lima, as shown in Figure 5.10.

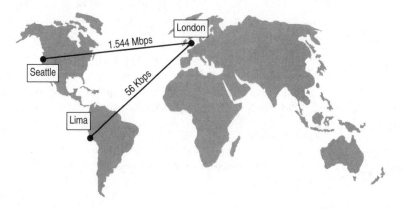

Figure 5.10   Wide Area Network for Contoso Ltd.

In London two servers are deployed for the Human Resources application. The HRLondon server contains most of the application data used by the Human Resources application. When a client queries the HRLondon server, the query will return only a response set that's allowed by the credentials. When Kerberos delegation is used, all queries are run in the security context of the calling user.

Exercise 1: Designing Security Groups

This exercise looks at designing the security groups required for Contoso's Human Resources application deployment. Answers to these questions can be found in the appendix.

1. What factors would make you choose an A-G-DL-P methodology for creating groups for Contoso's Human Resources application?

2. If you use A-G-U-DL-P to define security for the HR application, what must you do to reduce WAN replication?

3. Assuming that you use A-G-DL-P as your security group methodology, in the following table define all global groups that you must create for the Human Resources application. Use existing groups if possible.

Category	Global Group(s)	Membership
Application Managers		
HR Managers		
HR Department		
Employees		

4. Assuming that you use A-G-DL-P as your security group methodology, in the following table define all domain local groups that must be defined at the London domain. Include the membership of each group and where the domain local group will be used.

Domain Local Group	Membership	Where Deployed
■		
■		
■		
■		

5. Assuming that you use A-G-DL-P as your security group methodology, in the following table define all domain local groups that must be defined at the Lima domain. Include the membership of each group and where the domain local group will be used.

Domain Local Group	Membership	Where Deployed
■		
■		
■		
■		

6. Assuming that you use A-G-DL-P as your security group methodology, in the following table define all domain local groups that must be defined at the Seattle domain. Include the membership of each group and where the domain local group will be used.

Domain Local Group	Membership	Where Deployed
■		
■		
■		
■		

7. If you used A-G-U-DL-P, which additional group memberships would you need to define?

8. If universal groups are deployed, what can you do to reduce the amount of WAN traffic related to global catalog replication?

Exercise 2: Designing User Rights

The Human Resources application requires a service account that will be used at all application servers involved in running the HR application. Answers to these questions can be found in the appendix.

1. What must you ensure when you choose the name of the Human Resources service account?

2. In which domain would you create the service account to prevent administrators at regional offices from modifying the service account's properties?

3. Does the decision on which domain to create the service account in affect the usage of the service account?

4. Assuming that all Human Resources application servers are installed as nondomain controllers, what Active Directory design must you use to apply the service account user rights?

5. What user rights must you apply to the Human Resources application service account?

Review

Answering the following questions will reinforce key information presented in this chapter. If you are unable to answer a question, review the appropriate lesson and then try the question again. Answers to the questions can be found in the appendix.

1. Your organization is trying to determine whether to implement universal groups or global groups for the purpose of combining user accounts with identical security requirements. What factors will cause you to choose global groups over universal groups?

2. The newly hired network administrator is testing the ability to convert group types in Active Directory Users And Computers. A group named Payroll is currently defined as a universal group. When testing conversion, the network administrator found she can convert the group to a domain local group, but she is unable to convert the group to a global group. What might be the reason?

3. Eva Corets, a summer intern in the Information Technology (IT) department at company.tld has found that she is unable to log on locally at the servers in the marketing department. Figure 5.11 shows the current OU structure for the organization.

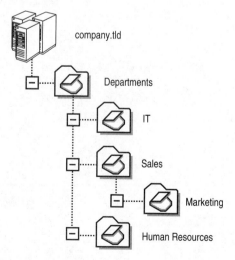

Figure 5.11   Active Directory structure for company.tld

To allow herself to log on locally, Eva has edited the local policy at each of the marketing servers to grant her account the user right to log on locally. But she's still unable to log on at the console of any servers in the marketing department. What has Eva done wrong? What must she do to allow her account to log on locally at the Marketing member servers?

4. To assist with the deployment of Windows 2000 Professional, an outside contractor has been assigned an account on the local network. To allow the contractor to install new Windows 2000 Professional computers and make them members of the domain company.tld, you've assigned the contractor's account the user right of Add Workstations To A Domain. After the first few days, the contractor suddenly loses the ability to make the newly installed Windows 2000 Professional computers members of the company.tld domain. What must you do to allow the contractor to continue adding computers to the domain?

C H A P T E R   6

Securing File Resources

About This Chapter

Microsoft Windows 2000 uses share permissions and NTFS permissions to protect file and print resources on a network. Your goal is to combine both sets of
permissions so that only intended users or groups can access network resources.
This chapter will show you how to do that, and it will also examine the design
requirements for deploying Encrypting File System (EFS) to encrypt stored data.

Before You Begin

To complete this chapter, you must read the chapter scenario. This scenario is
used throughout the chapter to apply the design decisions discussed in each lesson.

Chapter Scenario: Wide World Importers

This chapter will apply decision matrices to Wide World Importers, a North American corporation with distribution centers and service centers across the continent. You will be designing security for the deployment of five software applications: Adobe Acrobat Reader, Microsoft Office, WinZip, Adobe Photoshop, and QuarkXPress. Due to misconceptions about how EFS works, Wide World Importers wants to disable EFS within the wideworldimporters.tld domain.

Planning Security for Software Deployment

Wide World Importers is rolling out new software packages at various locations on its network. The Information Technology (IT) department wants to ensure that security is designed for the installation folders so that only required users can install the software and that only authorized users can modify the installation points.

Storage Locations

Wide World Importers has defined the following directory structures for the storage of the software applications. In Washington the following directory structure shown in Figure 6.1 has been defined for the installation points for Adobe Acrobat Reader, Microsoft Office, and WinZip.

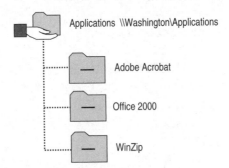

Figure 6.1   Washington applications directory hierarchy

In Dallas, the directory shown in Figure 6.2 has been defined for the installation of Adobe Photoshop and QuarkXPress.

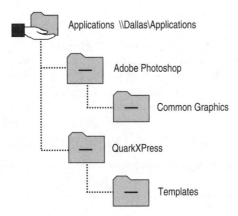

Applications \\Dallas\Applications

Adobe Photoshop

Common Graphics

QuarkXPress

Templates

Figure 6.2   Dallas applications directory hierarchy

In addition to storing the application installation points, each application also has a folder used to store common graphics (in the case of Photoshop) and templates (for QuarkXPress). These folders require some users to have elevated privileges to allow them to create, modify, and delete template and graphic files.

Software Requirements

Wide World Importers wants to deploy the following software packages, and you've been asked to design security for the applications:

- Administrators of the network must be able to manage permissions and apply patches to the software distribution points at all offices.

- Office 2000 will be installed on all corporate desktops. All users must have access to the centralized distribution point so they can run the installation program.

- All staff must be able to install commonly used utilities. These utilities include WinZip and Adobe Acrobat Reader.

- The Graphics department in Dallas uses Adobe Photoshop and QuarkXPress to create marketing flyers. Only members of the Graphics department should be able to install the software packages from the distribution point in Dallas.

- Two users in the Graphics department (Lisa Jacobson and David Jaffe) are responsible for maintaining the default graphics stored in the Common Graphics folder. Lisa and David must be able to create new default graphics and to modify existing default graphics. If new designs are introduced, they must also be able to delete the former versions of the graphics.

- When producing marketing literature, the Graphics department uses templates within QuarkXPress to ensure that all literature has the same look. Stefan Knorr and Linda Kobara are in charge of modifying the templates. The other users in the Graphics department should only be able to read the templates.

Print Security

Wide World Importers recently purchased an Agfa Proset 9800 film printer for the Graphics department. The department uses it to print color separations for magazine layouts. Due to the cost of printing to film, Wide World Importers wants to ensure that only members of the Graphics department can print to the Agfa Proset 9800.

Planning for Protection of Confidential Data

Wide World Importers wants to prevent users from encrypting local data by using EFS. Twice in the last month, a user has rebuilt a computer and was unable to access previously encrypted data.

Lesson 1: Securing Access to File Resources

When you design security for file resources, consider

- The design of share permissions
- The design of NT file system (NTFS) permissions
- The effect of combining share and NTFS permissions

The key to ensuring secure file access is to plan your share and NTFS permissions before you deploy resources.

After this lesson, you will be able to

- Design security for local and network-based files by combining share and NTFS permissions

Estimated lesson time: 45 minutes

Designing Share Security

Share permissions are used to secure network access to data stored on a server. Share permissions are flexible in that they aren't limited to a specific file system. You can establish shares for folders located on file allocation table (FAT), FAT32, NTFS, and CD-ROM file system (CDFS) volumes.

Although they're flexible, share permissions are limited in that they have no effect on a user who is logged on locally at the computer hosting the shared folder. For example, if share permissions for the Project folder are configured to deny Read access to members of the Sales group, the share permissions would only come into effect if the Sales group is connecting to the Project folder over the network. If seated at the server itself, a user could read and execute any file in the Project folder. It's only by combining share permissions with NTFS permissions that you achieve a totally secure file access solution.

Configuring Share Permissions

You can enable a shared folder by editing the folder properties. In the Properties dialog box, configure the share permissions in the Sharing tab, as shown in Figure 6.3.

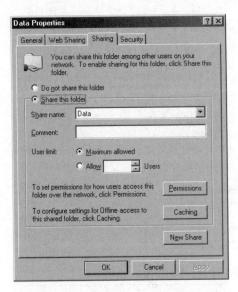

Figure 6.3   Enabling a shared folder

When you enable a shared folder, you can limit the maximum number of sessions that are allowed. To configure more precise permissions, click Permissions. The standard permissions for a share are

- **Full Control.** This permission allows the assigned security principal to create, delete, and modify any content within the shared folder. In addition, if it's located on an NTFS partition, Full Control permission allows the security principal to take ownership of files and folders and to change permissions on the files or folders within the shared folder.

- **Change.** This permission allows a security principal to read, write, create, or modify any content within the shared folder.

- **Read.** This permission allows a security principal to read, copy, or execute any content within the shared folder.

Changes to Shares in Windows 2000

In Windows 3.1, Windows 95, Windows 98, and Windows NT, if you assigned a logical drive letter to a file share, you could only establish a fake root directory at the folder that was shared. For example, if you used the command `net use h: \\server\home\brian`, the drive mapping when you connect to the H drive would be `h:\brian>`. If you wanted the Brian folder to appear as the root folder, you had to share the Brian folder separately. In organizations with large numbers of users, this created an impossibly long listing of available shared home folders.

In Windows 2000 the default behavior is different. Typing the above net use command results in the root being established at the Brian folder. In other words, if you switched to drive H, you'd see `h:\>` as the command prompt. This provides additional security because the user won't be able to navigate to any folders above or at the same level in the folder hierarchy.

This doesn't affect down-level clients. They still require separate shares to be established for each user home directory.

Making the Decision

When you design share permissions, use the following guidelines to increase security of share permissions:

- Remove the default share permission that assigns Everyone the Full Control permission. For higher security networks, you can consider the default permission assignment an excess assignment of permissions. Users should usually not require more than Change permission.

- Assign share permissions to domain local groups, not user accounts. By assigning permissions to domain local groups, you can manage share permissions by modifying group memberships rather than by editing the permissions of each shared folder.

- Assign the maximum permission that a security principal will require for the folder hierarchy below the shared folder. The assigned share permissions should never exceed the required level of access for all folders within the shared folder. When you define share permissions, inspect the entire folder hierarchy contained within the shared folder.

Applying the Decision

You need to establish two separate shares for Wide World Importers: one for the default applications in Washington and a second for the Graphics department in Dallas.

To meet the current requirements, you need to establish the following share permissions for the \\Washington\Applications share:

- **Users: Read.** Users don't require any permissions other than Read permissions to find and run application software.

- **Administrators: Full Control.** Administrators require Full Control permissions to modify permissions on files and to update files. If Administrators aren't required to change permissions, you could implement Change permissions for Administrators instead of Full Control.

These permissions allow all users to read and install the applications. Administrators are able to modify files and change permissions on the files.

To meet the security requirements for share permissions in Dallas, the need to assign elevated privileges to Lisa Jacobson, David Jaffe, Stefan Knorr, and Linda Kobara requires you to define a different set of share permissions for \\Dallas\Applications. You must define the following permissions to meet security requirements:

- **Graphics Users: Change.** Members of the Graphics department must have Change permissions assigned. This is because all members of the Graphics department need to be allowed to submit new graphic files to the Common Graphics folder.

- **Graphics Admins: Change.** This domain local group contains four users: Lisa, David, Stefan, and Linda. Lisa and David would be in a global group named Common Graphics and Stefan and Linda would be in another global group named Template Admins.

- **Administrators: Full Control.** Administrators require Full Control permissions to modify permissions on files and to update files. If Administrators aren't required to change permissions, you could implement Change permissions for Administrators instead of Full Control.

Planning NTFS Security

While share permissions affect only network users, NTFS permissions affect both network users and users who are at the computer console. In addition to providing local folder security, NTFS allows permissions to be set for individual files within a folder. The ability to set permissions on files gives you more flexibility when you design your security model for file access.

Note   This raises the question of why share permissions are even required. Remember that to connect to a network resource, you must have an entry point. The share provides this entry point, and you can secure it by using share permissions.

Changes in the Windows 2000 NTFS File System

Windows 2000 introduces functionality in the NTFS file system that isn't found in Windows NT. (Unless otherwise indicated, "Windows NT" refers to versions 3.51 and 4.0.) This functionality includes

- **Encryption.** File-level and directory-level encryption is supported in Windows 2000 through the Encrypting Files System (EFS). EFS allows files and folders to be encrypted so that only the user who performed the encryption (or a designated EFS recovery agent) can decrypt the protected files.

- **Quotas.** NTFS allows storage space restrictions to be set on a per volume basis. You can apply these quotas on a per user basis to limit the amount of disk space in which a user can store data on a volume.

- **Permission inheritance.** Permissions configured at a parent folder propagate to subfolders and file objects within the parent folder. This feature reduces the effort required to modify the permissions of multiple files and subfolders.

Note   If permissions for a resource are inherited, you can't remove them directly. You must copy the inherited permissions to the folder, thus breaking the inheritance, and then remove the individual Access Control Entry (ACE) from the Discretionary Access Control List (DACL).

Assessing NTFS Permissions

You can define NTFS permissions at either the folder or file level. For folders, you can assign the following permissions in the Security tab of the folder's Properties dialog box: Full Control, Modify, Read & Execute, List Folder Contents, Read, and Write. Likewise, you can set permissions for individual files to Full Control, Modify, Read & Execute, Read, and Write.

The predefined NTFS permissions are compilations of several special permissions, including

- **Traverse Folder/Execute File.** Traverse Folder allows or denies navigating through folders, even though the user doesn't have permissions to access files or folders within that folder. This permission applies to folders only. Execute File allows or denies running program files and applies to files only.

- **List Folder/Read Data.** List Folder allows or denies viewing file names and subfolder names within the folder and applies to folders only. Read Data allows or denies viewing data in files and applies to files only.

- **Read Attributes.** Allows or denies viewing the attributes of a file or folder, such as read-only and hidden attributes.

- **Read Extended Attributes.** Allows or denies viewing the extended attributes of a file or folder. Specific programs define the extended attributes.

- **Create Files/Write Data.** Create Files allows or denies creating files within a folder. Write Data allows or denies making changes to a file and overwriting existing content.

- **Create Folders/Append Data.** Create Folders allows or denies creating folders within a folder. Append Data allows or denies making changes to the end of the file but not changing, deleting, or overwriting any existing data in the file.

- **Write Attributes.** Allows or denies changing the attributes of a file or folder, such as read-only and hidden attributes.

- **Write Extended Attributes.** Allows or denies viewing the extended attributes of a file or folder. The extended attributes are defined by specific programs.

- **Delete Subfolders and Files.** Allows or denies deleting subfolders and files when applied at a parent folder, even if the Delete permission hasn't been granted on the specific subfolder or file.

- **Delete.** Allows or denies the deletion of a file or folder.

- **Read Permissions.** Allows or denies reading permissions assigned to a file or folder.

- **Change Permissions.** Allows or denies modification of the permissions assigned to a file or folder.

- **Take Ownership.** Allows or denies taking ownership of the file or folder.

Note   The owner of a file or folder can always change permissions, even if the current permissions explicitly deny access to the owner of the file or folder.

- **Synchronize.** Allows or denies a thread to synchronize with another thread that may signal the original thread. This permission applies only to multi-threaded, multiprocessed programs.

Table 6.1 outlines how the special permissions map to the default folder and file NTFS permissions.

Table 6.1 Special Permission Composition

Special Permissions	Full Control	Modify	Read & Execute	List Folder Contents	Read	Write
Traverse Folder/Execute Files	✓	✓	✓	✓		
List Folder/Read Data	✓	✓	✓	✓	✓	
Read Attributes	✓	✓	✓	✓	✓	
Read Extended Attributes	✓	✓	✓	✓	✓	
Create Files/Write Data	✓	✓	✓	✓	✓	✓
Create Folders/Append Data	✓	✓				✓
Write Attributes	✓	✓				✓
Write Extended Attributes	✓	✓				✓
Delete Subfolders and Files	✓					
Delete	✓	✓				
Read Permissions	✓	✓	✓	✓	✓	✓
Change Permissions	✓					
Take Ownership	✓					
Synchronize	✓	✓	✓	✓	✓	✓

In general, you can define most permissions by choosing the predefined permissions. Remember that you must create security groups that will be included in each ACE in the DACL. The DACL will have one ACE for each level of access you define for an object.

Making the Decision

The following factors will affect your NTFS permission design:

- Assign only necessary permissions. By ensuring that excess permissions are never granted, you increase your network's security and prevent accidental use of excess permissions, such as the deletion of a document.

- If multiple access rights are required to a resource, create a custom domain local group for each type of access. By creating custom domain local groups, you can create separate ACEs for each type of required access. The level of access for any user will be based on that user's group memberships.

- ACEs defined directly to an object are evaluated before any inherited ACEs. Consider, for example, a folder that inherits an ACE that denies write access to the Finance domain local group. While at the folder, Sally, a member of the Finance domain local group, is allowed write access. She can then modify the document's contents because the write ACE is evaluated before the deny ACE. The processing of the ACEs terminates when it's determined that Sally has the necessary permissions to modify the folder's contents.

- Within a group of explicit ACEs, access-denied ACEs are placed before access-allowed ACEs. This order of processing ensures that deny ACEs take precedence over allow ACEs when applied in the same grouping.

- If there are multiple inherited ACEs, the ACEs are evaluated from closest to the object to farthest. This ensures that any explicit ACEs applied to the file or folder containing the file are evaluated before any inherited ACEs.

- Use security templates and Group Policy to standardize NTFS permissions. You can define security templates that set prescribed NTFS permissions for specific folders in a Windows 2000 installation. You can then import these security templates into Group Policy to ensure that they're applied to all computers within the container where the Group Policy is applied.

Note   For more information on using security templates to define security configuration, see Chapter 8, "Securing Microsoft Windows 2000–Based Computers."

Applying the Decision

For the software deployment at the Washington office, the NTFS permissions are going to be consistent for the entire directory structure. This allows you to define NTFS permissions at a higher level in the directory structure. You could deploy the following NTFS permissions to meet the security requirements:

- **Users: Read & Execute.** You don't need to implement separate NTFS permissions for individual files in the Microsoft Office folder. The Read & Execute permissions allow users to read the data in the folder and to execute programs.

- **Administrators: Full Control.** Administrators require Full Control permissions.

The NTFS permissions for the Dallas office will be more complex. This is because you need to provide additional permissions for the Corporate Graphics and Templates folders. By taking advantage of NTFS permission inheritance, you can make the permission assignments shown in Figure 6.4.

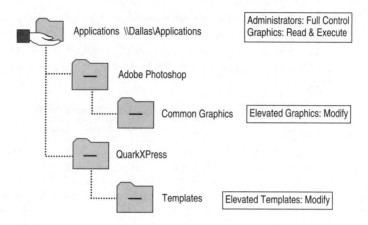

Figure 6.4   Recommended NTFS permission assignments

These permission assignments take advantage of NTFS permission inheritance in that all subfolders of the Applications folder inherit the permissions assigned at the Applications folder.

Combining Share and NTFS Security

An important aspect of securing file access is understanding the interaction of share and NTFS permissions. One set of permissions doesn't necessarily take precedence over the other. Instead, the most restrictive set becomes the effective permissions for the resource. Use the decision tree in Figure 6.5 to determine effective permissions of each security principal.

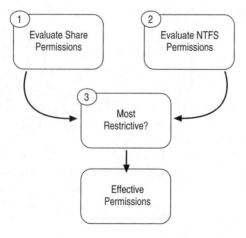

Figure 6.5   Combining share permissions and NTFS permissions

Because individual share permissions or NTFS permissions may vary depending on the group memberships of the security principal, you should perform this evaluation separately for each security principal. For example, the share and NTFS permissions shown in Table 6.2 have been assigned to a folder named Data.

Table 6.2   Share and NTFS Permissions Assigned to the Data Folder

Share Permissions	NTFS Permissions
▪ Users: Read ▪ Administrators: Full Control	▪ Users: Read & Execute ▪ Users: Write ▪ Marketing: Modify ▪ Administrators: Modify

If a member of the Marketing department attempts to access a file in the Data folder over the network, the permissions are evaluated as follows:

1. Determine share permissions. All user accounts are members of the Domain Users group. The Domain Users group is a member of the Users group. Based on membership, the user account would be assigned a share permission of Read.

2. Determine NTFS permissions. The member of the Marketing department is a member of the Users group and the Marketing group. The NTFS permission for the Data folder would be Modify.

3. Determine the most restrictive permissions. In this case, the share permissions are the most restrictive, so the user's effective permissions would be Read. This prevents members of the Marketing department from modifying or deleting documents in the Data folder when they connect over the network.

Likewise, the effective permissions for an administrator would be Modify because the NTFS permissions would be the most restrictive.

In general, your strategy should be to designate either share permissions or NTFS permissions as the primary permissions when you set your security. To define a more granular level of security, designate your effective security through NTFS permissions. Evaluate all folders below a shared folder to determine the highest level of permissions that a security group requires and set the share permissions at that level. This ensures that the share permissions won't become the most restrictive permissions and prevent the NTFS permissions from being the effective permissions.

Should I Just Leave the Default Share Permissions in Place?

Probably not. When you create a new share, the default share permissions include a single entry that assigns Full Control permission to the Everyone group. In a secure Windows 2000 network, modify this share permission to prevent granting excessive privileges if NTFS permissions aren't monitored.

The Full Control permission under NTFS includes three additional abilities over the Modify permission:

- Delete files and folders you don't have permissions to
- Take ownership of a file
- Change permissions of a file

In most networks, these permissions are restricted to the network's administrators. If this is the case in your network, a more effective set of default permissions to use for a shared folder are

- Administrators: Full Control
- Users: Change

Note If users require only Read access to a folder, you should change the Users permissions to Read rather than use Change.

These permissions allow users to create, read, delete, and modify any files in the share, but they can't redefine security settings within the folder.

Making the Decision

Use the following guidelines when planning for combined share permissions and NTFS permissions:

- Set share permissions as the highest level of permissions required for the tree below. This ensures that if NTFS permissions are changed, share permissions won't provide excess privileges to a security principal.

- Use NTFS permissions to define precise access control to file resources. Because NTFS permissions allow protection of both files and folders, define your security by using NTFS permissions. Share permissions don't provide the required flexibility and should only be considered as an entry point to the file system.

- Always use the NTFS file system for data. If you don't use NTFS as your file system, you're limited to share permissions. This prevents you from defining more specific security for files and subfolders within shared folders.

- Evaluate whether Full Control is appropriate. The Full Control permission allows security principals to redefine security for a resource. In general, assign Full Control permission only to administrators and never assign permissions greater than Modify to non-administrators.

Applying the Decision

In reviewing the initial share permissions and NTFS permissions applied to the Applications folders in Washington and Dallas, you see that neither share permissions nor NTFS permissions assign excess permissions.

While you could have left share permissions for Wide World Importers at the default of Everyone being assigned Full Control permissions, doing so could have resulted in excess permissions if any of the NTFS permissions were applied incorrectly.

To troubleshoot any potential problems with NTFS and share permissions, Wide World Importers must complete the design by documenting all initial permission assignments. The documentation should include all folders where permissions are assigned, details on group memberships, and the rationale for each permission assignment. The documentation will assist in troubleshooting permissions later.

Lesson Summary

You must perform the design of share and NTFS permissions by inspecting both sets of permissions. The effective permissions for any resources are based on the most restrictive settings when comparing the share permissions to the NTFS permissions. When designing file security, always base the share permissions on the maximum level of permissions required by a security principal for the directory structure. This ensures that share permissions never restrict access that NTFS permissions are attempting to provide.

Activity: Evaluating Permissions

Your organization has created a Projects share that will contain subfolders created for each ongoing project within the organization. Currently these folders exist within the Projects share, as shown in Figure 6.6.

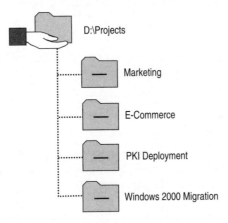

Figure 6.6   Projects folder contents

Table 6.3 outlines the NTFS permissions that have been assigned to the folders within the Projects share.

Table 6.3   NTFS Permissions Assigned to the Projects Folder Tree

Folder	Permissions
\Projects	▪ Administrators: Full Control
\Projects\Marketing	▪ Marketing Department: Read ▪ Marketing Project: Modify ▪ Management: Read
\projects\E-commerce	▪ IT Department: Read ▪ E-commerce Project: Modify ▪ Management: Read
\Projects\PKI Deployment	▪ PKI Project: Modify ▪ IT Department: Read ▪ Management: Read
\Projects\Windows 2000 Migration	▪ IT Department: Read ▪ Migration Project: Modify ▪ Management: Read

The share permissions for the Projects share are configured as follows:

▪ Users: Read

▪ Administrators: Full Control

Based on this information, answer the following questions. The answers can be found in the appendix.

1. If Megan is a member of the IT Department, PKI Project, and E-commerce department, what would be her effective rights for each of the four subfolders within the Projects share?

2. What must you do to the share permissions of the project folder to allow Megan the modify permissions that she requires for the E-commerce and PKI Deployment folders?

3. If at the Projects share, Megan's account was assigned Deny Read permissions for the NTFS permissions, how would this affect her effective rights for the E-commerce and PKI Deployment folders?

Lesson 2: Securing Access to Print Resources

When you design secure access to print resources, consider not only who is allowed to print to a particular printer but also the security of data as it's transmitted to the printer. You need to protect traffic to restricted printers, such as check printers, and prevent users from printing sensitive or confidential material to public printers.

After this lesson, you will be able to

- Plan secure access to print resources

Estimated lesson time: 30 minutes

Assessing Printer Security

You assign printer security by defining permissions when a printer is shared. The permissions you can assign for a printer include

- **Print.** A security principal assigned this permission can submit print jobs to a printer and have the printer process the jobs.

- **Manage Documents.** A security principal assigned this permission can change the order of documents and pause or delete documents in the print queue. By default, this permission is assigned to the special group named Creator Owner. This assignment allows all users to manage their own print jobs submitted to a printer.

- **Manage Printers.** A security principal assigned this permission can share a printer and change a printer's properties.

Many times, though, security requirements for a printer may be more encompassing than simply defining print permissions. In some cases security of the printer output becomes just as important. In the case of confidential documents, this may include the physical security of the printers and the protection of the print job as it's transmitted to the network printer.

For physical security, print devices can be located in a secure place that may require security cards or biometric input to access the device.

To prevent transmission interception of a print job by a network sniffer, you can deploy Internet Protocol Security (IPSec) to protect data print streams to the server hosting the printer, as shown in Figure 6.7. Network sniffers are able to view the contents of data packets as they are transmitted across the network if the packets are not encrypted.

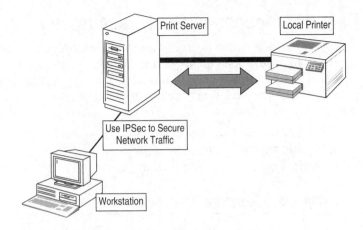

Figure 6.7   Protecting printer data transmissions

To implement IPSec, you must define IPSec policies that require IPSec for any data transmissions sent to the print server. At this time you can't use IPSec to print to a physical print device, so the print device must be locally attached to the print server (using a parallel, USB, or serial port) to ensure end-to-end security of the print transmission.

Note   For more information on planning IPSec, see Chapter 12, "Securing Data with Internet Protocol Security."

Making the Decision

Table 6.4 shows how to secure printing in your organization.

Table 6.4   Print Security Design Decisions

To	Do the Following
Restrict access to the printer to specific groups of users	■ Change the default permissions to only allow the specific domain local groups Print permissions. You'd make the users members of the domain local group by placing the users in a global group that's a member of the domain local group.
Delegate administration of a printer	■ Make the security principal a member of the Print Operators group. ■ To restrict to a specific printer, assign the Manage Printers permissions to the security principal.
Prevent inspection of print jobs	■ Use IPSec between the clients and the print server. ■ Locate printers that print confidential data in restricted areas of the office. ■ Attach the printers directly to the print server. Network-attached printers currently are incapable of performing IPSec operations.

Applying the Decision

The only security that Wide World Importers requires is to prevent employees who aren't members of the Graphics department from using the Agfa Proset 9800 printer. You can easily accomplish this by changing the default share permissions for the printer. Figure 6.8 shows the recommended print permissions that limit usage to the Graphics department.

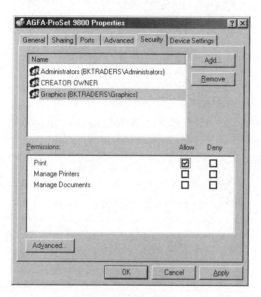

Figure 6.8   Recommended print permissions for the Agfa Proset 9800

Because the jobs sent to the printer are all magazine layouts and graphics that will be for public consumption, you don't need to protect data transmissions to the film printer.

Lesson Summary

While configuring print security may not seem as important as configuring file security, sometimes confidential documents must be secured to prevent inspection of the output. Print security design must include restricting who can access the printer, planning printer placement, and using IPSec where required to prevent inspection of the print job stream.

Lesson 3: Planning EFS Security

Encrypting File System (EFS) allows you to secure files that are stored locally. In addition to encrypting files, you must develop a plan for recovering data in the event recovery keys are lost. Poor EFS planning can result in permanent loss of data.

After this lesson, you will be able to

- Plan the deployment of EFS encryption for a network

Estimated lesson time: 30 minutes

Overview of the EFS Process

Before planning an EFS deployment, it's important to understand how EFS encrypts data stored on NTFS volumes. Knowing how the EFS process takes place will help you in the following cases:

- Determining which user has encrypted a file by using EFS
- Determining who can recover an EFS encrypted file

To the user, the process of encrypting a stored file is as simple as selecting the Encrypt Contents To Secure Data check box for a file or folder, as shown in Figure 6.9.

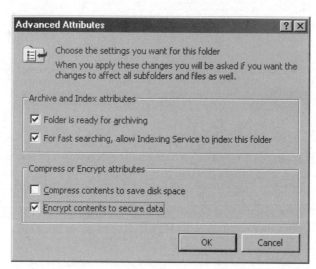

Figure 6.9 Enabling encryption of a file through the interface

Alternatively, an administrator may have configured it so that all content within a specific folder is encrypted on a laptop computer to ensure the security of confidential data.

Encrypting EFS Data

The data encryption process takes place any time a user sets the encryption attribute on a file or folder or when the user saves a file that has the encryption attribute enabled. The process (shown in Figure 6.10) takes place as follows:

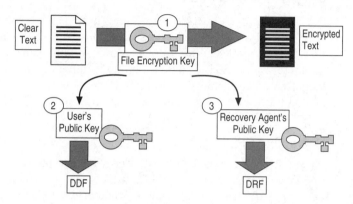

Figure 6.10   The EFS encryption process

1. A File Encryption Key is generated for each file that is to be encrypted. This File Encryption Key is then used to encrypt the clear text document into an encrypted text format.

Note   The encrypted document now has two additional header fields, the Data Decryption Field (DDF) and the Data Recovery Field (DRF). The DDF contains an encrypted copy of the File Encryption Key that only the user who encrypted the file can decrypt. The DRF contains an encrypted copy of the File Encryption Key that only the designated EFS recovery agent can decrypt.

2. The File Encryption Key is encrypted with the User's EFS Encryption public key. This ensures that only the user who holds the matching EFS Encryption private key can decrypt the File Encryption Key. The encrypted File Encryption Key is then stored in the DDF.

Warning   EFS encrypted files can't be shared between users because of the way the File Encryption Key is protected. Only the user who encrypted the file will have the private key required to decrypt the File Encryption Key. This prevents the sharing of EFS encrypted files.

3. The File Encryption Key is encrypted with the EFS recovery agent's EFS Recovery public key. This action ensures that only the user who holds the matching EFS Recovery private key can decrypt the File Encryption Key. The encrypted File Encryption Key is then stored in the DRF.

It's possible to have more than one EFS recovery agent defined for a domain or Organizational Unit (OU). In this case, multiple DRFs are associated with a file. The File Encryption Key is encrypted once for each EFS recovery agent. Each recovery agent will only be able to decrypt the DRF encrypted with her EFS Recovery public key.

Warning   EFS only protects data stored on an NTFS partition. It doesn't provide network transport security. In other words, if you open an EFS-encrypted file on a remote server, the file contents are transmitted to you over the network in clear text. To protect the transmission of the file, you must use IPSec to protect the contents as they are transferred to your computer.

Decrypting EFS Data

Once a file is encrypted, only the user who encrypted the file or a designated EFS recovery agent can open the file and view its contents. The process of decrypting the file differs based on whether it's done by the user or the EFS recovery agent.

Decryption by the Original User

When the user who encrypted the file attempts to open the file, the following process takes place, as shown in Figure 6.11.

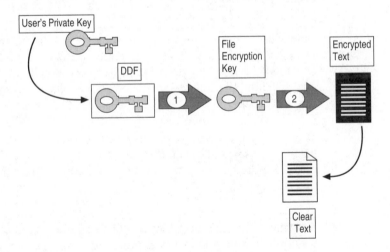

Figure 6.11   EFS decryption by the original user

1. The user's EFS Encryption private key is used to decrypt the File Encryption Key stored in the DDF.

2. The File Encryption Key is used to decrypt the encrypted document.

Note   The decrypted clear text document is then opened with the application associated with the document. To the user it appears that the document "just opened." The user doesn't see any different behavior when opening an encrypted or nonencrypted file.

Decryption by an EFS Recovery Agent

When an EFS recovery agent attempts to open an EFS-encrypted file, the following process takes place, as shown in Figure 6.12.

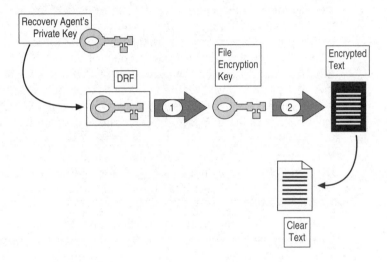

Figure 6.12   EFS decryption by the EFS recovery agent

1. The EFS recovery agent's EFS Recovery private key is used to decrypt the File Encryption Key stored in the DRF.

2. The File Encryption Key is used to decrypt the encrypted document.

Designating an EFS Recovery Agent

A major design issue when you deploy EFS is selecting the account that will be the EFS recovery agent. In other words, you must define the public/private key pair that the EFS process will use to encrypt the File Encryption Key into the DRF of each EFS encrypted file. If you don't define the EFS recovery agent, EFS recovery attempts might fail.

The Initial EFS Recovery Agent

If a Windows 2000–based computer isn't a member of the domain, the default behavior is to configure the initial Administrator account as the EFS recovery agent.

Note The initial Administrator account might not be named Administrator, depending on what name is provided during setup for the initial account at the member server or workstation.

The EFS recovery certificate is *self-issued*, which means that it isn't acquired from a certificate authority but is created by the operating system.

If the Windows 2000–based computer is a member of a domain, the Default Domain Policy is applied to that computer. The Default Domain Policy configures the Administrator account of the domain as the EFS recovery agent. When you log on as Administrator, you may or may not have the necessary private key to perform the EFS recovery. The public key for EFS encryption is the public key associated with the Administrator account of the first domain controller (DC) installed into the domain. This DC's former Security Account Management (SAM) database is used to initially populate the Active Directory directory service domain. During this process, the Administrator's EFS recovery certificate is reconfigured as the EFS recovery agent in the Default Domain Policy.

Note The EFS recovery agent is defined in the following location of the Default Domain Policy: Computer Configuration\Windows Settings\Security Settings \Public Key Policies\Encrypted Data Recovery Agents.

Initially, the only computer that has the associated private key is the initial DC in the domain. Unless you export the private key to a safe location or configure the Administrator account to have a roaming profile and then populate the roaming profile with the contents of the Administrator's profile from the initial DC, you could lose the private key. Losing the private key will prevent you from recovering EFS encrypted files.

The private key is stored in the local user profile in secured storage. Only when you configure a roaming profile is information stored in the user profile shared among multiple computers.

Warning If you configure the roaming profile for the Administrator account and populate the information for the account from a DC other than a member server or the initial DC, you will lose the initial EFS recovery agent private key permanently, which will prevent you from decrypting any files encrypted with the EFS recovery agent's public key.

Configuring a Custom EFS Recovery Agent

A more effective method of configuring the EFS recovery agent is to define a new account as the EFS recovery agent. The newly created EFS Recovery Agent account requires an EFS Recovery certificate but doesn't have to be a member of the Administrators group in the domain. This certificate template is available from a Windows 2000 Enterprise Certification Authority (CA).

Note For more information on deploying Certificate Services in Windows 2000, see Chapter 10, "Planning a Public Key Infrastructure."

You can import the EFS recovery certificate into the Default Domain Policy as the domain's encrypted data recovery agent. The imported public key is used to encrypt the File Encryption Key stored in the DRF. In fact, you can import multiple EFS recovery certificates into Group Policy so that you have multiple EFS recovery agents.

Configuring an Empty Encrypted Data Recovery Agent Policy

You may also choose to prevent EFS encryption on your network by deleting all current EFS recovery agent certificates in the Encrypted Data Recovery Agent policy. Without defined encrypted data recovery agents, it's impossible to use EFS encryption.

When the Encrypted Data Recovery Agent policy exists, but there are no recovery agents included in the policy, this is known as an *empty policy*. The policy exists and is applied, but no values are assigned from it. This differs from the case where no Encrypted Data Recovery Agent policy exists. If there's no policy applied within the site, domain, or OU, then the local policy defined at each computer would take precedence. The creation of an empty policy ensures that local policy doesn't take precedence.

Making the Decision

Use the decision matrix shown in Table 6.5 when planning EFS recovery agents for a domain.

Table 6.5   Decision Factors for EFS Recovery Agents

To	Do the Following
Ensure the recoverability of all EFS-encrypted files in a domain	Define an encrypted data recovery agent in the default domain policy.
Prevent EFS encryption from being used	Delete all existing recovery agent certificates in the Encrypted Data Recovery Agent policy.
Prevent specific computers from using EFS encryption	Place all computers that can't use EFS encryption in a separate OU or OU structure. At the OU or the parent OU, define a Group Policy object that has an empty policy. This is accomplished by initializing an empty policy from encrypted data recovery agents in the Group Policy object.
Restrict EFS encryption to specific users	You can't do this unless all users have only one computer where they log on to the network. EFS recovery agents are a property of the computer, not the user.

Applying the Decision

Wide World Importers wants to prevent the use of EFS encryption. You can do this by deleting the default EFS recovery agent from the Default Domain Policy. By removing all entries from the Default Domain Policy, but not deleting the policy, Wide World Importers can prevent users from using EFS to encrypt files. If there's no defined EFS recovery agent, EFS encryption is disabled on the domain member computers.

Recovering Encrypted Files

When you develop your security plan for encrypted files, you must set up a process for recovering encrypted files. The process must include the use of the EFS recovery private keys and defining where EFS recovery operations can take place on the network.

Assessing Recovery of Encrypted Files

To decrypt an encrypted file, you must be the user who encrypted the file or be a designated recovery agent. In other words, you must hold the private key for the EFS encryption public key of the user who encrypted the File Encryption Key or you must hold the private key for the EFS recovery public key used to encrypt the File Encryption Key.

The best way to deploy an EFS recovery solution is to complete the following steps:

1. Create a new account to perform the request for the EFS recovery certificate.

2. Configure the permissions on the EFS Recovery certificate template to allow the new account to have Enroll permissions in Active Directory Sites And Services.

Note Changing the permissions for a certificate template requires that the Services node is exposed in the Active Directory Sites And Services console. This is done by selecting Show Services Node from the View menu. The certificate templates can be found in the Active Directory Sites And Services\Public Key Services \Certificate Templates folder.

---

3. Request an EFS recovery certificate when logged on as the new account. You can request certificates by using a Web browser and connecting to http://*certsrvname*/certsrv/ (where *certservname* is the server issuing the certificate) or by loading the Certificates MMC console focused on the current user.

4. Export the key and the corresponding private key to a PKCS#12 file and protect the file with a strong password. The PKCS#12 file is a format that allows the private key to be exported. The PKCS #12 file should then be stored on a removable medium, such as a Jaz drive, floppy disk, or writable CD-ROM.

5. Store the PKCS#12 file in a secure location, such as a safe.

6. Import the public key into the Default Domain Policy in the Encrypted Data Recovery Agent policy.

7. Delete the new account.

When you perform an EFS recovery, determine the private key that can perform the EFS recovery and then import the private key into the certificate store of any user account. The user can decrypt the file because the user account now holds the corresponding private key to the public key used to encrypt the File Encryption Key.

Determining the Required Private Keys

Use the Efsinfo utility from the *Microsoft Windows 2000 Server Resource Kit* to determine which private key is required to decrypt an EFS encrypted file. Efsinfo has the following parameters:

```
EFSINFO [/U] [/R] [/C] [/I] [/Y] [/S:dir] [pathname [...]]
```

Where

- /U displays user information (Default option).
- /R displays Recovery Agent information.
- /C displays certificate thumbprint information.

Warning Don't confuse the certificate thumbprint with the certificate serial number. You can view the certificate thumbprint by viewing the properties of the certificate and inspecting the details page. You access the properties of a certificate by double-clicking an issued certificate in the Certificates MMC.

- /I continues performing the specified operation even after errors have occurred. By default, Efsinfo stops when an error is encountered.
- /Y displays your current EFS certificate thumbprint on the local PC. The files you specified might not be on this PC.
- /S performs the specified operation on directories in the given directory and all subdirectories.

For example, to recover the file c:\license.txt, you could type **EFSINFO LICENSE.TXT /R /U /C**. The output from the command shows the thumbprint of the user private key and the recovery private key that you can use to decrypt the License.txt file.

Note The Cipher.exe command allows the launching of bulk encryption and decryption processes.

Making the Decision

Use the decision matrix shown in Table 6.6 when planning recovery of encrypted files.

Table 6.6   Planning EFS Recovery

To	Do the Following
Restrict the ability to recover encrypted files	Export the private key of the defined recovery agent to a PKCS#12 file. Import the file only when it's necessary to recover an encrypted file.
Restrict recovery to a specific workstation	Create a new account to perform the recovery and restrict the account to the desired workstation. Import the PKCS#12 file to restore the private key for recovery.
Allow more than one private key to perform EFS recovery	Designate more than one certificate in the encrypted data recovery agent policy.
Determine which users can decrypt a file	Use Efsinfo /U /C to determine which private key is required to decrypt the DDF and decrypt the File Encryption Key.
Determine which recovery agents can decrypt a file	Use Efsinfo /R /C to determine which private key is required to decrypt the DRF and decrypt the File Encryption Key.

Applying the Decision

The files that were encrypted before the computers were rebuilt may still be recoverable. A network administrator should run the Efsinfo utility from the *Microsoft Windows 2000 Server Resource Kit* to determine the thumbprint of the private key that can decrypt the DRF of the encrypted files.

Because Wide World Importers hasn't configured the EFS recovery agent, chances are the default EFS recovery agent was previously configured. In this case, the holder of the EFS recovery agent private key is probably the Administrator account from the first DC installed in the wideworldimporters.tld domain. As long as a roaming profile hasn't been implemented for the Administrator account, the private key for EFS recovery of this account might be able to decrypt the data recovery field and decrypt the encrypted data files.

Lesson Summary

While the process of performing EFS encryption is relatively easy, when you draw up your design you must be careful to ensure the recoverability of EFS encrypted files. Your security design must contain provisions for the designation of an EFS recovery agent and outline the preferred process for performing EFS recovery.

Lab 6-1: Securing File and Print Resources

Lab Objectives

This lab prepares you to secure file and print resources by meeting the following objectives:

- Design share and NTFS permissions to provide required security for file resources
- Design print permissions to secure data submitted to a printer
- Design EFS encryption for a domain

About This Lab

This lab looks at three topics:

- Designing security for user's home directories and a shared data store location
- Securing the printing of confidential documents by the legal department that must not be intercepted when sent to the printer
- Designing EFS security for mobile computer users

Before You Begin

Make sure that you've completed reading the chapter material before starting the lab. Pay close attention to the sections where the design decisions were applied throughout the chapter for information on building your administrative structure.

Scenario: Contoso Ltd.

Contoso Ltd., an international magazine sales company, wants to design security for all user home directories, security for a transfer file location, print security for the legal department, and EFS security for the mobile sales people.

Folder Structure

The following folder structure will exist on a DC located at either the Seattle, Lima, or London location. The user's home folder is stored on a DCat his location.

You will create a folder structure on each of the DCs, as shown in Figure 6.13.

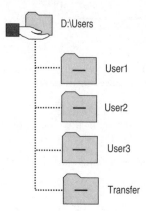

Figure 6.13   The users' directory structure

The d:\Users folder will be located on an NTFS partition to allow local file security to be defined for all folders in the hierarchy.

Shared Folders

You will define the following shared folders on the network to allow administrators to access all folders and to allow users to access their home folders and the shared folder.

Shared Name	Location	Purpose
Users	D:\users	To provide an entry point that allows access to all user home directories and the shared folder (subject to NTFS permissions). Must be accessible by all users of the network.
User#	D:\users\User#	The personal home folder for User#. In practice, User# would be replaced with the user's logon name. Should only be accessible by the user associated with the personal home folder.

NTFS Permission Requirements

To provide more specific security, Contoso has defined the following NTFS permissions requirements:

- The Users share should allow users to see only the subfolders that they have permissions to. For example, if User1 is the current user, he should only see the User1 and Transfer folders when connected to the Users share.

- Administrators of the network must have Full Control of all folders in the d:\Users folder hierarchy.

- In the Transfer folder, the following requirements have been defined:

    - A global group named SharedFilesAdmins exists. This group must be able to modify and read any documents stored in the d:\Users\Transfer folder.

    - The creator of the document must be able to modify or delete the document once it's placed in the folder.

    - All other users should be able to read only documents posted by other users. This allows the users to copy a file posted by another employee to their personal folder.

Print Security for the Legal Department

In a separate case, the legal department is concerned that highly confidential documents related to the acquisition of another company may have been compromised when a printed copy of a document went missing.

The legal department wants to have a printer available that can be used only by itself, that's physically accessible only by its members, and that isn't subject to inspection as the print job is sent to the printer.

Mobile Computer Security

Contoso has several salespeople who use a laptop computer as their primary computer. The salespeople connect to the network every day to download their latest pricing database. This database is key to the salespeople because it sets the pricing for that day for the products that they will sell.

The Driving Force

Over the past few months laptops have been stolen from some of Contoso's salespeople. While it may be just a coincidence, a competing magazine sales company has released a pricing strategy that undercuts all Contoso pricing.

Management is concerned about the effects of the stolen laptops and wants to better secure the pricing database and other key documents found on the salespeople's laptops. Management isn't concerned about desktop computers located at Contoso offices.

IT's Perspective

The IT department must design local file security for the pricing database so that only the laptop's user can access the data. In addition, a folder must be provided to allow documents to be encrypted when placed within the folder. The IT department wants to ensure that only salespeople have this ability. They want to prevent all other users from using EFS to encrypt data on their computers until they develop a recovery strategy for the EFS encryption.

Additional Requirements

For each domain, you must define a recovery agent account that allows recovery of encrypted data on the salespeople's laptops. The recovery agent must not exist as an account on the network. If data must be recovered from a user's laptop, the user must go into her home office in London, Seattle, or Lima. A network administrator then uses the recovery key to recover any encrypted files. The administrator must work with another administrator to attach the EFS recovery private key to the administrative account. Once the recovery is performed, a second administrator must verify the removal of the EFS recovery private key from the administrator's account.

Exercise 1: Planning File Security

This exercise looks at the design of Share and NTFS permissions to protect the d:\Users folder hierarchy based on the design requirements outlined in the lab scenario.

Planning Share Security

This exercise looks at designing the share permissions necessary for meeting Contoso's requirements for providing user home folders and a transfer folder. Answers to these questions can be found in the appendix.

1. What share permissions must be established on the Users folder to allow users to access their personal folder and the transfer folder?

2. What share permissions must you establish for each user name share?

3. Under what circumstances would you not need to create individual user shared folders?

Planning NTFS Security

This exercise looks at designing the NTFS permissions necessary for meeting Contoso's requirements for providing user home folders and a transfer folder. Answers to the questions can be found in the appendix.

1. Will default NTFS permissions meet all security requirements, or must you define special permissions?

2. Complete the following table to define NTFS permissions for each folder in the D:\Users folder hierarchy. Assume that the global group named SharedFileAdmins is a member of the domain local group named TransferAdmins.

Folder	Permissions
D:\Users	
D:\Users\User1	
D:\Users\User2	
D:\Users\User3	
D:\Users\Transfer	

3. Where would the home folders be defined for each user account?

Exercise 2: Planning Print Security

This exercise looks at planning security for the legal department to secure the printing of highly confidential legal documents. Answers to these questions can be found in the appendix.

1. What can you do to limit who can print to the Legal printer?

2. Complete the following table to document the required permissions for the Legal printer.

Group	Permissions
Administrators	
Print Operators	
Legal Department	
Creator Owner	

3. What planning is required to prevent output to the Legal printer from being viewed by unauthorized personnel?

4. What can you do to protect documents as they are sent to the Legal printer?

Exercise 3: Planning EFS for Laptops

This exercise looks at planning the EFS deployment to provide local file encryption to laptop users. Answers to these questions can be found in the appendix.

1. What must you do to provide EFS capabilities only to laptop computers at Contoso?

2. Assuming that you've created the OU structure for Contoso's London domain as shown in Figure 6.14, where would you apply the Group Policy object that designates the EFS recovery agent?

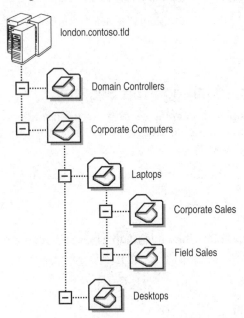

Figure 6.14　The OU structure of Contoso's London office

3. What must you do to prevent all other computers in the domain from using EFS encryption?

4. How can you enforce the requirement to have two administrators verify the attachment of the EFS recovery private key to an administrator's account?

5. What's another method you could use to protect the private key in addition to storing it in a safe?

Review

Answering the following questions will reinforce key information presented in this chapter. If you are unable to answer a question, review the appropriate lesson and then try the question again. Answers to the questions can be found in the appendix.

1. Scott Culp is concerned about the security of his contacts database. The database is in a shared folder on his computer named Contacts. He has set share permissions to allow only members of the Scott Contacts group Read permissions to the share and to ensure that only his account has Full Control permissions. Scott's computer is configured to dual boot with Windows 98 and the Contacts folder is stored on his c:\ drive. Are Scott's concerns valid?

2. Bob has created a new folder on his desktop that he wants to share with Brian. If Bob enables only sharing and doesn't configure permissions, what security risks may exist?

3. Your organization wants to secure the transmission of print jobs to a network printer. All client computers are using Windows 2000 Professional. The plan is to use IPSec to protect the transmission of print jobs between the client computer and the print server and from the print server to the physical network print device. Is this strategy feasible? If not, what can you do as an alternative?

4. What security concerns result from leaving the domain's EFS recovery agent as the default EFS recovery agent?

5. Two users in the Marketing department are working on a new ad campaign, and other members of the marketing department shouldn't know the details. Only the two user accounts must be able to open the document. An outside consultant has recommended using EFS to encrypt the file so that only the two users can access the document. Explain whether this proposal will work. If it won't, provide an alternative solution.

CHAPTER 7

Designing Group Policy

About This Chapter

Group Policy defines and controls the behavior of applications and network resources for an organization's users and computers. This chapter explores the planning issues involved when applying Group Policy. You learn how to design Group Policy to ensure that inheritance works as expected. This chapter also illustrates how to override the default inheritance model by using the Block Policy Inheritance and No Override attributes.

Before You Begin

To complete this chapter, you must read the chapter scenario. This scenario is used throughout the chapter to apply the design decisions discussed in each lesson.

Chapter Scenario: Wide World Importers

In this chapter you will apply design decisions to Wide World Importers, a North American corporation with distribution and service centers across the continent. Your task is to design a Group Policy deployment for the installation of application software that enforces specific restrictions of the Microsoft Windows 2000 desktop settings.

Proposed OU Structure

A consultant has recommended the Organizational Unit (OU) structure depicted in Figure 7.1 to Wide World Importers for the deployment of Group Policy.

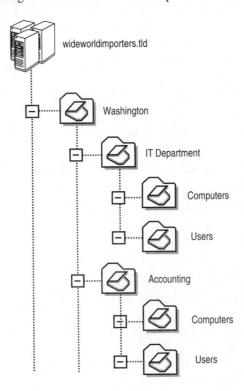

Figure 7.1   Proposed OU structure for Wide World Importers

In addition to the Washington, D.C., office (shown in Figure 7.1), the regional offices in Vancouver, Toronto, Portland, Dallas, and Mexico City each need to have its own OU structures. Departments within each regional office also have separate OUs. Each office might have additional departments besides IT and Accounting.

Existing Site Definitions

Each city has been defined as a site within Active Directory directory service. The IP addressing scheme has been defined to associate the IP subnet at each office with the site name, as shown in Figure 7.2.

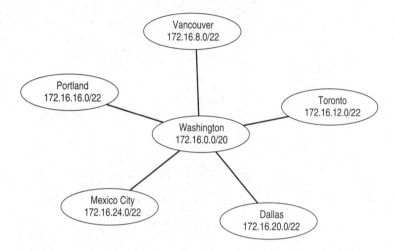

Figure 7.2 Site and IP subnet addressing for Wide World Importers

All computers at a site will use addresses from the subnets assigned to each site. The site information for each computer will be determined by its IP address. Regional offices will be assigned a subset of the site's IP address range to ensure that they connect to a domain controller (DC) at the nearest regional office.

Application Installation Requirements

Wide World Importers wants to use Group Policy to assign Microsoft Office to all full-time employees. Contingent staff will have Office manually installed to ensure that licensing information is maintained. To perform the automatic installation, Wide World Importers wants to assign Office to all full-time employees in the wideworldimporters.tld domain.

The Accounting department wants to assign the accounting software to all of its computers. Because Wide World Importers has purchased only a limited number of licenses, the software must be available only on the Accounting department's computers.

Engineering Requirements

As mentioned in Chapter 2, the Engineering department has its own requirements for account policies that require a separate domain for the department. Figure 7.3 shows the OU structure required by the Engineering department.

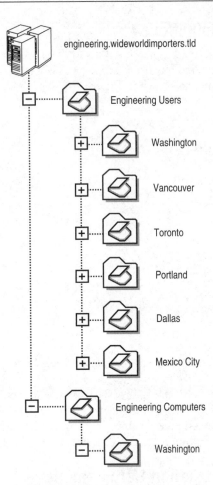

Figure 7.3   OU design for engineering.wideworldimporters.tld

The Engineering department has implemented an OU structure using the type of security principal (Engineering Users and Engineering Computers) as the top level of the OU hierarchy. Below this level are six OUs based on the six regional office locations. The Engineering department needs to have Office automatically installed on the desktop computers of all users, including full-time and contingent staff.

The New Employee

Don Funk was hired by Wide World Importers' Accounting department after working two years as an on-site contractor in the Toronto office. When Don logged on to the network on his first day as a full-time employee, he found that the accounting software was installed and available but Office wasn't installed.

Lesson 1: Planning Deployment of Group Policy

When designing Group Policy for an organization, consider the default inheritance model to ensure that you take full advantage of Group Policy inheritance. In certain circumstances you may want to deviate from the default behavior by implementing Block Policy Inheritance or the No Override attribute.

After this lesson, you will be able to

- Plan the deployment of Group Policy objects in Active Directory

Estimated lesson time: 30 minutes

Group Policy Overview

Group Policy allows centralized control of user and computer configuration settings. Rather than applying security settings at each computer in an organization, Group Policy uses Active Directory to centralize management and standardize security settings.

Note   For more information on how Group Policy works within a Windows 2000 network, see the white papers "Introduction to Group Policy" and "Windows 2000 Group Policy" on the Supplemental Course Materials CD-ROM (\chapt07\Group Policy Introduction.doc and \chapt07\Group Policy White Paper.doc) that accompanies this book.

Planning Group Policy Inheritance

Inheritance simplifies Group Policy administration by allowing administrators to apply widespread policy settings only to higher-level OUs. You can apply Group Policy at different levels within Active Directory by defining Group Policy objects that are linked to sites, domains, or OUs. The Group Policy is applied to all computer or user objects within the container where you define the Group Policy object.

If you define Group Policy using the default inheritance model; Group Policies are applied in the order shown in Figure 7.4.

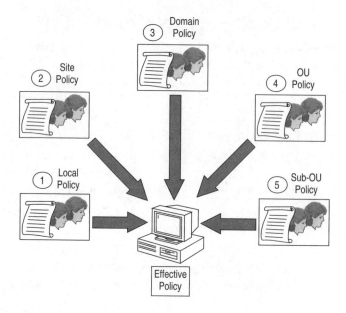

Figure 7.4   Group Policy application order

1. **Local Group Policies.** If you apply local Group Policies first, centralized Group Policy settings always take precedence, since they are applied later.

2. **Site Group Policies.** In general, don't define site Group Policies. The reason you shouldn't is because they're stored in the system volume of the DCs in the domain where the site Group Policy was defined. If you define a site Group Policy, the Windows 2000 client must connect to a DC where the site Group Policy was defined in order to download the Group Policy. If the DCs aren't located at the local site, logon times might be slow.

3. **Domain Group Policies.** Domain Group Policies are often used to define standard settings that apply to all computers in the domain. For example, account policy settings are domain-level settings that must be defined at the domain.

Note   For more information on account policies and their effect on designing domain structures, see Chapter 2, "Designing Active Directory for Security."

---

4. **OU Group Policies.** The effective range of OU Group Policies is greater when you apply them higher up the OU structure. Group Policy settings that affect a larger number of computers or users are applied at top-level OUs.

5. **Sub-OU Group Policies.** You apply sub-OU Group Policies last. In general, the lower in the OU structure, the more specific the Group Policy settings will be, as the Group Policy settings will affect a smaller number of users or computer objects.

The effective permissions for a computer or user are based on the preceding inheritance model. If you apply different settings, the settings you apply to an OU where the user or computer object is located typically take precedence.

Assessing Group Policy Application

When you design Group Policy, make sure that your design meets security requirements without significantly affecting logon performance. Use the following design strategies to optimize the application of Group Policy:

- Disable unused portions of Group Policy. If the Group Policy object defines only computer settings, disable the user portion of Group Policy to ensure that the user settings aren't processed, as shown in Figure 7.5. Disabling the unused portions of Group Policy results in faster processing of the Group Policy object.

Figure 7.5   Preventing user Group Policy application

- Minimize the levels at which you apply Group Policy. The more Group Policies that you apply to a user or computer, the slower the logon process will be. If you apply a Group Policy at each level of the OU structure, the logon time increases as each of the Group Policies is processed.

Note A common misconception is that the number of OU levels affects logon performance. In fact, logon performance is affected by the number of levels at which Group Policy is applied.

- Avoid cross-domain Group Policy object assignments. If you define the Group Policy in a different domain, the user or computer must contact a domain controller from the domain containing the Group Policy object. If the domain is accessible only over a slow WAN link, logon performance suffers.

Block Policy Inheritance

Sometimes you don't want to apply a Group Policy that was defined at a higher-level OU. For example, a policy that enables the auditing of directory service access at a parent OU may not be desired for computers located in an OU under the parent OU. In this situation you can use the Block Policy Inheritance attribute to prevent application of the higher-level Group Policies, as shown in Figure 7.6.

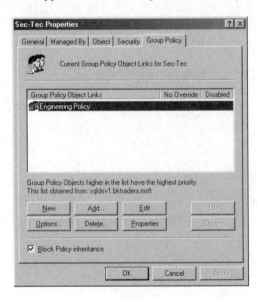

Figure 7.6 Configuring the Block Policy Inheritance attribute

Use the Block Policy Inheritance attribute sparingly because it complicates the troubleshooting of Group Policy application problems. In most cases adding new OUs or redesigning your OU structure removes the need to apply Block Policy Inheritance.

Configuring No Override

Sometimes an administrator doesn't want administrators of lower-level OUs to
be able to block critical Group Policy settings. For example, if a standard has
been developed that all computers in the domain must enable success and failure
auditing for account logon events, an administrator could enable the No Override
attribute on the Group Policy object so that lower-level OUs can't block inheritance, as shown in Figure 7.7.

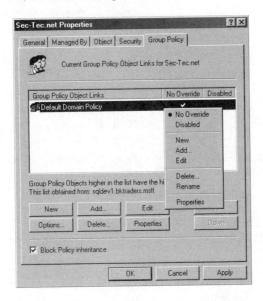

Figure 7.7   Configuring the No Override attribute

When you apply the No Override attribute, lower-level Group Policy objects
can't override higher-level Group Policy settings. When you configure No Override Group Policies, include only those settings that you specifically wish to prevent Block Policy Inheritance from affecting. Don't include other settings that
can be overridden in the Group Policy. A recommended best practice is to create
a separate Group Policy object containing only those settings that you wish to
apply to all objects within the container structure.

Making the Decision

Use the decision matrix shown in Table 7.1 to assist in designing Group Policy
application for your organization.

Table 7.1   Designing Group Policy Application

To	Do the Following
Simplify the troubleshooting of Group Policy	■ Allow only default inheritance to take place, rather than implementing Block Policy Inheritance or No Override settings. This action might require extensive reworking of your OU design.
Minimize the time spent processing Group Policy during logon	■ Minimize the number of levels where Group Policy is applied in the OU structure. ■ Avoid cross-linking Group Policy objects between domains.
Prevent blocking of key Group Policy settings	■ Break the key settings into a separate Group Policy object and apply the No Override attribute to the Group Policy object.
Prevent users from changing configuration by applying Local Group Policies	■ Ensure that important settings are defined in Group Policy. Group Policy settings always take precedence over local Group Policy settings.
Apply central Group Policy that will affect all users	■ Apply the Group Policy object higher in the Active Directory hierarchy. These Group Policy objects are commonly applied at the domain or at a top-level OU.
Apply specific Group Policy to a limited number of computers or users	■ Apply the Group Policy object at the OU where the user or computer objects are located in Active Directory.

Applying the Decision

In the Wide World Importers case study, you've been asked to design a targeted deployment of Office and an accounting software application. Making the following decisions will help you deploy these applications:

■ Create separate Group Policy objects for the engineering.wideworldimporters.tld and wideworldimporters.tld domains. If you define the Group Policy object to install Office in the wideworldimporters.tld domain and then cross-link it to the engineering.wideworldimporters.tld domain, the Engineering department will have slower logons. You will achieve better performance by defining two Group Policy objects, one in the wideworldimporters.tld domain and one in the engineering.wideworldimporters.tld domain.

■ Apply the Group Policy that assigns Office to all employees at the wideworldimporters.tld domain and the engineering.wideworldimporters.tld domain. This ensures that the application is available to all users in each domain.

- Remove the computer component of the Office installation Group Policy object. You don't need to enable the computer component of the Group Policy object because the application will be user-assigned.

- Apply the Group Policy object to assign the accounting software at the OU=Computers, OU=Account, OU=*cityname*, DC=Wideworldimporters, DC=tld containers (where *cityname* is the name of the city represented by the OU). The Group Policy will be linked to six separate OUs (one for each of the six regional offices).

- Remove the user component of the accounting software installation Group Policy object. You don't need to enable the user component of the Group Policy object because the application will be computer-assigned.

This Group Policy design ensures that all required computers or users have the necessary software that Group Policy applies. This design also ensures that you don't have to implement the No Override or Block Policy Inheritance settings.

Filtering Group Policy by Using Security Groups

Group Policy isn't applied to security groups. Instead, Group Policy is based on the location of objects within the Active Directory hierarchy. By default, Group Policies apply to all users and computers within a site, domain, or OU.

Note   If you want to apply a Group Policy to a user or computer, that user or computer must belong to a security group that has both the Read permission and the Apply Group Policy permission.

You can use security groups to filter Group Policy application so that it applies only to specific users and groups within a given object. When defining a Group Policy object, you can define which security groups will be able to Read and Apply Group Policy. You do this in the Group Policy object's Security tab.

Note   A common misconception is that the security group must be located in the OU where the Group Policy is applied. In fact, the security group can exist anywhere in the Active Directory structure.

Another Use for Group Policy Filtering

How can you prevent OU administrators from implementing the Block Policy Inheritance attribute? The following example walks you through an alternate design that you can use.

Figure 7.8 shows a typical Group Policy deployment strategy.

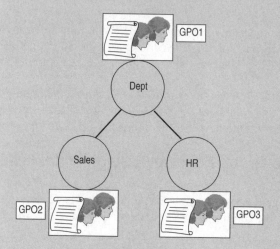

Figure 7.8   A typical strategy for Group Policy deployment

In this case GPO1 is applied at the Dept OU and by default affects both the Sales and Human Resources OUs through Group Policy Inheritance. GPO2 affects only objects in the Sales OU, and GPO3 affects only objects in the Human Resources OU. It's possible that at the Sales OU or at the Human Resources OU an OU Administrator could implement the Block Policy Inheritance attribute. If this happened, the Group Policy settings in the Dept OU wouldn't be applied.

As an alternative, rather than deploying separate OUs for the Sales and Human Resources departments, you could use Group Policy filtering at the Dept OU and remove the need for the separate Sales and Human Resources OUs, as shown in Figure 7.9.

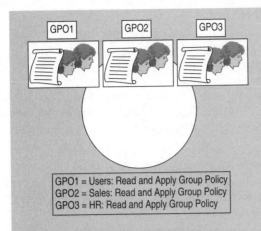

GPO1 = Users: Read and Apply Group Policy
GPO2 = Sales: Read and Apply Group Policy
GPO3 = HR: Read and Apply Group Policy

Figure 7.9 An alternate strategy for Group Policy deployment

Rather than creating sub-OUs, you define three separate Group Policy objects at the Dept OU. You then use Group Policy filtering to determine which security groups apply the Group Policy objects. In this example, you apply GPO1 to the Users group. You apply GPO2 only to members of the Sales group and you apply GPO3 only to members of the Human Resources group. This design keeps users who can modify GPO2 and GPO3 from blocking inheritance, since GPO1 is applied at the same OU level.

Making the Decision

Use the design matrix shown in Table 7.2 to design filtering strategies for Group Policy application.

Table 7.2 Designing Group Policy Filtering

To	Incorporate the Following into Your Design Plan
Ensure that a Group Policy is applied to a security group	• Assign both the Read and Apply Group Policy permissions to the security group.
Prevent an OU administrator from blocking inheritance	• Don't assign the OU administrator the Write permission for the Group Policy object. • Apply the Group Policy object at the parent OU and filter the Group Policy object so that it's applied to only the computers or users in the child OU.
Prevent application of a Group Policy object to a specific group of users or computers	• Create a security group with those users or computers as members. • Assign the security group the Deny permission for Apply Group Policy. This security assignment prevents the Group Policy object from being applied to the security group.

Applying the Decision

You can meet the requirement to install Office software only on the desktop computers of full-time employees by using Group Policy filtering. Include the following procedures in your Group Policy deployment plan:

- Create two custom domain local groups named FullTimeGP and ContingentGP. Assign Read and Apply Group Policy permissions to these domain local groups. You do this in the Office Group Policy object's Security tab.

- Create two custom global groups named FullTimeEmployees and ContingentStaff that contain all full-time staff and all contingent staff. You will make these global groups members of the FullTimeGP and ContingentGP domain local groups.

- Configure the security for the Office Group Policy so that only the FullTimeGP domain local group has Read and Apply Group Policy permissions. This ensures that only the full-time staff has the Office software assigned by using Group Policy.

The network administrators could also configure the Office Group Policy to have the No Override attribute. This would prevent regional office administrators from blocking the installation of Office. Since this isn't a security setting, this option wouldn't be required for the Office Group Policy.

Lesson Summary

Your Group Policy design allows for the default Group Policy object inheritance model. The inheritance model ensures that settings applied higher in the Active Directory hierarchy will be applied to all computers or users lower in the Active Directory hierarchy. The default behavior changes only when you apply the Block Policy Inheritance or No Override attributes.

Lesson 2: Troubleshooting Group Policy

Sometimes the application of Group Policy doesn't occur as expected. For example, a Group Policy object might apply unexpected restrictions to a computer or user. This lesson outlines a methodology you can use to troubleshoot Group Policy application and locate the undesired Group Policy object.

After this lesson, you will be able to

- Troubleshoot Group Policy application to find the Group Policy object that's applying the undesired setting

Estimated lesson time: 30 minutes

Assessing Group Policy Troubleshooting

One common reason that Group Policy application doesn't always work as expected is that there's been a misapplication of the Block Policy Inheritance or No Override attributes to Group Policy. Take the following steps to troubleshoot Group Policy application:

- Inspect the Active Directory hierarchy. Because there's a default inheritance order for Group Policies, you can inspect the Active Directory hierarchy to determine the location of Group Policy objects that affect the user or computer.

- Inspect applied Group Policies by using Gpresult. The Gpresult utility from the *Microsoft Windows 2000 Server Resource Kit* shows which Group Policies were applied to the computer or user.

Using Gpresult

The Gpresult utility shows which Group Policy objects were applied to a user or a computer. The Gpresult utility uses the following parameters:

```
gpresult [/V] [/S] [/C | /U] [/?]
```

where:

/V runs Gpresult in verbose mode

/S runs Gpresult in super verbose mode

/C displays only the Group Policy objects applied to the computer

/U displays only the Group Policy objects applied to the user

(continued)

In addition to showing which Group Policy objects were applied, the Gpresult utility also lists all group memberships of the user or computer being analyzed. The group membership information is useful in troubleshooting security group filtering, as demonstrated in Figure 7.10.

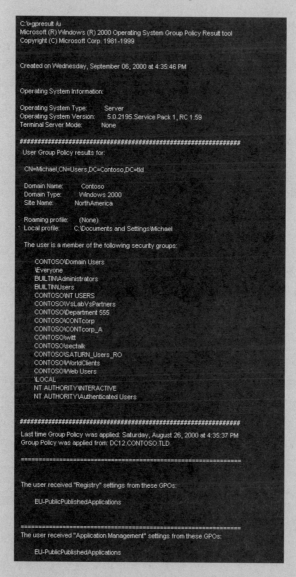

Figure 7.10   Gpresult output for a user named Michael

Making the Decision

Use the decision matrix shown in Table 7.3 to troubleshoot Group Policy application.

Table 7.3   Troubleshooting Group Policy Application

To	Do the Following
Determine all possible locations where Group Policy objects may be defined	▪ Inspect the Active Directory structure to determine the site, domain, and OUs that could have Group Policy applied to the user or computer.
Determine whether the Group Policy that was applied is a user or computer configuration setting	▪ Use the Gpresult utility from the *Microsoft Windows 2000 Server Resource Kit* to determine which Group Policies were applied to the computer or user.
Determine why a higher-level Group Policy isn't applied	▪ Look for Block Policy Inheritance settings or conflicting settings at an OU closer to the user or computer object than where the higher-level Group Policy is defined. ▪ Alternatively, determine if any Group Policy filtering has been configured. If the affected computer or user isn't a member of a security group that has the Read and Apply Group Policy permissions assigned, the Group Policy object won't be applied.
Determine why a lower-level Group Policy isn't applied	▪ Look for a Group Policy object with the No Override attribute set at an OU, domain, or site higher in the hierarchy. ▪ As an alternative, determine if any Group Policy filtering has been configured. If the affected computer or user isn't a member of a security group that has the Read and Apply Group Policy permissions assigned, the Group Policy object won't be applied.
Determine why a Group Policy doesn't apply to all computers or users within a site, domain, or OU	▪ Inspect the Group Policy object's Security tab to determine which security groups have been assigned the Read Group Policy and Apply Group Policy permissions. To apply Group Policy, you must assign both permissions.

Applying the Decision

As a member of the Accounting department, Don Funk should have the accounting software assigned to his computer and should have had Office assigned to his user account. Because the accounting software is working as expected, there's no reason to troubleshoot the associated Group Policy objects. Assuming that Don is now a member of the Accounting department in Toronto, perform the following tasks:

- Verify the location of Don's user account in Active Directory. Don's user account should be located in the following container in Active Directory: OU=Users, OU=Accounting, OU=Toronto, DC=Wideworldimporters, DC=tld.

- Determine where Group Policies may exist that could affect Don's user account for application of Group Policy. Group Policy could be applied to Don's user account from the following locations: the Toronto site, the wideworldimporters.tld domain, the Toronto OU, the Accounting OU, or the Users OU. Assume that your inspection finds no additional Group Policy objects (other than the Office and accounting software Group Policy objects).

- Run Gpresult to determine all user Group Policies that were applied to Don's user account at logon. To determine which user Group Policy objects were applied when Don logged on to the network, run Gpresult /u /s at Don's computer. The results would show that the Office Group Policy object wasn't applied.

- Determine if filtering is affecting the Group Policy application. The Office Group Policy object is applied only to full-time employees in the wideworldimporters.tld domain. The most likely reason that Don doesn't have Office assigned to his user account is that his account wasn't made a member of the FullTimeEmployees global group and is still a member of the ContingentStaff global group. Until he's made a member of the FullTimeEmployees global group and then logs off and back onto the network to repopulate his Access Token, Don won't have the Office Group Policy applied to his user account.

Lesson Summary

When Group Policy application doesn't take place as expected, you must have a methodology for determining the reason. Using the Gpresult utility and inspecting the Active Directory hierarchy allows you to determine where Group Policy objects have been applied to a user or computer. Once you identify *where* Group Policy objects can be applied, you can identify *which* Group Policy objects are applied.

Activity: Troubleshooting Group Policy Application

This activity uses the Active Directory structure shown in Figure 7.11.

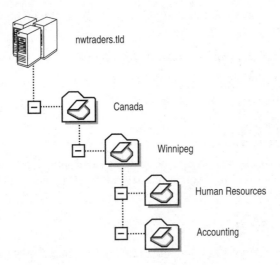

Figure 7.11   The nwtraders.tld Active Directory hierarchy

Don Funk recently transferred to the Accounting department from the Human Resources department at the Washington office. He found that applications that should be available only to the Human Resources department are still being installed on his computer.

Based on this information, answer the following questions. The answers to these questions can be found in the appendix.

1. Is the application of software a user or computer configuration option in Group Policy?

2. If the Human Resources application Group Policy object is applied at the Human Resources OU, what could be the reason that the Human Resources application is being installed to Don's computer?

3. If the Human Resources application Group Policy object is applied at the Washington OU to users in the Human Resources Domain Local group, what could be a reason for the Human Resources application being installed to Don's computer?

Lab 7-1: Planning Group Policy Deployment

Lab Objectives

This lab prepares you to design Group Policy deployment by meeting the following objectives:

- Design placement of Group Policy objects
- Design filtering for Group Policy application
- Troubleshoot Group Policy application errors

About This Lab

This lab looks at the Group Policy deployment plan for Contoso Ltd. It covers designing Group Policy creation, and the filtering and troubleshooting Group Policy application.

Before You Begin

Make sure that you've completed reading the chapter material before starting the lab. Pay close attention to the sections where the design decisions were applied throughout the chapter for information on designing your administrative structure.

Scenario: Contoso Ltd.

Contoso Ltd., an international magazine sales company, wants to design standardized security configuration by using Group Policy. This lab looks specifically at the Group Policy assignments required for the Seattle, Lima, and London domains.

Group Policy Requirements

The Group Policy design must meet the following business requirements:

- All users in the network must have Entire Network removed from My Network Places to reduce the amount of browsing that takes place on the network. This setting shouldn't apply to any members of the Information Technology (IT) department or the Administrators group.
- All client computers in the domain must have their Administrator and Guest accounts renamed to reduce attacks involving the default account names.

- Many users have been tinkering with the Control Panel programs. Unless the user is a member of Server Operators or Administrators, you should prevent access to the Control Panel.

- The Accounting department requires that all client computers with the Accounting software have a drive mapping assigned the letter M: that points to the \\Accounting\Shareddata folder. The accounting software is installed only on desktop computers to ensure that no accounting data can be removed from the premises on a laptop computer.

Group Policy Objects

To meet the requirements, the following Group Policy objects are defined and can be used in each of the three domains:

- **Hide Entire Network.** This Group Policy object hides the Entire Network icon when a user opens My Network Places. The setting is configured in \User Configuration\Administrative Templates\Windows Components \Windows Explorer\No "Entire Network" In My Network Places.

- **Rename Default Accounts.** This Group Policy object renames the Administrator and Guest accounts with alternate names provided in the Group Policy object. This Group Policy object contains two separate settings:

  - Computer Configuration\Windows Settings\Security Settings \Local Policies\Security Options\Rename Administrator Account

  - Computer Configuration\Windows Settings\Security Settings \Local Policies\Security Options\Rename Guest Account

- **Disable Control Panel.** This Group Policy object disables the Control Panel for any users that the Group Policy setting is applied to. This Group Policy setting is configured in \User Configuration\Administrative Templates \Control Panel\Disable Control Panel.

- **Accounting Logon Script.** This Group Policy object applies a machine-based logon script that runs a startup. The script contains the command NET USE M: \\ACCOUNTING\SHAREDDATA. This setting is configured in \Computer Configuration\Windows Settings\Scripts\Startup.

Active Directory Structure

This lab focuses on the Seattle deployment of the Group Policy objects. For this lab, assume that the Group Policy objects will be applied to the Active Directory hierarchy shown in Figure 7.12.

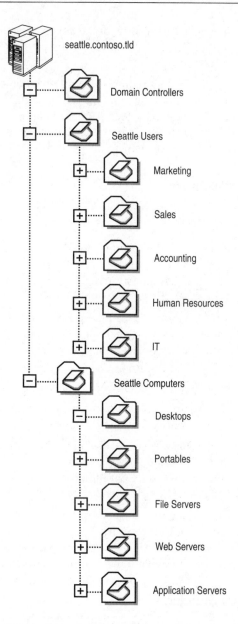

Figure 7.12 The seattle.contoso.tld Active Directory hierarchy

You need to answer questions on the design implications for applying the same types of Group Policies to the london.contoso.tld and lima.contoso.tld domains.

Exercise 1: Applying Group Policy

This exercise looks at how to decide where to apply Group Policy objects in the Contoso Active Directory to meet security requirements. The answers to these questions can be found in the appendix.

1. Based on the design requirements, where would you apply the Hide Entire Network Group Policy object to meet the requirements to hide the Control Panel for all network users?

2. Where would you apply the Group Policy object to rename the Administrator and Guest accounts on all client computers?

3. Where would you apply the "Disable Control Panel" Group Policy object to meet design requirements?

4. Where would you apply the Accounting Logon Script Group Policy object to meet design requirements?

5. Do you need to configure any other properties for these Group Policy objects to meet design requirements?

Exercise 2: Designing Group Policy Filtering

This exercise looks at using the Group Policy object Security tab to filter Group Policy application to specific security groups. The answers to these questions can be found in the appendix.

1. What security group filtering must you apply for the application of the Hide Entire Network Group Policy object? Assume that the Group Policy object is applied at the Seattle Users OU.

2. What security group filtering must you apply for the application of the Disable Control Panel Group Policy? Assume that the Group Policy object is applied at the Seattle Users OU.

3. You can apply both the Disable Control Panel and the Hide Entire Network Group Policy objects at the Seattle Users OU. Why can't you combine these two Group Policy objects into a single Group Policy object?

4. What issues would you face if you applied the Rename Default Accounts Group Policy object at the Seattle Computers OU?

5. What can you do to prevent the need for filtering for the Accounting Logon Script Group Policy object?

Exercise 3: Troubleshooting Group Policy Application

This exercise looks at the Group Policy application deployment to determine where the Block Policy Inheritance, No Override, or security group filtering may be affecting Group Policy application. All examples in this exercise are based on the Active Directory structure introduced at the beginning of this lab. The answers to these questions can be found in the appendix.

Determining Effective Group Policy Settings

Assume that the Hide Entire Network, Disable Control Panel, and Enable Control Panel Group Policies have been applied to the following locations in the seattle.contoso.tld domain.

Policy	Location	Permissions	Optional Attributes
Enable Control Panel	Domain	▪ Users: Read ▪ Users: Apply Group Policy	None
Disable Control Panel	Seattle Users	▪ Users: Read ▪ Users: Apply Group Policy	None
Hide Entire Network	Marketing	▪ Marketing: Read ▪ Marketing: Apply Group Policy ▪ Administrators: Deny Apply Group Policy	None
Hide Entire Network	Sales	▪ Sales: Read ▪ Sales: Apply Group Policy ▪ Administrators: Deny Apply Group Policy	None
Enable Control Panel	IT	▪ IT: Read ▪ IT: Apply Group Policy	None

1. If Julie is a member of the sales force and her user account is in the Sales OU, would she be able to use the Control Panel?

2. Would Julie be able to view the Entire Network in My Network Places?

3. Jackson is a member of the IT department. Would Jackson be able to access the Control Panel?

Determining the Effect of Blocking Policy Inheritance and No Override

Assume that the Hide Entire Network, Disable Control Panel, and Enable Control Panel Group Policies have been applied to the following locations in the seattle.contoso.tld domain. The optional attributes indicate whether Block Policy Inheritance or No Override has been applied.

Policy	Location	Permissions	Optional Attributes
Enable Control Panel	Domain	■ Users: Read ■ Users: Apply Group Policy	None
Disable Control Panel	Seattle Users	■ Users: Read ■ Users: Apply Group Policy	None
Hide Entire Network	Marketing	■ Marketing: Read ■ Marketing: Apply Group Policy ■ Administrators: Deny Apply Group Policy	Block Policy Inheritance
Hide Entire Network	Sales	■ Sales: Read ■ Sales: Apply Group Policy ■ Administrators: Deny Apply Group Policy	Block Policy Inheritance
Enable Control Panel	IT	■ IT: Read ■ IT: Apply Group Policy	None

1. If Julie is a member of the sales force and her user account exists in the Sales OU, would she be able to use the Control Panel?

2. Would Julie be able to view the Entire Network in My Network Places?

3. What could the network administrator for the seattle.contoso.tld domain do to prevent the Block Policy Inheritance settings for the Sales and Marketing OUs from affecting the Disable Control Panel Group Policy applied at the Seattle Users OU?

4. If the No Override attribute was enabled for the Disable Control Panel Group Policy applied at the Seattle Users OU, what additional security configuration must you perform to ensure that the IT department could use the Control Panel?

Review

Answering the following questions will reinforce key information presented in this chapter. If you are unable to answer a question, review the appropriate lesson and then try the question again. Answers to the questions can be found in the appendix.

1. If the Group Policy settings applied at the domain conflict with the Group Policy settings at the OU where the user's object is located in Active Directory, which settings take precedence?

2. A Group Policy object is applied at the Employees OU that hides My Network Places from the desktop. The following permissions for the Group Policy object are configured:

   - Authenticated User: Read (Allow)
   - Users: Apply Group Policy (Allow)
   - NetAdmins: Apply Group Policy (Deny)

   If Jonas, a member of the NetAdmins group, logs on to the network, would he see the My Network Places icon on his desktop?

3. You're a network administrator for your company's network. You have two separate domains in your Active Directory located at the same physical site. Both domains will require the same account policy settings to ensure that all network users implement complex passwords that have at least eight characters. Could you apply the account policy settings at the site?

4. Figure 7.13 shows the Active Directory hierarchy for abc.tld. A computer in the Accounting department doesn't need CTRL+ALT+DEL to log on. The computer automatically logs on with a default account when it's restarted.

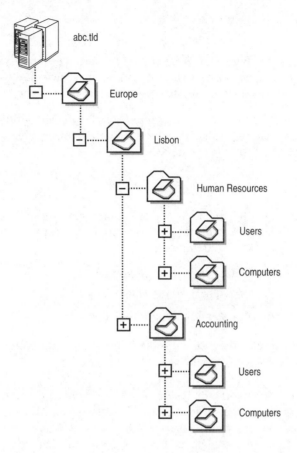

Figure 7.13   The abc.tld directory hierarchy

Assuming that the computer is located in the corporate site and is located in the OU=Computers, OU=Accounting, OU=Lisbon, OU=Europe, DC=abc, DC=tld OU, what locations would you have to inspect to find the Group Policy object that's applying the rogue setting?

5. What utility from the *Microsoft Windows 2000 Server Resource Kit* could you use to narrow the search? What parameters do you need to know in order to troubleshoot the problem?

C H A P T E R   8

Securing Microsoft Windows 2000–Based Computers

About This Chapter

To secure a network effectively, you must plan security for the individual computers on that network. Security configurations for computers or a group of computers are represented in special files called *security templates*. This chapter discusses how to plan, analyze, and deploy Windows 2000 security templates to establish baseline security on your network.

Before You Begin

To complete this chapter, you must read the chapter scenario. This scenario is used throughout the chapter to apply the design decisions discussed in each lesson.

Chapter Scenario: Market Florist

Market Florist, an Internet-based company, plans to design the application of consistent security settings to all Windows 2000–based computers on its network. A recent attack on its Web site revealed that some of the servers in the Web farm weren't properly secured. An attacker used the vulnerable servers to falsify flower orders.

Market Florist Domain Structure

Market Florist has three domains within their Active Directory directory service structure, shown in Figure 8.1: marketflorist.tld, ca.marketflorist.tld, and mx.marketflorist.tld. Computers in the Seattle and San Francisco locations have their computer accounts stored in the marketflorist.tld domain, the computers in the Winnipeg office are in the ca.marketflorist.tld domain, and the computers in the Monterrey office are in the mx.marketflorist.tld domain.

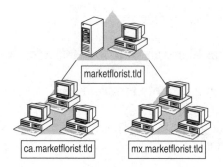

Figure 8.1   The Market Florist domain structure

Market Florist Computers

Market Florist is moving toward a pure Windows 2000 network. The progress of the migration is as follows:

- All servers on the Market Florist network are running fresh installations of Windows 2000. All previous servers have been removed from the network.

- All client computers are being upgraded to Windows 2000 from previous operating systems. The upgrades to the remaining computers are expected to be completed within the next month.

- All new computers will arrive with Windows 2000 preinstalled to ensure that the network has only Windows 2000–based computers.

- All laptop computers were acquired in the last month and were shipped with Windows 2000 preinstalled.

Computer Roles

Market Florist has identified the following roles that Windows 2000–based computers will play on the network, shown in Table 8.1.

Table 8.1   Windows 2000–Based Computer Roles for Market Florist

Computer Type	Numbers and Locations
Domain controllers (DCs)	▪ Three DCs for the marketflorist.tld domain in Seattle. ▪ Two DCs for the marketflorist.tld domain in San Francisco. ▪ Three DCs for the ca.marketflorist.tld domain in Winnipeg. ▪ Two DCs for the mx.marketflorist.tld domain in Monterrey.
File and print servers	▪ Four file and print servers in the Seattle office. Configured as members of the marketflorist.tld domain. ▪ Two file and print servers in the San Francisco office. Configured as members of the marketflorist.tld domain. ▪ Two file and print servers in the Winnipeg office. Configured as members of the ca.marketflorist.tld domain. ▪ One file and print server in the Monterrey office. Configured as a member of the mx.marketflorist.tld domain.
SQL servers	▪ Three SQL servers are in the Seattle office. Two are used for internal database applications and the third is used as the database for the Internet Web site.
External Web servers	▪ The *www.marketflorist.tld* Web site is hosted by four Web servers configured as a Windows 2000 Network Load Balancing Service (NLBS) cluster to provide high availability. These Web servers are members of a workgroup.
Client computers running Windows 2000 Professional (new installations)	▪ 700 client computers in the Seattle office configured as members of the marketflorist.tld domain. ▪ 100 client computers in the San Francisco office configured as members of the marketflorist.tld domain. ▪ 300 client computers in the Winnipeg office configured as members of the ca.marketflorist.tld domain. ▪ 100 client computers in the Monterrey office configured as members of the mx.marketflorist.tld domain.
Client computers running Windows 2000 Professional (upgraded from Microsoft Windows 95)	▪ 200 client computers in the San Francisco office configured as members of the marketflorist.tld domain. ▪ 300 client computers in the Monterrey office configured as members of the mx.marketflorist.tld domain.
Client computers running Windows 2000 Professional (upgraded from Windows NT 4.0)	▪ 300 client computers in the San Francisco office configured as members of the marketflorist.tld domain. ▪ 200 client computers in the Winnipeg office configured as members of the ca.marketflorist.tld domain.
Laptop computers running Windows 2000 Professional (new installations)	▪ 300 client laptop computers in each of the three domains used by the remote sales force.

Security Requirements

Market Florist wants to ensure the highest level of security on the internal network. Once the upgrades to Windows 2000 are completed on the client computers, Market Florist wants to prevent down-level clients' computers from accessing resources on the network.

For the external Web site, Market Florist wants to ensure that only necessary services are running on the Web servers in the NLBS cluster. Market Florist wants to use security templates to disable unnecessary services on the Web servers.

The Flower Power Application

Market Florist has developed an application that allows customers to create and then reference user accounts when purchasing flowers over the Internet. To access the software, the customer must complete a form on the *www.marketflorist.tld* Web site and provide credit card information. Once the form is completed and the customer information is verified, the customer is able to download the Flower Power application. The application, an ActiveX Control launched within the Web page, allows customers to order flowers quickly without providing credentials other than their customer numbers.

The Flower Power back-end application is installed on the external Web servers. The application requires additional NT file system (NTFS) permissions to be defined for the Flower Power folder structure and for the registry entries created by the Flower Power application.

Additionally, the Flower Power application provides the ability to change the port that the application listens on for connections. Periodically, Market Florist will want to change the port that the Flower Power application listens on for connections. The change will only be made in conjunction with an update to the ActiveX control. Once clients have downloaded the updated ActiveX control, they will connect using the newly defined port.

The port definition is stored in the registry in the following location:

```
HKEY_LOCAL_MACHINE\Software\MarketFlorist\FlowerPower\Parameters
```

Within the Parameters key, the value Port will be used to define the listening port for the Flower Power application. The Port value is a REG_DWORD value type.

Security Requirements for the Internal Network

Although computers with different roles on the network require different security settings, the Market Florist IT department wants all computers with similar roles to have the same security configurations. They don't want inconsistent security configurations like those discovered on the external Web site.

Lesson 1: Planning Microsoft Windows 2000 Security Templates

Security templates allow you to define baseline security for computers that share similar security requirements. Using security templates ensures that security can be applied consistently to multiple computers.

After this lesson, you will be able to

- Plan the use of security templates to ensure that consistent security is applied to all computers performing similar roles in your network

Estimated lesson time: 60 minutes

Introducing Windows 2000 Security Templates

Windows 2000 has made it easier to apply consistent security by introducing security templates. Security templates define security based on seven categories of configuration. You use each category to apply specific computer-based security settings. These categories include

- **Account Policy.** Defines account authentication configuration settings. For domain accounts, account policy settings must be consistent across the domain. You can't define individual account policy settings for users within a specific organizational unit (OU). Within account policies, there are three subcategories of configuration:
  - **Password Policy.** Defines password restrictions. These restrictions include minimum password length, password history maintenance, minimum and maximum password age, password complexity, and the use of reversible encryption for storing passwords.
  - **Account Lockout Policy.** Defines what action is to be taken when a user enters incorrect passwords. This policy includes the threshold when account lockout takes place, the response to take, and how frequently to reset counters associated with account lockout.
  - **Kerberos Policy.** Defines Kerberos v5 protocol settings. These settings include lifetimes for Ticket Granting Tickets (TGTs), Service Tickets (STs), maximum clock deviance, and the verification of group memberships and account lockout status.

Note   Account policy settings applied at the OU level affect the local Security Accounts Management (SAM) databases but not the user accounts within the OU. This is because the user accounts apply their account policy settings from the Default Domain Policy.

- **Local Policy.** Defines security settings only for the computer on which the security template is applied. Local computer policies are applied to the local computer account database and are composed of the following three categories:

  - **Audit Policy.** Defines the events that will be audited. The audited events will be stored in the local computer's security log. You can configure each auditing event to include either success or failure audits (or both if necessary).

  - **User Rights Assignment.** Defines which security principals will be assigned user rights on the local computer. These user rights supersede any NTFS permissions defined for an object.

  - **Security Options.** Define a wide variety of settings that are configured in the Windows 2000 registry. Common security options include whether to display the last user name used to log on to a computer or to rename the Administrator's account name.

- **Event Log.** Defines the properties of the application, security, and system logs. These properties include the maximum log sizes, who can view the logs, retention periods for the logs, and what action to take if the security log reaches the defined maximum size.

- **Restricted Groups.** Used to define memberships of security groups. The creator of the security template selects the security groups. Common groups that are included in this policy are Power Users, Enterprise Admins, and Schema Admins. Memberships include which security principals can be members of the restricted group. The policy also defines what other groups the restricted group can be a member of.

- **Systems Services.** Allows you to define restrictions for services installed on a computer. These restrictions include defining whether a service is enabled or disabled and which security principals can start or stop the selected service. For example, you could configure this policy to disable the Routing and Remote Access service on all client workstations to prevent users from configuring their desktop computers as dial-up servers.

- **Registry.** Allows you to define security for registry keys and their subtrees. For each defined registry key, you can define security settings for the registry key, configure whether the current permissions are replaced, and configure whether subtrees will have their permissions replaced. Security settings for the registry key include defining which security principals can modify security settings and auditing attempts to modify the registry settings.

- **File System.** Defines discretionary access control list (DACL) and system access control list (SACL) settings for any folders included within this policy. This policy requires NTFS to be used as the file system where the folders exist.

You can define the security template settings by loading the Security Templates Microsoft Management Console (MMC), shown in Figure 8.2.

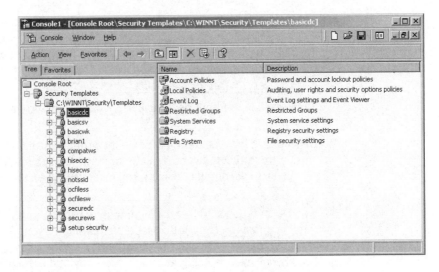

Figure 8.2   The Security Templates MMC console

The Security Templates MCC console allows you to create new templates or modify existing templates to meet your security needs.

Determining Common Security Requirements

Before defining security templates, you must identify computers on your network that require similar security configurations. You usually do this by determining the specific role that each Windows 2000–based computer will play on the network and by identifying each role's unique security requirements.

Each role will ultimately be associated with a security template that identifies the baseline (or required) security for that class of computer. Some of the more common roles that you can define for computers include

- **DCs.** These Windows 2000–based computers maintain the Active Directory database. The security requirements for securing Active Directory will be more stringent than any other security requirements on the network.

- **Application servers.** These Windows 2000–based computers host various client server applications, such as Web-based applications, structured query language (SQL) databases, and Microsoft Exchange mail servers. In some cases you may want to further categorize each application server by its primary application. Within each category you can define the required security baselines for that application.

- **File and print servers.** These Windows 2000–based computers host data that's shared among network users. Within the security definition, you may have specific DACLs defined for specific data stores.

- **Extranet servers.** These Windows 2000–based computers aren't members of your Active Directory. While authentication may take place, these servers are most likely located in a Demilitarized Zone (DMZ) and will have only limited access to internal network resources.

- **Workstations.** Windows 2000–based client computers that won't leave the premises. There might be a further breakdown based on department or business unit.

- **Laptops.** Windows 2000–based client computers that may be either inside or outside the office network. Users who have laptops might require elevated privileges to accomplish some tasks when disconnected from the corporate network.

- **Kiosks.** Windows 2000–based computers used in public locations that run a single application for public usage. For example, you might secure kiosks to prevent access to any other applications or network resources. Settings might also include automatic logon using a preconfigured account to run the application.

Making the Decision

When you determine the roles of Windows 2000–based computers within your organization, use the following guidelines:

- Categorize computers into three general categories: workstations, servers, and DCs. This breakdown matches the Default templates included with Windows 2000.

- Within each category, identify groups of computers that require similar security configurations. You can base the subcategories on the applications that the servers host or the resources that the server makes available on the network.

- Have someone else review the categories and identify further subcategories. Be careful not to get too specific. You don't want to identify separate templates for each computer on the network.

Note   You can apply Windows 2000 security templates only to Windows 2000–based computers. Therefore, consider only Windows 2000–based computers in your role definitions.

Applying the Decision

Based on the information given in this scenario, Market Florist could use the following categories of computers:

- **DCs.** This group contains all DCs in each of the three domains.

Note   Because the marketflorist.tld forest has three separate domains, you have to deploy the security templates in each of them.

- **File and print servers.** Each file and print server requires similar security configuration. If you use similar file structures on the servers, you can also set NTFS permissions by using security templates.

- **Internal SQL servers.** The internal SQL servers require unique security configuration based on internal usage only.

- **External SQL server.** Because one SQL server stores data from the external Web site, you might need additional security configuration for this SQL server.

Note   You might be able to use a single security template for all SQL servers. It depends on your analysis of the security requirements for the two roles played by SQL servers. Despite the different data stored on the servers, they may use identical security configuration.

- **Web servers.** The four Web servers require identical security configuration to ensure that the Web site has consistent security applied no matter which Web server in the NLBS cluster is contacted.

- **Client computers.** All client computers require the same security configuration. It doesn't matter whether the client computer was upgraded from a previous version of the operating system.

- **Laptop computers.** All laptop computers have unique security requirements for the deployment of Windows 2000.

Analyzing Default Security in Windows 2000

One of the common complaints about Windows NT 4.0 was that the operating system wasn't secure after a default installation was performed. Windows 2000 addresses this concern by defining default security to increase the security applied to the operating system. These default settings are applied in one of two ways:

- **Newly installed computers.** A newly installed Windows 2000–based computer will have the default security template applied during installation. This security template defines the security environment and includes elevated security for NTFS permissions and registry permissions.

Warning   For the default security settings to be fully applied, Windows 2000 must be installed to an NTFS partition.

- **Upgraded computers.** Upgraded computers maintain their previous Windows NT 4.0 settings. You can apply the Basic template to an upgraded computer to ensure that the default Windows 2000 security settings are also applied to upgraded computers. The Basic template does differ from the default template in that certain security settings aren't modified. For example, any user rights assigned to existing accounts are maintained so that applications that depend on these services continue to operate correctly.

Note Windows 2000–based computers that have been upgraded from Microsoft Windows 95 or Microsoft Windows 98 have the default security settings applied, with the exception that all local user accounts are configured to be members of the local Administrators group if the current file system is converted to NTFS. When upgrading from Windows 95 or Windows 98, always review the membership of the local Administrators group to ensure that excess privileges aren't being assigned to the local computer.

Securing Newly Installed Computers

As mentioned earlier, newly installed Windows 2000–based computers will have the Default security template applied during the computer's installation. There are actually three Default security templates, depending on the role the computer plays on the network:

- **Defltwk.inf.** Applied to all workstations running Windows 2000 Professional
- **Defltsv.inf.** Applied to all servers running Windows 2000 Server, Windows 2000 Advanced Server, and Windows 2000 Data Center
- **Defltdc.inf.** Applied to all DCs running Windows 2000

Note The Default security templates are stored in the *systemroot*\inf directory (where *systemroot* represents the folder where Windows 2000 is installed). Once a Default template is applied to a computer, the applied template is stored in *systemroot*\security\templates as "Setup security.inf."

Securing Upgraded Computers

When Windows 2000–based computers are upgraded from previous versions of Windows NT, they won't have the Default template applied. In this situation the existing security configuration is maintained. You can still increase the security of the computer by applying the Basic templates. The Basic templates will apply the same settings configured in the default security templates with the exception of restricted groups and user rights. This ensures that any existing user rights (for example, user rights assigned to allow service accounts to operate) aren't removed. You can apply the following Basic templates to upgraded Windows 2000–based computers:

- **Basicwk.inf.** Can be applied to workstations running Windows 2000 Professional

- **Basicsv.inf.** Can be applied to servers running Windows 2000 as long as they're not functioning as DCs
- **Basicdc.inf.** Can be applied to DCs running Windows 2000

Note You can find the three Basic templates in the *systemroot*\security\templates folder.

Making the Decision

Use the design matrix shown in Table 8.2 to ensure that the default settings are applied to all Windows 2000–based computers.

Table 8.2 Applying Windows 2000 Default Security Configuration

If the Computer Is	Do the Following
Upgraded from Windows 95 or Windows 98 to Windows 2000 Professional	▪ Ensure that during the upgrade you choose to convert the file system to NTFS. ▪ Do nothing else. The Defltwk.inf security template will be applied automatically.
Upgraded from Windows NT 4.0 Workstation to Windows 2000 Professional	▪ Ensure that the file system is converted to NTFS. ▪ Apply the Basicwk.inf security template to ensure that default security is applied.
A member server upgraded from Windows NT 4.0 to Windows 2000	▪ Ensure that the file system is converted to NTFS. ▪ Apply the Basicsv.inf security template to ensure that default security is applied.
A DC upgraded from Windows NT 4.0 to Windows 2000	▪ Ensure that the file system is converted to NTFS. ▪ Apply the Basicdc.inf security template to ensure that default security is applied.
A new install of Windows 2000	▪ Ensure that the system and boot partitions are configured to use NTFS. ▪ Do nothing else. The default security templates will be applied automatically and stored in the Setup Security.inf file.

Applying the Decision

To ensure consistent default security on the Market Florist network, use Table 8.3, which shows whether the Default or Basic security templates are used to apply Windows 2000 default security.

Table 8.3   Ensuring Default Security for Market Florist

DCs	The default DC security template (Defltdc.inf) is automatically applied at installation.
File and print servers	The default server security template (Defltsv.inf) is automatically applied at installation.
Internal SQL servers	The default server security template (Defltsv.inf) is automatically applied at installation.
External Web servers	The default server security template (Defltsv.inf) is automatically applied at installation.
Client computers running Windows 2000 Professional (new installations)	The default workstation security template (Defltwk.inf) is automatically applied at installation.
Client computers running Windows 2000 Professional (upgraded from Windows 95)	The default workstation security template (Defltwk.inf) is automatically applied during the upgrade. The upgrade process must convert the file system to NTFS for all security settings to be applied.
Client computers running Windows 2000 Professional (upgraded from Windows NT 4.0)	The basic workstation security template (Basicwk.inf) must be manually applied as part of the upgrade process to ensure that default security is applied to the upgraded computers.
Laptop computers running Windows 2000 Professional (new installations)	The default workstation security template (Defltwk.inf) is automatically applied at installation.

Additionally, you should inspect the membership of the local Administrators group of the Windows 2000 Professional clients that were upgraded from Windows 95. By default, an upgrade from Windows 95 to Windows 2000 Professional places any existing user accounts into the local Administrators group. You must modify the membership of the local Administrators group to ensure that excess privileges aren't assigned to user accounts.

Using Incremental Security Templates

Although the default Windows 2000 security configurations provide adequate security for many situations, sometimes additional security configuration is required. To help you define additional security, Microsoft has included several incremental security templates. These incremental templates provide security settings that are best applied in specific scenarios, such as when Terminal Services is deployed on a Windows 2000 Server.

Note   The incremental templates are effective only if the default or basic templates have already been applied.

Windows 2000 provides the following incremental security templates:

- **The No Terminal Server Security Identifier (SID) (Nottssid.inf) template.** This template removes the Terminal Server Users SID from all DACLs. By default, Terminal Services applies consistent security settings to all Terminal Services users by defining resource access for the Terminal Server Users security group. By removing the Terminal Server Users SID from a DACL, all security is applied based on the individual user's SID and group memberships.

- **The Windows NT 4.0 Compatible Security (Compatws.inf) template.** With the increased security in Windows 2000, some older applications may not function correctly. These applications generally attempt to write to areas that are now restricted to members of the Administrators or Power Users groups on the computer. A normal user running the applications won't have the permissions to write to the registry or to the file system. The Compatws.inf template weakens default security so that noncertified applications can run under Windows 2000.

Alternative Methods of Providing Application Compatibility

When you upgrade to a new operating system such as Windows 2000, some older applications might fail to operate correctly in the new environment. For example, Microsoft Office 97 isn't a Windows 2000–certified application. Under default security, the spelling checker doesn't operate because it attempts to write to folders that aren't accessible to normal user accounts.

When designing security templates, consider using the following methods to ensure that the applications run in a Windows 2000 environment:

- Add all users to the Power Users group. In Windows 2000, the Power Users group is the equivalent of the Users group in Windows NT 4.0. Adding all users to the Power User group isn't recommended because membership in Power Users provides some administrative capabilities, such as adding local users or managing NTFS permissions on the local computer.

- Apply the Compatws.inf security template. As mentioned earlier, the compatible workstation template weakens the default security to match Windows NT 4.0 security. Applying the Compatws.inf security template isn't recommended because default security is very important to a secure network.

- Use the Apcompat.exe utility included in the Windows 2000 Support Tools. In some cases the reason an application won't run isn't due to security restrictions, but that it doesn't recognize the Windows 2000 operating system. In these cases, use the Apcompat.exe utility to have Windows 2000 emulate a previous Windows operating system, as shown in Figure 8.3.

(continued)

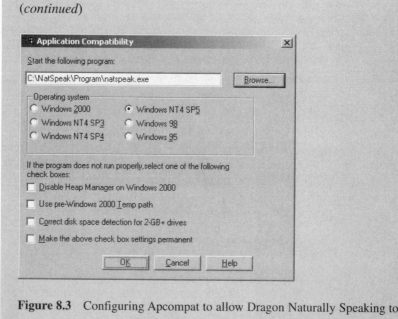

Figure 8.3   Configuring Apcompat to allow Dragon Naturally Speaking to execute

- Upgrade to a newer version of the application. Consider upgrading to a Windows 2000–certified version of the application. This may involve an upgrade or may only require the installation of a patch to the application.

- **The Initial DC Configuration template (DC security.inf).** When a Windows 2000–based server is promoted to a DC, you must apply specific file and registry permissions to ensure security in the new role. These settings are contained within this template.

Note   This incremental security template is always applied when a member server is promoted to a DC. This isn't truly an optional security template. You can use this security template to ensure that initial DC security is still applied.

- **The Optional Components templates (Ocfilesw.inf and Ocfiles.inf).** These templates increase the local security for optional components that might be installed on Windows 2000 Professional or Windows 2000 Server–based computers, including applications such as Microsoft Internet Explorer, Microsoft NetMeeting, and Internet Information Services (IIS) 5.0.

- **The Secure templates (Securews.inf and Securedc.inf).** These templates provide security beyond DACLs on the registry and the file system. The Secure templates force the operating system to behave more securely and include modifications for account policy. For example, the Secure templates prevent security principals from being members of the Power Users security group. Membership in this group is considered an excess privilege for normal user accounts.

- **The High Secure templates (Hisecws.inf and Hisecdc.inf).** These templates offer increased security over the Secure templates for higher security networks. While the Secure template only sends NTLM responses for file sessions using the NTLM protocol, the High Secure template only responds using NTLMv2. In addition, a server configured with the High Secure template will ignore all LAN Manager and NTLM requests.

Warning Implementing the High Secure templates may prevent down-level Windows clients from participating in the network. Only deploy the High Secure templates when all client computers are running Windows 2000.

Comparing the Secure and High Secure Options

Table 8.4 shows the differences between the Secure and High Secure templates.

Table 8.4 Comparing the Secure and High Secure Templates

Setting	Secure Template (Securedc.inf)	High Security Template (Hisecdc.inf)
Additional restrictions for anonymous connections	Don't allow enumeration of SAM accounts and shares	No access without explicit anonymous restrictions
Clear virtual memory pagefile when system shuts down	Disabled	Enabled
Digitally sign client communications (always)	Disabled	Enabled
Digitally sign client communications (when possible)	Enabled	Enabled
Digitally sign server communications (always)	Disabled	Enabled
Digitally sign server communications (when possible)	Enabled	Enabled
Do not display last user name in logon screen	Disabled	Enabled
LAN Manager Authentication Level	Send NTLM responses only	Send NTLMv2 response only \ Refuse LM & NTLM
Secure channel: Digitally encrypt or sign secure channel data (always)	Disabled	Enabled

Table 8.4   Comparing the Secure and High Secure Templates (*continued*)

Setting	Secure Template (Securedc.inf)	High Security Template (Hisecdc.inf)
Secure channel: Digitally encrypt or sign secure channel data (when possible)	Enabled	Enabled
Secure channel: Digitally sign secure channel data (when possible)	Enabled	Enabled
Secure channel: Require strong (Windows 2000 or later) session key	Disabled	Enabled
Unsigned driver installation behavior	Don't allow installation	Don't allow installation
Unsigned nondriver installation behavior	Warn but allow installation	Silently succeed

As you can see, there isn't a great difference between the Secure and High Secure templates. The key differences is the enforcement of server message block (SMB) signing (digitally sign server communications) and secure channel session keys.

Making the Decision

Use the decision matrix shown in Table 8.5 to determine when it's appropriate to use each of the incremental security templates.

Table 8.5   Designing Incremental Security Template Usage

Use This Template	When You Have the Following Security Requirements
No Terminal Services ID	▪ You've deployed Windows 2000 servers with Terminal Services configured to use Application Mode. ▪ You wish to secure access to Terminal Services and the resources on the terminal server on a per user basis. ▪ You are deploying Terminal Services as a desktop replacement and want to provide maximum security for all users.
Compatible Workstation	▪ Your budget doesn't allow for an immediate upgrade to a Windows 2000–certified version of the application. ▪ You don't want to make all users members of the Power Users group. ▪ You can't identify which individual NTFS files or registry keys require modified permissions.
Optional Components	▪ You've installed additional components to Windows 2000 and want to maintain the highest level of security.

Table 8.5   Designing Incremental Security Template Usage

Use This Template	When You Have the Following Security Requirements
DC Security	■ You want to ensure that initial DC security is still applied to a DC.
Secure	■ You're in a mixed environment of Windows 2000 and down-level clients. ■ You wish to have the strongest security without excluding down-level clients.
High Security	■ No down-level clients remain on the network. ■ You want to provide the strongest form of security for all data usage.

Applying the Decision

Market Florist has decided that they want to prevent down-level clients from connecting to the network while maintaining the highest level of security on the internal network. By applying the High Security templates to all its Windows 2000–based computers, Market Florist will accomplish both goals.

You must apply High Security templates (Hisecws.inf and Hisecdc.inf) only to computers that have Windows 2000 default security applied, as mentioned earlier. You can apply the Hisecws.inf security template to all client computers, including those upgraded from previous versions of Windows, and you can apply the Hisecdc.inf to all Windows 2000 servers, including both DCs and file and print servers.

Creating Custom Security Templates

While the Default templates meet most security requirements, you may need to create modified templates to define security baselines for some computer roles. If the settings that you require are in the Security Templates interface, you can simply create custom security templates by using an existing template as the starting point for your custom security template.

When defining a custom security template, be careful to avoid applying too many settings. The security template should meet, but not exceed, the required security baseline.

Making the Decision

When designing custom security templates, consider the following points:

■ Identify an existing security template to be your starting point. You can save an existing security template under a new name in the Security Templates console. By saving an existing template with a different name, you ensure that you don't miss any settings that you may not be aware of in the initial template.

- Configure any additional settings. Add the additional settings that required you to define a custom security template. Document any additional settings so that you will know the reason for using the additional settings if you review them.

- Test the newly created security template against a new installation. This process ensures that you haven't missed any settings in your security template.

Applying the Decision

Market Florist must create a custom security template for the Web servers hosting the *www.marketflorist.tld* Web site and the Flower Power application. You must include the following items in the custom security template:

- **Disabling of nonrequired services.** You must analyze the Web servers to determine exactly which services must be present on the Web servers. Some of the services that you can disable include the FTP Publishing service, Telnet Service, Simple Mail Transfer Protocol (SMTP) service, and the Server service, which are common services that are exploited by attackers.

Note   Disabling the Server service would prevent Windows 2000 SMB file connections to the Web server from both the internal and external networks. An alternative would be to configure IPSec to protect connections to the server from the internal network. This would require defining IPSec on the Web servers. For more information, see Chapter 12, "Securing Data at the IP Level."

- **Custom NTFS permissions for the Flower Power folder structure.** You must determine what are the NTFS permissions required for the Flower Power folder structure to restrict access to the data to only authorized access. By applying the permissions through a security template, you can ensure that the required permissions are enforced.

- **Custom Registry permissions for the Flower Power application.** You must determine what security principals can modify registry settings related to the Flower Power application.

Extending the Security Configuration Tool Set

Although you can create custom security templates from existing settings, sometimes the settings you require might not be included in the Security Configuration Tool Set (SCTS). For example, you may want to use Group Policy to prevent Windows 2000 client computers from attempting to register the Host (A) and Pointer (PTR) resource records with Domain Name System (DNS) by using dynamic updates. You can extend the SCTS to include the registry entry to prevent dynamic updates for all network adapters.

Note   The registry value to prevent Windows 2000 client computers from perform-ing dynamic update of the A and PTR resource records is HKEY_Local_Machine \System\CurrentControlSet\Services\TcpIp\Parameters\DisableDynamicUpdate. By setting this REG_DWORD to a value of 1, you can prevent the client com-puter from performing dynamic updates. This is useful in a network where the dynamic updates are restricted to DHCP servers.

To add registry entries, complete the following steps:

1. Identify the required registry settings including the registry path, the registry data type, and the acceptable values for the registry setting.

2. Edit the *systemroot*\inf\sceregvl.inf file. This is the source file used by the Security Templates console for all available security options.

3. Reregister the security configuration client dynamic link library (Scecli.dll) by running **REGSVR32 SCECLI.DLL**. This reads the changed Sceregvl.inf file and creates a compiled version that alters the Security Options settings listed in Security Templates.

Warning   The next section is relevant if you wish to extend security templates to include additional registry values in the Security Options settings. You won't have to know the parameters within the Sceregvl.inf file for the 70-220 exam.

The Sceregvl.inf File

The Sceregvl.inf file is a setup file provided with Windows 2000. The Sceregvl.inf file is split into three distinct sections:

- **Version.** Defines the version of the file. Any time you edit the file, you should change the last edited date. This isn't required, but it's useful when you're trying to audit or manage changes to the file.

- **Register Registry Values.** Contains all registry values that are listed in Secu-rity Options with the Security Templates console. For each entry, you have to define the following:

  - **Registry path.** The full path indicating where the value is set in the Windows 2000 registry.

  - **Data type.** The data type of the new registry path. Supported types include REG_SZ (1), REG_EXPAND_SZ(2), REG_BINARY(3), REG_DWORD(4), REG_MULTI_SZ(7).

  - **Display name.** The name that's displayed in the listing of Security Op-tions in the Security Templates console.

  - **Display type.** Indicates how the user interface appears in order to allow the registry value to be manipulated within the Security Templates con-sole. Display type options include Boolean(0), Number(1), String(2), and Choices(3).

Note   Choices is commonly used for registry values that allow specific entries. The Choices data type allows for any number of options and their display string to be included for a security option.

- **Strings.** Used to expand any variables that may have been used in the [Register Registry Values] section. Strings are commonly used when display names or value lists contain strings that include spaces " ".

The best way to show the syntax is to show the specific entries for one of the security options. A commonly set security option is to suppress the last user's logon name from the Windows 2000 security box. This prevents a user from knowing who previously used the console. For this option, the following values exist in the [Register Registry Values] and [Strings] section of the Sceregvl.inf file:

```
[Register Registry Values]

MACHINE\Software\Microsoft\Windows\CurrentVersion\Policies\System
    \DontDisplayLastUserName,4,%DontDisplayLastUserName%,0

[Strings]

DontDisplayLastUserName = Do not display last user name in logon screen
```

The line in the [Register Registry Value] section can be broken down as follows:

- The path to the registry value is HKEY_LOCAL_MACHINE\Software\Microsoft \Windows\CurrentVersion\Policies\System\DontDisplayLastUserName.
- The DontDisplayLastUserName value is a REG_DWORD value type.
- Within the list of security options in the Security Templates console, this option is listed as "Do not display last user name in logon screen." The value %DontDisplayLastUserName% indicates that the expanded string is found within the [Strings] section of the Sceregvl.inf file.
- The 0 indicates that the dialog box presented to an administrator when the administrator configures this option should be for a Boolean setting. This means that the dialog box gives the user the choice of either enabling or disabling the option.

Note   When you're adding a custom registry entry to the Sceregvl.inf file, it's a good idea to copy an existing registry value within the text file and modify as required to reduce the possibility of incorrect syntax being applied.

Making the Decision

When designing custom registry values to be included in the Security Templates console, use the decision matrix shown in Table 8.6.

Table 8.6   Extending the Security Configuration Tool Set

To	Do the Following
Determine what registry values need to be added	Identify registry values that are commonly modified at Windows 2000–based computers for security configuration as part of the installation process. The registry values may be defined in documentation or knowledge base articles.
Identify the properties of the registry value that must be added to the Sceregvl.inf file.	Identify the properties for a specific registry value by reviewing the Regentry.chm compressed help file included with the *Microsoft Windows 2000 Resource Kit*, or by reading knowledge base articles or the software documentation.
Protect the original Sceregvl.inf file	Save a copy of the original Sceregvl.inf file in a secure location before making any modifications.
Register the changes in the Security Templates console	Run **REGSVR32 SCECLI.DLL** at the command prompt. Ensure that the modified Sceregvl.inf file is located in the *systemroot*\inf folder.
Verify the configuration changes	Open the Security Templates console and verify that the new entry appears in the Security Options settings. Also attempt to apply the setting by using the Security Configuration And Analysis console.
Ensure that all required stations see the modified entries	Register the modified Sceregvl.inf file at all Windows 2000–based computers where the security template will be modified.

Applying the Decision

You must extend the security templates to allow the listening port for the Flower Power application to be changed. This change requires modification of the Sceregvl.inf file at any Windows 2000–based computers where the security templates will be modified.

You must make the following modifications to the Sceregvl.inf file to allow the listening port to be modified:

```
[Register Registry Values]

Machine\Software\MarketFlorist\FlowerPower\Parameters
    \Port,4,%ListenPort%,1

[Strings]

ListenPort= Configure the Flower Power Listening Port
```

Once you've made the modifications to the Sceregvl.inf file, you must reregister the file by running the command **REGSVR32 SCECLI.DLL** at the computer with the modified Sceregvl.inf configuration file. You must repeat this process at any workstations where the security template will be defined.

Lesson Summary

Windows 2000 has increased the base security settings from previous versions of Windows NT. By using security templates, you can ensure that consistent security is applied to all Windows 2000–based computers.

When planning the use of security templates, be sure to include decisions on applying default security to all Windows 2000–based computers, when to use the incremental security templates included with Windows 2000, and when to create custom security templates to meet your security goals. The creation of custom security templates may also require extending the Security Configuration Tool Set.

Activity: Evaluating a Security Template

You've been asked to review a proposed security template to determine if it meets the organization's security needs. You've reviewed all security settings with the exception of the password policy, shown in Figure 8.4.

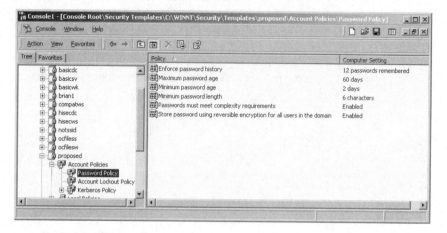

Figure 8.4 The proposed password policy

This activity reviews the password policy settings against the following requirements:

- Users must not be able to reuse a password for two years

- Passwords must be at least five characters long

- Passwords must be stored using only the securest format within Active Directory

- Passwords must contain a combination of lowercase letters, uppercase letters, numbers, or symbols to prevent easy determination of passwords

Taking into account these requirements and the proposed security template settings, answer the following questions. Answers can be found in the appendix.

1. Is it possible for a user to reuse a password within a two-year period?

2. What can you do to enforce the password reuse requirement?

3. Does the security template meet the minimum password length requirement?

4. If you implement the proposed security template, are passwords stored securely in Active Directory?

5. Is the requirement for password construction met?

6. Assuming that your proposed recommendations are accepted, where must you apply this security template to ensure that all DCs enforce the password policy?

Lesson 2: Analyzing Security Settings with Security Configuration and Analysis

Before deploying security templates, you need to compare a target computer's current security settings to the desired settings configured in the security template for that class of computer.

After this lesson, you will be able to

- Compare the existing security configuration to the desired baseline configuration stored in a certificate template

Estimated lesson time: 30 minutes

Comparing Security Settings to the Security Template

Once you've created your security template, it's valuable to compare the current security settings of a Windows 2000–based computer to the security template to determine how the current configuration differs from the desired configuration.

This comparison ensures that the template meets all security requirements. If the Security Configuration And Analysis console indicates that the current security matches the tested baseline and there are still security issues, further work is required on the template design.

Comparing current security to desired security helps you identify

- **Current security weaknesses on your network.** If the security template hasn't been deployed yet, you can identify where the current configuration is weak when compared to the desired baseline security.
- **Security template deficiencies.** You must perform the testing at a computer separate from the computer where the security template was created. Doing this ensures that any manually configured settings at the computer where the security template was created are identified during the analysis.
- **Modified security configuration at the testing station.** Because the settings won't match those in the security template, any manually configured security settings are identified during the security analysis.

Performing the Analysis

You use the Security Configuration And Analysis console to analyze a computer's current security settings against a security template. The console indicates whether a Windows 2000–based computer's current security configuration matches the defined configuration in the security template. To perform the analysis, complete the following steps:

1. Load the Security Configuration And Analysis console into an MMC console.

2. Create a new database locally for storing the imported security template and the analysis data.

3. Import the desired security template into the security database.

4. Analyze the current security against the security configuration now stored in the security database, as shown in Figure 8.5.

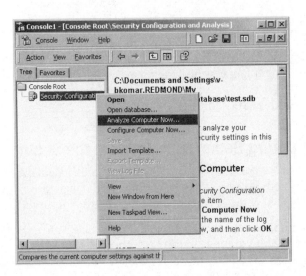

Figure 8.5   Performing an analysis of current security against a security template

5. Review the analysis information. The Security Configuration And Analysis console displays whether individual security options match (indicated by a green check mark) or don't match (indicated by a red x) the configured settings in the security template, as shown in Figure 8.6.

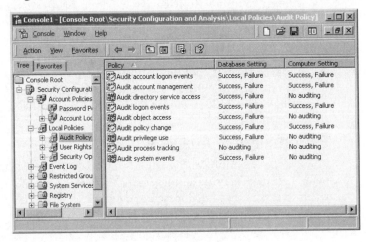

Figure 8.6   Reviewing the analysis of current security against a security template

6. Choose either to rework the security template or to apply the security template to the local security configuration.

Note The only time it's recommended to apply the security template at this point is when the computer being analyzed is in a workgroup or non–Windows 2000 network environment. In an Active Directory environment, it's better to import the security template into Group Policy to ensure the security template's continued application.

Automating the Continued Analysis of a Security Template

While the Security Configuration And Analysis console does allow one-time analysis of your computer's configuration compared to a security template, it doesn't allow for long-term analysis. You can perform long-term analysis by using the Secedit command line tool with the /ANALYZE option.

The syntax of the secedit command line is:

SECEDIT /ANALYZE [/DB *filename*] [/CFG *filename*] [/LOG *logpath*] [/VERBOSE]

where

- **/DB** *filename* provides the path to the database file that contains the stored configuration from the desired security template indicated in the /CFG option.

- **/CFG** *filename* provides the path to the security template that's imported into the database for analysis. If this option isn't provided, it's assumed that a security template has already been imported in the indicated database.

- **/LOG** *logpath* provides the path that's used to log the reports of the analysis.

- **/VERBOSE** indicates that the log file contains more detailed progress information than regularly recorded.

By creating a batch file that contains your preconfigured Secedit command line, you can use the Scheduled Tasks program in the Control Panel to provide automated analysis of the security configuration of select computers, as shown in Figure 8.7.

(continued)

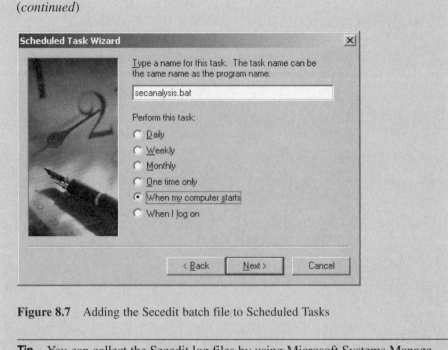

Figure 8.7   Adding the Secedit batch file to Scheduled Tasks

Tip   You can collect the Secedit log files by using Microsoft Systems Management Server (SMS) and then search for the phrase "Mismatch." Mismatch indicates that the current configuration of a computer doesn't match the security template.

Making the Decision

When determining whether a computer matches the security template, include the following in your security design:

- Analyze the security template before deployment. This ensures that the security template contains all required settings.

- Automate continued analysis of security baseline. By using the Secedit command and Schedule Tasks, you can ensure that a computer is regularly compared to the desired security baseline.

- Ensure that the continued analysis logs are collected and analyzed. By using a product such as SMS to collect the analysis logs, you can set regular intervals to search for the Mismatch phrase in the collected log files.

Note A mismatch doesn't indicate weaker security configuration. It only indicates that the current configuration doesn't match the setting in the security template. It's up to you to determine whether the mismatch has strengthened or weakened security. For example, if the template requires a minimum password length of six characters and your DCs are configured to require eight, is this a weakness? No, it's simply a longer minimum password length.

Applying the Decision

Market Florist must ensure that any custom security templates meet security requirements. There are a few ways that Market Florist can accomplish this. The easiest would be to create a test OU structure within the marketflorist.tld domain and apply the security templates to OUs within this structure, as shown in Figure 8.8.

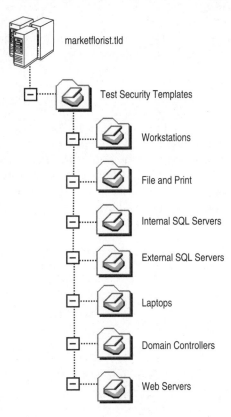

Figure 8.8 Developing an OU structure for testing security templates

To test the application of the Security Templates, you can define a Group Policy object (GPO) at each of the sub-OUs. You can import the security template associated with the sub-OU into the Group Policy object to apply the security template settings. Finally, you can move a computer to the OU to verify the security template settings.

For all of the Windows 2000–based computers, you can accomplish ongoing analysis of the security template application by running a batch file in the computer's startup script that runs Secedit with the /ANALYZE parameter. For example, the startup script for laptop computers could include the following line:

```
SECEDIT /ANALYZE [/DB Security.sdb ] [/CFG Laptop.inf ]
    [/LOG c:\Sectemp.log] [/VERBOSE]
```

Finally, you can use a product such as SMS to collect the c:\Sectemp.log files from each computer. You can examine these log files for the word Mismatch. If you find it, the effective security on the laptop computer doesn't match the security defined in the Laptop.inf security template.

Lesson Summary

Analyzing a Windows 2000–based computer current security configuration against the recommended settings in a security template allows you to determine how well security is configured on the Windows 2000–based computer. Scheduling regular analysis of security configuration will help prevent security weaknesses created by a user of the network modifying security configuration. Ongoing analysis will help in detecting the security configuration change before security weaknesses can be exploited.

Lesson 3: Planning the Deployment of Security by Using Security Templates

Once you've designed your custom security templates and determined that they meet the security baseline for your network, you must deploy the templates to the required computers. You may have to deploy several templates, one for each role that you've defined on the network. The decision on how to deploy the templates will vary depending on whether the underlying network uses Active Directory or is based on another network operating system or a workgroup environment.

After this lesson, you will be able to

- Plan the best way to deploy security templates to ensure consistent application of security to computers with similar roles on the network

Estimated lesson time: 30 minutes

Deploying Security Templates in a Workgroup

A workgroup or non-Microsoft network is unable to use Group Policy to provide continued deployment of the security template. The only way to ensure continued application of the security template is to import the security template into local computer policy.

You can apply the security template manually during the Windows 2000 installation. Once the operating system is loaded and the computer is ready to be deployed, you can apply the custom security template for that class of computer to the computer by using the Security Configuration And Analysis console.

You can also apply the security template automatically by saving the security template locally to the computer and using the Secedit command within a batch file to apply the security template. You do this by using Secedit with the /CONFIGURE parameter:

```
SECEDIT /CONFIGURE [/DB filename] [/CFG filename ] [/OVERWRITE]
    [/LOG logpath] [/VERBOSE] [/QUIET]
```

where

- **/DB** *filename* provides the path to the database file that contains the stored configuration from the desired security template indicated in the /CFG option.

- **/CFG** *filename* provides the path to the security template that's imported into the database for analysis. If this option isn't provided, it's assumed that a security template has already been imported in the indicated database.

- **/OVERWRITE** ensures that any previous security template imported into the security database is overwritten with the information in the indicated security template rather than having the security template information appended to the stored template.

- **/LOG** *logpath* provides the path that's used to log the reports of the analysis.
- **/VERBOSE** indicates that the log file contains more detailed progress information than is regularly recorded.
- **/QUIET** suppresses all log and screen output. This option is useful to prevent the user from realizing the continued application of the security template.

Note If your organization is using another network operating system, such as Novell, you can add the Secedit command to your network's logon scripts to ensure the regular application of the security template.

Making the Decision

In a workgroup or non-Microsoft networking environment, deploy security templates by performing the following tasks:

- Distribute the configured security templates to the client computers. If the template is defined in advance, include the template in the base image for the computer role. Otherwise, you could mail or manually install the template to each client computer or distribute it through the logon process in a networked environment.
- Configure the computer initially with the security template. You can set the installation process to include the application of the security template by using the Security Configuration And Analysis console.
- Ensure continued application of the security template. Use the SECEDIT /CONFIGURE command in batch files or network logon scripts. This ensures that the security template is regularly applied to the required computers.

Applying the Decision

Market Florist's Web servers won't participate in the domain structure. Because of this fact, you must use the Secedit command to ensure that the Web Server security template is applied to the Web server.

You can automate the application of the security template by using the Scheduled Tasks program in Control Panel. The best choice is to configure Scheduled Tasks to run Secedit daily to ensure continued application of the security template. Assuming that the template is named Webserv.inf, Market Florist must perform the following tasks:

1. The Webserv.inf file must be manually distributed to the four Web servers.

2. A batch file must be created that includes the following content:

```
SECEDIT  /CONFIGURE  /DB SECURITY.SDB  /CFG WEBSERV.INF
    /OVERWRITE  /LOG C:\SECTEMP.LOG   /QUIET
```

3. This batch file must be configured under Scheduled Tasks to be run daily. This ensures continued application of the security template settings.

Deploying Security Templates in a Windows 2000 Domain

An administrator of a Windows 2000 domain can leverage Active Directory for the continued application of security templates. Security templates can be imported into Group Policy objects defined at the site, domain, or OU. Importing the security template ensures that the settings defined in the template are applied with the application of Group Policy objects.

Note All security template settings are computer configuration settings and should only be applied at OUs that contain computer accounts. There is no benefit in applying the security templates to OUs that contain only user accounts because the settings aren't applied to the user configuration within Group Policy.

To facilitate the deployment of security templates, you must define an OU structure that reflects the categories of computers that you've defined for your network. You should have at least one OU for each security template that you wish to deploy. You can still create sub-OUs within an OU where you deploy the security template. For example, the OU structure in Figure 8.9 has the File Server security template at the File and Print OU, while the computer accounts are contained within the Sales and Accounting OUs.

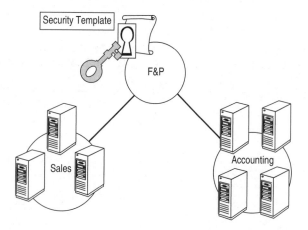

Figure 8.9 Group Policy allows for policy inheritance to be leveraged

Group Policy supports policy inheritance by default. This allows child OUs to inherit a Group Policy object applied at a parent OU. In this example, both the

Sales and Accounting OUs inherit the security template settings applied at the F&P OU.

Making the Decision

When using Group Policy to deploy security templates, consider the following factors in your security design:

- Your OU structure must reflect the categories of computers that require security templates. This is a one-to-one mapping, in that you only apply the security template directly to a single OU.

- Place all computers that require a security template in the same OU or OU structure. Doing this allows the Group Policy object to be applied only once in the Active Directory structure. It's best to minimize the areas where Group Policy is applied to ensure faster startup times for Windows 2000–based computers.

- Import the custom security template into the correct OU. Once you've tested the security template, you can import the completed security template into a Group Policy object. You must apply the Group Policy object at an OU that contains the computer accounts requiring the security template. Don't apply the Group Policy object to an OU that contains user accounts.

- Group Policy application isn't immediate. A computer that's in an OU where Group Policy is applied won't immediately receive the newly configured Group Policy settings. By default, a DC refreshes Group Policy settings every 5 minutes and a Windows 2000–based computer refreshes Group Policy settings every 90 minutes.

Note   You can force a Windows 2000–based computer to apply any computer-based security settings immediately by running the following command at a Command Prompt: **SECEDIT /REFRESHPOLICY MACHINE_POLICY /ENFORCE**.

Applying the Decision

Market Florist must develop an OU structure that meets their security template deployment needs. Because there are three domains, this process must be repeated for each of the three domains, with the exception of the SQL Server templates, which are applied only in the marketflorist.tld domain, and the Web Server templates, which are deployed in a workgroup environment.

Assuming that the OU structure has been defined for Market Florist as shown in Figure 8.10, you can make the assignments shown in Table 8.7.

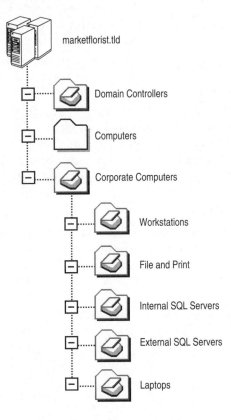

Figure 8.10   Proposed OU structure for the deployment of security templates

Table 8.7   Designing Security Template Deployment for Market Florist

Security Template	Apply to
Domain Controller.inf	OU=Domain Controllers, DC=marketflorist, DC=tld
FileandPrint.inf	OU=File and Print, OU=Corporate Computers, DC=marketflorist, DC=tld
InternalSQL.inf	OU=Internal SQL Servers, OU=Corporate Computers, DC=marketflorist, DC=tld
ExternalSQL.inf	OU=External SQL Servers, OU=Corporate Computers, DC=marketflorist, DC=tld
Workstn.inf	OU=Workstations, OU=Corporate Computers, DC=marketflorist, DC=tld
Laptop.inf	OU=Laptops, OU=Corporate Computers, DC=marketflorist, DC=tld

Within the OU=Workstations, OU=Corporate Computers, DC=marketflorist, DC=tld organizational unit, there may be further OUs that break out the departments for the computers. If this is the case, the Group Policy object with the imported Workstn.inf security template would still be applied at the Workstations OU because inheritance will apply the settings to all sub-OUs.

Lesson Summary

Once you've created security templates that enforce the required security configuration for Windows 2000–based computers, you must develop a method to ensure the continued application of the security templates. In an Active Directory environment, you can use Group Policy to ensure that the security template is regularly applied to Windows 2000–based computers. In a non–Active Directory environment, you can use the Scheduled Tasks program in Control Panel to regularly run the Secedit command to apply the desired security templates.

Lab 8-1: Planning Security Templates

Lab Objectives

This lab prepares you to plan the design and deployment of security templates by meeting the following objectives:

- Identify computer roles on the network
- Determine which standard security templates can be used in a given situation
- Design custom security templates
- Plan the deployment of security templates in workgroup and domain environments

About This Lab

This lab looks at the planning that Contoso Ltd. must do to ensure consistent security configuration for all Windows 2000–based computers by using security templates to define baseline security for a class of computers on its network.

Before You Begin

Make sure that you've completed reading the chapter material before starting the lab. Pay close attention to the sections where the design decisions were applied throughout the chapter for information on building your administrative structure.

Scenario: Contoso Ltd.

Contoso Ltd., an international magazine sales company, wants to ensure consistent security configuration of its Windows 2000–based computers by deploying security templates based on the function a computer provides on the network. The consistent security configuration will be deployed by using a combination of Group Policy (for domain members) and scheduled tasks (for workgroup members).

Windows 2000–Based Computer Deployment

The following table describes the types of Windows 2000–based computers in use on the Contoso corporate network.

Computer Type	Numbers and Locations
DCs	■ Eight DCs exist at the London location. There are two DCs for each of the four domains: contoso.tld, seattle.contoso.tld, lima.contoso.tld, and london.contoso.tld. The four Primary Domain Controller (PDC) emulators at the London office are upgraded Windows NT 4.0 PDCs. ■ Three DCs for the seattle.contoso.tld are located at the Seattle office. ■ Two DCs for the lima.contoso.tld are located at the Lima office.
File and print servers	■ There are two file and print servers at the London office that are members of the london.contoso.tld domain. ■ There are two file and print servers at the Seattle office that are members of the seattle.contoso.tld domain. ■ There are two file and print servers at the Lima office that are members of the lima.contoso.tld domain.
Mail servers	■ There are two Exchange 5.5 mail servers at the London office. One mail server functions as the Internet mail gateway and is a member of the contoso.tld domain. The second mail server hosts the mailboxes for all users at the London office and is a member of the london.contoso.tld domain. ■ There is one Exchange 5.5 mail server at the Seattle office that hosts mailboxes for the Seattle users. This mail server is a member of the seattle.contoso.tld domain. ■ There is one Exchange 5.5 mail server at the Lima office that hosts mailboxes for the Lima users. This mail server is a member of the lima.contoso.tld domain.
Terminal servers	■ There is a single terminal server deployed at each of the three offices. The terminal server in each office is a Windows 2000 member server in the domain.
Web servers	■ At the London office, there are two Web servers that host the contoso.tld external Web site.
Sales Force Operations servers	■ The London office hosts two servers that function as the Sales Force Operations application. These servers are members of the contoso.tld domain and store all data related to the Sales Force Operations application in a custom database.

Client Computer Details

The Contoso network has a mix of computers on the corporate network. Each office has Windows 2000, Windows NT 4.0, Windows 98, and Windows for Workgroups 3.11 client computers. The following table shows the statistics on operating systems at each office.

Location	Client Computers
London	■ 400 Windows 2000 Professional desktops (new installations) ■ 200 Windows 2000 Professional clients (upgraded from Windows NT 4.0) ■ 100 Windows 2000 Professional clients (upgraded from Windows 98) ■ 200 Windows NT 4.0 Workstation clients ■ 100 Windows 98 clients ■ 250 Windows 2000 Professional mobile laptop salespeople
Seattle	■ 400 Windows 2000 Professional clients (new installations) ■ 300 Windows 2000 Professional clients (upgraded from Windows NT 4.0) ■ 300 Windows 98 clients ■ 400 Windows 2000 Professional mobile laptop salespeople
Lima	■ 200 Windows 2000 Professional clients (new installations) ■ 200 Windows 2000 Professional clients (upgraded from Windows NT 4.0) ■ 200 Windows 2000 Professional clients (upgraded from Windows 98) ■ 100 Windows NT 4.0 Workstation clients ■ 75 Windows 98 clients ■ 10 Windows for Workgroups 3.11 clients ■ 100 Windows 2000 Professional mobile laptop salespeople

In addition, each office has 20 Wyse Winterm terminal services clients installed on the shop floor. These Winterm clients connect to the terminal server located at their office.

The Sales Force Operations Software

The remote sales force uses a custom software application to synchronize the salesperson's client database with the central database on the sales force operations servers. The salespeople will connect first thing in the morning to ensure that they have the latest client information and the current pricing information for today.

Security Requirements

The Contoso network team has developed the following security requirements for Windows 2000–based computers:

- All Windows 2000–based computers must be deployed initially with Windows 2000 default security.

- The DCs for each of the three domains must ensure that passwords are eight characters in length and complex.

- The DCs must audit all account management and logon attempts, whether they're successful or unsuccessful.

- File and print servers will have a common folder structure deployed on each computer's D drive. This folder structure will make it easier to configure NTFS permissions by using security templates. The folder structure is shown in Figure 8.11.

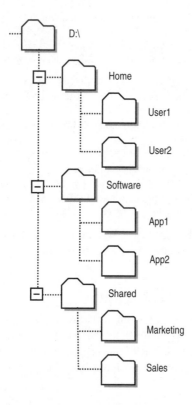

Figure 8.11   Default folder structure for Contoso's file and print servers

- The Web servers will host both internal and externally available data. You must configure NTFS permissions to ensure that only authenticated users are able to access internal data.

- All terminal server access must be based on the individual user accounts. A user should be allowed to connect to the server only if the user, or a group that the user belongs to, is directly assigned permissions to a resource.

- The Sales Force Operations servers require the periodic modification of specific registry entries. These registry settings enable SSL encryption for the Sales Force Operations application. The two registry values that must be configured are located in the following registry location:

```
HKEY_LOCAL_MACHINE\Software\Contoso\SFO\Parameters\
```

The parameter settings that need to be added are:

```
EnableSSL: REG_BINARY
```

```
SSLPort: REG_DWORD
```

- Contoso needs to support Windows 98, Windows NT 4.0, and Windows 2000 client computers on the network for a long time. Contoso wants to implement the strongest form of security without excluding the down-level clients from the network.

Exercise 1: Determining Computer Classifications

This exercise looks at the computer classes that Contoso will need to develop for their network security plan to ensure that security requirements are met for all computers. The exercise also determines which security template must initially be deployed to ensure that Windows 2000 default security is deployed to all Windows 2000–based computers. Answers to these questions can be found in the appendix.

1. Complete the following table with your proposed computer classifications for servers and the total number of computers that will require the template applied.

Server Classification	Total # of Computers
▪	
▪	
▪	
▪	
▪	
▪	

2. Complete the following table to indicate which security templates must be used to ensure that the default Windows 2000 security settings are applied to all Windows 2000–based computers. Indicate whether the template is applied automatically or must be applied manually.

Computer Type	Template	Installation Method
DCs (Windows NT 4.0 upgrades)		
DCs (new installations)		
Mail servers (new installations)		
Client computers (new installations)		
Client computers (upgrades from Windows NT 4.0)		
Client computers (upgrades from Windows 98)		

Exercise 2: Developing Custom Security Templates

This exercise has you identify which incremental security templates you must deploy to fulfill Contoso's security requirements. The exercise also discusses the custom configuration that will be required to extend the security templates to allow the application of settings for the Sales Force Operations application.

Determining Incremental Template Requirements

The following section identifies which incremental security templates you may use for configuring Windows 2000 computer security for Contoso. Answers to the questions can be found in the appendix.

1. Can you apply the High Security incremental security template to the Windows 2000–based computers at Contoso?

2. What incremental template can you apply to all Windows 2000–based computers to increase security over the default levels?

3. Which security template requires individual user and group membership to be used for securing terminal services access?

Designing Custom Templates for Server Classifications

The following section looks at the customization of security templates that are required for each classification of computer on the Contoso network. Answers to the questions can be found in the appendix.

1. How many security templates must be configured to meet DC security requirements?

2. What settings must be included in the DC's security template to meet Contoso's password security requirements?

3. Where would you apply the security template to ensure that all DCs enforce the password settings?

4. What settings must be included in the DC's security template to meet Contoso's audit security requirements?

5. Where would you apply the security template to ensure that all DCs enforce the audit settings?

6. Is it possible to create a security template to secure the file and print server folder structure shown in Figure 8.11?

Extending the Security Configuration Tool Set to Support the Sales Force Operations Application

The following questions involve the steps needed to extend security templates to include settings for the Sales Force Operations application. Answers to the questions can be found in the appendix.

1. Does the Security Configuration Tool Set currently have entries for the Sales Force Operations software within Security Options?

2. How can you extend the Security Configuration Tool Set to include the required registry settings?

3. What values must you add to the [Register Registry Values] section?

4. What values must you add to the [Strings] section?

5. Once the Sceregvl.inf file is edited, what must you do?

Exercise 3: Planning Deployment of the Security Templates

The following exercise helps you determine the best way to deploy the security templates in the Contoso network. Answers to the questions can be found in the appendix.

1. What security templates can you apply by importing the security templates into Group Policy objects?

2. Draw an OU structure that supports the deployment of security templates by importing the security templates into Group Policy objects.

3. What method can you use to ensure that the security template for Web servers is deployed to the Web servers?

Review

Answering the following questions will reinforce key information presented in this chapter. If you are unable to answer a question, review the appropriate lesson and then try the question again. Answers to the questions can be found in the appendix.

1. What are the differences between the default and basic security templates?

2. You're upgrading your Windows 95 computers to Windows 2000. What security template is applied to the upgraded computer to achieve default Windows 2000 security? Are there any security implications you should be aware of?

3. You've implemented Terminal Services on a Windows 2000 Advanced Server on your network. You notice that all users who access the terminal server are able to access common areas on the terminal server's local file system. What can you do to restrict access by the individual user accounts?

4. During your migration to Windows 2000, your testing has determined that one of your existing applications isn't on the Windows 2000–certified applications list. Due to budget constraints, you can't upgrade to the latest version at this time. What options do you have to allow the application to be used in the upgraded Windows 2000 network?

5. Your network uses Novell NetWare 4.11 as its operating system. You've deployed Windows 2000 Professional clients for the Engineering department and want to use security templates to ensure that consistent security configuration is applied to the Windows 2000 Professional clients. What can you do to ensure the consistent application of the security template?

6. Figure 8.12 shows the status of your DC after you perform an analysis of your DC's current settings against the settings in your security template.

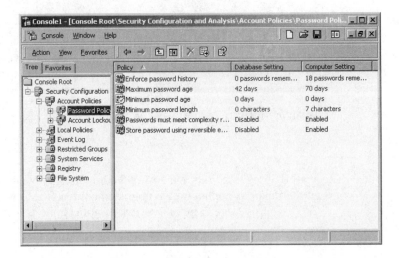

Figure 8.12   Analysis results for a DC

How would you rate the configuration of this computer against the settings in the security template? Give your answers in the following table.

Setting	Rating (Below, Meets, Exceeds)	Rationale
Enforce password history		
Maximum password age		
Minimum password age		
Minimum password length		
Passwords must meet complexity requirements		
Store passwords using reversible encryption		

7. Your organization has deployed Windows 2000 using a single domain forest for your Active Directory. Once you've created security templates for each configuration of computers in your network, what would be the most efficient way to ensure that the security template is applied to all computers in the same classification?

CHAPTER 9

Designing Microsoft Windows 2000 Services Security

About This Chapter

When you deploy common services in Microsoft Windows 2000, you should consider security issues. Without proper planning, these services may expose your network to certain vulnerabilities. Proper planning will lessen both the probability of these vulnerabilities and their effect and create a more secure network.

This chapter looks at design considerations for the following services:

- Domain Name Services (DNS)
- Dynamic Host Configuration Protocol (DHCP)
- Remote Installation Services (RIS)
- Simple Network Management Protocol (SNMP)
- Terminal Services

Before You Begin

To complete this chapter, you must read the chapter scenario. This scenario is used throughout the chapter to apply the design decisions discussed in each lesson.

Chapter Scenario: Lucerne Publishing

Lucerne Publishing is deploying a Web site that will allow customers to order books on the Internet. The Web site will be hosted on an Internet Information Services (IIS) server located at the company's Tokyo office.

Active Directory Design for Lucerne Publishing

Lucerne Publishing is an international publisher of reference materials headquartered in Tokyo. To improve book sales on the Internet and to increase network manageability, they have implemented several Windows 2000 network services.

Lucerne Publishing's Active Directory

Lucerne Publishing has deployed Active Directory directory service using an empty forest root domain design. The forest root (lucernepublishing.tld) doesn't host any client computers. Only the domain controllers (DCs) that support the forest root domain and provide DNS services are located in the forest root domain. The forest has four additional domains based on geographic regions, as shown in Figure 9.1.

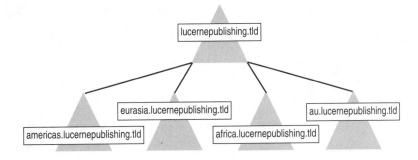

Figure 9.1   Lucerne Publishing forest design

Users and computers in each office are members of the domain that describes their geographic region.

DNS Services

Lucerne Publishing has deployed DNS to provide the necessary locator services for the internal network. In addition, Lucerne Publishing is hosting its DNS domain on the Internet (lucernepublishing.tld).

The DNS services for each domain in the forest are configured as shown in Table 9.1.

Table 9.1   DNS Services Deployment for Lucerne Publishing

Active Directory Domain	DNS Service
lucernepublishing.tld	▪ Active Directory–integrated zone on all DCs in the lucernepublishing.tld domain. ▪ This zone must also be available at each remote office.
americas.lucernepublishing.tld	▪ Active Directory–integrated zone on all DCs in the americas.lucernepublishing.tld domain. ▪ This zone must be available only at the Denver and Caracas offices.
africa.lucernepublishing.tld	▪ Active Directory–integrated zone on all DCs in the africa.lucernepublishing.tld domain. ▪ This zone must be available only at the Casablanca office.
eurasia.lucernepublishing.tld	▪ Active Directory–integrated zone on all DCs in the eurasia.lucernepublishing.tld domain. ▪ This zone must be available only at the Moscow and Tokyo offices.
au.lucernepublishing.tld	▪ Active Directory–integrated zone on all DCs in the au.lucernepublishing.tld domain. ▪ This zone must be available only at the Brisbane office.

DHCP Services

All client computers will be assigned IP addresses using local DHCP servers. The DHCP Service is installed on member servers at the Tokyo, Moscow, Denver, and Brisbane offices. Because the Caracas and Casablanca offices have a limited amount of server-class computers, DHCP is deployed on DCs at these offices.

Not all client computers are currently running Windows 2000. To allow the Host (A) and Pointer (PTR) DNS resource records to be registered using dynamic update, the DHCP server is configured to update DNS for DNS clients that don't support dynamic update. Lucerne Publishing wants to make sure that client computers can take over the registration of DNS resource records when they're upgraded to Windows 2000.

Remote Installation Services (RIS)

Lucerne Publishing wants to use RIS for the deployment of new client computers. Some of the existing client computers don't meet the minimum hardware specifications to run Windows 2000 Professional. Lucerne Publishing has decided to use RIS to deploy the new client workstations.

Lucerne Publishing wants to ensure that only approved computers are able to use RIS for operating system installation. Client computers should be installed to the domain at their geographic location. The network management team would like to have all computer accounts for RIS-installed computers stored in a separate OU.

Simple Network Management Protocol (SNMP)

Lucerne Publishing plans to use SNMP to manage their network infrastructure. By deploying SNMP agents on all network devices (routers, switches, and hubs) and on all servers and client computers, Lucerne Publishing believes they will be able to detect network failures more quickly.

Lucerne Publishing has purchased Unicenter TNG, manufactured by Computer Associates, for its SNMP management software. Each domain will manage its own SNMP environments to ensure prompt response to any network problems. Lucerne Publishing will use the SNMP software to detect network settings but not to reconfigure network devices.

Terminal Services

During the migration to Windows 2000, several desktop client computers will continue to use previous versions of Windows operating systems. However, some of the necessary software will run only in a Windows 2000 environment.

To allow these computers to use the newer software, Terminal Services is deployed at each office to allow clients to connect to the server by using the Terminal Services client software. Table 9.2 shows how the clients connect to the terminal servers on the network.

Table 9.2   Terminal Server Deployment for Lucerne Publishing

Office	Terminal Server
Denver	A Windows 2000 member server in the americas.lucernepublishing.tld domain
Caracas	A Windows 2000 DC in the americas.lucernepublishing.tld domain
Casablanca	A Windows 2000 DC in the africa.lucernepublishing.tld domain
Moscow	A Windows 2000 DC in the eurasia.lucernepublishing.tld domain
Tokyo	A Windows 2000 DC in the eurasia.lucernepublishing.tld domain
Brisbane	A Windows 2000 DC in the au.lucernepublishing.tld domain

Lucerne Publishing wants to ensure that all information sent to the terminal servers is encrypted so that password information and account information aren't compromised on the network.

Lesson 1: Designing DNS Security

Deploying Domain Name System (DNS) service is one of the key steps in designing your Active Directory. DNS acts as the locator service in a Windows 2000 network. When designing a DNS deployment, ensure that security is maintained so that the DNS Service doesn't expose excessive information about the internal network.

After this lesson, you will be able to

- Design security for your DNS deployment

Estimated lesson time: 45 minutes

Assessing Security Risks for the DNS Service

DNS gives you the ability to resolve host names to IP addresses on a Transmission Control Protocol/Internet Protocol (TCP/IP) network. DNS is the standard resolution service that the Internet uses for addressing and resolving Internet-based resources. Within a Windows 2000 network, DNS provides the locator service for Windows 2000 service through the implementation of Service (SRV) resource records as defined in RFC 2782, as well as standard DNS resource records such as Host (A), Canonical Name (CNAME), Mail Exchanger (MX), and Pointer (PTR) records.

Make sure that the DNS Service is properly configured so that client computers can easily query the DNS Service to resolve services and hosts to specific IP addresses on the network.

Determining Network Services with SRV Resource Records

The SRV resource records provide a mechanism for finding common services in a Windows 2000 network. The format of the SRV resource record is as follows:

```
_ldap._tcp.microsoft.com. 600 SRV 0 100 389 dc1.microsoft.com
```

The following components are defined in an SRV resource record:

- **_ldap._tcp.microsoft.com.** This component refers to three separate pieces of information:
    - **The advertised service (_ldap).** Valid options for Windows 2000 services include _ldap (the Lightweight Directory Access Protocol [LDAP] service), _Kerberos (the Kerberos Key Distribution Center), _gc (Windows 2000 global catalog servers), and _pdc (Windows 2000 primary domain controller emulators).
    - **The transport protocol (_tcp).** Each protocol uses either transmission control protocol (TCP) or user datagram protocol (UDP).

- **The domain (microsoft.com).** In this case the LDAP service will be able to resolve LDAP queries for the microsoft.com domain.
- **The time to live (TTL) (600).** This is the amount of time (in seconds) that the SRV resource record will be cached at a DNS server or DNS client in the resolver cache.
- **SRV.** This indicates that the resource record is a service resource record indicating the location of a network service on the network.
- **The priority and weight (0 100).** The combination of these two fields allows you to configure preference for one SRV resource record over another SRV resource record for the duplicate service.
- **The port that the service is listening on.** In this case the LDAP service listens on TCP port 389.
- **Network host where the LDAP service resides (dc1.microsoft.com).** In this case the LDAP service is hosted on dc1.microsoft.com. During the resolution process this host name would be resolved by querying DNS for the A resource record.

Since DNS can reveal the internal structure of your network to a potential attacker, security within your DNS infrastructure is an important design consideration. The potential risks of deploying the DNS Service with inadequate security include the following:

- Dynamic update can allow client computers to overwrite existing DNS resource records and hijack sessions.
- Without adequate security, an attacker can create a secondary DNS zone and obtain a read-only copy of your DNS zone data, which will reveal all resource records located within the source zone.
- DNS services available on the Internet could expose the internal IP addressing scheme of the internal network.

Securing Dynamic Updates

The DNS Service in Windows 2000 provides security through a new zone type known as an *Active Directory–integrated zone*. Active Directory–integrated zones store their resource records within Active Directory instead of standard DNS text files. When the data is stored in Active Directory, each resource record exists as an object in Active Directory and has a Discretionary Access Control List (DACL) that limits which computers can update the resource record.

Deploying Active Directory–integrated zones offers the following advantages:

- **Fault tolerance of zone data.** The DNS zone data can be shared between DCs in the same domain. If the DC has the DNS Service installed, you can query the DC for DNS resolution and read the resource records from Active Directory.

- **Reduction in replication topologies.** Rather than having to configure a standard DNS deployment involving zone transfers between master servers and secondary servers, Active Directory–integrated zones transfer their data using the existing Active Directory replication methods.

- **Security on resource records.** Because the resource records are stored in Active Directory, the resource records are treated as objects with DACLs that will protect the resource records. Only the resource record's owner can modify the resource record. To enable this feature, set the dynamic update option to only allow secure updates.

Note   Many networks implement Berkeley Internet Name Daemon (BIND) DNS servers for their DNS service. BIND 8.x DNS can restrict only dynamic updates to specific IP addresses. The BIND DNS Service doesn't have a mechanism to provide authenticated DNS updates using Active Directory authentication.

Restricting Zone Transfers

Zone transfers are used to transfer zone data to secondary DNS servers. The zone transfer ensures that any secondary DNS servers have current information for all resource records in the zone.

Note   Active Directory–integrated zones are limited to a single domain. If you need to have zone data available in multiple domains, you must still implement secondary DNS zones.

You can secure the zone transfer process by restricting zone transfers to approved DNS servers, as shown in Figure 9.2.

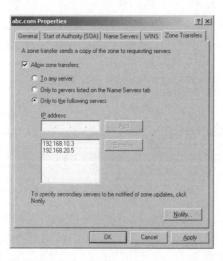

Figure 9.2   Restricting DNS zone transfers to authorized DNS servers

By restricting the DNS servers that can act as secondary DNS servers for your source zone, you ensure that only authorized DNS servers can perform zone transfers of the data.

Warning   A common method for acquiring all zone data from a DNS server is to use the command LS –d DOMAIN.COM within the NSLOOKUP command to cause a zone transfer. If you restrict zone transfers to specific DNS servers, attackers will fail to acquire the zone data if they run the LS –d DOMAIN.COM command.

Implementing Separate External DNS Servers

If your organization is hosting its DNS services on the Internet, the DNS server that processes requests from the Internet should be different from the DNS server used internally. Using separate DNS servers allows you to exclude all internal DNS resource records from the external DNS server and prevent an attacker from determining the internal addressing scheme, as shown in Figure 9.3.

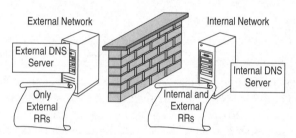

Figure 9.3   Ensuring that the external DNS server contains only externally available resource records

---

Note   Implementing separate internal and external DNS servers might require you to include external resource records in the internal DNS zone. You need to do this when the Active Directory forest root uses the same DNS domain name as the external network. In this situation you can't use forwarders to resolve the external DNS resource records because the internal DNS zone is authoritative for the DNS zone. If the resource record isn't found in an authoritative zone, DNS will report that the resource record doesn't exist and the DNS request won't be forwarded to the configured forwarder.

Restricting Membership in the DNS Admins Group

The DNS Admins group is assigned the right to create new DNS zones at a DNS server and to modify the properties of a DNS server. Only authorized user accounts should be members of the DNS Admins group. By using Restricted Groups in Group Policy, you can restrict DNS Admins group membership.

Making the Decision

Table 9.3 reviews the design decisions that you face when securing the DNS Service and the actions that you must perform.

Table 9.3   Securing the DNS Service

To	Do the Following
Protect the internal address space	Deploy separate DNS services for the internal and the external network. The external DNS server should never have internal resource records in the zone.
Prevent the failure of a single DNS server from stopping dynamic DNS updates	Design the DNS zones as Active Directory–integrated zones.
Prevent unauthorized DNS servers from hosting your DNS zone data	Configure zone transfers to take place only to authorized servers.
Prevent registration of unauthorized resource records	Use Active Directory–integrated zones. When using a BIND DNS server, restrict by IP address.
Prevent unauthorized membership in the DNS Admins group	Define the membership in the Restricted Groups Group Policy setting to include only authorized members.

Applying the Decision

To secure the DNS service, Lucerne Publishing needs to include the following components in its network security design:

- Establish both internal and external DNS servers to host the lucernepublishing.tld domain. Because lucernepublishing.tld is used both on the Internet and as the Active Directory forest root, the DNS zone must be provided on both an external and an internal DNS server. Using two servers will ensure that the SRV resource records and internal addressing information in the lucernepublishing.tld domain aren't exposed on the Internet.

- Configure secondary DNS servers for the lucernepublishing.tld zone on DNS servers in each of the child domains. The lucernepublishing.tld DNS zone is an Active Directory–integrated zone. Active Directory–integrated zones can be replicated only between DCs in the same domain. To provide access to the lucernepublishing.tld domain at each of the cities, configure a DNS server at each city as a secondary DNS server for the lucernepublishing.tld zone.

- Restrict zone transfers to approved secondary DNS servers. To ensure that only approved secondary DNS servers are able to perform zone transfers with the lucernepublishing.tld DNS zone, restrict zone transfers for the zone to the IP address of the DNS servers in the child domains. In addition, configure each secondary DNS server not to allow DNS zone transfers.

Lesson Summary

The DNS service is required for Windows 2000 Active Directory. Consider the security implications of the DNS service when you design your DNS zones. Use Active Directory–integrated zones to ensure that the owner of a DNS resource record is the only one who can update the resource record.

Activity: Designing DNS for Internal and External Use

This activity requires you to determine whether a resource record should be included on an internally accessible DNS server, an externally accessible DNS server, or on both DNS servers.

Your organization has the network infrastructure for its Windows 2000 deployment shown in Figure 9.4.

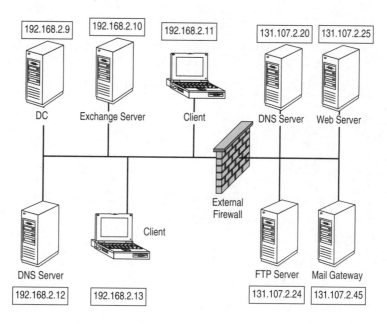

Figure 9.4   Your organization's network

Your organization's Active Directory forest root is deployed as a child domain of your current DNS namespace. The DNS name for your organization is organization.tld, and your Active Directory forest root is deployed as ad.organization.tld.

Your organization uses a mix of Microsoft Outlook 2000 clients configured to use the Exchange Server service and Outlook Express clients. The mail clients use Internet Message Access Protocol version 4.0 (IMAP4) and Simple Mail Transport Protocol (SMTP) to access e-mail services. When working at client sites, Outlook Express clients require e-mail access on both the internal network and the external network.

Outside clients have reported that they can't send mail to your organization. Messages are returned stating that a Mail Exchanger doesn't exist for your organization's domain name.

Answer the following questions about this situation. The answers to these questions can be found in the appendix.

1. What DNS zones must be hosted on the external DNS server?

2. Based on the information provided, complete the following table of resource records that must be included at the external DNS server.

Host	IP Address or Contents
▪	
▪	
▪	
▪	

3. Are there any additional resource records that you must manually configure on the external DNS server?

4. What DNS zones must be hosted on the internal DNS server?

5. Do you have to include externally available resources on the internal DNS server?

6. Assume that the internal DNS server is configured to host the organization.tld DNS zone. What resource records must be included for the Outlook Express clients to ensure that they communicate only with the internal mail server when they use the internal DNS server? Enter your answer in the following table.

DNS Resource Record	IP Address or Contents
mail.organization.tld	
MX record for organization.tld	

Lesson 2: Designing DHCP Security

Dynamic Host Configuration Protocol (DHCP) allows a client computer to lease an IP address from a DHCP server so that the client can participate in the network. Your DHCP design should include provisions for securing the DHCP process.

After this lesson, you will be able to
- Design security for the DHCP Service

Estimated lesson time: 30 minutes

Assessing the Security Risks of the DHCP Service

The DHCP Service provides IP address configuration to DHCP clients on the network. These clients depend on the DHCP Service to provide them with correct IP addressing information. If the client were to receive an incorrect IP address from the DHCP Service, the result could be a loss of connectivity on the network—and, in the worst case, provide connectivity to unauthorized servers on the network.

The DHCP Service's security risks can be broken down into three categories:

- The risk of an unauthorized DHCP server assigning incorrect IP addressing information.
- The ability of the DHCP server to overwrite static IP address information in DNS.
- Unauthorized DHCP clients leasing IP addresses on the network.

Preventing Unauthorized DHCP Servers

A common security concern is the possibility that an unauthorized DHCP server might provide incorrect IP addressing information to the DHCP clients. Windows 2000 has reduced the possibility of unauthorized Windows 2000–based DHCP servers by requiring the DHCP servers to be authorized in Active Directory. Only authorized DHCP servers can issue IP addresses for DHCP clients, as shown in Figure 9.5.

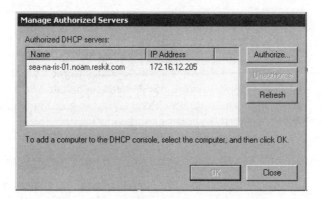

Figure 9.5   Identifying authorized DHCP servers

The DHCP server won't issue IP addresses to clients if it determines that it's not authorized to do so.

How DHCP Authorization Works

A DHCP server sends a DHCPInform message when the DHCP Service starts to the limited broadcast address (255.255.255.255). By using the 255.255.255.255 address, the DHCPInform message doesn't cross network routers to other network segments. The purpose of the DHCPInform message is to find the directory enterprise root that maintains information on authorized DHCP servers. Any DHCP servers that receive the DHCPInform message respond with a DHCPAck message, allowing the DHCP server to collect information on other active DHCP servers. The DHCP server also collects information on the directory service used by the other DHCP servers.

The newly started DHCP server queries the directory enterprise root to ensure that it's listed as an authorized DHCP server. If it's authorized to do so, the DHCP Service initializes and provides IP address information to DHCP clients. If it isn't, the DHCP services don't initialize. The DHCP Service also starts if it determines that there's no configured directory enterprise root and therefore no restrictions on the DHCP Service.

By default, only members of the Enterprise Admins universal group can authorize DHCP servers in Active Directory.

Warning   Non–Windows 2000 DHCP services can still be started on the network and issue incorrect IP addressing information to DHCP clients. Your security plan must include provisions for the detection of unauthorized DHCP servers on the network. One way to find the IP address of an unauthorized DHCP server is to run IPCONFIG /ALL at a client computer that has received incorrect IP addressing information.

Preventing DHCP Servers from Overwriting Static IP Addresses in DNS

Client computers that are running previous versions of Microsoft operating systems aren't able to perform dynamic updates to the DNS server. You can configure DHCP servers to perform the updates on behalf of these clients by selecting the Enable Updates For DNS Clients That Do Not Support Dynamic Update check box for a DHCP scope, as shown in Figure 9.6.

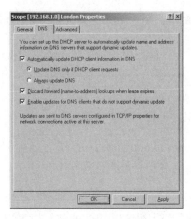

Figure 9.6   Configuring DHCP to perform DNS updates on behalf of
down-level clients

If the DNS update is sent to an Active Directory–integrated zone, the DHCP
server will become the owner of the DNS resource records in Active Directory.
This may cause problems if the non–Windows 2000 client is later upgraded to
Windows 2000. The default behavior for registration of DNS resource records for
Windows 2000 clients is as follows:

- The DHCP server updates the Pointer (PTR) resource records to the reverse
  lookup zone.

- The Windows 2000 client updates the Host (A) resource record to the forward
  lookup zone.

If the DHCP server is the owner of the DNS resource record, the Windows 2000
client won't be able to update the resource record.

You can change this behavior by adding the DHCP server to the DNSUpdateProxy
global group. Membership in this group changes the behavior of DNS updates to
Active Directory–integrated zones. If the DHCP server is a member of the
DNSUpdateProxy group, it won't take ownership of any DNS resource records
that it writes to the DNS Active Directory–integrated zone. The client is able to
register the resource records after upgrade and then take ownership of the resource records.

Warning   In one circumstance, preventing the DHCP server from taking ownership of a DNS resource record isn't the desired behavior. Never make the DHCP
server a member of the DNSUpdateProxy group if the DHCP Service is running
on a DC. Membership in the DNSUpdateProxy group doesn't differentiate
between resource records registered on behalf of another client and resource
records registered by that specific client. Membership in the DNSUpdateProxy
group allows any user or computer to modify resource records corresponding to
the DC, including all related SRV resource records.

Preventing Unauthorized DHCP Clients from Leasing IP Addresses

In higher-security networks, DHCP may introduce security weaknesses because any DHCP client can lease a valid IP address on the network. To prevent this, you must reserve all IP addresses in the scope to specific Media Access Control (MAC) addresses.

This practice requires that all approved client MAC addresses are documented and that reservations are created for each MAC address. Nonleased addresses in the DHCP pool of IP addresses must be reserved to nonexistent MAC addresses to prevent the assignment of these IP addresses until the IP address is assigned to a valid MAC address.

Warning This practice can be difficult to manage. In some cases it will be easier to deploy IP addressing using static IP addresses rather than using IP address reservations in DHCP.

Making the Decision

Table 9.4 reviews the design decisions that you face when you deploy the DHCP Service in a Windows 2000 network and want to ensure that security is maintained.

Table 9.4   Securing the DHCP Service

To	Include the Following in Your Design
Prevent unauthorized DHCP servers on the network	■ Upgrade all computers running DHCP services to Windows 2000. ■ Only authorize the required DHCP servers in Active Directory.
Protect DC-related DNS resource records	■ Don't install DHCP services on a Windows 2000 DC *and* make the DHCP server a member of the DNSUpdateProxy group.
Ensure that only authorized clients receive DHCP addresses from the DHCP server	■ Create reservations for all DHCP clients. Ensure that all addresses in the DHCP scope are associated with a MAC address to prevent unauthorized clients from receiving DHCP-assigned IP addresses.
Detect unauthorized non–Windows 2000 DHCP servers	■ Watch for pockets of misconfigured IP addresses. ■ Use IPCONFIG /ALL at the DHCP client to determine the IP address of the DHCP server that assigned the address.

Applying the Decision

Lucerne Publishing should move the DHCP services at the Caracas and Casablanca offices to member servers. Lucerne Publishing wants the client computers that have been upgraded to Windows 2000 to take over the registration of

DNS resource records. To do this, you must make the DHCP servers members of the DNSUpdateProxy group to prevent the DHCP server from taking ownership of the DNS resource records.

If the Caracas and Casablanca DHCP services remain on DCs, it's possible to overwrite the DC's DNS resource records or the static DNS resource records. Additionally, the DHCP servers should be configured to perform dynamic updates on behalf of all DNS clients that don't support dynamic updates.

Lesson Summary

DHCP is a key service on most Windows 2000 networks. If an unauthorized DCHP server is introduced on the network, the results can range from temporary loss of connectivity to the loss of data to an unauthorized server posing as the actual server.

Your DHCP deployment plan should include strategies for detecting and preventing unauthorized DHCP servers. You should also consider how the DHCP service will integrate with the DNS service.

Lesson 3: Designing RIS Security

To simplify the deployment of Windows 2000 clients, many organizations use RIS to help deploy Windows 2000 Professional images to desktop computers. The risk in using RIS to deploy clients is that if RIS isn't configured securely, an unauthorized user might be able to install an unauthorized computer on the network.

After this lesson, you will be able to

- Design secure deployment of Windows 2000 Professional by using RIS

Estimated lesson time: 30 minutes

Designing RIS Security

RIS is a collection of services that work together to allow remote installations of preconfigured Windows 2000 Professional desktop computers. The services that comprise RIS include the following, illustrated in Figure 9.7.

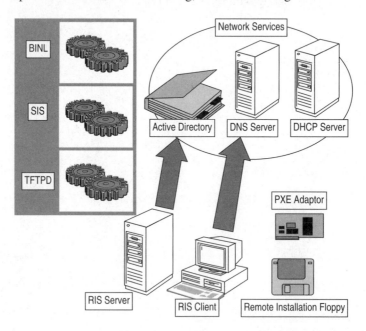

Figure 9.7   Components of Remote Installation Services

- **Boot Information Negotiation Layer (BINL).** The BINL service answers DHCP requests from Preboot Execution Environment (PXE) network adapters or clients using a remote installation floppy. If the network has multiple RIS images, the BINL service will direct the client computer to the correct installation files based on the credentials provided by the user when requesting the image. The BINL service determines whether the installation is a reinstallation that will use an existing computer account or a new installation that requires creation of a new computer account by inspecting the target computer and Active Directory.

- **Trivial File Transfer Protocol Daemon (TFTPD).** The files that initiate the RIS installation are transferred from the RIS server to the client by using Trivial File Transfer Protocol (TFTP).

Note TFTP is used instead of File Transfer Protocol (FTP) because a TFTP file transfer involves less overhead. TFTP provides a connectionless transfer by using User Datagram Protocol (UDP).

- **Single Instance Store (SIS).** The SIS allows multiple RIS images to be stored at a RIS server but reduces the duplication of files stored at the RIS server. If a file is duplicated between multiple images, the SIS keeps only a single instance of the file.

You configure and start these services with the Remote Installation Setup Wizard, RISetup.

Assessing Security Risks for Remote Installation

Consider the following practices whenever you implement RIS on your network:

- Prevent unauthorized RIS servers from being deployed on the network
- Determine whether the RIS server should respond only to specific client computers
- Restrict which users can create RIS image computers
- Limit user access to specific RIS images
- Ensure that proper security configuration is restored with a RIS image
- Address data transmission security during the initial RIS processing

Authorizing RIS Servers

The remote installation process requires the RIS server to be authorized in Active Directory. As with DHCP servers, only authorized RIS servers will respond to RIS clients requesting a RIS installation.

RIS servers are authorized in the DHCP console by members of the Enterprise Admins group. The RIS server will require authorization only if it doesn't have the DHCP Service installed. If the RIS server has already been authorized in Active Directory for the DHCP Service, there's no need to reauthorize the computer for RIS.

Note When a PXE client is started on the network, the DHCP discover packet sent by the PXE client will request both an IP address for the client and the location of a PXE boot server, also known as the RIS server. The RIS installation can't proceed unless both the client IP address and the RIS server are provided.

Defining Which RIS Servers Will Respond to Client Requests

By default, RIS servers won't respond to client installation requests until you enable the ability to respond at the RIS server. For higher-security networks, you should not only enable the RIS server to respond to installation requests, but you should also restrict the responses to prestaged clients, as shown in Figure 9.8.

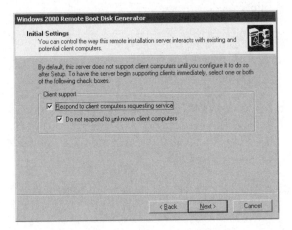

Figure 9.8 Configuring RIS to respond only to known client computers

Prestaged client computers are computers that have a computer account existing in Active Directory before RIS is installed. A common method of prestaging clients is to configure the globally unique identifier (GUID) attribute for the computer account in Active Directory, as shown in Figure 9.9.

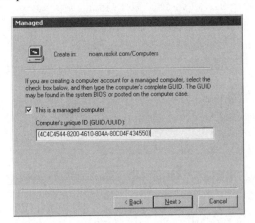

Figure 9.9 Configuring the GUID for a computer account

Tip If the client is a PC98 or NetPC-compliant computer, you can find the GUID either in the system BIOS or on the computer case.

In addition, the user account performing the installation must have read and write permissions for all properties of the prestaged computer object and rights to reset and change passwords for the computer account.

Restricting the Creation of Computer Accounts

In some cases you may want to grant network users the necessary permissions to create the computer account during the client installation. To do this, complete the following steps:

1. Determine the location in Active Directory where computer accounts will be created. You can determine that computer accounts will be created in one of three locations, illustrated in Figure 9.10.

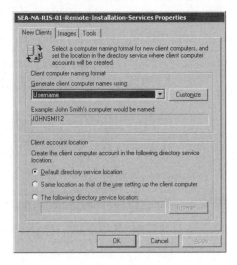

Figure 9.10 Configuring the directory service location for computer accounts

- The default location (the Computers container) in the same domain as the RIS server responding to the client request

- The same OU as the user account that's performing the client installation

- To a specific OU provided by an administrator

2. Grant the user accounts the necessary permissions to create the computer account. Grant Read permissions and Create Computer Object permissions for the OU where the computer account will be created. Grant these permissions with the Delegation Of Control Wizard by granting the Join A Computer To The Domain privilege in the Delegation Of Administration Wizard.

Once you complete these two steps, the users with the delegated permission can perform remote installation of the operating system.

Restricting Which RIS Images a User Can Load

If you plan for users to select from multiple RIS images, you can restrict which images are available to users by configuring DACLs to change the default permissions.

The default permissions for a RIS image allow all users to install the image. You can modify which groups can install a RIS image by defining the security on an image's Templates subfolder, as shown in Figure 9.11.

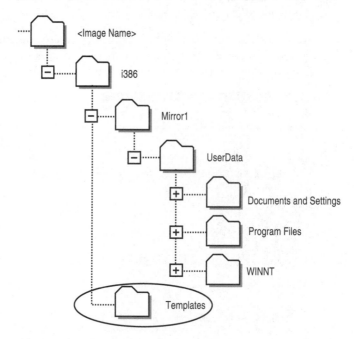

Figure 9.11   Changing NTFS permissions on the Templates subfolder to restrict who can load a RIS image

By creating a custom domain local group that contains the user accounts that can install a specific RIS image, you can restrict who can install each image and show users only images they are allowed to see when they perform a remote installation.

Ensuring Proper Security Settings on the RIS Image Computer

Before using the RIPrep utility to prepare a RIS image, make sure that you've installed all necessary applications and have configured all required security settings. This includes registry, NTFS settings, and all other security template–related settings. When the RIPrep image is downloaded to destination RIS clients, your security settings will be maintained.

You can't include EFS encrypted files in the RIS image. Files encrypted with EFS will be unusable at any destination RIS client computers because the clients won't have the EFS private key required to decrypt the file encryption key.

Protecting Data Transmissions Between RIS Clients and RIS Servers

RIS uses TFTP for the initial transfer of data from the RIS server to the RIS client. TFTP doesn't encrypt data transmitted between the client and the server. Make sure that you're not using an account with Administrator rights on the network for the RIS process. A network sniffer could capture the credentials and use them to launch attacks against the network. Instead, configure an account that has only the permissions to install the RIS image to the client computer.

Note Because you use RIS to install a client operating system, you can't implement IPSec to protect the TFTP data stream between the RIS server and the RIS client computers. Only the Windows 2000 operating system supports the use of IPSec.

Making the Decision

When you use RIS to deploy client computers, use the decision matrix shown in Table 9.5 to ensure that security is maintained on your network.

Table 9.5   Securing RIS Deployments

To	Do the Following
Prevent deployment of unauthorized RIS servers	■ Restrict membership in the Enterprise Admins group because only members of this group can authorize RIS servers. ■ Authorize only approved RIS servers. ■ Restrict installation of RIS services on existing DHCP servers since they are already authorized in Active Directory.
Restrict RIS-installed computer accounts to a specific OU	■ Allow only prestaged computer accounts to install RIS images. ■ Create the prestaged computer accounts in the desired OU. ■ Alternatively, configure a specific location in Active Directory where computer accounts will be created for remote installations.
Restrict who can perform remote installations	■ Assign only approved users the permission to create computer accounts in the OU where remote installation computer accounts will be created. ■ If using prestaged computer accounts, assign only approved users the permissions to modify the attributes of the prestaged computer accounts.
Restrict which images a user can load using remote installation	■ Change the DACLs on the RIS image's Templates subfolder to only allow authorized security groups READ permissions.
Maintain default security for RIS images	■ Preconfigure all security settings at the source computer before running the RIPrep utility to create the remote installation image.
Protect administrative permissions during RIS installations	■ Delegate the permissions to create computer accounts in Active Directory and never use an Administrator account for the remote installation because the TFTP protocol doesn't encrypt network data transmissions.

Applying the Decision

To meet their RIS security requirements, Lucerne Publishing can either prestage computer accounts for remote installation or change permissions to allow users to create the computer accounts. If Lucerne Publishing chooses to prestage the computer accounts, you must add the following tasks to the security plan:

■ Ensure that a member of the Enterprise Admins group authorizes all RIS servers in Active Directory.

■ Determine the GUIDs for each new computer and create the computer account in an OU named RIS Computers in the domain that will contain the new computer account. This action ensures that each computer is installed in the correct domain, because only RIS servers from that domain process the RIS request.

■ For the prestaged computer objects, create a domain local group that has the permissions to modify the attributes of the computer object. This action ensures that the users can perform the remote installation and make the necessary modifications to the computer account.

■ Configure the RIS server so that it doesn't respond to requests from unknown clients. This configuration restricts remote installation to prestaged computer accounts.

If Lucerne Publishing decides to allow users to create the computer accounts in Active Directory, add the following tasks to the security plan:

■ Ensure that a member of the Enterprise Admins group authorizes all RIS servers in Active Directory.

■ Configure the RIS server to create the computer accounts in the RIS Computers OU.

■ Delegate all authorized users with the ability to Join A Computer To The Domain at the RIS Computers OU.

■ Modify the DACL for the Templates folder of the remote installation package to allow only users from the domain to download the image.

The decision to use prestaged computers or grant users the ability to create computer accounts will depend largely on how many computers will be installed. The more computers, the less likely it will be that an administrator will want to precreate the computer accounts and manually enter GUID attribute information. Even using scripts will require the manual installation of each GUID.

Lesson Summary

RIS is a key component of change and configuration management within Windows 2000. You must design the ability to create and install RIS images carefully so that only authorized users can use this service.

Lesson 4: Designing SNMP Security

Many network administrators use Simple Network Management Protocol (SNMP) to provide a preemptive method of detecting network faults. This protocol allows SNMP agents to inform SNMP management stations when abnormal events take place on the network that the network administrator should address.

After this lesson, you will be able to

- Design security for deploying SNMP

Estimated lesson time: 30 minutes

Designing SNMP Security

SNMP allows a network administrator to proactively manage a network by providing early detection of network faults or incorrect network configuration. Network administrators use SNMP to do the following:

- **Monitor network performance.** SNMP can determine network throughput and determine if data is being transmitted successfully on the network. You can use the monitoring of network performance to detect network faults.
- **Detect network faults or unauthorized access.** You can configure SNMP alerts to inform the SNMP management station when specified events take place. These events can include a failed router, attempted management of an SNMP agent by an unauthorized management station, or the restart of a device.
- **Configure network devices.** Use SNMP to configure SNMP agents remotely.
- **Audit network usage.** Use SNMP to determine network usage. You can use this information to determine overused areas of the network.

An SNMP environment has several participants, including

- **SNMP management stations.** SNMP management stations run software capable of querying and managing SNMP agents on the network.

Note   Windows 2000 doesn't ship with an SNMP management station component. The Windows 2000 support tools includes a simple graphical SNMP manager called SNMPUtilg.exe. For an extended feature set, consider implementing third-party solutions such as HP OpenView from Hewlett-Packard or Unicenter TNG from Computer Associates.

- **SNMP agents.** SNMP agents run a service that's able to respond to SNMP management requests and to alert SNMP management stations when unauthorized management is attempted or when predefined events take place.

SNMP agents send status messages to the SNMP management station. The status messages include regular updates sent to an SNMP management station or responses to SNMP queries. In specific instances the SNMP agent will send an SNMP trap message to indicate that a defined event has taken place.

Note   Another difference between SNMP status messages and SNMP trap messages is that they're directed to different ports on the SNMP management station. SNMP status messages are sent to User Datagram Protocol (UDP) port 161 on the SNMP management station, and SNMP trap messages are sent to UDP port 162.

Assessing the Security Risks of SNMP

SNMP allows you to query network devices and clients for configuration information. In the wrong hands, this configuration information may reduce your network's security by exposing sensitive information, such as Active Directory account information or router configuration.

To provide security for your organization's SNMP deployment, you must consider the following design points:

- Configuration of SNMP communities
- Configuration of approved SNMP management stations
- Interception of SNMP status messages and SNMP trap messages

Restricting Management to Specific SNMP Communities

The SNMP protocol provides limited security through the configuration of SNMP communities. SNMP communities define a collection of SNMP agents that can be managed as a collection on the network. The SNMP community doesn't have to map to domains within your Active Directory, but it should map to areas of management within your network.

An SNMP agent can belong to multiple communities, and you can configure rights for each community. You can assign rights to be

- **None or Notify.** The SNMP agent does not process the request. When the agent receives an SNMP message from a management system in this community, it discards the request and generates an authentication trap.
- **Read Only.** The SNMP agent processes GET, GET-NEXT, and GET-BULK requests from the community but discards all SET requests.
- **Read Create or Read Write.** The SNMP agent processes all requests from the SNMP community including GET, GET-NEXT, GET-BULK, and SET requests. SET requests are limited to the addition of new objects in a Management Information Base (MIB) table.

Figure 9.12 shows an SNMP agent configured to belong to two communities, Corporate and Redmond. SNMP management stations have been assigned different rights for each community.

Within this dialog box, you can enable the option to send authentication traps. An authentication trap will inform a configured SNMP management station if an SNMP management station from a community that's not included in the approved communities list attempts to manage the SNMP agent.

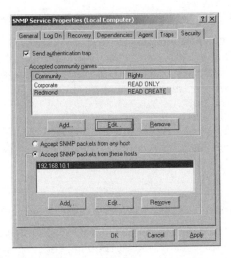

Figure 9.12   SNMP agent configured to respond to two communities

Restricting Management to Specific SNMP Management Stations

Figure 9.12 shows additional security configuration for the SNMP Service. You can configure each SNMP agent to respond only to specific SNMP management stations. If an SNMP message is received from an unapproved management station, the SNMP agent will send an SNMP trap message to a configured management station. In addition, you can configure SNMP agents to send messages only to a preconfigured management station. This configuration prevents unauthorized management stations from requesting data from SNMP agents. If an unauthorized management station attempts to manage the SNMP agent, you can configure an authorized management station as the host that SNMP trap messages are sent to indicating the unauthorized access, as shown in Figure 9.13.

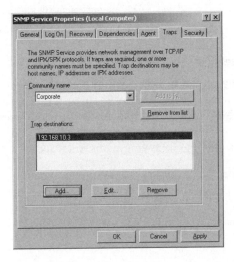

Figure 9.13   Configuring the destination for SNMP trap messages for the
Corporate community

Protecting SNMP Messages from Interception

Because SNMP status messages and SNMP trap messages are sent in clear text across the network, a network sniffer can intercept the SNMP messages and read the information in them. You can configure IPSec to require that SNMP status messages and SNMP trap messages be encrypted.

Be careful when implementing IPSec. All SNMP agents must support the use of IPSec. If a single SNMP agent doesn't support IPSec, you'll have to configure IPSec to only request and not require IPSec encryption. Otherwise you'll have to remove the SNMP agent that doesn't support IPSec from your management scheme.

Making the Decision

Table 9.6 outlines the design decisions that you face when designing a secure SNMP deployment for your Windows 2000 network.

Table 9.6   Securing the SNMP Service

To	Do the Following
Prevent SNMP management stations from modifying configuration by using SNMP SET commands	Configure the communities in which the SNMP agent participates to be Read-Only communities. This configuration prevents the SNMP agent from processing SNMP SET messages.
Prevent unauthorized SNMP management stations from managing SNMP agents	Change the community name from the default name of "Public." Be sure to choose a community name that's difficult to guess.
Track unauthorized management attempts	Configure the SNMP agent to send trap messages for authentication traps and to have the SNMP traps sent to a specific SNMP management station.
Protect SNMP messages from interception	Encrypt SNMP messages by using IPSec. This requires that all SNMP management stations and SNMP agents support IPSec encryption.

Applying the Decision

Lucerne Publishing wants to use SNMP to manage network devices, clients, and servers. As mentioned earlier, each domain will manage its own SNMP environments and SNMP will be used to query information, not to configure SNMP-enabled devices. To ensure security for its SNMP environment, Lucerne Publishing will include the following items in its security design:

- Deploy separate community names that map to the domains within the lucernepublishing.tld forest. The community names shouldn't be the actual domain names because this would be too easy to guess. Likewise, the names shouldn't include the default name Public, because this is a common target for SNMP attacks.

- Configure all SNMP communities as Read-Only. Lucerne Publishing plans to use SNMP to query SNMP agents and to respond to SNMP traps. These processes don't require write abilities to the SNMP agents. Configuring communities as Read-Only prevents the use of SNMP SET commands.

- Restrict management to occur only within the domain. Add the other community names to the list of community names for each SNMP agent and configure them with the NONE right to prevent management from other areas of the network.

- Detect unauthorized SNMP management attempts. Lucerne Publishing should configure each SNMP agent to send authentication trap messages to track unauthorized management attempts. Configure each SNMP agent with a listing of authorized management stations and an SNMP management station to which the SNMP trap messages will be sent.

Lucerne Publishing has to review its situation carefully to determine whether it should implement IPSec for SNMP messages. The company must find out if all network devices deployed on its network support IPSec. If they don't, it would be unwise to deploy IPSec because Lucerne Publishing would lose the ability to monitor the network devices.

Lesson Summary

SNMP is an excellent tool for proactively managing your network. If you configure it properly for security, you can prevent attackers from taking advantage of security weaknesses in the SNMP protocol. When you deploy SNMP in your environment, always make sure that you configure approved communities and SNMP management stations. Don't leave the default configuration because the default uses the Public community name and allows any SNMP management stations to manage SNMP agents on the network.

Lesson 5: Designing Terminal Services Security

Terminal Services allows users who don't have Windows 2000–based client computers to take advantage of Windows 2000 technology. You can load Terminal Services clients on Windows 3.1, Windows for Workgroups 3.11, Windows 95, Windows 98, and Windows NT–based clients. In addition, you can deploy the Terminal Services Advanced Client to allow any user with a Web browser that support ActiveX controls to connect to the terminal server. You can get the Terminal Services Advanced Client by going to *www.microsoft.com* and searching for "Terminal Services Advanced Client."

After this lesson, you will be able to

- Design security for a Terminal Services deployment

Estimated lesson time: 30 minutes

Designing Terminal Services Security

Terminal Services allows clients to run Windows 2000 compatible applications on a terminal server without loading Windows 2000 at the client computer. The terminal server hosts all client data processing, application execution, and data storage. The Terminal Services client sends only keyboard input and mouse movement to the terminal server. The terminal server performs all processing and returns only display information to the Terminal Services client.

Terminal Services gives a network administrator additional advantages. You can limit the Terminal Services sessions to a single application by changing the shell application from the default of Explorer.exe.

Assessing Security Risks of Terminal Services

When a Terminal Services client connects to a terminal server, it appears as if the client is sitting at the keyboard of the server. Securing Terminal Services may include configuring the terminal server or performing administrative tasks.

In your network design you must include security design for the following Terminal Services issues:

- The potential for remote administration of a terminal server.
- All Terminal Service clients require access to the local file system.
- To use Terminal Services, the Terminal Services client must have Log On Locally rights to the terminal server.
- By default, security is assigned to the terminal server Users group and isn't based on the individual group memberships of the Terminal Service clients.
- Data sent between the terminal server and the Terminal Service client could be intercepted.

- Two-factor authentication methods, such as smart card logon, aren't supported within Terminal Services.

Restricting Remote Administration

You can install Terminal Services in one of two modes: Remote Administration Mode or Application Server Mode. If you install Terminal Services to provide remote administration of a server, consider configuring the terminal server to use Remote Administration Mode. This mode allows only members of the Administrators group to connect to the terminal server. In addition, Remote Administration Mode restricts Terminal Service connections to a maximum of two simultaneous connections.

Restricting Access to the Local File System

Terminal Services clients see the file system on the terminal server as their local file system. To ensure that Terminal Services clients have access only to specific areas of the file system, configure all volumes as NTFS volumes. Also, configure NTFS permissions to restrict access to specific folders on the server.

Warning   Not only do the Terminal Service clients share the file system, but they also share any services related to the computer. For example, if one Terminal Service user were to implement a dial-up connection to the Internet, all Terminal Service clients would have access to that connection because the connection is associated with the computer, not the individual user.

Determining Where to Deploy Terminal Services

To connect to a terminal server, Terminal Service clients require the Log On Locally right. Don't deploy Terminal Services using Application Server Mode on a DC because all users require the Log On Locally right in order to connect to the terminal server. In a default Windows 2000 environment, this circumstance would allow Terminal Services users to log on locally at all DCs, not just the DCs with Terminal Services installed. For best security, install Terminal Services only on member servers so that you don't grant excess rights on DCs.

Implementing Individual User Security

By default, security for Terminal Services clients is based on membership in the Terminal Server Users group. Any user who is logged on at a terminal server, whether using a remote connection or logged on at the console, is automatically made a member of the Terminal Server Users group.

You can apply the incremental security template Notssid.inf to remove the Terminal Server Users group from all DACLs on the file system. By removing this group, you ensure that users gain access to the file system based on their user accounts and group memberships, not by the fact that they're connecting to a terminal server.

Tip To simplify the deployment of this security template, place all terminal servers in a common OU and import the Notssid.inf security template into the Group Policy object for that OU. This practice ensures the continued application of the security template.

Securing Transmissions Between Terminal Services Clients and the Terminal Server

You can encrypt data transferred between the Terminal Services client and the terminal server, as shown in Figure 9.14.

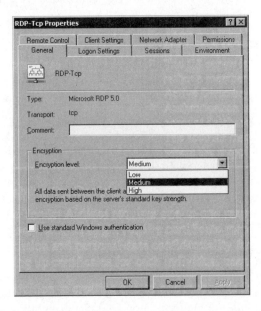

Figure 9.14 Configuring the encryption level for Terminal Services connections

You can deploy the following levels of encryption:

- **Low Encryption.** Low encryption encrypts only traffic sent from the client to the server. The data is encrypted using the RC4 algorithm and either a 56-bit or 40-bit key (Remote Desktop Protocol [RDP] 4.0 clients can only use 40-bit encryption). Low encryption provides protection for passwords and any data inputted by the user but doesn't encrypt the screen data sent from the server to the client.

- **Medium Encryption.** Medium encryption encrypts all data transmitted between the client and the server. The data is encrypted using the RC4 algorithm and either a 56-bit or 40-bit key (RDP 4.0 clients can only use 40-bit encryption). Medium encryption provides protection for passwords and any data inputted by the user and encrypts the screen data sent from the server to the client.

- **High Encryption.** High encryption encrypts all data transmitted between the client and the server. The data is encrypted using the RC4 algorithm and a 128-bit key. High encryption requires installation of the Windows 2000 High Encryption Pack. If the high encryption pack isn't installed at either the terminal server or the client computer running the Terminal Services client software, security will fall back to the medium encryption level.

Note For information on export regulations for encryption software, see *www.microsoft.com/exporting/*.

Planning for Loss of Strong Authentication Methods

Terminal Services doesn't support the use of two-factor authentication such as smart cards and Kerberos v5 protocol. If a user connects to the network using Terminal Services, you can't restrict the account to require a smart card for logon.

Making the Decision

Use the decision matrix shown in Table 9.7 to plan a secure deployment of Terminal Services in your organization.

Table 9.7   Securing Terminal Services Access

To	Do the Following
Limit access to administrators of the network	Configure Terminal Services to run in Remote Administration Mode. You must be a member of the Administrators group to connect with a Terminal Services client.
Restrict access to the local file system	Ensure that all volumes are formatted with NTFS and that permissions have been set to restrict access to the file system.
Prevent users from being assigned excess user rights	Don't install Terminal Services in Application Server Mode on a DC, because the user must be granted Log On Locally permissions to use the terminal server.
Determine if a user is connected to the network using Terminal Services	Inspect the user's environment variables for the %clientname% or %sessionname% environment variables. These environment variables only exist within a Terminal Services session.
Restrict access to a single application	Configure Terminal Services to use an alternate shell program. Configure the shell program to be the single application.
Protect data transmissions between the Terminal Services client and the terminal server	Implement either medium or high security for the Terminal Services session.
Restrict access to Terminal Services	Assign only the permission to use Terminal Services to the individual user accounts that require Terminal Services access.

Applying the Decision

The proposed Terminal Services deployment for Lucerne Publishing needs some modification to ensure that security is maintained. Consider the following for the Lucerne Publishing Terminal Services deployment:

- **Terminal Services mode.** Since Terminal Services must be configured to support network users, configure Terminal Services to use Application Server Mode to allow normal users to connect to the terminal server.

- **Excess rights assignments.** Move Terminal Services in Caracas and Casablanca to Windows 2000 member servers, rather than continuing to host the services on DCs. The users in Caracas and Casablanca require Log On Locally permissions, which would grant Log On Locally rights to all DCs in either the americas.lucernepublishing.tld or africa.lucernepublishing.tld domain.

- **Terminal server encryption.** Configure Terminal Services to use either medium or high encryption to ensure that Terminal Services traffic is encrypted in both directions between the terminal server and the Terminal Services client.

- **Additional configuration.** Configure each terminal server so that all file volumes use the NTFS file system to ensure local security of all files.

Lesson Summary

Terminal Services enables non–Windows 2000–based clients to operate applications in a full Windows 2000 environment. Your security plan should include strategies to ensure that security is maintained when you deploy Terminal Services. This includes ensuring that data is encrypted between the terminal server and the Terminal Services client and that only approved users can access the terminal server.

Lab 9-1: Planning Security for Network Services

Lab Objectives

This lab prepares you to design security for common Windows 2000 network services by meeting the following objectives:

- Design security for the DNS Service
- Design security for the DHCP Service
- Design security for RIS
- Design security for the SNMP Service
- Design security for Terminal Services

About This Lab

This lab looks at the design of the DNS, DHCP, RIS, SNMP, and Terminal Services for Contoso Ltd. to ensure that security is maintained for the deployment of these services.

Before You Begin

Make sure that you've read the chapter material before starting the lab. Pay close attention to the sections where the design decisions were applied throughout the chapter for information on building your administrative structure.

Scenario: Contoso Ltd.

Contoso Ltd., an international magazine sales company, wants to ensure that network services deployed on the corporate network don't compromise the security of the network. Specifically, Contoso wishes to design security for the following services:

- DNS
- DHCP
- RIS
- SNMP
- Terminal Services

The Planned DNS Environment for Contoso Ltd.

Contoso has deployed DNS to support Active Directory. The DNS deployment provides name resolution for both internal and external clients. This name resolution is accomplished in the following manner:

- The DNS servers at the London office host the contoso.tld DNS domain and are made available to both internal and external network users. The contoso.tld domain is configured as an Active Directory–integrated zone with the properties shown in Figure 9.15.

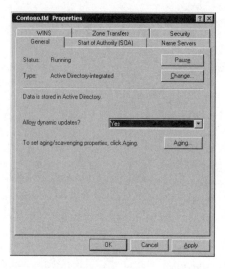

Figure 9.15   DNS configuration for the contoso.tld domain

- The subdomains london.contoso.tld, seattle.contoso.tld, and lima.contoso.tld are delegated to DCs located at the London, Seattle, and Lima offices. The subdomains are configured as Active Directory–integrated zones.

- Contoso uses the 172.28.0.0/16 network for their internal IP addressing scheme.

- During the design phase of the Contoso network, the network engineers developed the following security requirements for the DNS deployment:

  - Only authenticated clients will be allowed to register DNS resource records using dynamic update.

  - Only the following DNS resource records should be available to external clients connecting to contoso.tld Internet resources:

    - mail.contoso.tld. A host record that refers to the external mail address of the Internet gateway mail servers

    - www.contoso.tld. A host record that references the external Web server Network Load Balancing Service (NLBS) cluster address

    - contoso.tld. A host record that references the external Web server in case someone doesn't type the prefix *www*

    - vpn.contoso.tld. A host record that references the virtual private network (VPN) server used by the remote sales force to connect to the network

    - An MX record that indicates that mail.contoso.tld is the mail exchanger for contoso.tld

    - Standard Name Server (NS) and Start of Authority (SOA) resource records for the contoso.tld domain

  - Only approved DNS servers can host DNS zone information for contoso.tld, london.contoso.tld, seattle.contoso.tld, and lima.contoso.tld.

The following table shows the UP addresses of all approved DNS servers. By default, the DNS servers host only Active Directory–integrated zones for the domain that they are a member of.

DNS Server	IP Address
Ns1.contoso.tld	172.28.1.2
Ns2.contoso.tld	172.28.1.3
Ns3.london.contoso.tld	172.28.5.2
Ns4.london.contoso.tld	172.28.5.3
Ns4.seattle.contoso.tld	172.28.9.2
Ns5.seattle.contoso.tld	172.28.9.3
Ns6.london.contoso.tld	172.28.13.2
Ns7.london.contoso.tld	172.28.13.3

DHCP Usage at Contoso Ltd.

Contoso uses a centralized deployment for DHCP IP address assignment. DHCP services are installed on member servers in the london.contoso.tld andseattle.contoso.tld domains. The Lima office has the DHCP Service installed on a DC.

Only client computers in the london.contoso.tld, seattle.contoso.tld, and lima.contoso.tld domains are configured to be DHCP clients. The DHCP server is configured to update DNS clients that don't perform dynamic updates. The plan is to replace all legacy client computers with Windows 2000 Professional–based computers. Therefore, DHCP servers are configured as members of the DNSUpdateProxy group to prevent the DHCP server from taking ownership of any DNS resource records it registers on behalf of down-level clients.

Contoso has several distribution plants where magazine shipments originate. These sites are Barcelona, Yokohama, and Perth. The remote office routers are configured as DHCP Relay agents, and the DHCP requests are forwarded to the nearest central office.

Last month the Barcelona office was unable to communicate with other offices when a new employee studying for his Microsoft Certified Professional designation installed the DHCP Service on a Windows NT 4.0 server. The DHCP server issued incorrect IP addressing information to the Barcelona clients. To avoid such problems in the future, Contoso plans to prevent unauthorized DHCP servers from assigning incorrect IP address information.

Remote Installation Services Deployment

Contoso plans to use RIS to deploy updated client computers and reduce the time the Information Technology (IT) department spends installing the new computers. The new client computers all have PXE-enabled network adapters installed to facilitate the deployment of RIS images.

Separate RIS images will be created for the Sales, Marketing, IT, and Accounting departments. For offices where users choose the RIS image, only the image for their department should be presented when the user runs the RIS client installation.

Due to the large number of client computers (300) requiring upgrades to Windows 2000 at the London office, Contoso wants users to install the RIS images themselves. When the RIS image is installed, the computer account that is created should be placed into the correct OU structure, as shown in Figure 9.16.

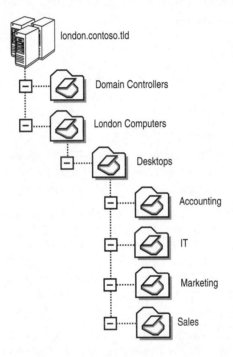

Figure 9.16   Proposed OU structure for RIS clients in the Seattle domain

The Seattle and Lima offices will use prestaged computer accounts and ensure that the computer accounts are precreated in the correct OU structure.

Network Management Plans for Contoso Ltd.

Contoso has purchased HP OpenView to enable SNMP network management on their network. Contoso will use SNMP to manage all servers, client workstations, and network devices on the network.

Contoso will deploy SNMP management using a hybrid model. The WAN management team at the London office must be able to query all network devices and reconfigure network devices on the network from the London office. All WAN management will take place from the HP OpenView UNIX console located at IP address 172.28.2.254. The London Windows 2000 deployment team also needs to be able to query information from all Windows 2000–based computers at all three office locations. The Windows 2000 deployment team requires only Read access to the Windows 2000–based computers. All management of the Windows 2000–based computers will take place from an HP OpenView console installed on a DC at IP address 172.16.3.254.

Note The routers currently used on Contoso's network don't support IPSec encryption.

Each of the three offices have network administrators who need to query all servers, clients, and network devices located at their offices. These network administrators require only Read access to all SNMP agents in their local network. The following table outlines the IP address for each of the HP OpenView consoles:

Office	Management Station
London	172.28.6.254
Seattle	172.16.10.254
Lima	172.16.14.254

If any unauthorized SNMP management stations attempt to manage SNMP agents, an SNMP trap should be sent to any configured SNMP management stations for the community in which the SNMP request is sent.

As part of the initial design, Contoso has developed four SNMP communities to meet the SNMP design requirements. The SNMP community design is shown in Figure 9.17.

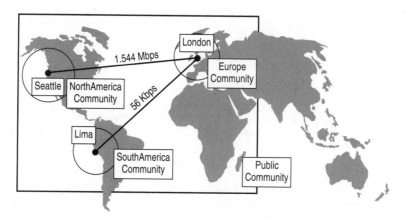

Figure 9.17   Proposed SNMP community names for Contoso Ltd.

Using Terminal Services

Terminal Services has been deployed at each of the three offices to allow both application access and remote network management.

At the London and Seattle offices, remote administration of the network is accomplished by using Terminal Services. No users require access to Terminal Services for running applications.

The Lima office requires both remote administration of the network and application support for clients. The clients who require access to Terminal Services in the Lima office include the 20 Wyse Winterm (hardware-based Terminal Services) clients on the shop floor and the 10 Windows for Workgroups 3.11 clients who require immediate use of Windows 2000–approved software.

The Winterm clients require only access to the Time Billing application. As the magazines are printed, the Time Billing application records how long it takes to produce each production run of a magazine and how many magazines are printed in the run. The Winterm clients won't require access to any other applications.

The Windows for Workgroups clients need to connect to the terminal server by using their Web browser. The 10 users who access the terminal server require distinct permission assignments because they're editing sensitive legal documents. Each user will be able to access only specific documents. The Windows for Workgroup clients must have access to the standard Windows 2000 Professional screen so that they can run Office 2000 in the Terminal Services session.

Figure 9.18 shows the initial Terminal Services environment proposed for the Lima office. All Terminal Services clients will connect to the Terminal Services member server at the Lima office.

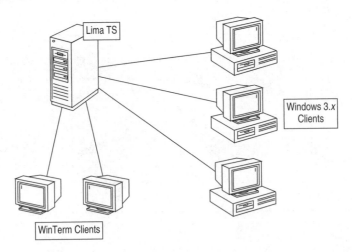

Figure 9.18   Proposed Terminal Services environment for the Lima office

Exercise 1: Designing DNS Security

In this exercise you will review the security of Contoso's DNS design. The answers to these questions can be found in the appendix.

1. Are there any security issues with the configuration of the contoso.tld Active Directory–integrated zone? If so, what change must you make to the DNS zone properties?

2. What security risks for exposure of resource records on the Internet does the current DNS configuration for contoso.tld have?

3. What modification is required to increase security for external DNS requests?

4. To ensure that the contoso.tld DNS domain is available at all locations even if a WAN link is unavailable, Contoso has decided to make the contoso.tld DNS zone available at all corporate DNS servers. What form of DNS zone must you configure in the London, Seattle, and Lima domains?

5. What must you do to secure the zone transfers of the contoso.tld DNS zone to the child domains?

6. What must you do to prevent unauthorized zone transfers from the DNS servers located in the London, Seattle, and Lima domains?

Exercise 2: Designing DHCP Security

In this exercise you will review Contoso's DHCP design and identify security weaknesses. You will complete the exercise by proposing alternatives that will increase security of the DHCP server. The answers to these questions can be found in the appendix.

1. What risks are there with the DHCP Service in Lima being installed on a DC?

2. How does membership in the DNSUpdateProxy group affect the SRV resource records registered by the DC hosting the DHCP Service?

3. What would you recommend to Contoso to improve the DHCP security at the Lima office?

4. Why was the DHCP server at the Barcelona office allowed to reply to DHCP requests even though the DHCP server wasn't authorized in Active Directory?

5. What could be done to prevent unauthorized DHCP servers on the Contoso network?

Exercise 3: Designing RIS Security

In this exercise you will review the RIS deployment plan for Contoso to determine whether any security configurations are missing. The answers to these questions can be found in the appendix.

1. During the pilot project, many users installed the incorrect image when they performed the RIS client setup. How can Contoso ensure that users in the London office install the correct image based on their departmental membership?

2. What security assignments must take place to limit users so that they can install only the RIS image associated with their department?

3. Can a single RIS server meet the security requirement to create the necessary computer accounts in the correct OU based on department?

4. What security configuration is required at the RIS servers at the Lima and Seattle offices to prevent unauthorized RIS client installations?

5. What permissions on computer objects will the user accounts require to install the RIS images at the Seattle and Lima offices?

Exercise 4: Designing SNMP Security

In this exercise you will review the proposed SNMP design for Contoso and modify it to meet the company's security requirements. The answers to these questions can be found in the appendix.

1. Do the four proposed communities, Public, NorthAmerica, SouthAmerica, and Europe, meet the SNMP security requirements?

2. What risks are involved with using the default community name Public? What permissions can you assign to this community to limit risk?

3. Complete the following table to show the required community names and permissions that must be assigned to each community name.

Community	Permissions
■	
■	
■	
■	
■	
■	

4. What SNMP configuration must you perform to restrict SNMP management tasks only to approved SNMP management stations?

5. Which communities and SNMP management station IP addresses should you configure Windows 2000 clients at the London office to send SNMP authentication traps to?

6. Could you use IPSec to protect SNMP status messages and SNMP trap messages for any of the communities? What must you configure in the IPSec rule?

Exercise 5: Designing Terminal Services

In this exercise you will review the proposed Terminal Services design for Contoso and modify the design to meet security requirements. The answers to these questions can be found in the appendix.

1. What mode must Terminal Services use on DCs in the London and Seattle domain to make sure that only administrators can use Terminal Services?

2. If you wanted to enforce that the shell is replaced with the Time Billing application for the Winterm clients at the terminal server, does the proposed Terminal Services deployment support both the Winterm and Windows for Workgroups Terminal Services clients?

3. What risks are there in configuring the shell replacement for the Winterm clients at the clients?

4. How would you ensure that the Windows for Workgroups clients are allowed access only to resources based on their individual and group membership permissions?

5. What minimum level of encryption is required for the Windows for Workgroups clients when connecting to the terminal server?

Review

The following questions are intended to reinforce key information presented in this chapter. If you are unable to answer a question, review the appropriate lesson and then try the question again. Answers to the questions can be found in the appendix.

1. You've found that certain DNS resource records in your DNS zone have been overwritten with incorrect information. When you inspect the domain controller that should own the resource records, you find that the IP configuration is correct. What could be causing the overwrite of the resource records?

2. Are there any circumstances in which a Windows 2000 DHCP server that hasn't been authorized is still able to issue IP addresses?

3. Your organization has deployed RIS servers to assist with the deployment of Windows 2000. Users are responsible for starting the remote installations. Clients have been selecting the incorrect images, and management wants to tighten security to allow only the user to install the correct image. What can you do to enforce installation of the correct image?

4. Your RIS deployment is working as expected. The users of the network are performing the RIS installations and the client computers are getting the correct RIS images applied. The only problem is that the computer accounts are all being created in the Computers container. What's wrong with your design?

5. After attending a Windows 2000 course, several of the help desk personnel have started using the SNMPutilg.exe utility from the Windows 2000 support tools to query SNMP agents on the network. What can you do to track which help desk personnel are attempting this unauthorized access?

6. You need to manage a DC at a remote site on your network, and you don't want any users of the network to use the terminal server. What can you do to ensure that only administrators can access the Terminal Services on the DC?

7. A branch manager's laptop isn't working. To allow the manager to continue working, the local network administrator has told him to use the terminal server as a desktop replacement for the rest of the day. The branch manager needs to check stock prices on the Internet. After he uses the local modem to connect to the Internet, you find that the Internet connection is also available to the Terminal Service clients. Is this expected behavior? What can you do to prevent this from happening?

CHAPTER 1 0

Planning a Public Key Infrastructure

About This Chapter

A Public Key Infrastructure (PKI) is a combination of technologies, protocols, standards, and services that allows an organization to provide strong authentication and encryption services on the network. Designing and deploying a PKI that meets your organization's business needs can be a time-consuming process.

This chapter describes the primary design decisions that you need to make when you deploy a PKI. These decisions include planning the structure of the CA hierarchy, planning management of the CAs in the hierarchy, and designing certificates for authentication.

Before You Begin

To complete this chapter, you must read the chapter scenario. This scenario is used throughout the chapter to apply the design decisions discussed in each lesson.

Chapter Scenario: Blue Yonder Airlines

Blue Yonder Airlines is a discount airline that serves the West Coast of the United States. Blue Yonder Airlines wants to use the Internet to give customers the ability to purchase airline tickets securely from the Blue Yonder Airlines Web site (*www.blueyonder.tld*).

Blue Yonder Airlines Destinations

Blue Yonder Airlines uses a fleet of Boeing 737s to carry passengers between several West Coast airports, as shown in Figure 10.1.

Figure 10.1 Blue Yonder Airlines destinations

The hub for Blue Yonder Airlines is Salt Lake City, and all airplane maintenance is performed at the Salt Lake City hangar. The central Information Technology (IT) department is also at the Salt Lake City office, and the Blue Yonder Airlines Web site and supporting infrastructure will be there as well.

The Ordering Web Site

Blue Yonder Airlines wants its customers to be able to order airline tickets directly over the Internet. The plan is to have potential customers provide customer information in a form on the Blue Yonder Airlines Web site and then to issue each customer a customer card and a smart card reader.

The customer card is a Schlumberger smart card imprinted with the Blue Yonder Airlines logo. For future transactions, customers will insert their smart card and enter their personal identification number (PIN) to confirm online ticket purchases.

Creating Customer Accounts

When the Blue Yonder Airlines customer service department receives a new request, a customer service representative verifies all information entered in the Web form. The representative's job includes verifying all address information and running a credit check.

If the customer information is accurate and the results of the credit check are satisfactory, a user account is created in the Active Directory directory service for the customer. Blue Yonder Airlines uses a single-domain model for its Active Directory, where the Active Directory forest root domain is ad.blueyonder.tld. Within the domain a dedicated OU for airline customers is maintained so that customer user accounts are maintained separately from employee user accounts, as shown in Figure 10.2.

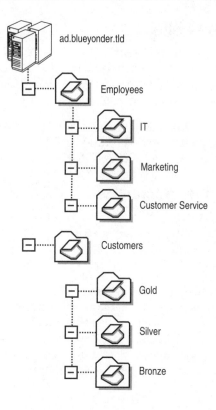

Figure 10.2   Blue Yonder Airlines Active Directory OU structure

Within the customer OU, accounts are organized according to the mileage the passenger flies each year with Blue Yonder Airlines. All customers are set initially as Bronze partners. If the customer flies 30,000 miles, her status is elevated to Silver. If the customer reaches 60,000 miles, she is elevated to Gold. The customer's user account is placed in the OU that matches her partner status.

The Active Directory schema for Blue Yonder Airlines is extended to include additional customer attributes, which ensures that credit card information can be included in the user object for each user account.

Certificate Management

Once the user account is created, a request form is sent to the smart card administrator, Jenny Sax, so that she can issue a personalized smart card to the new customer.

Jenny creates the smart card so that the private/public key pair is associated with the new customer. After creating and verifying the card, she ships it, along with a smart card reader, to the customer by overnight express.

A letter specifying the PIN for the smart card is sent to the customer separately. Blue Yonder Airlines decided to deliver the PIN and smart card in separate packages after an incident the previous year in which an unauthorized user ordered airline tickets.

Jenny also serves as the certificate administrator and is responsible for revoking certificates if a customer breaks the rules outlined in the Blue Yonder Airlines Certificate Practice Statement (CPS), which is available at *www.blueyonder.tld/Public/etiquette.html*. The CPS explains acceptable use of the smart card and the circumstances under which the certificate associated with the smart card will be revoked. The Blue Yonder Airlines CPS requires the certificate revocation to be effective within four hours of the revocation request.

Using the Smart Card

Customers use their new smart cards and smart card readers to access the Members section of the Blue Yonder Airlines Web site (*www.blueyonder.tld/members/login.asp*). The login page is configured to accept only certificate-based authentication. When customers attempt to access the *www.blueyonder.tld/members/login.asp* Web site, they will be prompted to insert their smart card into the reader and enter their PIN.

Because the smart card is associated with an Active Directory account, no additional information is required to purchase a ticket. Customers are able to request the ticket and have the ticket charged to their credit card.

All transactions are recorded in a structured query language (SQL) database on the Blue Yonder Airlines internal network. The SQL database is queried frequently to determine customer preferences for seating, to ascertain commonly traveled routes, and to track pricing information.

Other Uses for PKI at Blue Yonder Airlines

The employees of Blue Yonder Airlines also use smart cards. Both local users on the corporate network and users dialing into the network from remote locations use the cards to authenticate with the network. User authentication for remote access is configured to require the use of Extensible Authentication Protocol (EAP), and all client computers connect by using Layer 2 Tunneling Protocol over Internet Protocol Security (L2TP/IPSec) tunnels.

Lesson 1: Planning a Certification Authority Hierarchy

The primary part of your PKI deployment is the design of your Certification Authorities (CAs). The deployment of your PKI must include the following steps:

- Determine whether a public CA or a private CA meets your PKI-aware application's business needs. In some cases the design will call for a mix of public and private CAs.

- Design a CA hierarchy that allows all clients to recognize and verify all issued certificates.

- Determine whether to deploy an Enterprise or Standalone scope for your private CAs. Each scope offers advantages in specific scenarios that are outlined in this lesson.

- Plan security for the root CA of your CA hierarchy.

- Plan a disaster recovery for the potential failure of a CA.

After this lesson, you will be able to

- Plan and design a CA hierarchy to meet your organization's business needs while maintaining the highest level of security on the network

Estimated lesson time: 60 minutes

Reviewing PKI Components

A PKI is comprised of several services and components working together. A PKI's primary components include

- **Certificates.** Electronic credentials that are used to represent an entity on the network. The entity can be a user, a computer, or a network device. Possession of a certificate and its associated public and private keys provides authentication and encryption services. Certificates are the foundation of a PKI.

- **Certificate templates.** Define whether a certificate can be designed for a single usage (EFS Recovery) or for multiple purposes (User or Computer).

- **Certificate Revocation List (CRL).** A list of certificates that have been revoked before reaching the scheduled expiration date. The CRL includes both the certificate's serial number and the reason for the revocation.

- **Certification authority (CA).** A trusted entity or service that issues and manages digital certificates. In a Microsoft Windows 2000 network, you can define CAs by installing Certificate Services on a Windows 2000 Server or Windows 2000 Advanced Server.

- **Certificate management tools.** Provided through the Windows 2000 Certification Authority snap-in for the Microsoft Management Console (MMC) to allow management of the issued certificates. From the Certification Authority console you can revoke, issue, and audit all certificates that have been issued by the CA. You can also use the Active Directory Sites And Services console for certificate management. You can configure the permissions for individual certificate templates from the Active Directory Sites And Services console.

Note In addition to graphical tools, the *Microsoft Windows 2000 Server Resource Kit* includes text-based certificate tools, including Certutil and Dsstore. Certutil provides the same functionality as the Certification Authority console. Dsstore is used to manage CA certificates in Active Directory.

- **Certificate distribution point.** A location where certificates or CRLs can be retrieved by clients that participate in a PKI. Publication points include Active Directory, Web servers, FTP services, and the local file system.

- **Public key–enabled applications and services.** Applications that use certificate-based security. Examples of public key–enabled applications include Microsoft Outlook Express and Microsoft Internet Explorer. Examples of PKI-aware system services include Encrypting File System (EFS), Smart Card Logon, and Internet Protocol Security (IPSec).

Determining Whether to Use a Private or Public CA

One of the first decisions you need to make when you deploy a public key–enabled application is where to obtain the necessary certificates. In general, you must decide between a public CA (also known as a third-party CA) and a private CA.

Choosing a Public CA

Public CAs are managed by third-party companies such as Entrust or Verisign. You should obtain certificates from public CAs when the application requiring the certificates runs on a public network and when the use of a third-party certificate increases customer trust in the application. For example, most e-commerce sites obtain the certificate for their secured Web site from a public CA. Consumers may not trust a small or unknown organization when that same organization issues the certificate for the Web site.

Public CAs include an issuer statement that describes rules of conduct for the certificate. The issuer statement (or CPS) defines acceptable usage, conduct that results in the certificate's revocation, and the issuing company's liability. Public CA service isn't free. Any certificates acquired from a public CA have a price determined by the certificate's use.

Public CAs are also used for interorganization projects. Each organization can trust certificates from the other if they're acquired from a common root authority such as Verisign or Entrust. If you use a public CA, the CA hierarchy is simplified because certificates are acquired from a common CA structure.

Choosing a Private CA

For many internal applications a private CA may be beneficial. Windows 2000 provides all the tools needed to create and maintain a private CA within Certificate Services.

You should obtain certificates from private CAs when you need greater ability to manage and control certificates issued to clients. Rather than waiting for a third-party organization to revoke certificates, you're immediately able to implement the revocation process when you need to.

Consider whether participants will trust certificates issued by your CA and how you will make key certificate services publicly available. These resources include the CA's certificate and the Certificate Revocation List associated with the CA.

Should I Mix and Match Public and Private CAs?

Sometimes it's best to mix private and public CAs. For example, if you're hosting a Web-based application on your extranet that will be protected using Secure Hypertext Transfer Protocol (HTTP-S) and you also wish to implement certificate-based authentication, the best solution is a mix of public and private CAs.

For the Web server, you want to acquire a Web server certificate from a trusted public CA. This certificate allows encryption of all data transferred between the client and the Web server hosting the application. The public CA certificate inspires consumer confidence in your Web server because your Web-based application must follow the issuance policy of the public CA that issued the certificate.

For certificate-based authentication of users, it may be desirable to create a private CA to manage user certificates. The primary advantage of using a private CA is that your organization has much more control over the management of issued certificates. It can revoke a compromised certificate quickly if necessary.

Making the Decision

Use the decision matrix shown in Table 10.1 to determine whether to implement a public or a private CA for your application.

Table 10.1   Choosing Between Public CAs and Private CAs

Use a	When
Public CA	■ Your application requires verification from a trusted third party, such as selling products on the Internet.
	■ You don't have, and don't want to allocate, the resources to deploy an internal PKI.
	■ Time is limited. Public CAs already have the necessary infrastructure in place.
	■ A project requires certificate interoperability between organizations. Use of a public CA provides all issued certificates with a common root CA.
	■ Your application requires liability protection in case security is breached for your certificate-based application.
Private CA	■ Your organization wants to maintain management control of all client-associated certificates.
	■ The certificates will be used only for internal projects, applications, and services.
	■ You want to minimize the costs associated with issuing certificates.
	■ Your organization has PKI expertise that can manage and maintain Certificate Services.

Applying the Decision

Blue Yonder Airlines requires a mix of public and private CAs for its PKI deployment. The Web server that hosts the online booking Web site must have a public CA–issued certificate to ensure customer confidence in the security of sensitive data such as credit card information. As an added security feature, you also should configure the Web server to require 128-bit encryption to provide the strongest form of encryption available.

A private CA makes it possible to issue smart cards to customers while maintaining the ability to revoke certificates quickly (within four hours, for example, as described in the scenario). Likewise, a private CA provides internal employees with smart card logon and EAP authentication for remote access. Consequently, Blue Yonder Airlines requires a mix of private and public CAs.

Determining the Certification Authority Structure

Most PKI deployments require multiple CAs in the organization. The CAs are organized into either a rooted hierarchy or a cross-certification hierarchy, depending on business needs.

Deploying a Rooted Hierarchy

Rooted hierarchies are the most common CA structures. A rooted hierarchy has an initial CA, known as a *root CA*. The root CA is unique in that it issues itself a certificate. This certificate is also known as a *self-signed certificate*.

Below the root CA are one or more subordinate CAs. The root CA issues certificates to the subordinate CAs with the subject matching the name of the subordinate CA, as illustrated in Figure 10.3.

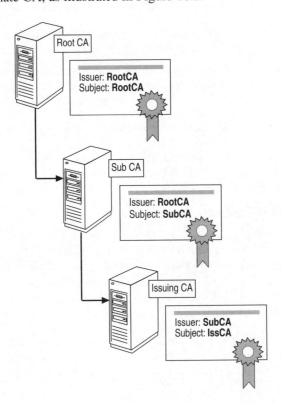

Figure 10.3   A rooted CA hierarchy

Additional levels of CAs might exist below a subordinate CA. These CAs are often referred to as *issuing CAs*. Rooted CA hierarchies enable the highest form of security because you can remove the root CA from the network, thus protecting it from attack.

Warning   There are far-reaching implications if a CA is compromised and the CA's certificate must be revoked. Not only is the CA's certificate revoked, but all certificates issued by the CA—including those issued by subordinate CAs that received their certificates from the compromised CA—are considered compromised and are invalidated. By removing the root CA from your network, you can ensure that all certificates are protected from key compromise of the root CA.

Deploying a Cross-Certification Hierarchy

In a cross-certification hierarchy, a CA acts as both a root CA and a subordinate CA. This structure is used when two organizations want to establish certificate trust between them.

Cross-certification is commonly deployed in business-to-business scenarios when the participating organizations have existing CA hierarchies. Cross-certification allows existing hierarchies to be maintained while allowing additional CAs to exist in the hierarchy.

Figure 10.4 shows an example of a cross-certification hierarchy.

Figure 10.4   A cross-certification CA hierarchy

In this hierarchy the Corp CA is the root CA for the corporation. In addition to the self-signed certificate signifying that the Corp CA is a root CA, the Corp CA also has a subordinate CA certificate issued by the Partner CA. This certificate indicates that the Root CA is a subordinate CA of the Partner CA. Following the same logic, the Partner CA is a subordinate CA of the Corp CA.

Figure 10.5 shows the logical structures that exist in the case of cross-certification.

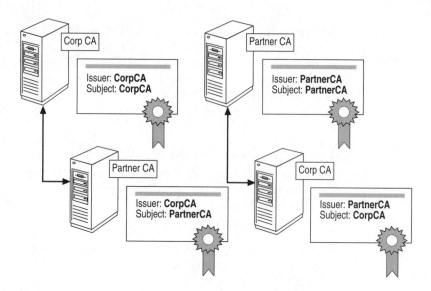

Figure 10.5   The logical view of a cross-certification CA hierarchy

The CA hierarchy on the left shows the CA structure from the Corp organization's perspective. The Corp CA is the root CA, and the Partner CA is the subordinate CA. The CA hierarchy on the right shows the CA structure from the Partner organization's perspective. For the partner organization, the Partner CA is the root CA and the Corp CA is a subordinate CA of the Partner CA.

The risk of cross-certification is that the existence of another organization's root CA means that all other CAs in the structure and the certificates issued by those CAs are also trusted. This circumstance often might be considered excess trust between organizations. You may want to trust only certificates issued by a specific CA located within a partner's CA hierarchy.

You can minimize this risk by implementing certificate trust lists (CTLs). A CTL is a group of CA certificates deemed trustworthy by a CA administrator. Only certificates issued by CAs in the CTL can be used. In a cross-certification scenario, only the CAs at the partner's site that you trust would be included in the CTL.

Making the Decision

Use the decision matrix in Table 10.2 to decide whether to implement a rooted CA hierarchy or a cross-certification hierarchy.

Table 10.2   Designing Certificate Hierarchies

To	Do the Following
Provide maximum security for the root CA	Deploy a rooted CA hierarchy. Only a rooted CA hierarchy allows the root CA to be removed from the network.
Limit trusted CAs to your organization's CAs	Deploy a rooted CA and remove all other CAs from the trusted root store.
Provide interoperability between organizations	Deploy a cross-certification hierarchy where the root CA from each organization is configured as a subordinate CA of the other organization.
Limit which CAs will be trusted from a partner organization	Deploy a cross-certification hierarchy and configure a CTL that contains only the trusted CAs from the partner organization.

Applying the Decision

Blue Yonder Airlines requires a CA hierarchy only for the internal network and for customers of its Web site. The company doesn't need to create cross-certification with another organization.

The rooted CA hierarchy allows Blue Yonder Airlines to increase security by removing the root CA from the network. Even though Blue Yonder Airlines will acquire a certificate for their Web server from a public CA such as Entrust, there's no business reason to create cross-certification between the Blue Yonder Airlines CA hierarchy and the Entrust CA hierarchy. The Entrust certificate will be trusted because the root certificate from Entrust CA will be included in the Trusted Root Certification Authorities container by default for all users of the network, as shown in Figure 10.6.

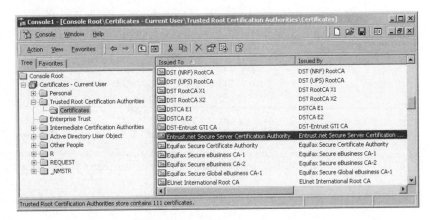

Figure 10.6   The Entrust root CA certificate included in the Trusted Root Certification Authorities store

Planning the Scope of a CA

Within Microsoft Services you can install two scopes of CAs: Enterprise and Standalone. The scope of the CA defines where the CA stores its database of issued certificates and how the CA issues certificates, as shown in Figure 10.7.

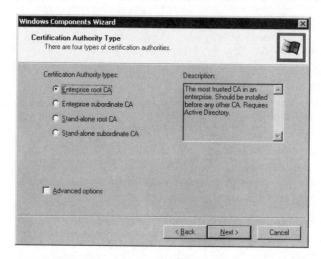

Figure 10.7   Configuring Certificate Services as either an Enterprise or Standalone CA

Deploying an Enterprise CA

An Enterprise CA must be a member of a Windows 2000 domain. Only members of the Enterprise Admins universal group can install an Enterprise CA. If you aren't a member, the Enterprise CA options will be unavailable.

Some of the reasons to consider deploying an Enterprise CA include

- **Certificate templates.** Enterprise CAs use certificate templates to restrict certificate usage. Each certificate template includes definitions of authorized purposes. A template can have either a single purpose or several purposes. A certificate can only be used for its defined purposes.

Note   Only Enterprise CAs support the use of certificate templates. Standalone CAs don't implement certificate templates to define certificate usage restrictions.

- **Integration with Windows 2000 security.** Enterprise CAs provide integrated Windows 2000 security by applying the Windows 2000 security model to certificate templates. Permissions for individual certificate templates are configured in Active Directory Sites And Services. You can access the available certificates within the Certificate Templates container, as illustrated in Figure 10.8. Only security principals with both Read and Enroll permissions can acquire specific certificate templates.

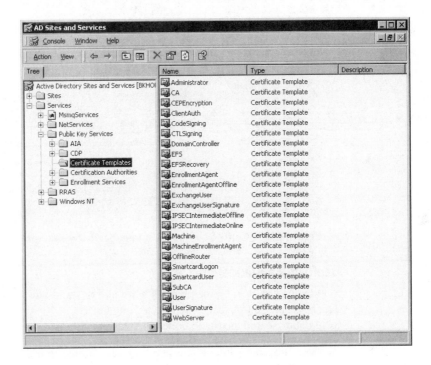

Figure 10.8   Configuring Enroll permissions for each certificate template

- **Storage of data in Active Directory.** Enterprise CAs use Active Directory to store the Certificate Services database, thus ensuring that the data is protected by Active Directory's multimaster replication model.

- **Some applications and services that require Enterprise CAs.** Enterprise CAs are required for smart card logon, and EFS encryption. If you want to deploy these technologies in your environment, you must deploy at least one Enterprise CA to issue the necessary certificates.

- **Reduction in management for certificate issuance.** Enterprise CAs issue certificates based on the credentials of the security principal requesting the certificate and the permissions assigned to the specific certificate template. Because the default issuance policy for Enterprise CAs is to automatically issue certificates, a certificate administrator doesn't need to approve certificate requests, as illustrated in Figure 10.9.

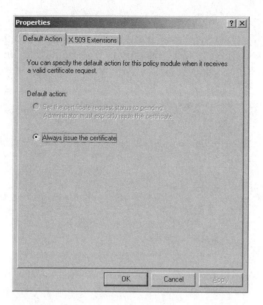

Figure 10.9   Certificates issued automatically by Enterprise CAs

Deploying a Standalone CA

Standalone CAs can be members of a domain or stand-alone servers in a workgroup. The Standalone CA differs from the Enterprise CA because all data is stored in a local database and the Standalone CA doesn't use certificate templates.

Because the Standalone CA doesn't use certificate templates, a security principal must complete a form when requesting a certificate. By default, the certificate request is then reviewed by a certificate administrator who accepts or rejects the certificate request in the Certification Authority console. All requests requiring a decision by a certificate administrator will be placed in the Pending Requests store until a certificate administrator either issues or denies the certificate request, as illustrated in Figure 10.10.

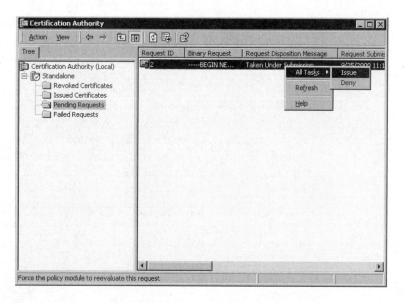

Figure 10.10   A Standalone CA issuing a certificate request

Note   The default behavior for a Standalone CA is to require the certificate administrator to issue or deny certificate requests. You can configure the issuance policy to automatically issue certificates for valid certificate requests to match the default behavior of an Enterprise CA.

Consider deploying a Standalone CA when

- You're establishing an offline root CA. Offline root CAs, by default, aren't attached to the network. This circumstance prevents the use of an Enterprise CA because Enterprise CAs store the Certificate Services database in Active Directory. With the root CA removed from the network, you'd be unable to access the certificate database. For all offline CAs, you must select a Standalone scope for the CA.

- You want to integrate Windows 2000 Certificate Services with an Exchange 5.5 Key Management Server (KMS). The Exchange 5.5 KMS requires that the issuing CA be a Standalone CA to run the Exchange 5.5 Policy. Certificate Service must be configured to run as a Standalone CA to support X509.3 certificates.

Note   X.509 is a standard for digital certificates defined by the International Telecommunication Union-Telecommunications Standardization Sector (ITU-T) and the ISO/International Electrotechnical Commission (ISO/ IEC). First published in 1988 and then extended in 1993, the current version (3.0) was released in 1996.

- You require a CA to run in the Demilitarized Zone (DMZ) where it can't contact Active Directory. If the CA isn't able to connect to Active Directory, then the CA must be configured as a Standalone CA.

Mixing and Matching CAs

A common question is whether you can mix Standalone and Enterprise CAs in the same CA hierarchy. The answer is Yes! When you design a secure CA hierarchy, one of your goals is to configure the root CA as an offline CA. You must use Standalone CAs for offline root CAs, due to Enterprise CAs' dependence on Active Directory.

Figure 10.11 shows a CA hierarchy that mixes both Standalone and Enterprise CA policies.

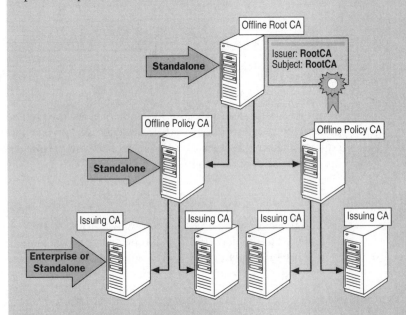

Figure 10.11   Enterprise and Standalone CAs existing in the same CA hierarchy

Note   Don't consider Enterprise to mean domain and Standalone to mean workgroup. The terms refer only to where the certificate services database information is stored.

Making the Decision

Use the decision matrix in Table 10.3 to determine when to implement an Enterprise CA or a Standalone CA in your certification authority hierarchy design.

Table 10.3   Deciding Between Enterprise and Standalone CAs

Use This CA Scope	When You Want To
Enterprise CA	■ Deploy Certificate Services for an internal deployment where the users will be providing their network credentials for authentication. ■ Deploy Windows 2000 services that require certificate templates provided only by Enterprise CAs. These include 　▪ EFS deployment 　▪ IPSec deployment 　▪ Smart card logon ■ Leverage the standard Windows 2000 security model to determine who can acquire specific certificate templates.
Standalone CA	■ Deploy offline CAs that must operate without communicating with the rest of the network. ■ Configure the Exchange 5.5 KMS to use x.509 v3 certificates, rather than the default x.509 v1 certificates. ■ Place the CA in a location where it can't connect to Active Directory.

Applying the Decision

The requirement to issue smart cards for both customers and internal user accounts requires you to deploy an Enterprise CA. Only an Enterprise CA supports certificates for smart cards. Each CA hierarchy should have an offline root CA to increase the security of the CA hierarchy. An offline root CA requires you to configure a Standalone scope for the CA.

For the internal network, Blue Yonder Airlines requires a mix of Standalone and Enterprise CAs.

Planning Offline CAs

An important step in protecting your CA hierarchy is to remove the root CA, and, potentially, a second level of CAs from the network. This action ensures that the CAs aren't compromised. Remember that if a CA is compromised, all certificates issued by the CA also are compromised.

The decision to remove a CA from the network isn't as simple as removing the network interface card or shutting down the server. The design of an offline CA also must include the following considerations:

■ **Storage location of the offline CA.** You should store the CA in a secure location that makes it extremely difficult to reattach the offline CA to the network. For example, many companies store an offline CA in a vault that's accessible only to authorized personnel.

■ **Use of a strong Cryptographic Service Provider (CSP).** Windows 2000 includes several default CSPs. CSPs are software modules that actually define how cryptography algorithms are used for authentication, encoding, and encryption. For the strongest form of encryption, consider using a hardware CSP that's physically attached to the offline CA. Hardware CSPs provide additional security by requiring two-factor authentication. For example, some hardware CSPs require the use of a smart card for generating private/public key pairs.

- **Publication of the CRL.** Issued certificates must be verified against the CRL even when the CA is removed from the network. Your design must define an accessible network location where the CRL will be published and define how frequently the CRLs will be updated.

- **Publication of the Authority Information Access (AIA).** As with the CRL, the certificate associated with the CA must also be available. Clients determine where to access the CRL through the certificate attributes. The AIA publication point must also be set to be a location that's always available.

- **Definition of certificate renewal period.** Avoid the need to continually update the root certificate for your CA hierarchy. In general, the root CA certificate should have the longest lifetime of any certificate issued on the network. This ensures that the remaining lifetime on the root CA certificate doesn't affect the lifetimes of any certificates issued by the root CA or CAs subordinate to the root CA.

Configuring an Offline Root CA

You perform the primary configuration of an offline root CA in a text configuration file known as *Capolicy.inf*. The Capolicy.inf file must be placed in the *Systemroot* folder before you install Windows 2000 Certificate Services. The Capolicy.inf file is read from the *Systemroot* folder during the installation of Certificate Services. The following code example shows the structure of the Capolicy.inf file:

```
[Version]
Signature="$Windows NT$"

[CAPolicy]
Policies=LegalPolicy

[LegalPolicy]
OID=1.2.840.113556.1.4.7000.233.28688.28684.8.189041.1105561.1861398.1661801.1
Notice="http://www.abc.tld/certificate/cps.doc"

[CRLDistributionPoint]
URL="http://www.abc.tld/Public/crlname.crl"
URL="ldap:///CN=EnterpriseCA,CN=CA-ROOT,CN=CDP,
    CN=Public%%%%20Key%%%%20Services,CN=Services,CN=Configuration,
    DC=abc,DC=tld?certificateRevocationList?base?
    objectclass=cRLDistributionPoint"
```

```
[AuthorityInformationAccess]
URL="http://www.abc.tld/Public/certname.crt"
URL="ldap:///CN=EnterpriseCA,CN=AIA,
    CN=Public%%%%20Key%%%%20Services,CN=Services,CN=Configuration,DC=abc,
    DC=tld?cACertificate?base?objectclass=certificationAuthority"

[Certsrv_Server]
RenewalKeyLength=4096
RenewalValidityPeriod=5
RenewalValidityPeriodUnits=Years
```

Note The four "%"s in a row aren't a typo. You must represent a space character with the string "%%%%20" when defining Lightweight Directory Access
Protocol (LDAP) paths in the Capolicy.inf configuration file. The "%" symbols
ensure that the space character is included in the LDAP URL.

The following sections are included in the Capolicy.inf configuration file:

- **The [Version] Section.** This section defines the configuration file as a Windows NT–compatible configuration file. This circumstance enables the use of
  pointers for referencing future sections in the configuration file.

- **The [CAPolicy] Section.** This section outlines all policies that are defined in
  the Capolicy.inf text file. It's possible to include multiple policies within a
  single Capolicy.inf configuration file.

- **The [*PolicyName*] Section.** This section defines the object identification
  number (OID) for the policy and the legal notice text that will appear when
  you click the Issuer Statement button in an issued certificate. The issuer statement is also known as a CPS. By clicking the Issuer Statement button when
  viewing the certificate's properties, the user will either see the text string entered in the Capolicy.inf text file or be redirected to an Internet URL. Using a
  URL is advantageous in that it allows an organization to modify the CPS
  without having to renew the CA's certificate.

- **The [CRLDistributionPoint] Section.** This section indicates alternative
  CRL distribution points for the CA. The CRL points must be set to locations
  that will be available when the CA is taken off the network. The CRL distribution point can be set to be an HTTP URL, an FTP URL, an LDAP URL, or
  a file reference. The example above shows both an HTTP and an LDAP URL.

- **The [AuthorityInformationAccess] Section.** This section is used to indicate
  alternative AIA distribution points for the CA. As with CRL distribution
  points, the AIA points must be set to locations that will be available when the
  CA is taken off the network. The AIA distribution point can also be set to be
  an HTTP URL, an FTP URL, an LDAP URL, or a file reference.

- **The [Certsrv_Server] Section.** This section outlines the settings for certificate renewal. Because the certificate for a root CA is self-issued, the renewal
  information must be read from the Capolicy.inf file. Options include the

length of the keys that are generated during the renewal process and the interval at which key renewal must be performed.

Do You Use Capolicy.inf Only for Root CAs?

In most cases, the answer is yes. The only time you use a Capolicy.inf configuration file for a nonroot CA is to define a CPS for an issuing CA. The Capolicy.inf text file is the only way you can enter information into a CPS for Windows 2000 Certificate Services.

A nonroot CA processes only the [CAPolicy] and [*Policyname*] sections of the Capolicy.inf configuration file. All other sections are ignored because they're defined by the issuing CA from which the subordinate CA received its subordinate CA certificate.

In addition to configuring the Capolicy.inf file with CRL and AIA publication points, you must also configure the certificate distribution points (CDPs) for the CRL and AIA associated with the CA. Configure the CDPs in the properties of the Certification Authority by defining the X.509 extensions for the CA's policy module, as shown in Figure 10.12.

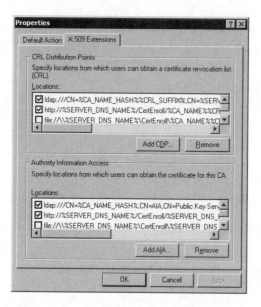

Figure 10.12   Defining certificate distribution points for the CRL and AIA

The URLs you define for the CRL and AIA distribution points will be included in the properties of any newly issued certificate by the CA.

Making the Decision

Include the design points featured in Table 10.4 in your security plan to ensure the security and functionality of an offline root CA.

Table 10.4   Securing Offline Root CAs

To	Do the Following
Allow the CA to be removed from the network for long periods of time	▪ Configure the CA to be a Standalone CA. Make sure that the CA is installed on a Windows 2000 Server that isn't a member of a Windows 2000 domain.
Provide the strongest form of encryption at the offline root CA	▪ Implement a hardware CSP for the offline root CA. ▪ Ensure that the associated CSP is installed before installing the offline root CA.
Make the CRL and AIA available to network users	▪ Configure the Capolicy.inf file to provide alternative locations for the CRL and AIA publication points. ▪ Configure the publishing schedule for the CRL to be a longer period of time than for issuing CAs. ▪ Configure the certificate distribution points for the CRL and AIA to be located at areas of the network that are available when the root CA is offline. ▪ Establish a manual process for placing the updated CRL or AIA into the public locations outlined in the certificate properties for offline CAs. ▪ Edit the registry to allow longer certificate lifetimes for the certificates issued by the root CA. The default of one year is too short for subordinate CAs.
Define a CPS	▪ Ensure that the Capolicy.inf file is edited and placed in the *Systemroot* folder before installing Certificate Services. ▪ To provide for updates, ensure that the Notice= line references a URL rather than just a text statement. Using a URL allows you to modify the CPS without having to renew the CA's certificate.
Provide the most security for your CA hierarchy	▪ Ensure that at a minimum, the root CA is removed from the network. For higher-security networks, also consider removing the second layer of CAs in the rooted hierarchy from the network.

Applying the Decision

Blue Yonder Airlines must use a Standalone CA for the offline root CA. Depending on the level of business expected for the Web site, Blue Yonder also can remove a second layer of subordinate CAs from the network.

Blue Yonder Airlines must configure a Capolicy.inf configuration file to issue a CPS that defines usage policy for all customers who receive Blue Yonder Airlines smart cards. The Capolicy.inf configuration file must also provide CRL and AIA publication points that will be available when the root CA is removed from the network.

For example, Blue Yonder Airlines could use the following Capolicy.inf file when installing Certificate Services on their offline root CA:

```
[Version]
Signature="$Windows NT$"

[CAPolicy]
Policies=BlueYonder

[BlueYonder]
OID=1.2.840.113567.1.4.6000.234.28697.28632.8.1325041.1005461.1934398.1223661.4
Notice="http://www.blueyonder.tld/Public/etiquette.html  "

[CRLDistributionPoint]
URL="http://www.blueyonder.tld/Public/crlname.crl"
URL="ldap:///CN=RootCA,CN=OfflineROOT,CN=CDP,
    CN=Public%%%%20Key%%%%20Services,CN=Services,CN=Configuration,
    DC=AD,DC=Blueyonder,DC=Tld?certificateRevocationList?base?
    objectclass=cRLDistributionPoint

[AuthorityInformationAccess]
URL="http://www.blueyonder.tld/Public/certname.crt"
URL="ldap:///CN=RootCA,CN=AIA,
    CN=Public%%%%20Key%%%%20Services,CN=Services,
    CN=Configuration,DC=AD,DC=Blueyonder,
    DC=Tld?cACertificate?base?objectclass=certificationAuthority"

[Certsrv_Server]
RenewalKeyLength=4096
RenewalValidityPeriod=5
RenewalValidityPeriodUnits=Years
```

In addition to configuring the Capolicy.inf configuration file, Blue Yonder must set the following attributes for the CA before removing the CA from the network:

- **CRL publication interval.** The CRL publication interval should be increased from the default of one week. Consider a value in the range of two to three months instead.

- **CRL and AIA distribution points.** Disable the default CRL and AIA distribution points because the root CA won't be available on the network. Ensure that the updated versions of the CRL and AIA are manually copied to the distribution points defined.

- **The default lifetime for issued certificates.** Edit the registry in HKLM \System\CurrentControlSet\Services\CertSvc\Configuration*CAName* to set the value ValidityPeriodUnits to be greater than the default of one year.

Designing the Certification Authority Hierarchy

Once you've determined your CA structure's security by implementing an offline root CA, you must design a CA hierarchy below the root CA. The CA hierarchy helps you deploy certificates to security principals in your organization. In general, your CA hierarchy falls into one of the following general structures:

- **Structure by usage.** In this structure, the issuing CAs will be configured to issue only specific certificate templates. The individual CAs are assigned to specific projects such as smart card logon, IPSec deployment, or secure e-mail, as shown in Figure 10.13.

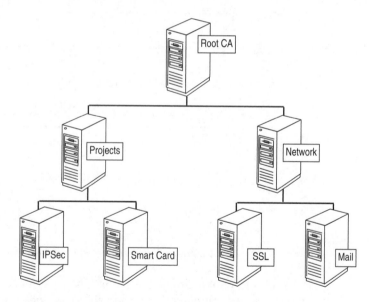

Figure 10.13   A CA hierarchy based on usage

You configure this structure by setting each CA to issue only the certificates that are required by the associated project. For example, in a smart card deployment, you might want to configure the CA to issue only Smartcard User, Smartcard Logon, Enrollment Agent, and Enrollment Agent (Computer) certificates. This action restricts the CA to issuing only certificates for the smart card deployment.

Note For more information on configuring a CA to support smart card authentication, see Lesson 3, "Using Certificates for Authentication," in this chapter.

- **Structure by administration.** An administrative structure attempts to distribute CAs to match the administration of the network. For example, Figure 10.14 shows two subordinate structures divided according to whether the certificate recipients are employees or partners of the organization.

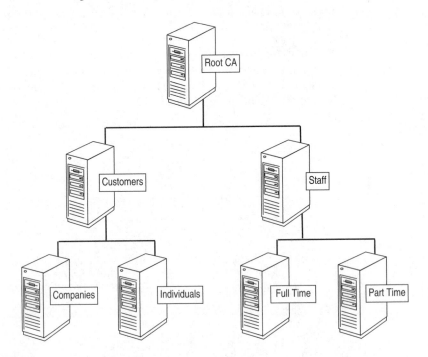

Figure 10.14 A CA hierarchy based on an administrative model

At the third level in the figure, different CAs exist for full-time and part-time personnel so that different certificate validity periods can be issued.

- **Structure by location.** In geographically distributed organizations you can delegate administration of certificates to IT personnel at each location. Figure 10.15 depicts an organization divided into Europe and North America. Below the subordinate CAs, you could configure the issuing CAs by usage or administration needs.

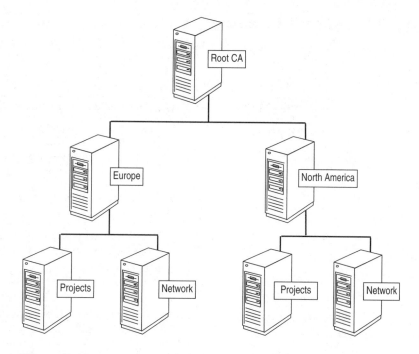

Figure 10.15   A CA hierarchy based on geographic location

Regardless of the structure, for maximum security you must configure the root CA as an offline CA. In higher-security networks, consider configuring the second-level CAs as offline CAs as well. For example, in the structure-by-location example in Figure 10.15, you could configure the Europe and North America CAs as offline CAs.

How Many Levels Do I Require?

The general goal is to create a CA hierarchy that's three to four levels deep. CA hierarchies with fewer than three levels are more vulnerable. If there are only two levels and the root level is compromised, all certificates also are compromised. Likewise, having a CA structure that's more than four levels deep introduces unnecessary complexity and might result in extra time being needed to verify the revocation status for each CA in the certificate chain.

Making the Decision

Use the decision matrix shown in Table 10.5 when deciding which CA hierarchy structure to deploy for your organization.

Table 10.5   Choosing CA Hierarchy Structures

Choose This CA Structure	When the Following Conditions Exist
Usage structure	■ There are several active projects within an organization and each project is managed by a separate team. ■ A pilot project requires that the CA related to the project be rebuilt when the project is launched for the entire organization. ■ You want CAs dedicated to issuing certificates related to specific projects.
Administrative structure	■ The organization requires different issuance policies based on the relationship of the security principal to the organization. ■ You must issue the same certificate template, but with differing validity periods.
Location structure	■ The organization is geographically distributed and management of certificates is delegated to each region.

The final CA hierarchy design might end up as a combination of these designs. You might need to implement a highly customized hierarchy to meet your business needs.

Applying the Decision

Blue Yonder Airlines could implement a CA hierarchy based on either usage or administration. Blue Yonder doesn't need to develop a CA hierarchy based on location because the smart card authentication for clients will be centralized at the Salt Lake City office.

Figure 10.16 shows one possible Blue Yonder Airlines CA hierarchy that meets both its customer and internal network needs.

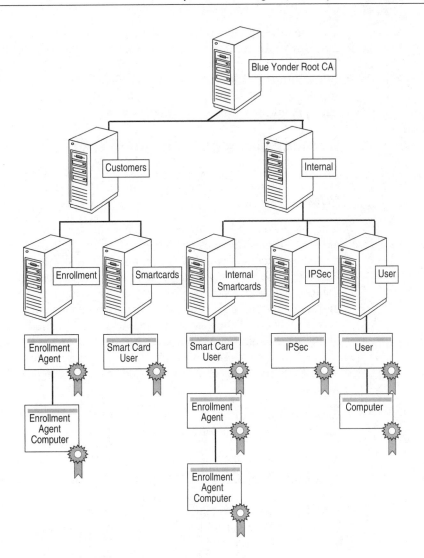

Figure 10.16   A CA hierarchy based on administration and usage

Blue Yonder Airlines can establish two separate CAs for outside customers ordering airline tickets. The Enrollment CA will issue only Enrollment Agent (Machine) certificates and Enrollment Agent certificates. This arrangement allows greater security for the Enrollment Agent server. The Smartcards CA issues the smart card user certificate template.

You can establish three CAs for the internal network. Use the Internal Smartcards CA to issue all certificates related to smart card logon. Use the IPSec CA to issue IPSec-specific certificates for all computers that perform IPSec, including L2TP/IPSec Virtual Private Network (VPN) clients. Finally, use a dedicated CA to issue other certificates (such as User and Computer certificates) for users and computers requiring certificates for other purposes on the network.

Planning Disaster Recovery of CAs

The final step in deploying CAs is planning for the recovery of the CAs in the event of disaster. Disaster can result from disk failure or accidental removal of Certificate Services.

You can prevent CA failure by implementing hardware solutions for fault tolerance. Certificate Services performs best when you place the Certificate Services database on a redundant array of independent disks (RAID) volume that combines multiple disks into what is known as a stripe set with parity or RAID-5 disk volume. A RAID-5 volume protects data by writing the data in a stripe across multiple physical disks. For each stripe, one disk contains parity information that allows recovery of the data stored in that stripe if a single disk fails in the RAID-5 disk set. In addition, you should store the Certificate Services log files on a RAID-1 mirror set. This ensures that the log files are also protected in the event of disk failure. A mirror set offers better performance than RAID-5 disk volumes for log files.

Ensure that the Certificate Services data stores are backed up regularly. You can accomplish this in one of two ways:

- Include the System State option in your Windows 2000 backup set
- Manually run backup from within the Certification Authority console

Warning   You must include Internet Information Services (IIS) in the backup set because the Web Enrollment Support pages included with Certificate Services update the IIS metabase.

In the case of an offline CA, you may want to consider backing up the server with disk imaging software. Some organizations store an exact duplicate of the offline CA at a remote location to protect against natural disasters. When the CA is updated (such as renewing the CAs certificate), a new image is created for remote storage.

Making the Decision

Consider the points in Table 10.6 in your disaster recovery plan for CAs.

Table 10.6   Planning Disaster Recovery of a CA

To	Do the Following
Prevent loss of data in the Certificate Services database	▪ Store the Certificate Services database on a RAID-5 disk volume. Hardware RAID-5 is preferable to software RAID-5 solutions for both performance and recoverability reasons. ▪ Store the Certificate Services log files on a RAID-1 disk volume. As with the Certificate Services database, hardware RAID-1 solutions are preferable to software RAID-1 solutions for both performance and recoverability reasons.
Ensure that a rebuilt CA is still valid for all issued certificates	▪ Ensure that all server keys are backed up. This allows the CA to reuse existing keys in the event of a failure.
Allow a CA to be recovered	▪ Ensure that the Certificate Service database is regularly backed up through the Certification Authority console or by including System State in the backup set.
Ensure recoverability	▪ Run a test recovery to a different server to ensure that your recovery procedures are adequate.

Applying the Decision

Blue Yonder Airlines must include a backup and restore strategy for all CAs in their organization. The company should purchase a common computer system that implements RAID-5 and RAID-1 disk sets for the Certificate Services database and log files.

In addition, you should schedule regular backups that include the system state backups. The backup sets must include the IIS directory structure so that the IIS metabase captures all changes made by Certificate Services.

To ensure recoverability in the event that you have to rebuild and restore a CA from backup, you should export the existing private and public keys associated with the CAs certificate to files and include those files in the regular backup set.

Finally, you should create an image of the root CA for the hierarchy on a CD. This CD allows you to restore the root CA quickly in the event of failure. You must update this image whenever additional certificates are issued or renewed at the root CA.

Lesson Summary

Developing your CA structure is a primary component of your PKI design. The CA structure must meet your business needs, ensure security, and, most of all, provide the necessary functionality to ensure success for your PKI-based applications.

Make sure that your design includes a decision on whether to use public or private CAs for specific scenarios. Once you decide on using a public or private CA, you must design the CA hierarchy structure. This process involves determining whether to use a rooted hierarchy or a cross-certification hierarchy. With rooted hierarchies, you must decide whether a CA will be taken offline to protect the Certificate Services database from vulnerabilities.

Finally, you must design a CA structure that mirrors your administrative model. Protect the CA structure in the event of failure so that you can restore the CA hierarchy without reissuing certificates.

Lesson 2: Managing Certification Authorities

When designing your CA hierarchy structure, consider designing the individual tasks that are performed at a CA. Plan all tasks involved during the lifetime of the certificate, including issuing certificates, revoking certificates, and renewing certificates.

After this lesson, you will be able to

- Design the management of certification authorities for the issuance, revocation, and renewal of certificates

Estimated lesson time: 45 minutes

Once you've established your optimal CA structure, plan the deployment, revocation, and renewal of certificates issued by the CA that you are managing.

Planning Certificate Issuance

The first step in managing certificates is issuing certificates to the necessary users, computers, and network devices. Issuing certificates involves either configuring permissions to establish which security principals have Enroll permissions for specific templates (in the case of Enterprise CAs) or appointing a certificate administrator who will review each certificate request and issue or deny the request based on the information provided.

Designing Automatic Issuance

You can design your PKI to perform certificate requests for computer accounts automatically. Within Group Policy, you can define which certificate templates will be requested automatically by computer accounts within the site, domain, or organizational unit (OU) where the Group Policy object is defined, as shown in Figure 10.17.

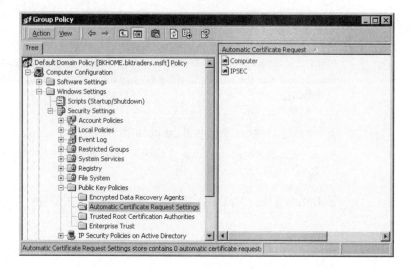

Figure 10.17   Issuing computer certificates by configuring automatic certificate requests in Group Policy

In addition to defining which certificate templates are automatically requested by computers in Group Policy, you must assign the required computers the correct permissions to acquire the certificate templates. The computers must have Read and Enroll permissions for each certificate template they require. Finally, you must configure at least one Enterprise CA in the forest to issue the required certificate templates.

Designing Manual Issuance

All user certificates, and some computer certificates, must be requested manually from a CA. If the issuing CA is an Enterprise CA, the request can be performed either from the Certificates MMC snap-in or from the Certificate Services Web registration page. If the issuing CA is a Standalone CA, you can use only the Certificate Services Web registration page.

You can't automatically assign user certificates. Users must be trained to perform the certificate request themselves. In most cases the certificate administrators need to create documentation that walks the user through the process of acquiring the certificate.

As with automatically assigned computer certificates, you must set permissions for each certificate template to ensure that only authorized security principals have Read and Enroll permissions for all manually registered certificates. In addition, you must designate a CA to issue the required certificate templates.

Making the Decision

Use the decision matrix shown in Table 10.7 when planning the issuing of certificates.

Table 10.7   Planning Certificate Issuance

To	Do the Following
Restrict access to specific templates	▪ Configure the Discretionary Access Control List (DACL) for each template in Active Directory Sites And Services so that only the required security principals have the Enroll and Read permissions for the desired template.
Restrict which CA issues a specific certificate template	▪ Configure the list of certificate templates that a CA issues. You configure the list of certificate templates in the Certification Authority console in the Policy Settings container.
Automate the deployment of computer certificates	▪ Configure Group Policy to automatically assign the necessary computer certificates by adding the certificate template to the Automatic Certificate Request Settings option in Group Policy.
Issue certificates to users	▪ Configure documentation on how to request a user certificate using the Web-based interface. This requires connecting to the CA server using the following URL: *http://CAName/certsrv/*. ▪ You can use the URL to request certificates from both Enterprise and Standalone CAs. ▪ Configure documentation on how to request a user certificate using the Certificates MMC console. You can use the MMC console only to request certificates from an Enterprise CA. ▪ Configure documentation on how to request a certificate using the Web-based interface. This requires connecting to the CA server using the following URL: *http://CAName/certsrv/*. ▪ Configure documentation on how to request a certificate using the Certificates MMC console.
Require a certificate administrator to approve or reject each certificate request	▪ Use a Standalone CA with the issuance policy configured to require a certificate administrator to approve or reject each certificate request.

Applying the Decision

Blue Yonder Airlines must develop an issuance policy for all internal certificates required on the network. Separate strategies are required for Computer certificates and User certificates.

For Computer certificates, Blue Yonder Airlines can take advantage of Group Policy. The computers require either IPSec-specific certificates, or they can use the multipurpose Computer certificates for IPSec authentication. To provide these certificates to all computers in the domain, configure the Default Domain Policy to issue both IPSec and Computer certificates by defining the Automatic Certificate Request Settings policy.

There's no way to issue certificates to internal users automatically. Blue Yonder Airlines must decide how to issue User certificates for internal users. The company can choose to use either the Web-based forms or the Certificates MMC console.

For external customers, Jenny Sax will make all certificate requests. Planning to request the necessary smart card certificates is discussed in Lesson 3, "Using Certificates for Authentication."

Planning Certificate Revocation

Sometimes you have to revoke a certificate before its expiration date. Reasons for the revocation may include termination of the employee, a compromise of the issuing CA, or dissolution of a partnership between organizations.

Your PKI deployment design must include considerations for certificate deployment. Just because a certificate has been revoked doesn't mean that the certificate is instantly unusable. When you revoke a certificate, the certificate's serial number is added to the Certificate Revocation List, as shown in Figure 10.18.

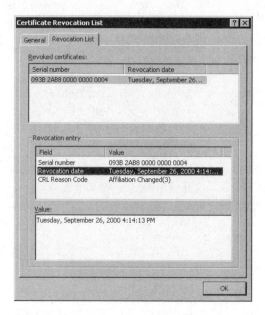

Figure 10.18   A certificate revocation list

When an application needs to verify a certificate, the application downloads the CRL referenced in the certificate to the client's local cache. The CRL won't be downloaded again until the lifetime of the downloaded CRL expires. This fact is an important design point. If you foresee frequent certificate revocations, you should shorten the publication period to minimize the time in which clients may have outdated CRLs in their cache. You can minimize the time by reducing the interval for publication of the CRL to a distribution point. Don't reduce the interval too much or the updated CRL will generate excess traffic. Consider implementing shorter duration CRL publication intervals only for CRLs that are frequently modified. If there's little modification, you can use longer publication intervals.

Another issue you must include in your CRL design is the CRL's availability. If the server hosting the CRL is unavailable, a client won't be able to access the CRL. In this case the client application will treat the certificate as if its status is set to be revoked. The client will be unable to use the certificate for authentication purposes until the CRL is available. When designing offline CAs, configure CRL distribution points that are always available on the network.

Making the Decision

Consider the following factors when planning CRL availability for the CAs in your organization:

- Create a central location for offline CA CRLs. Due to the removal of the CA from the network, the default locations for the CRLs won't be available. Use both the Capolicy.inf file (for root CAs) and the CDP configuration for subordinate CAs to change the publication point to an area of the network that's always available.

- Determine the optimal publication schedule for the CRL associated with a CA. If the CA has issued several certificates and the revocation process occurs frequently, publish the CRL on a more frequent schedule than the default of one week. For example, it may be more secure to publish the CRL every four hours. Likewise, for a root CA that only has two subordinate CAs, it may be better to publish the CRL every three months. You only have to worry about clients using an out-of-date cached version of the CRL when the CRL is actually changing.

- Ensure availability of the CRL. If you have Active Directory available on the network, ensure that each CRL includes an LDAP publication point. The CRL then is available from any domain controller in the forest. CRLs are stored in the configuration naming context, which is replicated to all domain controllers in the forest. Also be sure to include additional URLs for the CRL. You can define both HTTP and FTP URLs.

- Ensure that CRLs are available to external clients if they receive certificates from the internal network. If clients are to authenticate by using certificates issued by an internal CA, ensure that the CRL is published to an externally available resource. Consider using either HTTP or FTP publication points for the CRL to ensure external availability. Remember that if the CRL is unavailable, the application may treat the certificate as if it's revoked.

- Ensure that all necessary CRLs are available. Not only must the CRL for the CA that issued the certificate be available, but the CRL for each CA in the chain back to the root CA must be available to ensure that none of the CA's certificates are revoked. If any part of the CA chain doesn't have its CRL available, the certificate may be rejected.

Applying the Decision

Blue Yonder Airlines must ensure that the CRLs for all CAs related to the Enrollment CA are available. For smart card users, this requires the CRL for the Blue Yonder Root CA, the Customers CA, and the Smartcards CA to be available at the public Web site to ensure that CRL checking proceeds as required, as illustrated in Figure 10.19.

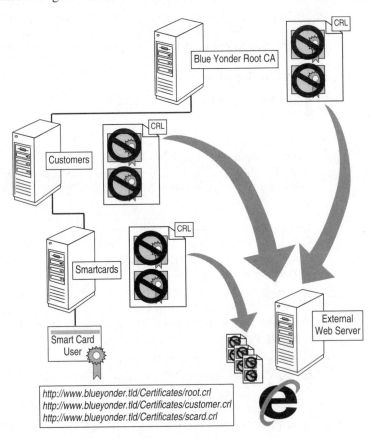

Figure 10.19   Designing CRL availability for Blue Yonder Airlines

Because the CRLs are published to a public location, some of the CRLs may have to be copied manually to the CRL distribution point (*http://www.blueyonder.tld/Certificates/*).

For the root CA, the publication interval should be infrequent. A range of three to four months may be sufficient. There are only two subordinate CAs below the root CA, and the chances of these certificates being revoked is minimal. Likewise, the publication schedule for the Customers CA doesn't have to be updated frequently—every two to three months would be sufficient.

The Smartcards CA requires more frequent publication. According to the scenario, the CRL must be updated every four hours to ensure that a revoked certificate is recognized quickly. Permissions must be defined on the external Web server to ensure that the CA can update the CRL stored on the Web server.

Planning Certificate Renewal

All certificates have a finite lifetime defined by the issuing CA. For Windows 2000 CAs, this lifetime value is defined by editing the registry. Two registry values define the lifetime for all issued certificates:

```
HKLM\System\CurrentControlSet\Services\CertSvc\Configuration\CAName\

ValidityPeriod: REG_SZ (values include Years, Days, Hours)

ValidityPeriodUnits: REG_DWORD (numeric value)
```

When a User certificate or Computer certificate is nearing the end of its lifetime, you must have a strategy for renewing it. In the case of User and Computer certificates, you can renew the certificate from the Certificates MMC console, as shown in Figure 10.20.

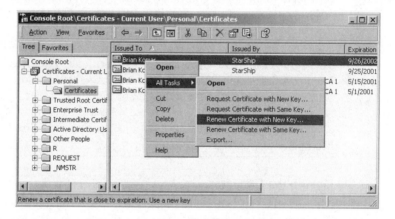

Figure 10.20   Renewing user and computer certificates with the same keys or with new keys

When you renew the certificate, you can either reuse the same private and public key or generate new private and public keys. For the highest security, you should always generate new private and public keys. Reuse the existing private and public key only if you're rebuilding a CA and don't wish to invalidate all issued certificates by changing the private key used to sign each issued certificate.

For CAs, you renew the CA certificate in the Certification Authority console, as illustrated in Figure 10.21.

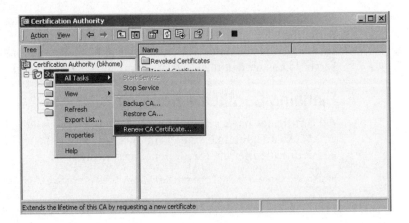

Figure 10.21   Renewing CA certificates in the Certification Authority console

The process varies depending on whether the CA that issued the certificate is online or offline. If the issuing CA is online, you can send the certificate renewal request directly to the issuing CA. If the issuing CA is offline, you must save the certificate request to a certificate request file and manually transport it to the offline CA.

Important   You should set the lifetime for CA and SubCA certificates significantly longer than the lifetime of other certificate templates. An issuing CA can't issue certificates with a lifetime that exceeds the remaining lifetime of the CA's certificate. You must include this factor in the certificate renewal design for your organization's CAs. You may wish to renew CA certificates earlier than user or computer certificates to ensure that the CA certificate lifetime doesn't affect the lifetime of any issued certificates.

Making the Decision

Consider the following design decisions when designing a renewal policy for certificates issued within your organization:

- Define certificate lifetimes based on renewal requirements. CA certificates generally have a longer lifetime than the certificates they issue. In general, CAs located closer to the root CA require longer lifetimes. You define the certificate lifetimes either during the installation of the root CA, in the Capolicy.inf for root CA renewal, or in the individual CA's registry settings.

- Define a process that users and computers will use to renew their certificates. User and computer certificates must be renewed in the Certificates MMC. Develop a plan for training users how to renew the certificates.

- Ensure that the CA certificate's remaining lifetime is never shorter than the lifetime for issued certificates. You can't issue certificates with a lifetime greater than the remaining lifetime of the issuing CA's certificate. If the CA's certificate were to expire, you couldn't verify the digital signature on the issued certificates, and this would invalidate all issued certificates.

- Plan for renewal dates far in the future. A well-planned PKI deployment defines how certificates will be renewed to avoid confusion as the renewal date approaches. By being proactive in the design of certificate renewal, you can ensure that the process takes place with little or no effect on the users and computers involved.

Applying the Decision

Blue Yonder Airlines must perform a few tasks involved with certificate renewal. The first is defining the certificate lifetimes for each issuing CA.

Install the root CA with the longest lifetime to ensure that the root CA doesn't limit the lifetime of any certificates issued by CAs lower in the CA hierarchy. For example, you could configure the root CA with a 10-year validity period and configure the subordinate CAs, the Internal, and Customers CA (as shown in Figure 10.16) with a 5-year validity period.

If you use this design, the root CAs certificate should be renewed before the initial five years. This ensures that the remaining certificate validity period on the root CAs doesn't affect the validity period for certificates issued by the subordinate CAs.

The issuing CAs for Blue Yonder Airlines require varying validity periods. The Smartcards CA probably requires the shortest period, which forces the customers to stay in touch with Blue Yonder Airlines and renew their Smart Card certificates frequently.

For the internal network, develop a plan for when certificates must be renewed. The plan should also include a defined process that details how the renewal takes place and sets the renewed validity period for the renewed certificate.

Lesson Summary

To ensure that security is maintained for the enrollment, revocation, and renewal processes, you must carefully define the management functions associated with a CA. All three processes make up the lifetime of a digital certificate. Your plan must ensure that only authorized security principals can acquire certificates from your CAs. If you revoke a certificate, make sure that the delay between the revocation process and the publication of the CRL is acceptable in your business operations. Finally, avoid allowing issued certificates to expire when the validity period ends. By planning a process for certificate renewal, you can ensure that newly established PKIs will continue to be used.

Activity: Planning Certificate Renewal Settings

An organization named Trey Research has deployed the CA hierarchy illustrated in Figure 10.22.

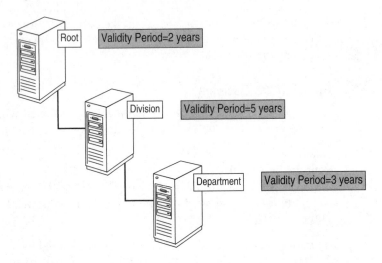

Figure 10.22   The Trey Research CA hierarchy

The Root CA is configured with a certificate validity period of two years, the Division CA has a certificate validity period of five years, and the Department CA has a certificate validity period of three years.

Based on this configuration, answer the following questions. Answers to these questions can be found in the appendix.

1. What is the longest validity period that can be configured for certificates issued by the Root CA?

2. What is the longest validity period that can be configured for certificates issued by the Division CA?

3. What is the longest validity period that can be configured for certificates issued by the Department CA?

4. What must be done to the validity period of the Root CA to allow the Division CA to issue certificates with a five-year validity period?

Lesson 3: Using Certificates for Authentication

One of the primary functions of certificates in a PKI is the mutual authentication of a client and a server. This lesson examines two of the most common deployments of certificates for authentication purposes: smart card logon and Web-based authentication.

After this lesson, you will be able to

- Design the necessary components to support smart card logon and Web authentication using certificates

Estimated lesson time: 40 minutes

Planning Smart Card Logon

Smart card logon provides stronger security than the default authentication process in Windows 2000 because password information isn't transmitted across the network. As a review, Figure 10.23 shows the smart card logon process:

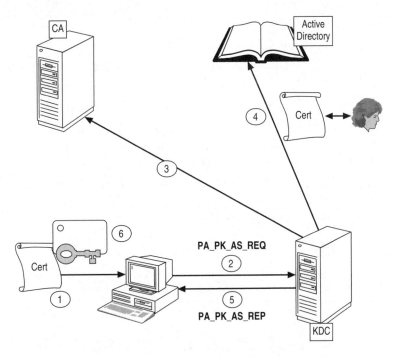

Figure 10.23   The smart card logon process

1. The user starts the logon process by inserting the smart card into the smart card reader and entering the PIN code. The smart card contains the user's public key credentials, private/public key pair, and certificate.

2. A modified Kerberos Authentication Service Request (PA_PK_AS_REQ) message is sent to the Key Distribution Center (KDC). This request contains the user principal name and time stamp and a copy of the user's certificate. The user's principal name and time stamp are signed by the private key.

3. The KDC validates the request by verifying the user's certificate and the digital signature with the CA that issued the certificate.

4. The KDC queries Active Directory to determine the mapping between the certificate included in the PA_PK_AS_REQ and a Windows 2000 security identifier (SID). When it determines the mapping, the KDC issues a Ticket Granting Ticket (TGT) for the corresponding SID.

5. The KDC sends the TGT back to the user in a modified Kerberos Authentication Service Response (PA_PK_AS_REP). Within the response, the session key is encrypted with the user's public key, ensuring that only the correct user can decrypt the session key.

6. The user retrieves the session key by decrypting the session key with the private key located on the smart card.

Planning Smart Card Deployment

Take the following steps to ensure that smart cards are integrated successfully into your organization's security model:

1. Define which users can enroll for the required types of certificates.

2. Define a CA to issue the required certificates.

3. Configure a computer and user account to function as the smart card enrollment station and smart card enrollment agent.

4. Define the physical process for smart card enrollment.

The following sections outline the design decisions you face during each step of the smart card deployment.

Defining Permissions for Certificate Templates

Smart card logon requires the use of several certificate templates. Define security for each of the required templates so that only the desired security groups have the permission to enroll for the required certificates. The required certificates include

- **EnrollmentAgent.** The person performing smart card enrollment on behalf of other users requires this certificate. Define the enrollment agent certificate permissions carefully so that only a designated administrator who performs smart card enrollment can acquire an EnrollmentAgent certificate. A user with this certificate might generate a certificate for another user and act as that user on the network.

- **MachineEnrollmentAgent.** The computer functioning as the smart card enrollment station requires this certificate. This certificate enables the enrollment station to prove its identity to a remote computer and ensure the identity of a remote computer. The computer account that enrolls for the MachineEnrollmentAgent certificate requires the Read and Enroll permissions for the MachineEnrollmentAgent certificate template.

Note You can also use a multipurpose certificate template in place of the MachineEnrollmentAgent certificate as long as you include the ability to provide mutual authentication in the certificate template definition.

- **SmartcardUser.** This certificate provides the user with the ability to authenticate with a smart card and to send encrypted e-mail. The enrollment agent and the user account that use the smart card must have Read and Enroll permissions for the SmartcardUser certificate template.
- **SmartcardLogon.** This certificate only gives the user the ability to authenticate with the network. The certificate can't be used for other purposes, such as secure e-mail. The intended user account and the enrollment agent account must have both the Read and Enroll permissions to acquire a SmartcardLogon certificate.

Important A smart card deployment requires either a SmartcardUser or a SmartcardLogon certificate to be issued. The choice of which one is issued depends on whether smart cards are used only for network authentication (SmartcardLogon) or also for e-mail purposes (SmartcardUser). You don't require both certificates to use a smart card on the network.

The permissions for each of the certificate templates is defined in Active Directory Sites And Services by exposing the Services node. You can find the certificate templates in Active Directory Sites and Services\Services\Public Key Services \Certificate Templates.

Warning Don't delete any certificate templates in Active Directory Sites And Services. This action removes the certificate template from your forest and makes it unavailable for all users in the forest. The only way to reinstall the templates is to uninstall and reinstall an Enterprise CA.

Configuring CAs to Issue the Required Certificates

After defining permissions for the required certificate templates, you must configure one or more CAs to issue the certificate templates. By default, CAs don't issue any of the required certificate templates for smart card logon. Only Enterprise CAs can issue the certificate templates. You should select an Enterprise CA that's located near the smart card enrollment station because all requests will be generated at this workstation.

Acquiring the Required Certificates

Once you've defined permissions for the certificates and configured a CA to issue the certificates, the enrollment agent and the enrollment station can acquire their required certificates.

The enrollment agent must acquire an EnrollmentAgent certificate. This certificate gives the user the ability to request certificates on behalf of other users of the network. The EnrollmentAgent certificate can be requested using either the Certificate Services Web page or the Certificates MMC console.

The smart card enrollment station computer requires a MachineEnrollmentAgent certificate to allow the computer to mutually authenticate with the issuing CA to ensure that only an authorized computer performs the smart card request.

Note   For details on the actual deployment of smart card logon, see "Q257480–Certificate Enrollment Using Smart Cards" on the Supplemental Course Materials CD-ROM (\chapt10\Q257480.mht).

Defining the Enrollment Process

You can build security into the smart card certificate distribution process. To ensure that the smart card is issued only to the required user, you can mandate that the user must meet face-to-face with the enrollment agent in order to obtain the card. By issuing smart cards only to validated users, the enrollment agent can define the validation criteria through Web-based questionnaires or personal interviews.

The enrollment process should include safeguards that ensure that only the smart card's user knows the associated PIN. Typically, the enrollment agent allows users to select their own PINs if the users are employees of the company and physically present during the certificate request. If the requestor isn't an employee, the enrollment agent can either reset the initial user PIN through smart card management software or assign a random PIN to each smart card and securely transmit the PIN to the required user.

Note   The organization should also include provisions for what to do when a smart card needs to be reset. In the worst case, you need to plan what to do when a user leaves the smart card at home.

Making the Decision

Use the decision matrix in Table 10.8 to ensure that security is maintained at the highest level during a smart card deployment.

Table 10.8   Planning Smart Card Deployment

To	Do the Following
Ensure that only authorized personnel can request certificates required for smart card authentication	■ Configure the DACLs on the required certificate templates to grant Read and Enroll permissions to only authorized users for the certificate templates. ■ Restrict which CAs are allowed to issue the smart card-related certificates.
Restrict the smart card enrollment process to specific workstations	■ Restrict which computers can Read and Enroll the MachineEnrollmentAgent certificate. ■ Install smart card readers only at workstations that act as the enrollment station or as workstations for smart card users.
Require smart card users to log on with smart cards	■ Edit the properties of a smart card user to require a smart card for logon. Remember that this could effectively prevent users from accessing the network if they misplace their smart card.
Ensure that only authorized users obtain a smart card	■ Allow smart cards to be issued only during face-to-face meetings.
Define what happens when a smart card is removed from the smart card reader	■ Define the smart card removal action property in Group Policy under Security Options. You can define this policy for the site, domain, or OU.

Applying the Decision

Blue Yonder Airlines won't be able to require face-to-face interviews with Jenny Sax in all instances because their customers reside in many locations on the West Coast of the United States.

To ensure that smart cards are issued only to authorized users, customers must request the cards by filling out an extensive form. Jenny Sax will have to review each request and determine whether to issue a smart card to the customer. If she issues the card, she should send the card, the smart card reader, and the PIN in separate packages to minimize an attacker's ability to intercept the delivery. If an attacker acquires the smart card and the associated PIN, the attacker can act as the user.

For internal requests, such as the requirement for EAP logon over Virtual Private Networks (VPNs), Jenny can require face-to-face meetings before issuing a smart card. This process can be safeguarded by having users show Jenny a form of photo ID to prove their identity.

Planning Certificate-Based Web Authentication

Certificates also can provide authentication through Web services. When a user is connecting to a Web site protected by a Secure Sockets Layer (SSL) protocol, you also can configure the Web site to require certificates for user authentication. This requirement helps prevent a user name and password from being intercepted as they are transmitted across the network. Only the certificate is transmitted across the network.

The Web server receives the certificate and looks either at its own mapping table or at the mapping table in Active Directory to determine the user account associated with (or mapped to) the certificate. The certificate proves the user's identity.

Certificate mapping allows either a single certificate or multiple certificates with similar properties to be mapped to a single user account. These mappings are known as either *one-to-one* or *many-to-one* mappings.

Your design for the mapping of certificates to user accounts includes the following decision points:

- Determine where to perform the mapping. Certificate mapping can be performed in both Active Directory and within the properties of the local Web server. If an administrator performs the mapping in Active Directory, the mapping is available to all other Web servers in the corporate network. If the administrator performs the mapping at the IIS server, the mapping is recognized only at the IIS server. If the same mappings are required at other IIS servers, the mappings must be repeated at each IIS server.

- Determine the type of mapping to implement. The certificate administrator has the option to perform either a one-to-one or a many-to-one mapping. One-to-one mappings are required whenever users have unique permissions or unique levels of access within a PKI-aware application. If there isn't a requirement to identify each participant in the PKI uniquely, a many-to-one mapping allows multiple certificates to be mapped to a single user account.

- Ensure that all certificates are issued from trusted root CA hierarchies. The Web servers that you deploy must trust the CAs that issue the certificates to the users. If the certificate isn't from a trusted CA, the Authentication dialog box won't present a certificate to choose for authentication.

When certificate-based authentication is enabled for an IIS Web site, you can change the Web site's authentication configuration to allow only certificate-based authentication. You do this by configuring the supported authentication methods, as shown in Figure 10.24.

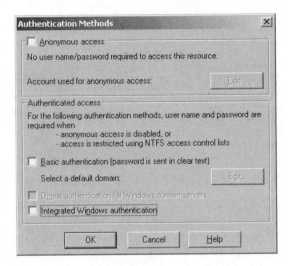

Figure 10.24   Restricting authentication to support only smart card authentication

Configuring authentication in this manner prevents IIS from presenting the user with an Authentication dialog box if certificate-based authentication fails. Therefore, only certificates can be used to authenticate users.

Making the Decision

Use the decision matrix shown in Table 10.9 when deciding how to implement account mapping to provide certificate-based authentication for Web applications.

Table 10.9   Mapping Certificates to User Accounts

Choose the Following Account-Mapping Strategy	When
One-to-one mappings	■ You must differentiate access levels based on different users. ■ All users who must access the Web-based application are assigned or will be assigned their own certificates. ■ Varying levels of access must be granted to the same Web site. ■ The number of users requiring account mappings is relatively small. You wouldn't want to define one-to-one mappings for a project that supports a million users. ■ All certificates must be issued by a trusted root CA hierarchy.
Many-to-one mappings	■ All users from the same business unit, partner organization, or department require the same level of access to a Web site. ■ The certificates involved in the mapping have similar attributes or similar values that can easily be mapped to a single user account. ■ The CA that issued the certificates is configured as a Trusted Root Certification Authority and all certificates from the CA will be trusted. ■ You can easily define a set of rules that describe all certificates that will be mapped to the single user account. ■ All certificates must be issued by a trusted root CA hierarchy.

> **Tip**   You can improve the process of performing one-to-one mappings by creating a custom Web enrollment page that automates the mapping process.

In addition to determining what type of mappings to perform, you also must decide where to perform the mappings. The design matrix shown in Table 10.10 will assist you in determining the best location to perform the account mappings.

Table 10.10   Planning Where to Configure Account Mapping

Choose	When the Following Conditions Exist
Active Directory mappings	■ The certificate mapping is required for more than one application. ■ You don't want to define identical certificate mappings at multiple servers.
IIS mappings	■ The IIS server isn't a member of any domain, but rather a member of a workgroup and can't access Active Directory to determine certificate mappings. ■ Authentication takes place against the IIS server's local account database, rather than against Active Directory. ■ The account mapping is used only at the IIS server where the mapping is defined.

Applying the Decision

Blue Yonder Airlines requires one-to-one mappings. Even though a large number of user accounts might require certificate mappings, the need for credit card information and personal data confidentiality far outweighs the costs involved in setting up certificates for each individual user.

In addition to creating one-to-one mappings for each user account, Blue Yonder Airlines must determine where to perform the mappings. The easiest place to perform the mappings is in Active Directory. Because each account acquires its certificate from an Enterprise CA, there's no need to redo the same mappings that exist in Active Directory at the IIS server.

If the certificates were acquired from a private CA on the Internet, you might decide to define the certificate mappings at the IIS server. Since the certificates are mapped only to a single smart card, there's no reason to input the data into the IIS server. By using Active Directory, you also ensure that the certificate mappings won't have to be reentered for an additional IIS server if the same certificate mappings are required for separate applications.

Lesson Summary

This lesson described two common methods of authentication. A major part of your security plan will be identifying where certificate-based authentication is used on the network. Identifying who uses PKI-based authentication will make your job easier when you design secure access to the network.

Lab 10-1: Planning a PKI Deployment

Lab Objectives

This lab prepares you to design a PKI by meeting the following objectives:

- Design a Certification Authority (CA) structure
- Design a PKI to support the certificate life cycle
- Design certificate-based authentication

About This Lab

This lab explores the design decisions you face when implementing a PKI in a Windows 2000 network.

Before You Begin

Make sure that you've completed reading the chapter material before starting the lab. Pay close attention to the sections where the design decisions were applied throughout the chapter for information on building your administrative structure.

Scenario: Contoso Ltd.

Contoso Ltd., an international magazine sales company, wants to deploy its own PKI to support certificate-based authentication and encryption on its network. Contoso wants to develop a CA hierarchy that matches its current administrative structure.

Defining the CA Requirements

Contoso wants to develop a CA structure that allows management of the certificate deployment at each of its regional offices in Lima, London, and Seattle. At each office, separate CAs will be established to support ongoing projects. Separate CAs must be established for each project to ensure that the CA design decisions for one project don't affect the availability of the CA associated with a different project.

Contoso doesn't want the actions of one regional office to affect the others. Likewise, the actions in one project's CA shouldn't affect the security of another project's CA. If the need arises to redeploy Certificate Services for one office, the redeployment shouldn't affect the others.

Contoso wants to ensure that the root CA is protected from attackers. The PKI design should provide protection from both hackers and natural disaster.

PKI-Aware Projects at Contoso

Contoso requires a PKI for three separate projects:

- The Contoso Web site will start to sell magazine subscriptions online. Each office will be responsible for allowing certificate-based authentication to its region's subscription Web site. The office's IIS server hosting the subscription Web site should be configured to allow both user-entered authentication and certificate-based authentication when someone places an online order. Customers will obtain their certificates for authentication by completing a Web-based form. A certificate administrator will review the form and either issue or deny the certificate.

- Contoso wants to allow employees of a partner organization named Northwind Traders to access data stored on an IIS server located in the Contoso extranet at the London office. The Northwind Traders employees involved in the project will acquire their certificates from a CA in the Northwind Traders CA hierarchy named Cooperation. Contoso has decided that all employees who are issued certificates from the Cooperation CA will have the same level of access to the project data. The Northwind Traders users will simply have to provide a certificate issued by the Cooperation CA to prove their identity before gaining access to the project Web site. Figure 10.25 shows the CA hierarchy for Northwind Traders.

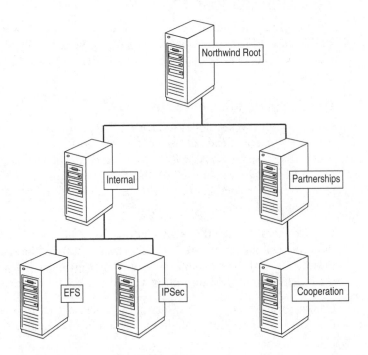

Figure 10.25   The Northwind Traders CA hierarchy

Exercise 1: Designing a CA Hierarchy for Contoso Ltd.

This exercise has you design a CA hierarchy that meets the design requirements defined by Contoso Ltd. Answers to these questions can be found in the appendix.

1. How many separate CA hierarchies does the Contoso Ltd. PKI deployment need?

2. What can you do to protect the root CA from attackers?

3. What can you do to protect the root CA from natural disaster?

4. To meet design requirements, what structure should you define for the second level of CAs in the Contoso CA hierarchy?

5. To meet design requirements, what structure should you define for the third level of CAs in the Contoso CA hierarchy?

6. To meet the security requirements, which levels of CAs should be offline CAs? Would the offline CAs be Standalone or Enterprise CAs?

7. What must you do to ensure the availability of the certificate revocation list for the root CA?

8. In the space below, draw a CA hierarchy for Contoso CA that meets all design requirements.

Exercise 2: Planning Security for Web-Based Subscriptions to Magazines

This exercise looks at the design required to secure subscriptions to Contoso's magazines using the subscription Web site. Answers to these questions can be found in the appendix.

1. From what type of CA should Contoso acquire the certificate for the Web servers hosting the subscription Web site? What purpose will the keys associated with this certificate be used for?

2. What must you do to allow customers to choose either certificate-based or user-entered authentication to the subscription Web site?

3. What type of CA should be used to allocate certificates to customers for accessing the subscription Web site?

4. Assuming that customers will connect only to the Web site in their locale, what type of certificate mapping must be defined to allow certificate-based authentication to the subscription Web site?

5. Would one-to-one or many-to-one certificate mappings be used for the subscription Web site project?

6. Assume that in an average day the WebSeattle CA certificate administrator revokes 10 certificates. What would you recommend as a CRL publication schedule if Contoso wants all certificate revocations to be effective within one business day of the revocation?

7. What problems would arise if the CRL publication schedule for the WebLondon CA were set to be one hour?

Exercise 3: Planning Partner Access

The following exercise looks at the design decisions that Contoso will face in providing certificate-based authentication to Northwind Traders' employees involved in the project shared by Contoso and Northwind Traders. Answers to these questions can be found in the appendix.

1. What type of hierarchy must be established to allow certificates issued by the Northwind Traders CA to be recognized by clients in the Contoso Ltd. forest?

2. If cross-certification is defined between the root CAs of the Contoso and Northwind Traders CA hierarchies, will the security requirements defined for the project shared by Northwind Traders and Contoso be met?

3. What can you do to trust only certificates issued by the Cooperation CA for the purpose of authenticating with the Web server and to reject all certificates issued from the Northwind Traders CA hierarchy?

4. What type of certificate mapping must you configure to allow Northwind Trader users access to the Project Web site?

5. Where should you define the account mapping? In Active Directory or in IIS?

6. What risks are there when a many-to-one mapping is defined and the certificates used in the many-to-one mapping aren't issued by a CA in your management control?

Review

Answering the following questions will reinforce key information presented in this chapter. If you are unable to answer a question, review the appropriate lesson and then try the question again. Answers to the questions can be found in the appendix.

1. A company has found that its offline root CA's hard disk has crashed. What must you include in the backup set to ensure that the root CA can be recovered?

2. Assume that after the restoration of the previous backup, Certificate Services refused to start. What can you do to get Certificate Services running without having to redeploy the organization's PKI?

3. The CRL publication interval for the CA that issues user certificates for authenticating with the Human Resources Web site is currently set to the default of seven days. The actual publication takes place every Sunday evening. On Tuesday morning, Amy Anderson was terminated from her position at the company and her user certificate was revoked immediately. When the administrator reset the password on Amy's account so that her supervisor could investigate Amy's My Documents folder, the supervisor found that she still could access the Human Resources Web site by authenticating with Amy's certificate. If the certificate was revoked, why is this happening?

4. The permissions for the EnrollmentAgent certificate template are defined in the following manner:

- Authenticated Users: Read, Enroll
- Domain Admins: Full Control
- Enterprise Admins: Read

Are there any security weaknesses with the defined DACL for the EnrollmentAgent certificate template? What modifications should be made to give only members of the SmartCardDeployment group the ability to perform smart card enrollments?

5. An organization has been approached as a consultant to design certificate mapping to allow secure access to a Web server located in the organization's DMZ. To prevent the internal network from being compromised, the Web server located in the DMZ isn't made a member of the domain. The Web server uses certificate-based authentication to ensure that only members of the IT infrastructure team can access the auditing Web pages. Where should the certificate mapping be defined—at the IIS server or in Active Directory?

6. An organization has been approached as a consultant to design certificate mapping to allow secure access to a series of Web servers located on the organization's internal network. The Web servers use certificate-based authentication to ensure that only members of the IT infrastructure team can access the auditing Web pages. Where should the certificate mapping be defined—at the IIS servers or in Active Directory?

C H A P T E R   1 1

Securing Data at the Application Layer

About This Chapter

In this chapter you will explore methods for applying security to transmitted data at the application layer. Once you make configuration changes, application security works seamlessly. The application, however, must support the application-layer security.

Before You Begin

To complete this chapter you must read the chapter scenario. This scenario is used throughout the chapter to apply the design decisions discussed in each lesson.

Learning Resources
Centre

Chapter Scenario: Fabrikam Inc.

Fabrikam Inc. is a defense contractor that develops weapon solutions for the U.S. military. The head office is in Washington, D.C., and research offices are in New York and San Francisco. Manufacturing plants are in Detroit and Albuquerque, and warehouses are in Houston and Miami. The company's various locations are illustrated in Figure 11.1.

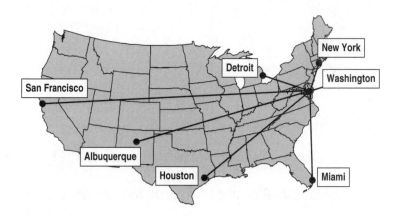

Figure 11.1   Fabrikam locations

Fabrikam has implemented a single domain model for their Microsoft Windows 2000 domain and is using corp.fabrikam.tld as their forest root domain. Each location is defined as a separate site and is connected to the head office in Washington with a 1.544 megabit-per-second (Mbps) link.

Client Operating Systems

The Fabrikam network is in the process of migrating all computers to Windows 2000. Currently only the Washington and San Francisco sites have completed the migration. Table 11.1 shows the progress of the upgrade at the other Fabrikam sites.

Table 11.1 Fabrikam's Client Operating Systems

Location	Client Operating Systems
Albuquerque	200 Windows 98–based clients 300 Windows NT 4.0–based clients 500 Windows 2000–based clients
Houston	35 Windows 95–based clients 250 Windows NT 4.0–based clients 100 Windows 2000–based clients
Miami	50 Windows 98–based clients 500 Windows 2000–based clients
Detroit	400 Windows 98–based clients 100 Windows NT 4.0–based clients 500 Windows 2000–based clients
New York	350 Windows NT 4.0–based clients 300 Windows 2000–based clients

At each location the operating systems have been well maintained. The latest service packs and critical updates are applied to all client computers within one month of their release.

The Department of Defense

The Department of Defense requires all contracting organizations to submit their bids for contracts using a Web-based system. To access the bidding system, the bidding agent for Fabrikam connects to the Department of Defense Web site and submits all proposals.

To ensure security, the Defense Department requires the bidding agent for each company to log on to its Web site by providing a user name and password. The Web site is configured to support any browser that supports Secure Sockets Layer (SSL) v3. Due to the nature of these projects, the Defense Department requires that the maximum level of security be applied.

Once a bid is submitted, the Defense Department requires that a price quote be e-mailed from the winning contractor. The e-mail must be protected to ensure that the pricing information hasn't been modified and that the contents aren't viewable during transmission over the Internet.

Ongoing Projects

Fabrikam is currently working on two unrelated projects with the Defense Department. The first project, involving an advanced radar system, is a joint project among the Washington, Albuquerque, Miami, and New York offices. The second project, involving a new sonar system for submarines, is a joint project among the Washington, San Francisco, Houston, and Detroit offices and another company named A. Datum Corporation.

The Radar System Project

The Radar System project stores all data for the project on a server located at the New York office. Fabrikam wants to ensure that only members of the project team can connect to the project server (named HELIOS) and that the client and server are mutually authenticated.

This project requires that detailed specifications be e-mailed among project members. Recently an e-mail was sent to the Defense Department by a former staff member masquerading as another staff member still on the project team. To prevent forged e-mails, Fabrikam wants to ensure that e-mails originate from the indicated source address.

The Sonar System Project

Due to the nature of the Sonar System project, the highest level of security is required. The following components are part of the required security design:

- All hours performed by A. Datum Corporation must be recorded to a Web-based time recording system located in the Fabrikam extranet.

- E-mail containing design specifications is considered sensitive and should be protected during the transmission between Fabrikam and A. Datum Corporation. In recent weeks an attacker falsified a message from an employee at A. Datum Corporation that resulted in classified documents being published to a public location on the Fabrikam network.

- A project server at the San Francisco office stores all data required for the project. All clients at the Washington, Houston, and Detroit offices must access the data securely and ensure that the data can't be intercepted as it's transferred across the network.

Lesson 1: Planning Authenticity and Integrity of Transmitted Data

A common security goal when designing application-level security is to prevent impersonation. Impersonation often involves an attacker who assumes the identity of a trusted individual on the network. Another form of impersonation is an unauthorized computer impersonating a trusted computer on the network. This lesson examines procedures implemented at the application layer to ensure the authenticity of all parties involved in a data transfer. These procedures also ensure that transmitted data isn't modified after being sent on the network.

After this lesson, you will be able to

- Plan application layer methods that provide authenticity and integrity to transmitted data

Estimated lesson time: 45 minutes

Providing Authenticity and Integrity of Transmitted Data

A Windows 2000 network has two distinct methods for providing authenticity and integrity of transmitted data at the application layer. Server message block (SMB) signing can help ensure that file transmissions between a client and a server aren't modified in transit. For e-mail, both Secure/Multipurpose Internet Mail Extensions (S/MIME) and Pretty Good Privacy (PGP) provide the ability to digitally sign e-mail messages to protect them from being modified in transit.

Planning SMB Signing

SMB signing, also known as Common Internet File System (CIFS) signing, ensures the authenticity and integrity of packets transmitted between a client and a server. It does this by signing each packet as it's transmitted and verifying the signature at the recipient computer.

What Protections Does Signing Provide?

Signing is accomplished by running a mathematical algorithm over specific fields in a packet and arriving at a mathematical result. The recipient will run the same algorithm against the received packet and compare the results. If the results match, the packet's contents weren't modified during transmission.

Warning   When SMB signing is implemented, the performance for transmitted data decreases. The overhead involved in signing and verifying each packet is roughly 10 to 15 percent more than when packets are transmitted without SMB signing.

SMB signing is negotiated between the client and the server when the initial SMB session is established, as shown in Figure 11.2. The process involves the following steps:

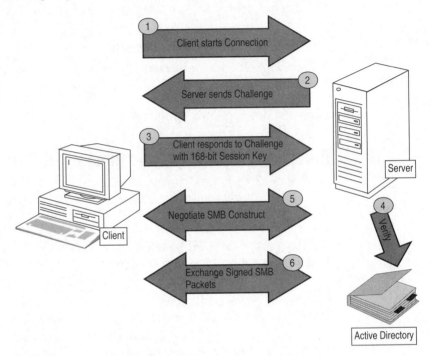

Figure 11.2   The SMB signing process

1. The client attempts to connect to a server that's configured to require SMB signing.

2. The server sends a challenge to the client. The challenge is the data that the client will encrypt to authenticate with the server.

3. The client responds by encrypting the challenge with a 168-bit session key computed from the user's password. The response and the algorithm used to encrypt the challenge is returned to the server.

4. The server validates the authentication attempt by performing the same algorithm on the challenge using the stored value of the user's password and comparing the results. If the results are the same, the user is authenticated.

5. The client and server negotiate which variation, or construct, of SMBs will be used by the client and the server. Which versions of SMBs are selected depends on the operating systems involved in the client/server exchange. The client and server always select the highest variation supported by both client and server.

6. Subsequent data exchange between the client and the server is protected by computing a digest for each message and including the digest with the message. The digest covers both the message text and the sequence number of the packet to ensure that a replay attack can't take place.

The key used to create the digests is created using the Message Digest v5 (MD5) algorithm. The MD5 message digest algorithm breaks the data into 512-bit blocks and produces a 128-bit message digest for each 512-bit block of the data. The key is computed from the session key established between the client and the server and the initial response sent by the client to the server's challenge.

SMB signing is commonly implemented in high-security networks to prevent impersonation of clients and servers. SMB signing authenticates the user and the server hosting the data. If either side fails the authentication, data transmission won't take place.

Consider using SMB signing in networks that implement both Windows 2000–based clients and down-level Windows clients. Internet Protocol Security (IPSec) Authentication Headers (AH) are supported only in pure Windows 2000 networks. SMB signing is supported by Windows 2000, Windows NT 4.0 (with SP3 or higher), and Windows 98–based clients.

Note For information on deploying IPSec to provide authenticity and integrity of transmitted data, see Chapter 12, "Securing Data with Internet Protocol Security (IPSec)."

Planning the Deployment of SMB Signing

SMB signing requires modification of the registry in Windows 2000, Windows NT 4.0 (SP3 or higher), and Windows 98. The method used to deploy the registry depends on the operating system.

Deploying SMB Signing for Windows 2000–Based Clients

In a Windows 2000 environment, which method you use to deploy SMB signing depends on whether the Windows 2000–based computers are participating in a workgroup or domain environment. In a workgroup environment, you deploy the security template file by using the Secedit command. In a domain environment, you can store the required modifications in a security template file and then deploy them by using Group Policy.

Note   For more information on deploying security templates in workgroup and domain environments, see Chapter 8, "Securing Microsoft Windows 2000–Based Computers."

When you configure a security template to use SMB signing, you can enable four separate options to tailor the SMB signing options to meet your organization's security requirements, as shown in Figure 11.3.

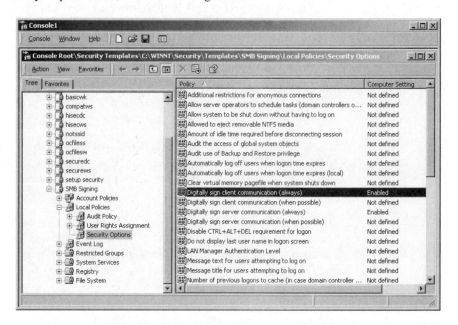

Figure 11.3   Configuring a security template to implement SMB signing

- **Digitally Sign Client Communications (Always).** When enabled, this security option requires the Windows 2000–based computer to always use SMB signing when acting as the client in a Windows 2000 file session.

- **Digitally Sign Client Communications (When Possible).** When enabled, this security option configures the Windows 2000–based computer to request the use of SMB signing when acting as the client in a Windows 2000 file session.

- **Digitally Sign Server Communications (Always).** When enabled, this security option requires the Windows 2000–based computer to always use SMB signing when acting as a server in a Windows 2000 file session.

- **Digitally Sign Server Communications (When Possible).** When enabled, this security option configures the Windows 2000–based computer to request the use of SMB signing when acting as the server in a Windows 2000 file session.

The choice of settings depends on the role that the Windows 2000–based computer plays on the network and the security requirements for SMB signing defined for your network.

In a domain environment you can import the security template to a specific domain, site, or OU Group Policy object. For example, you might want to require SMB signing when communicating with a specific group of servers hosting data for a sensitive project in your organization. You can create an OU for the servers, place all of the servers within the OU, and then import a security template that enables the Digitally Sign Server Communications (Always) security option, as illustrated in Figure 11.4.

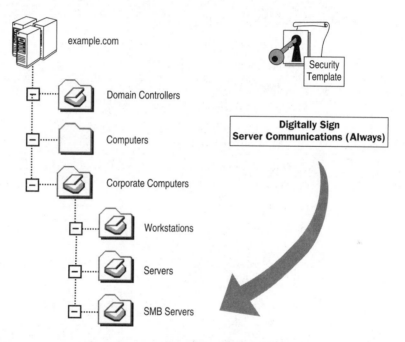

example.com

Domain Controllers

Computers

Corporate Computers

Workstations

Servers

SMB Servers

Security Template

**Digitally Sign
Server Communications (Always)**

Figure 11.4 Importing a security template enforcing SMB signing for servers to a specific OU

In a workgroup environment you must copy the completed security template locally to each Windows 2000–based computer that requires enabled SMB signing. The security template is then applied by creating a batch file that calls the Secedit command using the /configure option. For example, if the security template file were named Smbsign.inf, you could use the following batch file to apply the security template settings and store them in a database named Security.sdb:

```
secedit /configure /DB Security.sdb /CFG Smbsign.inf /overwrite
```

Deploying SMB Signing for Windows NT 4.0–Based Clients

Windows NT 4.0 introduced support for SMB signing in Service Pack 3. The ability to deploy SMB signing in Windows NT 4.0 requires editing the registry. To enable SMB signing in a Windows NT 4.0 environment, you must edit different registry values depending on whether the Windows NT 4.0–based client is acting as a client or a server.

If the Windows NT 4.0 client is functioning as a server, you must consider editing these two registry values to deploy SMB signing to match your organization's security requirements:

- Key: HKEY_LOCAL_MACHINE\System\CurrentControlSet\Services \LanManServer\Parameters
  - Value Name: EnableSecuritySignature
  - Data Type: REG_DWORD
  - Value: 0 (disable), 1 (enable)
  - Default: 0 (disable)
- Key: HKEY_LOCAL_MACHINE\System\CurrentControlSet\Services \LanManServer\Parameters
  - Value Name: RequireSecuritySignature
  - Data Type: REG_DWORD
  - Value: 0 (disable), 1 (enable)
  - Default: 0 (disable)

When the Windows NT 4.0 client is functioning as a client, you must edit two different registry values to meet your organization's security requirements:

- Key: HKEY_LOCAL_MACHINE\System\CurrentControlSet\Services \Rdr\Parameters
  - Value Name: EnableSecuritySignature
  - Data Type: REG_DWORD
  - Value: 0 (disable), 1 (enable)
  - Default: 1 (enable)
- Key: HKEY_LOCAL_MACHINE\System\CurrentControlSet\Services \Rdr\Parameters
  - Value Name: RequireSecuritySignature
  - Data Type: REG_DWORD
  - Value: 0 (disable), 1 (enable)
  - Default: 0 (disable)

You can deploy these settings by creating a custom template file and then applying them with the System Policy Editor. Assuming that the Windows NT 4.0 client is operating in a domain environment, you can apply the settings to a Ntconfig.pol configuration file. You can then place the modified Ntconfig.pol file in the Netlogon share to ensure that the settings are applied to all required clients.

Note For more information on deploying SMB signing in a Windows NT 4.0 environment, see Knowledge Base article Q161372 on the Supplemental Course Materials CD-ROM (\chapt11\Q161372.mht).

Deploying SMB Signing for Windows 98–Based Clients

Windows 98 also includes an updated version of the SMB protocol that allows Windows 98–based clients to participate in SMB signing. As with Windows NT 4.0–based clients, you enable SMB signing by editing the registry, but the registry keys are different.

You can enable SMB signing on Windows 98–based computers by configuring the following two registry values:

- In HKEY_LOCAL_MACHINE\System\CurrentControlSet\Services \VxD\Vnetsup
  - Value Name: EnableSecuritySignature
  - Data Type: REG_DWORD
  - Value: 0 (disable), 1 (enable)
  - Default: 1 (enable)
- In HKEY_LOCAL_MACHINE\System\CurrentControlSet\Services \VxD\Vnetsup
  - Value Name: RequireSecuritySignature
  - Data Type: REG_DWORD
  - Value: 0 (disable), 1 (enable)
  - Default: 0 (disable)

Note Once you've completed the registry modifications, you need to reboot the Windows 98–based computer before the modified settings take effect.

For Windows 98–based computers, the easiest way to deploy this setting would be to e-mail a .reg file containing the desired settings to all Windows 98–based clients. Users import the settings at their computers by double-clicking the .reg file. You can use system policies only if the network has no Windows 95–based clients. Windows 95–based clients don't support SMB signing.

Note   For more information on deploying SMB signing in a Windows 98 environment, see Knowledge Base article Q230545 on the Supplemental Course Materials CD-ROM (\chapt11\Q230545.mht).

Making the Decision

You must consider the decision points in Table 11.2 when you develop a design for SMB signing on a network.

Table 11.2   Planning SMB Signing Security

To	Consider the Following
Require that all communications to a server require SMB signing	■ Configure the server to enable the use of SMB signing and also to require the use of SMB signing. ■ Configure all required client computers to either enable or require SMB signing.
Allow SMB signing to take place but still allow fallback to unsigned communications	■ Configure the server to enable only SMB signing.
Deploy SMB signing configuration for Windows 2000–based clients	■ Create a security template that enables the required SMB signing configuration. ■ Place all computers that require the settings into a common OU structure. ■ Import the security template into a Group Policy object applied at the OU.
Deploy SMB signing configuration for Windows NT 4.0–based clients	■ Create a custom system policy template that contains the required SMB signing settings. ■ Modify the Ntconfig.pol file to apply the required SMB settings. ■ Ensure that all Windows NT 4.0–based clients have Service Pack 3 as the minimum service pack level.
Deploy SMB signing configuration for Windows 98–based clients	■ Create a .reg file that contains the required SMB settings for Windows 98–based computers. ■ Distribute the .reg file to all Windows 98–based computers. ■ Apply the .reg file to the Windows 98–based computers. ■ Restart the Windows 98–based computers.

Applying the Decision

To meet the requirement to mutually authenticate clients and servers, you must implement SMB signing at the HELIOS server for the Radar System project. The offices involved in the Radar System project use a mix of Windows 98, Windows NT 4.0, and Windows 2000. As discussed in this chapter, all of these operating systems support the use of SMB signing to ensure mutual authentication of clients and servers.

To deploy SMB signing, you have to use different methods based on the computer's operating system. There are four possible systems:

- **The HELIOS server.** You can place the Windows 2000–based server in an OU that has the Digitally Sign Server Communications (Always) security option enabled in Group Policy. This setting ensures that any clients that connect to the HELIOS server must use SMB signing. In addition, you must configure the share where the project files are stored with Share and NTFS permissions that give access only to authorized users.

- **Windows 2000 clients.** The Windows 2000–based clients at each office can be placed in the same OU as the HELIOS server or in a sub-OU based on the Windows 2000 client's office location, as shown in Figure 11.5.

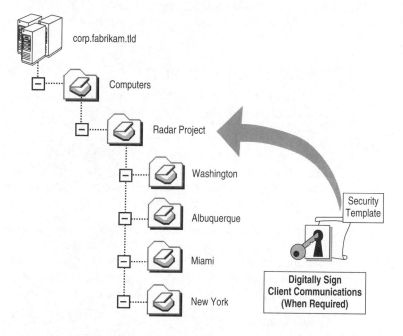

Figure 11.5   Proposed OU structure for Windows 2000-based clients for Fabrikam Inc.

The Group Policy object (GPO) should be set so that the computers digitally sign client communications, but only when required. This setting allows the computers to still communicate with other servers in the organization that may not require SMB signing but use SMB signing when connecting to the HELIOS server. When you apply the GPO at a parent OU, the GPO is inherited by all child OUs by default.

- **Windows NT 4.0 clients.** You can create a system policy template that enables the Windows NT 4.0–based clients to enable SMB signing. You can apply the template file to the file Ntconfig.pol stored in the Netlogon share of all domain controllers in the corp.fabrikam.tld domain. The Windows NT 4.0–

based computers then apply the system policy every time they're restarted and they authenticate with the network. To ensure that the system policy setting works, all Windows NT 4.0 clients must be configured with at least Service Pack 3.

- **Windows 98 clients.** You should create a .reg file that enables SMB signing for Windows 98 clients. Because Fabrikam uses a single-domain model and the domain has Windows 95 clients, you shouldn't deploy the registry setting for SMB signing by using system policy because the policy would also be applied to Windows 95–based computers. You could e-mail the .reg file to the Windows 98 users or apply it with a login script.

SMB signing isn't required for the Sonar System project. If the Sonar System project required integrity and authenticity of the data, an alternative method would be needed because the project involves Windows 95–based computers that don't support SMB signing.

Planning Digital Signing

While SMB signing protects file transmissions between a client and a server, digital signatures ensure authenticity and integrity of e-mail messages between clients.

Digital signatures differ from SMB signing in that a Public Key Infrastructure (PKI) is required to deploy the necessary public/private key pairs to participating clients. Once a participating client has acquired a private/public key pair, the client can implement digital signatures to protect e-mail messages.

Digital signatures ensure that the contents of e-mail messages aren't modified in transit. Additionally, the digital signature confirms that the message originated from the correct source. This feature works in two ways. First, it prevents someone from impersonating another e-mail user, and second, it prevents an e-mail user from denying that he sent a specific e-mail message.

Digital signatures function by applying a digest function to the contents of the message. The digest function creates a message digest as output. The message digest is a representation of the message. If the contents of the message are modified, the message digest output will also change. Both the sender and receiver of the message will run the same digest function against the e-mail message. The recipient's e-mail application will compare the two digests to determine if the contents have been modified. If the digests match, the contents haven't been modified.

Note   While it's theoretically possible to modify a message so that the message digest function returns the same value, it's highly improbable that this will happen.

Figure 11.6 shows the digital signature process that occurs when an e-mail client sends a digitally signed message to a recipient. The process involves the following steps:

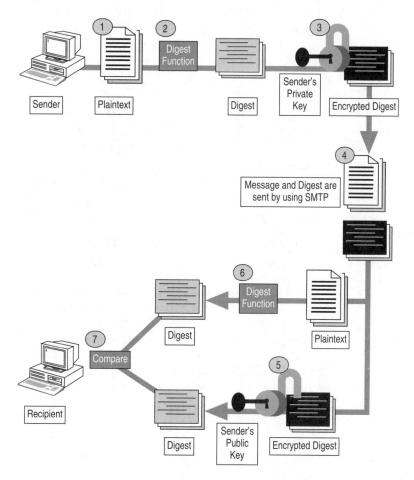

Figure 11.6   Digital Signatures preventing modification of an e-mail message

1. The sender creates a plaintext e-mail message. By default, Post Office Protocol v3 (POP3)/Simple Mail Transfer Protocol (SMTP) e-mail clients send their messages in plaintext format.

2. The sender will run a known algorithm against the plaintext message to create a digest of the message. Most commonly, either a Secure Hash Algorithm v1 (SHA1) or MD5 algorithm is used to create the digest.

Note   SHA1 and MD5 are both algorithms that produce a message digest when applied against the contents of an e-mail message. SHA1 is considered to be slightly stronger than MD5 because the digest for SHA1 is 32 bits longer than the digest for MD5.

3. The digest is encrypted using the sender's private key. The digest is securely transmitted to the recipient and only the sender's public key can be used to decrypt the encrypted digest.

4. The plaintext message and the encrypted digest are sent to the recipient by using SMTP. For digital signing, no protection is applied to the plaintext message. The message can be modified, but modification will invalidate the encrypted digest sent with the message.

5. The recipient decrypts the encrypted digest by using the sender's public key. The public key is retrieved either from a directory where the public key is stored (such as Active Directory directory service) or is included in the signed message.

6. The recipient runs the same algorithm used by the sender to create the recipient's own digest of the message. This digest is created against the plaintext message received from the sender.

7. The two digests are compared. If the digests differ, the message was modified during transmission. If the digest can't be decrypted, the sender was masquerading as another user.

Determining Protocol Choices for Digital Signing

Two protocols currently provide digital signatures for e-mail applications:

- **Secure Multipurpose Internet Mail Extensions (S/MIME).** An S/MIME extension provides the ability to encrypt and digitally sign e-mail messages by using public and private key pairs. The biggest benefit of implementing S/MIME is that S/MIME is an Internet Engineering Task Force (IETF) standard designed to extend the MIME standard to provide secure e-mail functions. S/MIME requires only that the e-mail applications support S/MIME. There's no requirement for the e-mail servers to support S/MIME.

- **Pretty Good Privacy (PGP).** PGP is also a protocol that provides the ability to encrypt and digitally sign e-mail messages. As with S/MIME, PGP provides this ability by using private/public key pairs. The main difference with PGP is that PGP isn't controlled by a centralized standard organization.

The decision on which protocol to use is often based on the e-mail applications deployed for an organization.

Important   While S/MIME and PGP provide the same functionality, they aren't interoperable. You can't send signed e-mail between e-mail applications that support different protocols. If you use S/MIME to sign a message, the recipient must also support S/MIME.

Deploying Public Keys

The main challenge that an organization faces when implementing digital signatures is ensuring the availability of public keys. Without a public key, the digest encrypted with the sender's private key can't be decrypted to verify message integrity.

To ensure the availability of public keys, do the following:

- Configure e-mail clients to include their certificate with all signed messages. Including the certificate in the signed message ensures that the recipient has the public key required to decrypt the message digest. The public key associated with the digital certificate is included as an attribute of the digital certificate.

Important   The digital certificate must be issued by a Certificate Authority (CA) that the recipient trusts. In addition, the certificate revocation list (CRL) must be accessible to any recipients so that the revocation status of the digital certificate can be verified. If the CRL can't be accessed, the certificate is assumed to be revoked.

- Implement the Key Management Service (KMS) in Microsoft Exchange Server 5.5 or Exchange 2000 Server. The KMS service manages private/public key pairs and ensures that the public keys are stored within the directory (Exchange Server 5.5 users use the Exchange directory and Exchange 2000 Server users use the Active Directory for storage of public keys).

Making the Decision

Table 11.3 discusses the design decisions that you need to make when implementing digital signatures for e-mail messages.

Table 11.3   Planning Digital Signature Design

To	Do the Following
Choose which protocol to use for digitally signing e-mail messages within your organization	- Determine which protocol is supported by your organization's e-mail application.
Ensure that important messages are digitally signed	- Train users on how and when to digitally sign messages.
Ensure that digital signatures are validated	- Configure e-mail applications to include the digital certificate in all signed messages. - Ensure that the CRL publication point for all CAs is available to recipients.
Limit which users can use digital signatures	- Deploy certificates that support digital signatures only to approved users.

Applying the Decision

Fabrikam must provide the ability to digitally sign messages for three scenarios:

- **Defense Department price quotes.** All price quotes to the Defense Department must be digitally signed to ensure that the contents aren't modified during transmission. The digital signature will also prove that the e-mail originated from the validated user at Fabrikam. For this process, the public key of the e-mail sender must be available publicly to allow a recipient at the Defense Department to acquire the public key and verify that the certificate associated with the private/public key hasn't been revoked. Either the certificates must be acquired from a public CA, or the issuing CA's CRLs must be published externally. Because the e-mails are being sent to another organization and security is a key requirement, the recommendation would be to acquire the certificates for these transactions from a public CA such as RSA or Verisign.

- **The Radar System project.** All e-mails regarding specifications must be digitally signed to ensure that the e-mail is from the correct source. Digitally signing the messages validate the sender of the specifications within the e-mail. Because the transmissions are internal, you could use a private CA to issue the certificates required for the digitally signed e-mail.

- **The Sonar System project.** E-mail exchanged between A. Datum Corporation and Fabrikam should be digitally signed to ensure the authenticity of the e-mail messages and to prevent changes to them. Fabrikam and A. Datum Corporation should either acquire certificates from a public CA or establish a cross certification between their two internal CA hierarchies to ensure that certificates from the other organization can be validated.

Fabrikam must determine which users need to acquire certificates for digitally signed e-mail. Based on requirements, only users involved with the three projects must acquire digital signatures. All the users at Fabrikam don't need to issue certificates for digitally signed e-mail.

Finally, for the digitally signed e-mail sent to outside organizations (the Defense Department and A. Datum Corporation), the network administrators must determine whether the partners use PGP or S/MIME for their e-mail packages. This decision determines which e-mail applications must be used at Fabrikam to ensure that the partner's e-mail application can validate the digital signatures.

Lesson Summary

The transmission of sensitive data such as contracts and ordering information across and between networks makes it necessary to verify that the original message hasn't been modified in transit and that the message originated from the true source. Implementing SMB signing in a network ensures that mutual authentication of client and server takes place and prevents an attacker from impersonating a client or server. Digital signatures ensure that the contents of e-mail messages aren't modified. Together, these two technologies help prevent attacks caused by someone impersonating an authorized user or computer.

Lesson 2: Planning Encryption of Transmitted Data

Protecting data from being modified during transmission is critical, but sometimes you must further protect the transmitted data by encrypting it. Encryption protects the transmitted data from inspection by unauthorized users.

After this lesson, you will be able to

- Design a strategy for encrypting transmitted data by using application layer technologies

Estimated lesson time: 30 minutes

Planning Secure E-Mail Encryption

Although digital signing protects e-mail messages from modification, it doesn't prevent someone from inspecting them during transmission across the network. The default protocol used for sending e-mail messages is Simple Mail Transfer Protocol (SMTP). SMTP doesn't include any extensions for the encryption of e-mail. As such, the contents of e-mail messages are vulnerable to inspection.

Figure 11.7 illustrates a plaintext e-mail message that has been intercepted during transmission.

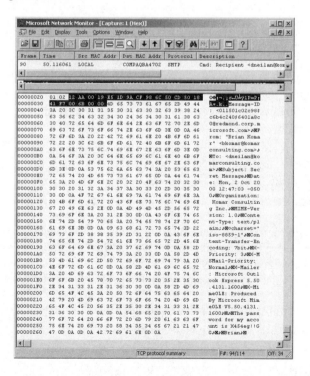

Figure 11.7   Network monitor capture of an e-mail message

The graphic shows that the contents of the e-mail message are transmitted in clear text. From the message we can determine that bkomar@komarconsulting.com sent his e-mail password to dneilan@komarconsulting.com and that the password is X454eg!!GG.

Note   The actual password isn't shown in the SMTP process. It's only because the user put the password in the text of the message that the password is exposed to the attacker using a network monitor. **Never share your password with another user under any circumstances.**

Analyzing the E-Mail Encryption Process

For e-mail encryption to be successful, the recipient requires a private/public key pair. The e-mail encryption process takes place as shown in Figure 11.8.

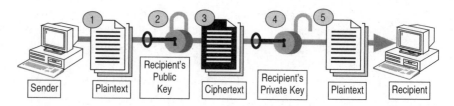

Figure 11.8   The e-mail encryption process

1. The sender of the e-mail creates a plaintext message.
2. The sender encrypts the message by using the recipient's public key. To perform the encryption, the sender must have access to the recipient's public key. The public key can be either retrieved from a directory or exchanged by having the recipient send a digitally signed message to the sender.
3. The encrypted message is sent to the recipient of the message using the SMTP protocol.
4. The recipient decrypts the message using the recipient's own private key. This use of the public and private keys ensures that only the holder of the private key (the recipient) can view the contents of an encrypted message.
5. The decrypted message is displayed in the recipient's e-mail application.

As with digital signatures, the recipient's public key has to be deployed for e-mail encryption to take place. The public keys must be made available either by exchanging digitally signed messages, or in the case of a Windows 2000 network, the public keys can be retrieved from Active Directory.

Determining Encryption Levels for E-Mail Encryption

E-mail messages can be encrypted by using different algorithms. Supported algorithms in Microsoft Outlook 2000 include

- **Rivest's Cipher v2 (RC2).**   RC2 is a secret-key block encryption algorithm developed by Ron Rivest at RSA Security that uses 64-bit input and output blocks. The key size can be varied up to 128 bits in length with most implementations using 40-bit or 128-bit length keys. RC2 is optimized for speed and encrypts messages faster than DES or 3DES on slower computers.

- **Data Encryption Standard (DES).** DES is the most widely used encryption algorithm in the world. DES takes 64-bit blocks of plaintext and applies a 56-bit key to each block of plaintext. This key is the recipient's public key. The encrypted package is decrypted using the recipient's private key.

- **Triple DES (3DES).** 3DES increases the strength of DES by using an encrypt-decrypt-encrypt process that uses three keys. The 64–bit plaintext message block is first encrypted with the first key. Then the encrypted result is decrypted using a second key. Finally, the result of the decryption process is encrypted using a third key. The formula to arrive at the encrypted packet is $E_{k3}[D_{k2}[E_{k1}[Plaintext]]]$ where E_{k3}, E_{k2}, and E_{k1} are the three separate encryption keys. The resulting encryption strength is 168 bits (3×56-bits).

Important Use of RC2 (128 bit) and 3DES require the Windows 2000 High Encryption Pack to be installed. The installation of the Windows 2000 High Encryption Pack is subject to your country's import and export laws. The United States allows the export of high encryption to nonembargoed nations. For more information, see *www.microsoft.com/exporting/*.

Select the e-mail encryption algorithm that meets your organization's security needs. The encryption algorithm you select must abide by all the laws on the export and import of strong encryption products that your organization uses.

Determining Protocol Choices for E-Mail Encryption

As with digitally signing messages, you have to choose between S/MIME and PGP for your encryption protocol. The decision is based on the e-mail applications implemented in your organization. You can't mix encryption protocols for e-mail. If you use S/MIME to encrypt the message, you have to use S/MIME to decrypt it.

Making the Decision

Include the following considerations in your security plan when deploying e-mail encryption:

- Determine all approved e-mail applications that are in use. The decision on whether to use S/MIME or PGP is determined by the security protocols supported by your primary e-mail system. You may not be able to support all e-mail applications deployed within an organization.

- Determine who can use secure e-mail. If you don't have a private/public key pair for e-mail encryption, you can't receive encrypted e-mail. Your organization must draft a set of criteria that, if met, qualifies an individual to acquire a private/public key pair for encrypting e-mail.

- Determine where the private/public keys will be acquired. You must choose between implementing your own internal CA for certificate distribution or purchasing certificates from a public CA such as Verisign or Thawte. If you choose your own CA, remember that the certificates may not be trusted by other organizations. If you choose a public CA, costs are associated with each certificate acquired from the CA.

- Establish guidelines for the distribution of public keys to recipients outside the organization. Recipients outside the organization won't have access to your Exchange or Windows 2000 directory.

- Establish an external public point for CRLs if using an internal CA. External e-mail recipients need to verify the revocation status of any encrypted messages. Ensure that the CRL is available to the outside world by publishing the CRL to an externally available service, such as your external Web server.

Note   For more information on designing CRL publication points, see Chapter 10, "Planning a Public Key Infrastructure."

- Train users on when to encrypt messages. You should set guidelines outlining the types of e-mail that should be encrypted when sent on the network. Guidelines reduce the risk of critical data being sent in an unencrypted format.

Note   While you could simply implement a policy that all e-mail messages be encrypted when sent, this isn't necessary in most cases and necessitates more processing at both the client and the recipient.

Applying the Decision

Fabrikam will require encryption of e-mail sent to the Defense Department and between project members on the Sonar System project. The same infrastructure that's required for digitally signing e-mail messages works for encrypting e-mail messages.

Because the encryption requirements are for e-mail messages sent to other organizations, it's recommended that you acquire the Mail certificates either from a public CA, such as Verisign or RSA, or ensure that the CAs that issue the certificates to the mail users have their CRLs available on the Internet for certificate revocation checking.

The users involved in the two projects should be trained in how to encrypt messages when the messages are sent to recipients in other companies. The process may require that a digitally signed message is first sent between the two users who require encrypted mail. If the message is digitally signed, it contains the certificate and public key that's used to encrypt messages. Remember that the public key of the recipient is used to encrypt messages sent to that recipient.

Planning Application-Level Encryption with SSL/TLS

Applications other than e-mail, such as Web pages containing sensitive data, also require encryption of data when it's transmitted. For example, Windows 2000 supports two forms of application-level encryption: SSL and Transport Layer Security (TLS).

- **SSL.** Provides encryption services to several applications by using public and private keys to encrypt data transmitted between a server and a client. While most commonly associated with Web browsers, SSL is also used to provide encryption services to Lightweight Directory Access Protocol (LDAP) queries, Network News Transfer Protocol (NNTP) authentication and news group transfers, Post Office Protocol v3 (POP3) authentication and e-mail retrieval encryption, and Internet Message Access Protocol v4 (IMAP4) authentication and e-mail retrieval encryption. As with secured Web browsing, the applications must support the use of SSL encryption.

Configuring an Application to Support SSL Encryption

Applications must include options to take advantage of SSL or TLS protection. For example, Microsoft Outlook Express supports the use of SSL encryption for POP3 by providing a check box to enable SSL encryption of POP3 credentials, as shown in Figure 11.9.

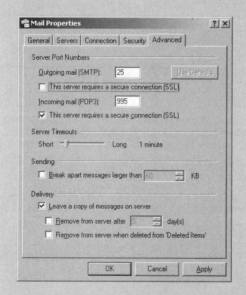

Figure 11.9   Enabling POP3 SSL protection in Outlook Express

If the application isn't enabled to recognize SSL encryption, you can't configure the application to do so. To use SSL, the application must be programmed to support SSL.

- **TLS.** TLS is very similar to SSL in that it provides communications privacy, authentication, and message integrity by using a combination of public key and symmetric encryption. TLS uses different encryption algorithms than SSL. TLS is an IETF draft standard. Windows 2000 uses TLS to encrypt smart card authentication information transmitted when using Extended Authentication Protocol (EAP).

Note   TLS also supports the option of reverting to SSL support if needed. TLS may replace SSL in the future.

Both SSL and TLS are implemented between the TCP and application layers, as illustrated in Figure 11.10.

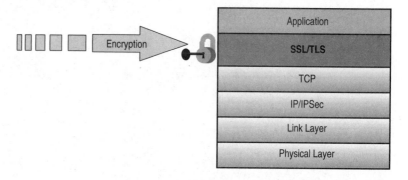

Figure 11.10   SSL and TLS encrypting data between the transport and application layers

When an application is SSL-enabled, the application listens for client connections on a different port than the usual port used by the application. Table 11.4 shows the ports used by protocols when SSL is implemented at the server.

Table 11.4   Standard and SSL Ports

Protocol	Standard Port	SSL Port
Hypertext Transfer Protocol (HTTP)	80	443
Internet Message Access Protocol v4 (IMAP4)	143	993
Lightweight Directory Access Protocol (LDAP)	389	636
Network News Transfer Protocol (NNTP)	119	563
Post Office Protocol v3 (POP3)	110	995
Simple Mail Transfer Protocol (SMTP)	25	465

Deploying SSL and TLS

Both SSL and TLS require the server hosting the application that uses SSL or TLS to acquire a private/public key pair for encrypting the data. Figure 11.11 shows the encryption process for Web applications.

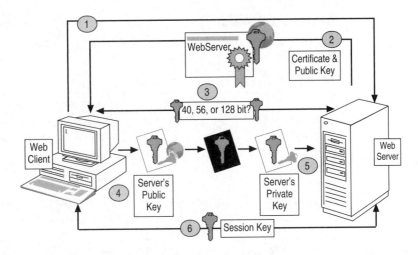

Figure 11.11   SSL Encryption for Web-based transactions

1. The Web client attempts to connect to the Web server by using SSL. No additional software is required for the client. The client simply changes the protocol in the URL from http: to https:.

2. The Web server returns the Web server's certificate and public key to the Web client. The Web client requires the public key to encrypt any transmissions sent to the Web server. The certificate is included so that the Web client can access the public key and determine CRL locations if revocation checking is enabled on the Web client computer.

3. The Web client and Web server enter into a negotiation to determine encryption levels. The Web server and Web client negotiate to determine if 40-bit, 56-bit, or 128-bit encryption will be used for the session key.

4. The Web client generates a session key and encrypts the session key with the Web server's public key. The session key is set to be the length negotiated between the Web client and the Web server. Once the session key is encrypted, the encrypted session key is transmitted to the Web server.

5. The Web server decrypts the session key using the Web server's private key. Only the Web server has access to this private key, ensuring that the connection attempt isn't intercepted by an attacker.

6. The session key is used to encrypt all further data exchanged between the Web client and the Web server.

The benefit of using application-level security is that the encryption requires no additional work by the user. The only noticeable change is that the user must use https: in the URL rather than http:.

Note   Only applications that are programmed to use SSL and TLS can implement the two forms of encryption. Only applications that recognize SSL and TLS can make the appropriate calls to programming interfaces to encrypt and decrypt data.

Making the Decision

Use the decision matrix shown in Table 11.5 to design application-level encryption of data when using SSL or TLS.

Table 11.5   Designing SSL and TLS Encryption

To	Include the Following in Your Design
Enable secure Web communications	▪ Acquire a Web server certificate from a trusted CA. The CA can either be a private CA or a public CA, depending on the application.
Enable secure Web communications for a public Web site	▪ Acquire a Web server certificate from a public CA such as Verisign or RSA. The use of a public CA certificate increases consumer confidence in your Web site.
Enable secure communications for a private Web site	▪ Acquire a Web server certificate from a private CA within your organization's PKI. This action reduces the costs of the Web site deployment.
Secure authentication to your Web site and support any browser	▪ Configure the Web server to use basic authentication and require SSL encryption for access. The SSL encryption encrypts the plaintext authentication used by basic authentication. ▪ In a Microsoft Internet Explorer deployment, consider deploying Windows Integrated Authentication, which isn't supported by other browsers. ▪ Deploy client certificates and configure the Web server to use certificate-based authentication.
Define the level of encryption to use for a Web site	▪ Determine the type of information that will be available at the Web site. ▪ Determine how export and import laws affect the use of strong encryption. Always use the strongest level of encryption allowed by law to ensure protection of the data.
To enable strong encryption at a Windows 2000 Web server	▪ Acquire a server certificate for the Web server to enable SSL communications. ▪ Configure the Web server to require 128-bit encryption to allow connections.
To enable strong encryption at a Windows client	▪ For Windows 2000 clients, install the Windows 2000 High Encryption Pack to enable 128-bit encryption at the Windows 2000–based computer. ▪ For older versions of Windows clients, install the strong encryption patch for the version of Internet Explorer installed on the computer. ▪ For other companies' browsers (such as Netscape), download the strong encryption patch for the browser.
Minimize reduction in performance due to encryption of transmitted data	▪ Enable SSL only for the Web pages that require encryption. To minimize excessive CPU utilization, reduce the amount of Web content being encrypted. In other words, don't automatically encrypt the entire Web site. ▪ Minimize the amount of graphics contained in secured Web pages. Typically, you don't need to encrypt graphics embedded in HTML pages.

Applying the Decision

You must protect three separate Web sites with SSL encryption to ensure that information entered into or downloaded from Web pages isn't compromised during transmission. These Web sites include the Defense Department Web site, the time input Web site for the Sonar System project, and a secured Web site for the Sonar System project server.

Defense Department Bidding Web Site

The first Web site that uses SSL encryption is the Defense Department bidding Web site. Although the Defense Department administers this Web site, the network administrators must ensure that any users who connect to the Web site from Fabrikam are enabled for strong encryption. If the computer used to connect to the Defense Department is a Windows 2000–based computer, the Windows 2000 High Encryption Pack must be applied to enable 128-bit encryption for the browser. If the computer runs Windows 95, Windows 98, or Windows NT 4.0, the 128-bit encryption patch for the current version of its browser must be installed to enable strong encryption.

Sonar Project Time Sheet Web Site

The Sonar System project members who work at A. Datum Corporation must enter the number of hours they work into a Web-based time recording system hosted in the Fabrikam extranet.

The Web server hosting the Time Sheet application must have a Web server certificate. Because only members from a partner organization are connecting to the Web site, an internal CA can issue the Web server certificate. If an internal CA is used, the CRL for the CA and any CAs that issued certificates in the certificate chain must be made available at a public location as indicated in the issued certificate. This action ensures that if the client Web browser is configured to perform certificate revocation checking, the checking won't cause the certificate to fail the revocation check.

You could configure the Web server to require 128-bit encryption, but you don't have to.

The Sonar System Project Server

The Sonar System project server at the San Francisco office requires that all communication with the server is protected from interception.

Making the data accessible by using a Web server allows the data to be accessed by a mix of Windows 95, Windows 98, Windows NT 4.0, and Windows 2000 clients. Web pages containing links for key files or directory browsing must be enabled at the Web server to allow access to the data.

The project server requires the acquisition of a Web server certificate. Because the server is required only for internal project use and the partners at A. Datum Corporation won't require access, you can use an internal CA to acquire the necessary Web server certificate to enable SSL encryption. The client computers may require additional configuration if the Web server is configured to require 128-bit encryption.

Lesson Summary

The encryption of data at the application layer allows data to be protected from inspection as it's transmitted across the network. Application-layer security benefits the network administrator because little configuration of the client computers is needed to deploy the application-layer security.

Activity: Determining Key Usage

This activity requires you to determine which keys are used to secure e-mail and Web transactions for the purposes of digitally signing and encrypting data transmissions.

Scenario

Eva Corets and Don Hall work for competing movie studios. They want to send encrypted and digitally signed messages to each other to prevent their e-mail administrators from reading the content of the e-mail messages. They are currently codeveloping a screenplay and want to ensure its authenticity, integrity, and protection as it's sent between their computers.

Questions

Here are some questions about this scenario. The answers to these questions are located in the appendix.

1. If Eva wants to digitally sign a message she is sending to Don, which key is used to encrypt the message digest that protects the message?

   a. Eva's private key

   b. Eva's public key

   c. Don's private key

   d. Don's public key

2. When Don receives Eva's digitally signed message, which key is used to decrypt the message digest that protects the message?

   a. Eva's private key

   b. Eva's public key

   c. Don's private key

   d. Don's public key

3. If Don wants to encrypt a message he is sending to Eva, which key is used to encrypt the contents of the e-mail message?

   a. Eva's private key

   b. Eva's public key

   c. Don's private key

   d. Don's public key

4. When Eva receives Don's encrypted e-mail message, which key does Eva use to decrypt the encrypted e-mail message?

   a. Eva's private key

   b. Eva's public key

   c. Don's private key

   d. Don's public key

5. Eva wants to both digitally sign and encrypt an e-mail message that she is sending to Don. Which two keys are used to digitally sign and encrypt the e-mail message?

   a. Eva's private key

   b. Eva's public key

   c. Don's private key

   d. Don's public key

6. When Don receives the digitally signed and encrypted e-mail message from Eva, which two keys does Don use to decrypt the message digest and the encrypted message from Eva?

   a. Eva's private key

   b. Eva's public key

   c. Don's private key

   d. Don's public key

Lab 11-1: Providing Application-Layer Security for Contoso Ltd.

Lab Objectives

This lab prepares you to plan the design application-layer security by meeting the following objectives:

- Design an SMB signing solution
- Design a digital signature solution for e-mail security
- Design an encryption solution for e-mail security
- Design SSL security for applications

About This Lab

This lab looks at the planning that Contoso Ltd. must do to ensure that security is deployed at the application layer to meet the organization's security needs. You need to make decisions on the configuration and deployment of the technologies that are required to meet the company's objectives.

Before You Begin

Make sure that you've completed reading the chapter material before starting the lab. Pay close attention to the sections where the design decisions were applied throughout the chapter for information on building your administrative structure.

Scenario: Contoso Ltd.

Contoso Ltd., an international magazine sales company, wants to use application-layer security in several future endeavors. Application-layer security is being considered to restrict data transmissions to members within a project team, protect e-mail messages, and secure a subscription and back issue ordering Web site.

Planning a New Publication

Contoso is currently in the research stage for a new magazine that will focus on the entertainment industry in North America. The Seattle office will handle all the work on the publication.

The magazine's project team consists of 20 employees led by the executive editor at the Seattle office. Of the 20 employees, 18 currently have Windows 2000 Professional desktops or laptop computers. The two summer interns are using older desktop computers running Windows 95.

Management has decided that only members of the project team should be able to connect to the project server named PHOENIX. Access to the PHOENIX server must be protected so that only members of the project team can connect to it. On a previous project, a former employee renamed his desktop computer to match the name of another server and gained access to documents that project members saved to their computers. This occurrence must be prevented in the new magazine project.

Taking Over a Competing Publisher

Contoso has been approached about buying a small U.S. publisher named Lakes & Sons. Both companies have agreed to the takeover, and the lawyers are drafting the final agreement.

Because information about the takeover has been reported in the local press, management is concerned that there is an internal leak. The article reported the impending takeover and discussed the possibility that Lakes & Sons would drop several titles after the takeover was completed.

Management can't determine if a staff member leaked the information or whether someone outside the organization intercepted an e-mail message regarding the takeover. Management wants to ensure that all future e-mails sent to the lawyers are protected against modification and inspection as the e-mail messages cross the Internet.

Establishing an E-Business

Contoso wants to offer subscription services and back-issue ordering services for all their magazine titles. Contoso sees two separate types of clients who will connect to their external web site (*www.contoso.tld*).

- **Frequent visitors.** Frequent visitors will establish a relationship with Contoso by joining the Contoso Club, which involves acquiring a digital certificate for authentication with the Contoso Web site. The digital certificate allows the customer to order subscriptions and back issues without providing any additional information. All required information will be provided during the certificate request process. The customers will be allowed to update their profile information (address, credit card, phone number) by accessing a profile Web page.

- **One-time visitors.** Through market research, Contoso has learned that some infrequent visitors to the Web site also want to purchase back issues of Contoso magazines. Contoso will make one-time purchases possible by having the customer input all required information, such as mailing address and credit card, and make the order directly over the Internet.

The Web site must be protected so that all visitors can be sure that any information entered into the site will be kept confidential. When a visitor accesses the Web site and wants to order a subscription or purchase a back issue, the visitor is offered the choice of logging on with the Contoso Club membership by using a digital certificate or accessing a secured Web page where the transaction can be completed by using a Web form.

Contoso wants to reduce the time it takes to revoke a customer's certificate. In the past year the company processed more than $10,000 worth of fraudulent sales that should have been rejected but weren't because certificate revocation was too slow.

Exercise 1: Planning SMB Signing for Contoso Ltd.

This exercise looks at the security design required to implement SMB signing to meet the requirements defined by Contoso for the new magazine project. The answers to these questions can be found in the appendix.

1. What application-layer security solution can you use to ensure that both the client and the server are mutually authenticated?

2. Are there any barriers that prevent the implementation of SMB signing to protect communications with the PHOENIX server?

3. With the current network configuration, how must SMB signing be configured for the PHOENIX server?

4. How should the Windows 2000–based computers be configured to allow access to the PHOENIX server yet not prevent access to other servers on the network?

5. What would be the best way to deploy the computer accounts in Active Directory to meet the security requirements for SMB signing?

6. If the Windows 95 computers were upgraded to Windows 98, how would this affect your design?

7. In addition to SMB signing, what other security should you consider at the PHOENIX server to restrict access to the project data?

Exercise 2: Designing Secure E-Mail for Contoso

This exercise looks at the security design required to implement secure e-mail for Contoso. The answers to these questions can be found in the appendix.

1. If e-mail sent to the lawyers' office is to be secured, what must you determine first to ensure that secure e-mail can be exchanged?

2. If the CA hierarchy that Contoso uses to issue certificates is self-hosted, what issues must you consider in the secure e-mail project?

3. If the certificates issued to Contoso employees are from an internal CA, what methods can be used to distribute the public keys associated with the certificates to the lawyers?

4. If the certificates issued to the lawyers are from a public CA, what method can be used to distribute the public keys associated with the certificates to the lawyers?

5. How will public keys be obtained for secure e-mail messages exchanged between employees of Contoso?

6. How should e-mail from Contoso to the lawyers be sent to meet security objectives?

Exercise 3: Planning a Secure Web Site

This exercise looks at the security design required for the subscription and back-issue pages on Contoso's Web site. The answers to these questions can be found in the appendix.

1. Do you need to apply SSL encryption to the entire Contoso Web site?

2. What can you do at the Contoso Web site to ensure that only strong encryption is used to secure the SSL-protected Web forms?

3. Where should you acquire the Web server certificate for the Contoso Web site?

4. For customers who want to authenticate by using digital certificates, from where should the certificate be acquired?

5. What must you include in the infrastructure design to support the customer certificates?

Review

Answering the following questions will reinforce key information presented in this chapter. If you are unable to answer a question, review the appropriate lesson and then try the question again. Answers to the questions can be found in the appendix.

1. You're the mayor of a small town and you would like to allow e-mail ballots for the upcoming general election. What security issues do you face in implementing a solution? What type of e-mail security will be required?

2. Your organization wants to implement mutual authentication for a sensitive project. The data is stored on a server named PROJECT1 and a mix of Windows 98, Windows NT 4.0, and Windows 2000 clients will connect to the share. How must you configure the PROJECT1 server to allow SMB signing to take place?

3. Your organization wants to implement mutual authentication for a sensitive project. The data is stored on a server named PROJECT1 and a mix of Windows 95, Windows NT 4.0, and Windows 2000 clients will connect to the share. How must you configure the PROJECT1 server to allow SMB signing to take place?

4. You're attempting to exchange encrypted e-mail messages with a business associate and the process isn't working. You've successfully exchanged public keys by exporting the public keys and including the export files as attachments. The certificates are from Verisign and haven't been revoked. What could be your problem?

5. You're attempting to exchange encrypted e-mail messages with a business associate and the process isn't working. You've successfully exchanged public keys by exporting the public keys and including the export files as attachments. Your certificate was issued from an internal CA and your business associate's was acquired from RSA. You're able to send encrypted e-mail to the business associate, but the business associate is unable to send encrypted e-mail to you. In addition, your business associate is unable to verify any digitally signed messages that you send. What could be the problem with your design?

6. The gas company has created a Web site for customers to pay their bills. The support desk is receiving calls from clients who say that they can't connect with their browsers. The error message states that their browsers don't support strong encryption. What must be done if the browsers are a mix of Windows 98, Windows NT 4.0, and Windows 2000 clients?

C H A P T E R   1 2

Securing Data with Internet Protocol Security (IPSec)

About This Chapter

In this chapter you will examine the design requirements for deploying Internet Protocol Security (IPSec) within a Microsoft Windows 2000 network. Specifically, you will look at the design decisions involved with

- Designing IPSec policies
- Planning IPSec deployment

Before You Begin

To complete this chapter, you must read the chapter scenario. This scenario is used throughout the chapter to apply the design decisions discussed in each lesson.

Chapter Scenario: Fabrikam, Inc.

Fabrikam, a defense contractor with offices located across the United States, is investigating the use of IPSec to improve security on their local network and on the network link to their business partner, A. Datum Corporation.

The Network

Fabrikam's Wide Area Network (WAN) is linked with 1.544 megabit-per-second (Mbps) private network links. Each office is assigned a class B address space, but not all addresses at the office are currently in use, as shown in Figure 12.1.

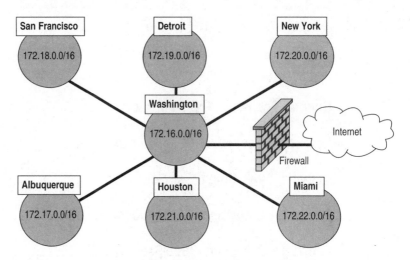

Figure 12.1   The Fabrikam WAN configuration

Fabrikam has deployed a firewall to protect the Washington office from attacks coming from the 45 Mbps link to the Internet. On the Internet, Fabrikam owns the 131.107.2.0/24 network range.

Connecting to A. Datum Corporation

Fabrikam is working with A. Datum Corporation to develop a new sonar system for the Department of Defense. Several Fabrikam employees are working at the A. Datum Corporation office in Chicago.

A. Datum Corporation wants to establish a secure WAN link between the two organization's networks using their existing Internet connections. Due to the sensitive nature of the projects, all data that's transmitted over the Internet must be encrypted to ensure that the data isn't compromised. Figure 12.2 shows the current network configuration for A. Datum Corporation and Fabrikam.

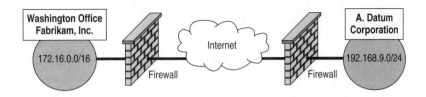

Figure 12.2   Connectivity between the Fabrikam and A. Datum Corporation offices

A. Datum Corporation and Fabrikam have had great difficulty configuring this WAN connection. Authentication has been failing between the two tunnel servers.

The Data Collection Package

Fabrikam is also involved in a project with the Department of Defense developing a new radar system. The radar's prototype is complete and they're testing it to determine if the prototype meets the Defense Department's design specifications. The testing is being performed at Fabrikam's Albuquerque office.

To test the design, Fabrikam has created a custom data collection application housed at the Washington office. The application's server portion is hosted on a Windows 2000 member server. The data collection software uses Transmission Control Protocol (TCP) and clients will connect to the application by connecting to port 5555 on the server. The server is located at IP address 172.16.100.123.

To collect and transmit test data, the radar prototype is connected to a Windows 2000–based laptop using a Universal Serial Bus (USB) connector. The client portion of the data collection software connects to the server at the Washington office to upload the latest data. The client uses a random port for the connection to the server. All data that's transmitted must be protected from impersonation and from inspection attacks. The data must also be protected from attacks, such as a source routing attack, that attempt to reroute the packets.

Fabrikam plans to test additional radar devices in the future. The testing will require multiple laptops configured to use IPSec to protect data streams to the server at the Washington office. All the laptops will be based at the Albuquerque office.

Lesson 1: Designing IPSec Policies

An understanding of the IPSec process will help you make the following IPSec policy design decisions:

- Decide which IPSec protocols to use.

- Decide whether to implement IPSec transport mode or IPSec tunnel mode.

- Design IPSec filters that identify which packets to protect with IPSec.

- Determine which actions will take place if the packets meet the IPSec filter criteria.

- Determine which encryption levels will be used if packets meet the IPSec filter criteria.

- Design how computers using IPSec protection authenticate each other.

After this lesson, you will be able to

- Design IPSec policies to protect data transmitted between Windows 2000–based computers

Estimated lesson time: 75 minutes

Before discussing the design of IPSec policies, let's examine how IPSec communications take place between two IPSec-enabled computers.

Describing IPSec Communications

IPSec implements encryption and authenticity at a lower level in the Transmission Control Protocol/Internet Protocol (TCP/IP) stack than application-layer protocols such as Secure Socket Layer (SSL) and Transport Layer Security (TLS). Because the protection process takes place lower in the TCP/IP stack, IPSec protection is transparent to applications. The applications require only a recognized port to be protected by IPSec. If the application uses random ports for all connections, it's almost impossible to define an IPSec filter that identifies the application's network data streams.

The application doesn't have to be IPSec-aware because the data transferred between the client and the server is normally transmitted in plaintext. The IPSec process encrypts the payload after it leaves the application at the client and then decrypts the payload before it reaches the application at the server.

For example, Telnet protocol transmits authentication and application data in plaintext. Figure 12.3 illustrates a scenario where both the client and server are configured to negotiate IPSec security whenever transmissions are sent using the Telnet protocol. At no point in this entire sequence of events is the Telnet protocol aware of the encryption process. The process is as follows:

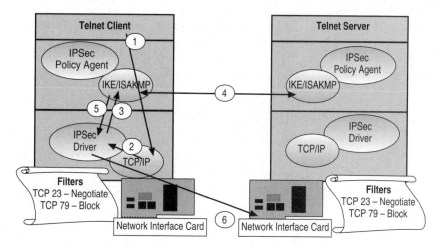

Figure 12.3   The IPSec process

1. The Telnet client sends a packet destined to the Telnet server. The packet is sent from a random source port at the client, but the data is always sent to TCP port 23 on the Telnet server.

2. The IPSec driver at the client computer intercepts the packet when it reaches the IP layer and compares the packet to the list of IPSec filters configured at the client. In this case, the filter matches TCP 23. This match initiates a negotiation between the client and the server that will establish a *security association* (SA) between the client and server. A security association defines the details of the IPSec session between the client and the server. The SA defines the IPSec protocol, encryption and integrity algorithms, and the authentication protocol for the connection.

3. The IPSec driver forwards the packet to the Internet Security Association and Key Management Protocol (ISAKMP) to negotiate a SA between the client and server. ISAKMP is used to determine the definition of the SA that's established between the client and the server.

4. The client and server proceed with the ISAKMP process using the Internet Key Exchange (IKE) protocol by connecting using User Datagram Protocol (UDP) 500. The ISAKMP process establishes the necessary SAs between the client and server. The SA includes the protocol and the encryption algorithms used to protect the data transmitted between the client and the server.

5. The results of the SA are returned to the IPSec driver so that the IPSec driver can perform all necessary tasks and make any security modifications to the data before it's transmitted from the client to the server.

6. The IPSec driver applies the required encryption or integrity algorithm or both to the data and then sends the data to the network interface card (NIC) for transmission to the client.

Note The process of encrypting and decrypting IPSec-protected packets can be processor intensive. To increase performance, consider purchasing IPSec-aware network cards (NICs) that will offload the IPSec encryption process from the computer's processor. Currently, IPSec-aware NICs are available from Intel and 3Com.

Planning IPSec Protocols

IPSec provides two protocols for protection of transmitted data, Authentication Headers (AH) and Encapsulating Security Payloads (ESP). In their simplest form, AH provides authentication and integrity services to transmitted data while ESP provides encryption services. Be aware that AH and ESP are separate protocols. You can use them individually or you can combine them to provide both integrity and inspection protection.

Assessing AH

AH provides authentication, integrity, and antireplay protection to transmitted data on the network. AH doesn't protect transmitted data from being read, but it does eliminate the possibility of the data being modified during transmission. Figure 12.4 shows the composition of an AH packet. It's important to know the fields of an AH packet to understand how the AH packet protects transmitted data.

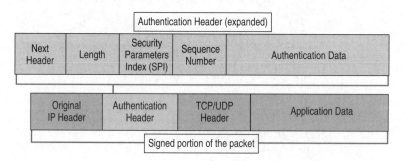

Figure 12.4 IPSec AH header fields

The fields in an AH packet include

- **Next Header.** This field indicates the protocol ID for the header that follows the AH header. For example, if the encrypted data is transmitted using TCP, the next header value would be 6, the protocol ID for TCP.

Note You can find a partial list of protocol IDs in the *systemroot*\system32 \drivers\etc\protocol configuration file, where *systemroot* is the folder where Windows 2000 is locally installed on your computer.

- **Length.** This field contains the total length of the Authentication Header.

- **Security Parameters Index (SPI).** This field identifies the security association that was negotiated in the ISAKMP protocol exchange between the source computer and the destination computer.

- **Sequence Number.** This field protects the AH-protected packet from antireplay attacks. For each packet issued for a specific SA, the sequence number is incremented by one to ensure that each packet is assigned a unique sequence number. The recipient computer verifies each packet to ensure that a sequence number hasn't been reused. The sequence number prevents an attacker from capturing packets, modifying them, and then retransmitting the packets later.

- **Authentication Data.** This field contains the *hash* created against the signed portion of the AH packet. The hash is the result of the integrity algorithm applied to the AH packet to determine if the packet has been modified. The recipient performs the same integrity algorithm and compares the result of the hash algorithm with the result stored within the authentication data field to ensure that the signed portion of the AH packet hasn't been altered in transit.

Deploying AH

AH packets are used to authenticate computers involved in data transmissions and to provide integrity to the transmitted packets so an attacker can't modify or replay the transmitted data.

Use AH when communications must be restricted to specific computers in a workgroup or project. AH ensures that mutual authentication takes place between the participating computers so that only authenticated computers can participate in data communications.

The advantage of AH is that it allows mutual authentication capabilities to protocols that don't support mutual authentication. If the authentication process is moved lower in the network protocol stack, all applications can support IPSec.

Important AH is supported only by Windows 2000 clients in a Microsoft networking environment. If you want to deploy mutual authentication in a mixed network containing Windows 98, Windows NT 4.0, and Windows 2000–based clients, consider using SMB signing as an alternative.

Assessing Encapsulating Security Payloads (ESP)

ESP packets are used to provide encryption services to transmitted data. In addition, ESP provides authentication, integrity, and antireplay services.

Note When designing an IPSec solution, you can combine AH and ESP protocols in a single IPSec SA. While both AH and ESP provide integrity protection to transmitted data, AH protects the entire packet from modification while ESP protects only the TCP/UDP header and the data payload from inspection.

The encryption provided by ESP encrypts the TCP or UDP header and the application data included within an IP packet. The encryption normally doesn't include the original IP header unless IPSec tunnel mode is used (discussed in the section "Planning IPSec Modes," later in this chapter).

As with the composition of an AH header, knowing the composition of an ESP packet helps you understand how ESP protects the contents of a transmitted data packet. An ESP packet contains an ESP header, an ESP trailer, and an ESP authentication trailer, as shown in Figure 12.5.

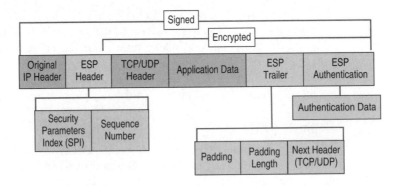

Figure 12.5 IPSec ESP fields

The ESP header has two fields that are inserted between the original IP header and the TCP or UDP header from the original packet:

- **Security Parameters Index (SPI).** This field identifies the SA that was negotiated between the source computer and the destination computer for IPSec communication. It's the combination of the SPI, the IPSec protocol (AH or ESP), and the source and destination IP addresses that identifies the SA used for the IPSec transmission within the ESP packet.

- **Sequence Number.** This field protects the SA from replay attacks. This field is increased incrementally to ensure that packets are never received more than once. If a packet is received with a previous sequence number, the packet is dropped.

The ESP trailer is inserted after the application data from the original packet and includes the following fields:

- **Padding.** This field is a variable length between 0 and 255 bytes that brings the length of the application data and ESP trailer to a length divisible by 32 bits so that they match the required size for the cipher algorithm.

- **Padding Length.** This field indicates the length of the padding field. After the packet is decrypted, this field is used to determine the length of the padding field.

- **Next Header.** This field identifies the protocol used for the transmission of the data, such as TCP or UDP.

Following the ESP trailer, the ESP protocol adds an ESP authentication trailer to the end of the packet. The ESP authentication trailer contains a single field:

- **Authentication Data.** This field contains the Integrity Check Value (ICV) and a message authentication code. The two components function as a digital signature that verifies the originating host that sent the message and ensures that the packet wasn't modified in transit. The ICV uses the defined integrity algorithm to digitally sign the packet. The integrity algorithm is applied to the ESP header, the TCP/UDP header, the application data, and the ESP trailer.

Important   The ICV isn't applied to any mutable fields in the ESP header, TCP/UDP header, application data, or ESP trailer. A mutable field is any field that changes value during transmission. For example, the value of the Time To Live (TTL) field decreases by one for every router that it crosses. If this field were included in the ICV, the ICV would be invalidated every time an ESP packet crossed a router.

ESP provides integrity protection by signing the ESP header, the TCP/UDP header, the application data, and the ESP trailer. ESP also provides inspection protection by encrypting the TCP/UDP header, the application data, and the ESP trailer.

Deploying ESP

ESP provides encryption services for transmitted data. ESP is necessary when the application doesn't recognize application-layer security, such as SSL. Because the IPSec encryption and decryption process takes place at the IP/IPSec layer, the application doesn't have to support IPSec. In fact, the application is unaware that IPSec protection is taking place, as illustrated in Figure 12.6.

Only operating systems and network devices that support IPSec can apply ESP encryption. If an operating system or network device doesn't support IPSec, either the IPSec SA must allow plaintext or you must implement an alternative encryption process.

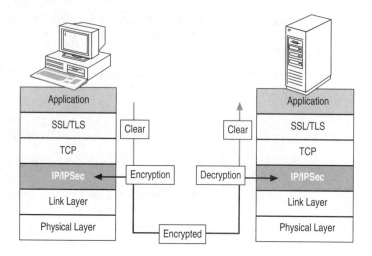

Figure 12.6   IPSec encryption not evident in applications

In addition to encryption support, ESP provides digital signing of the transmitted data. The only difference between AH and ESP is the portion of the data packet that's protected against modification. While AH protects the entire packet, ESP signing doesn't include protection for the IP header used to route the packet through the network. If you want to encrypt the data transmissions and ensure that all fields in the packet are protected, you must configure the SA to implement both IPSec AH and ESP protocols.

Note   To allow IPSec traffic to pass through a firewall, you must allow packets using UDP 500 and a protocol identifier (ID) of 51 for AH or a protocol ID of 50 for ESP to pass through the firewall. In addition, the firewall must not be performing Network Address Translation (NAT). IPSec packets can't pass through a NAT because the fields modified by the NAT process are protected by IPSec and can't be modified without invalidating the packet.

Making the Decision

The decision to use AH, ESP, or a combination of AH and ESP in your security design depends on the requirements for IPSec protection. Include AH in your IPSec design to meet the following security objectives:

- **To protect the entire packets against modification.** AH digitally signs the entire packet, including the original IP header, to ensure that the packet isn't modified during transmission. Use AH to sign the packet when your business requirements require protection of the entire packet to prevent attacks that attempt to modify the IP header and reroute packets on the network.

- **To provide mutual authentication of both client and server.** IPSec using AH requires that both hosts involved in the data transmission authenticate with each other. Authentication takes place between the hosts and not between the users working at the hosts.

- **To limit communications to authorized computers for a project.** AH requires mutual authentication of the hosts involved in a data transmission. If the hosts can't negotiate a SA, communications won't take place. You can use AH to ensure that only authorized hosts can communicate with each other.

Use ESP in your IPSec security design to meet the following security objectives:

- **To protect the application payload from being observed during transmission.** ESP packets encrypt the original data payload to ensure that the packet's contents aren't visible when transmitted across the network.

- **To protect the TCP/UDP header and application data from modification during transmission.** ESP can apply a digital signature to the data packet, but it doesn't protect the entire packet from modification. Only the ESP header, the TCP/UDP header, the application data, and the ESP trailer are protected from modification.

Warning IPSec using ESP may lead to a firewall losing the ability to inspect data as it's transmitted through the firewall. To pass ESP-protected traffic, you must configure a firewall to allow connections to UDP port 500 and protocol ID 50. Unfortunately, this allows all ESP-protected data to pass. There's no way to determine which protocol is encrypted within the packet. The inability to determine which protocols are encrypted can lead to unauthorized traffic passing through the firewall if both hosts can establish an IPSec connection.

Finally, apply both AH and ESP when you require encryption of transmitted data and protection of the entire packet against modification. To ensure total protection of transmitted data, you can negotiate a SA that requires both AH and ESP.

Applying the Decision

Fabrikam must design IPSec protocols for two distinct IPSec connections: the data collection software and the network link to A. Datum Corporation.

For the data collection software, the security specifications include requirements for protecting the data from inspection, proving the authenticity of the sender, and ensuring that data packets aren't modified during transmission. To meet these requirements, you must apply both AH and ESP protection to each packet. While ESP provides the ability to sign the data portion of a packet, it doesn't protect the entire packet against modification. Only AH protects the entire packet in this manner. Likewise, you must configure ESP to allow the data payload to be encrypted as it's transmitted from the client to the server.

For the network link between A. Datum Corporation, the security requirements specify only protection from inspection. Therefore, you only need to use ESP to encrypt all data transmitted over the Internet between the two networks.

Planning IPSec Modes

You can configure IPSec to use one of two modes: transport mode or tunnel mode. In some cases you require IPSec protection from the issuing client all the way to the destination server, as illustrated in Figure 12.7. This mode is referred to as IPSec transport mode.

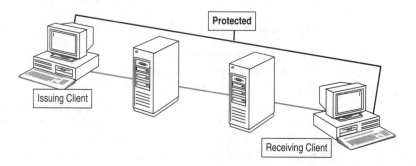

Figure 12.7   IPSec transport mode providing end-to-end protection

You protect the data sent between the two hosts by using AH, ESP, or both. The transmitted data is protected for the entire path between the two hosts.

In IPSec tunnel mode, shown in Figure 12.8, data is protected only between the two defined tunnel points or gateways. IPSec tunnel mode provides what is known as gateway-to-gateway protection of transmitted data.

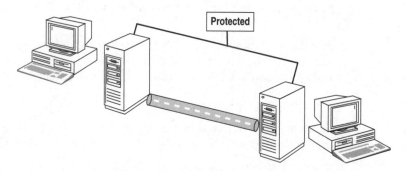

Figure 12.8   IPSec tunnel mode providing gateway-to-gateway protection

When the data is transmitted between the client and the server, it's sent in an unprotected state until it reaches the initial gateway. Then the protection specified in the SA, AH, or ESP is applied to the packets as they're transmitted to the destination network. The decryption and verification process takes place at the receiving gateway. Finally, the data is transmitted in plaintext to the destination host.

You commonly use tunnel mode when packets must traverse a public or unsecured network between two hosts. Tunnel mode is appropriate when it's unnecessary to protect the data at the local networks.

How Does Network Address Translation (NAT) Affect IPSec Configuration?

IPSec protected data can't pass through a firewall or perimeter server that performs NAT. This is because of the NAT process and its effect on fields protected by the AH and ESP protocols.

When a packet passes through a NAT service, the original source IP address is translated into a common IP address and the source port is translated to the actual port established by the server performing the translation, as illustrated in Figure 12.9.

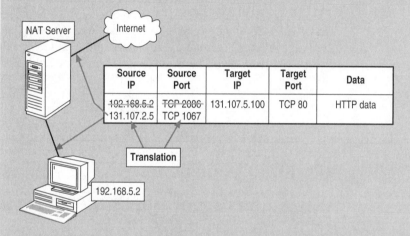

Source IP	Source Port	Target IP	Target Port	Data
~~192.168.5.2~~ 131.107.2.5	~~TCP 2086~~ TCP 1067	131.107.5.100	TCP 80	HTTP data

Figure 12.9   The NAT process

The client sends a packet with the source address of the client computer (192.168.5.2) and the source port used at the client computer (TCP port 2086). When the packet passes through the NAT service, the source IP address and port are translated to 131.107.2.5 port TCP 1067.

If the packets are protected with IPSec, the TCP/UDP header field is always protected by AH and ESP packets. The port information that's translated can't be changed without invalidating the packet in the case of AH-protected data and can't be read when implementing ESP-protected data.

You can identify NAT-protected networks by recognizing the use of private network addressing as defined in Request for Comment (RFC) 1918. In RFC 1918 the following IP address ranges have been reserved for private network usage and aren't in use on the Internet:

- 10.0.0.0 – 10.255.255.255
- 172.16.0.0 – 172.31.255.255
- 192.168.0.0 – 192.168.255.255

(continued)

If you see these addresses in use on a private network, some form of NAT is probably being used to protect the data that is transmitted to the Internet. NAT only takes place when a private network address space is connected to a public network address space. NAT isn't performed if the two network segments attached to the NAT server or firewall both use private network addressing.

Examining Tunnel Mode Packets

IPSec tunnel mode packets differ from transport mode packets in that a new IP header is added to the packet as it's transmitted between gateways. In Figure 12.10, the AH tunnel mode packet inserts the AH between the new IP header and the original IP header. There's no difference in the fields included in the Authentication Header.

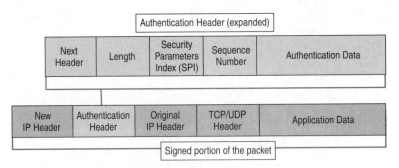

Figure 12.10   AH tunnel mode packet fields

Likewise, an ESP tunnel mode packet, shown in Figure 12.11, varies from an ESP transport mode packet in the location of the ESP header. As with the AH tunnel mode packet, the ESP header is placed between the new IP header and the old IP header.

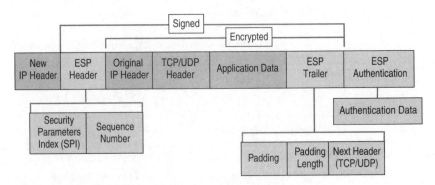

Figure 12.11   ESP tunnel mode packet fields

The fields included in the ESP header don't vary between transport mode and tunnel mode. The only difference is the location of the ESP header in the tunnel mode packet and the protection of the original IP header information.

Making the Decision

Table 12.1 shows the design decisions you need to make when choosing between IPSec transport mode and IPSec tunnel mode.

Table 12.1 Determining When to Use IPSec Transport Mode or Tunnel Mode

Use	Under These Circumstances
IPSec transport mode	■ Communications are taking place within a private network or on a single LAN segment where inspection of transmitted data must be prevented. ■ NAT isn't being performed on the packets as they're transmitted from the source computer to the destination computer. ■ Data must be encrypted over the entire path from the source computer to the destination computer. ■ The connection will be between only two computers.
IPSec tunnel mode	■ Data must be protected when being transmitted over a public portion of the network. There's no risk of data inspection in the private segments of the network. ■ Encryption can only take place between perimeter servers to avoid passing through a firewall or perimeter server implementing NAT.

Applying the Decision

Fabrikam requires the use of IPSec transport mode for the data collection software and IPSec tunnel mode for the network link between the Fabrikam and A. Datum Corporation.

For the data collection application, all data is being transmitted between the Windows 2000–based laptops and the server at the Washington office. The data must be encrypted as it passes across the network to ensure that no one can read it. The data must be signed to prove its authenticity.

Make sure that an IPSec tunnel can be established for the connection to the A. Datum Corporation office. Based on the IP addressing information provided in the scenario, the firewalls at the two organizations are performing NAT. Note that the IP address ranges used at each site are private network address ranges defined in RFC 1918.

Because NAT is being performed, IPSec tunnel mode is unable to pass through the firewall. To allow IPSec tunnel mode to connect the two networks, deploy a separate dual-homed server at each network to allow you to establish an IPSec tunnel that bypasses the firewall, as shown in Figure 12.12.

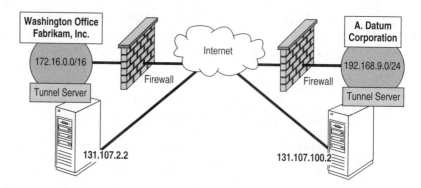

Figure 12.12   Implementing IPSec tunnel mode between the two organizations

To ensure that only IPSec tunnel mode packets are received at the tunnel servers, configure the IPSec filters to encrypt all traffic that is transferred between the 172.16.0.0/16 and the 192.168.9.0/24 networks using the two tunnel servers as tunnel endpoints.

Designing IPSec Filters

To identify the protocols that are to be protected with AH or ESP protocols, you must define IPSec filters that identify known characteristics of the protocols. For example, Figure 12.13 shows the IPSec filter properties required for protecting Telnet transmissions to a Telnet server.

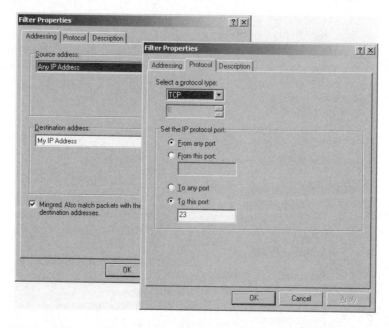

Figure 12.13   An IPSec filter for the Telnet protocol

The IPSec filter is defined to match data transmission from any IP address to the Telnet server's IP address where the source port is any port and the destination port is TCP port 23.

The characteristics that you can use to identify a protocol include

- **Source address information.** The source IP address can be a specific IP address, a specific IP subnet address, or any address.

- **Destination address information.** The destination IP address can be a specific IP address, a specific IP subnet address, or any address.

- **Protocol type.** The protocol ID or transport protocol used by the protocol. For example, Point to Point Tunneling Protocol (PPTP) uses Generic Routing Encapsulation (GRE) packets. GRE packets are identified by their protocol ID, which is Protocol ID 47. Telnet, on the other hand, uses TCP as its transport protocol, so an IPSec filter for Telnet would only define the protocol type as TCP.

- **Source port.** If the protocol were to use TCP or UDP, the source port could be defined for the protected connection. The source port is set to a specific port or to a random port depending on the protocol being defined. Most protocols use a random port for the source port.

- **Destination port.** If the protocol uses TCP or UDP, the protocol uses a specific port at the server to accept transmissions. For example, Telnet configures the server to listen for connections on TCP port 23.

Note A listing of the ports used by common services can be found by going to *www.isi.edu/in-notes/iana/assignments/port-numbers/.*

To ensure that response packets are also protected by IPSec, you should configure all defined IPSec filters as mirrored filters. A mirrored filter reverses the source and destination information so that response packets that originate at the server are also protected by IPSec when they're sent back to the client.

Important The only time you don't use mirrored rules is when you define filters for IPSec tunnel mode. In this case, you must design separate filters to reflect the tunnel endpoint that is used at each end of the tunnel.

Defining When IPSec Filters Aren't Required

There is only one circumstance in which IPSec filters don't have to be defined to enable IPSec protection in a Windows 2000 network. Whenever the Layer Two Tunneling Protocol (L2TP) is used to establish a virtual private network (VPN), Windows 2000 automatically enables IPSec protection for the L2TP tunnel. You don't have to define IPSec filters in this case because Windows 2000 automatically protects the data transmitted through the L2TP tunnel by enabling IPSec ESP protection.

(continued)

You can view the negotiated IPSec SA by running the Netdiag command line utility from the Windows 2000 Support Tools with the following parameters:

```
netdiag /test:ipsec /debug /v
```

The command's output shows all existing IPSec SAs when the L2TP tunnel is established including the applied IPSec filter. If other IPSec filters are defined, the output also includes any manually configured SAs and the filters used by those associations. For more information on planning and designing L2TP, see Chapter 13, "Securing Access for Remote Users and Networks."

Determining IPSec Exclusions

While you can use IPSec to protect most protocols, it can't protect some protocols due to the nature or use of the protocols. When designing your IPSec solution, you should be aware of the protocols that can't be protected and why you can't use IPSec to protect them. The protocols include

- **IP broadcast addresses.** You can define IPSec filters only for single recipients of packets. You can't define IPSec filters for packets destined to multiple recipients because SAs must be established between pairs of computers.

- **Multicast addresses.** As with broadcast messages, you can't secure packets sent to multiple recipients. Multicast addresses include all class D IP addresses (224.0.0.0 through 237.255.255.255).

- **Resource ReSerVation Protocol (RSVP).** A host uses the RSVP protocol (protocol ID 46) to request a specific Quality of Service (QoS) from the network. IPSec can protect the protocol for which RSVP is requesting the QoS, but not the RSVP packets used to request QoS settings.

- **Kerberos.** You can use Kerberos to authenticate two hosts participating in an IPSec exchange. Kerberos authentication is protected within the Kerberos protocol and doesn't require IPSec protection.

- **Internet Key Exchange (IKE).** IKE is used to negotiate the SA between two hosts participating in an IPSec transmission. You can't encrypt the negotiation process of IPSec. The negotiation must take place by using plaintext packets that define how future packets will be protected.

Making the Decision

To ensure that the IPSec filters you define meet all of your business needs, consider the following when you design them:

- You can assign only one IPSec policy per computer. If you're going to filter several different protocols, create a filter list of all the protocols and input them into a filter listing.

- You define policies for computers, not for users. You can define IPSec filters only for computers on the network. It doesn't matter which users are sitting at the computers.

- When possible, define the protocol requirements so that explicit filters can be defined. Determine the following attributes for each required filter:
  - Source IP address
  - Source port
  - Destination IP address
  - Destination port
  - Protocol type

Note In some cases, you only require the protocol type for an IPSec filter. Only when you define the protocol type as TCP or UDP do you need to define the source and destination ports. If the IPSec filter is based on a protocol other than TCP or UDP, you don't have to define the source port and destination port for the filter.

- You can't identify IPSec encrypted traffic if it's passed through a firewall. Once ESP is applied to a packet, you can't determine which protocol is encrypted within the packet. This can lead to unwanted traffic being allowed to pass through the firewall if the firewall is configured to pass IKE packets (UDP port 500) and ESP packets (protocol ID 50). Because the data within the packet is encrypted, the firewall can't determine which original protocol was protected by IPSec.

- If multiple filters are defined, the most specific filters are evaluated first and the least specific filters are evaluated last. The display order of the IPSec doesn't matter.

- Always mirror defined packet filters when using IPSec transport mode. Mirroring enables response packets to be encrypted when they're transmitted back to the source computer. The response packets will have the source and destination information reversed. Mirroring the rules ensures that the responses are also encrypted.

- Define an IPSec filter for each direction when defining IPSec tunnel mode connections. You can't use mirrored packet filters for IPSec tunnel mode because a different tunnel endpoint must be defined for traffic heading in each direction.

Applying the Decision

Fabrikam must define two IPSec filter listings, one for each IPSec policy. The first IPSec filter list they must define is for the data collection software. The data collection software requires separate IPSec policies to be implemented for the Windows 2000–based laptops running the client software and for the Windows 2000–based server hosting the server-side application.

Table 12.2 lists the necessary filters for the Windows 2000–based laptops to al-low the filters to identify transmissions to the data collection software application running on the server in Washington.

Table 12.2   Client-Side IPSec Filters for the Data Collection Software

Source IP	Source Port	Target IP	Target Port	Transport Protocol
My IP Address	Any	172.16.100.123	5555	TCP

Table 12.3 lists the necessary filters for the Windows 2000–based server to have the filters identify transmissions destined to the server-side of the data collection software running on the server in Washington.

Table 12.3   Server-Side IPSec Filters for the Data Collection Software

Source IP	Source Port	Target IP	Target Port	Transport Protocol
Any IP Address	Any	My IP Address	5555	TCP

Alternatively, if the laptop IP address remains constant, you could set the source IP address to be the IP address of the laptop or limit the connections to the Albuquerque office by accepting only packets with a source IP address in the 172.17.0.0/16 network address range.

You must establish filters at the two tunnel servers to ensure that IPSec ESP tun-nel mode is used for all communications between the A. Datum Corporation office and Fabrikam's Washington office. Because tunnel mode is being used, you must define two filters at each of the tunnel servers. The first filter will en-crypt traffic sent from the A. Datum Corporation network (192.168.9.0/24) to Fabrikam's Washington office (172.16.0.0/16) with the tunnel server at the Fabrikam office (131.107.2.2) as the tunnel endpoint. The second filter will en-crypt traffic sent from Fabrikam's Washington office to the A. Datum Cor-poration network with the tunnel server at the A. Datum Corporation office (131.107.100.2) as the tunnel endpoint. To block any other transmissions, you can configure a third filter at each tunnel server to block all other traffic. Table 12.4 shows the filters that you must define at the Fabrikam tunnel server.

Table 12.4   IPSec Filters Required for the Fabrikam Tunnel Server

Source IP	Destination IP	Protocol	Tunnel Endpoint
192.168.9.0/24	172.16.0.0/16	Any	131.107.2.2
172.16.0.0/16	192.168.9.0/24	Any	131.107.100.2

Finally, you must establish filters at the A. Datum Corporation tunnel server to establish an IPSec tunnel mode connection with the Fabrikam tunnel server. Table 12.5 shows the required IPSec filters.

Table 12.5   IPSec Filters Required for the A. Datum Corporation Tunnel Server

Source IP	Destination IP	Protocol	Tunnel Endpoint
192.168.9.0/24	172.16.0.0/16	Any	131.107.2.2
172.16.0.0/16	192.168.9.0/24	Any	131.107.100.2

Important   To ensure that all packets destined between the two networks are exchanged through the IPSec tunnel, you must add static routes manually at each tunnel server that defines the route to the other office's network through the IPSec tunnel. The tunnel server at Fabrikam's Washington office must add a static route that defines that the 192.168.9.0/24 network is reachable by the gateway at IP address 131.107.100.2. The tunnel server at the A. Datum Corporation office must add a static route that defines that the 172.16.0.0/16 network is reachable by the gateway at IP address 131.107.2.2.

Designing IPSec Filter Actions

Once you've defined which protocols will be protected with IPSec, you must then define what action is taken if the host sends or receives packets that match an IPSec filter, as shown in Figure 12.14. The IPSec actions that you can take include

- **Permit.** The permit action allows packets to be transmitted without IPSec protection. For example, Simple Network Management Protocol (SNMP) includes support for devices that may not be IPSec-aware. Enabling IPSec for SNMP would cause loss of network management capabilities for these devices. In a highly secure network, you could create an IPSec filter for SNMP actions and set the IPSec action to Permit to allow SNMP packets to be transmitted without IPSec protection.

- **Block.** You use the block action when the protocol that matches the associated IPSec filter should never be allowed to exist on the network. If the associated IPSec filter is matched, all packets with the block action defined are discarded. You can use this filter for Internet-accessible Windows 2000–based computers to prevent common attacks and probes, such as the Finger protocol.

- **Negotiate Security.** The negotiate security action allows an administrator to define the desired encryption and hash algorithms that must be used to secure data transmissions if an IPSec filter is matched. The Negotiate Security action allows an administrator to define the desired encryption and integrity algorithms to secure data transmissions if an IPSec filter is matched.

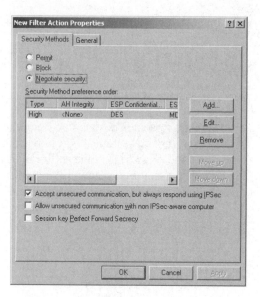

Figure 12.14   Defining IPSec filter actions

In addition to the three basic actions, you can define settings that define how the Windows 2000–based computer will react if non-IPSec protected data is received and how frequently new session keys are defined to protect the IPSec data. Options include the following:

- **Accept Unsecured Communication, But Always Respond Using IPSec.** You use this option when the IPSec protection is enforced only at the servers, not at the clients. In a typical IPSec deployment, clients are configured to use IPSec if requested by the server but never initiate an IPSec SA. This setting allows the initial packet to be received by the server, which then starts the IKE process to negotiate a SA between the client and the server. While it's riskier to have the initial packet of a data transmission accepted using plaintext, the response packet sent from the server won't be transmitted until a SA is established.

- **Allow Unsecured Communication With Non-IPSec-Aware Computers.** In a mixed network, this option allows non-IPSec aware clients to connect to the server. Windows 2000 clients, if configured to do so, will connect to the server and negotiate an IPSec SA. Non-IPSec aware clients will still be allowed to connect using unprotected data streams.

- **Session Key Perfect Forward Secrecy.** Data encryption for IPSec packets is provided by using session keys. The Perfect Forward Secrecy option ensures that an existing key is never used as the foundation of a new key. All keys must be generated without using existing keys. This reduces the risk of key compromise since previous keys can't be used to determine future keys.

Making the Decision

Table 12.6 shows the design decisions for selecting the IPSec actions to take when an IPSec filter is matched by an incoming data transmission.

Table 12.6   Designing IPSec Actions

Use	Under These Circumstances
Permit	■ You want to enable unencrypted data transmissions to be accepted by a client or server. You use this action when a protocol must not be encrypted. For example, in mixed environments you might require that all SNMP packets aren't encrypted. By assigning the Permit action to the IPSec filter that defines SNMP packets, you ensure that encryption isn't applied. ■ The protocol allows application-layer protection. For example, you don't need to apply IPSec encryption to HTTP transmissions because HTTP can be encrypted using SSL.
Block	■ You're required to drop all connection attempts using the protocol that matches the IPSec filter assigned the block action. ■ You want to prevent the visibility of commonly attacked ports for an Internet-accessible computer.
Negotiate Security	■ You want to provide IPSec-protected access to authorized computers while blocking unauthorized access if the connecting host fails to authenticate. For example, you might place a server in a Demilitarized Zone (DMZ) and want to access the server using NetBIOS from the internal network but block all NetBIOS connection attempts from the Internet. When you define the Negotiate action, only computers from the internal network can negotiate a SA and use IPsec. ■ You want to define the exact encryption and integrity algorithms that will be used for a SA between two network hosts.
Accept Unsecured Communication, But Always Respond Using IPSec	■ The server, rather than the client, is configured to initiate the use of IPSec. This setting allows the client to initially attempt to connect using unprotected transmissions, but allows the server to require IPSec protection.
Allow Unsecured Communication, with Non-IPSec-Aware Computer	■ The network contains non-IPSec-aware computers that will require access to a server . ■ You want to use IPSec if possible, but will accept unprotected sessions if the connecting computer doesn't support IPSec.
Session Key Perfect Forward Secrecy	■ You require maximum security for IPSec session keys. ■ Your security policy requires that previous session keys aren't used to generate new session keys.

Applying the Decision

Fabrikam must now match the IPSec actions to the filters that were previously defined. For the data collection software, the filter action would be set to Negotiate Security so that the client and the server can negotiate the encryption algorithm that will be used to secure the data transmission.

The scenario doesn't state whether the client or server will be used for other purposes. To allow or disallow other protocols, define another filter that's set to be any protocol. If the computers will be used for other purposes, you should set the additional filter action to Permit, so that all other traffic will be used without IPSec protection. If the client or server won't be used for any other purposes, you should set the filter action to Block or Negotiate Security. Negotiate Security is probably a better choice because it allows connections as long as IPSec is negotiated between the client and the server.

The tunnel servers used to create the IPSec tunnel between Fabrikam's Washington office and the A. Datum Corporation office will require two different IPSec actions for the list of filters. The filters that define the traffic that's transmitted between Fabrikam's Washington office and the A. Datum Corporation office require the Negotiate Security action so that ESP tunnel mode is used to encrypt the transmitted data.

In addition, you must establish a separate IPSec filter so that only authorized data received by the external interface card of the tunnel server at each office is allowed. This IPSec filter ensures that the IPSec tunnel mode transmissions—and other IPSec transmissions that are negotiated by the tunnel server—are accepted and all other connections are rejected. Table 12.7 shows the IPSec filters and actions that are required for the tunnel server at Fabrikam's Washington office.

Table 12.7   IPSec Filters and Actions for the Fabrikam Tunnel Server

Source IP	Destination IP	Protocol	Tunnel Endpoint	IPSec Action
192.168.9.0/24	172.16.0.0/16	Any	131.107.2.2	Negotiate Security
172.16.0.0/16	192.168.9.0/24	Any	131.107.100.2	Negotiate Security
Any	131.107.2.2	Any	N/A	Negotiate Security

Finally, you must establish filters and actions at the A. Datum Corporation tunnel server to establish an IPSec tunnel mode connection with the Fabrikam tunnel server. Table 12.8 shows the required IPSec filters.

Table 12.8   IPSec Filters and Actions for the A. Datum Corporation Tunnel Server

Source IP	Destination IP	Protocol	Tunnel Endpoint	IPSec Action
192.168.9.0/24	172.16.0.0/16	Any	131.107.2.2	Negotiate Security
172.16.0.0/16	192.168.9.0/24	Any	131.107.100.2	Negotiate Security
Any	131.107.100.2	Any	N/A	Negotiate Security

Designing IPSec Encryption and Integrity Algorithms

You configure IPSec filter properties to specifically define which algorithms IPSec uses when negotiating security. You can define separate algorithms for AH and ESP-protected data streams, as shown in Figure 12.15.

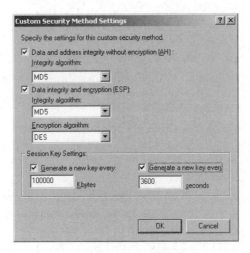

Figure 12.15   Defining encryption and integrity algorithms

Defining custom settings for IPSec protection enables you to define how IPSec protects transmitted data. If AH protection is required, define Message Digest v5 (MD5) or Secure Hash Algorithm v1 (SHA1) as the integrity algorithm.

If ESP encryption is required, set the digital signing algorithm to be MD5 or SHA1 and the encryption algorithm to be Data Encryption Standard (DES) or Triple DES (3DES).

You can define multiple algorithms for the Negotiate Security action. The listing of algorithms can be ordered so that the security administrator can define the desired IPSec protection while allowing less secure variations that are used only if negotiation fails for the higher-level encryption. For example, the security administrator may desire 3DES encryption of ESP packets. If either the client or server doesn't have the Windows 2000 High Encryption Pack installed, you can define a secondary IPSec security method that allows DES protection. The DES protection will be used only if 3DES protection isn't supported by one of the two hosts involved in the IPSec transmission.

In addition to defining the integrity and encryption algorithms, you can also define when new keys are generated to protect the data. You can define key generation based on the amount of data that's transmitted (in kilobytes) and the lifetime of the key (in seconds). Configuring these options can protect the key from compromise.

Making the Decision

Consider the following design factors when deciding on encryption and integrity algorithms for a SA:

- If configuring support for multiple algorithm support, sort the algorithms from strongest to weakest. The listing will be processed sequentially from top to bottom. By ordering the list in this manner, you ensure that the strongest mutual algorithms are always used.

Important   For integrity algorithms, SHA1 is considered stronger than MD5, and for encryption algorithms, 3DES is considered stronger than DES.

- Include security methods only for the required algorithms. If your IPSec design requires only AH protection, don't include ESP algorithms in the listing of supported security methods. This could result in the establishment of an unsupported IPSec SA.
- Use of strong encryption protocols such as 3DES requires the installation of the Windows 2000 High Encryption Pack. Consider including an additional security method to support DES encryption in case a connecting client doesn't have the High Encryption Pack installed. Alternatively, ensure that all authorized client computers have the Windows 2000 High Encryption Pack installed.
- Modify the default key generation settings in higher-security networks. You can configure the generation of new session keys based on the amount of data transmitted and the elapsed time in the transmission. The default settings are 100,000 kilobytes (KB) and every 3600 seconds.

Applying the Decision

In both scenarios Fabrikam will use ESP to protect their transmitted data. The security requirements call for authenticity for the data payload but not for the entire packet. To accomplish this, configure the ESP packets to enable both encryption and integrity algorithms.

Because the scenario doesn't mention whether the Windows 2000 High Encryption Pack is applied, you must make provisions to allow the clients to connect without it. To meet these requirements, establish the negotiation list shown in Table 12.9 for both scenarios to ensure that the highest form of encryption and integrity is achieved during the negotiation process.

Table 12.9   Defining Security Methods for Fabrikam

ESP Encryption Algorithm	ESP Integrity Algorithm
3DES	SHA1
3DES	MD5
DES	SHA1
DES	MD5

Designing IPSec Authentication

IPSec requires that the two network hosts using IPSec authenticate with each other before entering into SA negotiations. IPSec allows three methods for authenticating the two hosts involved in the SA:

- **Kerberos.** Kerberos authentication leverages the default Windows 2000 authentication mechanism. Kerberos provides a strong form of authentication that's easy to configure because all Windows 2000–based computers are able to authenticate with other Windows 2000–based computers in the forest with no further configuration. You can't use Kerberos as an authentication mechanism between forests.

- **Certificates.** You can use certificate-based authentication to authenticate network hosts using IPSec. To use IPSec, the certificates must be issued from a Certification Authority (CA) that's trusted by the two hosts using IPSec. Certificates provide strong authentication options for network hosts that don't belong to the same enterprise network. Certificate-based authentication requires both hosts using IPSec to have certificates for authentication before entering into an IPSec SA.

- **Preshared keys.** Preshared keys are text strings entered at the two hosts to prove their identities. You should use preshared keys only in circumstances where you can't use either Kerberos or certificates or when you're testing the IPSec filters before deploying the IPSec settings on the network.

Making the Decision

Use Table 12.10 to determine which authentication method to use for a specific IPSec scenario.

Table 12.10   Planning IPSec Authentication Protocols

Use	Under the Following Circumstances
Kerberos authentication	<ul><li>All computers using IPSec are members of the same Active Directory directory service forest.</li><li>You want to minimize the amount of configuration involved in authenticating hosts yet maintain security for authentication.</li></ul>
Public key authentication	<ul><li>You require strong authentication between hosts not in the same forest.</li><li>A common root CA exists for the two hosts using IPSec.</li><li>Each host has a valid machine certificate installed that can be used to authenticate the host.</li><li>You want to use L2TP/IPSec for a VPN solution. L2TP/IPSec requires a machine certificate to be used for authentication.</li></ul>

Table 12.10   Planning IPSec Authentication Protocols   *(continued)*

Use	Under the Following Circumstances
Preshared keys	<ul><li>You can't use Kerberos or public key authentication. Some third-party IPSec solutions may not be able to use Kerberos or public key authentication, and the only resort is to use preshared keys.</li><li>You're testing a new IPSec filter and want to make sure that authentication problems aren't causing the SA's failure.</li><li>You're establishing an IPSec SA between two hosts and the association will only be between the two hosts.</li><li>The preshared key is set to be complex and access to the IPSec configuration interface is secured to prevent inspection of the preshared key established between the two hosts.</li></ul>

Note   The choice between using Kerberos or public key authentication generally comes down to ease of configuration. In a Windows 2000 forest, Kerberos is the easiest authentication mechanism to use because it's already implemented at all computers in the forest. You more often use public key authentication when a Public Key Infrastructure (PKI) exists or when IPSec is required between organizations.

Applying the Decision

Fabrikam requires different authentication mechanisms for the two scenarios. For the data collection software, both the client laptop and the server are members of the corp.fabrikam.tld forest. The easiest authentication method that doesn't lessen security would be Kerberos because both computers have accounts in the corp.fabrikam.tld domain.

For the tunnel servers between the two organizations, the securest authentication method to use would be public key authentication. You can't use Kerberos authentication because the two tunnel servers are members of different forests and Kerberos isn't supported in this scenario. To ensure that the certificates for each tunnel server are recognized and trusted by the other organization, you must either acquire the certificate from a public CA such as Verisign or establish cross-certification between the two organization's CA hierarchies.

Lesson Summary

In most cases you have to define custom IPSec policies to meet your business needs. The process of designing the IPSec policy includes defining filters that identify the protocol, defining the IPSec mode and protocol that's to be used, identifying the authentication mechanisms to use, and defining the security algorithms.

You must test the IPSec policies to ensure that the computers continue to function and provide the necessary level of security for the transmitted data.

Activity: Evaluating IPSec Scenarios

This activity examines various network configurations. Through analysis, you will determine whether IPSec can be implemented in the given scenario. Answers to the following questions can be found in the appendix.

1. Figure 12.16 shows a client computer and a server located on your office's network. Can you use IPSec Authentication Headers to ensure the authentication and integrity of data transmitted between the two computers? If you can't use IPSec, can you use an alternate configuration to meet your business needs?

Figure 12.16   A proposed network infrastructure

2. Figure 12.17 shows a server located on a network segment that's protected by a firewall. In this configuration can you use IPSec to encrypt all traffic transmitted between the client and the server?

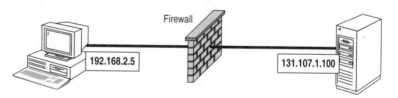

Figure 12.17   A proposed network infrastructure

3. Figure 12.18 shows a server located on a network segment that's protected by a firewall. In this configuration can you use IPSec to encrypt all traffic transmitted between the client and the server?

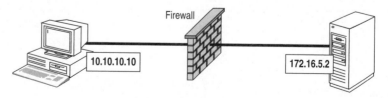

Figure 12.18   A proposed network infrastructure

The following two questions are based on Figure 12.19, which illustrates two office networks that are connected over the Internet. The client at IP address 192.168.5.2 wants to communicate securely over the Internet with the client at IP address 10.10.10.20.

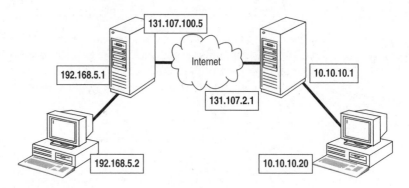

Figure 12.19   A proposed network infrastructure

4. Can you use IPSec transport mode to encrypt data transmitted between the two client computers?

5. How could you use IPSec tunnel mode to protect the data transmitted over the Internet?

Lesson 2: Planning IPSec Deployment

Once you've designed an IPSec policy that meets your needs, you must deploy the IPSec policy to all Windows 2000–based computers that require the security provided by the IPSec policy. This lesson begins with an overview of the default IPSec policies that ship with Windows 2000 and then examines the following topics:

- Deploying IPSec policies in a workgroup environment
- Deploying IPSec policies in a domain environment
- Planning the autodeployment of computer certificates
- Troubleshooting Group Policy application

After this lesson, you will be able to

- Plan and troubleshoot the deployment of IPSec policies to network clients

Estimated lesson time: 45 minutes

Assessing the Preconfigured IPSec Policies

Windows 2000 includes three default IPSec policies that may or may not meet your organization's security requirements. The default IPSec policies are available in both a domain or workgroup environment and you can apply them locally or by using Group Policy.

The predefined IPSec policies are

- **Secure Server (Require Security).** This policy secures all network traffic to or from the computer that the IPSec policy is applied to, with the exception of Internet Control Message Protocol (ICMP), better known as Packet InterNet Groper (PING) traffic. When you apply this policy, you must secure all communications with the affected computer. This policy rejects any connection attempts by non-IPSec aware clients.

- **Server (Request Security).** This policy differs from the Secure Server IPSec policy in that it only requests that IPSec security be applied. If the connecting client is non-IPSec aware, the Server (Request Security) policy allows unsecured communications to take place.

- **Client (Respond Only).** This policy doesn't enable IPSec for specific protocols, but it allows the affected computer to negotiate an IPSec SA with any servers that request or require IPSec protection. When you apply this IPSec policy, the client computer will never initiate IPSec protection but will participate in IPSec SAs when requested to do so by another computer.

In many cases you require custom IPSec policies. While the default policies enable IPSec protection for all network traffic, you may often need to add exclusions for specific protocols. For example, you don't need to enable IPSec protection for protocols, such as HTTP, that support application-layer security.

If modifications are required, create a custom IPsec policy instead of modifying the default policies. Modifying the default policies can result in unexpected behavior if you apply the modified IPSec policy and it doesn't function as expected.

Note   You can restore the default IPSec policies in an MMC console by right-clicking the IPSec Policies On Local Machine or IPSec Policies On Active Directory console and then clicking Restore Default Policies. This action restores the default settings for the three default IPSec policies.

Making the Decision

Table 12.11 shows the factors that influence your IPSec design to deploy the default IPSec policies.

Table 12.11   Choosing to Deploy the Default IPSec Policies

Use	When Any of the Following Business Requirements Exist
Secure Server (Require Security)	■ The highest level of default security is required. This IPSec policy requires IPSec to be used for all protocols, except those that can't be protected by IPSec. ■ All traffic sent to the server must be protected by using IPSec. ■ Fallback to unprotected data transmissions isn't desired. ■ Only Windows 2000–based computers are required to connect to the server. ■ You've placed all servers that require the IPSec configuration in the same organizational unit (OU) or OU structure.
Server (Request Security)	■ All traffic sent to the server should be protected by using IPSec. ■ Fallback to unprotected data transmissions will be supported for legacy clients. ■ The server must support a mix of Windows 2000 and non–Windows 2000–based clients. ■ You've placed all servers that require the IPSec configuration in the same organizational unit (OU) or OU structure.
Client (Respond Only)	■ Enable the Windows 2000–based computer to use IPSec protection when requested by a server. ■ You don't want the client computer to initiate IPSec protection. ■ You determine that all computers within an OU or OU structure are to be enabled for IPSec protection.

Applying the Decision

Fabrikam requires custom IPSec policies to meet its security objectives. The default IPSec policies don't meet the current security requirements. The one scenario where they could consider using a default IPSec policy would be for the data collection software.

If more than one laptop were used for data collection, the laptops could be assigned the Client (Respond Only) IPSec policy. This IPSec policy would enable the laptop computers to negotiate an IPSec SA when requested but still use unprotected transmissions to other servers.

If the Client (Respond Only) IPSec policy were enabled, you'd have to modify the IPSec policy applied to the server hosting the data collection software to accept unsecured communication but always respond using IPSec. This modification is required because the Client (Respond Only) IPSec policy would have the client send an unprotected packet initially to TCP port 5555. Only after the server responds would the IPSec SA be negotiated and established.

Deploying IPSec Policies in a Workgroup Environment

A workgroup environment can't depend on Active Directory for the consistent application of IPSec policies. In a workgroup environment, you can configure IPSec policies only by connecting to the local computer security settings.

You can achieve consistent IPSec configuration across similar computers by exporting properly configured IPSec settings to a .ipsec export file and importing the IPSec settings to all matching computers.

Important   Although you can configure the IPSec policies through the Local Computer Security console, you can't configure IPSec settings through security templates. Security templates don't contain information for IPSec policies. Because of this, you can't use the Secedit command to ensure consistent application of IPSec policy. You must manually inspect IPSec policies at periodic intervals.

Making the Decision

When designing IPSec deployment in a workgroup environment, include the following tasks in your IPSec deployment design:

- Define the required IPSec policies at a test machine. You should define and test the IPSec policy before you apply it to production computers.

- Create a lab environment that emulates the production network. Configuring the lab environment in this manner ensures that valid testing occurs and that network infrastructure issues, such as a NAT service, won't affect your IPSec deployment.

- Export the IPSec policies to an .ipsec export file. Use the IP Security Policy Management console in MMC to export the required settings so that the exported file can be imported into all required computers. Using an export/import method ensures consistent configuration of the IPSec policy.

- Store the exported IPSec policies in a secure location. This practice facilitates the reapplication of IPSec policies if they are modified or deleted by accident.

Applying the Decision

The two tunnel servers may not be members of the domain at Fabrikam or A. Datum Corporation. Because the tunnel servers aren't members of the domain, you must define the IPSec policy in the local computer policy for each tunnel server.

Because each site has only one tunnel server and the rules are different at each server, it would be best to deploy the IPSec policy by manually configuring the IPSec policy at each tunnel server.

Deploying IPSec Policies in a Domain Environment

Active Directory enables an administrator to standardize IPSec configuration by applying IPSec policies in Group Policy objects. You can define IPSec policies for the site, domain, or OU to ensure that all computer objects within the container have consistent IPSec policies applied.

The use of Group Policy ensures that a computer's administrator can't override the desired IPSec settings at the local computer. The settings inherited from Group Policy always supersede local policy settings.

Note   You can't use security templates to define IPSec policies. Security templates don't include settings for IPSec policy definition. To define IPSec policies, create the IPSec policy at a stand-alone computer and then export the settings to a .ipsec export file. The export file can then be imported into the Group Policy object where you wish to deploy the IPSec policy.

Making the Decision

In an Active Directory environment, consider the following when designing your IPSec deployment:

- Place computer accounts with the same IPSec requirements into the same OU or OU structure. By deploying the IPSec policy within the OU's Group Policy object, you ensure that the same IPSec policy is applied to all computer accounts in the OU structure.

- Know the processing order for Group Policies and local computer policies. The last policy applied will be the effective policy by default. By default, the policy processing order is first local computer policy, then site policy, then domain policy, and finally OU policies. The policy located closest to the computer account always takes effect unless the no override option is enabled.

- Assign the default Client (Respond Only) policy to the Default Domain Policy if you wish to enable IPSec for all Windows 2000–based computers in a domain. This ensures that all Windows 2000–based computers will respond to an IPSec negotiation request.

- Assign the default Client (Respond Only) policy to a specific OU if you wish to enable IPSec for only a subset of Windows 2000–based computers in a domain. Placing the computer accounts in the OU or within the OU hierarchy enables you to apply the default Client (Respond Only) policy to the highest-level OU in the OU hierarchy and only enable IPSec for the computer accounts in the OU hierarchy.

- A computer can have only a single IPSec policy assigned at any one time. If you require components from multiple IPSec policies, you must define a single IPSec policy that encompasses all IPSec settings in a single policy.

Applying the Decision

If Fabrikam were to deploy additional laptops, the best strategy would be to place all of the Windows 2000–based laptops in a common OU. By doing this, you can define a Group Policy object that applies the custom IPSec policy.

The Group Policy object takes precedence over any domain settings or local settings defined directly at the laptop computers and ensures that a consistent IPSec policy is applied to all laptops running the data collection client software.

At the Washington office, you could place the data collection server in a separate OU or have the Group Policy object that defines the IPSec policy applied with a filter so that only the data collection server applies the Group Policy object. This action ensures that the policy is consistently applied to the data collection server and that the local computer policy can't be changed to lessen the security for the data collection software.

Automatically Deploying Computer Certificates

IPSec gives two computers entering into a SA the ability to authenticate with certificates. In a Windows 2000 network, only domain controllers (DCs) acquire certificates by default. If you wish to use certificates for authentication, you must either manually configure each computer with the necessary certificate or enable automatic certificate enrollment.

You configure automatic certificate enrollment within Group Policy objects, as shown in Figure 12.20.

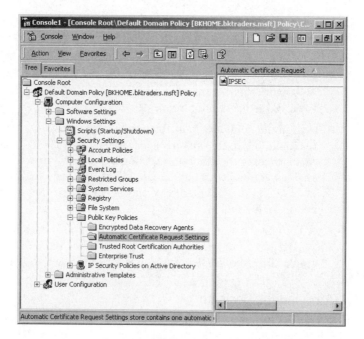

Figure 12.20   Configuring automatic certificate enrollment for an IPSec certificate

You can apply the Group Policy object at the site, the domain, or the OU to deploy the certificate automatically to all computer accounts within the container. A CA trusted by both computers in the SA must issue the certificates. In other words, the issuing CA must be a trusted intermediate CA and the root CA in the CA hierarchy must be a trusted root CA.

To enable IPSec, you can choose one of three certificate templates:

- **IPSec.** A single-use certificate template that allows only the computer associated with the certificate to use IPSec.

- **Computer.** A multipurpose certificate template that can also be used for IPSec authentication. You should assign the computer certificate template to nondomain controllers.

- **Domain Controller.** A multipurpose certificate template that allows IPSec authentication. You should assign the Domain Controller certificate template only to DCs.

Making the Decision

Consider the following points when designing certificate-based authentication for IPSec:

- Determine which certificate template to issue. Depending on how you use certificates for authentication in your organization, you need to choose between a single use (IPSec) or multipurpose (computer or DC) certificate.

- Ensure that a CA is configured to issue the certificate template. IPSec certificate templates aren't issued by default. You will have to configure a CA to issue the IPSec certificate by adding the IPSec certificate template to the CA's policy settings.

- Ensure that all required computers have the Read and Enroll permissions for the certificate template. The automatic certificate request will fail if the computer account performing the request doesn't have the necessary permissions. Consider placing all IPSec-aware computers into a domain local group and assigning the Read and Enroll permissions to the custom domain local group.

- Configure a Group Policy object to perform the automatic certificate request. Configure the automatic certificate request at the Group Policy container that contains all computer accounts that require the certificate.

- Distribute certificates to all client computers requiring L2TP tunnel connectivity. L2TP over IPSec is the one instance where only certificate-based authentication is allowed. For L2TP clients, both the remote access server and the VPN client must have a certificate installed to authenticate the IPSec SA.

Applying the Decision

In the Fabrikam scenario described at the beginning of the chapter, the tunnel servers probably wouldn't be members of the organization's domains, so you couldn't configure automated certificate deployment. But if you decided to use certificate-based authentication for the data collection software IPSec solution, then you could configure automatic certificate requests.

As with the IPSec policies, you could apply Group Policy at the OU containing the laptops and at the OU containing the data collection server. For the laptops, you could define the autoenrollment certificate request to issue either IPSec or computer certificates. Because no other projects are defined that require a PKI for Fabrikam, the securest solution would be to issue an IPSec certificate to the computers. This would require ensuring that the Discretionary Access Control List (DACL) for the IPSec certificate template is modified to allow the laptops the Read and Enroll permissions for the IPSec certificate template. Additionally, an existing CA must be configured to issue the IPSec certificates. With this configuration, all laptops located in the OU will automatically request an IPSec certificate when the computer account is authenticated at startup or when Group Policy settings are refreshed at the regular interval.

Troubleshooting IPSec Problems

Sometimes an IPSec design doesn't work as expected. When this occurs, you can use several tools use to determine why an IPSec SA isn't being established. These tools include

- **Ping.** Use Ping to ensure that the SA is being correctly established between two computers. Ping uses the Internet Control Message Protocol (ICMP), and when IPSec is enabled for ICMP packets, you will initially see that IPSec is being negotiated before the ICMP packets work as expected.

- **IPSec Monitor.** The IPSec Monitor (Ipsecmon.exe) shows any currently active IPSec SAs that are established with your computer and the current IPSec statistics for your computer, as illustrated in Figure 12.21. Use the IPSec Monitor to detect whether any errors are occurring during IPSec transmissions.

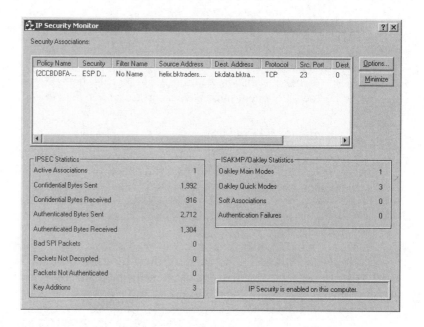

Figure 12.21   Current SAs as shown in the IPSec monitor

- **Netdiag.** The Netdiag utility, included in the Windows 2000 Support Tools, allows you to verify the current SAs active on your computer. By using the /debug option, you can verify the actual IPSec policy applied, the filter that was applied, and the authentication protocol used. The command used to show the information is NETDIAG /TEST:IPSEC /DEBUG.

- **System Management Server (SMS) Network Monitor.** The SMS Network Monitor allows you to inspect data packets as they're transmitted across the network. You can use the Network Monitor to determine if the IKE negotiation takes place (look for ISAKMP packets) and whether the negotiation succeeded (look for AH or ESP packets). You can't use the Network Monitor to inspect the contents of an ESP packet because the contents are encrypted.

- **Oakley logs.** As a last resort, you can enable Oakley logs to look at detailed debugging of an IPSec connection. Oakley logs provide detailed reporting on the ISAKMP negotiation process, and a security technician can use them to identify incorrect configuration information.

Important   By default, Oakley logs aren't enabled. You must add the value EnableLogging to the registry in the HKEY_LOCAL_MACHINE\System \CurrentControlSet\Services\PolicyAgent\Oakley key. The REG_DWORD value must be set to a value of "1" to enable Oakley logging.

Making the Decision

Table 12.12 lists some potential IPSec connection problems and the tools you use to troubleshoot them.

Table 12.12   Troubleshooting IPSec Connection Problems

Use This Strategy	To Perform These Actions
Ping	■ Determine if authentication is working between the two IPSec hosts. Change the IPSec filter to encrypt only ICMP packets. If the encryption of ICMP packets works, you probably have a filter definition problem and must edit your original IPSec filter settings.
A preshared key	■ Determine if the filter is working correctly. A preshared key is the least complex form of authentication and ensures that you only have to troubleshoot your filter definition.
IPSec Monitor	■ Determine if a SA is established between your computer and the target computer. ■ Determine which protocol is protected with IPSec. ■ Review statistics for IPSec usage to determine if errors are occurring.
Netdiag	■ Determine which IPSec policy is currently assigned to the computer. ■ Determine which filters are in use for the IPSec SA. ■ Determine which authentication protocol is used for the SA.
SMS Network Monitor	■ Look at the packet level to determine if the ISAKMP process is taking place. ■ Determine if the ISAKMP process is successful. You determine this by looking for AH and ESP protocol packets.
Oakley logs	■ Determine errors found during the ISAKMP negotiation between two computers. ■ Only use as a last resort for troubleshooting IPSec configuration errors.

Applying the Decision

The scenario mentions that the tunnel servers were suffering from authentication errors during testing of the tunnel. This could be because the certificates issued to the tunnel servers aren't being recognized by the other organization's tunnel server. To troubleshoot the problem, complete the following steps:

1. Configure the authentication mechanism to use a preshared key and see if the connection succeeds. If the connection succeeds, a certificate trust problem is probably causing the connection to fail. Make sure that the certificates are issued by a CA that's trusted by both the organizations.

2. If the authentication continues to fail, run the IPSec Monitor to see if a SA is established and determine if any errors are occurring during the session.

3. If no session is established, review the IPSec policy assigned to each computer. Make sure that the correct policy is assigned to each of the tunnel servers.

4. Run the SMS Network Monitor to ensure that ISAKMP packets are being received at each of the tunnel servers. This identifies whether network connectivity problems are causing the packets to fail to reach the destination server. Also review the network design at this point to ensure that the packets aren't crossing any servers or network devices that perform NAT.

5. Enable the Oakley logs to record detailed information about the ISAKMP process. In the Oakley logs, determine what settings, if any, are incorrectly set at the tunnel servers.

Lesson Summary

After defining your IPSec policies, you must deploy the IPSec policies to the necessary computers in your network. Take advantage of Active Directory to ensure that IPSec policies are applied consistently to similar computers on the network. Group Policy ensures that the proper IPSec policies are applied and that local computer settings don't change the IPSec policies assigned to a computer.

Once you have the policies assigned, ensure that the IPSec SA is functioning as expected. If it isn't, know what tools you can use to troubleshoot the problem. Ensure that you use a structured approach to troubleshooting so that each step of the way you eliminate potential configuration issues and narrow the problem down to a likely source.

Lab 12-1: Designing IPSec Security

Lab Objectives

This lab prepares you to design an IPSec solution for Contoso Ltd. The lab meets the following objectives:

- Design IPSec filters to apply IPSec only to desired network traffic
- Plan IPSec deployment

About This Lab

This lab looks at the planning that Contoso must do to protect their Web server that's exposed to the Internet and to secure a server that hosts a sales tracking application on the internal network. The lab outlines security requirements that will act as design inputs for your solution.

Before You Begin

Make sure that you've completed reading the chapter material before starting the lab. Pay close attention to the sections where the design decisions were applied throughout the chapter for information on building your administrative structure.

Scenario: Contoso Ltd.

Contoso Ltd., an international magazine sales company, wants to design an IPSec solution to protect two servers on its network. The first server that requires protection is the Web server. The Web server has been the focus of several attacks from the Internet and management wants to lock down the server to reduce the chance of a successful attack.

The second server that requires additional security is the Sales Tracking application server. Salespeople at the London office use the Sales Tracking application to record all sales activity during the day. The application also provides a query engine that allows salespeople to query the stored data to determine sales patterns and quota status.

Protecting the External Web Server

The Web server that's hosting the subscription and back-issue ordering site has been the target of several attacks. The Web administrator installed an intrusion detection application at the Web server and found that most attacks start with a port probe that determines which ports are open on the Web server. The attacks then target known vulnerabilities with each open port.

Management would like to lock down the Web server to expose only the ports that are necessary to the Internet. If a port probe is launched against the Web server, all other ports should be configured to appear as if they don't exist.

The Information Technology (IT) department plans to deploy the Web server in a DMZ, as shown in Figure 12.22.

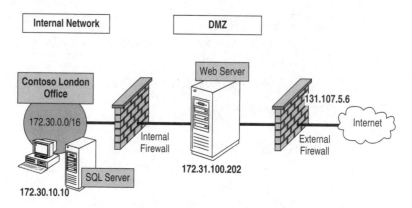

Figure 12.22   The Contoso Web server security configuration

The Web server is located in the DMZ. On the Internet, the Web server is advertised to be at the IP address 131.107.5.6. All incoming traffic to the address 131.107.5.6 is translated to the internal IP address 172.31.100.202. In researching the security of the Web server, the IT department has identified the following business objectives that your design must meet:

- The Web server allows connections from the Internet only to the HTTP (TCP port 80) and HTTPS (TCP port 443) services. All other services must be hidden from Internet users.

- The Web server must store subscription and back-issue orders information on the Microsoft SQL server located on the London network at IP address 172.30.10.10. The Web server will connect to the SQL server using the TCP protocol connecting to the SQL-Data port (TCP 1433). Due to the confidential information that's inputted at the Web server, all data that's transmitted to the SQL server must be encrypted using 3DES. The data that's entered must be protected against modification as well.

- The Web server's administrators are located at the London office in the 172.30.0.0/16 subnet. Administrators need to be able to connect to all services on the Web server. The connections require full encryption. In addition, the entire data packet should be protected against modification to prevent source routing attacks that may compromise the Web server. Source routing attacks attempt to modify the IP header to change the routing of an IP packet.

- Any other connection attempts to the Web server should be prevented.

- Only computers that support strong forms of encryption will be allowed to connect to the Web server for administrative tasks.

- The computers designated for Web server administration are all members of a global group named Web Server Administrators.

Securing the Sales Application Server

The Sales application server is stored on a secure network segment at the London office. All traffic that enters the secured segment must pass through a firewall that separates the secure segment from the public segment. The client-side application is installed on Windows 2000–based computers at each of the three offices, as illustrated in Figure 12.23.

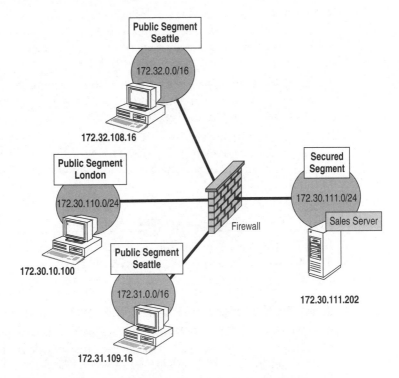

Figure 12.23   Contoso's Sales Tracking application deployment

Management requires you to meet the following business objectives when you design secure access to the Sales server:

- The Sales application server listens for sales updates on TCP port 77889.

- All updates to the server must be encrypted to ensure that other salespeople don't see the data included in the update.

- The update must ensure that both the client computer and the server are mutually authenticated.

- The update packet must be entirely protected from modification of any sort. The sales program uses the IP address of the client computer to identify which salesperson sent the update. Last month a salesperson attempted to re-play another salesperson's updates in an attempt to claim the sales as his own. You must prevent attacks of this kind.

- The Sales application server listens for sales queries on TCP port 77890.

- All query information must be protected against inspection when the data is transmitted from the server to the computer. The data payload must be protected against modification as well.

- Connection attempts to the Sales application server must be limited to salespeople. All salespeople are assigned to the global group named Sales Staff that's created in each of the three domains: seattle.contoso.tld, lima.contoso.tld, and london.contoso.tld.

- The Sales application server is dedicated to running the Sales application. No other applications are running on the server. All management of the server is performed locally at the server.

- You must configure the firewall protecting the secure segment to ensure that only updates and queries are passed to the Sales application server in the secure segment. All other requests to the Sales application server must be blocked at the firewall.

Exercise 1: Designing IPSec Policies for Contoso Ltd.

This exercise looks at the design of the IPSec policies required to meet the business objectives outlined for the two projects. Answers to these questions can be found in the appendix.

Designing IPSec Policies for the Web Server

The Contoso Web server is located in the DMZ of the company's network. Assume that the Web server isn't a member of the contoso.tld forest but is a stand-alone server in the workgroup named Internet. The Web server is configured in this manner to prevent attacks from revealing account information from the internal network.

1. Does the network architecture prevent you from implementing an IPSec solution? Provide details on why the network architecture does or doesn't allow you to deploy IPSec.

2. Could an administrator connect to the Web server and perform administrative tasks from a computer connected directly to the Internet? Why or why not?

3. What IPSec protocols are required to meet the business objectives drafted by the IT department?

4. What IPSec mode is required to meet the business objectives drafted by the IT department?

5. In the following table, enter the required filters and actions that must be assigned to the Web server to meet the defined business objectives.

Protocol	Source IP	Destination IP	Protocol	Source Port	Destination Port	Action
HTTP						
HTTPS						
SQL-Data						
Any	172.30.0.0/ 16					
Any	Any					

6. What must you configure to allow response packets to be secured when returned to connecting client computers?

7. To maintain the highest level of security, what authentication protocol must be used to authenticate the computers used by the administrators at the London office with the Web server?

8. What encryption algorithm(s) must be supported to meet the business requirements?

9. What must you install at all client computers to support 3DES encryption?

Designing IPSec Policies for the Sales Order Server

Answer the following questions based on the scenario presented at the beginning of the lab. Answers to these questions can be found in the appendix.

1. Does the network architecture prevent you from implementing an IPSec solution? Provide details on why the network architecture does or doesn't allow IPSec to be deployed.

2. What IPSec protocols are required to meet the business objectives drafted by the IT department?

3. What IPSec mode is required to meet the business objectives drafted by the IT department?

4. In the following table, enter the required filters and actions that must be assigned to the Sales server to meet the defined business objectives.

Protocol	Source IP	Destination IP	Protocol	Source Port	Destination Port	Action
Sales Updates						
Sales Queries						
Any						

5. If Contoso wants to authenticate the computer accounts with no additional configuration, what authentication protocol must be used?

6. What filters must be applied at the firewall to allow Sales Application server updates and to allow queries to pass between the public network segments and the secured segment?

7. What risk is there in passing IPSec packets through a firewall?

Exercise 2: Planning Deployment of the IPSec Policies

This exercise looks at the deployment of the IPSec policies required to protect data transmission to the Web server and the Sales server. Answers to these questions can be found in the appendix.

1. How can you use the default IPSec Policies to protect access to the Web server?

2. Assuming that public key authentication will be used to authenticate the IPSec connection, what planning is required for certificate deployment?

3. Assume that the OU structure shown in Figure 12.24 exists for the london.contoso.tld domain. The computers that will manage the Web server are located in the IT OU, but the IT OU has other computers that shouldn't be allowed to connect to the Web server.

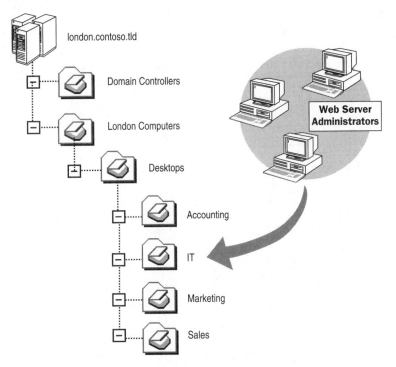

Figure 12.24   Locating the Web server administrator computers in the IT OU

What strategy can you use to ensure that designated computers can negotiate IPSec agreements with the Web server without moving the computer accounts to a different OU?

4. If Contoso intends to use IPSec certificates for authentication, what additional design modifications must you make to the PKI to support the automatic issuance of IPSec certificates?

5. A new administrator is assigned to manage the Web server. The administrator was just issued a newly installed computer and the computer account for the computer is placed in the IT OU. You've verified that an IPSec certificate is installed to the computer account and that the Client (Respond Only) IPSec policy is assigned to the computer. But the IPSec SA fails to be established. How would you troubleshoot this problem? What's the probable cause?

Review

Answering the following questions will reinforce key information presented in this chapter. If you are unable to answer a question, review the appropriate lesson and then try the question again. Answers to the questions can be found in the appendix.

1. As security administrator for your organization, you discover that an attacker has successfully authenticated onto the network using your personal credentials. You suspect that the attacker captured and replayed one of your earlier remote sessions. In an effort to prevent further attacks (and clear your name) you implement IPSec using ESP. Will this address the problem? Why or why not?

2. The Payroll department shares sensitive data with an internal Accounting department. Data includes the salaries of every employee in your organization. To maintain confidentiality of this data and prevent possible manipulation during transmission, you decide to implement IPSec using the AH protocol. Will this address your concerns?

3. The same Payroll department decides to outsource its accounting needs to an external accounting company. They set up IPSec using AH and ESP in tunnel mode between the tunnel servers in the perimeter networks of the two organizations. Files are copied between the two organizations and transmitted in the tunnel. Does this solution prevent inspection of the files as they're transmitted from the Payroll department to the external accounting company?

4. Last year you successfully thwarted a well-known hacker who was using a Telnet attack against your organization's FTP server. You did this by blocking the Telnet protocol at your firewall. Now it appears that the attacker has again gained access to the computer by launching the Telnet attack from another computer in your organization's DMZ. What could you do to prevent any Telnet connections to the FTP server?

5. What security risks exist when preshared keys are used to authenticate IPSec SAs?

6. When data is protected using IPSec AH, are there any fields in the IP packet that aren't protected from modification? Why or why not?

CHAPTER 13

Securing Access for Remote Users and Networks

About This Chapter

When external users and networks connect to an organization's wide area network (WAN), you must address additional security issues in your security design. Design decisions range from choosing allowed protocols to providing single sign-on capabilities.

Before You Begin

To complete this chapter, you must read the chapter scenario. This scenario is used throughout the chapter to apply the design decisions discussed in each lesson.

Chapter Scenario: Hanson Brothers

Hanson Brothers, a hockey equipment manufacturing company based in Warroad, Minnesota, requires a remote access solution for its employees. Hanson Brothers must address the following three remote access scenarios:

- **Providing access to network resources for employees at the Boise, Calgary, and Warroad offices.** Due to the increasing demand that the company implement telecommuting, employees will be allowed to work from home one day a week. Employees require access to all network resources. Some employees have asymmetric digital subscriber line (ADSL) and cable connections to the Internet at home and wish to use these technologies to connect to their local office network.

- **Providing access to a production server at the Warroad office for a partner organization.** Adventure Works is a major distributor of Hanson Brothers hockey equipment. Only a single specified computer at Adventure Works will be allowed to dial up to the production server at the Hanson Brothers Warroad office to determine stock availability.

- **Providing network connectivity to a new office in Montréal.** Hanson Brothers plans to open a new office in Montréal. Due to the high cost of establishing a dedicated network link across national borders, Hanson Brothers plans to investigate a virtual private networking (VPN) solution.

All domain controllers operating in the Hanson Brothers network are running Microsoft Windows 2000. No more Windows NT 4.0 backup domain controllers (BDCs) are running on the network.

Business goals and network infrastructure proposals for the three projects are detailed in the following sections.

Providing Access to Home Users

Hanson Brothers management plans to meet the following business objectives when granting remote access to employees:

- Before receiving remote network access, employees must be approved on an individual basis. Approved employees will be placed in a security group named Remote Users. Only members of the Remote Users group will be granted dial-up access to the network.

- Only administrators will be allowed to connect to the network remotely on Saturday evenings. Remote access to employees will be blocked between the hours of 6:00 P.M. and midnight so that network backups and administrative tasks can be processed.

- Employees must authenticate with the network using the strongest authentication protocol supported by both the remote client computer and the Routing and Remote Access Service (RRAS) computer.

- Connections must use 128-bit encryption to ensure that sensitive data is protected from inspection attempts.

- One server will be used for both dial-up and VPN access at each of the three offices. The remote access server will be placed in a Demilitarized Zone (DMZ) (also known as a perimeter network) at each office. Figure 13.1 shows how the connection will exist at the Warroad office.

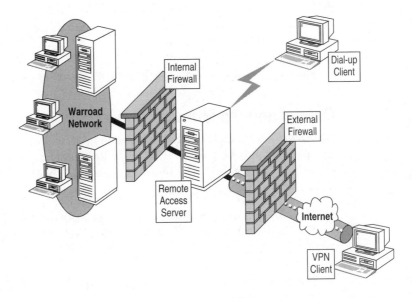

Figure 13.1   Remote access server placement for the Warroad office

- Users connecting to the remote access server will use their domain accounts and passwords for authentication.

- Employees use a combination of Windows 98, Windows NT 4.0, and Windows 2000–based computers to connect to the network.

- All remote access servers will be installed as Windows 2000 stand-alone servers, not as members of the hansonbrothers.tld domain.

- All remote access policy for employees will be maintained at the Warroad office. It's important that the three offices don't have different remote access policies.

Providing Access to the Partner Organization

While Adventure Works is a trusted partner, Hanson Brothers management wants to ensure that users connecting from Adventure Works have restricted access to the Hanson Brothers corporate network.

- Connections from Adventure Works will be granted only if strong encryption of account and password is used.

- Connections from Adventure Works will be limited to a single phone number. Connections from any other phone number will be disallowed.

- Connections from Adventure Works will be limited to the remote access server hosting the stock application. Connections to any other server on the network must be prevented.

- The computer accessing the stock application from Adventure Works is running Windows NT 4.0 Workstation as the operating system.

Connecting the Montréal Office

Due to the cost of establishing a dedicated network link between the Montréal and Warroad offices, Hanson Brothers will establish a VPN solution to connect the two offices securely. The following constraints will affect the design of the VPN connection:

- The Montréal office has acquired a third-party firewall to protect their office. The third-party firewall supports Internet Protocol Security (IPSec) but doesn't support Point to Point Tunneling Protocol (PPTP) or Layer Two Tunneling Protocol (L2TP).

- The third-party firewall doesn't support certificate-based authentication.

- Users at the Montréal office access corporate resources through the VPN connection to the corporate office.

- The VPN connection must provide the strongest encryption of the data encapsulated within the VPN.

- The Warroad office must ensure that the VPN server accepts only connections from the Montréal office.

Lesson 1: Planning Remote Access Security

Allowing remote access to your network enables your organization's employees to access corporate information from anywhere in the world. It empowers users in remote offices to access valuable network resources as if they were in the main office. However, allowing remote access introduces an entirely new set of security risks. Your job as a security professional is to configure dial-up and VPN connections so that they allow only carefully defined traffic to flow between offices and users without exposing sensitive data or granting unauthorized access.

After this lesson, you will be able to

- Plan the components involved in remote access security

Estimated lesson time: 30 minutes

Choosing Between Dial-Up and VPN Solutions

Windows 2000 offers two methods for remote users to connect to the local network: dial-up remote access, where the user connects to the network by using a modem, or VPN, where the user connects through a tunnel that's running over an existing network connection. The existing network connection may be the local network or an Internet connection.

Dial-up connections offer access to the greatest number of users because the client requires only a modem and a phone number to connect to a remote access server. The client connects to the remote access server over the Public Switched Telephone Network (PSTN) and establishes a virtual circuit to a listening port on the remote access server, as shown in Figure 13.2.

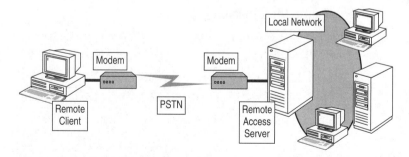

Figure 13.2   Remote access over a PSTN

In addition to the virtual circuit, the client and server negotiate link control protocol (LCP) parameters that define the authentication protocol and other connection parameters.

Dial-up access is most often used when the dial-up connections are to local phone numbers or toll-free numbers. Dial-up connections are also used to initially access the Internet when establishing VPN connections.

An existing Internet Protocol (IP) connection must exist before you can establish a VPN. The VPN client connects to a listening Transmission Control Protocol (TCP) port on the remote access server using a tunneling protocol such as L2TP or PPTP, as shown in Figure 13.3.

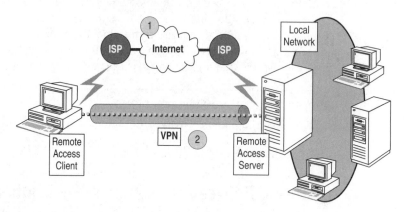

Figure 13.3   Remote access over a VPN

The figure shows that the VPN connection (item 2) requires an existing connection to an IP network (item 1). The connection could be either a dedicated connection, such as a T1 link at the office, or a dial-up connection to an Internet Service Provider (ISP) by the remote access client.

VPN access is commonly implemented to reduce the costs associated with support modem pools for an organization and the long distance costs associated with remote employees.

Making the Decision

Table 13.1 shows important factors you should consider when choosing between a dial-up or VPN solution for remote access to a network.

Table 13.1   Choosing Between Dial-Up and VPN Access

Use	Under the Following Circumstances
Dial-up access	■ Your organization maintains an existing modem pool. ■ Most remote connections to the network are through local access numbers and don't require long distance or toll-free charges. ■ Your organization requires an alternative connection method between offices if a dedicated network link fails.
VPN access	■ Your organization wants to outsource modem support to an ISP. ■ Users have existing Internet access. ■ Your organization wants to reduce the costs associated with long distance and toll-free numbers. ■ Your organization requires faster access speeds than are possible with dial-up networking solutions.

Applying the Decision

Hanson Brothers requires a combination of dial-up and VPN support for the scenarios presented in this chapter's case study.

Hanson Brothers will provide both dial-up and VPN access to their employees. Providing both forms of access ensures that users with modems and users with high-speed Internet connections can connect to their local office.

The computer connecting to the stock application from Adventure Works requires a dial-up connection. A dial-up connection will allow Hanson Brothers to restrict the connection to a specific phone number.

Finally, the new office in Montréal will require a VPN solution to provide connectivity to the corporate office in Warroad. For redundancy, Hanson Brothers could create a demand-dial connection between the two offices that use telephone lines in case either of the ISP connections at the Warroad or Montréal offices are unavailable. The demand-dial connection would be established only if the VPN were unavailable. Packets destined to the other network would initiate the dial-up connection if the VPN were unavailable.

Planning Remote Access Authentication

When a remote user connects to the network, the user must provide credentials to authenticate with the network.

Windows 2000 RRAS supports the following authentication methods:

- **Password Authentication Protocol (PAP).** PAP offers the most flexibility among the authentication protocols because it's supported by almost all dial-up network services. The danger is that PAP sends the user password as a plaintext string. Accordingly, the use of PAP isn't recommended under any circumstances in security-aware networks.

- **Shiva Password Authentication Protocol (SPAP).** SPAP uses a reversible encryption method supported by Shiva remote access servers and Windows 2000 remote access servers. The encryption algorithms are stronger than those used in PAP, but SPAP doesn't provide protection against server impersonation.

- **Challenge Handshake Authentication Protocol (CHAP).** CHAP sends the password and a challenge from the server through a hashing algorithm. The recipient identifies the user, obtains the password from the directory, and performs the same hashing algorithm against the challenge and password. If the results match, the user is authenticated.

Important   CHAP authentication requires that the user's password be stored in plaintext or in reversibly encrypted format at the domain controller for comparison purposes. When this attribute is set, the storage of the plaintext password format doesn't take place until the user changes the password after the attribute is enabled.

- **Microsoft Challenge Handshake Authentication Protocol (MS-CHAP).**
  MS-CHAP increases security by dropping the requirement to store the user's
  password in a plaintext format at the domain controller. MS-CHAP creates
  the challenge response by passing the challenge and the user's password
  through the Message Digest v4 (MD4) hashing algorithm rather than the
  MD5 algorithm. Because the algorithm is well known, MS-CHAP is also vulnerable to dictionary attacks if short passwords or passwords that are found in
  a dictionary are used. MS-CHAP uses Microsoft Point-to-Point Encryption
  (MPPE) Protocol to encrypt all data transmitted between the remote access
  client and the Network Access Server (NAS).

- **Microsoft Challenge Handshake Authentication Protocol Version 2
  (MS-CHAPv2).** MS-CHAPv2 improves security by supporting mutual
  authentication, stronger data encryption keys, and separate encryption keys
  for sending and receiving data.

- **Extensible Authentication Protocol (EAP).** EAP provides extensions to
  dial-up and VPN connections. These extensions provide two-factor authentication by using devices such as smart cards to provide network credentials.
  EAP uses Transport Layer Security (TLS) to secure the authentication process. EAP provides mutual authentication, negotiation of encryption methods,
  and secured key exchange between the NAS and the remote access client.
  EAP requires that both the remote access client and the NAS run Windows
  2000 and that a Public Key Infrastructure (PKI) is deployed to provide certificates for both the NAS and the remote access clients.

The Advantage of Two-Factor Authentication

Two-factor authentication adds security to the authentication process by
requiring two forms of identification when users are authenticating with
the network. For example, smart cards require you to have the physical
smart card and know the PIN to access the private key on the smart card.
If you don't have both the smart card and the PIN, you can't authenticate
with the network.

Note The same authentication protocols are available for both dial-up and VPN
scenarios.

Making the Decision

When choosing between remote access authentication protocols, consider the desired level of security and the type of remote access clients that your solution
must support. Table 13.2 lists the design decisions you need to consider when
choosing whether to implement a remote access authentication protocol.

Table 13.2   Choosing Remote Access Authentication Protocols

Use	Under the Following Conditions	Level of Protection
PAP	■ No other authentication methods are possible for the remote access connection. ■ All connections are dial-up connections. No VPN connections are supported. ■ Remote access clients don't support any other authentication methods.	Low
SPAP	■ You're using Shiva Remote Access servers as NASs. ■ You don't require strong encryption methods for access.	Low
CHAP	■ Your organization doesn't consider the storage of passwords in reversible encrypted format on the domain controller a security risk. ■ Remote access clients are a mix of Microsoft and other operating systems.	Medium
MS-CHAP	■ You don't wish to store passwords in reversible encrypted format. ■ You only need to support Microsoft operating systems for dial-up and VPN connectivity. ■ You require encryption of data between the remote access client and the NAS.	Medium
MS-CHAPv2	■ You're using Windows 2000– and Windows NT 4.0–based clients for both dial-up and VPN authentication. ■ You're using Windows 95 and Windows 98 clients for VPN authentication only. ■ Your organization requires mutual authentication of the remote access client and the NAS. ■ You require encryption of data between the remote access client and the NAS.	High
EAP-TLS	■ Your organization wants to implement two-factor authentication for dial-up and VPN access. ■ You're using only Windows 2000 or other operating systems that support smart card authentication. ■ You require encryption of data between the remote access client and the NAS. ■ You have a PKI deployed within your organization. ■ Your organization requires mutual authentication of remote access client and NAS to prevent impersonation of either the user or the NAS.	High

Note If you choose multiple authentication protocol support, the authentication protocol that provides the highest level of security supported by both the NAS and the remote access client will automatically be selected by the initial negotiation process.

Applying the Decision

To provide the strongest form of authentication acceptable to both the remote client and the RRAS server, configure the RRAS server to support MS-CHAP and MS-CHAPv2. While it would be best to support only MS-CHAPv2, Windows 98 clients require MS-CHAP to provide authentication for dial-up connections. Windows 98–based clients only support MS-CHAPv2 for VPN connections. To ensure security, you should enforce strong passwords for all user accounts. Strong passwords help prevent successful dictionary attacks.

Hanson Brothers will implement strong encryption of the user account and password on the remote access connection from Adventure Works. Strong encryption requires you to use MS-CHAPv2 or EAP. Because the Windows NT 4.0 client doesn't support smart card authentication, MS-CHAPv2 is the only authentication protocol that meets this objective.

Because Montréal's third-party firewall won't support PPTP or L2TP/IPSec, IPSec tunnel mode is the only choice for connecting the Montréal office securely to the Warroad office over the Internet. The Montréal office won't be able to implement user authentication for the VPN connection between the offices because IPSec tunnel mode doesn't support user authentication.

Planning Dial-Up Protocols

You must configure remote access clients and NASs to support a dial-up remote access protocol when using dial-up connections. Windows 2000 supports three remote access protocols for dial-up connectivity:

- **Point-to-Point Protocol (PPP).** PPP has the ability to negotiate security requirements between a remote access client and a NAS. PPP offers support for multiple protocols (NetBEUI, IPX/SPX, and TCP/IP) and interoperability with other operating systems.

- **Serial Line Internet Protocol (SLIP).** SLIP is an older dial-up framing protocol that uses plaintext authentication and supports only TCP/IP protocol connections. Because of the use of plaintext authentication, only Windows 2000 remote access clients can use SLIP. RRAS can't use SLIP to authenticate remote access connections.

- **Asynchronous NetBEUI (AsyBEUI).** AsyBEUI, also known as Microsoft RAS protocol, was used by Windows NT 3.1, Windows for Workgroups, MS-DOS, and LAN Manager. Use this protocol only to support these down-level remote access clients.

Making the Decision

Table 13.3 shows the design decisions you need to make for choosing remote access protocols supported by Windows 2000.

Table 13.3   Choosing a Remote Access Protocol

Use	Under the Following Conditions
PPP	■ You need to deploy remote access services for Windows 95, Windows 98, Windows NT 3.5, Windows NT 3.51, Windows NT 4.0, Windows 2000, and most third-party dialers. ■ You require negotiation of authentication protocols and remote access session characteristics, such as requiring mutual authentication or encryption of transmitted data.
SLIP	■ Your remote access clients must connect to third-party NAS's that support only SLIP communications.
AsyBEUI	■ Your organization must support Windows NT 3.1, Windows for Workgroups, MS-DOS, or LAN Manager–based remote access clients.

Applying the Decision

Hanson Brothers will use Windows 2000 RRAS to provide remote user and office connectivity. Because all connecting computers use Windows 98, Windows NT 4.0, or Windows 2000, PPP meets all needs for connectivity.

Because it uses plaintext password transmission, SLIP is supported only for remote access clients. Because there are no UNIX remote access servers involved in the design, you don't need to configure the remote access clients to support SLIP connections. Likewise, there are no Windows NT 3.1, Windows for Workgroups, MS-DOS, or LAN Manager clients. Therefore, you don't need to support AsyBEUI remote access connections.

Planning VPN Protocols

Windows 2000 supports VPN solutions for both client-to-server and network-to-network connectivity. For client-to-server connections, Windows 2000 supports both PPTP and L2TP/IPSec solutions. In addition, Windows 2000 supports IPSec tunnel solutions for providing network-to-network connectivity. The design decisions don't vary for client-to-network and network-to-network scenarios, although network-to-network solutions can include IPSec tunnel mode.

Analyzing VPN Protocol Selections

As mentioned earlier, there are three protocols for VPN connections: PPTP, L2TP/IPSec, and IPSec tunnel mode. The following sections provide an analysis of each VPN protocol choice.

Point to Point Tunneling Protocol (PPTP)

PPTP is supported by Windows 95, Windows 98, Windows NT 4.0, and Windows 2000 remote access clients. Like all VPN protocols, PPTP requires an IP connection to exist before the VPN can be established. PPTP uses MPPE to provide encryption of the transmitted data. MPPE can use 40-bit, 56-bit, or 128-bit encryption keys.

Note   MPPE using 128-bit encryption requires the Windows High Encryption Pack to be installed on Windows 2000–based computers. For legacy clients, the strong encryption patch must be installed. Strong encryption is available only to nonembargoed countries.

PPTP is commonly used to meet the following requirements:

- **If support for down-level clients is needed.** Windows 95, Windows 98, and Windows NT 4.0 clients support PPTP only as a VPN protocol.

- **If the VPN must cross a firewall or perimeter network that performs Network Address Translation (NAT).** PPTP is the only VPN protocol that can pass through NAT because the fields modified by the NAT process aren't protected by the MPPE encryption.

- **If your organization requires the authentication only of the user account, not the machine account.** PPTP doesn't support the authentication of the computers used in the remote access connection. If MS-CHAPv2 is used, then the user account and the computer account of the remote access server are authenticated, but the computer account of the remote access client computer isn't authenticated.

What About the Security Weaknesses Related to PPTP?

The original implementation of PPTP used MS-CHAP as the authentication protocol. If a remote access client used weak user passwords, it was possible to determine the password by using a dictionary attack. The latest update to PPTP has added support for MS-CHAPv2 and EAP authentication to reduce the risk of password determination.

Configuring the tunnel server to allow only MS-CHAPv2 or EAP connections reduces the risk of weak passwords being determined by a dictionary attack. If weak passwords are a major concern, ensure that all remote access clients use Windows 2000 and issue smart cards to use EAP authentication.

If PPTP packets must pass through a firewall, you must configure the firewall to allow the PPTP packets to pass through the firewall. PPTP packets have a destination port of TCP port 1723 and use protocol ID 47 (Generic Routing Encapsulation or GRE).

Layer Two Tunneling Protocol over IPSec (L2TP/IPSec)

L2TP is an alternate method of providing VPN access to the network. As with PPTP, you can use L2TP to provide both client-to-server and server-to-server access. L2TP and PPTP have three major differences:

- L2TP doesn't include an encryption mechanism. To provide encryption, IPSec is automatically used to negotiate a security association between the two computers using the L2TP tunnel. Unlike other IPSec security associations, the L2TP security association isn't defined in the IPSec configuration for the computer's local policy.

- L2TP provides two forms of authentication. L2TP provides user authentication using standard dial-up authentication protocols, including MS-CHAP, MS-CHAPv2, and EAP. In addition, IPSec provides machine authentication.

- L2TP can't pass through a firewall or perimeter server performing NAT. NAT modifies the IP address and port information in an IP packet. Because these fields are protected by the IPSec encryption, the packets are discarded at the receiving tunnel server because the contents of the packets are modified. You must place the tunnel server accepting L2TP connections on a network segment where NAT isn't applied to incoming and outgoing packets.

Note L2TP is a proposed Internet standard defined in Request for Comment (RFC) 2661. You can obtain a copy of this RFC by going to *www.ietf.org/rfc* and searching for "RFC 2661."

If L2TP/IPSec packets must pass through a firewall, you must configure the firewall to allow IPSec packets destined to the tunnel server to pass through the firewall. The IPSec packets are destined to UDP port 500 on the tunnel server using IPSec Encapsulating Security Payload (ESP) protocol that is identified by protocol ID 50. You don't configure the firewall to pass L2TP packets (destined to UDP port 1701), because the packets are still encrypted when they pass through the firewall.

IPSec Tunnel Mode

IPSec tunnel mode uses Encapsulated Security Payloads (ESPs) to encrypt all traffic passing between the tunnel endpoints. The original IP packets are encrypted within the IPSec tunnel mode packet as they are transmitted across the unsecured network. The data is decrypted when it reaches the endpoint nearest the destination computer. You must consider the following factors when investigating an IPSec tunnel mode solution for network connectivity:

- IPSec tunnel mode is a highly interoperable solution. If you need to provide secure interoffice connectivity with third-party firewalls, routers or gateways that don't support L2TP/IPSec or PPTP VPN tunneling technology, consider deploying IPSec tunnel mode as a VPN solution.

- IPSec doesn't provide user authentication of the two endpoints involved in the IPSec tunnel. IPSec tunnel mode only provides machine authentication of the tunnel endpoints.

- IPSec tunnel mode doesn't support client-to-network VPN access. IPSec tunnel mode is supported only for network-to-network connectivity.

Note   IPSec tunnel mode doesn't provide end-to-end encryption of data. The data is only encrypted as it passes between the tunnel endpoints. You can provide end-to-end encryption by configuring IPSec transport mode to be passed through the IPSec tunnel.

- IPSec supports certificate-based authentication, Kerberos, and preshared key authentication for IPSec connections. If the connection is between organizations, consider using a preshared key or certificate-based authentication. Preshared keys are viable provided that you configure security associations to accept only connections from the other tunnel endpoint.

- Tunnel server placement can prevent IPSec tunnel mode communications. Don't place the tunnel servers behind firewalls or perimeter servers that perform NAT. You must place the tunnel servers on network segments where NAT doesn't take place for incoming or outgoing packets.

Making the Decision

Table 13.4 shows the design factors you should consider when choosing a VPN protocol.

Table 13.4   Selecting a VPN Protocol

Choose This VPN Protocol	When These Circumstances Exist
PPTP	<ul><li>You require client-to-gateway or network-to-network connectivity.</li><li>The VPN must pass through a firewall or perimeter server that performs NAT.</li><li>You require VPN support for legacy Windows clients.</li></ul>
L2TP	<ul><li>You require client-to-gateway or network-to-network connectivity.</li><li>Computer certificates are deployed to all client computers requiring L2TP connections.</li><li>You require authentication of the user accounts and authentication of the machine accounts.</li><li>The tunnel server isn't located behind a firewall or perimeter server performing NAT.</li><li>You plan to implement an IPSec-protected tunnel with the least amount of configuration.</li></ul>

Table 13.4   Selecting a VPN Protocol

Choose This VPN Protocol	When These Circumstances Exist
IPSec tunnel mode	• You require only network-to-network connectivity. • Only machine authentication is required for the tunnel endpoints. • If using certificate-based authentication, the certificates are issued from trusted CAs. • If using preshared keys, the IPSec security associations are configured to only allow connections from the tunnel endpoints.

If IPSec tunnel mode packets must pass through a firewall, you must configure the firewall to allow packets destined to UDP port 500 on the tunnel server. An additional packet filter must be added to restrict connections to using ESP packets (protocol ID 50).

Applying the Decision

Figure 13.4 shows how the Montréal office would connect to the Warroad office.

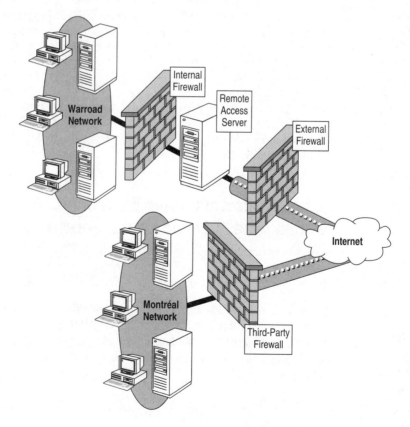

Figure 13.4   VPN solution for connecting the Montréal office to the Warroad office

You must configure the external firewall at the Warroad office not to perform NAT. This is required because the third-party firewall at the Montréal office doesn't support PPTP. IPSec tunnel mode can't pass through a firewall if NAT is performed on incoming traffic. To ensure that IPSec tunnel mode works, use an IP address range in the DMZ that's a public network address range.

Note   RFC 1918 describes the three pools of IP addresses reserved for private network usage. The ranges include 10.0.0.0/8, 172.16.0.0/12, and 192.168.0.0/16. You can obtain a copy of this RFC by going to *www.ietf.org/rfc* and searching for "RFC 1918."

For employees connecting to the network, you could use either PPTP or L2TP/IPSec. Although the scenario doesn't mention certificates being issued to the computers, it's possible to use L2TP/IPSec in the future based on the network configuration.

You must configure the connection between the Montréal office and the Warroad office to use IPSec tunnel mode because the third-party firewall at the Montréal office doesn't support PPTP or L2TP IPSec. IPSec tunnel mode allows full connectivity between the offices but requires additional configuration.

Because the third-party firewall doesn't support certificate-based authentication, you must configure a preshared key for use by the Windows 2000 tunnel server at the Warroad office and the third-party firewall at the Montréal office. To secure the preshared key, configure IPSec filters to allow only IPSec connections using the preshared key from the other tunnel endpoint. This configuration ensures that if the preshared key is compromised, an attacker will be unable to establish an IPSec tunnel mode connection to the network because the attacker won't be connecting from the correct IP address.

Planning Integration with Windows NT 4.0 Remote Access Service (RAS) Servers

If your network contains a mix of Windows NT 4.0 RAS servers and Windows 2000 remote access servers, you must make special considerations to allow authentication of clients connecting to the Windows NT 4.0 RAS servers.

Windows NT 4.0 RAS servers determine whether a connecting user has dial-in permissions by connecting to a domain controller with a NULL session. A NULL session is a security risk because it doesn't provide credentials for the connection. If you allow NULL sessions on the network, anyone connected to the network can query Active Directory directory service without the default security mechanisms in place.

If you don't allow NULL sessions, a remote access client being authenticated by a Windows NT 4.0 RAS server may face the following authentication results:

- If the Windows NT 4.0 RAS server connects to a Windows NT 4.0 BDC in a mixed-mode network, authentication will succeed because the Windows NT 4.0 BDC supports NULL sessions.

- If the Windows NT 4.0 RAS server is a Windows NT 4.0 BDC in a mixed-mode network, authentication will succeed because the BDC can determine dial-in permissions by looking at its versions of the domain database.

- If the Windows NT 4.0 RAS server connects to a Windows 2000 domain controller, the authentication will fail or succeed depending on the membership of the Pre–Windows 2000 Compatible Access security group. If the group contains the Everyone group, authentication will succeed because members of the Pre–Windows 2000 Compatible Access security group can query the domain controller with a NULL session. If the Pre–Windows 2000 Compatible Access security group doesn't contain the Everyone group, the authentication attempt will fail.

The membership of the Pre–Windows 2000 Compatible Access security group is determined by the user creating a new domain in the forest. When you run the Active Directory Installation Wizard (Dcpromo.exe), you're asked if you want to provide support for Windows NT 4.0 RAS servers. If you enable this support, the Everyone group is added to the membership of the Pre–Windows 2000 Compatible Access security group.

Important You can add the Everyone group to the Pre–Windows 2000 Compatible Access security group by using the command **NET LOCALGROUP "PRE–WINDOWS 2000 COMPATIBLE ACCESS"/ADD EVERYONE.** You can't add the Everyone group in Active Directory Users And Computers to the domain–local group.

Due to the security implications of allowing unsecured queries to Active Directory, your migration plan should include the early migration of remote access servers to Windows 2000. Once all remote access servers are upgraded to Windows 2000, remove the Everyone group from the Pre–Windows 2000 Compatible Access membership.

Making the Decision

When Windows NT 4.0 RAS servers exist on the network, add the following items to your remote access design:

- If the Windows NT 4.0 remote access server isn't a BDC, ensure that the membership of the Pre–Windows 2000 Compatible Access group contains the Everyone group.

- Upgrade the Windows NT 4.0 remote access servers to Windows 2000 as soon as possible or decommission the Windows NT 4.0 remote access servers and replace the servers with Windows 2000 servers running RRAS.

- Remove the Everyone group from the Pre–Windows 2000 Compatible Access group once all Windows NT 4.0 remote access servers are removed from the network or upgraded to Windows 2000.

Applying the Decision

There are no Windows NT 4.0 servers running remote access services in the Hanson Brothers network. To prevent excess rights from being granted to the network, inspect the membership of the Pre–Windows 2000 Compatible Access security group. If the Everyone group is a member, simply delete the group from the existing membership.

Lesson Summary

The decision to allow users to remotely connect to your organization's network requires careful planning to ensure that security is maintained. Make sure that you identify how the users will remotely connect to the network so that you can include authentication, protocol, and integration decisions in your remote access design.

Lesson 2: Designing Remote Access Security for Users

You can apply several settings to secure user connections to the network. These settings include user properties that allow or deny remote access, authorization based on the source or destination phone number, and preconfigured remote access connection objects using the Connection Manager Administration Kit (CMAK).

Planning User Settings for Dial-Up Networking Security

Windows 2000 allows an administrator to configure how dial-up security is applied at the user account property level, as shown in Figure 13.5.

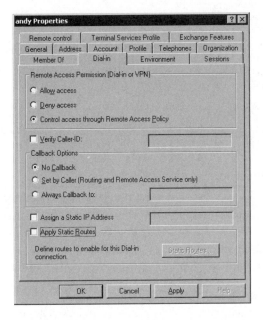

Figure 13.5   Dial-in properties for an Active Directory user account

For each user account you can define the following settings to secure remote access connections:

- **Remote Access Permission.** You can set permissions for each user to allow access, deny access, or control access through remote access policy. Even if allow access is selected, remote access policy will be evaluated to ensure that the connection attempt matches the defined profile settings.

- **Verify Caller-ID.** If caller ID is implemented on the phone system, the phone number from which the remote access connection originated can be verified against this attribute value. If the originating phone number doesn't match, the connection attempt is dropped.

- **Callback Options.** Callback allows phone charges to be applied to the remote access server rather than to the remote access client. You can choose to implement no callback security, have the remote access client provide the phone number to call back, or require callbacks to predetermined phone numbers. Configuring callback to call a specific number provides the highest form of security.

- **Assign a Static IP Address.** Some firewall software identifies connections by their IP address. Use the static IP address attribute to assign a specific IP address to a client connection. This attribute requires that the remote access client always connects to the same remote access server. If the connection is made to a remote access server on a different network, the IP addressing could be incorrect.

- **Apply Static Routes.** You can restrict which networks a remote access client can access by applying static routes to the remote access connection. If a network segment isn't included in the static routes, access to that segment of the network is prevented.

Making the Decision

When designing remote access security, you want to include user property settings to secure remote access connections, as described in Table 13.5.

Table 13.5   Planning User Properties for Remote Access

To	Set the Following User Property Settings
Prevent remote access to the network	- Configure the remote access permission for the user account to Deny Access.
Use remote access policy settings to determine remote access permissions	- Configure the remote access permission for the user account to Control Access Through Remote Access Policy.
Restrict dial-up connections to a specific phone number	- In phone networks that support caller ID verification, configure Verify Caller–ID to the approved phone number.
	- In phone networks that don't support caller ID verification, configure the callback number to a specific phone number. Be careful with this option, because call forwarding could forward the callback to an unauthorized phone number.
Assign a specific IP address for all connection attempts by the user	- Set the Assign A Static IP Address attribute to the required IP address. Ensure that the remote access client connects only to a single remote access server or to remote access servers on the same network segment.
Restrict remote access clients to specific network segments	- Define static routes for the remote access client that define which network segments are accessible by the remote access client.

In addition to configuring individual attributes of a user account to secure remote access, you can also enable the remote access account lockout feature at the remote access server. Remote access account lockout denies remote access to a user account if a preconfigured number of failed authentication attempts occur during remote access connections. This setting helps prevent an attacker from attempting dictionary attacks over a remote access connection. The attacked account will be disabled for remote access once the number of failed attempts exceeds the configured threshold.

Note Remote access account lockout isn't related to user account lockout. Remote access account lockout only prevents an account from connecting to the network using remote access. Account lockout prevents all access to the network for the locked out account.

You must define two registry settings to enable remote access account lockout:

- Set HKEY_LOCAL_MACHINE\SYSTEM\CurrentControlSet\Services \RemoteAccess\Parameters\AccountLockout\MaxDenials to set the value for the failed attempts counter. If the counter exceeds the configured value, remote access will be locked out for the account. A successful authentication resets the failed attempts counter.

- Set HKEY_LOCAL_MACHINE\SYSTEM\CurrentControlSet\Services \RemoteAccess\Parameters\AccountLockout\ResetTime to the interval in minutes that you wish to reset the failed attempts counter to a value of zero. The default for this value is 2880 minutes or 48 hours.

If the remote access server is configured for RADIUS authentication, you must make the registry modifications at the server running Internet Authentication Services (IAS).

Warning Enabling the remote access account lockout settings leaves your network susceptible to an attacker. An attacker could lock out user accounts by attempting remote access connections for a user account until the account is locked out.

Applying the Decision

If Hanson Brothers chooses to deploy remote access security by using remote access policies, then the default option of Control Access Through Remote Access Policy is appropriate for all user accounts. If Hanson Brothers wants to ensure that certain accounts, such as the Guest account, can't be used for remote access, those accounts can be configured to Deny Access.

For Adventure Works you should define a dedicated user account for connecting to the Hanson Brothers network. You should configure the dial-in settings for the account to Verify Caller–ID, with the phone number being set to the predefined phone number at Adventure Works. If the calls were long distance, Hanson Brothers could cover the phone charges by using callback security to return the call to the specified phone number. Using both attributes ensures that the call originates at an authorized phone number and that the callback is made to an authorized phone number.

Authorizing Dial-Up Connections

In addition to authenticating remote access connections, you can also implement Windows 2000 remote access authorization techniques. Authorization techniques don't evaluate the account that's attempting the connection but instead examine the attributes of the connection attempt. In fact, it's reasonable to eliminate authentication from the dial-up connection attempt when using authorization methods.

Important   To use these authorization methods, the entire phone system must support the authorization method. This includes the telephone system that the caller uses, the telephone system between the caller and the remote access server, and all communications hardware used to complete the call. If any part of the connection doesn't support the authorization method, authorization will fail.

Windows 2000 supports the following remote access authorization methods:

- **Automatic Number Identification/Calling Line Identification (ANI/CLI).** ANI/CLI restricts a remote access connection to one or more originating phone numbers. If the remote access connection doesn't originate from the configured phone number, the connection attempt is denied.

- **Dialed Number Identification Service (DNIS).** DNIS identifies the phone number dialed by a remote access client. DNIS allows you to apply different remote access policies based on the phone number dialed by the remote access client. This is useful for organizations such as an ISP that provides different phone numbers to different clients even though all clients call the same modem pool. DNIS allows the ISP to identify which company the client is calling from and applies the correct remote access policy to the client.

What's the Difference Between ANI/CLI and Caller ID?

ANI/CLI doesn't require the remote access connection to provide user credentials. When you use ANI/CLI, the remote access connection is authorized based on the originating phone number. No user credentials are sent in the connection request.

Caller ID is an attribute of a user account. The caller ID attribute isn't verified until after the credentials are presented for a remote access connection.

Use caller ID when you wish to use the Windows 2000 access model to secure access to other resources on the network.

- **Third-Party Security Host.** You can configure remote access to the network to require the use of a third-party security host such as a SecureID security card. A SecureID security card prevents replay attacks by generating a new access code with each successful connection to the network. If a previous authentication attempt is replayed on the network, it will be using a previous code that's now invalid.

Making the Decision

Use Table 13.6 to determine when to implement authorization methods for remote access connections in a Windows 2000 network.

Table 13.6   Planning Authorization for Windows 2000 Remote Access Connections

Use	To Meet the Following Security Goals
ANI/CLI	- To restrict connections to a specific originating phone number. If the phone number doesn't match the configured originating phone number, the connection is dropped.
DNIS	- To host multiple phone numbers using the same bank of modems. DNIS allows you to create remote access policies based on the telephone number called by a remote access client.
Third-party security hosts	- Your network requires protection against replay attacks. - Unique session keys and access codes must be used for access to a high security network.

Applying the Decision

Hanson Brothers should consider using a combination of ANI/CLI and DNIS for the connection from Adventure Works. Adventure Works should use a different phone number when connecting to the Hanson Brothers network to query stock levels. DNIS can identify connection attempts to the network and apply the most restrictive remote access policy to the connection.

Alternatively, Hanson Brothers could use ANI/CLI to provide Adventure Works with unauthenticated, but authorized, access to the network. Only connections from the predefined phone number would be allowed to connect. The only problem with using ANI/CLI is that you can't use security for requests to the stocking application. The connection could use only the default security defined for the application because the Adventure Works user wouldn't be required to provide user credentials.

Securing Client Configuration

Dial-up networking for clients requires that the client computers are configured with dial-up connections to the remote network. The configuration and maintenance of dial-up connections objects at the remote access clients can cause administrative overhead if the configuration is modified incorrectly.

The CMAK, which is included with Windows 2000 Server, allows an administrator to create a dial-up networking connection that works with Windows 95,

Windows 98, Windows NT 4.0, and Windows 2000. A dial-up network connection object created using the CMAK provides the following advantages over user-defined dial-up networking objects:

- It defines a highly secure connection object. To remove the possibility of weakened security due to a remote access client modifying connection settings, you can define the connection object to block access to key configuration screens.

- It defines a package that launches a dial-up and VPN connection. The combined package simplifies the VPN process by requiring the end user to launch only a single connection object. The package will automatically launch the VPN once Internet connectivity is established.

- It defines a package that works on Windows 95–, Windows 98–, Windows NT 4.0–, and Windows 2000–based computers. The CMAK creates a package that can be deployed to most Windows operating systems.

- It removes saved password vulnerabilities. The CMAK allows you to prevent a user from saving his password within the network connection object.

- It deploys preset security configurations. You can predefine the connection object with the required authentication protocol, tunnel protocol, and encryption levels for both dial-up and VPN connections.

- It uses a standard phone book. You can update the connection object with a phone book that provides current local phone numbers.

Making the Decision

When defining a CMAK package, ensure that the options in Table 13.7 are configured to provide security.

Table 13.7   Configuring CMAK Packages to Secure Remote Access Connectivity

To	Configure the Following CMAK Package Settings
Provide local access numbers	- Define a phone book that provides local access numbers for all locations where employees will access the Internet.
Simplify the dial-up process when VPNs are deployed	- Configure the CMAK package to automatically launch the VPN connection once the Internet connection is established.
Prevent modification of security configuration parameters set in a dial-up connection	- Restrict access to the property pages where security parameters are configured. Consider including authentication protocols, encryption settings, and tunnel settings when using VPNs.
Prevent remote access connections by unauthorized personnel	- Configure the CMAK package to prevent users from saving their passwords. This prevents an unauthorized user from connecting to the corporate network.
Meet multiple dial-up configuration requirements	- Configure separate CMAK packages to match each dial-up configuration required.

Applying the Decision

Hanson Brothers can create a CMAK package that preconfigures desired settings to allow remote employees to connect to the office network. You can create separate CMAK packages for both the dial-up and VPN clients. Table 13.8 outlines the settings that you could design for the dial-up and VPN client CMAK packages.

Table 13.8 Designing CMAK Packages for Hanson Brothers

CMAK Package	Recommended Settings
Dial-up clients	■ Configure the phone book to provide local access numbers for the Calgary, Boise, and Warroad offices. ■ Configure the dial-up connections to use only MS-CHAPv2 to ensure mutual authentication of remote access client and remote access server. ■ Configure the dial-up connections to require the strongest encryption settings. ■ Prevent access to the Security tab to prevent users from modifying data encryption or authentication settings.
VPN clients	■ Configure the phone book to provide host names for the remote access servers at the Calgary, Boise, and Warroad offices or configure separate CMAK packages for each office. ■ Configure the VPN connections to only use MS-CHAPv2 to ensure mutual authentication of remote access client and remote access server. ■ Configure the VPN connections to require the strongest encryption settings. ■ Configure the VPN connection to use only PPTP. Before implementing L2TP/IPSec connections, you must deploy computer certificates to all remote access client computers. ■ Prevent access to the Security tab so users can't modify data encryption or authentication settings.

Lesson Summary

Your remote access security design defines whether it's more appropriate to allow connections based on user account or on phone number information. You can use a combination of the two, but be careful to make sure that the criteria are reasonable so that the appropriate users can access the network.

Finally, the CMAK lets you control the security settings of remote access connections by enforcing the settings that your organization requires and allowing you to restrict access to key configuration screens for the remote access connection objects. This ensures that the desired level of security is used for all remote users accessing the network.

Lesson 3: Designing Remote Access Security for Networks

When designing secure connectivity to remote offices, you must choose a method for connecting the remote office and develop a security plan for the remote office link.

Choosing Remote Office Connectivity Solutions

Your first decision when connecting a remote office to a corporate network is choosing which connection solution to use. You can deploy a dedicated (or private) WAN link or you can implement a VPN over a public network such as the Internet. Your decision will be based on your evaluation of the risks and costs associated with each deployment.

Private WAN links are typically implemented by purchasing or leasing a dedicated telecommunications line between the remote office and the corporate network, as shown in Figure 13.6.

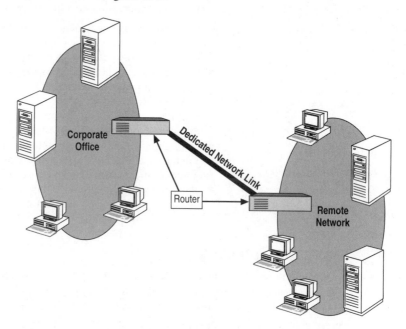

Figure 13.6   Connecting a remote network to the corporate office using a dedicated WAN link

The telecommunication links are typically technologies such as T1, T3, Frame Relay, or Integrated Services Digital Network (ISDN). Advantages of selecting a dedicated WAN solution include guaranteed bandwidth between sites and not sharing the network link with other organizations.

In a VPN solution the organization uses a public network to link the offices. The remote office and the corporate office will still require telecommunication links, but the links will be to the Internet rather than between the offices. Using a public network between the offices carries a risk of data interception. By creating VPNs between the two offices, you reduce the risk because the data is transmitted in an encrypted format.

Making the Decision

Table 13.9 shows the factors you need to consider when deciding whether to implement private or VPN methods for connecting a remote office to a corporate network.

Table 13.9   Choosing a Remote Office Connectivity Solution

Choose This Connection Solution	To Meet These Business Objectives
Dedicated WAN link	■ To restrict network traffic over the WAN link exclusively to traffic between the two offices. ■ To guarantee bandwidth between the two sites. ■ The cost of a dedicated link isn't prohibitive. ■ International boundaries or local laws don't prevent the establishment of a dedicated network link.
VPN over a public network	■ To leverage existing Internet links to provide network connectivity between sites. ■ To provide connectivity between hardware from different network vendors over public networks. ■ To reduce the costs associated with connecting offices across international boundaries.

Applying the Decision

Due to the high costs of establishing a dedicated WAN link between Canada and the United States, Hanson Brothers plans to implement a VPN solution. All data exchanged between the Montréal office and the Warroad office must be encrypted as it's transmitted over the Internet.

Securing Dedicated WAN Connections

Although dedicated WAN connections aren't exposed to the same vulnerabilities as VPN solutions, you should still take the following measures to ensure the security of transmitted data over the WAN connection:

■ Limit the types of data that can be transmitted over the WAN link. Configure routers at the remote network and corporate office with packet filters that define the types of network traffic that can cross the dedicated WAN link.

- Limit which computers can transmit data over the WAN link. Configure packet filters to define which IP addresses are allowed to transmit data over the WAN link. You can use this design to limit WAN link usage to servers and prevent unauthorized client computers from connecting to remote servers.

- Encrypt all traffic that's transmitted over the WAN link. You can configure some routers to encrypt data as it's transmitted over the WAN link. Consider encrypting traffic if you want to prevent the company that provides the WAN connection from viewing the transmitted data.

- Require mutual authentication of routers. In some network designs, such as frame relay networks, you can establish multiple connections in the WAN environment. Configuring mutual authentication of routers can limit the connections that can be established between routers.

Note   A Windows 2000 server configured with RRAS can act as a router for a dedicated network link. Windows 2000 supports common routing protocols such as Routing Information Protocol (RIP) and Open Shortest Path First (OSPF) protocol and can interoperate with many third-party routers.

Making the Decision

Table 13.10 outlines the design decisions you face when implementing a dedicated network connection between network offices.

Table 13.10   Designing Security for Dedicated WAN Links

To	Do the Following
Limit which protocols are allowed to traverse the network link	- Determine which protocols your organization will permit to traverse the WAN link. - Design packet filters to match the allowed protocols or to match the protocols that can't be transmitted over the WAN link. - Apply the packet filters at each router and test to ensure that the filters only allow the use of desired protocols.
Limit which computers can transmit data over the WAN link	- Identify which computers will be allowed to transmit data across the WAN link. - Develop packet filters at each router that enforce which computers can transmit data over the WAN link.
Ensure that confidential data can't be inspected as it's transmitted	- Configure the routers to encrypt data over the WAN link.
Limit which routers can connect to another router	- Enable mutual authentication between routers to limit which routers can establish connections.

Applying the Decision

Hanson Brothers plans to use a VPN solution for connecting the Montréal office to the corporate network in Warroad. Since a third-party firewall will be used at the Montréal office, many of the design decisions for dedicated network connections will be applied at the firewall.

Configure the third-party firewall to accept only connections from the remote access server at the Warroad office. This ensures that no other routers, remote access servers, or firewalls can establish connections to the firewall.

Designing VPN Solutions

VPNs allow an organization to leverage existing network links to a public network and use those links to connect remote offices. VPNs ensure that data is protected as it's transmitted over the public network.

VPN solutions between offices can use PPTP, L2TP/IPSec, and IPSec tunnel mode. Your choice depends on the remote access devices deployed at each office, the availability of a Public Key Infrastructure (PKI), and the placement of remote access devices.

For example, Figure 13.7 shows a typical remote access server deployment for securing access to a remote network. In this scenario, the remote access server, also referred to as a tunnel server, is located in the network's Demilitarized Zone (DMZ). The DMZ, or perimeter network, is used to store externally available resources. In this scenario the DMZ is implementing NAT. Since you can't use IPSec to connect through a firewall that's implementing NAT, this network infrastructure supports only a PPTP tunnel connection to the tunnel server.

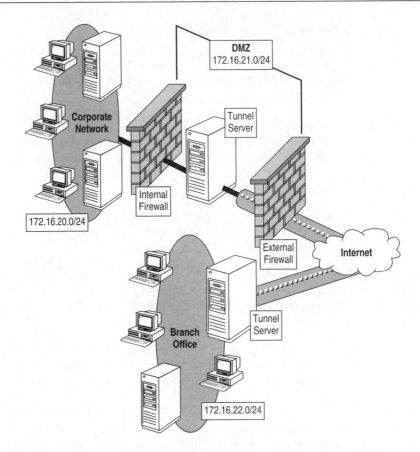

Figure 13.7   A VPN deployment in a DMZ using private network addressing

---

Note   You can identify when NAT is applied by inspecting the address ranges used on the interfaces of the firewall or perimeter server. If any of the interfaces use RFC 1918 addressing while others use public network addressing, the firewall or perimeter server is performing NAT services.

Alternatively, you could deploy the tunnel server in the network shown in Figure 13.8.

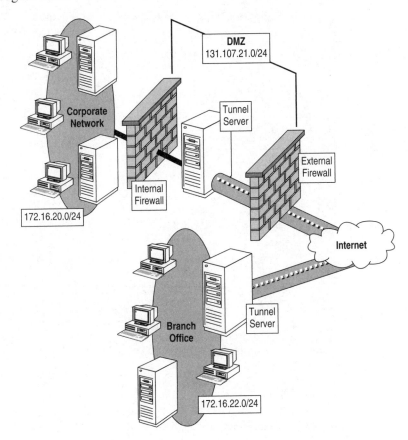

Figure 13.8 A VPN deployment in a DMZ not using private network addressing

In this network the tunnel server is located in a network segment that's using public network addressing. Because the firewall isn't performing NAT on traffic entering the DMZ, the VPN can use PPTP, L2TP/IPSec, or IPSec tunnel mode. The decision in this case will be based on other business factors.

What if the Tunnel Server is the Server Performing NAT?

You can deploy NAT and IPSec tunnels in one circumstance—when the tunnel server is also the server that performs the NAT process, as shown in Figure 13.9.

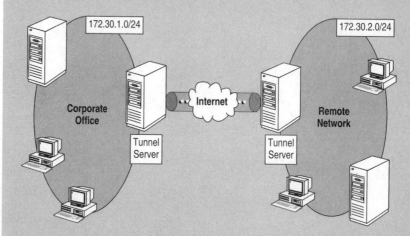

Figure 13.9   A scenario where IPSec and NAT can work together

In this scenario the tunnel servers at the corporate office and the remote network are both performing NAT services for the local networks. The external interfaces connected to the Internet use public network addresses.

If L2TP/IPSec or IPSec tunnel mode is configured between the two tunnel servers, the VPN connection will terminate before the NAT process is performed on any incoming or outgoing packets.

Making the Decision

Table 13.11 shows a decision matrix for determining when to use PPTP, L2TP/IPSec, or IPSec tunnel mode to connect remote offices with a VPN over a public network.

Table 13.11   Determining When to Deploy Tunneling Protocols

Use the Following VPN Protocol	When
PPTP	<ul><li>Either tunnel server is located in a network segment where NAT is performed.</li><li>Creating VPNs with Windows NT 4.0 RAS servers. Windows NT 4.0 RAS servers only support the use of PPTP. Windows NT 4.0 doesn't support IPSec encryption.</li><li>You require only user authentication for the VPN connection. PPTP connections are established by authenticating the user accounts provided for the connection.</li></ul>

Table 13.11   Determining When to Deploy Tunneling Protocols

Use the Following VPN Protocol	When
L2TP/IPSec	■ Stronger encryption is required for the connection between sites.
	■ Authentication of both a user account and machine account is required.
	■ The tunnel servers aren't located behind a firewall or perimeter server that performs NAT.
IPSec tunnel mode	■ The tunnel servers aren't located behind a firewall or perimeter server that performs NAT.
	■ Connecting to a third-party firewall or firewall that doesn't support PPTP or L2TP/IPSec.
	■ You only require machine authentication between the two tunnel endpoints.

Applying the Decision

Hanson Brothers will use IPSec tunnel mode for the connection between the Montréal office and the corporate office in Warroad. Hanson Brothers must either ensure that the DMZ uses public network addressing or deploy the tunnel server as a perimeter server so that the NAT process takes place after the tunnel has terminated.

To secure the tunnel server, include the following tasks in the security design plan:

■ Configure the IPSec security association to use preshared key authentication. The third-party firewall doesn't support certificate-based authentication. You can't use Kerberos authentication because the third-party firewall can't be a member of the domain. Therefore, preshared key authentication is your only option.

■ Configure the third-party firewall to accept only connections from the Windows 2000 tunnel server. This ensures that only the tunnel server can connect to the third-party firewall.

■ Configure the third-party as a tunnel endpoint for IPSec communications. The IPSec security association requires two packet filters: a packet filter describing network traffic directed from the Warroad office to the Montréal office using the third-party firewall as the tunnel endpoint and a packet filter describing network traffic from the Montréal office to the Warroad office using the Warroad office tunnel server's external network interface card (NIC) as the tunnel endpoint.

■ Configure the tunnel server as a tunnel endpoint for IPSec communications. The IPSec security association requires two packet filters: a packet filter describing network traffic directed from the Warroad office to the Montréal office using the third-party firewall as the tunnel endpoint and a packet filter describing network traffic from the Montréal office to the Warroad office using the Warroad office tunnel server's external NIC as the tunnel endpoint.

- Ensure that the Windows 2000 High Encryption Pack is installed on the tunnel server and that the third-party firewall allows 3DES encryption. This allows the IPSec security association to negotiate the use of 3DES as the encryption algorithm for transmitted data.

Lesson Summary

If your organization requires connectivity to remote offices, you must ensure that security is maintained so that network communications to the remote office don't weaken the overall network security.

Define security to protect all data transmitted between the remote office and the corporate network. This may be as simple as providing authentication between the connecting devices, or it may require the encryption of all data transmitted between the networks. Whatever solution you choose, make sure that it meets your business objectives without weakening network security.

Lesson 4: Designing Remote Access Policy

Remote access policy provides more control to remote access connections than was previously available in Microsoft network solutions. With remote access policy, instead of defining whether a user account has dial-in permissions, you can define conditions and profiles that must be met before the connection is established. This allows you to define the criteria for allowing remote access and ensure that security is maintained at the desired level.

After this lesson, you will be able to

- Design remote access policies to provide secure connectivity for remote clients

Estimated lesson time: 45 minutes

Designing Remote Access Policy Condition Attributes

You can define remote access policies to grant or deny remote access based on several specified conditions. The remote access server evaluates the existing conditions of the remote access request and compares it to the conditions defined in the remote access policy. If all conditions are matched, the remote access policy is applied to the request.

You can define the following condition attributes to identify which remote access policy to apply to a remote access connection.

- **Called-Station-ID.** The phone number of the network access server connected to by the remote access client. This condition allows you to identify which remote access policy to apply if a specific phone number is dialed by the remote access connection.

- **Calling-Station-ID.** The phone number from which the call originated.

- **Client-Friendly-Name.** The name of the RADIUS client that's forwarding the authentication request. This condition allows you to apply differing remote access policies based on the RADIUS client connected to by the remote access client.

Note   Designing RADIUS security for a network is discussed in Lesson 5, "Planning RADIUS Security."

- **Client-IP Address.** The IP address of the RADIUS client that forwarded the authentication request. This condition is used to identify RADIUS clients for VPN authentication requests.

- **Client-Vendor.** Identifies the manufacturer of the RADIUS client that forwarded the authentication request. You can use this condition to apply manufacturer-specific remote access policies.

- **Day-And-Time-Restrictions.** Allows you to restrict connections to specific days of the week or times of day.

- **Framed Protocol.** Allows you to define which remote access protocols are allowed for connections. For example, you could restrict connections to use only PPP and X.25 while preventing SLIP connections.

- **NAS-Identifier.** Allows you to identify the RADIUS client that forwarded the request by comparing the string sent by the RADIUS client to a string defined in the remote access policy.

- **NAS-IP-Address.** Allows you to identify the RADIUS client by its IP address. This is useful if you want to apply different remote access policies to a specific VPN server.

- **NAS-Port-Type.** Allows you to identify the medium used by the remote access client. You can indicate dial-up, ISDN, or VPN connections.

- **Service-Type.** Allows you to identify the service requested by the client. For remote access clients, the type of service will typically be framed.

- **Tunnel-Type.** Allows you to restrict which protocol a client uses for a VPN connection. You can restrict the connection to use PPTP or L2TP subject to the existing network infrastructure.

- **Windows-Groups.** Allows you to restrict access by Windows 2000 group membership. It's recommended to use Windows 2000 Universal groups as the group type.

Warning   You can't use groups from the remote access server's local security account management (SAM) database in the Windows-Groups condition. All groups must be from the domain.

Making the Decision

When designing conditions for remote access policy, make sure that you consider the following design points in the development of your remote access policy:

- Don't include too many conditions in the remote access policy definition. For the remote access policy to be applied, all conditions in the remote access policy must be met. If a single condition isn't met, the remote access policy isn't applied.

- Remote access policies are processed in order from the top of the list to the bottom. Make sure that you apply the correct conditions to each remote access policy and order the remote access policies so that remote access policies with more specific conditions are evaluated before ones with more general conditions.

- Remote access policies can be defined to both allow and deny remote access to the network. It may be easier to develop a set of condition that, if matched, result in remote access being denied. If you design a remote access policy that implements a deny action, make sure that you place a less-restrictive remote access policy below the remote access policy that defines a deny access condition.

- If no remote access policies exist, all remote access is denied. By default, a remote access policy exists that allows connections 24 hours a day. If you delete this default remote access policy and don't define additional remote access policies, all remote access attempts are denied.

- Don't define a remote access policy condition that can't be met. For example, don't require all connections to use L2TP as the tunnel type if the RADIUS client is located behind a firewall or perimeter server that performs NAT.

Applying the Decision

Different remote access policies are required for the three remote access scenarios presented for Hanson Brothers. Table 13.12 outlines the conditions required for each remote access policy.

Table 13.12   Designing Remote Access Policies for Hanson Brothers

Remote Access Policy	Required Conditions
Employees	■ Windows Groups: Member of the Remote Users group. ■ Day-and-Time Restrictions: Access for all hours except 6 P.M. to midnight on Saturdays.
Administrators	■ Members of the Administrators group. ■ Day-and-Time-restrictions: Allow access at all hours and on all days of the week.
Adventure Works	■ Calling-Station-ID: Must match the phone number used at Adventure Works to connect to the remote access server.
Montréal office VPN	■ You can't set conditions for the Montréal office VPN because IPSec tunnel mode connections don't utilize RRAS.

Designing Remote Access Policy Profiles

Once a remote access connection attempt is found to match the conditions defined for a specific remote access policy, the remote access policy profile is applied to the connection. While conditions are used to identify a remote access connection attempt, the profile defines the security settings that the remote access connection must implement. These security settings can include the authentication method and encryption level required to proceed with the connection. You can define the following properties for a remote access policy profile to secure remote access connection attempts, as shown in Figure 13.10.

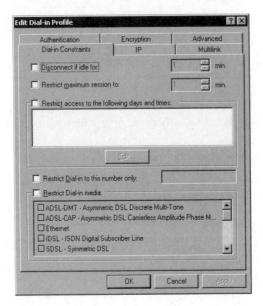

Figure 13.10   Defining remote access policy profile settings

- **Dial-in Constraints.** You can define how long a connection can remain idle before it's disconnected, the maximum time for session lengths, day and time limits, dial-in number constraints, and dial-in media. Commonly, you use the dial-in constraints to ensure that remote access sessions are terminated if they're idle for a long time.

- **IP.** You can define packet filters to restrict access to the network for the remote access client. You can define the packet filters on an Allow All Except For The Listed Protocols or a Deny All Except For The Listed Protocols basis.

- **Multilink.** No security-related settings can be defined for multilink attributes.

- **Authentication.** Allows you to define the authentication protocols required for a connection. If the connection doesn't support the defined authentication protocols, the connection will be dropped.

- **Encryption.** Allows you to define the required encryption levels. You can choose no encryption, basic encryption (40-bit keys for DES and MPPE), strong protection (56-bit keys for DES and MPPE), or strongest encryption (3DES and 128-bit MPPE).

Note MPPE provides encryption services for dial-up and PPTP-based VPN connections. DES and 3DES provide encryption for L2TP/IPSec connections.

- **Advanced.** Allows you to define advanced RADIUS attributes that are used when remote access connections use RADIUS authentication.

Making the Decision

Table 13.13 outlines scenarios in which you can use remote access policy profile settings to restrict remote access to the network.

Table 13.13   Using Remote Access Policy Profiles to Restrict Connections

To	Use the Following Profile Settings
Prevent idle remote access connections from using up the available remote access ports	■ Configure dial-in constraints to drop idle connections after a specified time has passed. ■ Configure dial-in constraints to define maximum session lengths. This requires the remote client to reconnect after the maximum session length is reached.
Restrict remote access connections to a specific phone number	■ Configure dial-in constraints to limit connections to a specific phone number and to require that the connection uses dial-in, referred to as asynch, media.
Restrict a remote access connection to a single computer or specific computers	■ Define IP packet filters that restrict access to specific IP addresses. Define the filters to deny all access except for the filters defined in the packet filter list.
Restrict a remote access connection to specific protocols	■ Define IP packet filters to allow only the protocols defined in the packet filter listing.
Require a specific authentication mechanism	■ Configure the profile to accept only connections using the desired authentication protocols. A connection attempt using a different authentication protocol will be dropped.
Require a specific level of encryption	■ Configure the profile to use the desired encryption level settings. Remember that the use of strongest encryption requires the Windows 2000 High Encryption Pack to be installed at both the remote access server and the remote access client.

Applying the Decision

Hanson Brothers must configure profiles for each of the client's remote access policies. Table 13.14 outlines the profile configuration required for each remote access policy.

Table 13.14   Designing Remote Access Policies Profiles for Hanson Brothers

Remote Access Policy	Required Profile Configuration
Employees	▪ Only accept MS-CHAPv2 or EAP authentication protocols to ensure mutual authentication of user and server. ▪ Allow both asynch and virtual network connections under dial-in constraints. This will provide support for both dial-up and VPN clients. ▪ Prevent connections on Saturdays between 6:00 P.M. and midnight under dial-in constraints.
Administrators	▪ Only accept MS-CHAPv2 or EAP authentication protocols to ensure mutual authentication of user and server. ▪ Allow both asynch and virtual network connections under dial-in constraints. This provides support for both dial-up and VPN clients.
Adventure Works	▪ Only accept MS-CHAPv2 or EAP authentication protocols to ensure strong authentication of the remote user account. ▪ Require that MPPE 128-bit encryption is required for the connection by requiring that only strongest encryption be accepted. ▪ Only accept connections from the phone number supplied by Adventure Works by configuring the dial-in number under dial-in constraints. ▪ Only accept asynch connections in the dial-in media property of dial-in constraints. This ensures that VPN connections will fail. ▪ Limit access to the remote access server by configuring IP filters that only allow access to the remote access server. ▪ If the stock application listens for connections on a known port, limit connections to that port only so that the remote access client can connect only to the stock application on the remote access server.
Montréal office VPN	▪ No conditions can be set to match the Montréal office VPN because IPSec tunnel mode connections don't use RRAS.

Planning Remote Access Policy Application

Remote access policy application varies depending on whether the domain is in native or mixed mode.

Note   If your organization wants to centralize remote access policy management, consider using RADIUS servers. Details on RADIUS design are covered in Lesson 5, "Planning RADIUS Security."

Remote Access Policy Application in Mixed Mode

In a mixed-mode domain you don't have the Control Access Through Remote Access Policy option available in a user account's properties. By default, every user is set to Allow Access, but remote access policy is still applied.

Important   The default remote access policy, Allow Access If Dial-In Permission Is Enabled, will grant access to all users if left unmodified. You must delete or modify the default remote access policy if you need to be able to restrict remote access to the network.

Whenever a connection attempt occurs, the remote access policy whose conditions match the attempt evaluates the remote access policy profile to determine whether to allow the connection. The connection attempt will end in one of two outcomes.

- The connection attempt will succeed. Success occurs when the user's account is configured to allow dial-in access and the remote access client meets the remote access policy profile settings.

- The connection attempt will fail. Failure occurs in the following circumstances:

  - The user is denied dial-in permissions in her user properties.

  - The connection attempt matches the conditions of a policy but not the profiles settings for the remote access policy.

  - The connection attempt doesn't match the conditions of any of the existing remote access policies.

Remote Access Policy Application in Native Mode

In a native mode domain, user accounts are configured to Control Access Through Remote Access Policy in the user account property pages. With this setting, all remote access permissions are determined through remote access policy settings. The connection attempt will result in one of three outcomes.

- **Allowed by policy.** The connection attempt will succeed if the remote access connection attempt matches the conditions and the remote access policy profile settings for a remote access policy that's set to Grant Remote Access Permission.

- **Denied by policy.** The connection attempt will fail if the remote access connection attempt matches the conditions and the remote access policy profile settings for a remote access policy that's set to Deny Remote Access Permission.

- **Denied implicitly.** If the connection attempt doesn't match the conditions defined for any of the existing remote access policies, the connection attempt will be denied.

Making the Decision

To provide remote access to the network, you must determine how you will apply remote access policy. Although remote access policy is applied in mixed mode, native mode provides the most flexibility.

When deciding how to use remote access policy in your domain, consider the following design points:

- In mixed mode, you should delete or modify the default remote access policy. By default, all users are allowed dial-in access. The only exceptions are the built-in Guest and Administrator accounts.

- If you don't want to allow all users dial-in permissions in a mixed mode domain, modify the default remote access policy or change the dial-in permissions for the user accounts that should not have dial-in permissions.

- To prevent specific connection attempts in a native mode domain, configure a remote access policy that defines the conditions of the remote access policy. Configure the remote access policy to deny access if the connection attempt is met.

- In mixed mode or native mode, remote access policy is evaluated to determine whether remote access should be granted to the network.

- To prevent all remote access to the network in mixed mode or native mode, remove all remote access policies from the remote access server.

Applying the Decision

To take full advantage of remote access policy, Hanson Brothers should ensure that their domain is in native mode. Native mode allows Hanson Brothers to take full advantage of remote access policy for dial-up access determination.

Hanson Brothers should verify that each user account that requires dial-up access to the network is configured to Control Access Through Remote Access Policy. This ensures that remote access policy is used to determine access settings. In addition, all other accounts should be configured to Deny Access.

Lesson Summary

Remote access policy provides more flexibility for securing remote access policies than was ever possible in a Windows NT 4.0 network. Make sure that your design includes refining the conditions and profiles that must be matched for remote access to the network. By spending the time to properly define remote access policy, you ensure that security is maintained when access to the network is extended to remote users and networks.

Activity: Designing Remote Access Policy

This activity examines troubleshooting a remote access policy configuration that isn't working as expected. You will determine which setting is incorrect and modify the settings to allow connectivity.

Providing VPN Access

Your organization plans to allow remote users to connect to the network only by using VPNs. The following configuration has been performed at the remote access server:

- The VPN server is configured with a single remote access policy named "VPN Client Access."

- The VPN server is a perimeter server for the network with network interfaces attached both to the internal network and to the Internet, as shown in Figure 13.11.

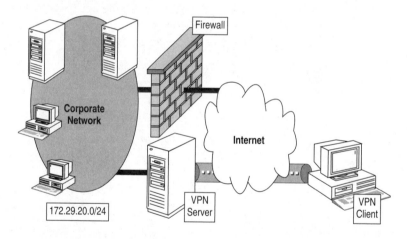

Figure 13.11   VPN server placement for your organization

- The VPN Client Access remote access policy is configured with a condition to accept only PPTP connections.

- The VPN server is assigned a computer certificate from the internal network's issuing Certificate Authority (CA) for machine authentication purposes.

The network connection on the VPN client computer is configured to automatically select a VPN protocol when connecting to the VPN server. The VPN client computer is a laptop running Windows 2000 Professional. The laptop has a computer certificate installed for the purpose of machine authentication.

It appears that the current remote access policy configuration has a flaw. Connections to the remote access server are consistently failing.

Answer the following questions about this situation. Answers to the questions can be found in the appendix.

1. Why is the connection to the remote access server failing?

2. What could you do at the VPN client to allow the connection to succeed?

3. What could you do at the VPN server to allow the connection to succeed?

4. Without modifying the existing remote access policy or the network connection object at the client computer, how can you ensure that the connection attempt uses PPTP as the tunneling protocol?

Lesson 5: Planning RADIUS Security

The Internet Authentication Service (IAS) in Windows 2000 allows centralized application of remote access security. IAS is Microsoft's deployment of the Remote Authentication Dial-In User Service (RADIUS) protocol. RADIUS allows centralized authentication, accounting, and management of remote access policy.

After this lesson, you will be able to

- Design a RADIUS deployment to allow single sign-on and provide centralized remote access policy deployment

Estimated lesson time: 30 minutes

Introducing RADIUS Authentication

In a Windows 2000 network, RADIUS allows single sign-on capabilities to remote users by allowing them to authenticate with the domain account and password. Single sign-on allows access to all resources on a network with a single user account and password, rather than having to provide different account/password combinations for connecting to the ISP and to the corporate network through a VPN connection. This single user account and password can be used at any remote access server or network device that's configured as a RADIUS client to the IAS server.

This lesson examines the components required for deploying RADIUS and explains how RADIUS enables centralized management of remote access policy.

Designing RADIUS Deployments

A RADIUS infrastructure requires servers that play different roles in the RADIUS authentication process. The servers required for a RADIUS deployment include

- **RADIUS server.** The RADIUS server provides remote access authentication, authorization, and accounting services. Rather than each remote access server providing these services, the services are centralized at a single RADIUS server.
- **RADIUS clients.** RADIUS clients include remote access servers, tunnel servers, and network access servers that can accept remote access client connections. A RADIUS client does *not* perform authentication, authorization, or account services. Instead, the requests are forwarded to the configured RADIUS server.
- **Remote access clients.** Remote access clients connect to the network using dial-up or VPN connections. Remote access clients may have to provide a prefix or suffix to identify the RADIUS server that a RADIUS proxy must forward the RADIUS authentication request to.

- **RADIUS proxy.** In some circumstances an organization such as an ISP may have network access servers that forward authentication requests to RADIUS servers from multiple organizations. A RADIUS proxy is able to determine the correct RADIUS server by inspecting prefixes and suffixes appended to the user name provided by the remote access clients.

Note Windows 2000 does *not* provide a RADIUS proxy service. If you require a RADIUS proxy in your RADIUS deployment, you must deploy either a third-party RADIUS server or the RADIUS proxy that's included in the Internet Connection Services for RAS for Windows NT 4.0.

RADIUS authentication provides single sign-on capabilities to remote access clients. In other words, when connecting to the network by using a VPN, a single password can be used to authenticate with both an ISP and the corporate network. Understanding how RADIUS authentication takes place will help you design server placement for a RADIUS deployment. Figure 13.12 shows how RADIUS authentication proceeds when a user connects to the corporate network by first connecting to an ISP.

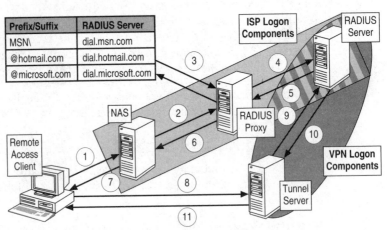

Figure 13.12   The RADIUS authentication process for a VPN client

1. The remote access client connects to an ISP by dialing the phone number of the ISP's modem. The modem is attached to the ISP's NAS.

2. The NAS is configured as a RADIUS client to the RADIUS proxy server located at the ISP. The NAS sends the authentication request to the RADIUS proxy server in a RADIUS authentication message format.

3. The RADIUS proxy server looks at its table of known suffixes and prefixes. For example, if the user name provided was cott.culp@hotmail.com, the RADIUS proxy would forward the authentication request to the dial.hotmail.com RADIUS server.

4. The RADIUS proxy forwards the authentication request to the appropriate RADIUS server. This request is known as a proxied RADIUS authentication message.

5. The RADIUS server verifies the credentials in the proxied authentication request and accepts or rejects the request. The request is compared to remote access policy to determine if the connection attempt should be accepted or rejected. If the attempt is accepted, the RADIUS response is sent to the RADIUS proxy in a RADIUS authentication acknowledge message.

6. The RADIUS proxy forwards the RADIUS authentication message as a proxied RADIUS authentication acknowledge message to the NAS.

7. The NAS informs the user that she is successfully authenticated on the network. In addition to authentication, the NAS then assigns TCP/IP configuration information to the remote access client. This TCP/IP configuration information includes the client's IP address, default gateway, and subnet mask.

   Now that the connection to the Internet is authenticated and established, the client can begin the process of connecting to the corporate network by establishing a VPN to the corporate office.

8. The remote access client sends the user's authentication request to the configured tunnel server at the user's local office using either PPTP or L2TP/IPSec as the VPN protocol.

9. The tunnel server, configured as a RADIUS client, creates a RADIUS authentication message and sends it to the RADIUS server.

10. The RADIUS server verifies the user's credentials in the authentication request and accepts or rejects the authentication request. The request is compared to remote access policy to determine if the connection attempt should be accepted or rejected. If the attempt is accepted, the RADIUS response is sent to the tunnel server.

11. The tunnel server passes the authentication message and any IP configuration details to the remote access client.

All authentication requests are passed to the directory source utilized by the RADIUS server. In the case of IAS, the authentication requests are forwarded to Active Directory.

Making the Decision

When designing a RADIUS solution for your organization, you must determine which RADIUS roles are required to provide single sign-on capabilities. Table 13.15 outlines when to include the various RADIUS components in your remote access design.

Table 13.15   Planning RADIUS Component Use

Use	To Perform the Following Tasks
RADIUS servers	■ To centralize remote access policy application in a Windows 2000 network ■ To centralize authentication requests to a single directory store ■ To centralize accounting information for remote access at a single location
RADIUS clients	■ To forward all authentication and accounting requests to the configured RADIUS server ■ To receive centralized remote access policy from the configured RADIUS server
RADIUS proxies	■ To allow the hosting of authentication services for multiple organizations through the same phone number or tunnel server IP address ■ To provide informed routing of RADIUS authentication packets to the correct RADIUS server based on either a prefix or suffix provided by the remote access client

Applying the Decision

To provide centralized management of authentication, you must configure the remote access servers at the Warroad, Boise, and Calgary offices as RADIUS clients to a RADIUS server at the Warroad office, as shown in Figure 13.13.

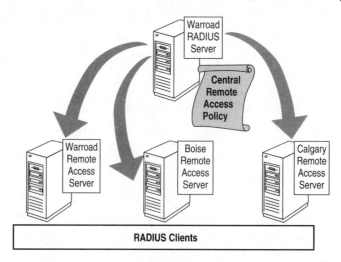

Figure 13.13   The RADIUS authentication process for a VPN client

The RADIUS server allows all users to authenticate by using their domain account and password. In addition, the RADIUS server allows centralized management of remote access policy and centralized collection of accounting information for all remote access connectivity.

Planning Centralized Application of Remote Access Policy

Decentralized application of remote access policy can result in inconsistent configurations at each remote access server. Figure 13.14 illustrates a situation commonly caused by decentralized application of remote access policy.

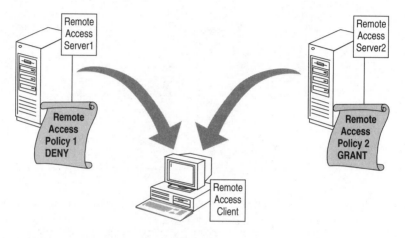

Figure 13.14   Decentralized application of remote access policy

In this situation clients are denied remote access if they connect to the remote access server1 but gain access if they connect to the remote access server2. Such inconsistent application of remote access policy can result in authorized users being denied access and unauthorized users gaining access to the network.

RADIUS servers allow the centralization of remote access policy. When the remote access servers are configured as RADIUS clients, they no longer configure remote access policy locally. Instead the remote access policy is obtained from the RADIUS server, which acts as the repository for remote access policy, as shown in Figure 13.15.

With the remote access servers configured as RADIUS clients, the remote user gains access to the network no matter which remote access server she accesses. Both servers have the same remote access policy, which is stored locally at the RADIUS server.

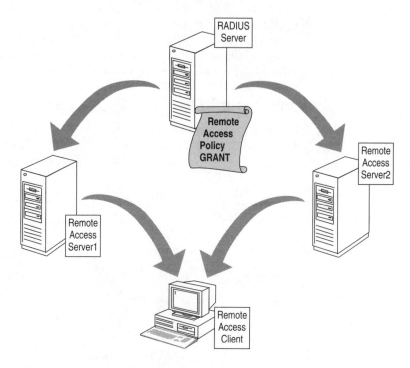

Figure 13.15   Centralized application of remote access policy with RADIUS

Important   RADIUS does expose a single point of failure if the server hosting the IAS service were to fail. Make sure that the configuration is backed up using the Netsh utility.

RADIUS servers allow you to centralize remote access policy at a single location for editing purposes. When a server running RRAS is configured as a RADIUS client, it receives its remote access policy from the RADIUS server. Remote access policy won't appear in the Routing And Remote Access console when the remote access server is configured as a RADIUS client.

In addition to configuring the existing remote access servers as RADIUS clients, you must prevent the deployment of new remote access servers that aren't configured as RADIUS clients. You can do this by using Group Policy to either enable or disable RRAS for Windows 2000–based computers. In addition to enabling or disabling RRAS, you can also change the permissions for the service to restrict who can start, stop, or pause the service.

To ensure that only the approved remote access servers are running RRAS, you can place the remote access servers in a dedicated organizational unit (OU). You can create a Group Policy object that enables RRAS. In addition, at the domain you can configure the Default Domain Policy to disable RRAS. Group Policy inheritance applies the service setting to all other OUs in the domain, as illustrated in Figure 13.16.

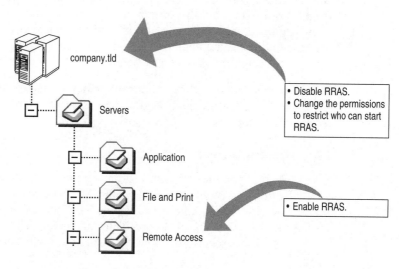

company.tld

Servers

• Disable RRAS.
• Change the permissions
  to restrict who can start
  RRAS.

Application

File and Print

• Enable RRAS.

Remote Access

Figure 13.16   Configuring Group Policy to enable RRAS only for authorized servers

Making the Decision

To ensure that only centralized application of remote access policy takes place, you must include the following items in your security design:

- Ensure that a server on the network is configured with the IAS service. The IAS server will host the centralized remote access policy to be deployed to RADIUS clients.

- Configure all authorized remote access servers as RADIUS clients. Remote access servers configured as RADIUS clients will receive their remote access policy from the RADIUS server. The remote access policy option won't exist within the MMC console once the remote access server is configured as a RADIUS client.

- Ensure that RRAS is disabled on all unauthorized remote access servers. Use Group Policy to ensure that RRAS is disabled on all unauthorized remote access servers. Configure permissions to restrict the ability to start, pause, and start RRAS to Domain Admins.

Applying the Decision

Hanson Brothers requires centralized management of remote access policies from the Warroad office. To prevent unauthorized remote access servers from being deployed, you can configure the default domain Group Policy to disable RRAS on all domain computers. In addition, you can place the remote access servers for each office in an OU where Group Policy enables RRAS.

To ensure that centralized remote access policy is applied, the remote access servers must be configured as RADIUS clients to the RADIUS server located at the Warroad office as shown previously in Figure 13.13.

Lesson Summary

RADIUS gives you the ability to centralize remote access security management. By configuring servers running RRAS as RADIUS clients to a common RADIUS server, you ensure that remote access policy design and deployment is centralized at the RADIUS server. Centralized management of RADIUS policy prevents inconsistent security from being applied to remote access connections.

Lab 13-1: Designing Security for Remote Access Users

Lab Objectives

This lab prepares you to design a remote access solution for Contoso Ltd. The lab meets the following objectives:

- Design a secure remote access solution for remote users
- Design a secure remote access solution for remote networks

About This Lab

This lab examines the planning required to provide remote connectivity to the Contoso Ltd. network and explores solutions for providing secure connectivity to remote users and remote networks.

Before You Begin

Make sure that you've completed reading the chapter material before starting the lab. Pay close attention to the sections where the design decisions were applied throughout the chapter for information on designing your administrative structure.

Scenario: Contoso Ltd.

Contoso Ltd., an international magazine sales company, plans to provide network access for their remote sales force. Currently, the sales force connects to the regional office by using toll-free numbers, but the costs are increasing to the point that alternative solutions must be found.

In a separate but related project, the company plans to open a new market research office in Barcelona, Spain, in two months. Rather than implementing a dedicated network link from the London office to the Barcelona office, Contoso wants to research the design requirements for implementing a VPN between the two offices.

The following sections outline the business goals for the two projects.

Providing Remote Access to the Remote Sales Force

Contoso must develop an alternative for remote network connectivity for the remote sales force. Your proposed solution must meet the following objectives:

- It must reduce the costs associated with long-distance calls. Currently the sales force connects to the London, Seattle, and Lima offices by calling a toll-free number. With the expansion of markets, the cost of the toll-free lines has increased rapidly.

- It must reduce the costs associated with maintaining a modem pool at each office. With the current growth of the remote sales force, the modem pool has been steadily increasing each quarter. In the last quarter more than 100 modems were added to the pool between the three offices.

- It must utilize smart card logon. Several remote sales force personnel were recently issued laptops running Windows 2000 Professional with built-in smart card readers. Contoso wants to ensure that all sales force personnel running Windows 2000 are required to log on with smart cards.

- It must provide remote access from laptops running both Windows 98 and Windows 2000 Professional. The remote sales force in South America is running older laptops with the Windows 98 operating system. The solution must allow connectivity from these laptops.

- It must simplify logon procedures. Remote access clients should select a local access phone number for their current location, provide their domain credentials, and log on to the network. The use of additional account and password combinations is unacceptable.

- It must provide mutual authentication of both the remote access user and the remote access server. Contoso wants to minimize the risk of an unauthorized remote access server accepting remote connections from the sales force.

- It must be restricted exclusively to the remote sales force. The solution must be restricted so that only members of the remote sales force can connect to the network. In the previous model this was accomplished by informing only the remote sales force of the toll-free number used to connect to the office.

- It must ensure the strongest form of encryption. Due to fears of confidential sales information being compromised, Contoso wants all authentication and data transmissions to be encrypted using only the strongest encryption algorithms. If the strongest form of encryption *can't* be used, the network connection must not be allowed.

- It must terminate connections if idle for more than 30 minutes. Due to the volume of remote sales force and the limited number of connections to the network, a connection that's idle for more than 30 minutes should be disconnected.

- The ability to save the user's password within the remote access network connection must be removed. An unauthorized person recently used a stolen laptop to connect to the network and access confidential documents. Users must be required to enter their passwords when connecting to the network remotely.

- All network traffic originating at remote clients must be inspected at a firewall. This allows the firewall to apply packet filters that prevent unauthorized network traffic from entering the corporate network.

Connecting the Barcelona Office to the Corporate Network

As mentioned earlier, Contoso wants to connect the Barcelona office to the London office using a VPN solution. The VPN solution must meet the following business objectives:

- All data that's sent between the two offices must be encrypted using the strongest form of encryption available for VPNs. Because the data will be transmitted over the Internet, there's a risk that the data could be inspected by unauthorized sources. Requiring the strongest form of encryption ensures that all data transmitted by the VPN solution is protected.

- The VPN servers must use dual authentication for network access. Both the computer accounts and the user accounts associated with the VPN must be authenticated.

- The tunnel server at the London office must be located in the DMZ behind an external firewall. Contoso wants to place the tunnel server behind the external firewall to prevent hackers from directly accessing the tunnel server. To allow this, you must configure the firewall to only allow VPN access to the tunnel server and prevent all other access attempts.

Exercise 1: Securing Access for the Remote Sales Force

This exercise examines providing secure access to the Contoso network for the remote sales force. Your design must meet the business objectives introduced in the lab scenario. Answers to these questions can be found in the appendix.

Determining a Solution

1. What can Contoso do to reduce the costs associated with toll-free phone lines for remote access connectivity and still provide remote connectivity to the corporate network?

2. If Contoso wants to implement the same VPN protocol for all remote access connections by the sales force, what VPN protocol must be deployed?

3. If the remote access server for the remote sales force is deployed as shown in Figure 13.17, will anything prevent the use of PPTP or L2TP/IPSec VPN connections?

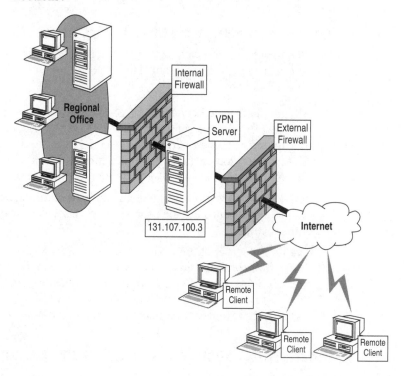

131.107.100.3

Figure 13.17   Proposed network configuration for the remote sales force VPN server

4. How can the requirement for logging on with the user's domain account and password be accomplished if the user is initially connecting to an ISP?

5. By using remote access policy, how can Contoso manage a sales force that runs different operating systems on their laptops?

Designing the Firewall

1. How should you configure the firewall to support both PPTP and L2TP so that VPN traffic reaches the VPN server?

2. Will the external firewall be able to inspect the data sent through the VPN tunnel to the tunnel server?

3. Will the internal firewall be able to inspect the data sent through the VPN tunnel to the tunnel server?

Designing Remote Access for Laptops Running Windows 2000 Professional

The following questions deal with the design decisions associated with the laptops running Windows 2000 Professional.

1. How can you develop a remote access policy that's applied only to remote access client computers running Windows 2000 Professional?

2. How would you enforce the use of smart card logon for sales force personnel running Windows 2000?

3. What PKI design is required to allow smart card logon?

4. If L2TP/IPSec is used by the Windows 2000 Professional laptops, are any additional certificates required?

5. What can you do in remote access policy to ensure that the required authentication protocol, encryption algorithm, and idle disconnect settings are applied to all remote access clients?

6. What settings must you configure in the remote access policy to meet the design objectives for connections from laptops running Windows 2000 Professional?

7. What can you do at the remote access clients to ensure that the required authentication protocol, encryption algorithm, and idle disconnect settings are used?

Designing Remote Access for Laptops Running Windows NT 4.0 Workstation

The following questions deal with the design decisions associated with the laptops running Windows NT 4.0 Workstation.

1. How can you develop a remote access policy that will only be applied to remote access client computers running Windows NT 4.0 Workstation?

Identifying RADIUS Design Decisions

The following section examines the RADIUS design required for the providing remote access to the sales force users.

1. What RADIUS component is required at the ISP to allow sales force users to connect using their domain account and password?

2. How will the ISP know where to forward authentication requests from the remote access clients? How would you configure this setting?

3. Where on the Contoso network would you place the RADIUS server to provide the maximum level of security?

4. What computers would you configure as RADIUS clients on the Contoso
   network?

5. What happens to remote access policy design when RADIUS is deployed?

Exercise 2: Securing the Connection to the Barcelona Office

The following exercise examines the design decisions that you must address
when designing network connectivity for the Barcelona office. Answers to these
questions can be found in the appendix.

1. What protocol must you use for the VPN between the London and Barcelona
   offices?

2. Could you use the same VPN server for both the network connection to the
   Barcelona office and for the sales force users? What must you configure if the
   VPN server can support both connection requests?

3. What must you include in the remote access policy to identify the connections
   from the Barcelona VPN server?

4. What PKI design is required to meet the business objectives?

5. Figure 13.18 shows the proposed network configuration to connect the Barcelona office to the London office. What packet filters are required at the Barcelona server to only allow connections from the London VPN server?

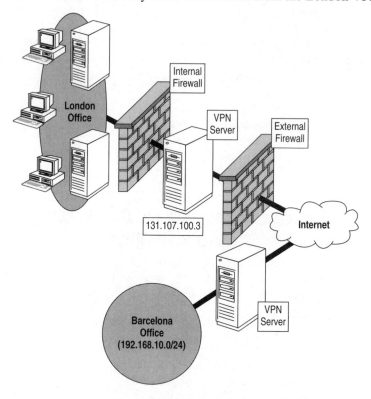

Figure 13.18   Connecting the Barcelona office to the London office

Review

Answering the following questions will reinforce key information presented in this chapter. If you are unable to answer a question, review the appropriate lesson and then try the question again. Answers to the questions can be found in the appendix.

1. Baldwin Museum of Science is designing several herbicide solutions for farmers. Many of the herbicides are highly toxic and require that any clothing exposed to the chemicals be destroyed. To access the testing laboratory, scientists must be authenticated with a retinal scan. The retinal scanner established a dial-up connection to a Windows 2000 remote access server and the retinal scan is compared to an extended attribute in Active Directory to validate the authentication. What authentication protocol would be used in this scenario?

2. Your organization has standardized on using L2TP/IPSec VPN connections for employees connecting to the corporate office from home. The remote access server doesn't support any other VPN protocols. A member of the help desk was terminated about an hour ago and you've been asked to prevent the employee from connecting to the network using a VPN connection. You're certain that the former employee may know several user accounts and passwords in use on the network. What can be done to prevent the former employee from connecting to the network?

3. You've discovered by reviewing log files that several employees have been accessing the network through remote access connections, even though the remote access project team hasn't authorized them for remote access permissions. It appears that the users are connecting through a server in their department that they have configured with RRAS. What can you do to prevent the installation of unauthorized remote access servers?

4. Sensitive data seems to be leaking from your organization. After eliminating all other possibilities, you suspect that the local telephone company that provides your WAN link may be the culprit. What can you do to protect data on the WAN?

5. Your salespeople tend to lose their laptops. In addition to your considerable hardware expenses, more and more unauthorized users have appeared on the network. Besides renewing user passwords, how can you prevent salespeople from leaving their passwords in their dial-up networking objects?

6. Your organization has started a short-term project that requires a temporary office to be connected to the corporate network. Because of deployment costs, you decide to use a VPN to connect to the corporate office. How does the configuration of your organization's DMZ at the corporate office affect your VPN protocol decision?

C H A P T E R   1 4

Securing an Extranet

About This Chapter

This chapter examines the security design requirements for hosting network resources that are accessible to users on the Internet. The challenge is to configure
firewalls in such a way as to allow Internet users into a portion of the private network without granting them access to the entire network. The area of a private
network that hosts Internet-accessible resources is called an *extranet*.

Web server content is the most common network resource that organizations
make available on the Internet. This chapter covers methods for securing Internet
Information Services (IIS) and describes how to secure network traffic and services within an extranet. The text concludes by discussing the design of packet
filters to protect extranet resources.

Before You Begin

To complete this chapter, you must read the chapter scenario. This scenario is used
throughout the chapter to apply the design decisions discussed in each lesson.

Chapter Scenario: Market Florist

Market Florist, an Internet-based florist, plans to manage its Web site at the head office in Seattle. The company is currently hosting the *www.marketflorist.tld* Web site off-site at its Internet Service Provider (ISP). Market Florist plans to move all Internet-based resources to its own network by the end of the year. The company believes that managing its own Internet site will allow it more flexibility in the services it offers on the Internet.

The decision to host the Internet services at the Seattle office has taken a long time. Senior management is concerned that hosting the Web site locally could result in a security breach that affects the private network. Management has authorized the purchase of a new firewall device but has approved funds for the purchase of only a single firewall.

You've been hired to design a secure Internet presence for Market Florist that provides accessibility to all Internet-accessible resources while maintaining the security of the private network. Additionally, the firewall must protect the private network users by hiding their true IP addresses from the public network.

Market Florist's DNS Services

Market Florist will use marketflorist.tld as its Active Directory directory service forest root and as its namespace on the Internet. The security design for the extranet must allow private network users to connect to the Internet and to Internet-accessible resources without exposing the internal IP addressing scheme to the public network.

Currently an internal DNS server that forwards Internet requests to the ISP's DNS server is located at IP address 10.10.10.3. The new security design calls for the DNS server to forward internal DNS requests to an external DNS server located in the extranet. The external DNS server will forward Internet requests to the ISP's DNS server at IP address 131.107.199.56.

Market Florist's FTP Server

John Coake and Pat Coleman, two members of the IT department, are responsible for maintaining the files available to external users at Market Florist's FTP server. To ensure that no files are uploaded to the FTP server, the FTP server is configured to allow file downloads only. John and Pat use Telnet to connect to the Internet-accessible FTP server and modify the files that are available for download.

Market Florist's Internet-Accessible Resources

Market Florist has designated a specific number of Microsoft Windows 2000–based computers to be accessible from the Internet. Table 14.1 outlines the Windows 2000–based servers and the role they will play in Market Florist's extranet.

Table 14.1 Market Florist Extranet Server Roles

Server Name	IP Address	Role
MFDNS	192.168.77.254	▪ External DNS server, located in the extranet for Market Florist, to allow public network client computers to resolve marketflorist.tld resources. ▪ Contains only externally accessible resource records. None of the addresses contain internal IP addressing information.

MFWEB	192.168.77.2	▪ A Network Load Balancing Services (NLBS) Web cluster consisting of four identically configured Web servers:
		  ▪ MFWeb1 (192.168.77.3)
		  ▪ MFWeb2 (192.168.77.4)
		  ▪ MFWeb3 (192.168.77.5)
		  ▪ MFWeb4 (192.168.77.6)
		▪ The Flower Power application, an application that allows customers to purchase floral arrangements on the Internet, will connect to a Microsoft SQL server on the private network for storing order details.
		▪ The port at which the Flower Power application listens for connection will be changed every six months.

MFFTP	192.168.77.7	▪ File Transfer Protocol (FTP) server used by client computers for downloading brochures on floral arrangements available from Market Florist. ▪ The FTP server must only allow downloads. All requests to upload data must be terminated immediately. ▪ John Coake and Pat Coleman can access the FTP server by using Telnet from the private network to manipulate the files located in the FTP folder. ▪ Only John and Pat should be allowed to connect to the MFFTP server using Telnet.
MFMAIL	192.168.77.8	▪ The server running Microsoft Exchange Server 5.5 accepts incoming e-mail and allows remote salespeople to retrieve their e-mail using Post Office Protocol v3 (POP3) client software.
MFTUNNEL	192.168.77.9	▪ This server, running Routing and Remote Access service (RRAS), allows employees to connect to private network resources.

All the servers available in the Market Florist extranet must allow administrators to manage the servers remotely using Terminal Services. Only administrators should be allowed to connect to the server by using Terminal Services.

External DNS Resource Records

All the Windows 2000 servers in the extranet are advertised on the Internet with public network addresses to allow external client computers to connect to the Market Florist resources. Table 14.2 shows the public network addresses and host names for the externally accessible resources.

Table 14.2   Market Florist Externally Available Resources

Hostname	IP address	Private Network Server
www.marketflorist.tld	131.107.88.254	MFWEB
ftp.marketflorist.tld	131.107.88.253	MFFTP
mail.marketflorist.tld	131.107.88.252	MFMAIL
vpn.marketflorist.tld.	131.107.88.251	MFTUNNEL
client.marketflorist.tld	131.107.88.2	All private network client computers accessing the Internet

The Flower Power Application

To support online ordering, Market Florist uses an ActiveX control named Flower Power. The Flower Power application allows customers to order floral arrangements over the Internet by providing nothing more than their customer number. When an order is made, the customer number and the floral arrangement order are recorded on a server named MFSQL that's located on the private network. The IP address of the internal MFSQL server is 10.10.10.20.

To acquire a Flower Power customer number, the customer must connect to *https://www.marketflorist.tld/newcustomer* and enter customer and credit card information. A Flower Power administrator will e-mail the customer number to the client to allow easy ordering on the Internet. There are concerns that the Flower Power application is suspect to data interception attacks. To reduce the risk of these attacks, the listening port for the Flower Power server-side application is changed every six months. The current port is User Datagram Protocol (UDP) 6834, but the security plan must provide a strategy for handling the port changing at regular intervals. The firewall solution must ensure that Flower Power connections aren't hijacked by an attacker.

Lesson 1: Identifying Common Firewall Strategies

A common way of providing security for the extranet is to deploy firewalls between the public network and the extranet. Being aware of common firewall features will help you design secure access to the resources in your extranet.

In addition to deploying a firewall between the public network and the extranet, many organizations deploy a firewall between the private network and the extranet. This configuration is commonly referred to as a *Demilitarized Zone* (DMZ), *perimeter network*, or *screened subnet*. This internal firewall ensures protection of the private network if the external firewall or resources in the extranet are compromised.

After this lesson, you will be able to

- Design a network infrastructure to secure your organization's extranet
- Identify the firewall features that you can use to protect the resources exposed in the extranet

Estimated lesson time: 45 minutes

Identifying Firewall Features to Protect the Extranet

In the simplest deployment, a firewall is placed between the private and public networks to secure the private network from the public network. This configuration is shown in Figure 14.1.

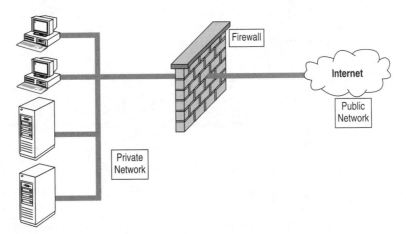

Figure 14.1 A firewall restricting public network access to the private network

A firewall acts as a barrier against attacks launched from the public network. A firewall can be a physical hardware device or a software application that executes on a computer.

To protect the private network, firewalls can offer a suite of services, including

- **Network Address Translation (NAT).** Translation of the source address of all outbound packets from a private network address to a public network address.

- **Packet filtering.** Configuration of rules at a firewall that define which protocols are allowed to pass through the firewall.

- **Static address mapping.** Configuration of how incoming packets are rerouted to servers using private network addressing.

- **Stateful inspection of network traffic.** Verification that protocols are following basic rules of communications. Stateful inspection ensures that sessions aren't hijacked by an attacker.

- **Advanced features that detect common attacks against the private network.** These include setting time-outs for incomplete session establishment and inspecting the content of incoming packets.

The following sections describe how these services function and the security threats they address.

Protecting Private Network Addressing with NAT

NAT prevents exposure of the IP addressing scheme used on your private network. An attacker with knowledge of the IP addressing scheme can attempt an IP spoofing attack by sending packets to the network with the falsified IP source address of a trusted private network address.

NAT protects against this form of attack by replacing the source IP address in all outgoing packets with a common IP address, as shown in Figure 14.2.

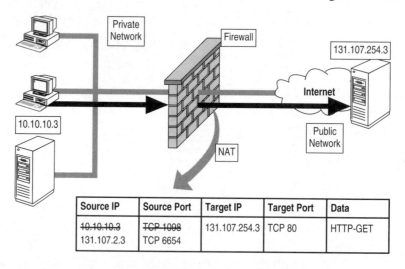

Source IP	Source Port	Target IP	Target Port	Data
~~10.10.10.3~~	~~TCP 1008~~	131.107.254.3	TCP 80	HTTP-GET
131.107.2.3	TCP 6654			

Figure 14.2   How NAT replaces the source IP address and source port fields for all outgoing packets

In addition to replacing the source IP address, NAT replaces the source port to prevent duplicate port requests by outgoing packets. The NAT device tracks all managed connections so that return packets are returned to the correct computer on the private network.

The private network commonly uses Request for Comment (RFC) 1918 addressing. RFC 1918 reserves three ranges of IP addresses for private network addressing:

- 10.0.0.0 – 10.255.255.255 (10.0.0.0/8)
- 172.16.0.0 – 172.31.255.255 (172.16.0.0/12)
- 192.168.0.0 – 192.168.255.255 (192.168.0.0/16)

These pools of IP addresses aren't used on the Internet and aren't included in Internet routing tables. The NAT process replaces the private network addresses with an IP address assigned to the organization by the Internet Corporation for Assigned Names and Numbers (ICANN).

Note Windows 2000 provides a native NAT service in RRAS.

Packet Filters

Once you've deployed a firewall, you must establish firewall rules to define what data is allowed to enter and exit the private network. Firewall rules are made up of individual packet filters. A firewall uses a packet filter to profile a protocol so that data transmitted using the protocol is identified. Packet filters allow a firewall administrator to prevent unauthorized protocols from entering the private network. Alternatively, administrators can apply packet filters to outbound data to restrict which protocols are available to private network computers.

A packet filter is typically composed of fields that profile a protocol and identify what action to take if the protocol attempts to pass through the firewall. The fields used by packet filters include

- **Source address.** The individual IP address or network IP address from which the data originates.
- **Source port.** The port from which the data is transmitted. Every IP-based protocol originates from a port at the source host. The source port for a client computer connection is often a random port.
- **Destination address.** The individual IP address or network IP address to which the data is sent.
- **Destination port.** The port that the server uses to listen for connections. IP-based services and applications listen for connections on a predefined port.

Tip   To determine what ports are used by specific services and applications, view the Services text file in the *systemroot*\system32\drivers\etc folder, where *systemroot* denotes the folder where Windows 2000 is installed. To view a listing of all well-known port numbers, go to *www.isi.edu/in-notes/iana/assignments /port-numbers*.

- **Protocol.** Application and Services use a specific protocol ID or a transport layer protocol for transporting application data. If the application or service uses a transport layer protocol, it will be either Transport Control Protocol (TCP) or UDP.
- **Action.** Defines what action to take if the other fields are matched and the data transmission is identified. Options include Allow or Deny. In addition, many firewalls also allow logging to identify any attempts to use the protocol.

Many firewalls include an option to mirror all packet filters. Mirroring is necessary to allow response packets to return to the source client computer. Mirroring simply switches the source and destination information to allow the response packets to cross the firewall, as shown in Figure 14.3.

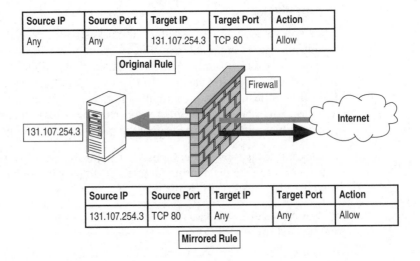

Source IP	Source Port	Target IP	Target Port	Action
Any	Any	131.107.254.3	TCP 80	Allow

Original Rule

Source IP	Source Port	Target IP	Target Port	Action
131.107.254.3	TCP 80	Any	Any	Allow

Mirrored Rule

Figure 14.3   How mirroring switches the source and destination information within an IP packet

Typically, you will implement one of the following firewall strategies at your firewall:

- Specify allowed protocols and prohibit everything else
- Specify prohibited protocols and allow everything else

The strategy you choose will be based on your organization's risk level. Typically, higher security networks specify the allowed protocols and prohibit everything else. This ensures that only authorized protocols are allowed to pass through the firewall.

Static Address Mapping

Use static address mapping at a firewall to redirect incoming traffic to Internet-accessible resources hidden behind the firewall. The resources are advertised on the Internet with publicly accessible IP addresses. When the firewall receives the packets, the firewall translates the destination address to the true IP address of the resource behind the firewall and redirects the data to the resource, as shown in Figure 14.4.

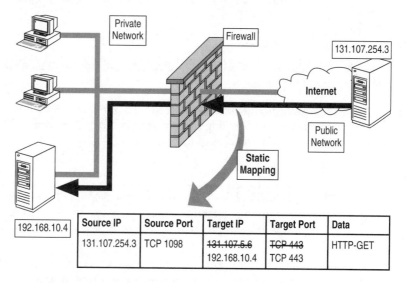

Source IP	Source Port	Target IP	Target Port	Data
131.107.254.3	TCP 1098	~~131.107.5.6~~ 192.168.10.4	~~TCP 443~~ TCP 443	HTTP-GET

Figure 14.4 How static address mapping redirects requests to Internet-accessible resources on the private network

In the figure the external DNS advertises the Web server as the IP address 131.107.5.6. Static address mapping translates the external IP address to 192.168.10.4 on the private network.

The advantage of using static address mapping is that it conceals the true IP address of Internet-accessible resources from potential attackers. Combined with packet filtering rules, static address mapping allows you to define authorized protocols and redirect the protocols to servers located in a DMZ.

Stateful Inspection

In higher-security networks, simple packet filters may not provide enough security. Packet filters define which ports are left open at the firewall to redirect network traffic to Internet-accessible resources. Many protocols utilize random ports above port 1024 at the client computer side. Opening up all ports above 1024 can leave both the firewall and the private network resources susceptible to attack. Stateful inspection allows the firewall to inspect which ports are used for an initial connection, open those ports, and then close the ports when the connection is terminated. If any suspect ports are requested, such as when a session hijack attempt takes place, the firewall can recognize the attack and drop the connection.

Stateful inspection allows firewall rules to be established so that UDP-based protocols such as Simple Network Management Protocol (SNMP) can pass through firewalls successfully. The firewall tracks client and server port information and allows only response packets to a valid host to pass through the firewall. The firewall does this by tracking the original ports used by a client application and ensuring that the server-side application only sends responses to the port used by the client application.

Advanced Techniques

In addition to these services, firewalls provide advanced security through the following features:

- **Configuring time-out tolerance.** Some attacks attempt to lock up the firewall by flooding it with incomplete TCP sessions. The time-out tolerance allows the firewall to disconnect these sessions before the synchronize (SYN) queue overflows.

Note This attack is commonly known as a *SYN flood attack*. By flooding the firewall with SYN packets, the attacker can prevent further connections from being established.

- **Content scanning.** Although packet filtering can restrict protocols, it can't inspect commands within a protocol. Content scanning allows the firewall to inspect the commands transmitted within a session. For example, you may want to disable the ability to upload data by using FTP. You can configure content scanning to allow FTP GET commands while preventing FTP PUT commands. Content scanning can also scan all incoming content for known virus signatures.

Making the Decision

When deciding which firewall features to implement, you should be aware of the benefits that each firewall feature provides. A knowledge of these benefits will assist you in utilizing the features to protect your network. Table 14.3 shows how you can use each firewall feature to protect your network.

Table 14.3   Designing Firewall Features to Protect Internet-Accessible Resources

Use This Firewall Feature	To Do the Following
NAT	▪ Prevent the private network addressing scheme from being revealed ▪ Hide the true IP address of private network resources when accessing Internet-based resources
Packet filters	▪ Manage what protocols are allowed to cross between the private network and the public network ▪ Define what action to take if a protocol is identified when crossing the firewall ▪ Define a default action to take if a protocol doesn't meet any of the defined packet filters
Static address mapping	▪ Advertise Internet-accessible resources that have private network addresses using public network addressing ▪ Hide the true IP address of Internet-accessible resources
Stateful inspection	▪ Protect UDP-based protocols that must enter the private network ▪ Detect session hijacking attempts ▪ Detect application-level attacks that attempt to bypass the packet filters established for a protocol
Time-out tolerances	▪ Prevent SYN flood attacks by closing sessions that have timed out ▪ Free up connections for new connection attempts if the connection is left idle
Content scanning	▪ Prevent specific application commands from being issued within a protocol ▪ Detect viruses within incoming packets

Applying the Decision

The new firewall purchased by Market Florist should provide the following features to meet its security needs:

▪ **NAT.** The private network client computers require access to the Internet. To provide the ability to hide the true IP network addressing scheme used on the private network, NAT will replace all outgoing IP addresses with the NAT common address. In the Market Florist network scenario, all private network IP addresses will be replaced with the *client.marketflorist.tld* IP address of 131.107.88.2.

▪ **Packet filters.** You must define packet filtering at the firewall to allow only the authorized protocols to connect to each network resource. The specific filters will be discussed in Lesson 3, but Table 14.4 outlines the authorized protocols for connecting to each computer in the extranet.

Table 14.4   Protocols Allowed to Enter the Market Florist Extranet

Server	Protocols
MFDNS	▪ DNS. Public network users require access to the DNS server to resolve host names in the *marketflorist.tld* domain to IP addresses. ▪ Terminal Services. All administrators require the ability to remotely manage the MFDNS server.
MFWEB	▪ Hypertext Transfer Protocol (HTTP). All Web pages require HTTP access. ▪ HTTPS. Customers requesting a customer number require encryption of credit card and personal information. ▪ Flower Power application. The Flower Power application listens for connections on a dedicated port. ▪ Terminal Services. All administrators require the ability to remotely manage the MFWEB server. Additionally, you should configure the firewall to allow Terminal Services connections to each of the component servers, or nodes, in the NLBS cluster. ▪ The MFWEB server also requires access to the MFSQL server on the private network.
MFFTP	▪ FTP. The MFFTP server allows FTP clients to enter FTP commands to access FTP data. ▪ FTP-DATA. FTP client software opens an FTP-DATA session when transferring data from the FTP server. ▪ Telnet. John and Pat require Telnet access to manipulate the files available on the FTP server. ▪ Terminal Services. All administrators require the ability to remotely manage the MFFTP server.
MFMAIL	▪ POP3. Remote Sales users must connect to the mail server using POP3 to retrieve their mail. ▪ SMTP. Remote Sales users connect to the MFMAIL server to send e-mail and customers connect to the MFMAIL server to deliver mail to Market Florist e-mail users. ▪ Terminal Services. All administrators require the ability to remotely manage the MFMAIL server.
MFTUNNEL	▪ PPTP. Employees require PPTP to connect to private network resources from the Internet. Layer 2 Tunneling Protocol over Internet Protocol Security (L2TP/IPSec) can't be supported because the MFTUNNEL server is located behind a firewall that performs NAT. ▪ Terminal Services. All administrators require the ability to remotely manage the MFTUNNEL server.

▪ **Static address mapping.** To make the extranet servers accessible to customers on the public network, configure static address mapping for each server. Table 14.5 lists the necessary static address mappings.

Table 14.5 Market Florist Static Address Mapping Table

Hostname	External IP Address	Private Network IP Address
www.marketflorist.tld	131.107.88.254	192.168.77.2
ftp.marketflorist.tld	131.107.88.253	192.168.77.7
mail.marketflorist.tld	131.107.88.252	192.168.77.8
vpn.marketflorist.tld.	131.107.88.251	192.168.77.9

- **Stateful inspection.** The Flower Power application uses UDP as its transport protocol. UDP-based applications do not establish sessions. A firewall must support stateful inspection to ensure that Flower Power connections aren't hijacked. The stateful inspection feature ensures that all response packets are using the same IP addresses and UDP ports that were used by the initial request packets.

- **Time-out tolerance.** To protect the Web site and other extranet resources from a denial of service attack, the firewall should support time-outs for disconnected sessions. This feature prevents SYN flooding attacks against the network.

- **Content scanning.** To prevent uploads of data to the MFFTP server, the firewall should deploy content scanning and prevent all attempts to use the FTP PUT command. This strategy provides greater protection by scanning the FTP transmissions for disallowed commands.

Comparing DMZ Configurations

When an organization hosts Internet-accessible resources, it's generally unadvisable to place those resources within the private network. Instead, place all Internet-accessible resources in a network segment commonly known as a DMZ between the private network and the public network.

What Are Some Other Terms for DMZ?

DMZs have a variety of common names, including screened subnet and perimeter network. Screened subnet refers to the function of a DMZ in network security. All network traffic that attempts to enter or exit the DMZ is screened by packet filters to determine whether they're allowed. Perimeter network refers to the DMZ's location. Typically, a DMZ exists between the private and the public network on the perimeter of the private network.

All three terms refer to the same area of your network and are configured identically to provide network security to Internet-accessible resources.

Networks use one of the following DMZ designs: a three-pronged firewall DMZ, a mid-ground DMZ, or a hybrid (or multizone) DMZ.

Designing a Three-Pronged Firewall DMZ

A three-pronged firewall DMZ consists of a firewall with three network interfaces. One interface is connected to the private network, another is connected to the public network, and the final interface is connected to the DMZ, as shown in Figure 14.5.

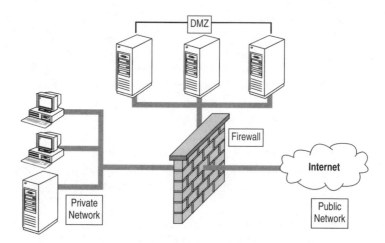

Figure 14.5   A three-pronged firewall DMZ

So Is the DMZ Part of the Private Network or the Public Network?

A DMZ is part of the private network *and* part of the public network. As you can see in Figure 14.5, the DMZ is separate from both the private and public networks.

In a sense, the DMZ is part of the public network, because resources that are accessible to the public network are placed in the DMZ. But the DMZ is also part of the private network because packet filters enforce which protocols can be used to connect to each server located in the DMZ.

An administrator establishes packet filters that are enforced by the firewall to restrict what traffic is allowed between each of the three zones. All Internet-accessible resources are placed in the DMZ to ensure that data connections originating from the public network can establish connections only to resources in the DMZ. They aren't allowed to establish connections to any resources on the private network.

When deploying a three-pronged firewall, ensure that your firewall solution supports three network interfaces. Each interface will be assigned to a zone and you must establish packet filters that define the interaction allowed between each zone.

When deciding whether the DMZ will use private or public network addressing, consider whether IPSec will be used from the public network to the DMZ. Since IPSec can't pass through a NAT service, you must use public network addressing in the DMZ whenever you require IPSec connections from the public network.

Mid-ground DMZ

You establish a mid-ground DMZ by using two firewalls. You place the first firewall between the public network and the DMZ and the second firewall between the DMZ and the private network, as shown in Figure 14.6.

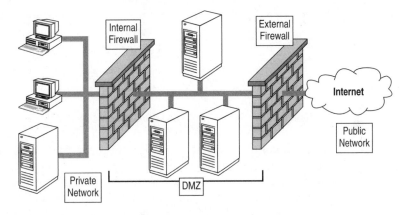

Figure 14.6   A mid-ground DMZ

While a three-pronged firewall DMZ can result in a single point of failure, the use of two firewalls provides additional protection to the private network because an attacker has to breach two firewalls before gaining access to the private network. By using two different firewall products, you can increase the protection offered to the private network because different methods may be required to breach the two firewalls.

As with a three-pronged firewall DMZ, the IP addressing used in the mid-ground DMZ can be either private or public network addressing. Generally you will use private network addressing in the DMZ unless there's a requirement to establish IPSec connections through the external firewall.

Hybrid DMZ

Sometimes a single DMZ may not meet your business requirements. In these cases, you can deploy a *hybrid DMZ*. A hybrid DMZ is a network where more than one zone exists between the private and the public networks.

Figure 14.7 depicts a hybrid DMZ configuration using a single firewall.

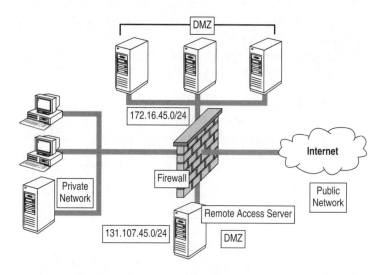

Figure 14.7   A hybrid DMZ with a single firewall

In this scenario you create two DMZs to support the need for IPSec connections and for protection of the private network addressing configuration for all other Internet-accessible resources. One DMZ, containing the remote access server that will accept IPSec connections, uses public network addressing. The second DMZ uses private network addressing and contains all other Internet-accessible resources. The firewall prevents static address mapping for all incoming traffic to the network segment. Likewise, NAT is performed on all outgoing traffic originating in the zone using private network addressing.

Alternatively, you can use multiple firewalls to establish two or more DMZs between the private network and the public network, as shown in Figure 14.8.

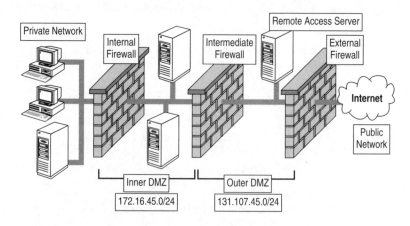

Figure 14.8   A hybrid DMZ with multiple firewalls

In this scenario the outermost DMZ uses public network addressing to allow IPSec connections to the remote access server. The innermost DMZ uses private network addressing to protect the remaining Internet-accessible resources. While more difficult to configure, the hybrid DMZ offers the most flexibility and allows a security administrator to group Internet-accessible resources based on the confidentiality of the data stored on the resource. Additionally, the administrator can configure each firewall with a set of packet filters to define exactly what traffic can enter and exit each DMZ.

Making the Decision

When network resources are exposed to the Internet, you should isolate the resources from the private network by deploying a DMZ. Table 14.6 discusses the design decisions for the three DMZ configurations that you must choose between.

Table 14.6   Choosing Between DMZ Configurations

Use	To Meet These Business Objectives
Three-pronged firewall DMZ	▪ To reduce the costs associated with deploying firewalls. Only a single firewall is required for this design. ▪ To maintain a single packet filter list. The packet filter rules determine which interface a packet filter is applied to.
Mid-ground DMZ	▪ To provide physical separation of the private network from the public network with the DMZ being placed between the private and public networks. An attacker must breach two firewalls to access the private network. ▪ To reduce the chance that the breach of the external firewall will lead to access of the private network. If you use two different manufacturers for the internal and external firewalls, you gain security because different methods must be used to breach the second firewall.
Hybrid	▪ To provide both private network and public network addressing to DMZ segments. ▪ To categorize Internet-accessible resources into different levels of access that can be protected by firewall strategies.

Applying the Decision

Market Florist is limited by its budget and must develop a DMZ configuration that uses only a single firewall. Figure 14.9 shows a three-pronged firewall DMZ configuration that will meet Market Florist's security needs and support the proposed IP addressing scheme for all servers on the network.

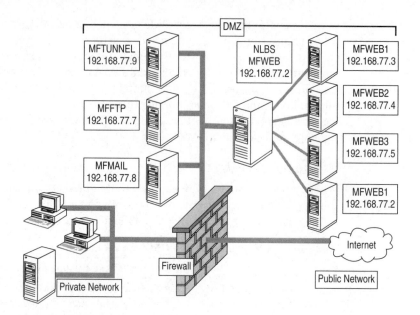

Figure 14.9   Proposed configuration for the Market Florist DMZ

Notice that each server in the NLBS cluster for the MFWEB server must be located in the DMZ. The NLBS listens on the IP address 192.168.77.2 but redirects the requests to one of the four servers in the cluster. The firewall is only required to redirect incoming HTTP or HTTPS packets to the NLBS cluster. The NLBS cluster service determines which node receives the incoming packets.

Lesson Summary

Knowing the features of firewalls and how they are commonly deployed will assist you in ensuring access to Internet-accessible resources is secure. Your design should take advantage of your firewall's configuration options to ensure that only authorized data transactions can take place.

Activity: Identifying Firewall Features

Your organization has purchased a new firewall, and the network administrator has asked you to help configure the firewall to meet the organization's security needs.

Identify the firewall features that will provide the necessary level of protection for your organization's network. For each question, implement one of the following firewall features:

- NAT
- Static address mapping
- Packet filtering
- Stateful inspection
- Content filtering
- Time-out tolerance

For each question, identify the firewall feature or features that are required to provide the necessary level of security and explain how you would configure the feature. Answers can be found in the appendix.

1. Last year your network was down for three days when an e-mail attachment virus attacked the network. The firewall that you implement must detect virus-infected attachments in e-mail messages arriving from the Internet and remove the content before it's delivered to the recipient.

2. When you initially placed your Web server on the Internet, you assigned the Web server an address from the public pool of IP addresses provided by your ISP. Now that the Web server is in a DMZ, the external firewall must translate all incoming traffic from the public network address advertised on the Internet to the actual IP address used on the private network.

3. The Web server was compromised last month when a hacker connected to the Web server and scanned the available ports. The hacker was able to connect to the Web server's Server service and browse shares located on the Web server. What firewall feature will limit connections only to authorized protocols?

4. An application server in the extranet must send SNMP trap messages and re-spond to SNMP requests from an SNMP management station located on the private network. The firewall must ensure that an attacker can't impersonate the application server and access information by using the SNMP protocol. What feature will provide this protection?

5. Last year several commercial Web sites were shut down by distributed denial of service (DDoS) attacks that used a SYN flooding attack. Your Web server is a key component of your e-business strategy, and your Web site's being un-available for any length of time would be catastrophic to your income and reputation. What firewall feature can lessen the effect of DDoS attacks?

6. Several computers on the private network must connect to servers on the Internet that belong to competitors in your industry. Management doesn't want these connections to provide information on the configuration of your organization's private network. What firewall feature would prevent outbound traffic from revealing your network's private network IP address scheme?

Lesson 2: Securing Internet-Accessible Resources in a DMZ

Within the DMZ you must secure resources to ensure that only authorized access takes place. This lesson explores methods for securing Internet Information Server (IIS) and other services commonly located within a DMZ. In addition, the lesson discusses ways of securing data transmissions between resources located in the DMZ.

After this lesson, you will be able to

- Design a secure configuration for all services and servers located within a DMZ

Estimated lesson time: 60 minutes

Securing IIS

The most common network resource exposed to the Internet is the content on a Web server. Internet Information Server (IIS) 5.0 is included with Windows 2000 Server and allows an organization to host Web sites. This lesson examines the additional configuration that's required to fully secure an IIS server when it's exposed to the Internet.

Although Windows 2000 has increased the default security level from Windows NT 4.0 for computers, you should consider additional security configurations for securing an IIS server. By applying the following recommendations to your Internet-accessible Web servers, you ensure that maximum security is applied to prevent attacks against the Web servers:

- Change all default account names. Attackers commonly attempt to connect to a Web server using the default account names included with Windows 2000. Make sure that the Administrator and Guest accounts are renamed, but don't choose names that are easy to guess when you rename them.

- Ensure that the Web server isn't a member of the same forest as the private network. If the Web server is compromised, your Active Directory could become compromised, too. By placing the Web server as a stand-alone server or as a member of a separate forest, you ensure that a compromised Web server won't compromise your organization's internal or private Active Directory.

- Separate available content into different folders by type. By separating the Web site by content type, you can apply security specific to each content type. For example, you can create the folder structure shown in Figure 14.10 to separate content into the categories of executables, scripts, include files, images, and static Web pages.

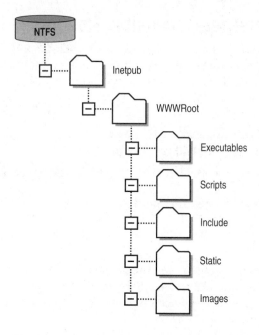

Figure 14.10   Proposed folder structure to secure Web content

- Secure available content by type. Once you've separated the Web content by type, you can then apply discretionary access control lists specific to the Web content type, as shown in Table 14.7.

Table 14.7   Securing Web Content by Content Type

Content Type	Recommended DACL Settings
Executables (.exe, .dll, .cmd, and .pl)	■ Everyone (Execute) ■ Administrators (Full Control) ■ System (Full Control)
Scripts (.asp)	■ Everyone (Execute) ■ Administrators (Full Control) ■ System (Full Control)
Includes (.inc, .shtm, and .shtml)	■ Everyone (Execute) ■ Administrators (Full Control) ■ System (Full Control)
Images (.jpg, .gif)	■ Everyone (Read) ■ Administrators (Full Control) ■ System (Full Control)
Static content (.htm, .html)	■ Everyone (Read) ■ Administrators (Full Control) ■ System (Full Control)

- Remove all sample applications from the Web server. The sample application files that are included with IIS 5.0 are installed by default and could provide tools to an attacker. Be aware of the sample applications shown in Table 14.8.

Table 14.8 Sample Files Included with IIS 5.0

Sample Name	Folder	Virtual Directory
IIS Samples	C:\Inetpub\Iissamples	\IISSamples
IIS Documentation	C:\Winnt\help\Iishelp	\IISHelp
Data Access	C:\Program Files\Common Files\System\Msadc	\MSADC

- Disable unnecessary services. If the Web server is dedicated to hosting Web applications, disable all unnecessary services, such as the Telnet or FTP service. If the service isn't being used to connect to the Web server, disable it to protect against attacks.

- Block commonly attacked ports with IPSec. A block policy drops all connection attempts to the port described by an IPSec filter.

Note   Alternatively, you can assign a negotiate policy so that computers from the private network that match the IPSec filter based on their connection attempt can still connect to the IIS server. All other connection attempts would fail as if a block policy had been applied.

- Enable IIS logging. IIS logging will help you determine whether your IIS server has been attacked. By using the World Wide Web Consortium (W3C) Extended logging you choose exactly which properties will be logged for each connection attempt to the IIS server. Consider storing the log results in an Open Database Connector (ODBC)–enabled database to improve the ability to query the log results.

Important   IIS logging is resource intensive and can affect the performance of your IIS server. If you plan to implement logging, make sure that you enable IIS logging when testing the performance of your IIS server. Also, consider changing the IIS log storage location to move the IIS logs from the Windows 2000 boot partition where the operating system files are stored.

- Implement Secure Socket Layer (SSL) protocol to protect secure areas of the Web server. Any areas of the Web server that require visitors to enter confidential information such as addresses, credit cards, or password information should be protected by using application-layer SSL protection. SSL encrypts all data transferred between the customer on the public network and the Web server.

- Deploy an intrusion detection system. Intrusion detection systems look for tell-tale signs of a hacking attempt aimed at your Web server. The intrusion detection system should inform you when the attack occurred, what kind of attack was attempted, and whether the attack was successful.

- Disable the use of parent paths. Parent paths allow you to use ".." in function calls to view a parent folder. This could lead to an attacker gaining access to a folder on the IIS server that wouldn't normally be accessible. You disable parent paths in the properties of the Web site in the Internet Services Manager MMC console.

- Apply the IIS 5.0 security checklist. Microsoft has developed a security checklist for IIS 5.0 servers. You can obtain it by going to *www.microsoft.com* and searching for "Secure Internet Information Services 5 Checklist." The IIS 5.0 security checklist includes a high-security Web server security template (Hisecweb.inf) that you can apply to secure the Web server.

- Mitigate against successful attacks. By configuring the Web server to participate in an NLBS cluster, you can host the Web site on multiple servers simultaneously. When a public network user connects to the shared address of the NLBS cluster, the connection is directed to one of the nodes in the cluster. If a server in the NLBS cluster is rendered inaccessible by an attack, the NLBS cluster recognizes that the node is down and directs future traffic to the remaining servers in the cluster.

Note NLBS allows weighting of nodes. This means that you can direct a higher percentage of the incoming traffic to the server with the most resources. For example, if your NLBS cluster is comprised of a Pentium 166 MHz server and a Pentium 933 MHz, you'd want a higher percentage of the connections to be established with the higher performance Web server.

- Maintain the latest service packs and hot fixes for the Web server. Ensure that regular updates to the operating system are applied so that security fixes included in the updates are applied to the Web server.

Making the Decision

Table 14.9 outlines the design decisions you need to make when securing an IIS server that's exposed to the Internet.

Table 14.9   Securing a Web Server

To	Do the Following
Track all access to the Web server	■ Implement auditing at the Web server and ensure that the logs are stored in a format that facilitates inspection of the log files.
Provide the strongest security to Web-accessible data	■ Separate the data by content type and apply the most restrictive permissions that still allow functionality.
Prevent an attacker from accessing unauthorized areas of the disk subsystem	■ Disable the use of parent paths in the Web site's property pages.
Prevent port scans against common attacked ports	■ Apply an IPSec block policy to commonly attacked ports that shouldn't be available on the Web server. This prevents a port scanner from detecting the status of the port. ■ Remove all unnecessary services from the Web server to eliminate ports from inspection.
Detect hacking attempts	■ Deploy intrusion detection software to detect hacking attempts. Be aware that some normal traffic patterns may appear as hacking attempts.
Prevent a successful attack against the Web server from compromising other data stored on the network	■ Don't make the Web server a member of the private network forest. ■ Don't store confidential documents on the disk subsystem of the Web server.
Ensure that the latest security fixes are applied to the Web server	■ Ensure that the latest service packs and hot fixes are applied to the Web server. ■ Periodically connect to the Windows Update Web site *(windowsupdate.microsoft.com/)*.
Limit the effect of a successful hacking attempt	■ Configure the Web server to participate in an NLBS cluster. If one node is brought down, all incoming traffic will be redirected to the remaining servers in the cluster.
Apply the recommended security configuration for your Web server	■ Use the IIS 5.0 security checklist tool.

Applying the Decision

Configure the Web server for Market Florist as an NLBS cluster. Because all of the component servers in the cluster use an identical hardware configuration, you can configure the NLBS cluster to load balance equally between the four nodes.

To ensure consistency to public network users, you must apply any additional security configurations uniformly against all four servers. Apply the following configurations to the four Web servers:

- Enable auditing on each of the four Web servers. To allow searching on the audited information, the four Web servers could store their data on the SQL server located on the private network. Storing the auditing information on the SQL server will facilitate searching for specific information in the log files and allow for the consolidation of the log material into a single source location.

- Separate the content from the rest of the Web site. You should break out the Web servers' folder structure to separate the Flower Power application from the rest of the Web site. The Flower Power application requires custom security to allow customers to download the Flower Power client-side application.

- Implement SSL on the Web server. This will protect the customer registration portion of the Web site. Likewise, program the Flower Power ActiveX control to use SSL to encrypt customer orders and prevent interception of customer numbers.

- Apply IPSec to restrict public network access to the Web server. Connections should only be allowed to the ports that are accessible by public network users. Block all other ports with IPSec by using a Negotiate IPSec policy. Negotiate allows connections from the private network while blocking connections from the external network. This would require the IPSec filters in Table 14.10 to be applied to the MFWeb1 server. Each server requires separate IPSec filters based on the cluster member's local IP address.

Table 14.10   Recommended IPSec Filters for the Market Florist Web Server

Protocol	Source IP	Source Port	Target IP	Target Port	Transport Protocol	Action
HTTP	Any	Any	192.168.7.3	80	TCP	Permit
HTTPS	Any	Any	192.168.7.3	443	TCP	Permit
Flower Power	Any	Any	192.168.7.3	6834	UDP	Permit
Terminal Services	Any	Any	192.168.7.3	3389	TCP	Permit
Any	Any	Any	Any	Any	Any	Negotiate

- Apply the IIS 5.0 Security Checklist recommendations to the IIS servers. The IIS 5.0 checklist enables recommended registry and file permission settings to ensure the secure configuration of the Web server.

Securing Other Services Within the DMZ

Within a DMZ you can expect to find several common resources. These include external FTP servers, Telnet servers, and DNS servers. Each service requires specific configuration to allow you to restrict access to these services.

- **FTP services.** The FTP service isn't loaded by default in a Windows 2000 installation. If you install the FTP service, be aware that the C:\Inetpub\Ftproot folder allows the Everyone group Full Control by default. This default setting could allow an attacker to upload data and fill up the drive partition of the FTP server if Write access is configured in the FTP service property pages in the Internet Services Manager console. Consider changing the permissions and enabling disk quotas to limit the amount of data that can be written to the FTP root.

- **Telnet servers.** Telnet provides text-based access to a server's disk subsystem. If it's enabled, all users could access the Telnet service by default. You can restrict access to Telnet servers by creating a group named TelnetClients in either the local Security Account Management (SAM) database of the Telnet server or, if the Telnet server is a member of a domain, within Active Directory. When the TelnetClients group exists, only members of the group will be able to access the server.

Note In addition, to ensure that authentication credentials aren't transmitted in plaintext, you should configure the Telnet service to accept only NTLM authentication. Additionally, if confidential data is accessed in the Telnet session, you can use IPSec to encrypt the data transmitted between the Telnet client and the Telnet server.

- **DNS services.** Only externally accessible DNS resource records should be stored on a DNS server located in the DMZ. The external DNS server should expose only the externally registered IP addresses to public DNS clients. This practice will ensure that DNS doesn't reveal your private network addressing scheme. To prevent an attacker from obtaining all zone information from the DNS server, consider restricting zone transfers to preconfigured DNS servers.

- **Terminal Services.** Restrict Terminal Services to administrators of the network by configuring Terminal Services to operate in Remote Administration mode. Remote Administration mode allows only members of the Administrators local group to connect using Terminal Services.

- **All services.** All services listen for client connections on a well-known port. Use IPSec to limit access to these well-known ports by creating IPSec block policies that will block access to other ports found on the server. For example, if you wanted to only allow HTTP, HTTPS, and Telnet connections to a Web server at IP address 10.10.10.10 in the DMZ, you could set the IPSec filters shown in Table 14.11.

Table 14.11   An IPSec Filter that Allows Only Connections for HTTP, HTTPS, and Telnet

Protocol	Source IP	Source Port	Target IP	Target Port	Transport Protocol	IPSec Action
HTTP	Any	Any	10.10.10.10	80	TCP	Permit
HTTPS	Any	Any	10.10.10.10	443	TCP	Permit
Telnet	Any	Any	10.10.10.10	23	TCP	Permit
Any	Any	Any	Any	Any	Any	Block

The first two packet filters in Table 14.11 allow any IP clients connecting to the HTTP and HTTPS services on the Web server at IP address 10.10.10.10. The third packet filter allows Telnet connections to the Web server. The final packet filter blocks any other protocols from connecting to the Web server.

Important   If you want private network computers to connect to other ports on the server, change the IPSec action to negotiate and define the encryption protocols that must be used for the connection. Only members on the private network should be able to negotiate a security association (SA) with the Web server.

In addition to securing the individual servers within the DMZ, you can also use IPSec to configure the security of transmitted data between the servers located in the DMZ. IPSec protects against an attacker's computer intercepting data transmissions between the servers located in the DMZ. You can configure an IPSec SA between two servers in the DMZ to apply Encapsulating Security Payloads (ESP) to all data transmitted between the two servers. For example, you can secure a Web front-end application and an SQL server so that IPSec encrypts data transmitted between the two servers by negotiating a SA between the two servers. This association is shown in Figure 14.11.

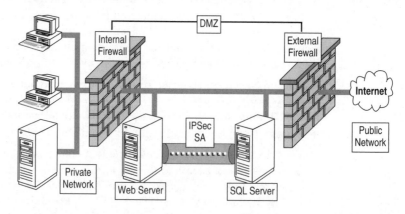

Figure 14.11   How IPSec SAs protect transmitted data between computers in the DMZ

Making the Decision

Table 14.12 outlines the security configuration options that should be included to protect Internet-accessible resources.

Table 14.12   Protecting Internet-Accessible Resources

To Protect	Include the Following in Your Design
FTP services	■ Change NTFS permissions to match the allowed transactions. For example, if only FTP downloads are allowed, configure permissions to allow only the anonymous FTP account Read permissions. ■ To prevent password interception, allow only anonymous connections.
Telnet services	■ Create a local security group named TelnetClients to restrict Telnet access to authorized users.
DNS services	■ If using the same namespace internally and externally, ensure that the external DNS server doesn't contain private network IP addressing. ■ Restrict zone transfers at the external DNS server to only approved DNS servers to prevent an attacker from retrieving the entire zone data file.
All services	■ If allowing only specific protocol connections, block all other protocols with an IPSec block action. This will prevent any other ports from responding to port scans or access attempts. ■ If you require private network access to the restricted ports on a server in the DMZ, change the IPSec action to negotiate so that private network client computers can establish an IPSec SA with the server in the DMZ.
Interaction between servers	■ Configure servers in the DMZ to use IPSec transport mode for data transmitted between the servers. IPSec transport mode encrypts all data exchanged between the servers and prevents unauthorized connections to the server. IPSec transport mode can pass through a firewall as long as NAT isn't performed against the data.

Applying the Decision

Market Florist can implement additional security configuration within the DMZ to ensure the security of the services located in the DMZ. Include the following in the Market Florist security design:

■ **FTP service.** Market Florist customers use the FTP service to download product brochures. Modify the permissions for the Ftproot folder to assign only Read permissions to the anonymous FTP account. Permissions should allow John Coake and Pat Coleman to modify the contents of the Ftproot folder.

■ **DNS service.** Configure the external DNS server to only allow zone transfers to configured secondary DNS servers. This configuration prevents attackers from dumping the zone database from the DNS server. In addition, the external DNS server should only refer to the public network addresses of the available services. There should be no references to the private network addresses used in the DMZ.

- **Telnet service.** Configure the MFFTP server with a local security group named TelnetClients. Make John Coake and Pat Coleman members of the group to restrict Telnet access to only John and Pat and exclude access to all other users.

- **Terminal Services.** To restrict Terminal Services to only network administrators, install Terminal Services using Remote Administration mode on each server in the DMZ. Install Terminal Services on each component server of the MFWEB NLBS cluster to allow administrators to connect to the individual component servers.

- **Interaction between servers.** Establish an IPSec SA between the MFWEB NLBS cluster servers and the MFSQL server on the private network to encrypt all data exchanged between the servers. The IPSec agreement can take place because NAT isn't performed between the DMZ and the private network.

Lesson Summary

Don't depend exclusively on firewalls to protect resources exposed to the Internet. When designing your security, imagine each server being exposed on the Internet without the protection of a firewall. Ensure that each server in the DMZ is properly configured so that security will be maintained even if a firewall is compromised.

Lesson 3: Securing Data Flow Through a DMZ

Firewalls can regulate which protocols are allowed to enter and exit the DMZ. By configuring the firewall to allow only the authorized protocols to connect to each server in the DMZ, you can prevent hackers from attaching to the servers using alternative protocols.

After this lesson, you will be able to

- Determine a strategy for configuring packet filters on a firewall
- Design packet filters for commonly accessed services in a DMZ configuration

Estimated lesson time: 60 minutes

Determining a Firewall Strategy

When configuring a firewall, decide between the following basic firewall strategies based on your desired security level:

- Specify allowed protocols and prohibit everything else. In this strategy the packet filters identify all protocols that are allowed to pass through the firewall. If a packet arrives that isn't identified by the packet filter listing, the packet is assumed to be disallowed and is dropped. This strategy is typically used at external firewalls to define which protocols are allowed to enter the DMZ and the private network and in high-security networks where only authorized protocols are allowed to enter the DMZ and the private network.

- Specify prohibited protocols and allow everything else. In this strategy the packet filters identify all protocols that must be dropped at the firewall. If a packet arrives that isn't identified by the packet filter listing, the packet is allowed to pass through the firewall. This strategy is often used at an internal firewall to block private network users from specific protocols or in lower security networks where only unauthorized protocols are blocked at the firewall.

What About the Order of the Packet Filters?

The order in which packet filters are processed depends on the specific firewall product. Firewalls typically process the packet filters using one of two common methods.

The first method is to process the packet filters in the order in which they're entered. In other words, the packet filters are processed from the top to the bottom of the packet filter list. If your firewall uses this strategy, ensure that the most important packet filters are placed at the top of the list. For example, place a packet filter that restricts access to the Web server using HTTP and HTTPS above a rule that denies access to any servers in the DMZ.

(*continued*)

The second method is to process the most specific packet filters before the more general packet filters. In other words, a packet filter that restricts access to a specific server will be processed before a packet filter that defines traffic between network segments. For example, a packet filter that allows the DNS server in the DMZ to connect to a DNS server at an ISP will be processed before a packet filter that allows any computer on the public network to connect to the DNS server.

Making the Decision

Table 14.13 outlines the factors you need to consider when deciding between the common firewall strategies.

Table 14.13   Choosing Between Firewall Strategies

Use This Strategy	In These Circumstances
Specify allowed protocols and prohibit everything else.	■ Your strategy defines exactly which protocols are allowed to enter the DMZ ■ You're defining packet filters for an external firewall
Specify prohibited protocols and allow everything else.	■ You must prevent specific protocols, such as Finger, from entering or exiting the network ■ You're defining packet filters for an internal firewall

These aren't the only strategies. Nothing prevents you from using "Specify allowed protocols and prohibit everything else" and creating packet filters that deny specific protocols. This is commonly done to log attempts to use the prohibited protocols since you can log an event only if a packet filter is matched.

Applying the Decision

For Market Florist, the "Specify allowed protocols and prohibit everything else" firewall strategy best meets the security needs of the network. This strategy enables Market Florist to define only authorized protocols that can enter the DMZ and the private network. If a protocol isn't included in the packet filter list, the protocol is assumed to be denied access to the DMZ or private network.

Securing DNS Resolution Traffic

The DNS service is used as a locator service in a Windows 2000 network. In addition, DNS is also used as the locator service for the Internet. When designing security for the DNS service, define how DNS traffic will move through your private network and through the DMZ to the Internet.

The key to securing DNS is separating the internal DNS service from the external DNS service. This allows separation of the internal DNS namespace from the external DNS namespace so that private network IP addressing schemes aren't exposed to the Internet.

Figure 14.12 shows a typical DNS deployment that's used when both internal and external DNS services are deployed in a network.

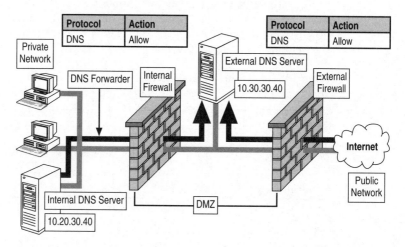

Protocol	Action
DNS	Allow

Protocol	Action
DNS	Allow

Figure 14.12   DNS traffic flow in a DMZ

In this configuration the internal firewall is configured to allow only DNS packets from the internal DNS server to be sent to the external DNS server in the DMZ through a DNS forwarder. This configuration limits internal DNS clients to connecting to the internal DNS server. The internal firewall prevents the internal DNS clients from connecting to any other external DNS server.

Based on the IP address information shown in the figure, Table 14.14 lists the packet filters that you must apply at the internal firewall to restrict DNS traffic between the two DNS servers.

Table 14.14   Internal Firewall Rules to Restrict DNS Usage

Protocol	Source IP	Source Port	Target IP	Target Port	Transport Protocol	Action
DNS	10.20.30.40	Any	10.30.30.40	53	TCP	Allow
DNS	10.20.30.40	Any	10.30.30.40	53	UDP	Allow
DNS	10.20.30.0/24	Any	10.30.30.40	53	TCP	Deny
DNS	10.20.30.0/24	Any	10.30.30.40	53	UDP	Deny

The first two packet filters allow the internal DNS server (10.20.30.40) to connect to the external DNS server (10.30.30.40) using either UDP-based or TCP-based DNS connections. The last two packet filters deny all other clients on the 10.20.30.0/24 network from connecting to any DNS servers beyond the firewall using UDP-based or TCP-based DNS queries.

Note   All firewall rules in this lesson assume that the firewalls support packet filter mirroring. As discussed in Lesson 1, packet filter mirroring allows response packets to be passed successfully through the firewall.

At the external firewall, create additional packet filters to allow external client computers to connect only to the DNS server using the DNS protocol. All other requests sent to the DNS server should be prevented (unless the DNS server is hosting other authorized services).

Table 14.15 lists the packet filters that you must establish at the external firewall to allow public network users to query the DNS server located in the DMZ and to allow the external DNS server to forward DNS requests to other DNS servers on the Internet.

Table 14.15   External Firewall Rules to Restrict DNS Usage

Protocol	Source IP	Source Port	Target IP	Target Port	Transport Protocol	Action
DNS	Any	Any	10.30.30.40	53	TCP	Allow
DNS	Any	Any	10.30.30.40	53	UDP	Allow
DNS	10.30.30.40	Any	Any	53	TCP	Allow
DNS	10.30.30.40	Any	Any	53	UDP	Allow

The first two packet filters allow any computers on the Internet to connect to the external DNS server (10.30.30.40) using either TCP-based or UDP-based DNS requests. The last two packet filters allow the external DNS server to forward DNS queries to any DNS server on the Internet.

Note   Packet filters will always refer to the true IP address of the server, not the advertised address on the Internet. Static address mapping converts the destination address before the packet filter is applied to determine if the data is allowed to reach the destination server.

Making the Decision

When configuring a firewall to allow DNS traffic, include the following items in your security design:

- Establish packet filters at the external firewall to allow only TCP port 53 and UDP port 53 packets to reach the DNS server.
- Establish packet filters at the internal firewall to allow only the internal DNS server to send TCP port 53 and UDP port 53 packets to the external DNS.
- Configure the internal DNS server to forward all irresolvable DNS queries to the external DNS server. In the same way, configure the external DNS server to forward irresolvable DNS queries to the ISP's DNS server. This strategy

focuses DNS resolution traffic to specific hosts and makes it easier to define packet filters.

Applying the Decision

Market Florist must configure the internal DNS server to forward irresolvable DNS requests to the external DNS server in the DMZ. Because there's only a single firewall, the firewall rules are included in a single packet filter listing. Table 14.16 shows the packet filters necessary to restrict DNS traffic for Market Florist.

Table 14.16   DNS Packet Filters for Market Florist

Protocol	Source IP	Source Port	Target IP	Target Port	Transport Protocol	Action
DNS	10.10.10.3	Any	192.168.77.254	53	TCP	Allow
DNS	10.10.10.3	Any	192.168.77.254	53	UDP	Allow
DNS	10.10.10.0/24	Any	Any	53	TCP	Deny
DNS	10.10.10.0/24	Any	Any	53	UDP	Deny
DNS	Any	Any	192.168.77.254	53	TCP	Allow
DNS	Any	Any	192.168.77.254	53	UDP	Allow
DNS	192.168.77.254	Any	131.107.199.56	53	TCP	Allow
DNS	192.168.77.254	Any	131.107.199.56	53	UDP	Allow

The first two packet filters allow the internal DNS server (10.10.10.3) to forward DNS queries to the external DNS server (192.168.77.254). The third and fourth packet filters prevent any other internal network clients (10.10.10.0/24) from querying DNS servers beyond the internal firewall. The fifth and sixth packet filters allow any DNS clients on the Internet to query the external DNS server. And the final two packet filters allow the external DNS server to forward DNS queries to the ISP's DNS server (131.107.199.56).

Note   The rules that deny access to hosts on the 10.10.10.0/24 network prevent private network client computers from connecting to Internet-based DNS services and bypassing the internal DNS server. These rules force private network client computers to use the internal DNS server.

Securing Web Traffic

A Web server is one of the most common network resources made available for Internet access. A Web server listens for connections from external client computers on TCP port 80 for HTTP connections and on TCP port 443 for HTTPS connections.

Figure 14.13 depicts a Web server located in a DMZ that allows internal and external access to the Web server.

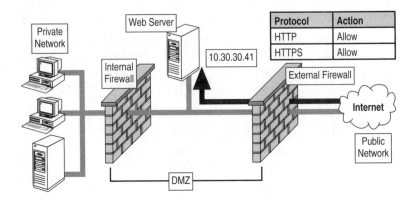

Protocol	Action
HTTP	Allow
HTTPS	Allow

Figure 14.13   Web server placement in a DMZ

Configure access to the Web server in the DMZ at both the internal and external firewalls to ensure that only authorized protocols are allowed to connect.

At the external firewall, establish packet filters that limit connections to the Web server to the HTTP and HTTPS protocols. Table 14.17 lists the required packet filters for Figure 14.13.

Table 14.17   External Packet Filters for a Web Server

Protocol	Source IP	Source Port	Target IP	Target Port	Transport Protocol	Action
HTTP	Any	Any	10.30.30.41	80	TCP	Allow
HTTPS	Any	Any	10.30.30.41	443	TCP	Allow

The first packet filter allows Internet users to connect to the Web server (10.30.30.41) using HTTP, and the second packet filter allows Internet users to connect to the Web server using HTTPS.

Note   Establishing packet filters at the internal firewall to restrict access to the Web server from the private network is optional. The packet filters are required only if connections to the Web server must be limited to HTTP and HTTPS connections.

Making the Decision

When configuring a firewall to allow Web server traffic, include the following items in your security design:

- Establish packet filters at the external firewall to only allow TCP port 80 and TCP port 443 packets to reach the Web server.

- Implement SSL protection for any Web pages that require input of sensitive data from external users.

- When authentication is required to a Web site, use either Windows Integrated Authentication or Basic Authentication with SSL encryption to protect credentials from interception.

Applying the Decision

Market Florist must ensure that the customer registration portion of the *www.marketflorist.tld* Web site is protected by SSL encryption to ensure that credit card information isn't intercepted. In addition, Market Florist must establish packet filters to restrict external access to the Web server. Table 14.18 lists the required packet filters.

Table 14.18   Web Server Packet Filters for Market Florist

Protocol	Source IP	Source Port	Target IP	Target Port	Transport Protocol	Action
HTTP	Any	Any	192.168.77.2	80	TCP	Allow
HTTPS	Any	Any	192.168.77.2	443	TCP	Allow

These two packet filters enable Internet users to connect to the Market Florist Web server (192.168.77.2) using only HTTP and HTTPS protocols.

Note   The firewall rules have to be established only for the NLBS Web server cluster IP address. Once the packets reach the Web cluster, the NLBS service determines which node receives the packets.

Securing FTP Traffic

FTP allows data to be transferred to and from a central location. When designing packet filters for FTP connections, it's helpful to understand how FTP transmissions work.

FTP uses two separate channels for FTP sessions. FTP uses a control stream (a connection to TCP port 21) to send FTP commands from the FTP client software to the FTP server and a data stream (a connection to TCP port 20) for transferring data. The two channels are used to allow a data transmission to be interrupted through the control stream.

Some FTP clients, known as active FTP clients, require the FTP server to initiate the data transfer. You must establish packet filters that allow the FTP server to initiate FTP data sessions.

To restrict FTP connections from the Internet, you typically place the FTP server in a DMZ, as shown in Figure 14.14.

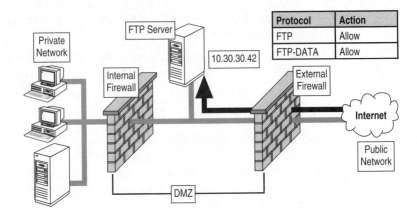

Figure 14.14 Providing FTP access in a DMZ

Table 14.19 shows the packet filters that you need to establish at the external firewall to allow access to the FTP server in the DMZ.

Table 14.19   FTP Server Packet Filters

Protocol	Source IP	Source Port	Target IP	Target Port	Transport Protocol	Action
FTP Data	Any	Any	192.168.77.7	20	TCP	Allow
FTP	Any	Any	192.168.77.7	21	TCP	Allow
FTP Data	192.168.77.7	20	Any	Any	TCP	Allow
FTP	192.168.77.7	21	Any	Any	TCP	Allow

The first two packet filters allow any Internet users to connect to the FTP server (192.168.77.7) for FTP connections. The last two packet filters enable the FTP server to establish connections to active FTP clients.

Note The packet filters listed in Table 14.19 assume that active FTP clients exist on the network. The last two packet filters allow data transfers initiated by the FTP server to pass through the external firewall. If the FTP clients were passive, you could remove the last two filters from the packet filter listing.

Making the Decision

When configuring a firewall to allow access to an FTP server, include the following items in your security design:

- Establish packet filters at the external firewall to allow only TCP port 20 and TCP port 21 packets to reach the FTP server.

- If active FTP clients exist, or if you aren't sure they exist, establish reverse packet filters that originate at the FTP server for TCP port 20 and TCP port 21.

- To provide maximum password security, allow only anonymous access to the FTP server. FTP uses plaintext authentication and is subject to password interception.

Applying the Decision

Market Florist must allow external client computers to only use the FTP protocol to connect to the MFFTP server in the DMZ. To accomplish this, apply the packet filters shown in Table 14.20 at the external firewall.

Table 14.20   FTP Server Packet Filters for Market Florist

Protocol	Source IP	Source Port	Target IP	Target Port	Transport Protocol	Action
FTP Data	Any	Any	192.168.77.7	20	TCP	Allow
FTP	Any	Any	192.168.77.7	21	TCP	Allow
FTP Data	192.168.77.7	20	Any	Any	TCP	Allow
FTP	192.168.77.7	21	Any	Any	TCP	Allow

The first two packet filters allow Internet users to connect to the MFFTP server (192.168.77.7) using FTP sessions. The last two packet filters allow the MFFTP server to initiate data transfers with active FTP clients.

Configure the FTP server to accept only anonymous connections. The FTP server is used to download floral arrangement brochures and authenticated access isn't required. Anonymous access ensures that credentials can't be intercepted. John and Pat will use Telnet from the private network to manage the data in the Ftproot folder.

Note   To allow Telnet access from the private network, the internal firewall must either allow all access or restrict access to TCP port 23 on the MFFTP server.

Securing Mail Traffic

Many organizations use e-mail to communicate within the organization and with other organizations. Ensure that mail servers are secured against attacks by allowing only authorized protocols to connect to the mail server.

Figure 14.15 shows a typical mail server deployment in a DMZ environment.

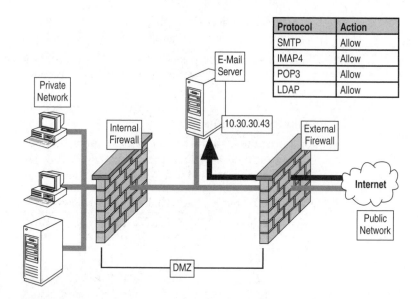

Protocol	Action
SMTP	Allow
IMAP4	Allow
POP3	Allow
LDAP	Allow

Figure 14.15   Providing e-mail access in a DMZ

Carefully plan mail access for an organization so that e-mail doesn't cause security problems. Typically, a mail server must support several protocols for e-mail access. Common protocols supported by mail servers include

- **Post Office Protocol v3 (POP3).** Used by e-mail users to retrieve their messages from the mail server. POP3 introduces a security risk because authentication is performed using plaintext.

- **Internet Mail Access Protocol v4 (IMAPv4).** Used by newer e-mail client software to retrieve messages from the mail server. IMAPv4 gives access to all folders on the mail server, not just the Inbox. Like POP3, IMAPv4 uses plaintext authentication.

- **Simple Message Transfer Protocol (SMTP).** Used by e-mail client software to send messages to other e-mail recipients. SMTP is subject to spamming attacks where unsolicited messages are relayed using an unprotected e-mail server.

Note   You can prevent SMTP relaying on a server so that only e-mail messages destined to a mailbox hosted on the mail server can be received. Alternatively, you can place restrictions to allow only SMTP relaying to authenticated users or to specific IP addresses or network IP addresses.

- **Lightweight Directory Access Protocol (LDAP).** Used by e-mail client software as a directory for the e-mail server. LDAP provides the ability to find e-mail addresses on a mail server. LDAP uses plaintext authentication by default.

Important   You can protect POP3, IMAPv4, and LDAP by implementing SSL. The protocols will use SSL encryption to protect user account and password verification during the authentication process.

Table 14.21 lists the packet filters that you must establish at the external firewall to allow access to the mail server in the DMZ by external client computers.

Table 14.21   Mail Server Packet Filters

Protocol	Source IP	Source Port	Target IP	Target Port	Transport Protocol	Action
POP3	Any	Any	10.30.30.43	110	TCP	Allow
POP3-SSL	Any	Any	10.30.30.43	995	TCP	Allow
IMAP4	Any	Any	10.30.30.43	143	TCP	Allow
IMAP4-SSL	Any	Any	10.30.30.43	993	TCP	Allow
LDAP	Any	Any	10.30.30.43	389	TCP	Allow
LDAP-SSL	Any	Any	10.30.30.43	636	TCP	Allow
SMTP	Any	Any	10.30.30.43	25	TCP	Allow
SMTP	10.30.30.43	Any	Any	25	TCP	Allow

The first two packet filters allow POP3 clients and POP3 clients using SSL to connect to the mail server (10.30.30.43). The third and fourth packet filters allow IMAP4 clients and IMAP4 clients using SSL to connect to the mail server. The fifth and sixth packet filters allow LDAP clients and LDAP clients using SSL to connect to the mail server. The seventh packet filter allows the mail server to accept SMTP messages from the Internet, and the final packet filter allows the mail server to send SMTP messages to any SMTP servers on the Internet.

Note   Some mail servers, such as Exchange Server 5.5 and Exchange 2000 Server, support HTTP-based access to user mailboxes. To support HTTP-based access, you can add additional packet filters to allow HTTPS to access the mail server.

Making the Decision

When configuring a firewall to allow access to a mail server, include the following items in your security design:

- Determine which protocols will be allowed to access the mail server from the public network. In many cases the only protocol allowed to connect to the mail server from the public network is SMTP. The organization can't allow e-mail to be retrieved from the public network.

- Establish packet filters at the external firewall to allow only the necessary ports to connect to the mail server. Ports to be opened can include POP3 (TCP port 110), POP3-ssl (TCP port 995), IMAP4 (TCP port 143), IMAP4-ssl (TCP port 993), LDAP (TCP port 389), LDAP-ssl (TCP port 636), and SMTP (TCP port 25).

- Establish restrictions on SMTP relaying to prevent the mail server from becoming a source for unsolicited bulk e-mail.

- Restrict which protocols can be used to connect to the mail server from the private network. Strategies include

  - Restrict access to specific protocols, such as allowing only POP3 and SMTP protocol access.

  - Restrict access to specific servers. Use this strategy if the organization has multiple mail servers and the mail server in the DMZ only acts as a gateway to the other e-mail system.

  - Allow private network client computers to connect using any protocol, provided they're located on the private network.

Applying the Decision

Market Florist must restrict which protocols can connect to the mail server in the DMZ. According to the scenario, only POP3 and SMTP will be used to connect to the mail server from the public network. To allow only these protocols, create the packet filters in Table 14.22 at the external firewall.

Table 14.22   Mail Server Packet Filters for Market Florist

Protocol	Source IP	Source Port	Target IP	Target Port	Transport Protocol	Action
POP3	Any	Any	192.168.77.8	110	TCP	Allow
POP3-ssl	Any	Any	192.168.77.8	995	TCP	Allow
SMTP	Any	Any	192.168.77.8	25	TCP	Allow
SMTP	192.168.77.8	Any	Any	25	TCP	Allow

The first two packet filters allow e-mail clients to retrieve mail from the MFMAIL server by using POP3 or POP3-ssl clients. The third packet filter allows the MFMAIL server to receive SMTP messages from the Internet. And the final packet filter allows the MFMAIL server to send SMTP messages to any mail server on the Internet.

In addition, configure the mail server to allow only SMTP relaying if the user authenticates with the MFMAIL server before the e-mail client attempts the SMTP relay action. Because the remote sales force will be connecting from unknown IP addresses, you can't establish restrictions using network IP addresses.

Securing Application Traffic

Servers in the DMZ are often required to store or access data from an application server, such as an SQL server, in the private network. You can protect the transfer of data by configuring the internal firewall to allow only specific protocols to pass between the server in the DMZ and the application server in the private network.

It's too risky to place the application server in the DMZ because data stored on the application server might be compromised. When you make use of the internal firewall's packet filtering abilities, only authorized connections between the server in the DMZ and the application server in the private network can take place.

You can manage the connection between the two servers by using one of three methods:

- Attach the server in the DMZ directly to the computer on the private network using a crossover cable and a protocol other than TCP/IP. This strategy works only when the two servers are near each other. But it offers little control over what data can be transmitted between the two servers.

- Open the firewall to allow the native protocol to transfer between the server in the DMZ and the application server in the private network, as shown in Figure 14.16. The risk with this configuration is that the data transmitted between the two servers may be passed in plaintext and allow confidential data to be inspected by a network sniffer. Network sniffers are able to view the contents of any unencrypted data packets transmitted on the network.

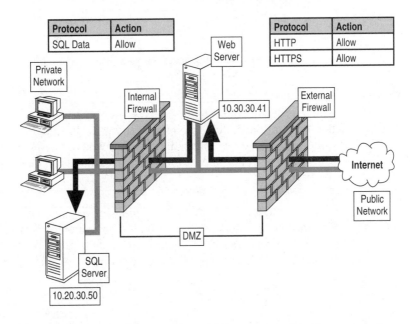

Figure 14.16   Securing access to an SQL server on the private network

- Use IPSec to encrypt the data transmitted between the server in the DMZ and the application server in the private network. As long as the internal firewall isn't performing NAT on the transmitted data, you can use IPSec to encrypt all data transmitted between the two servers. For example, if the application server is an SQL server, the connection to the server would be TCP port 1433. All data sent to that port on the SQL server could be encrypted as shown in Figure 14.17.

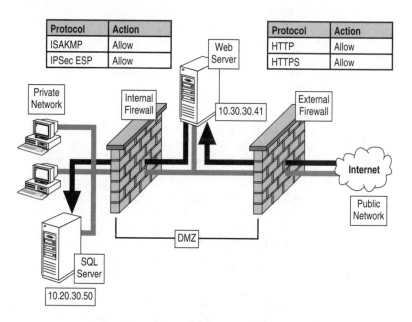

Figure 14.17   Securing access to an SQL server on the private network by using IPSec

---

Note   IPSec encryption prevents the firewall from inspecting the actual protocol that's being transmitted through the firewall. Be sure to set up your rules so that only server-to-server connections are allowed to pass using IPSec. This prevents other servers from establishing IPSec agreements and attempting to pass through the firewall.

Once you've identified the participating servers and the necessary protocols, define the packet filters necessary to allow communications to take place. Table 14.23 lists the packet filter required to write data to an SQL server using TCP/IP socket connections from a Web server in the DMZ as shown in Figure 14.16.

Table 14.23   SQL Server Packet Filters for the Internal Firewall

Protocol	Source IP	Source Port	Target IP	Target Port	Transport Protocol	Action
SQL Data	10.30.30.41	Any	10.20.30.50	1433	TCP	Allow

The packet filter permits the Web server (10.30.30.41) to connect to the SQL server (10.20.30.50) using only an SQL data connection. No other computers in the DMZ are allowed to connect to the SQL server. Also, the Web server can't use any other protocols to connect to the SQL server.

In this case the external firewall would use the same filters defined in Table 14.15. Public network clients are only allowed to connect to the Web server. The public network clients don't query the SQL server on the private network. It's the Web server that actually performs the query on behalf of the external customer. For the transaction to occur, the external customer only needs to connect to the Web server using HTTP or HTTPS.

If the connection between the Web server and the SQL server uses IPSec to encrypt all transmitted data, set up the packet filters at the internal firewall to allow both Internet Key Exchange (IKE) packets and IPSec ESP packets to pass, as shown in Table 14.24.

Table 14.24   IPSec Packet Filters for the Internal Firewall

Protocol	Source IP	Source Port	Target IP	Target Port	Transport Protocol	Action
IKE	10.30.30.41	500	10.20.30.50	500	UDP	Allow
ESP	10.30.30.41		10.20.30.50		ID 50	Allow

The first packet filter allows the Web server (10.30.30.41) to negotiate an IPSec SA with the SQL server (10.20.30.50). The second packet filter assumes that only ESP will be used to protect the IPSec packets and enables any packets encrypted with ESP (protocol ID 50) sent between the Web server and the SQL server to pass through the firewall.

Note   An ESP packet filter only describes the protocol ID. Port information isn't required for an ESP packet filter.

Making the Decision

When configuring a firewall to allow access to an application server on the private network, configure the firewall rules to match how data transmissions take place. Your design should include the following:

- Determine which protocols are required to access the server-based component in the DMZ. In many cases the server-based component will be a Web-based application running on a Web server.

- Configure the external firewall to allow only public network client computers to connect to the server in the DMZ using the protocols required for the server-based component.

- Determine which protocols the server-based component uses to connect to the application server in the private network.

- Determine the securest method to connect the server in the DMZ to the application server in the private network. Be sure to include a strategy to prevent inspection of data in the DMZ.

- Define the necessary packet filters at the internal firewall to allow only the required protocols to exchange data between the DMZ and the private network.

Applying the Decision

Market Florist must allow customers to connect to the SQL server on the private network using both a Web interface for customer registration and the Flower Power application to store order information. Because the customer registration information requires transmission security, all data transmitted between the Web server (MFWEB) and the SQL server (MFSQL) must be encrypted using IPSec transport mode, as shown in Table 14.25.

Table 14.25   Flower Power Packet Filters for Market Florist

Protocol	Source IP	Source Port	Target IP	Target Port	Transport Protocol	Action
HTTP	Any	Any	192.168.77.2	80	TCP	Allow
HTTPS	Any	Any	192.168.77.2	443	TCP	Allow
Flower Power	Any	Any	192.168.77.2	6834	UDP	Allow
IKE	192.168.77.3	500	10.10.10.20	500	UDP	Allow
IKE	192.168.77.4	500	10.10.10.20	500	UDP	Allow
IKE	192.168.77.5	500	10.10.10.20	500	UDP	Allow
IKE	192.168.77.6	500	10.10.10.20	500	UDP	Allow
ESP	192.168.77.3		10.10.10.20		ID 50	Allow
ESP	192.168.77.4		10.10.10.20		ID 50	Allow
ESP	192.168.77.5		10.10.10.20		ID 50	Allow
ESP	192.168.77.6		10.10.10.20		ID 50	Allow

The first two packet filters allow public network users to connect to the MFWEB server (192.168.77.2) using either HTTP or HTTPS. The third packet filter allows public network users to connect to the Flower Power server-side application listening on UDP port 6834 on the MFWEB server. The next four packet filters allow IPSec SAs to be negotiated between each component server in the NLBS Web cluster and the MFSQL server (10.10.10.20). You must establish separate packet filters for each Web server in the NLBS cluster because IPSec SAs are established between two computers, not between a computer and an NLBS cluster. The last four packet filters allow each component server in the NLBS cluster to send ESP-encrypted SQL-data packets to the MFSQL server.

Warning   The last eight packet filters allow the MFSQL and MFWEB server to transmit data in any protocol between the two servers. As long as the IPSec SA doesn't use Authentication Headers (AH), the firewall will allow the packets to pass. To prevent unauthorized protocols, you must inspect IPSec packet filters regularly at each server to ensure that they encrypt only authorized protocols.

Securing Terminal Server Traffic

Terminal Services allows an administrator to connect to servers on the network by using Remote Desktop Protocol (RDP). You can restrict Terminal Services to be used for administrative purposes only by configuring Terminal Services to run in Remote Administration mode rather than Application Services mode.

To restrict access to a terminal server, configure the external firewall to allow only RDP connections to the terminal server. As shown in Figure 14.18, configure the external firewall to allow only connections using RDP to pass through to the terminal server.

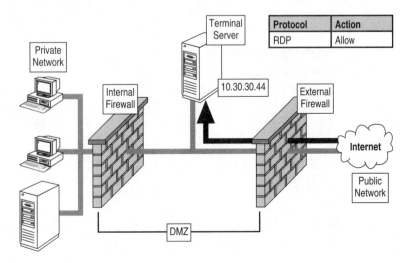

Figure 14.18   Securing access to a terminal server in the DMZ

Configure the terminal server to require strong encryption of the connection. If the Windows 2000 High Encryption Pack is installed at both the Terminal Services client computer and the server running Terminal Services, 128-bit RC4 encryption is used to protect transmitted data. If either the client or the server doesn't have the High Encryption Pack, 40-bit or 56-bit encryption is used.

To allow the RDP to pass through the external firewall, you must define the packet filter in Table 14.26.

Table 14.26   Terminal Services Packet Filters

Protocol	Source IP	Source Port	Target IP	Target Port	Transport Protocol	Action
RDP	Any	Any	10.30.30.44	3389	TCP	Allow

This packet filter allows any computer to connect to the terminal server (10.30.30.44) with the RDP protocol. Any attempts to connect to the terminal server with other protocols are denied.

Making the Decision

When configuring a firewall to allow access to a terminal server located in the DMZ, consider the following design points:

- Configure the firewall to allow only connections to TCP port 3389, the RDP protocol, to pass through the firewall.

- Configure the terminal server to use the highest level of encryption supported by the client computers, subject to local import and export laws.

- If you only require administrative access to the terminal server, configure the terminal server to user Remote Administration mode. This action prevents nonadministrative users from connecting to the terminal server.

Applying the Decision

Market Florist wants to use Terminal Services to manage all servers in the DMZ from the private network. To restrict access to Terminal Services to administrators only, configure Terminal Services to use Remote Administration mode at all computers in the DMZ. In addition, establish the packet filters shown in Table 14.27.

Table 14.27   Terminal Services Packet Filters for Market Florist

Protocol	Source IP	Source Port	Target IP	Target Port	Transport Protocol	Action
RDP	10.10.10.0/24	Any	192.168.77.3	3389	TCP	Allow
RDP	10.10.10.0/24	Any	192.168.77.4	3389	TCP	Allow
RDP	10.10.10.0/24	Any	192.168.77.5	3389	TCP	Allow
RDP	10.10.10.0/24	Any	192.168.77.6	3389	TCP	Allow
RDP	10.10.10.0/24	Any	192.168.77.7	3389	TCP	Allow
RDP	10.10.10.0/24	Any	192.168.77.8	3389	TCP	Allow
RDP	10.10.10.0/24	Any	192.168.77.9	3389	TCP	Allow
RDP	10.10.10.0/24	Any	192.168.77.254	3389	TCP	Allow

The packet filters configured in Table 14.27 limit RDP access to the servers located in the DMZ from the private network (10.10.10.0/24). All other connections are implicitly denied.

Note   You don't need to establish a separate packet filter for the NLBS cluster IP address. Each node of the NLBS cluster service allows Terminal Services connections from the private network.

Securing VPN Traffic

When an organization wants its network to permit VPN traffic, they must consider how the protocol they use affects their firewall and network infrastructure design. Remember that L2TP and IPSec tunnel mode both use IPSec to provide encryption services to the tunnel. IPSec is unable to pass through a firewall that performs NAT on incoming and outgoing packets.

This section examines the design decisions you face when deploying PPTP, L2TP/IPSec, and IPSec tunnel mode servers in a DMZ.

Securing PPTP Tunnel Traffic

You don't have to take any special considerations into account when placing a PPTP tunnel server in your network. It doesn't matter if the external firewall performs NAT on incoming and outgoing packets. The only requirement is to place the tunnel server in the DMZ, as shown in Figure 14.19.

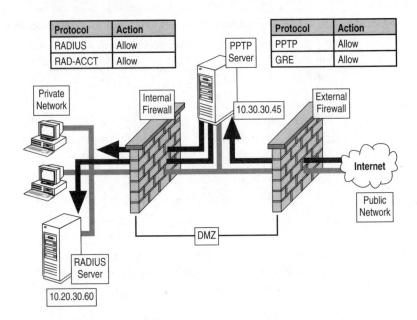

Protocol	Action
RADIUS	Allow
RAD-ACCT	Allow

Protocol	Action
PPTP	Allow
GRE	Allow

Figure 14.19   Securing access to a PPTP tunnel server in the DMZ

To support the placement of the PPTP tunnel server in the DMZ, configure the external firewall to allow connections to the tunnel server using PPTP (TCP port 1723) and the Generic Routing Encapsulation (GRE) protocol (protocol ID 47). Table 14.28 lists the packet filters that you must establish at the external firewall to support the network shown in Figure 14.19.

Table 14.28   PPTP Packet Filters at the External Firewall

Protocol	Source IP	Source Port	Target IP	Target Port	Transport Protocol	Action
PPTP	Any	Any	10.30.30.45	1723	TCP	Allow
GRE	Any		10.30.30.45		ID 47	Allow

The first packet filter allows PPTP connections from any computer on the public network to the PPTP Server (10.30.30.45). The second packet filter allows GRE packets, which are used by PPTP to encapsulate the original data packets, to pass through the external firewall to the PPTP server.

To protect the Active Directory database, you can deploy the PPTP server as a member of a workgroup rather than as a member of the domain. To support domain authentication, configure the tunnel server as a RADIUS client to a RADIUS server on the private network. To support this, configure the internal firewall to allow RADIUS authentication (UDP port 1812) packets and RADIUS accounting (UDP port 1813) packets to pass from the tunnel server to the RADIUS server on the private network. No additional encryption is required because the RADIUS protocol provides encryption services.

To support RADIUS authentication to a RADIUS server in the private network, configure the internal firewall with the packet filters listed in Table 14.29.

Table 14.29   RADIUS Authentication Filters at the Internal Firewall

Protocol	Source IP	Source Port	Target IP	Target Port	Transport Protocol	Action
RADIUS Auth	10.10.10.45	Any	10.20.30.60	1812	UDP	Allow
RADIUS Accting	10.10.10.45	Any	10.20.30.60	1813	UDP	Allow

The first packet filter allows the PPTP server (10.10.10.45) to forward RADIUS authentication requests to the RADIUS server (10.20.30.60) on the private network. The second filter allows RADIUS accounting packets to be sent from the PPTP server to the RADIUS server for centralized collection of accounting information.

Note   An L2TP tunnel server uses the same filters to provide authentication to a remote access client. Once the data has entered the DMZ, authentication takes place in the same manner.

Securing L2TP/IPSec Tunnel Traffic

L2TP tunnel connections require that the tunnel server not be placed behind a firewall that performs NAT. You can modify the configuration of the DMZ to meet this requirement.

Figure 14.20 depicts the most basic configuration in which the DMZ uses public network addressing. Because the firewall doesn't perform NAT, you can place the L2TP tunnel server in the DMZ like a PPTP tunnel server.

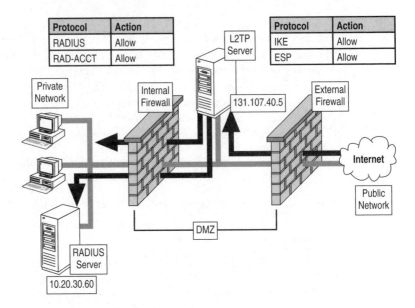

Protocol	Action
RADIUS	Allow
RAD-ACCT	Allow

Protocol	Action
IKE	Allow
ESP	Allow

Figure 14.20   Securing access to an L2TP Tunnel server in the DMZ using public network addressing

Alternatively, you can establish a hybrid DMZ that consists of an outer DMZ and an inner DMZ, as shown in Figure 14.21.

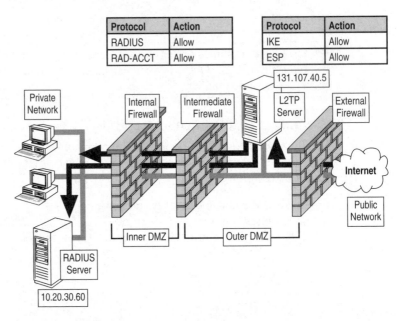

Protocol	Action
RADIUS	Allow
RAD-ACCT	Allow

Protocol	Action
IKE	Allow
ESP	Allow

Figure 14.21   Securing access to an L2TP Tunnel server in the hybrid DMZ

In this configuration the outer DMZ uses public network addressing so that NAT isn't performed on any of the packets destined for the L2TP tunnel server. Once the packets reach the tunnel server and are decrypted, they can pass through the intermediate firewall that's performing NAT to the inner DMZ. The packets can also pass all the way to the private network through both the intermediate and internal firewalls.

Finally, Figure 14.22 shows an L2TP tunnel deployment where the L2TP tunnel server is parallel to the firewall at the public network boundary.

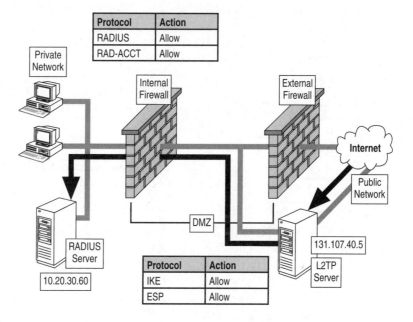

Figure 14.22   Securing access to an L2TP perimeter server

In this configuration the L2TP tunnel server is a dual-homed server with the external network interface card (NIC) on the public network, and the internal NIC is attached to the DMZ.

Important   To protect the external NIC, you must establish packet filters to allow only L2TP/IPSec connections. All other connection attempts must be denied.

The L2TP tunnel server is configured to use the NAT service included in Windows 2000 to translate private network addresses in the DMZ to public network addresses.

In each of these scenarios you must apply the packet filters in Table 14.30 at the external firewall to allow only L2TP/IPSec connections to pass through to the tunnel server. In the case of the L2TP perimeter server, you apply the packet filters to the L2TP perimeter server's external NIC.

Table 14.30   L2TP/IPSec Filters at the External Firewall

Protocol	Source IP	Source Port	Target IP	Target Port	Transport Protocol	Action
IKE	Any	500	131.107.40.5	500	UDP	Allow
ESP	Any		131.107.40.5		ID 50	Allow

The first packet filter allows any remote client computer to negotiate an IPSec SA with the L2TP server (131.107.40.5). The second packet filter allows the remote client computer to exchange ESP-encrypted data with the L2TP server.

Note   Even though L2TP is defined to use UDP port 1701 for connections, the external firewall or external NIC of the L2TP perimeter server doesn't require a packet filter for this protocol. It's only after the transmission is accepted at the tunnel server that the L2TP packet is decrypted from the IPSec ESP packet. Only the IPSec ESP packet must be allowed to pass through the firewall.

Making the Decision

When configuring a firewall to allow access to an L2TP tunnel server located in the DMZ, consider the following:

- Use public network addressing if the L2TP tunnel server is placed in the DMZ.

- If the DMZ uses private network addressing as defined in RFC 1918, consider establishing an outer DMZ that uses public network addressing or configuring the L2TP server as a perimeter server with an interface on the public network to accept tunnel connections.

- Configure the external firewall to pass the tunneling protocol used by the tunnel server in the DMZ. For PPTP, this requires that packet filters for PPTP (TCP port 1723) and GRE (protocol ID 47) be permitted to pass to the tunnel server. For L2TP, this requires the external firewall to allow IKE (UDP port 500) and ESP (protocol ID 50) packets to pass through to the tunnel server.

- Configure the internal firewall to allow RADIUS authentication to a RADIUS server on the private network. RADIUS authentication provides domain logon capabilities for remote access when the tunnel server is located in a DMZ. Configure packet filters for RADIUS authentication (UDP port 1812) and RADIUS accounting (UDP port 1813) that allow RADIUS transmissions only from the tunnel server to the RADIUS server.

Applying the Decision

The MFTUNNEL server is assigned an IP address of 192.168.77.9, which is an RFC 1918–defined private network address. This address indicates that the firewall for Market Florist is using NAT to protect the private network IP addressing scheme. The only tunneling protocol supported in this network infrastructure is PPTP.

To meet all design objectives for the Market Florist remote access solution, configure the firewall to allow the MFTUNNEL server to pass RADIUS authentication and accounting packets to the Internet Authentication Services (IAS) server at IP address 10.10.10.200. Table 14.31 shows the packet filters that you must create at the firewall to allow the necessary traffic to pass.

Table 14.31   Tunnel Packet Filters at the Market Florist Firewall

Protocol	Source IP	Source Port	Target IP	Target Port	Transport Protocol	Action
PPTP	Any	Any	192.168.77.9	1723	TCP	Allow
GRE	Any		192.168.77.9		ID 47	Allow
RADIUS Auth	192.168.77.9	Any	10.10.10.200	1812	UDP	Allow
RADIUS Accting	192.168.77.9	Any	10.10.10.200	1813	UDP	Allow

The first two filters allow remote clients to connect to the MFTUNNEL server (192.168.77.9) using only PPTP connections. Because the MFTUNNEL server is behind a firewall that performs NAT, you don't need to include packet filters for IPSec traffic. The last two filters allow RADIUS authentication and RADIUS accounting packets to be passed from the MFTUNNEL server to the RADIUS server (10.10.10.200) on the private network.

Lesson Summary

Creating packet filters at external and internal firewalls takes careful planning and design. After deciding on a firewall strategy, you must define the packet filters to fit your strategy. Packet filters must allow only authorized protocols to pass through the firewall. If additional protocols can pass through the firewall, you may be leaving your network vulnerable to an attacker.

Lab 14-1: Designing Firewall Rules

Lab Objectives

This lab prepares you to design security for Internet-accessible resources in a DMZ by meeting the following objectives:

- Determine a DMZ configuration that meets all business needs
- Design firewall packet filters to allow authorized traffic to enter and exit the DMZ

About This Lab

This lab looks at designing a DMZ for the Contoso Ltd. extranet to expose services to the Internet in a secure manner. Once you've established a DMZ configuration, you will design the internal and external firewalls packet filters to allow only authorized protocols to enter and exit the DMZ and private network.

Before You Begin

Make sure that you've completed reading the chapter material before starting the lab. Pay close attention to the sections where the design decisions were applied throughout the chapter for information on building your administrative structure.

Scenario: Contoso Ltd.

Contoso Ltd., an international magazine sales company, wants to design a DMZ to protect Internet-accessible resources by allowing only authorized protocols to enter and exit the DMZ.

Your DMZ design must meet the following business objectives:

- Contoso has a limited budget for the DMZ project and can afford only two firewalls for the creation of the DMZ.
- The DMZ configuration must prevent private network addressing from being exposed to the Internet. Only IP addresses from the 131.107.100.0/24 and 131.107.99.0/24 networks should be revealed to the Internet.
- The firewalls must ensure that only authorized traffic can enter and exit the DMZ. All other data must be dropped at the firewalls.

Internet-Accessible IP Addresses

Contoso owns the contoso.tld domain on the Internet. While this is the same domain as the Active Directory forest root, the two namespaces are maintained separately to ensure that the private network IP addresses aren't exposed to the Internet. On the Internet the following DNS resource records are available to public network users:

```
@                IN SOA ns.contoso.tld. admin.contoso.tld. (
                 6              ; serial number
                 900            ; refresh
                 600            ; retry
                 86400          ; expire
                 3600        ) ; minimum TTL

@                NS ns.contoso.tld.

@                MX 10 mail.contoso.tld.
mail             A 131.107.99.3
ns               A 131.107.99.2
vpn              A 131.107.100.3
www              A 131.107.99.4
```

Server Roles

Each server in the DMZ plays a specific role in Contoso's extranet services. The following list defines each role:

- **ns.contoso.tld.** Acts as the authoritative name service for contoso.tld on the Internet. This server resolves all queries from the Internet for resources in the contoso.tld domain. The private network DNS servers for contoso.tld (ns1.contoso.tld and ns2.contoso.tld) are configured to forward irresolvable DNS queries to ns.contoso.tld in the DMZ. ns.contoso.tld uses root hints to resolve resource records for other DNS domains and forwards DNS requests to any DNS server on the Internet for resolution.

- **mail.contoso.tld.** Acts as the mail gateway for e-mail sent to recipients in the contoso.tld domain. Public network access to the mail server should be limited to SMTP. All users with mailboxes hosted on the mail.contoso.tld server connect to the mail server either directly from the private network or remotely through a VPN to the DMZ.

- **vpn.contoso.tld.** Acts as the tunnel server for both PPTP and L2TP/IPSec VPN clients. VPN clients must be able to access the mail.contoso.tld server with Microsoft Outlook 2000 using the native Exchange client. Additionally, VPN clients must be able to access all resources on the London network.

- **www.contoso.tld.** The NLBS Web cluster that hosts the Contoso Web site. Public network users should only be able to connect to the Web cluster using HTTP or HTTPS protocols. From the private network, the same restriction applies except for the two Web administrator computers located at IP addresses 172.30.110.10 and 172.30.110.11. These computers must be able to connect to the component Web servers directly using IPSec ESP packets. Additionally, the servers in the www.contoso.tld NLBS Web cluster must be able to connect to the SQL server at IP address 172.30.10.10 with an IPSec ESP connection to encrypt all SQL-data transmissions. The SQL connection is for storing data on new subscriptions and back issue orders.

Exercise 1: Planning the DMZ Configuration

An external consultant has proposed the DMZ configuration shown in Figure 14.23. In this exercise you will evaluate the DMZ configuration, and, if necessary, modify the DMZ configuration to meet Contoso's business needs. Answers to these questions can be found in the appendix.

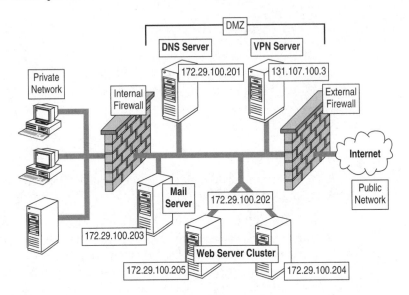

Figure 14.23 Proposed DMZ configuration for Contoso Ltd.

1. Are there any problems with the proposed DMZ configuration?

2. If the IP address of the VPN server were changed to 172.29.100.206, would this meet Contoso's security requirements and validate the DMZ configuration?

3. Given that Contoso has funds for only two firewalls, what modifications can you make to the DMZ to meet all security design objectives? What features must be supported by the external firewall to meet these objectives?

4. Draw your proposed DMZ configuration.

Exercise 2: Designing Packet Filters for the DMZ

This exercise looks at the specific packet filters required at both the internal and external firewall to secure public network access and private network access to resources in the DMZ. You must design the packet filters based on the DMZ configuration shown in Figure 14.24.

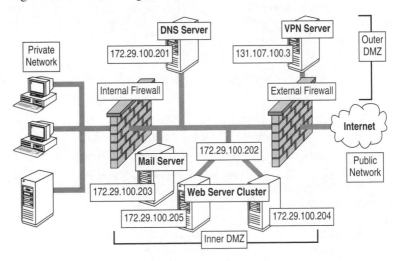

Figure 14.24 Modified DMZ configuration for Contoso Ltd.

When you design the necessary packet filters, assume that both the internal and external firewalls support mirroring of packet filters.

Securing DNS Access

You must secure DNS so that only the traffic patterns shown in Figure 14.25 are allowed to enter and exit the DMZ.

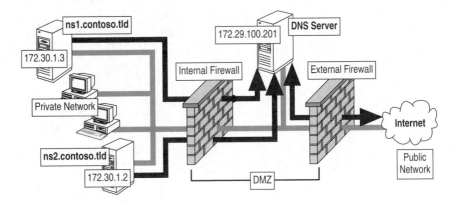

Figure 14.25 Allowed access to and from the DNS servers in the private network and the DMZ

- Only the ns1.contoso.tld and ns2.contoso.tld DNS servers may forward DNS requests to the ns.contoso.tld DNS server. The internal firewall must block all other DNS requests sent to any DNS server on the Internet from the private network.

- The ns.contoso.tld DNS server resolves DNS queries by using root hints and sending queries to the authoritative DNS servers on the Internet.

- DNS queries from the Internet for contoso.tld must be passed only to the external DNS server.

Answer the following questions based on this situation. Answers can be found in the appendix.

1. In the following table, enter the packet filters that you must enter at the internal firewall to allow only the ns1.contoso.tld and ns2.contoso.tld DNS servers to forward DNS queries to the ns.contoso.tld DNS server in the DMZ.

Protocol	Source IP	Source Port	Target IP	Target Port	Transport Protocol	Action
DNS						
DNS						
DNS						
DNS						
DNS						
DNS						

2. In the following table, enter the packet filters that you must enter at the external firewall to allow the ns.contoso.tld DNS servers to query other DNS servers on the Internet and to allow public network users to query the ns.contoso.tld DNS server for contoso.tld resource records.

Protocol	Source IP	Source Port	Target IP	Target Port	Transport Protocol	Action
DNS						
DNS						
DNS						
DNS						

3. Can you perform any other configuration changes at the external DNS server to increase security?

Securing Web Access

You must configure the externally accessible Web NLBS cluster to allow only the traffic patterns shown in Figure 14.26 to pass through the internal and external firewalls.

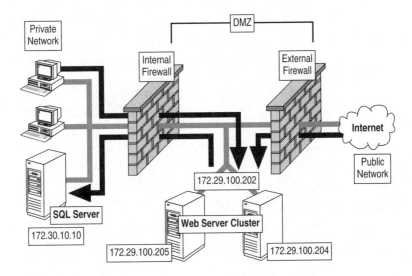

Figure 14.26   Allowed access to and from the Web cluster

- Public network users should be able to connect to the NLBS cluster address (172.29.100.202) only by using HTTP or HTTPS protocols.

- The individual Web server nodes in the NLBS cluster must be able to connect to the SQL server on the private network at IP address 172.30.10.10 using IPSec encrypted packets to securely store new subscription and back issue orders.

- The Web administrator's workstation, located at 172.30.10.200, must be able to connect to the Web cluster nodes using any protocol. All transmissions must be protected with IPSec encryption.

- Private network users from the London office (172.30.0.0/24) can connect to the Web cluster only by using HTTP or HTTPS. No other protocols are allowed.

Answer the following questions based on this situation. Answers can be found in the appendix.

1. In the following table, enter the packet filters that you must configure at the internal firewall to secure Web-related transmissions between the private network and the DMZ.

Protocol	Source IP	Source Port	Target IP	Target Port	Transport Protocol	Action
IKE						
ESP						
IKE						
ESP						
IKE						
ESP						
IKE						
ESP						
HTTP						
HTTPS						

2. Why must you create separate entries for the nodes in the NLBS cluster for IPSec connections from the Web administrator's computer?

3. In the following table, enter the packet filters that you must configure at the external firewall to secure Web-related transmissions between the public network and the DMZ.

Protocol	Source IP	Source Port	Target IP	Target Port	Transport Protocol	Action
HTTP						
HTTPS						

4. What can you apply to the node servers in the NLBS cluster to ensure that maximum security is applied to the Web server?

5. Complete the following table of static address mapping that you must config-ure at the external firewall.

Host Name	External IP Address	Internal IP Address
▪		
▪		
▪		

Securing VPN Server Access

You must secure the VPN server located in the DMZ, as shown in Figure 14.27, so that only the following traffic patterns are allowed to interact with the DMZ and the private network:

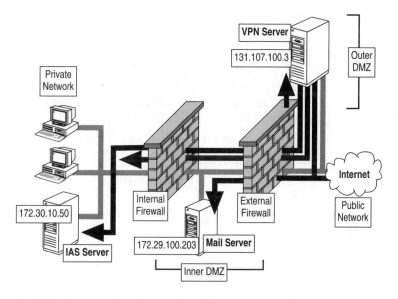

Figure 14.27   Allowed access to and from the VPN server

- Public network user connections must be allowed only to the VPN server using L2TP/IPsec and PPTP.

- The VPN server authenticates users with the RADIUS authentication proto-col by forwarding authentication requests to the IAS server at IP address 172.30.10.50 on the private network.

- The VPN server logs all accounting information locally.

- VPN users are assigned an IP address from the 131.107.100.128/25 network range (131.107.100.129 – 131.107.100.254).

- VPN users must be allowed to connect to the mail server in the DMZ using any protocol.

- VPN users must be able to connect to any server in the private network using any protocol.

Answer the following questions based on this situation. Answers can be found in the appendix.

1. In the following table, enter the packet filters that you must configure at the internal firewall to allow VPN users to connect to any server in the private network.

Protocol	Source IP	Source Port	Target IP	Target Port	Transport Protocol	Action
RADIUS-Auth						
Any						

2. In the following table, enter the packet filters that you must configure at the external firewall to allow VPN users to connect to the tunnel server and to the mail server once they authenticate with the network.

Protocol	Source IP	Source Port	Target IP	Target Port	Transport Protocol	Action
PPTP						
GRE						
IKE						
ESP						
RADIUS-Accting						
Any						

3. Why do you have to establish rules at the external firewall for allowing access to resources on the private network?

Securing Mail Access

The mail server located in the DMZ is running Exchange Server 5.5. Figure 14.28 shows the traffic patterns that must be allowed to access the Exchange Server from the public network, the external DMZ, and the private network.

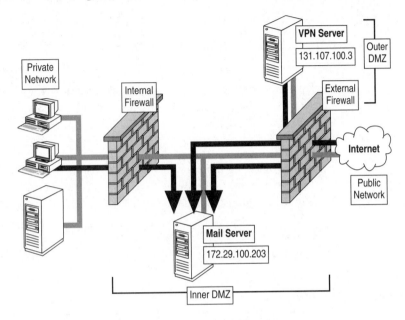

Figure 14.28   Allowed access to and from the mail server

- The mail server only accepts incoming e-mail messages from the public network.

- The mail server must be able to connect to any other mail server on the Internet to deliver Internet e-mail messages.

- Private network users (172.30.0.0/16) must be able to connect to the mail server using any protocol.

- VPN users connecting to the mail server are assigned IP addresses from the 131.107.100.129 – 131.107.100.254 range of IP addresses. All VPN users must be able to connect to the mail server using any protocol.

Answer the following questions based on this situation. Answers can be found in the appendix.

1. In the following table, enter the packet filters that you must configure at the internal firewall to allow private network users to access the mail server.

Protocol	Source IP	Source Port	Target IP	Target Port	Transport Protocol	Action
Any						

2. Do you need to create a separate packet filter to allow private network mail servers on the London network to connect to the mail server in the DMZ?

3. In the following table, enter the packet filters that you must configure at the external firewall to allow VPN users to access the mail server and to allow Internet e-mail to be exchanged with the mail server in the DMZ.

Protocol	Source IP	Source Port	Target IP	Target Port	Transport Protocol	Action
SMTP						
SMTP						
Any						

4. If public network users were allowed to access the mail server using Outlook Web Access (OWA) by connecting to the URL *https://mail.contoso.tld/exchange/*, what additional packet filter would be required at the external firewall?

Protocol	Source IP	Source Port	Target IP	Target Port	Transport Protocol	Action
■						

Review

Answering the following questions will reinforce key information presented in this chapter. If you are unable to answer a question, review the appropriate lesson and then try the question again. Answers to the questions can be found in the appendix.

1. Your organization compiles data for the local blood bank. How should you configure your database server so that certain fields (such as blood type and quantity) are accessible to external hospitals and emergency response organizations while other fields (such as disease screening and donor identity) are kept confidential?

2. You're the manager for your organization's new firewall. You must restrict access to a Web server (10.10.10.10) in your DMZ to allow only HTTP and HTTPS protocol access, but your attempts to do that have been unsuccessful. The following table shows the list of packet filters that you configured at the external firewall to protect the servers located in your DMZ. What's wrong with the packet filter list?

Protocol	Source IP	Source Port	Target IP	Target Port	Transport Protocol	Action
HTTP	Any	80	10.10.10.10	Any	TCP	Allow
HTTPS	Any	443	10.10.10.10	Any	TCP	Allow

3. In the following table, enter the correct packet filters for your organization's firewall to allow HTTP and HTTPS connections to your Web server located at 10.10.10.10 in your DMZ.

Protocol	Source IP	Source Port	Target IP	Target Port	Transport Protocol	Action
▪						
▪						

4. Contoso uses a DMZ to protect resources exposed to the Internet. What security weaknesses do you see in the DMZ configuration proposed in Figure 14.29?

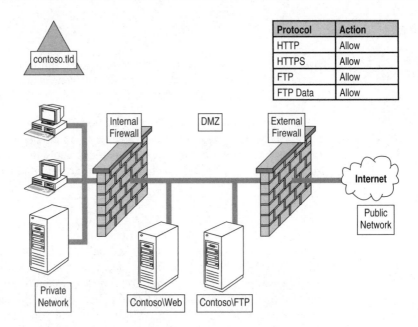

Figure 14.29   Proposed DMZ configuration for Contoso Ltd.

5. The news has just reported that computer intruders have taken control of an army of remote "zombie" computers. The bandwidth of all those computers will be targeted at a single target Web site, "flooding" the Web site with partial connections and effectively shutting it down. List two ways you can protect your e-business Web site.

6. During a routing inspection of the Web server in your DMZ, you discover that an unauthorized software application is installed on your Web server. The software application is a Trojan horse that collects passwords. What could you do to prevent this sort of attack? What measure must you take for private network security because of this attack?

CHAPTER 15

Securing Internet Access

About This Chapter

Internet access is an essential resource for many organizations and their employees. Your network design must include provisions to maintain network security when employees connect to the Internet. An important part of this design is your organization's Internet acceptable use policy, which defines how employees should and should not use the Internet. The policy serves as the blueprint for security mechanisms that will protect the private network as employees access the Internet.

Finally, the chapter examines strategies for auditing connections to the Internet. Auditing allows an organization to verify that its employees are following the Internet acceptable use policy.

Before You Begin

To complete this chapter, you must read the chapter scenario. This scenario is used throughout the chapter to apply the design decisions discussed in each lesson.

Chapter Scenario: Wide World Importers

Wide World Importers has acquired a T3 connection to the Internet for its Washington, D.C. corporate office. All Internet access from Wide World Importers employees must pass through the firewall located at the Washington office to ensure that only authorized protocols and computers access the Internet. This design is shown in Figure 15.1.

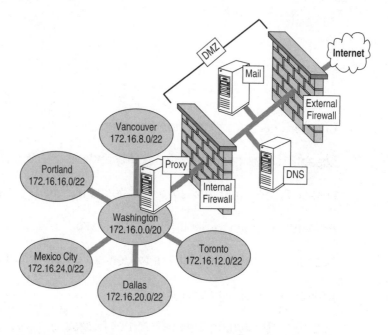

Figure 15.1   Internet access for Wide World Importers

Wide World Importers Domain Model

The Wide World Importers forest consists of two domains: wideworldimporters.tld and engineering.wideworldimporters.tld, as shown in Figure 15.2.

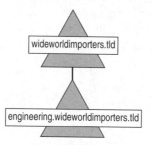

Figure 15.2   The Wide World Importers Active Directory directory service forest

The corporate Information Technology (IT) department will manage Internet access. The IT department plans to apply the Internet access policy equally for both domains. The same rules will apply to all users in the forest.

Computers Permitted to Access the Internet

Wide World Importers uses the network infrastructure shown in Figure 15.3 to provide secure Internet access to employees.

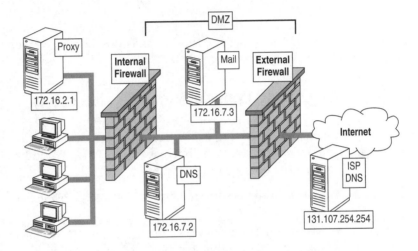

Figure 15.3   The Wide World Importers network infrastructure

Wide World Importers requires all client computers accessing the Internet to use Microsoft Proxy Server 2.0 located on the private network at the Washington office. The IP address of the Proxy Server is 172.16.2.1. The following servers, located in the Demilitarized Zone (DMZ), also send outgoing traffic to the Internet:

- **Domain Name System (DNS) server.**   The external DNS server forwards DNS requests to the DNS server of Wide World Importers' Internet Service Provider (ISP), located at IP address 131.107.254.254. The external DNS server's IP address is 172.16.7.2. The external DNS server resolves Internet requests for hosts in the wideworldimporters.tld domain.

- **Mail server.**   The mail server acts as a Simple Mail Transfer Protocol (SMTP) gateway to the Internet. All outgoing e-mail messages go through the mail server in the DMZ. All incoming e-mail messages for mailboxes in the wideworldimporters.tld domain also go to the mail server in the DMZ. The IP address of the mail server is 172.16.7.3.

Wide World Importers Computers and Applications

Wide World Importers must provide Internet access to a mix of Microsoft Windows 95–, Windows 98–, Windows NT 4.0–, and Windows 2000–based computers.

- Some of the Windows 98–based computers in the Toronto office continue to use Netscape Navigator for Internet browsing.
- News and FTP clients vary by site. Most offices are using third-party versions of the applications.
- A mix of Microsoft Internet Explorer versions is deployed throughout the network. The company plans to standardize on the most recent release of Internet Explorer soon.

Wide World Importers Internet Use Policy

Before deploying Internet access, Wide World Importers plans to develop an Internet acceptable use policy. This document will clearly define expectations for employees who access the Internet through Wide World Importers' Internet connection. The policy will specify that

- Only employees who sign the Internet acceptable use contract will be granted Internet access.
- Not all employees will have Internet access. Only employees who use the Internet in their day-to-day business affairs will have access.
- All employees will be able to send Internet e-mail messages through the corporate e-mail system. Outbound mail will be scanned periodically to ensure that the e-mail service is being used only for authorized business.
- Because all Internet access is through the single connection to the Internet, protocols will be limited to only authorized protocols. The Proxy Server will be configured to allow only authorized protocols through to the Internet.
- Logs will be maintained of all Internet usage and scanned monthly to minimize personal Internet use.
- Access to a popular Internet gaming site, nwtraders.tld, is prohibited.
- Access to sites that display pornography or violence must be prevented.

Wide World Importers Internet Restrictions

The following restrictions will be applied uniformly to all computers and users in the wideworldimporters.tld forest:

- Wide World Importers plans to use the Content Advisor in Internet Explorer to prevent access to inappropriate Internet sites. Content rating must be included in Internet Explorer's configuration and applied during the installation of the Windows 2000–based computers. When installed on Windows 95 and

Windows NT–based computers, Internet Explorer will be manually configured by the network administrators at each office during a maintenance visit.

- The Mexico City site will be restricted from using the Internet, except for e-mail services. The manager at the Mexico City site is unwilling to have the employees there sign the Internet acceptable use contract.

- Users who are granted Internet access will be allowed to use only the following protocols: Hypertext Transfer Protocol (HTTP), Hypertext Transfer Protocol Secure (HTTPS), Network News Transport Protocol (NNTP), and File Transfer Protocol (FTP).

- Users in the IT departments at each office will be allowed to use any available protocol. This includes IT departments for both the wideworldimporters.tld and engineering.wideworldimporters.tld domains.

Security Concerns for Wide World Importers

Wide World Importers' management is concerned that employees will introduce threats to corporate network security through the Internet connection. Specifically, management is concerned about

- **The introduction of viruses to the network.** Due to recent and highly publicized Internet viruses, management wants to deploy a comprehensive virus detection program that detects viruses at all network entry points.

- **The installation of unlicensed software downloaded from the Internet.** Another company in the same business as Wide World Importers was recently taken to court for using illegal software on client computers. Management wants to ensure that users won't be able to install software downloaded from the Internet.

- **Internet hackers gaining access to private network resources.** One of the managers read about an Internet hacker and was alarmed to find that hackers can gain access to the network if it's connected to the Internet. Management wants to ensure that the hackers won't have easy access to the corporate network.

Lesson 1: Designing an Internet Acceptable Use Policy

Before securing Internet access for private network users, your organization should consider drafting an Internet acceptable use policy. This policy will define what is acceptable employee usage of the Internet.

After this lesson, you will be able to

- Develop an Internet acceptable use policy that defines the required security mechanism for allowing private network users to access the Internet

Estimated lesson time: 30 minutes

It's important to define your organization's policy before designing the network infrastructure and services that will enforce and monitor that policy.

Determining Contents of the Policy

An Internet acceptable use policy must contain the following elements to ensure that private network users understand the rules when they access the Internet using corporate resources:

- The policy must contain descriptions of the available services. You must clearly define the specific services that are available to designated users. Defining the available services will help you determine whether a new service meets the standards defined in the Internet acceptable use policy.

- The policy must define user responsibility specifically. For example, the policy needs to state whether the user is responsible for the account and password if an attacker gains the account information. Some Internet acceptable use policies state that users are responsible for any actions performed with their user account.

- The policy must define what constitutes authorized use. The policy must define the tasks that are acceptable when a user accesses the Internet. A security policy could allow the following:

    - Users can access the Internet with authorized protocols. Include a list of acceptable protocols for accessing the Internet. This list may be defined for individual cases based on the organization's security model.

    - Users can send and receive e-mail for business purposes.

    - Users can send e-mail messages with attachments less than 2 megabytes (MB) in size.

    - Users can connect to any Web pages that are related to business purposes.

    - Users can download files for business purposes as long as the organization's virus scanner is running at all times.

    - Users can access Usenet newsgroups subject to business purposes. The policy may prohibit all access to all alternative newsgroups (alt.*).

- The policy must define unauthorized use of the Internet. A security policy could prohibit the following:

    - Users could be prevented from accessing the Internet with unauthorized protocols. Include a comprehensive list of unacceptable protocols.

    - Users could be preventing from exposing sensitive company information to persons outside the company.

    - Users could be prevented from attempting to bypass the organization's security mechanisms.

    - Users could be prevented from portraying the organization in a derogatory or nonprofessional manner in public discussion groups.

    - Users could be prevented from accessing the Internet for personal use.

    - Users could be prevented from accessing Web sites that have no business purposes. These can include Web sites related to sex, hate speech, online gambling, online merchandising, gaming, or job search engines.

    - Users could not use e-mail inappropriately. Examples include forwarding unsolicited bulk e-mail messages or forwarding chain letters.

    - Users could not install unauthorized software on their local disk.

Note The Internet acceptable use policy must also make provisions for new technologies. For example, a new technology could be defined as unauthorized use until management reviews it.

- The policy must define who has ownership of resources stored on the organization's computers. Clearly defining that the organization owns all data stored on company-owned hardware makes it easier for an organization to search for unauthorized data.

- The policy must define the consequences of performing unauthorized access. The policy must clearly define what actions the organization will take should an employee violate the Internet acceptable use policy. The consequences may include

    - Removal of Internet access privileges

    - Termination

    - Referring the employee's actions to local legal authorities

After defining the Internet acceptable use policy, create a document outlining the policy. The document should include a contract that employees sign before gaining access to the Internet. Your organization's legal representatives should review the contract and the policy to ensure that the contract is legally binding and in accordance with federal and local government policies.

Making the Decision

Table 15.1 outlines the decisions you will make when designing an Internet acceptable use policy for your organization.

Table 15.1   Design Decisions for an Internet Acceptable Use Policy

To	Do the Following
Develop a fair Internet acceptable use policy	■ Accept input from all potential users of the Internet. Getting input from all sources will help develop a secure but fair policy.
Determine which protocols will be allowed for Internet access	■ Poll users for the protocols that they require, or are currently using, for business use. Asking employees for a business case ensures that the protocols are screened.
Verify authorized usage and identify unauthorized usage	■ Implement auditing to track all Internet access originating from the private network. Logging can take place at the Proxy Server or at an internal firewall.
Enforce the Internet acceptable use policy	■ Clearly define the actions that will be performed if the Internet acceptable use policy is violated. ■ Ensure that all employees as well as management sign the acceptable use contract.

Applying the Decision

Wide World Importers' Internet acceptable use policy is missing a key component. The document needs to describe the consequences of violating the policy. There's no mention of whether employees can provide input during the drafting of the Internet acceptable use document. If Wide World Importers includes its employees in the decision process, the company would have a better chance of developing a policy that's accepted by both management and employees. General acceptance will make it easier to enforce the Internet acceptable use policy.

Lesson Summary

The first step in designing security for internal users is defining which actions are allowed when accessing the Internet. A clear definition of authorized and unauthorized actions in an Internet acceptable use policy will allow network administrators to design a security infrastructure that enforces acceptable Internet usage.

Lesson 2: Securing Access to the Internet by Private Network Users

When designing network security, consider the security risks of allowing private network users to connect to the Internet.

After this lesson, you will be able to

- Design secure access to the Internet for private network users

Estimated lesson time: 30 minutes

Identifying Risks When Private Network Users Connect to the Internet

When private network users access resources on the Internet, several risks are introduced to your network's overall security. If they're not carefully managed, these risks can result in reduced security for your network. Typical risks include

- **Introducing viruses.** To prevent virus attacks, deploy a virus scanning solution for your network. The virus scanning solution should include all client computers, servers, and entry points to the network.

Important   The absence of an Internet connection doesn't mean that there's no threat from viruses. Viruses can be introduced through floppy disks and shared files on the network.

- **Installing unauthorized software.** In highly secure networks you can control software installation through a central network authority. By ensuring that users are members of the local Users group, you can restrict users to writing data to their hard disk only in common shared areas and their personal profile directory. This strategy requires the installation of the Dfltwk.inf or Basicwk.inf security templates to apply default Windows 2000 security configuration.

- **Exposing private network addressing.** Outbound Internet traffic could expose the IP addressing scheme used on the internal network. A network address translation (NAT) service at a firewall or perimeter server will replace all outgoing source address information with a common address configured at the NAT server, as shown in Figure 15.4.

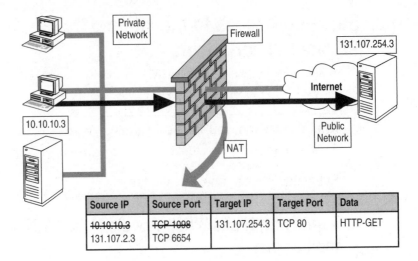

Source IP	Source Port	Target IP	Target Port	Data
~~10.10.10.3~~	~~TCP 1008~~	131.107.254.3	TCP 80	HTTP-GET
131.107.2.3	TCP 6654			

Figure 15.4   Using NAT to replace the source IP and source port information with a common IP address and random source port

- **Users attempting to bypass the established security.** Once restrictions are placed on Internet access, employees might attempt to bypass the configured security mechanisms. One of the most common methods is to use a modem to call directly to an ISP, as shown in Figure 15.5. This method bypasses firewall security.

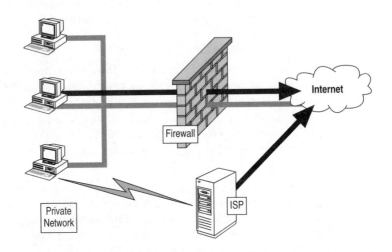

Figure 15.5   Using a modem to bypass firewall security

You can prevent modem usage by using Group Policy to disable the Remote Access Connection Service. This service must be running for Windows 2000 client computers to connect to a remote network by using a dial-up or VPN connection.

Making the Decision

You can reduce the risk of threats introduced to the private network by Internet access by implementing the recommendations in Table 15.2.

Table 15.2   Reducing Risks When Providing Internet Connectivity

To	Do the Following
Reduce the risk of viruses	■ Deploy virus scanning software at each client computer to detect locally introduced viruses. ■ Deploy virus scanning software at common targets, such as e-mail servers, so that viruses are detected before they enter the e-mail system. ■ Deploy virus scanning software at perimeter servers such as firewalls to detect virus-infected data before it enters the private network. ■ Ensure that virus signatures are regularly updated at all deployed locations.
Prevent the installation of unauthorized software	■ Restrict installation to signed software when installing from the Internet. ■ Configure Internet Explorer security settings to restrict what content can be installed. ■ Don't include users in Power Users or local Administrators group. This will restrict user access to specific areas of the local disk system where they can install software.
Prevent Internet users from revealing the private network addressing scheme	■ Deploy a NAT service at a firewall between the private network and the public network so that all source IP address information is replaced with a common browsing IP address configured at the firewall. ■ Have all internal client computers access the Internet by connecting to the Proxy Server. All requests will appear as if they were requested by the Proxy Server.
Prevent users from bypassing network security when accessing the Internet	■ Don't deploy modems to the desktop unless required for another application. ■ Use Group Policy to disable the Remote Access Connection Manager and thereby prevent dial-up sessions. ■ Configure the firewall to allow only authorized computers to connect directly to the Internet.

Applying the Decision

To dispel management's fears of risks introduced when employees connect to the Internet, the following items will be included in the Wide World Importers network security plan:

■ Install virus scanning software at multiple locations on the network. Install an antivirus plug-in at the mail server that scans incoming (and outgoing) messages for virus-infected attachments. If the firewall supports content scanning, load a plug-in that scans incoming data transmissions for viral content.

Finally, install virus scanning software on each computer in the organization to ensure that all incoming and outgoing traffic on the client computers is scanned for viruses. To ensure that virus signatures are current, Wide World Importers should acquire a virus scanning software solution that includes automatic update features for virus signatures.

- Preconfigure Internet Explorer to ensure that security settings are set to restrict download of specific content. Use Group Policy to enforce this setting on Windows 2000–based computers. In addition, apply the default or basic security templates to the client computers to ensure that users can only update their personal folders and portions of the registry. This should prevent several forms of software from being installed. You can't prevent a user from installing software, but these settings help restrict many software packages from being installed.

- Configure the external firewall for Wide World Importers with a NAT service to ensure that the private network addressing scheme isn't exposed on the Internet. The DMZ and private network should be assigned addresses from the network addresses defined in Request for Comment (RFC) 1918. The NAT service ensures that all outgoing packets are translated so that the original source IP address and source port fields are replaced with a common outgoing IP address and a unique source port.

Restricting Internet Access to Specific Computers

One method of restricting access to the Internet is to allow only specific computers to access the Internet. By assigning users to computers, you can limit Internet access to users who are authorized to log on to specific computers.

Granting computers access to the Internet involves more than configuring client computers. You must also configure Internet permissions for network servers that send data transmissions to the Internet. Resources in a DMZ must be allowed to respond to queries from the Internet. Some servers must initiate connections to the Internet. Servers that require access to the Internet through an external firewall to initiate connections include the following:

- **DNS servers.** DNS is a distributed database of all hosts on the Internet. To resolve a host name to an IP address, the DNS server may have to contact other DNS servers on the Internet.

- **Mail servers.** Internet e-mail is sent to recipients using SMTP. Your mail server must be able to determine which mail server to deliver mail to for a specific recipient by querying a DNS server for the recipient's domain Mail Exchange (MX) resource record. Once the mail exchange is determined, the mail server uses SMTP to send the e-mail message to the recipient.

- **FTP servers.** Active FTP clients require data transfers from the FTP server to the FTP client to be initiated by the FTP server. Once the FTP client the request to download a file, the FTP server initiates a connection to the FTP client.

- **Proxy Servers.** Proxy clients forward all of their Internet-bound requests to their configured Proxy Server and the Proxy Server sends the requests to the Internet. The Proxy Server must have nearly unlimited access to the Internet.

You can restrict access by internal computers to the Internet by configuring the firewall to limit which computers are allowed to connect to the Internet. You can further restrict each computer by defining outbound packet filters that define which protocols a computer can use to connect to the Internet. Figure 15.6 shows a firewall that limits the mail server to sending and receiving only SMTP packets.

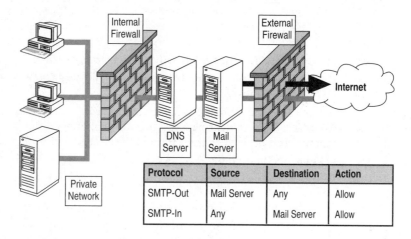

Protocol	Source	Destination	Action
SMTP-Out	Mail Server	Any	Allow
SMTP-In	Any	Mail Server	Allow

Figure 15.6   A firewall configured to allow the mail server to send and receive SMTP packets

Note   The mail server doesn't require DNS access to the Internet because all DNS requests are passed to the DNS server that's also located in the DMZ.

Making the Decision

You must make the following decisions when determining the design of your firewall's packet filters to allow Internet access.

- Determine which computers are required to respond directly to incoming requests. Typically, all computers located within your DMZ provide secure access from public network users. Configure your firewall to allow only the required protocols into the DMZ. Additionally, the packet filters should be mirrored to allow the server to send response packets.

- Determine which computers are required to initiate data exchange with computers on the Internet. Identify all computers that require direct connection (not through the Proxy Server) to resources on the Internet.

- Determine if the computers that require access to the Internet have a static IP address or a Dynamic Host Configuration Protocol (DHCP)–assigned IP address. If a computer is required to have direct access to the Internet, consider assigning a static IP address to the client computer, rather than using DHCP for IP addressing. If you use DHCP-assigned addresses, you may have to update the firewall packet filters to reflect changes in IP addressing.

Note You can even assign static IP addresses to remote access clients by configuring the user's dial-up properties to request a static IP address.

- Determine which protocols the computers use when accessing the Internet. Identifying the protocols will assist you in defining the required packet filters at the firewall.

Making these four decisions will help you design the necessary outgoing packet filters at your firewall. In a DMZ you may have to establish rules at the internal and external firewall.

Note If NAT is performed at a firewall, you must establish the packet filters at that specific firewall to limit protocols and destination IP addresses. Once the data passes through the NAT service, other firewalls will be unable to identify the packet's original source.

If you're channeling all Internet bound traffic through the Proxy Server, you can restrict specific subnets from using the Proxy Server by excluding their subnet network addresses from the Local Address Table (LAT) table. Figure 15.7 shows the default network ranges that are loaded into the LAT table. By excluding any addresses from these ranges, you effectively block those subnets from using the Proxy Server.

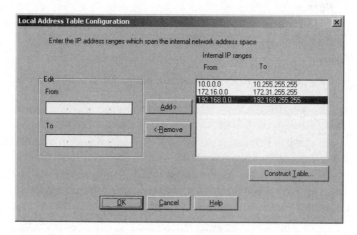

Figure 15.7 Configuring which subnets are included in the LAT table

Applying the Decision

The network security design for Wide World Importers must include the following items:

- Apply the following packet filters to the internal firewall to allow the Proxy Server to access the Internet using any protocol. Although Internet users are restricted to using HTTP, HTTPS, FTP, and NNTP, administrators have no restrictions on the protocols that they can use. Table 15.3 shows the required packet filter.

Table 15.3   Packet Filter Required for the Internal Firewall

Protocol	Source IP	Source Port	Target IP	Target Port	Transport Protocol	Action
Any	172.16.2.1	Any	Any	Any	Any	Allow

Note   The internal firewall requires additional filters to define network traffic from the private network to the servers in the DMZ. Specifically, filters are required to allow the internal DNS server to connect to the external DNS server and all internal clients require access to the mail server. The required packet filters are discussed in Chapter 14, "Securing an Extranet."

- Configure the Proxy Server to restrict computers at the Mexico City office from using Proxy services because the manager of the office refuses to allow employees to sign the Internet acceptable use policy. Assuming that only network addresses in the 172.16.0.0–172.31.255.255 network range will ever be used, configure the LAT table shown in Figure 15.8 to exclude the Mexico City office from using LAT services.

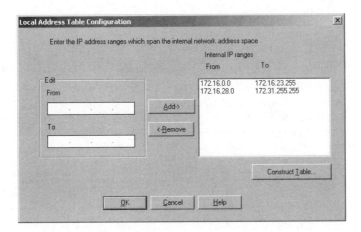

Figure 15.8   LAT definition that excludes the 172.16.24.0.0–172.16.27.255 network range

- The external firewall must have the packet filters defined in Table 15.4 to allow Internet access for the Proxy Server, mail server, and DNS server.

Table 15.4   External Firewall Packet Filters

Protocol	Source IP	Source Port	Target IP	Target Port	Transport Protocol	Action
DNS	172.16.7.2	Any	131.107.254.254	53	TCP	Allow
DNS	172.16.7.2	Any	131.107.254.254	53	UDP	Allow
DNS	Any	Any	172.16.7.2	53	TCP	Allow
DNS	Any	Any	172.16.7.2	53	TCP	Allow
SMTP	172.16.7.3	Any	Any	25	TCP	Allow
SMTP	Any	Any	172.16.7.3	25	TCP	Allow

Note   The first two packet filters allow the external DNS server (172.16.7.2) to forward DNS queries to the ISP's DNS server (131.107.254.254). The third and fourth packet filters allow DNS clients on the Internet to connect to the external DNS server to resolve host names for the wideworldimporters.tld Internet domain. The fifth packet filter allows the mail server to send e-mail to any SMTP server on the Internet, and the final packet filter allows the mail server to accept incoming SMTP messages.

Restricting Internet Access to Specific Users

Although it's possible to restrict Internet access to specific computers, sometimes it's more appropriate to restrict access based on user accounts. By defining which users and groups can access the Internet, you can extend the standard Windows 2000 security model of assigning permissions to groups for resource access. In this case the resource is simply Internet access.

Providing Proxy Services

To manage Internet access based on user accounts, you need a service capable of enforcing which users or groups can access the Internet. This service must provide an authentication mechanism that can identify users and evaluate group memberships. Proxy Server 2.0 provides this functionality through the following services:

- **Web Proxy service.** Allows users to connect to Internet resources by using HTTP, HTTPS, Gopher, and FTP through a Conseil Europeén pour la Recherche Nucléaire (CERN) compliant Web browser. The Web Proxy requires that the user authenticate with the Proxy Server to determine whether the user may use the Web Proxy service.

- **Windows Socket (WinSock) Proxy service.** Allows applications that make use of Windows sockets to connect to servers through the Proxy Server. This type of connection, known as a circuit-level connection, requires that the client computer install Proxy Client software so that all WinSock requests are redirected to the Proxy Server.

- **Socks Proxy service.** Allows the establishment of a SOCK 4.3 protocol data channel between a client and server with the Socks Proxy acting as an intermediary. The Socks Proxy service support TCP-based protocols such as Telnet, FTP, Gopher, and HTTP. The Socks Proxy service doesn't support RealPlayer, streaming video, or NetShow. The Socks Proxy is defined according to protocol connections and can't be restricted by users. Restrictions can only be defined based on IP addresses and ports.

Note Microsoft's next generation firewall and proxy server, known as Internet Security and Acceleration (ISA) Server, will provide firewall services to a Microsoft network. ISA will provide the same proxy services with more firewall services than were available in Proxy Server 2.0. For more information on Microsoft ISA Server, please see *www.microsoft.com/isaserver/*.

You can configure each proxy service to restrict access to specific Windows 2000 security groups. Group membership is determined by the access token presented by the user connecting to the proxy service. The access token contains the user's Security ID (SID) and the user's group SIDs.

When the user attempts to access an Internet resource through a proxy service, the user's SID and group SIDs are compared to the Access Control List (ACL) configured for the protocol the user is attempting to use. If the SID is allowed access, the Proxy Server completes the connection.

Authenticated access must occur in order to determine the user's SID and the SIDs of their group memberships. Only if anonymous access is enabled can a user connect to Internet resources without authenticating with the Proxy Server.

Authenticating Proxy Server Requests

Proxy Server 2.0 supports three methods of authenticating users: anonymous access, basic authentication, and Windows Integrated Authentication. The authentication methods supported by Proxy Server 2.0 are configured in the Directory Security tab of the Default Web site in the Internet Services Manager MMC console, as shown in Figure 15.9.

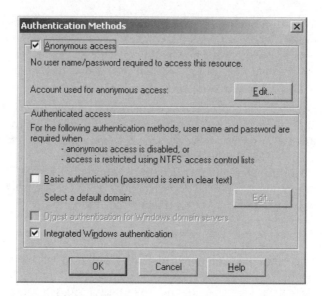

Figure 15.9   Configuring authentication mechanisms for the Proxy Server

- **Anonymous Access.** Allows anyone to use the Proxy Server services. When anonymous authentication is enabled, the Proxy Server doesn't request user credentials. All users are granted access to the proxy services.

- **Basic Authentication.** Allows authentication with the Proxy Server using clear text. While this is considered a security risk, it's sometimes the only way authentication can take place if non-Microsoft Web browsers are deployed.

- **Integrated Windows Authentication.** The user's access token is checked to obtain the user's SID and any group SIDs on the access token in a process that's transparent to the user. In previous versions of Windows this authentication mechanism was referred to as Windows Challenge/Response authentication.

Note   Because Proxy Server 2.0 was originally written to operate in a Windows NT 4.0 environment, you must download the Proxy Server update to configure the software to authenticate with Active Directory directory service. You can obtain the Proxy Server update from *www.microsoft.com/proxy/*.

Making the Decision

When designing Internet access by user account, include the design decisions in Table 15.5.

Table 15.5   Restricting Which Users Can Access the Internet

To	Include the Following in Your Security Design
Allow all users to access the Internet	▪ Configure anonymous authentication and don't configure ACLS for the proxy services. ▪ Allow the Users group for the domain to use any protocols available in the proxy services and to use any of the available authentication mechanisms.
Simplify the process of granting users access to Internet protocols	▪ If the Proxy Server is installed on a domain controller, create domain local groups in the domain where the Proxy Server resides to represent each level of access to Internet protocols required. ▪ If the Proxy Server is installed on a member server or stand-alone server in a workgroup, create local groups in the local Security Account Management (SAM) database to represent each level of access to Internet protocols required. ▪ Create global groups in each domain that will allow users to access the Internet. ▪ Place the global groups within the domain local group or local groups previously created.

Distinguish users connecting to the proxy service	▪ Plan which authentication mechanisms are required for the network.
	  ▪ Microsoft clients can use Integrated Windows Authentication.
	  ▪ Non-Microsoft clients may use basic authentication, which is a security risk.

Specify which users can use the Web Proxy service	▪ Configure the ACL for the Web Proxy service in the Internet Services Manager console to permit only specific groups to use protocols enabled through the Web Proxy service. Protocol choices include HTTP, HTTPS, Gopher, and FTP through the browser interface.
Specify which users can use the WinSock Proxy service	▪ Configure the ACL for the WinSock Proxy service in the Internet Services Manager console to allow only specific groups access to each protocol defined for the service.

Applying the Decision

Wide World Importers has identified two groups of employees who require access to the Internet.

▪ **Members of the IT department.** IT department employees require access to the Internet using all available protocols. Create a local group in the local Security Accounts Manager (SAM) database of the Proxy Server and global groups containing the members of the IT department in the wideworldimporters.tld and engineering.wideworldimporters.tld domains. Then make the two global groups members of the local group, as shown in Figure 15.10.

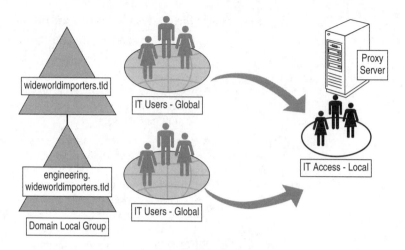

Figure 15.10   Creating groups to provide the IT department Internet access

- **Employees allowed to access the Internet.**   Create a global group in each domain that contains all users who have signed the Internet acceptable use policy.
  Create a local group in the local account database of the Proxy Server that contains the two global groups as members. This group is shown in Figure 15.11.

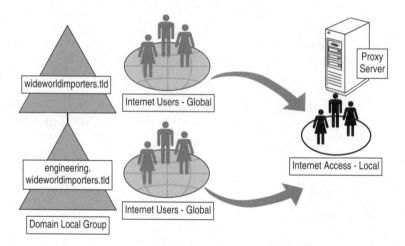

Figure 15.11   Creating groups to provide Internet access to employees granted
access to the Internet

Note   Regularly audit membership of the Internet Users global groups in the
wideworldimporters.tld and engineering.wideworldimporters.tld domains to ensure that users from the Mexico City office aren't included in the membership.
This prevents users from the Mexico City office from connecting to the Internet
if they connect to the network from another office.

To determine membership in the groups, authenticate the users with the Proxy Server. To provide authentication, configure the Proxy Server to support basic authentication and Windows Integrated Authentication. Basic authentication is required to authenticate the Netscape Navigator users because Netscape doesn't support Windows Integrated Authentication. Netscape Navigator uses only basic authentication for Proxy Server access. Disable anonymous authentication on the Proxy Server because Internet access is restricted to members of the IT Access and Internet Access domain local groups. You will use these groups to assign permissions in the Web Proxy and WinSock Proxy permission pages.

Restricting Internet Access to Specific Protocols

Once a user is authenticated, configure the proxy services available in Proxy Server 2.0 to allow access only to specific protocols. For each available protocol, assign permissions to allow only specific groups to use the protocol through the Proxy Server.

Note Only the Web Proxy and the WinSock Proxy support permissions based on user accounts. The Socks Proxy permissions are based on the connection attempt's properties. Much like a packet filter, Socks Proxy permissions define the source and destination IP address and port information for identifying permitted connections.

Restricting Protocol Access in the Web Proxy

The Web Proxy allows you to define permissions for the four protocols available in the Web Proxy through the Permissions tab for the Web Proxy service properties, as shown in Figure 15.12.

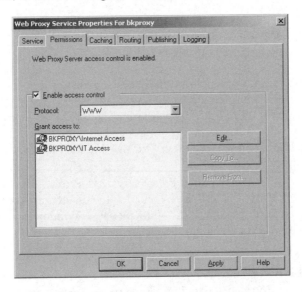

Figure 15.12   Setting Web Proxy permissions in the Permissions tab of the Web Proxy property pages

You can set permissions separately for the Web (HTTP), Secure (HTTPS), Gopher, and FTP Read services to allow only authorized groups to use the designated protocol. For each protocol, you can define which groups are allowed access to the protocol. You can't assign partial permissions to the protocols.

Restricting Protocol Access in the WinSock Proxy

As with the Web Proxy, you can set permissions for individual protocols in the WinSock Proxy on a per protocol basis. Because the list is extensive, an additional option exists to grant unlimited access to all protocols supported by the Proxy Server, as shown in Figure 15.13.

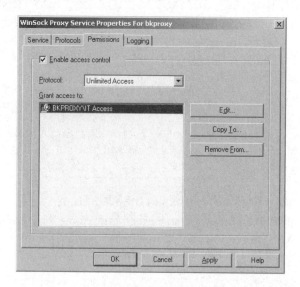

Figure 15.13   Using the WinSock Proxy to grant unlimited protocol access to security groups

The WinSock Proxy not only provides support for most popular protocols but also allows you to provide access to newer protocols by adding the protocol definitions to the WinSock Proxy. If you're defining a new protocol, you must know exactly what ports are used during a connection attempt that uses the protocol so that you can define the protocol for the WinSock Proxy.

Note   Use of the WinSock Proxy service in Proxy Server 2.0 requires the WinSock Proxy client to be installed at the client computer. The proxy client can be installed on Windows 95–, Windows 98–, Windows NT 4.0–, and Windows 2000–based client computers.

Making the Decision

Use Table 15.6 when deciding which protocols you will allow for Internet access.

Table 15.6   Determining Which Protocols Can Access the Internet

To	Do the Following
Determine what protocols are required	▪ Survey all employees to determine which applications they use or wish to use to access the Internet. ▪ Audit all Internet traffic that originates on the private network to determine protocols currently in use. ▪ Identify whether any protocols introduce risks to the private network. For example, Telnet typically uses clear text authentication. Ensure that domain passwords aren't used to access Internet resources.
Determine who requires protocol access	▪ Ensure that logging contains information on the user or IP address that uses the protocol. This helps you design your groups for restricting access to a specific protocol.
Define allowed protocols	▪ Configure the Web Proxy, WinSock Proxy, and Socks Proxy to permit only authorized protocols through the Proxy Server.
Add new protocols	▪ Provide a protocol definition in the WinSock Proxy that accurately describes the ports used by the new protocol.
Allow access to the WinSock Proxy	▪ Install the WinSock Proxy client on all computers that require access to the Internet using the WinSock Proxy service.

Applying the Decision

Wide World Importers must include the following permissions in their Web Proxy and WinSock Proxy configuration:

▪ Configure the Web Proxy to grant access permissions to the Internet Access local group and the IT Access local group for the Web (HTTP), Secure (HTTPS), and FTP Read protocols.

▪ Configure the WinSock Proxy to grant unlimited access to the IT Access local group.

▪ Configure the WinSock Proxy to grant access permission to the Internet Access group for the FTP and NNTP protocols.

Wide World Importers must also develop a strategy for the deployment of the WinSock Proxy client to enable the use of FTP and NNTP client software for accessing the Internet.

Lesson Summary

Your organization may need to configure restrictions on the computers, users, or protocols that can access the Internet. Your design must ensure that all computers and users that require access to the Internet can have it without exposing the network to additional risks. Develop your security plan so that it controls which computers and users can access the Internet. For each scenario that you develop, identify the required protocols so that you can restrict access to the correct protocols.

Activity: Identifying Security Design Risks

You've been hired by an organization to maintain network security when their employees access the Internet. To deploy a solution based on the user's group memberships, you've decided to deploy Proxy Server 2.0 on the network and require that all Internet-bound communications be performed by Proxy Server 2.0 on behalf of the employees.

This activity examines how your security design changes according to the location of the Proxy Server within your organization's network. In this activity the design must meet the following requirements:

- All access from the private network to Internet–based resources must be performed through the Proxy Server.
- All access to the Web server in the DMZ must bypass the Proxy Server.
- Client computers can send DNS requests only to the DNS server located in the private network. The DNS server in the private network is the only computer that may contact the DNS server in the DMZ.
- The DNS server in the DMZ forwards all Internet-related DNS queries to the ISP's DNS server located at IP address 131.107.1.1.

Locating the Proxy on the Private Network

The first proposal for the network configuration places the Proxy Server on the private network, as shown in Figure 15.14.

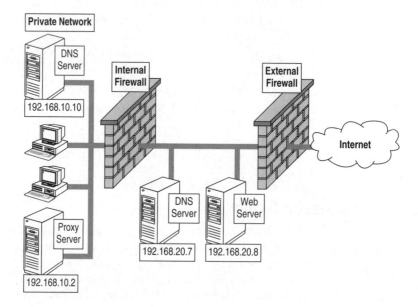

Figure 15.14   Placing the Proxy Server for your organization on the private network

Based on the proposed location of the Proxy Server, answer the following questions. Answers to these questions can be found in the appendix.

1. Assuming that the internal firewall processes packet filters in the order that they're listed in the packet filters list, which packet filters are required at the internal firewall to accomplish the following tasks?
   - Allow private network client computers to access the Proxy Server
   - Allow private network client computers to access the Web server in the DMZ using HTTP and HTTPS
   - Restrict access to the DNS server in the DMZ to only the DNS server in the private network
   - Allow the Proxy Server to access any resources on the Internet
   - Prevent private network client computers from directly accessing the Internet

Protocol	Source IP	Source Port	Target IP	Target Port	Transport Protocol	Action
HTTP						
HTTPS						
DNS						
DNS						
Any						
Any						

2. What packet filters are required at the external firewall to allow only the Proxy Server to connect to Internet resources and to allow the external DNS server to forward DNS requests to the ISP's DNS server?

Protocol	Source IP	Source Port	Target IP	Target Port	Transport Protocol	Action
DNS						
DNS						
Any						

3. Does the external firewall require a packet filter to prevent the private network clients from connecting to the Internet?

Locating the Proxy in the DMZ

The second proposal for the network configuration places the Proxy Server in the DMZ, as shown in Figure 15.15.

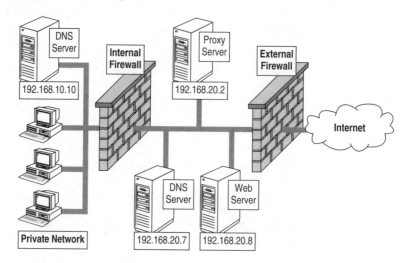

Figure 15.15   The Proxy Server location for your organization

Based on the proposed location of the Proxy Server, answer the following questions. Answers to the questions can be found in the appendix.

1. Assuming that the internal firewall processes packet filters in the order that they're listed in the packet filters list, what packet filters are required at the internal firewall to accomplish the following tasks?

   ▪ Allow private network client computers to access the Proxy Server

   ▪ Allow private network client computers to access the Web server in the DMZ using HTTP and HTTPS

   ▪ Restrict access to the DNS server in the DMZ to only the DNS server in the private network

   ▪ Allow the Proxy Server to access any resources on the Internet

   ▪ Prevent private network client computers from directly accessing the Internet

Protocol	Source IP	Source Port	Target IP	Target Port	Transport Protocol	Action
HTTP						
HTTPS						
DNS						
DNS						
Any						
Any						

2. Does the internal firewall require a packet filter for outbound traffic from the Proxy Server?

3. What packet filters are required at the external firewall to allow only the Proxy Server to connect to Internet resources and to allow the external DNS server to forward DNS requests to the ISP's DNS server?

Protocol	Source IP	Source Port	Target IP	Target Port	Transport Protocol	Action
DNS						
DNS						
Any						

Lesson 3: Restricting Access to Content on the Internet

Some organizations restrict Internet access based not only on users and computers, but also on the content of the Internet resources. Restrictions may be required for

- Denying access to specific domains on the Internet
- Preventing the download of harmful Web content
- Restricting what types of content can be downloaded from the Internet

If you employ these strategies, you will also require a way to ensure that your employees can't bypass or modify the required settings.

After this lesson, you will be able to

- Develop strategies for blocking access to unauthorized sites and content on the Internet

Estimated lesson time: 30 minutes

Preventing Access to Specific Web Sites

Once you've granted access to a specific protocol, you might wish to restrict access based on the Web site's host. For example, your organization's Internet acceptable use policy may not permit access to an Internet gaming site. You configure Web site restrictions by defining domain filters in Proxy Server 2.0. Domain filters block all access to Web sites and Internet resources that are located within the blocked domains. For example, Figure 15.16 shows a domain filter list that prohibits access to any resources in the hansonbrothers.tld Internet domain.

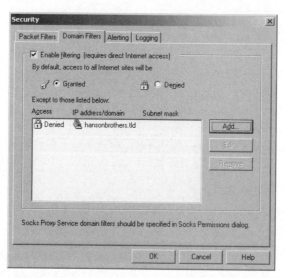

Figure 15.16 Using domain filters to block access to specific URLs

This domain filter blocks access to any resource within the hansonbrothers.tld domain, including first-level hosts such as *www.hansonbrothers.tld/* or hosts in child domains such as mail.east.na.hansonbrothers.tld.

Note All fully qualified domain names (FQDNs) in the domain filter list are converted to IP addresses before they're applied. This ensures that access is prevented to blocked Web sites even if the user attempts to connect to the Web site using the IP address instead of the Universal Resource Locator (URL).

Making the Decision

When designing security for private network users accessing the Internet, you can prevent access to specific Web sites by

- **Identifying Web sites that will always be unauthorized for access.** You generally do this by identifying types of Web sites that aren't authorized. For example, access to online casino sites may be restricted in your organization. You can identify the URLs for many well-known casinos.

- **Including the domain names in the domain filter list.** By including the domain in the domain filter list, you prevent access to any Web site within the domain.

Applying the Decision

Wide World Importers must configure a domain filter for nwtraders.tld to prevent the Proxy Server from allowing access to any Web sites for nwtraders.tld. The filter will prevent access to any Web site within nwtraders.tld.

Using the Internet Explorer Administration Kit to Preconfigure Settings

The Internet Explorer Administration Kit (IEAK) allows you to preconfigure Internet Explorer settings before deploying Internet Explorer to the desktops in your organization and to update deployments on an ongoing basis.

Note The IEAK is available for download by going to *www.microsoft.com* and searching for "IEAK."

The IEAK consists of two applications: the Internet Explorer Customization Wizard and the IEAK Profile Manager. The Internet Explorer Customization Wizard allows an administrator to define custom settings for all security settings in Internet Explorer. The IEAK Profile Manager allows modifications to be applied to existing installations by storing the modified configuration settings in a .ins file. Internet Explorer clients will detect the .ins file and apply those settings when Internet Explorer is configured to Automatically Detect Settings.

You can configure the following security related options within the IEAK Customization Wizard:

- **Enable Automatic Configuration.** You must enable automatic configuration to allow modified configuration settings to be downloaded from the .ins file created by the IEAK Profile Manager.

- **Proxy Settings.** If Proxy Server 2.0 is available on the network, you can preconfigure the proxy settings for Internet Explorer.

- **Define Certification Authorities.** Enables the addition or deletion of Certification Authorities (CAs) trusted by Internet Explorer.

- **Define Security Zones.** Allows you to define default security settings based on the zone in which a Web site is located.

- **Enable Content Rating.** Prevents access to Web sites based on the Content Advisor settings.

Making the Decision

You must consider the following items when planning consistent security configuration of Internet Explorer within an organization:

- Determine the desired configuration of Internet Explorer. The configuration must ensure that security is maintained by meeting the objectives defined in the organization's Internet acceptable use policy.

- Define an installation package that applies the standard configuration. Use this installation package to deploy the configured version of Internet Explorer to all desktop computers.

- Determine how modifications will be deployed. You can use the IEAK Profile Manager to create a .ins file that's automatically downloaded to Internet Explorer clients if the browser has the Automatically Detect Settings setting enabled.

- Prevent modification of the standard configuration. Use Group Policy to restrict access to the Internet Explorer Properties dialog box for Windows 2000–based computers. If users can't connect to the property pages, they can't modify the standard settings and weaken security.

Applying the Decision

Wide World Importers is currently supporting both Internet Explorer and Netscape Navigator. If Wide World Importers moves to a pure Internet Explorer environment, using the IEAK will reduce the cost of deploying the latest version of Internet Explorer and ensure that consistent security settings are deployed to all computers in the organization. The IEAK will work in the Wide World Importers network because the IEAK supports Windows 95, Windows 98, Windows NT, and Windows 2000 installations.

To ensure that modified settings are deployed to the desktop, use the IEAK Profile Manager to create a modified .ins file and post it on an accessible share on the network. If Internet Explorer is configured to autodetect Proxy settings, the .ins file will be read from the network location and used to apply any modifications to the Internet Explorer configuration.

Managing Content Downloads

Internet Explorer allows you to use security zones to manage what content can be downloaded from Web sites. Each security zone is configured with a security setting that defines what content can be downloaded from Web sites in the security zone.

The predefined security zones that are included with Internet Explorer are

- **My Computer.** Includes all resources stored on the local computer except for cached Java classes and content in the Temporary Internet Files folder.

- **Local Intranet.** Includes all Web resources located on the private network. The local intranet zone will contain all sites that are bypassed by the Proxy Server, all Universal Naming Convention (UNC) names, and URLs that don't have domain extensions, such as http://web.

- **Trusted Sites.** A list of all Internet sites that are determined to be trustworthy for downloading content. Typically, this includes business partners and common download sites such as *www.microsoft.com/* or *www.netscape.com/*.

- **Restricted Sites.** A list of sites that a private network user can view but can't use to download specific forms of content.

- **Internet.** All sites on the Internet that aren't included in the Trusted Sites or Restricted Sites zones.

Note   You can't add additional zones to the predefined zones included with Internet Explorer.

For each zone you can define the security settings by associating a security level with each zone. Four security levels are predefined, but you can also define custom settings if the defaults don't meet your organization's security needs. The default security levels include

- **Low.** Allows most content to be downloaded and executed without prompting the user. Due to the lack of safeguards, you should apply this setting only to the Local Intranet or Trusted Sites zone.

- **Medium-Low.** Allows most content to be downloaded and executed without prompting the user but prompts before downloading signed ActiveX controls and prevents the downloading of unsigned ActiveX controls.

- **Medium.** Attempts to download content that's potentially unsafe cause the user to be prompted before the content can be downloaded. This setting is commonly used for the Internet zone because it allows download but provides warning when caution should be applied.

- **High.** Disables most Internet Explorer features that introduce risks to the network, including the ability to download Java and ActiveX controls. This setting provides the most security, but it may result in a loss of functionality.

An organization can ensure that correct settings are applied to all Internet Explorer clients by using a mix of the IEAK and Group Policy. The IEAK allows default security settings to be defined for Internet Explorer and allows settings to be modified from a central location by defining configuration (.ins) files. Group Policy allows Windows 2000–based computers to secure Internet Explorer by preventing the display of configuration property pages. If users can't access the property pages, they won't be able to modify the default settings.

Making the Decision

Table 15.7 lists the actions that you must include in your security design to meet common objectives related to preventing harmful Web content from the Internet.

Table 15.7   Designing Content Rules by Internet Zone

To	Do the Following
Allow download of safe content from trusted sites	■ Add all trusted sites to the Trusted Sites zone. ■ Configure the security settings for the Trusted Sites zone to Medium-Low.
Allow unrestricted access to content on the private network	■ Ensure that Internet Explorer is configured to bypass the proxy for local intranet access. ■ Configure the security settings for the Local Intranet zone to either Low or Medium-Low.
Prevent download of harmful content from all Internet sites	■ Add sites that may contain harmful content to the Restricted Sites zone by adding the URLs to the list of sites. ■ Configure the security settings for the Restricted Sites zone to High.
Apply security settings that match the Internet acceptable use policy for your organization	■ Define custom settings for the security zone where you require the custom settings.
Ensure consistent security settings on all client computers	■ For all operating systems running Internet Explorer, define the required settings in the IEAK and ensure that all clients use automatic configuration so that the settings are updated whenever required. ■ For Windows 2000–based computers, define a Group Policy object that restricts access to the Internet Explorer's properties to prevent modification of the security settings.

Applying the Decision

Wide World Importers wants to place restrictions that make it difficult to download software from the Internet. Configuring the Internet zone to use the High security setting prevents the download of most harmful content from the Internet. Combining the High security settings with a deployment of a security template limits users to creating files in their personal folders and common shared files locations. This makes it difficult for a user to download and install unauthorized software from the Internet.

Note Make sure that the users aren't members of the Power Users group on the local computer, because membership in that group would elevate privileges and allow the users to install software in other locations on the disk.

Preventing Access to Specific Types of Content

Many Web sites contain content that isn't appropriate for business purposes. Content that falls into this category can include nudity, sex, language, and violence.

You can block access to Web sites that contain unauthorized content by using plug-ins that allow content scanning at the Proxy Server. If any inappropriate content is discovered, the Proxy Server won't load the materials and instead inform the user that the content is blocked.

Note A list of plug-ins for content scanning is available at *www.microsoft.com /proxy/*.

Another method is to use the Internet Explorer Content Advisor in Internet Explorer. The Content Advisor controls which content can be displayed in the browser window by using the Recreational Software Advisory Council on the Internet (RSACi) rating system. RSACi categorizes Internet content into four categories based on language, nudity, sex, and violence. When the Content Advisor is enabled, Internet Explorer scans the Hypertext Markup Language (HTML) source code for RSACi ratings contained in HTML metatags. If the rating is one that's blocked for access, the Web page won't be loaded in the browser window. You must also define what action to take if a site is unrated. If the Content Advisor doesn't find an RSACi metatag, you can choose to either prevent or grant access to the Web site HTML source code.

Note Deciding whether to block unrated sites is difficult. It isn't compulsory to include RSACi metatags in a Web site. Blocking access to unrated sites may deny access to sites that aren't offensive.

If you use the Content Advisor, you can prevent users from changing the content ratings. You can do this either by locking the Content Advisor settings with a supervisor password or by preventing access to the Content tab in the Internet Explorer Properties dialog box.

Making the Decision

Take the following actions when designing a strategy to block specific types of Internet content:

- Define your organization's policy on obscene content. The security that you implement to block forms of content must match your organization's Internet acceptable use policy.

- Define what content must be blocked. Each Internet acceptable use policy will define different levels of filters that must be applied. For some organizations, the filters may block only nudity and sex-related content. Other organizations may include restrictions on vulgar language.

- Define what action to take when an unrated Web site is accessed. The Content Advisor determines the rating for a Web site by reading HTML metatags in the source data. You can choose to either deny or allow access to unrated Web sites. The decision should match your organization's Internet acceptable use policy.

- Prevent users from changing content settings. Ensure that the supervisor password for content settings is a password that's difficult for the end users to guess. This ensures that users can't modify settings.

- Ensure that all settings for Internet Explorer installations are consistent. Use the IEAK to define the required content settings and lock the content settings with a common supervisor password.

Applying the Decision

Wide World Importers wants to prevent employees from connecting to sites that contain pornography and violence. Wide World Importers must enable content ratings for all Internet Explorer clients to ensure consistent application of the restrictions. In the Content Advisor, define restrictions to prevent access to sites that contain nudity, sex, and violence. To ensure that the settings aren't modified by employees, configure the settings using the IEAK so that the required settings are configured as the default settings. The IEAK can also ensure that Internet Explorer clients are configured to autoconfigure settings and will download any modified content settings. Finally, configure Group Policy to prevent access to the Content tab of the Internet Explorer Properties dialog box.

Lesson Summary

Creating restrictions on the content that can be accessed from the Internet ensures that the Internet isn't abused by an organization's employees. You can configure restrictions to block access to specific Web sites or to block access based on a Web site's contents. Additionally, you can use the IEAK to ensure that consistent configuration is applied to all the computers in the organization.

As with most security settings, Group Policy provides added control by restricting user access to certain property pages. By removing the ability to modify configurations, you can ensure that the desired default settings are maintained.

Lesson 4: Auditing Internet Access

To ensure that the Internet acceptable use policy is followed in an organization, you can enable Proxy Server 2.0 auditing to track all Internet access performed by the Proxy Server. Auditing enables an administrator to review the Internet resources that are accessed from the private network and ensure that only authorized resources are accessed. If unauthorized access is performed, the logs provide evidence and allow the administrator to implement restrictions to block further access.

After this lesson, you will be able to

- Develop an auditing strategy for tracking Internet access by private network users

Estimated lesson time: 30 minutes

Designing Proxy Server Auditing

Proxy Server 2.0 enables logging of actions performed by the Web Proxy, WinSock Proxy, and Socks Proxy services. The log data allows an administrator to review all Internet access. Unless logging is enabled, there's no way to ensure that the Proxy Server is properly configured and that employees are obeying Internet acceptable use policy.

By default, audit logs are written text files stored in the *systemroot*\system32\MSPlogs folder, where *systemroot* is the folder where Windows 2000 is installed. Proxy Server maintains the following logs for auditing Internet access:

- **Web Proxy log (W3yymmdd.log).** Audits all access performed by the Web Proxy service

- **WinSock Proxy log (Wsyymmdd.log).** Audits all access performed by the WinSock Proxy service

- **Socks Proxy log (Spyymmdd.log).** Audits all access performed by the Socks Proxy service

Note Depending on the amount of logging, you can choose to create new log files every day, week, or month. The interval that you select will be based on the amount of data being logged and the amount of disk space available for storing the log files.

You can configure logging to use either regular logging or verbose logging. Verbose logging provides the most detail but requires more disk resources due to the additional information that's logged. Each of the three logs uses the same fields. Table 15.8 shows the data that's logged by the Proxy Server services when either regular logging or verbose logging is enabled.

Table 15.8   Fields Included in Proxy Server Logging

Field Name	Regular Logging	Verbose Logging
Authentication Status (ClientAuthenticate)		✓
Bytes Received (BytesRecvd)		✓
Bytes Sent (BytesSent)		✓
Client Agent (ClientAgent)		✓
Client Computer Name (ClientIP)	✓	✓
Client Platform (ClientPlatform)		✓
Client User Name (ClientUserName)	✓	✓
Destination Address (DestHostIP)		✓
Destination Name (DestHost)	✓	✓
Destination Port (DestHostPort)	✓	✓
Log Date (LogDate)	✓	✓
Log Time (LogTime)	✓	✓
Object MIME (MimeType)		✓
Object Name (Uri)	✓	✓
Object Source (ObjectSource)	✓	✓
Operation (Operation)		✓
Processing Time (ProcessingTime)		✓
Protocol Name (Protocol)	✓	✓
Proxy Name (ServerName)		✓
Referring Server Name (ReferredServer)		✓
Result Code (ResultCode)	✓	✓
Service Name (Service)	✓	✓
Transport (Transport)		✓

Alternatively, you can log the proxy services to an Open Database Connectivity (ODBC)–compliant database such as a Microsoft SQL server. The advantage of using SQL Server is its improved search and management capabilities to review the logged data. The disadvantage is that ODBC logging uses more processor time than text-based logging. Before you implement ODBC logging you must determine whether the Proxy Server has any resource issues related to the processor.

Note   Proxy Server 2.0 includes SQL scripts for creating the SQL database tables required to store the Proxy Server logs.

Whatever method you choose for auditing, you must ensure that review of the logs is included in the Proxy Server administrator's regular actions. Unless the logs are reviewed, there's no way to ensure that the Proxy Server is functioning as expected. If you use ODBC logging, the database product provides query mechanisms to find data related to a specific user or protocol. If you use text logging, consider purchasing a third-party product, such as Seagate Crystal Reports, that provides reporting options for text-based log files.

Making the Decision

Table 15.9 outlines the design decisions that you face when implementing logging of Internet access.

Table 15.9   Designing Proxy Server Logging

To	Do the Following
Examine Internet usage from the private network	■ Enable logging at the Proxy Server for the proxy services enabled on your network.
Conserve disk space related to logging at the Proxy Server	■ Implement regular logging rather than verbose logging. ■ Use a daily interval for logging and move the older log files to other computers. ■ Use ODBC logging and configure the logging to take place at a remote server.
Ensure that all information of a proxied session can be analyzed	■ Enable verbose logging to record more details about the proxied sessions. ■ Configure the Proxy Server to stop all services if the log files are full.

Applying the Decision

Wide World Importers must enable logging of the Web Proxy and WinSock Proxy services to meet the objective of logging all Internet usage. They will log to an ODBC data source such as SQL Server to facilitate the viewing of the logs. This allows the Proxy administrator to query for specific information within the log files, such as the protocol or user that requested the service, and to produce better reports of Internet usage.

To record the greatest amount of information, configure the Proxy Server to use verbose logging. Verbose logging records additional fields, such as Authentication data and the amount of data transmitted by the session.

Lesson Summary

Implementing a proxy service isn't enough to maintain security when private network users connect to the Internet. You must perform regular auditing of Internet usage to ensure that existing policies are being followed. Auditing will reveal the first indications of whether the Internet acceptable use policy needs updating. Auditing allows an administrator to secure the network by analyzing existing traffic patterns.

Lab 15-1: Designing Secure Internet Access

This lab requires you to develop a design for providing secure Internet Access to the private network users of the Contoso Ltd. network.

Lab Objectives

This lab prepares you to develop a security design that provides secure Internet access to private network users by meeting the following objectives:

- Develop a security plan to restrict access to Internet resources based on an Internet acceptable use policy

- Limit access to the Internet to only authorized users

- Limit access to the Internet to only authorized protocols

- Restrict the types of content that can be downloaded to private network computers

- Design an auditing strategy for Internet access

About This Lab

This lab examines the process of securing Internet access for Contoso Ltd. private network users. In this lab you will develop an Internet acceptable use policy that matches the risk levels that Contoso deems appropriate. You will then develop a network design that enforces the Internet acceptable use policies.

Before You Begin

Make sure that you've completed reading the chapter material before starting the lab. Pay close attention to the sections where the decisions are applied throughout the chapter for information on designing your administrative structure.

Scenario: Contoso Ltd.

Contoso Ltd., an international magazine sales company, wants to provide Internet access for their private network users. Figure 15.17 shows the network infrastructure that's been approved for the Contoso network.

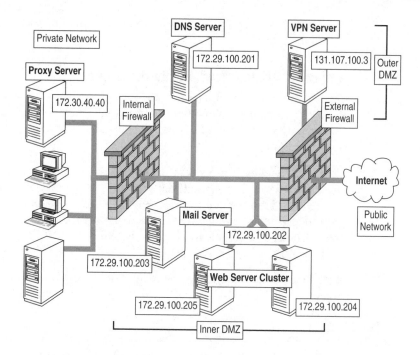

Figure 15.17   The Contoso Ltd. private network and DMZ configuration

The Proxy Server is located on the private network so that the internal firewall can limit which protocols are allowed to exit the private network.

Firewall Configuration

You must configure the firewalls for Contoso to meet the following business objectives:

- The internal firewall must only allow private network users to connect to the mail server and the Web server cluster in the DMZ. They should be restricted from connecting to any other servers in the DMZ or the Internet.

- The internal firewall must restrict connections to the Web server cluster from the private network to use only HTTP or HTTPS protocols.

- The internal firewall must allow the private network client computers to connect to the mail server in the DMZ by using any protocol.

- The firewalls must allow the Proxy Server to access the Internet by using any protocol.

- The Proxy Server must be configured to use the DNS server located in the DMZ as its primary DNS service.

- The DNS server in the DMZ must be allowed to forward DNS requests to any DNS server on the Internet.

- The mail server must be allowed to send e-mail messages to any mail server on the Internet.

Concerns About Providing Internet Access

The decision to allow Internet access has been a hard one for Contoso's CEO, Brian H. Valentine. Valentine is worried that access to the Internet will result in the employees using the Internet for nonbusiness purposes, which could lead to decreased productivity.

The original cause for concern occurred during a pilot project at the Seattle office. After a long series of all-day meetings, some pornographic Web content was viewed and left on a computer screen for all to see the next morning. A complaint was filed with the Human Resources department, but no action could be taken since Contoso hadn't clearly defined how the users of its private network should and should not use the Internet.

Valentine has developed the following preliminary set of guidelines that he wants to enforce through the secure Internet access solution developed by Contoso's IT department.

- All access to the Web site that led to the complaint to the Human Resources department, *www.southridgevideo.tld/*, must be blocked. Any attempts to connect to the Web site must be logged and reported to Valentine within 24 hours.
- All access to Web sites that contain pornography must be blocked.
- Any employees who access unauthorized Web sites will be terminated if a committee composed of management and staff finds that the employee knowingly performed the prohibited action.
- The IT department will determine authorized protocols in discussions with each department's technology specialist. The technology specialist will propose a list of required protocols to be approved or denied by the IT department.
- All personnel who access the Internet must sign a document that defines the Internet acceptable use policy. The signature ensures that Contoso has a record that the employee has accepted all the conditions of the agreement.
- The Internet acceptable use policy must clearly outline what is authorized and what is unauthorized when an employee connects to the Internet.

Proposed Restrictions for Internet Access

The IT department has spent several months investigating policy restrictions on which protocols, departments, and content can be accessed on the Internet. The following are the results of their research:

- In investigating preliminary logs, the IT department found that the Web site *www.adatum.tld/* downloads an unauthorized ActiveX control that reports disk and port information to an attacker on the Internet. In response to this incident, the IT department wants to prevent all access to this site and any sites associated with *adatum.tld/*.

- As a result of the *www.adatum.tld/* incident, ActiveX downloads

  - Must be limited to the Web server cluster in the DMZ and to trusted Web sites defined by the IT department

  - Should not display any prompts to the user when ActiveX controls are downloaded from the trusted sites.

- Table 15.10 outlines which protocols each department will be allowed to use when accessing the Internet. ·

Table 15.10   Protocols Allowed by Each Department

Protocol	Marketing	HR	Accounting	IT	Training
HTTP	✓	✓	✓	✓	✓
HTTPS	✓	✓	✓	✓	✓
Telnet				✓	
NNTP	✓			✓	✓
POP3				✓	
SMTP				✓	
NetMeeting	✓			✓	

- You must configure Internet Explorer to prevent access to Web sites that contain pornography.

- Updates and configuration changes to Internet Explorer must be managed centrally from the London office. The changes must be pulled by the clients as soon as they're available.

Exercise 1: Evaluating the Internet Acceptable Use Policy

This exercise evaluates the proposed Internet acceptable use policy developed by Valentine. Answers to these questions can be found in the appendix.

1. Do the guidelines proposed by Valentine define what is authorized and unauthorized for Internet access?

2. Do the guidelines include provisions for disciplinary actions?

3. Is anything missing from the guidelines?

Exercise 2: Designing Firewall Packet Filters for Secure Internet Access

This exercise examines the packet filters required by the internal and external firewalls to allow private network users and computers to connect securely to the Internet. Answers to these questions can be found in the appendix.

1. What packet filters are required at the internal firewall to implement the following restrictions at the internal firewall?

   ■ Allow internal computers to connect to the mail server when using any protocol

   ■ Allow internal computers to connect to the Web server cluster address to use only HTTP or HTTPS

   ■ Require the internal computers to access the Internet only by using the Proxy Server

   ■ Have the internal client computers bypass the Proxy Server for services on the private network and in the DMZ

   ■ Allow the Proxy Server to use the DNS server in the DMZ as its primary DNS server

   ■ Allow the Proxy Server to access any resources on the Internet

Protocol	Source IP	Source Port	Target IP	Target Port	Transport Protocol	Action
Any						
HTTP						
HTTPS						
Any						
Any						

2. What configuration is required on the client computers to bypass the firewall for services on the private network and in the DMZ?

3. How can you protect this configuration from being changed by users at the computers?

4. What packet filters are required at the external firewall to allow the following outgoing data transmissions?

- The Proxy Server must be able to forward Internet requests to any server on the Internet

- The mail server must be able to send e-mail messages to any mail server on the Internet

- The DNS server must be able to send DNS requests to any DNS server on the Internet

Protocol	Source IP	Source Port	Target IP	Target Port	Transport Protocol	Action
Any						
SMTP						
DNS						
DNS						

Exercise 3: Restricting Access to Content

This exercise examines the configuration required to prevent Contoso employees from accessing unauthorized Internet content. Answers to these questions can be found in the appendix.

1. What must you do to prevent access to any resources in the adatum.tld domain?

2. How would you allow signed ActiveX controls only from sites in the DMZ and from sites deemed trustworthy by the IT department?

3. What permission assignments are required for the Web Proxy service?

4. What groups are required for this?

5. What protocols require the use of the WinSock Proxy service? What group strategy could you use to secure use of these protocols?

6. What additional configuration is required at the client computers for the WinSock Proxy service?

7. How would you prevent access to Web sites that contain pornography? What measures must you take to prevent access if the Web site doesn't include RSACi metadata in their HTML source files?

8. How would you enforce any settings required in the Internet Explorer configuration for Windows 2000–based clients?

9. How would you enforce any settings required in the Internet Explorer configuration for non-Windows 2000–based clients?

Review

Answering the following questions will reinforce key information presented in this chapter. If you are unable to answer a question, review the appropriate lesson and then try the question again. Answers to the questions can be found in the appendix.

1. The lead IT administrator from Wide World Importers' Vancouver branch office decides to direct traffic from his network directly to the Internet without going through the firewall and the Proxy Server at the head office in Washington, D.C. As the head security administrator for all of Wide World Importers' enterprise network, how could you enforce the organization's policy that traffic must pass through the firewall at the Washington office?

2. As the head security administrator for Wide World Importers, you decide to grant limited Internet access to employees at the Mexico City branch office. How could you apply a different security policy (enforcing the High security setting for all Internet browsing) to employees at that office?

3. A new protocol has been developed that allows Internet users to search for pirated DVD-format movies and trade them with any of thousands of participating users on the Internet. As security administrator for a movie distribution company, list some reasons that you might want to prohibit this activity in your Internet acceptable use policy.

4. How could you have prevented the widespread use of the new protocol for downloading DVD-format movies on your network, given that your security policies were written before this protocol even existed?

5. An employee at your software company picks up a worm virus from the Internet that allows hackers to penetrate the corporate firewall and steal source code for your next major product release. The employee wasn't running the most current virus scanning software. How can you help prevent similar attacks in the future?

6. A network administrator has found that several people in the marketing department have received new computers in the last month and have lost the ability to connect to an NNTP news server that they used to use. The users are still able to connect to Web pages. What's the probable cause of this problem?

7. A laptop user in your organization reports that she can no longer access the Internet when she connects from home to her personal ISP. When she's connected to the corporate network, everything works as required, whether she's connected locally or connected to a modem at the corporate office. What's a possible reason for this?

CHAPTER 16

Securing Access in a Heterogeneous Network Environment

About This Chapter

This chapter examines the security issues that you need to address when non-Microsoft, or *heterogeneous*, clients require access to resources in a Microsoft Windows 2000 network. The chapter begins by discussing the process of authenticating heterogeneous clients. Without authentication, the Windows 2000 security model can't determine which account to use for a user who's connecting from a heterogeneous client.

The chapter continues with an examination of the security issues that arise when multiple directory services are implemented in a network. Microsoft Metadirectory Services (MMS) allow multiple directories to work together to produce a single directory for an organization. An important security consideration is determining which directory service is authoritative for a specific attribute in the metadirectory.

The chapter concludes with a discussion of the security issues related to resource access when heterogeneous clients access resources secured by a Windows 2000 network and when Windows 2000–based clients access resources in a heterogeneous network environment. In this scenario you can consider a heterogeneous network environment to be an environment in which Windows 2000 isn't the primary network operating system.

Before You Begin

To complete this chapter, you must read the chapter scenario. This scenario is used throughout the chapter to apply the design decisions discussed in each lesson.

Chapter Scenario: Blue Yonder Airlines

Blue Yonder Airlines is a North American airline that serves the West Coast of the United States. Blue Yonder uses a combination of Microsoft, Macintosh, and UNIX clients and servers for its corporate networking solution. Blue Yonder management is concerned that the combination of operating systems might create security vulnerabilities. You've been hired to ensure that the inclusion of these heterogeneous operating systems in the existing Windows 2000 network doesn't weaken the airline's network security.

Macintosh Deployment at Blue Yonder Airlines

Blue Yonder Airlines publishes a monthly magazine, *Into the Wild Blue Yonder*, that's given to all passengers. It's published by the Marketing department.

The Marketing department uses QuarkXPress on Macintosh computers to do the magazine's development and layout. The Macintosh computers access the Windows 2000 network when downloading digital photos and stories written by contributors using Microsoft Word. The stories and photos are stored on a Windows 2000 file server named BYDATA. Authentication of the Macintosh clients must not allow the inspection of user passwords as the passwords are transmitted to the BYDATA server.

The magazine is printed from an AGFA 9000 film printer located in the Marketing department. Because of the high costs associated with printing to a film printer, access to the printer should be restricted to the Macintosh users in the Marketing department.

UNIX Deployment at Blue Yonder Airlines

The flight scheduling system used by Blue Yonder Airlines stores its data in a database running on a UNIX server. The server hosting the UNIX database also stores analysis reports that are available through a Network File System (NFS) server share running on the UNIX server. Windows 2000 users need to access the UNIX database for scheduling flights and storing analysis reports on the NFS server share. Windows 2000 users must authenticate with the NFS server.

The UNIX database uses Kerberos v5 for authentication. Active Directory directory service user accounts must be able to authenticate with the UNIX KDC to provide access to the UNIX database using the UNIX database client. The Windows 2000 users shouldn't have to provide alternate credentials when they connect to the UNIX database.

The UNIX server must periodically connect to the BYDATA server to access scheduling projection reports. These reports record statistics for departures and arrivals that are used to determine modifications to the flight schedule. All access to the BYDATA server must be authenticated to ensure that security is maintained.

A Recent Acquisition

Blue Yonder Airlines recently acquired a smaller company that delivers cargo in the Pacific Northwest. The smaller airline, Consolidated Messenger, uses a NetWare 4.11 network. The accounting department in the Salt Lake City office must access data stored on the NetWare network that's related to the acquisition.

The network security design must meet the following objectives:

- All members of the accounting department require the same level of access to the data stored on a NetWare server named AIRDATA1. The data to which the accounting department requires access is stored on the DATA: volume in a folder named Accounting. The accounting department requires permission to read the data stored on the NetWare server, but they must not modify any data.

- As the Consolidated Messenger network is merged into the Blue Yonder network, the directories of the two networks must be integrated so that user accounts are maintained within the operating systems of both networks.

- NetWare users must be able to connect to the BYDATA server using native NetWare client software.

- Eventually, all data stored in the NetWare environment must be migrated to the Windows 2000 environment and maintain all current security settings.

Lesson 1: Providing Interoperability Between Windows 2000 and Heterogeneous Networks

Microsoft offers three services that allow Windows 2000 to provide both authentication and resource access capabilities to heterogeneous networks. They are the following:

- AppleTalk Network Integration Services
- Services for NetWare 5.0
- Services for UNIX 2.0

Note Services for NetWare 5.0 and Services for UNIX 2.0 are add-on products that you have to purchase from Microsoft. You can find more information on them by going to *www.microsoft.com* and searching for "Services for NetWare v5.0" and "Services for UNIX 2.0."

The following sections outline the features that each service provides and describes where to use these services in your network security design to allow secure access between the network systems.

After this lesson, you will be able to

- Identify the additional Windows 2000 services that are required to provide secure access between Windows 2000 and heterogeneous clients.

Estimated lesson time: 30 minutes

AppleTalk Network Integration Services

You can use AppleTalk Network Integration Services to allow Macintosh client computers to securely access resources in a Windows 2000 network. The services that provide this functionality are included with Windows 2000 and are named File Services for Macintosh and Print Services for Macintosh.

Note File Services for Macintosh and Print Services for Macintosh were formerly known as Services for Macintosh. File Services for Macintosh allow Macintosh users to authenticate with the network and access file resources by creating Macintosh-accessible volumes. Print Services for Macintosh allow Macintosh users to access print servers in a Windows 2000 network.

Microsoft Services for NetWare 5.0

Microsoft Services for NetWare 5.0 is an add-on product that allows integration of Windows 2000 and Novell NetWare networks through the following utilities:

- **Microsoft Directory Synchronization Services (MSDSS).** Allows two-way synchronization between Active Directory and Novell Directory Services (NDS). This synchronization allows users to maintain the same password in the two directory services.

Note MSDSS also allows synchronization between Active Directory and Novell Bindery Services available in NetWare 3.*x* and older.

- **Microsoft File Migration Utility.** Allows the migration of files from NetWare file resources to a Windows 2000 server. The File Migration Utility translates the NetWare trustee rights to NTFS permissions during the migration process.
- **File and Print Services for NetWare (FPNW).** Enables computers running Windows 2000 to emulate a NetWare 3.*x* server and provide file and print services to NetWare clients.

Microsoft Services for UNIX 2.0

Microsoft Services for UNIX version 2.0 is an add-on product that allows the integration of Windows 2000 and UNIX clients in a single network. Services for UNIX 2.0 includes the following components.

- **NFS software.** Includes an NFS client, NFS server, and NFS gateway. The NFS client allows Microsoft clients to connect to UNIX NFS servers. The NFS server allows UNIX NFS clients to connect to a Windows 2000 server for file access using the NFS protocol. The NFS gateway allows a Windows 2000 server to publish UNIX NFS data as a Windows 2000 share so that Microsoft clients can connect to NFS resources without installing NFS client software.
- **Telnet services.** Includes a Telnet server that allows up to 64 connections and a Telnet client for connecting to Telnet services on a UNIX computer.
- **Management tools.** Includes the Services for UNIX MMC console for managing various services for UNIX utilities and the ActivePerl script engine. ActivePerl allows UNIX scripts to take advantage of the Windows Management Instrumentation (WMI) and automate routine network administration tasks.
- **Network Information Services (NIS).** Includes the NIS to Active Directory Migration Wizard and the Server for NIS. The migration wizard allows the import of UNIX NIS source files into Active Directory to provide a single directory service. Server for NIS allows a Windows 2000 domain controller (DC) to act as a primary server for NIS.
- **Two-Way Password Synchronization.** Provides the ability to synchronize passwords between Active Directory and UNIX systems.

- **User Name Mapping.** Allows Windows 2000 account names to be mapped to UNIX User Identifiers (UIDs) so that a user connecting to an NFS resource doesn't have to provide alternate credentials for the UNIX system.

Making the Decision

When designing secure integration between a Windows 2000 network and a non-Microsoft operating system, consider the points shown in Table 16.1 when using additional services to provide interoperability.

Table 16.1   Planning Services for Heterogeneous Connectivity

Use	In These Circumstances
File Services for Macintosh	■ To allow Macintosh clients to access file resources stored on a Windows 2000 Server ■ To securely authenticate Macintosh users accessing the network
Print Services for Macintosh	■ To allow Macintosh users to print to Windows 2000 hosted print servers
Microsoft Directory Synchronization Services	■ To securely synchronize password information between Active Directory and a NetWare NDS or NetWare Bindery directory
File and Print Services for NetWare	■ To allow NetWare clients to authenticate with a Windows 2000 Server and access resources on the Windows 2000 Server using native NetWare utilities
NIS Services	■ To allow UNIX clients to authenticate with Active Directory when accessing NFS resources ■ To import existing UNIX NIS source files into Active Directory
NFS Services	■ To allow UNIX clients to access Windows 2000 resources using native NFS clients ■ To allow Windows 2000 clients to access NFS resources on a UNIX NFS server directly using the NFS client or indirectly using the NFS gateway
Two-Way Password Synchronization	■ To synchronize user passwords between the UNIX and Windows 2000 environments
User Name Mapping	■ To allow Windows 2000 users to connect to UNIX NFS resources using their Windows 2000 credentials

Applying the Decision

The Blue Yonder Airlines network requires services to integrate Macintosh, NetWare, and UNIX users into their network while maintaining security.

For Macintosh users, Blue Yonder must use File Services for Macintosh to ensure that Macintosh users have access to the data stored on the BYDATA server by authenticating with the Windows 2000 network.

The NetWare resources at Consolidated Messenger should eventually be migrated to Windows 2000. You can use MSDSS during the premigration stage to ensure that user account passwords between NDS and Active Directory are synchronized. You must install FPNW on the BYDATA server so that NetWare clients at Consolidated Messenger can connect to resources using native NetWare clients.

Deploy the NFS components from Services for UNIX 2.0 to ensure interoperability for the UNIX installations. The NFS client allows Windows 2000 users to access scheduling and status reports on the UNIX NFS server. The NFS Server allows UNIX clients to connect to the BYDATA server using UNIX NFS clients. To ensure interoperability, deploy Two-Way Password Synchronization to maintain the same password on both systems and User Name Mapping to allow UNIX UIDs to be associated with Windows 2000 user accounts for providing authorization to data stored on the BYDATA server.

Lesson Summary

A number of services allow Windows 2000 networks to interoperate with heterogeneous networks in a secure manner. By deploying AppleTalk Network Integration Services, Microsoft Services for Netware, or Microsoft Services for UNIX, you ensure that authentication and resource access by heterogeneous clients use the same security model as Windows 2000 clients.

Lesson 2: Securing Authentication in a Heterogeneous Network

When designing access to Windows 2000 networks by heterogeneous, or non-Microsoft clients, you must ensure the integrity of the authentication process. Authentication associates users with a security principal within Active Directory. The credentials provided by the user authenticate the user with the network. Once the user is authenticated, authorization can take place to limit access to specific authorized resources.

After this lesson, you will be able to

- Design secure authentication for Macintosh, Novell, and UNIX clients

Estimated lesson time: 30 minutes

Securing Authentication for Macintosh Clients

File Services for Macintosh supports users authenticating with Active Directory from Macintosh client computers. File Services for Macintosh requires that Macintosh clients authenticate using accounts stored in Active Directory.

When authenticating with the Windows 2000 network, Macintosh users can use any of the following authentication methods:

- **No authentication.** If guest access is enabled on the Windows 2000 Server, a Macintosh user can connect using the Guest account. Using the Guest account allows the user to connect without providing a password for authentication.

- **Apple Clear Text.** Passwords are passed in clear text from the Macintosh client to the Windows 2000 Server. Clear text authentication is available for Macintosh users who use the standard Apple Share client software or System 7 File Sharing.

- **Apple Standard Encryption.** Passwords up to eight characters are enabled. The encrypted password isn't transmitted on the network. Instead, a hash algorithm is executed against a random number using the user's password. At the server, the same password is used to perform the hash algorithm and the results are compared.

Note   This process requires the password to be stored in reversibly encrypted format at the server.

- **Microsoft User Authentication Module (MS-UAM).** Allows encrypted passwords up to 14 characters in length. MS-UAM also requires reversibly encrypted format. MS-UAM requires the MS-UAM to be installed at each Macintosh client to support the stronger encryption of authentication credentials.

Note   If your Windows 2000 network has multiple domains, the user should provide his account in the format *domain*\username, where *domain* denotes the domain where the user's account is located, to ensure that the logon request is forwarded to the correct domain. Not providing the domain prefix can lead to different results if the same username exists in multiple domains.

To maintain a minimum security level in your network, configure the File Services for Macintosh properties to limit authentication to specific methods. For example, you could limit authentication to MS-UAM.

You can also configure Macintosh-accessible volumes with a volume password that forces Macintosh users to provide the associated password before accessing the volume.

Making the Decision

Use Table 16.2 when authenticating Macintosh clients in a Windows 2000 network.

Table 16.2   Securing Macintosh User Authentication

To	Include the Following in Your Security Plan
Allow unauthenticated access to Macintosh users	■ Enable the Guest account at the server hosting File Services for Macintosh. ■ Enable Guest access for the Macintosh-accessible volume. ■ Have Macintosh users connect to the volume as a guest.
Allow all Macintosh clients to connect to the Windows 2000 server	■ Enable File Services for Macintosh to access Apple Clear Text authentication or enable Apple Clear Text or Microsoft authentication.
Require encrypted authentication	■ Configure all user accounts for Macintosh users to store passwords in reversible encrypted format. ■ Configure File Services for Macintosh properties to require Apple Encrypted authentication or Microsoft authentication.
Restrict supported authentication methods	■ Configure File Services for Macintosh properties to accept only authentication requests using authorized methods.
Limit access to a volume	■ Create a volume password that must be provided in addition to user credentials to gain access to a volume.

Applying the Decision

Blue Yonder Airlines requires that Macintosh user authentication not allow interception of user passwords. To enforce this, configure File Services for Macintosh to only allow Apple Standard Encryption or the MS-UAM, as shown in Figure 16.1.

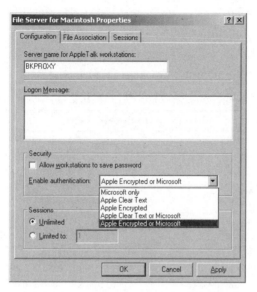

Figure 16.1   Configuring File Server for Macintosh to require encrypted authentication

The MS-UAM provides support for 14-character passwords but requires the installation of the MS-UAM at each Macintosh computer. Because all Macintosh computers are located in the same department, this shouldn't be difficult.

Securing Authentication for Novell Clients

A Windows 2000 Server running FPNW emulates a NetWare 3.*x* server and allows NetWare clients to authenticate with the Windows 2000 server. NetWare clients can access file and print services hosted by the Windows 2000 server using native NetWare commands and utilities.

Note   FPNW requires that the NetWare clients connect to the FPNW server using IPX/SPX protocols. Configure the FPNW server to use the same frame type and internal network number to ensure connectivity by NetWare clients. Failure to do so can result in the FPNW server being unavailable to NetWare clients.

To allow users to authenticate with Active Directory by using a NetWare client, configure user accounts as NetWare-enabled accounts in Active Directory Users And Computers. A NetWare-enabled account allows you to define NetWare-specific properties, such as the NetWare logon script for the user. You can limit which user accounts can authenticate using NetWare clients by enabling only the required accounts to Maintain NetWare Compatible Login in Active Directory

Users And Computers. By configuring the Concurrent Connections option for a user account, you can also limit the number of sessions that a NetWare client can establish.

Making the Decision

Table 16.3 lists the design decisions you need to make when securing NetWare client authentication with a Windows 2000 network.

Table 16.3   Securing NetWare User Authentication

To	Do the Following
Allow NetWare clients to authenticate with a Windows 2000 Server	■ Install FPNW on a Windows 2000 server. ■ Enable each required user account to maintain NetWare compatible login. ■ Install the IPX/SPX Compatible transport on the Windows 2000 server running FPNW.
Limit the number of simultaneous connections by a single user account	■ Limit the number of concurrent connections in the NW Compatible tab of the Properties dialog box of a user account.
Allow authentication by Windows for Workgroups 3.11, Windows 95, Windows 98, or Windows NT client computers	■ Windows for Workgroups 3.11, Windows 95, Windows 98, and Windows NT clients allow the installation of multiple network clients. Rather than install FPNW, consider deploying the Microsoft and NetWare clients to all client computers.

Applying the Decision

Blue Yonder Airlines must install FPNW on the BYDATA server to allow NetWare clients to connect to the file server using native NetWare clients. Before installing FPNW, Blue Yonder Airlines should determine what operating systems are in use for the client computers at the Consolidated Messenger office. If the client computers are running Windows 95 or later, consider installing both Microsoft and NetWare clients on the computers. This would allow file access and authentication to both the Windows 2000 and NetWare networks. You could remove the NetWare client software once the NetWare server data is migrated to Windows 2000.

Securing Authentication for UNIX Clients

UNIX clients can use several methods to authenticate with a Windows 2000 network. The choice will depend primarily on the application that's used to access data on the Windows 2000 server.

- **Clear text.** Several Windows Sockets (WinSock) applications use clear text authentication when authenticating with a Windows 2000 domain controller. Among the common applications, Telnet, Post Office Protocol version 3 (POP3), File Transfer Protocol (FTP), and Internet Mail Access Protocol version 4 (IMAP4) all use clear text authentication. The risk of using clear text authentication must be weighed against the needs for using these WinSock applications.

Note   These applications can use either Secure Socket Layers (SSL) or Internet Protocol Security (IPSec) to encrypt transmissions between the client and the server and protect clear text authentication.

- **Network Information Service (NIS).** Used to authenticate UNIX clients with NFS servers. NIS allows user logon information and group information to be centrally acquired from the NIS database. Windows 2000 can host the NIS database in Active Directory when Services for UNIX 2.0 is installed on the Windows 2000 server. The NIS service maps the provided UID and Group Identifier (GID) to a corresponding user account in Active Directory.

- **NT LAN Manager (NTLM).** Samba, a NetBIOS server for UNIX workstations, allows file access using Server Message Blocks (SMBs). If the UNIX clients are running Samba version 2.0.6 and later, NTLM authentication can be used for authenticating the user accounts. Samba versions earlier than version 2.0.6 use clear text authentication.

Warning   To allow access to UNIX Samba servers, you must configure Group Policy to enable the Send Unencrypted Password To Connect To Third-Party SMB Servers setting. You have to carefully consider implementing this setting because it results in passwords being passed on the network in clear text format.

- **Kerberos.** Used to authenticate UNIX users by using accounts in Active Directory. To use Kerberos, you must either configure the UNIX clients to use Active Directory domain controllers as their Kerberos Key Distribution Center (KDC) or implement inter-realm trust relationships between the Kerberos realm and the Windows 2000 domain. Both methods require you to create an account in Active Directory and map the account to its related UID.

Making the Decision

When you design secure authentication for UNIX clients, you should include the following in your security plan:

- Identify the applications that UNIX clients will use for accessing resources on the Windows 2000 network. Each application will have a specific form of required authentication. By identifying the supported applications, you can define what forms of authentication to provide on the network.

- Design an authentication infrastructure to support the deployed applications. The infrastructure you design will vary based on the required authentication mechanisms.

- For Kerberos authentication, determine whether the UNIX clients will authenticate with a Windows 2000 domain controller or use inter-realm trusts to allow integration of the Kerberos realms with the Windows 2000 domain structure.

- For NIS access, determine whether a UNIX NIS server or Server for NIS will provide NIS authentication services.

- For Samba access, determine what version of Samba is used by UNIX clients. UNIX clients running versions 2.0.6 or higher can use NTLM for authentication, while older clients require Group Policy to be modified to allow unencrypted password authentication.

- For WinSock application access, determine whether the applications support SSL encryption for authentication. If they do, ensure that the server hosting the server-side application is configured to support SSL. For example, to use SSL to encrypt POP3 authentication, the mail server must acquire a server-side certificate. If SSL isn't supported, consider using IPSec to encrypt all data transmitted between the WinSock client application and the server-side WinSock application.

- Create accounts in Active Directory where necessary. Kerberos authentication and NIS authentication associate UNIX UIDs with Active Directory user accounts. When credentials are provided by a UNIX user, account mapping determines what Active Directory account to use when accessing resources stored on a Windows 2000–based server.

Applying the Decision

Blue Yonder Airlines must use NIS authentication to provide NFS access to UNIX users connecting to the BYDATA server. The NFS Server software requires you to configure Active Directory to act as an NIS server by using Server for NIS. You can import the existing NIS source files from the UNIX NIS servers by using the NIS To Active Directory Migration Wizard. Finally, configure User Name Mapping so that the UID provided by a UNIX client when accessing the resources on the BYDATA server is translated to a Windows 2000 security principal. Use Two-Way Password Synchronization to synchronize the passwords used for UNIX and Windows 2000 so that users won't have to reenter credentials.

Blue Yonder Airlines must establish a Kerberos inter-realm trust between the blueyonder.tld domain and the UNIX Kerberos realm to allow Active Directory users to authenticate with the UNIX database. Only an inter-realm trust allows the UNIX KDC to recognize user credentials from Active Directory.

Lesson Summary

Until a non-Microsoft user authenticates with the Windows 2000 network, there's no way to apply the Windows 2000 security model to the heterogeneous client sessions. You must ensure that your design doesn't weaken Windows 2000 security by allowing heterogeneous clients to authenticate using clear text. By using Windows 2000 add-on services, you can ensure that authentication is encrypted to protect the Windows 2000 user credentials.

Activity: Identifying Authentication Risks in a Heterogeneous Network Environment

You've been hired by an organization to evaluate authentication risks in their network. For each scenario described in this activity, identify any authentication risks and describe what you could do to decrease these risks. Answers to these scenarios can be found in the appendix.

1. A Macintosh client computer connects to a Windows 2000 server running File Services for Macintosh using System 7 File Sharing to access graphic files stored on the Windows 2000 server.

2. A UNIX client uses Samba version 2.0.5 to connect to SMB file resources on a Windows 2000 server.

3. A UNIX user implements Telnet to run batch processes on a Windows 2000 server.

4. A NetWare client connects to a Windows 2000 server running FPNW for accessing accounting files.

5. A NetWare 3.12 user uses a server named RED312 as her preferred NetWare server. Due to changes in her job function, she must now access budget reports stored on a Windows 2000 server running FPNW. To reduce the number of credentials entered during authentication, the user has modified her NetWare login script to attach to the FPNW server.

6. A UNIX client retrieves data from a Windows 2000 FTP server. An IPSec security association protects all data that's transmitted between the FTP client and the FTP server using IPSec Authentication Headers (AH).

7. A UNIX client retrieves data from a Windows 2000 FTP server. An IPSec security association protects all data that's transmitted between the FTP client and the FTP server using IPSec Encapsulating Security Payloads (ESPs).

Lesson 3: Designing Directory Synchronization and Integration

When designing a secure network that includes multiple directories, consider how the directories will integrate. The goal is to allow a user to authenticate to the heterogeneous network using a single user account and password. All network operating systems and services should recognize the single set of credentials.

You also must plan directory integration to prevent changes in one directory service from overwriting directory modifications in another directory service. By defining which directory service is authoritative for a specific attribute, you can decentralize the management of directory data to specific departments.

Finally, you must plan for the integration of authentication mechanisms that are supported in multiple operating systems. Kerberos v5 is used by both Active Directory and several UNIX deployments. Configuring Kerberos realms to interoperate with Active Directory domains allow single sign-on capabilities in the mixed network.

After this lesson, you will be able to

- Design directory service interoperability in a Windows 2000 network

Estimated lesson time: 30 minutes

Synchronizing Active Directory with a Novell Directory

User accounts in a NetWare environment can synchronize their passwords with an Active Directory user account by using the MSDSS application included in Windows Services for NetWare 5.0. The MSDSS application allows passwords to be synchronized between Novell Directory Services (NDS) user accounts and Active Directory user accounts based on mappings configured in MSDSS.

Note   You can also use MSDSS to synchronize account information between Active Directory and a NetWare Bindery service from NetWare 3.*x*.

Making the Decision

Table 16.4 shows the design decisions you face when synchronizing NetWare NDS with Active Directory.

Table 16.4   Securing Directory Synchronization Between NetWare NDS and Active Directory

To	Do the Following
Synchronize passwords between NDS and Active Directory	■ Install MSDSS on a Windows 2000 domain controller.
Limit which attributes are synchronized	■ Modify the mapping table in MSDSS to map only the attributes required.
Perform password synchronization between NDS and Active Directory	■ The Windows 2000 client computer must have the Novell Client for Windows 2000 installed. You can't use Gateway Services For NetWare (GSNW).

Applying the Decision

MSDSS simplifies migration from NetWare 4.11 to Windows 2000 by ensuring that the same user credentials are used in both networks. By ensuring that passwords are the same for user accounts in both network operating systems, Blue Yonder Airlines will reduce the costs associated with migrating to Windows 2000. When the migration is complete, users will continue to authenticate using the same user name and password that they used in the NetWare environment, thus reducing security issues related to modifying passwords during a migration.

Securely Synchronizing Multiple Directories

Microsoft Metadirectory Services (MMS) 2.2 allows integration of identity information from multiple directory services. By using MMS, you ensure that the organization has a single authoritative directory store that collects all of its information from multiple existing directories.

MMS establishes a single directory by deploying a *metadirectory*. A metadirectory is a service that collects directory information from multiple directories, as shown in Figure 16.2.

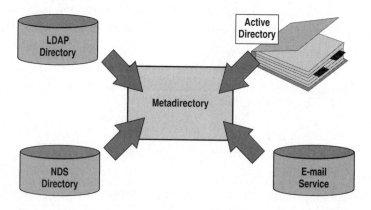

Figure 16.2   A metadirectory merging directory information from multiple sources

The metadirectory not only merges information from multiple directories into a single source, but it can also synchronize those changes to all directory services in an organization.

A metadirectory allows you to define ownership rules. You can designate which directory is authoritative for each attribute. For example, you could configure all Human Resources (HR)–related information in a directory to be maintained in Lotus Notes. If two directory services differ in an HR-related attribute, such as Manager, the Lotus Notes directory attribute value would be propagated to all other directories in the organization.

Management agents maintain synchronization between the metadirectory and the source directories. Management agents import data into the metadirectory and export metadirectory data to the connected directory assigned to the management agent. This process ensures that the directory service is synchronized with the metadirectory. MMS provides management agents for several common directories, including Windows NT, Novell NDS, cc:Mail, Banyan Vines, and Lotus Notes.

Making the Decision

MMS allows the coexistence of multiple directories in an organization. So that the multiple directories can interact, be sure to include the decision points in Table 16.5 when designing MMS.

Table 16.5   Planning Integration of Directories

To	Do the Following
Merge multiple directories into a common directory	■ Design an MMS solution that uses management agents to connect multiple directory services into a single metadirectory.
Connect a directory to an MMS metadirectory	■ Define a management agent that will manage the synchronization of the directory service with the metadirectory.
Maintain which directory service is authoritative for a specific attribute	■ Define ownership rules that define which directory service is authoritative for a specific attribute. The ownership rule will publish information to the metadirectory if the directory service is authoritative or roll the data back to the metadirectory value if another directory service is authoritative.

Applying the Decision

While MSDSS allows password synchronization between NetWare NDS directories and Active Directory, MMS provides you with greater flexibility of when deciding how attribute control is delegated. For example, imagine that user modifications performed in NDS are being overwritten with previous data stored in Active Directory during the migration from NetWare to Windows 2000. MMS allows you to configure NDS as the authoritative directory service for the OU and ensure that any updates performed in the NDS environment are propagated to Active Directory. The management agent also prevents any attempts by Active Directory to update objects stored in the OU. Because of the ability of MMS to delegate management of specific attributes, it may be desirable for Blue Yonder Airlines to use MMS instead of MSDSS.

Integrating Active Directory with Kerberos Realms

Windows 2000 uses Kerberos v5 authentication as the default authentication mechanism. Kerberos allows Windows 2000 and UNIX clients to interoperate and authenticate with each other. There are three common strategies for integrating UNIX and Windows 2000 networks for authentication services.

- **Using Active Directory as the Kerberos realm.** Configure UNIX clients to use Windows 2000 domain controllers as Kerberos Key Distribution Centers (KDCs). All authentication of UNIX Kerberos clients is performed using accounts stored in Active Directory.

- **Using Windows 2000 Professional in an existing Kerberos realm.** Configure Windows 2000 Professional client computers to authenticate with a UNIX KDC in a Kerberos realm. If this is required, configure the Windows 2000 Professional computer to be a member of a workgroup. In addition, you must configure the Kerberos realm for the Windows 2000 Professional computer and establish the necessary local account mappings.

- **Creating a Kerberos inter-realm trust.** Establish an inter-realm trust relationship between a Windows 2000 domain and a Kerberos realm. This trust relationship allows ticket granting tickets (TGTs) to be issued for resources located in another Kerberos realm or Windows 2000 domain. The inter-realm trust is established in the Active Directory Domains And Trusts console, as shown in Figure 16.3.

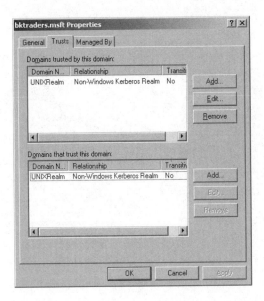

Figure 16.3   Establishing trust relationships between Windows 2000 domains and Kerberos realms

Note   For more information on Windows 2000 and UNIX interoperability, see the white paper "Windows 2000 Kerberos Interoperability" found on the Supplemental Course Materials CD-ROM (\Chapt16\Windows 2000 Kerberos Interoperability.doc) that accompanies this book.

While all three methods provide Kerberos authentication, creating a Kerberos inter-realm trust is the only method that allows true interoperability and cross-authentication. Figure 16.4 shows how Kerberos authentication takes place for a user account in a UNIX realm when the user account accesses resources in a Windows 2000 domain.

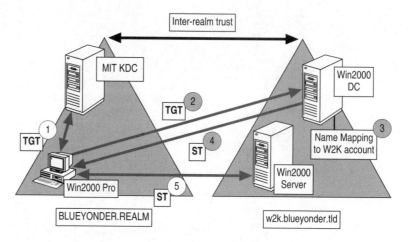

Figure 16.4   Establishing trust relationships between Windows 2000 domains
and Kerberos

1. The server must access resources on the server.w2k.blueyonder.tld domain.
   To authenticate, a Kerberos authentication request is sent to the computer's
   configured KDC, the MIT KDC. The MIT KDC responds with a TGT for the
   w2k.blueyonder.tld KDC, a Windows 2000 domain controller.

2. The client computer sends the TGT to the Windows 2000 KDC asking for a
   Service Ticket (ST) for the server.w2k.blueyonder.tld server.

3. The Windows 2000 DC performs a name mapping operation to determine
   what Active Directory account is associated with the submitted UID.

4. The Windows 2000 KDC issues an ST containing the user and group information of the Windows 2000 account mapped to the submitted UNIX UID.

5. The user submits the ST to the server.w2k.blueyonder.tld computer and is
   granted or denied access based on the Windows 2000 credentials included in
   the ST by comparing the account information to the resource's discretionary
   access control list (DACL).

Note   This process requires the passwords in the UNIX realm and Windows
2000 domain to be synchronized.

Making the Decision

When determining what form of Kerberos interoperability to use in a mixed network, consider the following design issues:

- Determine what version of Kerberos is used in the UNIX network. Only
  Kerberos v5 is supported by Windows 2000. If the UNIX network uses
  Kerberos v4, you can't configure Kerberos interoperability.

- Identify any Kerberos realms that exist in the UNIX environment. Determine whether you will continue to use the Kerberos realms. If you do, decide what will be the primary Kerberos service.

    - If the UNIX network is your organization's core network, consider configuring Windows 2000 Professional to authenticate with the Kerberos realm.

    - If Active Directory must become the primary Kerberos environment, configure all UNIX Kerberos clients to authenticate with Windows 2000 as their Kerberos realm.

    - If you support both Active Directory and the Kerberos realm, consider configuring a Kerberos inter-realm trust to allow authentication between the two Kerberos systems.

- If UNIX clients authenticate with a Windows 2000 domain controller, define name mappings so that a UNIX UID is associated with an Active Directory user account. The Active Directory user account SID and associated group SIDs will be placed in Service Tickets when UNIX clients are accessing Windows 2000–based servers.

Applying the Decision

Blue Yonder Airlines must establish a Kerberos inter-realm trust between the blueyonder.tld domain and the UNIX Kerberos realm. Active Directory user accounts can obtain Kerberos service tickets for access to the UNIX database server only if you establish inter-realm trusts. To be safe, establish a two-way trust relationship so that UNIX user accounts can access Windows 2000 resources. Granting access to Windows 2000 resources requires you to define Kerberos name mapping that will associate a UNIX UID with an Active Directory user account.

Lesson Summary

Consolidating directories allows you to maintain a single uniform directory within an organization. The implementation of a uniform directory requires planning to ensure that attributes modified in one directory aren't changed by entries in another directory. The security plan must define what directories are authoritative for specific attributes.

Alternatively, you may require two different directories to cross-authenticate users. Your security design must determine whether only one of the directories should provide the authentication or whether the directories must coexist and allow the forwarding of authentication requests between the multiple directories.

Lesson 4: Securing Access to Windows 2000 Resources

To make Windows 2000 network resources available to heterogeneous clients, you must be sure that only authorized users access those resources. The methods for making resources available to heterogeneous clients will depend on which operating system the clients use.

After this lesson, you will be able to

- Design secure access to Windows 2000 resources by heterogeneous clients

Estimated lesson time: 30 minutes

Securing Macintosh Access to Windows 2000 Resources

Windows 2000 supports resource access for Macintosh clients through Microsoft's File Services for Macintosh and Print Services for Macintosh. These services allow Macintosh clients to securely access resources stored on Windows 2000–based servers without installing additional software on the Macintosh clients.

Note For the highest level of security, install the MS-UAM on each Macintosh client to allow 14-character encrypted passwords for authentication.

Securing File Access

The File Services for Macintosh service in Windows 2000 provides user access to Macintosh clients. Macintosh clients are able to connect to the Windows 2000–based server using either AppleTalk Phase 2 protocol or, if AppleShare client version 3.7 or later is installed on the Macintosh clients, Apple Filing Protocol (AFP) over TCP/IP.

Windows 2000 allows the Macintosh clients to access the server by using Mac-accessible volumes that are predefined at the Windows 2000 server. The Mac-accessible volume is an entry point to an NTFS volume on a Windows 2000–based server. The Macintosh client can connect to the Mac-accessible volume by selecting the volume in the Macintosh Chooser.

Security for Mac-accessible volumes is defined by the permissions set on the Mac-accessible volume and the NTFS permissions set on the folders and files within the Mac-accessible volume. The user's effective permissions for the Mac-accessible volume will be defined by their Active Directory user account and primary group.

Comparing Macintosh and Windows 2000 Permissions

File Services for Macintosh translates permissions between Macintosh and Windows 2000 permissions. When permissions are defined at the Macintosh client, the permissions are translated to NTFS permissions for the files stored on the Mac-accessible volume. Likewise, Macintosh permissions set on the files and folders stored in the Mac-accessible volume are translated into NTFS permissions.

- NTFS Read permissions are translated to See Files and See Folders permissions for Macintosh clients.

- NTFS Write and Delete permissions are translated to the Make Changes permission for Macintosh clients.

Macintosh permissions differ from Windows 2000 permissions because permissions are assigned only to folders and permissions can't be assigned to multiple users and groups. Macintosh permissions are assigned to three categories of users for all folders.

- **Owner.** The user who creates the folder.

- **Primary Group.** Each folder is associated with a specific Macintosh group. The group can be any global group in the domain.

- **Everyone.** All other users who have permissions to access the folder. This includes users connecting with Guest credentials.

Securing Print Access

AppleTalk provides no native mechanisms for securing printer access in a Macintosh network. Because of this, Macintosh clients assume that security isn't required for access to printers and don't send user credentials when printing.

You can implement print security by changing the service account associated with the MacPrint service to a specific user account rather than the default of the System account. You can then restrict access to specific printers by assigning the new service account Print permissions only to the printers accessible to Macintosh users.

Making the Decision

When designing resource access for Macintosh clients, consider the points in Table 16.6.

Table 16.6   Securing Windows 2000 Resource Access for Macintosh Clients

To	Include the Following in Your Design
Allow Macintosh clients to access NTFS volumes	▪ Install File Services for Macintosh on any servers to which Macintosh clients require access. ▪ Ensure that all Macintosh clients are running System 6.0.7 or later as their operating system. ▪ Define Mac-accessible volumes in the Computer Management console.
Ensure the highest level of security for Macintosh users	▪ Deploy the MS-UAM to all Macintosh clients to enable 14-character encrypted passwords.
Restrict access to Mac-accessible volumes to authorized users	▪ Disable guest access to the Mac-accessible volume. ▪ Configure a volume password and distribute the password only to authorized users. ▪ Define NTFS permissions on files and folders in the Mac-accessible volume to restrict access for Macintosh users.

Applying the Decision

Blue Yonder Airlines must install File Services for Macintosh on the BYDATA server to allow Macintosh users in the Marketing department to access stories and digital photos.

Blue Yonder must establish a process that lets Microsoft clients store the stories and digital photos within the folder structure designated as the Mac-accessible volume. Define the permissions for the Mac-accessible volume to allow both Windows and Macintosh users to access the data. For the Macintosh users, create a global group to contain all the Macintosh users. To allow Macintosh computers to define permissions on the Mac-accessible volume, designate this global group as the users' primary group in Active Directory Users And Computers.

Restrict access to the AGFA film printer by creating a custom user account to act as the service account for the MacPrint service on the BYDATA server. By configuring the permissions for the AGFA film printer to assign only Print permissions to the custom user account, you limit access to the Macintosh users.

Securing NetWare Access to Windows 2000 Resources

FPNW allows a Windows 2000–based server to provide secure access to file and print resources to NetWare clients using NetWare Core Protocol (NCP). FPNW emulates a NetWare 3.*x* server and allows NetWare clients to connect to Windows 2000 resources by using NetWare clients and utilities.

Securing File Access

You can provide file access to NetWare clients by defining Novell volumes in the Computer Management console. Setting permissions on the NetWare volume can restrict access to authorized users. Defining NTFS permissions on folders and files within the NetWare volume also affects effective permissions. As with Windows 2000 native access, the most restrictive volume and NTFS permissions are the effective permissions for resources.

Note   The user account named FPNW Service Account must have Read permission for the directory that's the root of a NetWare volume.

Only user accounts that are NetWare-enabled accounts can access the NetWare volumes on the Windows 2000–based server.

Securing Print Access

All shared printers hosted by the Windows 2000–based server running FPNW are accessible to both Windows and NetWare client computers. NetWare clients use the share name defined for the printer as the queue name for the printer. You can control printer access by assigning Print permissions to groups that contain the NetWare-enabled user accounts.

Note   Within File and Print Services for NetWare, you can define a default queue to which NetWare clients will connect for printing.

Making the Decision

Table 16.7 outlines the design decisions you face when securing NetWare client access to Windows 2000 resources.

Table 16.7   Securing Windows 2000 Resource Access for NetWare Clients

To	Include the Following in Your Design
Allow NetWare clients to access NTFS volumes	■ Install File and Print Services for NetWare on any servers to which NetWare clients require access. ■ Ensure that all NetWare clients have the FPNW server configured as their preferred server. ■ Define NetWare volumes in the Computer Management console.
Restrict which user accounts can access NetWare volumes stored on a Windows 2000–based server	■ Define authorized accounts to be only NetWare-enabled user accounts. ■ Configure volume and NTFS permissions to restrict access to authorized user accounts.
Restrict access to printer resources	■ Assign Windows 2000 print permissions to groups consisting of NetWare-enabled accounts.

Applying the Decision

Blue Yonder Airlines must install FPNW on the BYDATA server to allow NetWare clients at Consolidated Messenger to connect and access data on the

BYDATA server. Define a NetWare volume that contains the folders where NetWare-accessible data is stored. Set NTFS and volume permissions that limit access to authorized users.

Securing UNIX Access to Windows 2000 Resources

UNIX clients can use several methods to access resources stored in a Windows network. UNIX clients can use NFS, WinSock applications, and SMB clients to access file resources on a Windows 2000–based server. By installing Print Services for UNIX, Windows 2000 can support UNIX clients using Line Printer Remote (LPR) print commands to send print jobs to Windows 2000 printers.

Securing File Access

Services for UNIX 2.0 provides an NFS Server service that allows UNIX clients using NFS client software to access file resources. The Server for NFS provided with Services for UNIX 2.0 allows a Windows 2000–based server to provide access to UNIX NFS clients. The UNIX clients see the Windows 2000–based server as a native NFS server and connect using NFS protocols.

The UNIX client doesn't have to provide alternate credentials when connecting to Server for NFS. Instead, Services for UNIX uses the User Name Mapping console to map UNIX UIDs and GIDs to Windows 2000 user accounts and group accounts. When the UNIX client connects, the client provides a User ID and Group ID from the UNIX environment. Server for NFS uses the defined user name mappings to determine the associated Windows 2000 user and group accounts. The Windows 2000 user and group accounts are used to determine whether access should be granted to the UNIX client.

Note If a mapping can't be found, the UNIX UID will be mapped to an anonymous logon account.

Once the Windows 2000 user account is identified, access to the NFS data is determined using the DACLs defined for the NFS folders.

Alternatively, you can use a WinSock application such as FTP or Telnet to access file resources. Typically, WinSock applications allow easy access to Windows 2000 resources, but authentication is generally weaker than NFS or SMB authentication. In many cases clear text authentication is used, which increases the risk of password interception.

Note You can protect authentication by using either SSL (if supported by the application) or IPSec to encrypt all the data that's transmitted.

Finally, Samba and other SMB clients for UNIX allow Server Message Block (SMB) access to Windows 2000 resources. SMB clients authenticate by submitting user accounts and passwords that exist in Active Directory. Depending on the version of the SMB client software, the authentication is either presented in a clear text or NTLM transmission.

Securing Print Access

You can support print access by UNIX clients by installing Microsoft Print Services for Unix. Print Services for UNIX installs a Line Printer Daemon (LPD) service on the Windows 2000–based server that allows UNIX clients running the LPR service to send documents to the LPD service.

Note The LPD service isn't set to start automatically. You must configure the startup options to start automatically to ensure that UNIX clients are still able to submit print jobs if the Windows 2000–based server hosting the LPD service is restarted.

Making the Decision

Table 16.8 outlines the design decisions you face when allowing UNIX clients to access resources stored on a Windows 2000–based server.

Table 16.8   Securing UNIX Client Access to Windows 2000 Resources

To	Include the Following in Your Design
Provide NFS access to file resources by UNIX clients	■ Install Services for UNIX 2.0 on the Windows 2000 Server providing UNIX client access. ■ Configure Server for NFS to provide access to UNIX NFS clients. ■ Configure User Name Mappings to associate UNIX UIDs and GIDs to Active Directory user and group accounts.
Provide SMB access to file resources by UNIX clients	■ Install Samba client software on all UNIX clients requiring SMB access to a Windows 2000–based server.
Secure WinSock application access to Windows 2000 resources	■ Enable SSL or IPSec encryption of all data transmitted between the client and the server.
Secure all file resources access by UNIX clients	■ Store all data accessible by UNIX clients on NTFS partitions. ■ Configure NTFS permissions to restrict access to only authorized users. Ensure that the user accounts assigned to UNIX users are included in groups assigned access to the resources.
Allow UNIX clients to print to Windows 2000 printers	■ Install Microsoft Print Services for UNIX to allow LPR connections to Windows 2000 printers. ■ Configure the LPD service to start automatically.

Applying the Decision

Blue Yonder Airlines must install Services for UNIX 2.0 on the BYDATA server. Services for UNIX 2.0 will allows Server for NFS to be configured to allow a user at the UNIX server to connect to the BYDATA server to access statistical reports. By mapping the UID and GID of the user account used at the UNIX server to a user and group account in Active Directory, all access by the UNIX user account can be secured.

Lesson Summary

Windows 2000 provides several services that allow heterogeneous clients to authenticate and access resources stored on a Windows 2000–based server. Although different protocols are used, you can implement standard Windows 2000 security once the heterogeneous client user authenticates with the Windows 2000–based server. By defining NTFS permissions for all resources accessed by heterogeneous clients, you can ensure that only authorized users gain access to the resources.

Lesson 5: Securing Windows 2000 User Access to Heterogeneous Networks

When designing access to resources stored in heterogeneous networks by Microsoft clients, you can provide secure access by using one of two methods: native clients or gateway services.

The native clients method requires that additional client software be loaded at the Microsoft clients. The client software allows the Microsoft client to make native connections to the heterogeneous server hosting the data.

The gateway services method requires that client software be loaded on a single gateway computer. The gateway then publishes resources from the heterogeneous network so that Microsoft clients can access the data through the gateway.

After this lesson, you will be able to

- Design secure access to data stored on heterogeneous networks from Microsoft clients

Estimated lesson time: 30 minutes

Securing Access to NetWare Resources

Many networks use NetWare servers for file and print services. You can provide Windows 2000 Professional–based computers with access to NetWare resources by installing Client Services for NetWare (CSNW) or by installing Novell Client v4.8 for Windows NT/2000 from Novell NetWare, as shown in Figure 16.5.

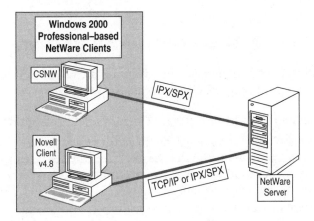

Figure 16.5   Windows 2000 Professional–based computers accessing NetWare resources with NetWare client software

Both clients require a user account in the NetWare environment that allows the user to authenticate with the NetWare environment.

Note   CSNW requires the installation of the NWLink IPX/SPX Compatible transport. Novell Client v4.8 for Windows NT/2000 can use TCP/IP when connecting to NetWare 5 network resources.

Alternatively, Windows 2000 Professional–based computers can access NetWare resources through a server with GSNW installed, as shown in Figure 16.6.

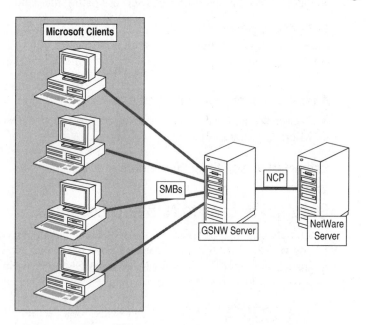

Figure 16.6   Accessing NetWare resources through a server running GSNW

Both methods require planning to ensure that security of the resources is maintained when Microsoft clients access NetWare resources.

Providing Access to NetWare Resources by Using a Native Client

Windows 2000 Professional–based computers can access NetWare resources by installing either CSNW or the NetWare Client v4.28 for Windows NT/2000. These client services act as a redirector for Windows 2000, allowing the Windows 2000–based computer to access resources in a Novell NetWare environment.

Both clients will recognize access attempts to access NetWare resources and translate the requests to use NCP so that the NetWare servers can authenticate the user and provide access.

To use the native NetWare clients, include the following in your network security deployment plan:

- Deploy the client software. Neither CSNW nor the NetWare Client are installed by default. Install the selected software at all clients that require access to the NetWare resources.

- Create user accounts in the NetWare environment. Create user accounts in the NetWare Bindery (for NetWare 3.*x* and older networks) or in NDS for NetWare 4.*x* and later networks. The user will use the user account and password to authenticate with the NetWare directory.

Comparing NetWare Trustee Rights to NTFS Permissions

NetWare assigns trustee rights to directories and files to determine what permissions are assigned to a user or group accessing the resources. NetWare trustee rights are composed of the following individual rights:

- **Read.** Allows users to read data in an existing file

- **Write.** Allows users to add data to an existing file

- **Create.** Allows users to create new files or new directories

- **Erase.** Allows users to delete existing files or directories

- **Modify.** Allows users to rename or change the attributes of files or folders

- **File Scan.** Allows users to view the contents of a directory

- **Access Control.** Allows users to modify trustee rights for folders

- **Supervisor.** Allows users all rights to folders or files

NetWare trustee rights are similar to NTFS permissions in their deployment. Only users with Supervisor rights (similar to Full Control in a Windows 2000 environment) or Access Control (similar to the Permissions permission) can modify the security for a file or directory.

Table 16.9 lists the NetWare trustee rights that are equivalent to NTFS folder permissions in Windows 2000.

Table 16.9   Comparing NTFS Permissions with NetWare Trustee Rights

NTFS Folder Permissions	NetWare Trustee Rights
List Folder Contents	File Scan
Read	Read, File Scan
Write	Write, Create, Modify
Modify	Read, Write, Create, Erase, Modify, File Scan
Full Control	Supervisor

- Configure the NetWare client. Configure the client software to connect the user to the correct *naming context* in NDS or to a preferred server in a Bindery environment. The naming context indicates where the user's account is located in the NDS directory structure.

- Implement a strategy to manage user passwords. Users now have two user accounts: one for Active Directory and one for NDS. Develop a strategy for the users to maintain the two accounts. The strategy can involve entering two separate sets of credentials or using MSDSS to synchronize passwords between NDS and Active Directory.

- Design NetWare permissions to restrict access. Access to NetWare resources is controlled entirely through the definition of trustee rights to the NetWare volume resources.

Providing Access to NetWare Resources by Using a Gateway

Windows 2000 can also allow access to NetWare resources through a single computer running GSNW. The Windows 2000–based server running GSNW authenticates with the NetWare server using an account in NDS or the NetWare Bindery. The GSNW server then publishes NetWare resources as if they were shares on the GSNW server. Microsoft clients access the resources using SMB or Common Internet Files System (CIFS) protocols without having to connect directly to the NetWare server.

If you plan to use GSNW to provide access to NetWare resources, consider the following items when designing your security plan:

- The user account that GSNW uses to connect to the NetWare environment must be a member of the Ntgateway group on the NetWare server. Only members of the Ntgateway group can provide gateway services to the NetWare resources.

- All trustee rights must reference the gateway account to secure access by users connecting through GSNW. All access to the NetWare server is performed using the credentials defined for the gateway.

- Individual users aren't identified when accessing NetWare resources through the GSNW gateway. If you require varying levels of access to NetWare resources, consider configuring multiple GSNW servers, as shown in Figure 16.7. Each GSNW server will have a unique gateway user account. As indicated in the figure, both the Gateway1 and Gateway2 accounts must be members of the Ntgateway group on the NetWare server. But you can assign different trustee rights to each gateway account.

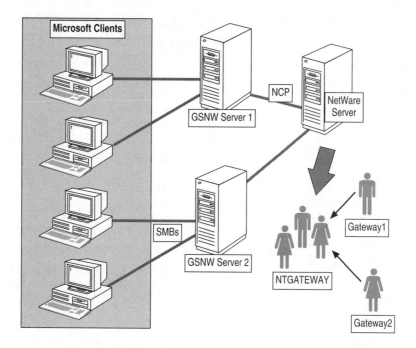

Figure 16.7 Providing different levels of access by implementing multiple
GSNW servers

- Define Share permissions at the GSNW server at the maximum level of
  trustee rights granted to the gateway account on the NetWare server. The most
  restrictive Share permissions and NetWare trustee rights will be the effective
  permissions. Because the resources are stored on a NetWare server, defining
  access permissions will commonly be the duty of the NetWare administrator.

- IPX/SPX must be run in the NetWare environment. GSNW requires that
  IPX/SPX be used for connecting to the NetWare server.

- Drive letters limit the number of GSNW shares. You can connect to NetWare
  servers only if available drive letters exist at the GSNW server. If no drive letters are available, you can't establish further connections.

Making the Decision

Use Table 16.10 to determine whether you should provide access to a NetWare
environment by installing NetWare clients at the Windows 2000–based client
computers or through GSNW.

Table 16.10   Designing Access to NetWare Resources

Use	When
Client Services for NetWare	▪ User-level security is required in the NetWare environment. CSNW requires that each user has an account in the NetWare environment. ▪ Your network allows protocols other than TCP/IP to be installed at client computers.
Novell Client v4.8 for Windows NT/2000	▪ All connectivity with the NetWare environment requires TCP/IP protocols. ▪ Administration of the Novell environment must take place from the Windows 2000 Professional–based computer. ▪ Synchronization of passwords between Active Directory and NDS using MSDSS is required.
Gateway Services for NetWare	▪ Users must have only a single account in the enterprise network. Instead of the user having two accounts, one in Active Directory and one in NDS, the gateway account will be used to access NetWare resources. ▪ Both Windows 2000 and NetWare administrators will manage security for NetWare resources. ▪ Limit deployment of the IPX/SPX protocol in the Microsoft network.

Applying the Decision

All members of the accounting department require the same level of access to the data stored on the NetWare server. The NetWare server is named AIRDATA1 and the data to which the accounting department requires access is stored on the DATA: volume in a folder named Accounting. The accounting department needs only to read the data stored on the NetWare server, they must not have permission to modify the data.

Blue Yonder Airlines can use GSNW to meet the security objectives for accessing data stored on the AIRDATA1 NetWare Server. To secure the access of the accounting department, include the following in your security plan:

▪ Install GSNW on a server that's accessible by the accounting department.

▪ Create an account for the GSNW service in NDS and make it a member of the Ntgateway group. This account will be the account that the GSNW service uses to authenticate with NetWare.

▪ Assign trustee rights at the NetWare server to allow only the gateway account Read and File Scan trustee rights to the Accounting directory on the DATA volume.

▪ Establish a GSNW share at the GSNW server connecting to \\AIRDATA1\DATA\Accounting.

- Configure share permissions for the GSNW share to allow only the accounting department Read permissions. No other groups should be allowed access to the GSNW share.

Securing Access to UNIX Resources

In some mixed networks Windows 2000 users have to access resources stored on UNIX servers. As with NetWare resources, you can provide access either directly to users or through a gateway service.

Providing Access to UNIX Resources with UNIX Client Software

To allow Windows–based computers to connect to NFS resources in a UNIX environment, Services for UNIX 2.0 provides the Client for NFS. A Windows 2000–based computer with the Client for NFS installed is able to connect to NFS shares on UNIX servers by using the same methods used to connect to Windows 2000 shares.

Client for NFS works in conjunction with User Name Mapping. When a client initially connects to the UNIX NFS server, User Name Mapping determines what UNIX UID and GID are mapped to the current Active Directory user account. User Name Mapping sends the associated UID and GID to Client for NFS, which submits the account information to the NFS server for authentication and authorization.

When planning to provide secure Windows 2000 client access to NFS shares on UNIX servers, include the following tasks in your design:

- Distribute Services for UNIX 2.0. Install the Client for NFS software from Services for UNIX 2.0 on each client computer that requires access to the NFS share.

- Configure security at the NFS server. The NFS server must configure security to only allow access to the authorized UIDs and GIDs.

- Define user name mappings. Deploy User Name Mapping to associate Active Directory accounts with a UID and GID in the UNIX environment. This includes defining which accounts must be mapped from Active Directory and defining which NIS server is authoritative in the UNIX environment.

- Define what action to take when a mapping isn't defined. Within User Name Mapping, you can either define that all nonmapped accounts are mapped to a common UID and GID or you can perform no mapping. The act of not defining a mapping blocks access to the NFS share.

Providing Access to UNIX Resources by Using a Gateway

Gateway for NFS allows Windows 2000 users to connect to UNIX NFS shares without installing NFS client software at each Windows 2000–based client computer. The Windows 2000–based client computers send file requests to the Gateway for NFS server using SMBs, and the gateway performs the file access request using the NFS protocol. Because all access is through a single point to the NFS server, the gateway server can become a bottleneck.

When planning a Gateway for NFS deployment to allow access to UNIX NFS share, address the following issues in your design:

- Define what account will be used by the Gateway for NFS service. The account will be used to authenticate all access to the UNIX NFS share.

- Define a user account mapping for the gateway account. Deploy User Name Mapping to map the gateway account to a UNIX UID and GID for authenticating with the NFS server.

- Define security at the UNIX NFS server. Define security at the UNIX NFS server to avoid providing excessive permissions to the gateway account.

- Limit which users can access the gateway. Share permissions for the gateway should limit access to authorized users. Ensure that the permissions are equivalent to the UNIX permissions so that access control is managed at the UNIX NFS server.

Making the Decision

Use Table 16.11 to determine whether you should provide access to a UNIX NFS environment by installation of Client for NFS at the Windows 2000–based client computers or through Gateway for NFS.

Table 16.11   Designing Access to UNIX NFS Resources

Use	When Your Security Design Requires
Client for NFS	<ul><li>User-level security in the UNIX environment.</li><li>Preventing the gateway from becoming a bottleneck and limiting access to the NFS server.</li><li>All security management of the NFS data to be performed at the UNIX server.</li></ul>
Gateway for NFS	<ul><li>No need to differentiate between user accounts when accessing the NFS share.</li><li>Security for NFS resources to be managed by both Windows 2000 and UNIX administrators.</li></ul>

Applying the Decision

Blue Yonder Airlines could use either Client for NFS or Gateway for NFS to provide access to the UNIX NFS server to store status reports. The requirements don't indicate whether varying levels of access are required. You must deploy the following to provide secure access to the NFS server:

- If Client for NFS is deployed to all Windows 2000–based client computers to provide access to the UNIX NFS share, then you should

- Create a user name mapping for each Active Directory account that requires access to the UNIX NFS server. Each user account that requires access to the UNIX NFS server must have a user name mapping created that associates its Active Directory account with a UNIX UID and GID.

- Configure User Name Mapping to perform only name mappings for defined user accounts. If a user account that doesn't have a mapping defined is presented, User Name Mapping won't apply a default mapping.

- Define security at the NFS server to limit access to only authorized users.

- If Gateway for NFS is deployed to provide Windows 2000–based client computers access to the NFS share, then you should

  - Create a user name mapping for the gateway account that requires access to the NFS server. The gateway account must have a user name mapping created that associates the Active Directory account with a UNIX UID and GID.

  - Configure User Name Mapping to only perform name mappings for defined user accounts. If a user account that doesn't have a mapping defined is presented, User Name Mapping won't apply a default mapping.

  - Define security at the NFS server that restricts access to the gateway account.

  - Define security at the gateway computer to allow only authorized users to connect to the NFS share.

Lesson Summary

When Windows 2000 clients require access to resources stored on NetWare or UNIX servers, you must decide whether to provide individual access or collective access. Whatever method you choose, ensure that Active Directory accounts are associated with UNIX UIDs and GIDs so that the connecting user doesn't have to provide additional credentials.

Lab 16-1: Securing Heterogeneous Clients

Lab Objectives

This lab prepares you to secure access between Windows 2000 and heterogeneous networks by meeting the following objectives:

- Design secure access to Windows 2000 resources by Macintosh users
- Design secure access to Novell NetWare resources by Windows 2000 users
- Design secure access to Windows 2000 resources by UNIX users

About This Lab

This lab looks at the design decisions you must make in order to allow heterogeneous clients to participate securely in a Windows 2000 network.

Before You Begin

Make sure that you've completed reading the chapter material before starting the lab. Pay close attention to the sections where the design decisions were applied throughout the chapter for information on designing your administrative structure.

Scenario: Contoso Ltd.

Contoso Ltd., an international magazine sales company, must design methods to securely integrate Windows 2000, Macintosh, NetWare, and UNIX resources that exist in the corporate network.

The Contoso Network

Contoso's Windows 2000 network uses an empty forest root named contoso.tld with three domains based on their geographic locations, as shown in Figure 16.8.

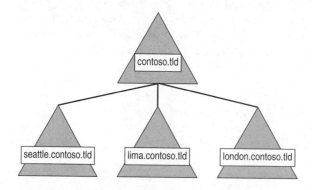

Figure 16.8   The contoso.tld forest structure

Users and computers at the Seattle, Lima, and London offices have their accounts located in the domain associated with their home office. This model is used both for users who access the network using only Microsoft clients and for users who access the network using Macintosh, NetWare, and UNIX clients.

Providing Access to Macintosh Clients

Several of the graphics personnel at Contoso use iMAC computers for creating graphics used in Contoso's magazine layouts. While some users use Macintosh computers exclusively, several users split their time between a Windows 2000 Professional workstation and an iMAC computer.

Contoso wishes to meet the following objectives when providing file and print access to the Windows 2000 resources on the network:

- All authentication information must be encrypted as it's transmitted across the network.

- Only authorized users will be allowed to log on from Macintosh computers.

- Three file servers are designated for access by Macintosh users: SFMLima, SFMSeattle, and SFMLondon. On each server, Macintosh users will have access only to the D:\Data and D:\Graphics folders.

- Macintosh users will require access to either the Data folder or the Graphics folder. No users will require access to both folders.

- Users must use the same password whether connecting to the network from Windows 2000 Professional computers or from Macintosh computers.

- All Macintosh users must be able to create, modify, delete, and read existing documents in the folders.

Providing Access to NetWare Resources

At the London office an older accounting software package runs on a NetWare 4.11 server named BIGRED. The data stored on the NetWare server is historical data that the accounting department frequently queries when it produces sales forecasts for the upcoming year. Members of the accounting department at each of the three offices must access the NetWare server to query the historical data.

Access to the NetWare 4.11 server must be secured so that only authorized members of the accounting department can access the data. Because the data is historical, members of the accounting department should have only read access to the data on the NetWare server. This configuration prevents any attempts to modify the data.

Sue Jackson, who's the administrator of the NetWare server, must have full access to the NetWare server from her Windows 2000 Professional client computer. Sue must be able to manage the NDS structure and assign trustee rights to all data stored on the NetWare server.

Your security design must consider the following issues faced by Contoso:

- The routers providing the WAN links to the London office from Seattle and Lima support only TCP/IP transmissions, as shown in Figure 16.9.

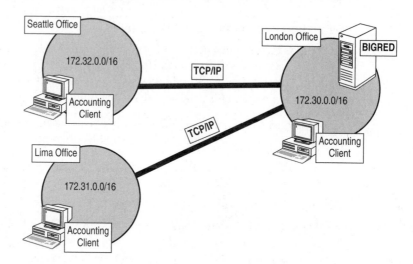

Figure 16.9   Accounting clients at all three offices accessing the BIGRED NetWare server

- The user accounts that are used by Windows 2000 Professional users to access the NetWare server are stored in the naming context OU=accounting.OU=london.O=contoso.

- Access to the historical accounting stored on the BIGRED server must be limited to members of the accounting department.

Providing Access to UNIX Clients

The multimedia office at the Seattle office develops Internet-based Java content that advertises product offerings on the Internet. The graphic components of the Web presence are developed on Silicon Graphics, Inc. (SGI) UNIX workstations.

The SGI UNIX workstations must store the graphics and multimedia files that they create on a Windows 2000 server named GRAPHICS that's located at the Seattle office. You must develop a secure method for the graphics and multimedia files to be stored on the Windows 2000 server that meets the following business objectives:

- The UNIX users must place the graphics in the FromUNIX folder on the GRAPHICS server. The UNIX users must be able to create, read, modify, and delete any files in the folder.

- The UNIX users must use authenticated protocols to transfer data to the GRAPHICS server.

- Due to management concerns, authentication must not use plaintext when transmitted on the network.

- UNIX users shouldn't have to provide alternate credentials. The UNIX users should have to provide only the credentials stored at the UNIX NIS server named NISCONTOSO.contoso.tld, which is at the London office.

Exercise 1: Securing Macintosh User Access

This exercise looks at the design required to provide secure resources access to Macintosh users. Answers to these questions can be found in the appendix.

1. If some Contoso employees who use both Windows 2000 Professional and Macintosh computers implement passwords greater than eight characters, what must you include in your network design to allow the employees to authenticate at both of their computers?

2. Assuming that different users will require access to the Data and Graphics folders, how many Mac-accessible volumes must you create on each server hosting File Services for Macintosh?

3. How can you limit access to the data stored on the three servers to only authorized Macintosh users?

4. What file system is required on the D drive of the SFMLima, SFMSeattle, and SFMLondon servers?

5. What permissions must you assign to the global groups in each domain to allow required access to the data in the D:\Data and D:\Graphic folders?

6. Contoso has two employees named Francisco Ramirez. Each has a user account named FRamirez, but the two accounts are located in separate domains. Francisco Ramirez, a graphics artist at the Lima office, has an account in the lima.contoso.tld domain, and Francisco Ramirez, the Director of Marketing in London, has an account in the london.contoso.tld domain. Both users have found that they can log on to the network at their home offices, but when they travel to other offices, network authentication fails on their iBook Macintosh laptop computers. What must you do to ensure that they can log on to the network at all offices?

Exercise 2: Securing Access to NetWare Resources

This exercise looks at the design required to give secure resources access to resources stored on the NetWare network. Answers to these questions can be found in the appendix.

1. Can CSNW be installed on all Windows 2000 Professional computers to provide the accounting department members access to the historical accounting data stored on the BIGRED NetWare server?

2. The solution shown in Figure 16.10 has been proposed to allow the accounting personnel to access data on the BIGRED NetWare file server.

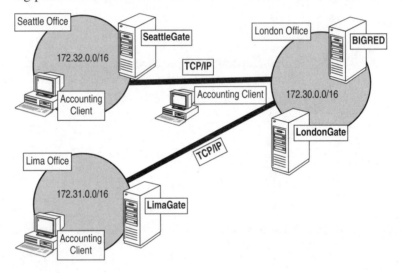

Figure 16.10   Proposed solution to access historical accounting data on the BIGRED NetWare server

■ A GSNW server will be set up at the Seattle office to connect to the BIGRED NetWare server. All accounting clients at the Seattle office will access the data through the SeattleGate GSNW server.

■ A GSNW server will be set up at the Lima office to connect to the BIGRED NetWare server. All accounting clients at the Lima office will access the data through the LimaGate GSNW server.

■ A GSNW server will be set up at the London office to connect to the BIGRED NetWare server. All accounting clients at the London office will access the data through the LondonGate GSNW server.

■ The LondonGate, SeattleGate, and LimaGate GSNW servers will have both TCP/IP and NWLink IPX/SPX installed.

Will this proposed solution work in the existing network environment? If not, what must you do to make the solution work?

3. The solution shown in Figure 16.11 has been proposed to allow the accounting personnel to access data on the BIGRED NetWare file server.

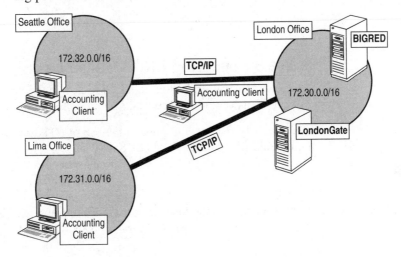

Figure 16.11   Proposed solution to access historical accounting data on the BIGRED NetWare server

- A GSNW server named LondonGate will be set up at the London office to connect to the BIGRED NetWare server. All accounting clients at the Lima, Seattle, and London offices will access the data through the LondonGate GSNW server.

- The LondonGate GSNW server will have both TCP/IP and NWLink IPX/SPX installed.

Will this proposed solution work in the existing network environment? If not, what must you do to make the solution work?

4. Can Sue Jackson use a GSNW solution to manage the NetWare server from her Windows 2000 Professional client computer? If not, what must you do to provide her administrative access?

5. What must you do at the GSNW server to ensure that only the accounting department can access the BIGRED NetWare server?

6. What naming context must you define in GSNW to authenticate the gateway account?

7. What must you do at the BIGRED server to grant the GSNW server access to the historical accounting data?

Exercise 3: Securing UNIX User Access

This exercise looks at the design required to provide secure resources access to UNIX users. Answers to these questions can be found in the appendix.

1. What security risks would prevent the use of FTP to transfer the graphics and multimedia files to the GRAPHICS server?

2. What service from the Services for UNIX 2.0 suite will allow the UNIX users to securely transfer data to the FromUNIX folder on the GRAPHICS server?

3. What must you do to provide single sign-on capabilities to the UNIX users so that they don't have to enter alternate credentials when they access the GRAPHICS server?

4. What permissions must be configured at the FromUNIX folder to meet security requirements?

5. What can you do to ensure that the passwords for the Active Directory accounts match the passwords for the UNIX UIDs?

Review

Answering the following questions will reinforce key information presented in this chapter. If you are unable to answer a question, review the appropriate lesson and then try the question again. Answers to the questions can be found in the appendix.

1. A computer game company creates versions of the same software for PCs, Linux, and Macintosh. Each version of the software is managed at separate branch offices, while the primary source code is stored on the corporate head office's Windows 2000 network. How would you authenticate Macintosh users and provide secure access to source code in the corporate office?

2. The branch office that develops the Linux version of games uses a NetWare 5.0 network to store all common data. All data related to the Linux branch office is stored on a NetWare 5.0 server named LINDATA. Assuming that all accounting users will require the same level of access, how would you provide users in the corporate accounting office with secure access to payroll data stored on the LINDATA server?

3. An organization currently uses both NetWare 4.11 and Windows 2000 Active Directory in the networking environment. User accounts are defined for all employees in both network operating systems. Many users are locked out of the network due to password violations related to maintaining two separate user accounts. What can you include in your design to limit password violations?

4. An organization maintains user information in several directory services in the enterprise network. Human Resources uses Lotus Notes to track personal employee information such as home addresses, Information Technology uses Active Directory for managing user accounts on the network, and Payroll uses NDS for managing payroll information. Many employees have complained that address updates aren't being uniformly performed across the directory services. Assuming that the organization wants each department to control user attributes pertaining to their department, how can you secure the integration of the directory services?

5. Several users in your organization use both Macintosh computers and Windows 2000 Professional computers to access the corporate network. Your organization recently implemented a new password policy that requires passwords to be a minimum of nine characters. Once the password policy came into effect, several of the multioperating system users could authenticate only on the Windows 2000 Professional computers. They lost the ability to log on to the network from the Macintosh computers. What might be causing this problem? What can your organization do to enable the users to continue using their Macintosh computers?

C H A P T E R   1 7

Designing a Security Plan

About This Chapter

Up to this point we have examined procedures and techniques for deploying security to different areas of a network. However, security across a network is only as strong as its weakest point. To deploy security consistently across an organization's network, you must create a comprehensive security plan for each project that requires protection. The security plan serves as a guide for configuring the network to meet an organization's security policy.

Before You Begin

To complete this chapter, you must read the chapter scenario. This scenario is used throughout the chapter to apply the design decisions discussed in each lesson.

Chapter Scenario: Fabrikam Inc.

Fabrikam Inc. is a defense contractor that develops weapon solutions for the U.S. military. The head office is located in Washington, D.C., and research offices are located in New York and San Francisco. Manufacturing plants are located in Detroit and Albuquerque, and warehouses are located in Houston and Miami. The company's office locations are illustrated in Figure 17.1.

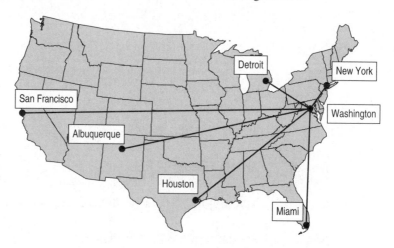

Figure 17.1   Fabrikam locations

Fabrikam has implemented a single-domain model for its Microsoft Windows 2000 domain and is using corp.fabrikam.tld as its forest root domain. Each location is defined as a separate site and is connected to the head office in Washington with a 1.544 megabit-per-second (Mbps) link.

Fabrikam has recently been the victim of a hacking attack. Plans for an advanced radar system that Fabrikam is developing were published in a technology magazine. Both upper management and the U.S. government are furious. Several business partners, including the Department of Defense, are questioning whether Fabrikam has implemented sufficient security to allow them to continue working together. The source of the hacking attack isn't yet known.

The Internal Audit

To determine the cause of the break-in, Fabrikam has hired an Internet security firm to evaluate the current network and determine the cause of the hacking attack. The Internet security firm has determined the following:

- Several projects were deployed before the security configuration was completed. Pressure from outside vendors to complete projects on time forced Fabrikam to deploy certain projects before all security was in place.

- Fabrikam was involved in several projects. Members of one project were unaware of the security issues and designs that were being developed for the other projects. In several circumstances security configuration design was duplicated, and the security implemented for one project weakened the security for another project.

- Fabrikam didn't have a clear corporate policy on security. The security firm couldn't determine the acceptable level of security for Fabrikam because Fabrikam had no company literature describing its acceptable risk level.

- The delays in security projects were related to Public Key Infrastructure (PKI) design issues. Upon further inspection, the security firm found that the tasks related to the PKI design were unassigned. When questioned, the Information Technology (IT) manager revealed that no one had ever been hired to design the organization's PKI. Fabrikam doesn't have any staff personnel with the necessary skills to design a PKI solution.

The Radar System Project

Fabrikam is developing an advanced radar system for the Department of Defense. The radar system can detect stealth-class aircraft.

The radar system designs are stored on a server named HELIOS located at the New York office. Due to the data's confidential nature, you must include the following in the security design:

- Only members of the Radar System project team can access the project server share, named Radar.

- All access to the project server requires mutual authentication of both the user and the HELIOS server. Members of the Radar System project team are using a combination of Windows 98–, Windows NT 4.0–, and Windows 2000–based computers.

- E-mail sent between members of the project team must be protected against inspection and modification.

- All attempts to access the data stored at the HELIOS server must be logged for subsequent review by administrators.

- Members of the project team require varying levels of access to the data stored on the HELIOS server. You need to configure security to allow varying levels of access without granting excess privileges to any member of the project team.

The Team

The following personnel have volunteered to help develop the security plan for the Radar System project:

- John Chen, manager of the IT department
- Scott Cooper, systems technologist for the New York office
- Kaarin Dolliver, technical lead of the Radar System project
- Beth Parsons, manager of the Radar System project
- Claus Romanowsky, administrative assistant, New York office
- Lani Ota, security manager, Fabrikam Inc.
- Shelly Szymanski, Human Resources manager
- Jeffrey Weems, graphic artist at the New York office
- Rob Young, developer of the Radar System software

Lesson 1: Defining a Security Policy

Defining an organization's security policy is the first step in designing an organization's security. The security policy defines the attitude that the organization will take toward security of its resources. This includes the value placed on resources held by the company and what the organization deems to be acceptable risk for the protection of those resources.

After this lesson, you will be able to

- Define the function of a security policy

Estimated lesson time: 30 minutes

A security policy defines an organization's security expectations. Once a security policy is developed, an organization can use it as a guideline for developing future security plans.

The security policy defines the security needs of an organization by identifying the following:

- **Resources to be protected.** Several resources in an organization may require protection, including hardware, software, and data. In some situations resources may include the people who know the security designs implemented for an organization.

- **Threats faced by the resources.** By identifying the threats that an organization's resources face, an organization can assign a value to the potential loss if the resource is compromised. Typical threats include unauthorized access to a resource and denial of service where the resource can't be accessed.

- **Probability of the threat occurring.** Before developing a security plan to minimize the effect of a specific threat, an organization must evaluate how likely the threat is.

By identifying the resources, the threats, and the probabilities of the threats, your organization will be able to design a security policy that addresses each threat and recommends a course of action to take if the threat occurs.

While it seems that organizations would assign maximum security to all their resources, costs often limit security implementations. These costs aren't only financial costs, but also performance and ease-of-use costs.

Evaluating the True Cost of a Threat

You determine the true cost of a threat by comparing the cost of the resource and the probability of the threat for each resource that must be secured. For example, say that an organization has two resources: a processing machine worth $20 million and an information database valued at $2 million. At first glance, resources should be directed to securing the more expensive processing machine.

If you then add in the probability of a threat taking place against the two resources, you get a better idea of the true costs associated with each resource. If the probability of an attack against the processing machine is 4 percent and the probability of an attack against the database is 50 percent, the values of the resource risks change. In this case the processing machine's value would be $800,000 and the database's value would be $1 million.

When comparing the value of resources in order to determine the threats those resources face, always factor in the probability that the threat will occur.

Generally, you define the security policy based on trade-offs between

- **Functionality versus security.** Sometimes an organization requires the use of a service on the network. The service provides some form of functionality to the organization even though the service introduces security risks. In this case the security plan costs must not outweigh the benefit received by the service's added functionality.

- **User convenience versus security.** The policy must identify when security becomes a barrier to users performing their jobs. For example, if smart cards are required for logon and a user forgets her smart card, the user won't be able to connect to the network.

- **Cost and functionality.** The policy must propose security plans that fall into the organization's budget. If the security level required by the policy isn't affordable, the policy can't be followed and must be revised.

After defining a security policy, you must make the policy visible throughout the organization. All employees in the organization must be aware of the policy so that they can help ensure that the principles outlined in the security policy are upheld. Employees must feel that management supports the security policy. If management doesn't appear to support the policy, employees will hesitate to follow the policy guidelines.

The organization must use the security policy for guidance when designing all security plans. If the policy doesn't provide this guidance, the organization should reevaluate its security policy to ensure that it reflects its security goals.

For example, if your organization's security policy dictates that the strongest forms of encryption must be used to protect all transmitted data, you should design Secure Socket Layer (SSL) configuration to require 128-bit encryption in your security design.

Note RFC 2196 contains best practices for designing security policies. You can obtain a copy of this RFC by going to *www.rfc-editor.org/rfc.html* and searching for "RFC 2196."

Making the Decision

You make the following decisions when designing a security policy for an organization:

- Identify resources that require protection. You must identify which resources are critical to the organization's operation or contain sensitive data that shouldn't be revealed to outside entities.

- Determine the value of the resources. Sometimes a resource's value is more than its actual worth in dollars. If a resource is the only product that a company produces, the loss or exposure of this resource's details could lead to the company's demise.

- Determine the acceptable level of risk for the organization. Each organization has different levels of acceptable risk. Generally an organization determines an acceptable risk by weighing the risk's probability and the cost associated with mitigating the risk.

- Develop recommendations for mitigation. The security policy should include actions that must be taken if a threat occurs.

- Ensure that the policy is distributed throughout the organization. For the policy to be effective, all personnel in an organization must be familiar with it.

Applying the Decision

Fabrikam has problems because it doesn't have a security policy. Fabrikam must develop a security policy that defines the methods the company will use to protect its resources. For example, Fabrikam's security policy should clearly define what levels of encryption must be used to encrypt stored and transmitted data. The resources that require protection are the data related to the projects that the company develops with its clients, including the Department of Defense. Fabrikam must ensure that its security policy defines how it will handle break-ins. Whatever security policy it develops, the company must ensure that its employees receive that information so they know what actions to take to uphold the policy.

Without a security policy, it's difficult to develop a functional security plan. The policy guides the security plan's developers to ensure that the organization's security goals are met.

Note   For Microsoft's recommendations on what to include in a security policy, please see the Security Planning white paper by going to *www.microsoft.com /technet* and searching for "Security Planning."

Lesson Summary

An organization must develop a security policy that defines the organization's view on security issues. The policy helps the organization define appropriate levels of security for all security plans. Without such a policy, there's no conformity in the security configuration of resources. And the lack of conformity brings the potential for security weakness.

Lesson 2: Developing a Security Plan

For each project that requires security in your organization, you must develop a security plan, or a security component to the project plan, that defines how you must configure security for the project.

After this lesson, you will be able to

- Design the steps required to develop a security plan for your organization

Estimated lesson time: 30 minutes

A security plan requires careful design to ensure that the plan reflects the organization's security policy and provides the framework for deploying security for the organization. Consider the following when designing a security plan:

- Define the scope. The most common problem with a security plan is that its scope is too great. By defining the scope of the security plan before developing it, you can easily determine whether a component proposed for the security plan is within the scope. Defining the scope prevents the project from being expanded during the project duration to include items that aren't related to the security plan's intent.

- Define the project team. You must put together a project team that represents the organization's views and ensures that the project is successfully completed. The project team can include both members from the organization and personnel from third-party organizations that supplement any skills deficiencies. When determining membership of the project team, consider the following participants:

  - Management representatives who can approve the project for both content and cost

  - Members of the IT department who will deploy the project plan

  - Representatives of the user groups affected by the security plan

  - Training personnel who will implement training for new technologies introduced by the security plan

  - Support personnel who will maintain the deployed security plan

  - Outside consultants who lend their expertise to the security plan's design

- Collect security requirements. The security plan must ensure that interviews are performed with all stakeholders in the project. Involving all stakeholders, including management and the users affected by the security project, helps ensure the proper balance between security and ease.

- Define security baselines. After collecting the security requirements, you must define the security baselines. Security baselines define the minimum level of security required for deployment. In some cases you can maintain the baseline through the use of Windows 2000 security templates. In other cases you can define the security baseline only by documenting the desired settings for future deployments.

Note You can set security baselines only when the desired results can be measured or documented. If it's impossible to measure or document the baseline, it's impossible to define what the baseline security must be. You can't define security baselines in an esoteric manner.

- Deploy the project plan. After completing the security plan design, you must develop a project plan that includes the following:

  - **Project timeline.** Establish a proposed timeline for the project. The timeline drives the project forward toward completion. You should be aware that you may have to adjust the timeline if unforeseen events occur.

Note In the plan, the project manager should identify tasks that will affect the project's completion date. The *critical path* tasks will affect the entire schedule if their due dates slip. The critical path for a project includes any tasks that will cause a project's completion date to slip if the tasks aren't completed on time.

  - **Define responsibilities.** Assign each task within the project timeline to a specific person or specific team. If you don't assign responsibility for each task, it's more likely that the task won't be completed on time.

Making the Decision

Table 17.1 outlines the design decisions you must make when developing a security plan for a project.

Table 17.1   Designing a Security Plan

To	Do the Following
Prevent a project from growing beyond its initial goals	<ul><li>Define the scope of the project before the project begins.</li><li>Compare any proposed additions to the project to the original scope to determine if the addition is within the scope.</li></ul>
Ensure that all aspects of the project are included in the security plan	<ul><li>Interview participants to determine the expected ease of use and security goals. Determine the appropriate balance based on the organization's security policy.</li></ul>
Ensure that management supports the project	<ul><li>Include management representation on the project team.</li><li>Develop the security plan to reflect the organization's security policy.</li></ul>
Define security baselines	<ul><li>Identify each resource that must be protected by the security plan.</li><li>Design security requirements for each resource and document the level of security required for each resource based on the organization's security policy.</li><li>Document all security requirements. Use documentation or security templates to define the security configuration settings.</li></ul>
Ensure that the project is completed on schedule	<ul><li>Ensure that all tasks in the project plan are assigned to a project team member.</li><li>Periodically reevaluate the project's timeline to ensure that the estimated time reflects the project's actual progress.</li></ul>

Applying the Decision

Fabrikam Inc. must ensure that the design decisions fit its security policy. To accomplish this, you must do the following:

- Define the scope. The plan must contain only security planning that's related to the Radar System project. Any tasks in the security plan that aren't related to the Radar System project should be considered out of scope and should be removed.

- Define the project team. Not everyone who has volunteered for the project team is appropriate for the Radar System project. Jeffrey Weems, the graphic artist at the New York office, doesn't need to be on the project team. All other proposed members, however, could play a part in the plan's design. Also, the proposed team doesn't include upper-level management. Without adequate representation, upper-level management may reject the proposed plan.

The current project team lacks expertise in the PKI infrastructure that's required to support encrypted and digitally signed e-mail messages. If these technical skills aren't available from employees, Fabrikam may have to hire a consulting firm.

- Collect security requirements. The security plan must define the levels of access that are required to the Radar share on the HELIOS server. The definition of the security requirements will facilitate the definition of group memberships and NT file system (NTFS) and share permissions. Collect the security requirements from all participants in the Radar System project, from the project manager to the data entry clerks.

- Define security baselines. The security plan must document the required settings for the Radar System project. This documentation includes the following:

  - Security groups required in Active Directory directory service

  - Organizational unit (OU) structure required for Group Policy deployment and delegation of administration

  - NTFS permissions that must be established for all data stored on the HELIOS server

  - Share permissions required for the Radar share on the HELIOS server

  - Group Policy settings required to ensure that Server Message Block (SMB) signing is enforced for all connections to the HELIOS server

  - SMB signing configuration settings for all Windows 98 and Windows NT 4.0 clients

  - E-mail client configuration to allow digital signatures and e-mail encryption

  - PKI design to allow the deployment of digital certificates, private keys, and public keys to e-mail participants

  - Audit policy that must be deployed at the HELIOS server to track all access to the Radar System project

- Deploy the project plan. Develop a plan that identifies all the tasks that must be completed in order to deliver it. Assign the tasks to the project team to ensure that each member is responsible for the completion of each task in the defined time frame.

Lesson Summary

A security plan must reflect an organization's security policy. All decisions made in the security plan must address the balance between security and ease of use. By defining the scope of the plan before development takes place, an organization can keep it within the scope and ensure that its focus isn't diverted from its primary goal.

Ensure that all participants affected by the security plan play a role in its development so that it addresses all employee concerns.

Lesson 3: Maintaining a Security Plan

The process doesn't stop after you design and implement your security plan. You must determine a strategy for maintaining the plan so that it's updated to address new risks.

After this lesson, you will be able to

- Develop a strategy for maintaining an existing security plan

Estimated lesson time: 15 minutes

A security plan's value continues even after it's implemented. You must revisit the security plan periodically to make sure that it still meets the organization's security needs. Some events that can lead to the modification of a security plan include

- **Organizational structure change.** Companies change their structures periodically. A change from a centralized administrative model to a decentralized model can result in modification of an existing security plan to match the new security model.

- **Mergers and acquisitions.** The scope of an existing security plan may have to be expanded due to an organization's growth. The security plan may have to be modified so it can work in the larger network environment.

- **Change in security policy.** As an organization changes, its security policy might change too. The existing security plan should then be modified to reflect the organization's new views on security. For example, after an Internet hacking attack, the organization might want to implement encryption of all confidential information entered at the corporate Web site. The security policy should be modified to reflect this change in opinion.

- **Recent security updates to deployed software.** Microsoft regularly issues updates that address recently discovered security threats against the Windows 2000 operating system. You can determine the required updates for a Windows 2000–based computer by connecting to the *windowsupdate.microsoft.com* Web site.

Important   To deploy updates with a more centralized method, Microsoft regularly issues service packs for Windows 2000. These service packs include all security and operating system updates that were issued before the service pack's release. You can deploy the service packs to all Windows 2000–based computers by using either Microsoft System Management Server (SMS) or Windows 2000 scripting solutions.

Not all forces that influence a security plan come from within the organization. An organization's network security personnel must stay informed of the latest issues that affect network security. To keep an organization secure, the security personnel must ensure that the security plan addresses the current risks and threats that affect the network's resources.

Some sources that the security personnel can use to monitor the latest security issues include

- **Web–based security bulletins.** Several security services offer e-mail bulletins that are issued when new security risks arise. For example, you can subscribe to the Microsoft security bulletin service at *www.microsoft.com/ technet/security/notify.asp*.

- **Security newsgroups.** There are several newsgroups related to Windows 2000 security including *news://msnews.microsoft.com/microsoft.public. win2000.security*.

- **Checking hacker Web sites.** Several Web sites contain information on the latest hacking strategies that are used to compromise network security. Examples include *www.2600.com/* and *www.insecure.org/*.

Note   Many network security resources are available on the Internet. Always make sure that the sites are trustworthy before downloading utilities and installing them on your network. What may be promised as a security solution may turn out to be a security weakness after you install it. The software that you download to protect your network may actually open up your network services to a hacking attack.

Making the Decision

Table 17.2 outlines design decisions you face when ensuring that a security plan remains effective after the security plan is fully deployed.

Table 17.2 Design Decisions for Maintaining a Security Plan

To	Do the Following
Stay current with the latest security vulnerabilities	■ Subscribe to security bulletins that alert you of any recent security vulnerabilities for the software implemented at your organization. ■ Read industry trade magazines. ■ Visit Web sites related to network security and hacking.
Ensure that security plans continue to reflect security policy	■ Review all security plans at regularly scheduled intervals to determine if the plans still reflect the organization's security policy. ■ Update the security plan to reflect any changes in security policy.
Stay current with the latest fixes	■ For Windows–based software, use the *windowsupdate.microsoft.com* Web site to review your system for required updates. ■ Ensure that the latest hot fixes and service packs are applied to all computers in the organization. ■ Perform auditing of all deployed systems to ensure that the required updates and hot fixes are applied.

Applying the Decision

Fabrikam must appoint a representative from the security team who will determine if the security plan requires modification in the event new hacking vulnerabilities are found. This person must have the ability and the permission to modify the plan.

Lesson Summary

The process of securing a network doesn't end when a security plan is completed and deployed. Security is an ongoing, iterative process. You should review the security of all deployed resources periodically to ensure that security configuration still meets the organization's security needs and security policy.

Review

Answering the following questions will reinforce key information presented in this chapter. If you are unable to answer a question, review the appropriate lesson and then try the question again. Answers to the questions can be found in the appendix.

1. What role does an organization's security policy play in the design of security plans?

2. Most design decisions are a trade-off between competing forces. What are some of the competing forces that are affected when security is increased for a resource?

3. What are some methods a security manager can use to ensure that security is maintained after the plan is deployed?

4. To maintain current network security, you decide to install service packs as soon as they're released. Will this ensure that you're protected against the latest security vulnerabilities?

5. If your organization is bought out by a larger organization, how could this affect your existing security plans?

APPENDIX

Answers

Chapter 1

Page 20 ## Answers to Review Questions

1. Implementing multiple security protocols allows a wide array of client operating systems to interact securely with a Windows 2000 network.

2. The UNIX client can use multiple security protocols for authentication. In a default installation, the UNIX client could use Kerberos (if an interrealm trust is established between the Kerberos realm and an Active Directory domain) and secure channel (if using a Web browser) as security protocols for authentication.

3. A decentralized account management strategy can lead to several different Active Directory designs. The common characteristic in the designs is that the ability to create and manage accounts isn't restricted to a small group of administrators. Possible solutions include the deployment of child domains or the creation of an OU structure that allows account management to be delegated to required personnel.

4. When a network has a global presence, import/export rules may affect the deployment of strong encryption solutions. The United States currently restricts the export of strong encryption software to embargoed countries. Additionally, laws in foreign countries could require local managem ent of network resources. These laws can affect your Active Directory design for domain structure.

5. In order for you to determine whether the design meets the technical requirements, the technical requirements must be measurable. If they're not measurable, determining whether the security design meets the technical requirements can be difficult.

6. The lab environment must emulate the production network. This includes emulating any WAN links and possible bottlenecks that exist on the production network. If the lab environment doesn't emulate the production network, any performance measurements are invalid because they don't reflect the actual performance that will occur in production.

Chapter 2

Page 56

Answers to Activity Questions

1.

Policy	Success	Failure
Audit account logon events		✓
Audit account management	✓	✓
Audit directory service access		
Audit logon events		
Audit object access	✓	✓
Audit policy changes	✓	✓
Audit privilege use	✓	
Audit process tracking		
Audit system events	✓	✓

2. The only additional settings that must be completed would be setting the object audit settings on the \\server\budget folder. This would include determining whether to audit the entire folder, all subfolders, or just specific files. It would also include auditing the Everyone group or specific user groups.

3. You should apply the audit policy to the Domain Controllers OU. If you want the same auditing to take place at all Windows 2000 computer accounts, you could also apply the settings at the domain.

Page 59

Answers to Exercise 1 Questions

1. The amount of bandwidth available on the WAN link between London and Lima may require you to deploy a separate forest at the Lima location. You can determine this only by analyzing the amount of traffic involved with global catalog, schema, and configuration replication to the Lima location from London.

2. The requirement to restrict administrative management of the forest-wide administration groups would require duplication of effort if multiple forests are deployed. This would require the monitoring of membership of duplicate Enterprise Admins and Schema Admins groups.

3. Based on the current specifications, the Contoso network would require only a single forest. You have to implement separate forests only when multiple organizations want to prevent access to a common global catalog or when the schema must be different between locations. The replication traffic issue for the Lima site must be monitored because the WAN link could require a second forest to be deployed at the Lima site.

4. Contoso may decide to deploy multiple forests in the case of a merger with or acquisition by a second corporation. If the other organization has an existing Windows 2000 forest, the initial merger might require more than one forest. In time, the migration would lead to the merger of the two forests.

   Another scenario where it would be appropriate to deploy a second forest is for testing schema modifications. Because schema modifications are permanent, using a separate forest to test the schema modification routines and scripts will reduce the occurrences of incorrect schema modifications being applied to Active Directory.

Page 60

Answers to Exercise 2 Questions

1. The requirement to reduce the amount of replication traffic to the Lima location, Seattle's desire to implement a different minimum password length than the other offices, and the requirement to limit modification to the Enterprise Admins and Schema Admins groups are all business factors that will require separate domains.

2.

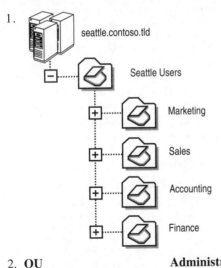

3. It would eliminate the need for a separate domain for Lima users.

Answers to Exercise 3 Questions

Page 60

Designing an OU Structure for Administration

1.

seattle.contoso.tld

Seattle Users

Marketing

Sales

Accounting

Finance

2.

OU	Administrators	Permissions
Seattle Users	Helpdesk	Reset Password
Seattle Users	Human Resources	Edit specific attributes
Seattle Users\Marketing	MarketAdmins	Edit User Objects
Seattle Users\Sales	SalesAdmins	Edit User Objects
Seattle Users\Accounting	AccountAdmins	Edit User Objects
Seattle Users\Finance	FinanceAdmins	Edit User Objects

Page 61   ## Designing an OU Structure for Group Policy Deployment

1.

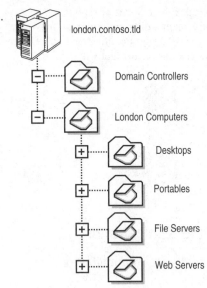

2.

OU	Apply the Security Template
London Computers\Desktops	Desktops
London Computers\Portables	Portables
London Computers\File Servers	File Servers
Domain Controllers	Domain Controllers
London Computers\Web Servers	Web Servers

Page 62   # Answers to Review Questions

1. In most cases a single organization will wish to implement only a single forest. Design factors that will require multiple forests include recent mergers or acquisitions and the need to maintain varying versions of the schema within an organization.

2. An empty forest root domain limits the number of users who can modify membership in the Enterprise Admins and Schema Admins groups. By default, a member of the forest root Domain Admins group is capable of changing membership in these forest-wide administration groups. By minimizing the accounts implemented in the forest root domain, you can better manage membership of the Domain Admins group.

3. If Group Policy isn't being applied in the standard order of local, site, domain, and then OU policy, it's likely that a Group Policy has been configured to block inheritance. You can prevent this by configuring higher-level OUs and containers to override any blocking attempts. To troubleshoot Group Policy application problems, you can use the Gpresult.exe tool from the *Microsoft Windows 2000 Resource Kit* to determine which group policies are applied to a computer or user at logon.

5. Enabling all audit options can cause the security log to fill with events very quickly. This can result in the computer being shut down due to a full event log if the security options are configured to do so. If you do enable a large amount of audit settings for a computer or an OU, you should consider increasing the default size of the security log and configuring what should take place when the security log fills.

Chapter 3

Page 101

Answers to Activity Questions

1. There's no global catalog server at the remote office. If the WAN link is down, the authenticating DC won't be able to access a global catalog server to enumerate universal group membership.

2. There must be at least two domains in the network. If it had just one domain, the authenticating domain controller would be able to determine universal group membership by looking at the domain naming context.

3. At the remote network, the lone domain controller must be configured as a global catalog server. In addition, the domain controller must also be configured as a DNS server so that SRV resource records can be found if the network link goes down.

4. If the DSClient software is loaded on the down-level clients, the down-level clients will require access to a DNS server to determine a domain controller in their site for authentication. The down-level clients will be able to find the local domain controller as long as they're set to include broadcast for NetBIOS name resolution.

   If system policy is enabled and the load-balancing option isn't enabled within system policy, Windows 95 and Windows 98 clients won't be able to contact the PDC emulator to load system policy.

Answers to Exercise 1 Questions

Page 104

Analyzing Server Placement

1. Windows 2000 client computers aren't PDC dependent. A Windows 2000 client can connect to any domain controller in the domain for password changes and for Group Policy application. But there are some WAN issues for processes that depend on the PDC emulator. For example, if administrators in Seattle are editing Group Policy, the MMC console connects to the PDC emulator of the domain by default.

2. The only office that doesn't have sufficient domain controller placement is Tampa. All authentication for the Tampa office must take place at the Seattle or London offices (where the domain controllers for the seattle.contoso.tld are located). At least one domain controller (two for fault tolerance) should be deployed at the Tampa office.

3. The Tampa and Lima offices don't have a local global catalog server. If the WAN link to the Seattle or London offices is unavailable, the authenticating DC won't be able to contact a global catalog server to determine universal group membership. This results in the user being logged on with cached credentials. At least one domain controller at each site should be configured as a global catalog server to ensure that logging on with cached credentials doesn't occur.

4. All DNS services are currently located at the London site in the contoso.tld domain. At least one server at each remote site should be configured as a secondary DNS server for the contoso.tld zone. Because all domain information for the four domains is contained in one zone, only the single zone must be created as a secondary at the remote sites. This ensures that if the WAN links are down, clients can locate network services on the local site.

Page 105

Analyzing Default Trust Relationships

1. Two-way transitive trust relationships are established between each child domain and the contoso.tld domain by default. These two-way transitive trust relationships provide access to all resources in the forest.

2. You could establish shortcut trusts between the London and Seattle domains to reduce the authentication process when accessing resources between the two domains. This results in one less referral ticket being issued, because the contoso.tld domain is bypassed during the authentication process.

Page 105

Answers to Exercise 2 Questions

1. All the down-level clients are using either LM or NTLM authentication, which isn't as secure as NTLMv2 authentication. The Windows for Workgroups 3.11 and Windows 98 clients use LM authentication, and the Windows NT 4.0 clients use NTLM authentication.

2. You must immediately upgrade the Windows for Workgroups clients to at least Windows 98. If the computers don't meet the minimum hardware requirements, remove them from the network. The Windows 98 and Windows NT 4.0 clients must have the DSClient software installed to ensure that NTLMv2 is used for authentication. The Windows NT 4.0 workstation clients should also have the latest service pack applied.

3. The DSClient software reduces the dependency on the PDC emulator for down-level clients. Rather than sending password changes to the PDC emulator, password changes can now be performed at a local domain controller. This is a great performance gain for Contoso because the PDC emulators are located at the London office.

   The DSClient software also makes the clients site-aware so that the clients can locate domain controllers on their own site, rather than using remote domain controllers. This reduces the dependency on WINS for remote logons.

4. The domain controllers must change the LMCompatibilityLevel setting to restrict authentication to NTLMv2 and disallow LM and NTLM authentication. This step also requires the removal of the Windows for Workgroups 3.11 clients from the network because they don't support NTLMv2 authentication.

Page 106

Answers to Review Questions

1. Kerberos authentication uses the time stamp as authorization data during an authentication process. The time stamp is encrypted using the long-term key shared between the KDC and the client computer. If the time stamp varies by more than 5 minutes with the current time at the KDC, the KDC assumes that a replay attack is taking place and the authentication attempt results in failure. The client can run **:NET TIME *domaincontroller* /SET"** (where *domaincontroller* is a variable representing the domain controller in question) to set the computer's clock to match that of the domain controller.

2. The Kerberos Authentication Service Exchange (KRB_AS_REQ) is used when a client initially authenticates on the network. The KRB_AS_REP that the KDC sends back to the client contains the TGT that the client uses to identify itself with the KDC when requesting service tickets. The Kerberos Ticket Granting Exchange (KRB_TGS_REQ) occurs when the client presents the TGT for the purpose of acquiring a service ticket in a Kerberos Ticket Granting Exchange Response (KRB_TGS_REP).

3. Smart card logons use the PKINIT extensions to the Kerberos protocol. Rather than using a long-term key to encrypt authentication data between the client and the KDC, the private key/public key pair is located on the user's smart card instead. Rather than using the standard KRB_AS_REQ and KRB_AS_REP messages, a smart card logon uses the PA_PK_AS_REQ and PA_PK_AS_REP messages. Because Kerberos is the authentication mechanism, smart card logons are only available to Windows 2000 client computers and can't be implemented at Windows 95, Windows 98, or Windows NT 4.0 client computers.

4. Kerberos protocol allows service tickets to have a forwardable flag. This indicates that a server can request a service ticket on behalf of a client computer. When the KDC issues the ticket to the server, it allows the server to run processes in the user's security context.

5. As an interim solution, you can deploy the DSClient to the Windows 98 computers. The DSClient makes the following enhancements to a Windows 98 client: NTLMv2 protocol, site awareness, the ability to search Active Directory for objects, a reduction in the dependency on the PDC, ADSI support, a DFS fault-tolerant client, and the ability to edit Active Directory objects using the WAB.

6. If the domain is in native mode, the authentication domain controllers must contact global catalog servers to expand universal group membership. Clients also contact global catalog servers when they authenticate using a UPN. The global catalog associates the UPN with a domain and user account. If either a global catalog server or a DNS server is unavailable, this can result in cached credentials being used. The DNS server must be available because DNS is used as the service locator service for finding domain controllers and global catalog servers.

Chapter 4

Page 134

Answers to Activity Questions

Tasks	Remote Administration Method
Create a new user account by using Active Directory Users And Computers	✓ a. RUNAS command b. Telnet Service ✓ c. Terminal Services d. Can't use Remote Administration in this scenario

To create a new user account, you can use either the RUNAS command to launch Active Directory Users And Computers under the security context of a user with the right to create user accounts. You could also use Terminal Services to connect to a domain controller using an administrative user account to run Active Directory Users And Computers.

Recover an encrypted file
using the domain's EFS
Recovery account

    a. RUNAS command
    b. Telnet Service
✓ c. Terminal Services
    d. Can't use Remote Administration in this scenario

To perform an EFS Recovery, you must load the profile of the user account where the private key for the EFS Recovery certificate is stored. Only by using Terminal Services could you remotely perform this task and still keep your current nonadministrative session active.

Run a batch file command
that requires administrative
access to the network

    a. RUNAS command
✓ b. Telnet Service
    c. Terminal Services
    d. Can't use Remote Administration in this scenario

Because the administrative process is a batch command, you can use the Telnet service to launch the batch file as an administrator of the network. If the computer where the Telnet Client is located is a Windows 2000–based computer, you can use NTLM authentication to secure the administrative credentials. If protection of all commands and output is required, you must implement IPSec.

Manage a Certification
Authority from a Windows
95 or Windows 98 computer

    a. RUNAS command
    b. Telnet Service
✓ c. Terminal Services
    d. Can't use Remote Administration in this scenario

Windows 2000 administrative MMC consoles can be run only from a Windows 2000–based computer. By using the Terminal Services client, a Windows 95 or Windows 98 client computer can remotely run the Certification Authority MMC.

Run an administrative process
by using an account that
requires a smart card for
authentication

    a. RUNAS command
    b. Telnet Service
    c. Terminal Services
✓ d. Can't use Remote Administration in this scenario

Remote administration doesn't support the use of smart cards for authentication. If the account requires a smart card for authentication, the process must be launched at a computer with a smart card reader.

Verify whether a user account
is locked out without inter-
rupting an application that's
running an hour-long process

✓ a. RUNAS command
    b. Telnet Service
    c. Terminal Services
    d. Can't use Remote Administration in this scenario

When you don't want to stop current processes from executing, the RUNAS command allows you to launch Active Directory Users And Computers without logging off the current user or stopping any currently executing processes.

Answers to Exercise 1 Questions

Page 138

Analyzing Administrative Group Membership

1. You must establish separate accounts for each of the administrators that are to be used when performing administrative tasks. These accounts must be separate from the accounts they use for day-to-day activities.

2. Peter Connelly must be made a member of four separate groups. Because he wants to be able to back up and restore data in the four domains that make up the Contoso Ltd. Active Directory—contoso.tld, london.contoso.tld, seattle.contoso.tld, and lima.contoso.tld—he must be a member of the Backup Operators group in each of the domains.

3. Scott Gode must be made a member of the DNS Admins group. If the DNS design for Contoso has all of the domains within a single Active Directory–integrated zone (contoso.tld), then Scott will require membership only in the forest root domain's DNS Admins group. If each of the subdomains has a delegated DNS subdomain that's managed locally, then Scott must be a member of the DNS Admins group in each of the domains where Active Directory–integrated zones exist.

4. Kate Dresen must be a member of the Schema Admins group in the forest root domain (contoso.tld).

5. Only if the contoso.tld domain is in mixed mode. In that case the Schema Admins group would be a global group, rather than a universal group. This would require that Kate's administrative account be located in the contoso.tld domain.

6.
User	Group Membership
Elizabeth Boyle	Lima\Account Operators
Suzan Fine	Seattle\Account Operators
Thom McCann	London\Account Operators

7. Each of the three accounts could have been delegated administrative rights for the domain that it is responsible for. This delegation would require only administrative permissions for user and computer objects.

8. Jörg must be made a member of the Group Policy Creators Owners group in each of the four domains. Membership in this group allows the creation of new Group Policy objects as well as management of existing Group Policy objects.

9. Because the forest-wide administration accounts (Enterprise Admins and Schema Admins) are located in the forest root domain, making Lisa a member of the contoso\Domain Admins group gives her the ability to manage membership of the forest-wide administrative groups.

Page 139

Protecting Administrative Group Membership

1. The Restricted Groups policy must be applied to each of the four domains, because there are groups that require protection in each of the four domains. In each domain the Restricted Groups policy will be applied to the Domain Controllers OU.

2. It's still possible to change a group's membership when a Restricted Groups policy is applied. The group membership change will last only until the next time the Group Policy is applied. By default, this period is every 5 minutes for domain controllers.

3. Enable both success and failure auditing for Account Management at the Domain Controllers OU for each of the four domains.

4.

Group	Members	Member of
Enterprise Admins	London\Administrator London\Domain Admins	Contoso\Administrators, Lima\Administrators, London\Administrators, Seattle\Administrators
Schema Admins	London\Adminstrator	None
Contoso\Domain Admins	Contoso\Administrator	Contoso\Administrators
Lima\Domain Admins	Lima\Administrator	Lima\Administrators
London\Domain Admins	London\Administrator	London\Administrators
Seattle\Domain Admins	Seattle\Administrator	Seattle\Administrators
Contoso\Administrators	Contoso\Domain Admins	N/A
Lima\Administrators	Lima\Domain Admins	N/A
London\Administrators	London\Domain Admins	N/A
Seattle\Administrators	Seattle\Domain Admins	N/A

5. Contoso should perform manual audits of the administrative group memberships at regular intervals. At these intervals Contoso can review and, if necessary, define memberships for the Restricted Groups policy.

Page 140

Answers to Exercise 2 Questions

1. In addition to their day-to-day user accounts, each user can also be assigned a second account for administrative functions. To differentiate between the two accounts, you could use a prefix such as "a-" or "a_" to identify the administrative account.

2. You can't require that the default administrator account in a domain have a smart card or be restricted to a specific workstation.

3. You could create an additional account that would be a member of the Enterprise Admins group. You could then restrict this newly created account to log on at londondc1 and londondc2 by using either workstation restrictions, smart card restrictions, or a combination of the two.

4. The newly created account would have to be included in the Member Of box of the Enterprise Admins group in restricted groups.

5. The two account operators could either use the RunAs service to launch Active Directory Users And Computers under the security context of their administrative account or they could use Terminal Services to connect to a domain controller and run Active Directory Users And Computers within the terminal sessions.

6. Because Elizabeth's primary workstation is a Windows 98 computer, she can't use the RunAs service or a custom MMC console. Elizabeth would have to use the Terminal Services client to connect to a Windows 2000–based server to perform administrative functions.

7. The Seattle administrator could use Telnet to run administrative scripts. The security risk in this form of management is that authentication, all typed commands, and all returned responses are sent on the network in clear text. The UNIX workstation wouldn't be able to use NTLM authentication, so IPSec must be considered to protect this sensitive data.

Page 142

Answers to Review Questions

1. Just because you're an administrator doesn't mean that you require administrative access to all functions within a domain. This can result in excess privileges being assigned to an account.

2. No. Restricted Groups policy is applied at regular intervals when Group Policy is applied. At a domain controller, the default interval is every 5 minutes. There's a brief window of opportunity where the membership of a restricted group can be modified before Group Policy resets the membership to the desired membership.

3. This is an excess allocation of rights. With Windows 2000, you could delegate the ability to reset the password on user accounts for a domain only to a Help Desk group. This provides only the help desk with the required permissions.

4. Smart card logon can't be used in conjunction with the RunAs service or Terminal Services. If an account requires the use of a smart card, the administrative user will be forced to log on as that user at the workstation using the smart card to perform administrative tasks. This assumes that the user has a smart card reader at her computer.

5. To determine what security context a process is running under, an administrator can display the account associated with a process by using Pulist.exe from the *Microsoft Windows 2000 Server Resource Kit*. Or if Terminal Services are loaded, the Task Manager can display the User Name column.

6. The administrator at a UNIX workstation would be restricted to running text-based administrative utilities. With the installation of the *Microsoft Windows 2000 Server Resource Kit* at the Telnet server, several utilities can actually be used. The security risks of doing Telnet administration include the exposure of user account and password information in clear text on the network. Additionally, all screen display and keyboard input is transmitted in clear text by default.

Chapter 5

Page 157

Answers to Activity Questions

1. The three domains in the technology.tld forest are running in mixed mode. The domains must be in native mode to allow global group in global group memberships and the use of domain local groups at a Windows 2000 member server. If you don't convert the domains to native mode (which isn't possible with Windows NT 4.0 BDCs), this proposal won't work.

2. This strategy will work because in mixed mode, global groups from the domain can be made members of a computer local group stored in the application server's local account database.

3. The three domains in the technology.tld forest are running in mixed mode. The domains must be in native mode to allow universal security groups. If you don't convert the domains to native mode (which isn't possible with Windows NT 4.0 BDCs), this proposal won't work.

4. Although this proposal looks similar to the second proposal, member servers are unable to recognize domain local groups in a mixed-mode environment. Domain local groups are shared among domain controllers only when in native mode.

Page 168

Answers to Exercise 1 Questions

1. The slow WAN link between London and Lima could be a bottleneck for global catalog membership. If universal groups were to be used in securing resources for the Human Resources application, this could affect it.

2. Your security design must ensure that universal groups don't contain user accounts but global groups. Doing this prevents the membership of the universal groups from frequently changing and creating WAN traffic due to global catalog replication.

3.

Category	Global Group(s)	Membership
Application Managers	■ Lima\AppManagers ■ Seattle\AppManagers ■ London\AppManagers	All Application managers. One global group for each domain.
HR Managers	■ Lima\HRManagers ■ Seattle\HRManagers ■ London\HRManagers	All HR managers. One global group for each domain.
HR Department	■ Lima\HRDept ■ Seattle\HRDept ■ London\HRDept	All members of the HR department. One global group for each domain.
Employees	■ Lima\Domain Users* ■ Seattle\Domain Users* ■ London\Domain Users*	Makes the assumption that all domain users are employees.

* As an alternative, you could use a custom global group that contains all employees if Domain Users contains some non-employee accounts.

4.

Domain Local Group	Membership	Where Deployed
London\AppMgrAccess	■ Lima\AppManagers ■ Seattle\AppManagers ■ London\AppManagers	■ HRLondon ■ Web
London\HRMgrAccess	■ Lima\HRManagers ■ Seattle\HRManagers ■ London\HRManagers	■ HRLondon ■ Web
London\HRAccess	■ Lima\HRDept ■ Seattle\HRDept ■ London\HRDept	■ HRLondon ■ Web
London\HRAppEEAccess	■ Lima\Domain Users* ■ Seattle\Domain Users* ■ London\Domain Users*	■ HRLondon ■ Web

* If custom global groups were created to represent employees, these global groups would be a member of the HRAppEEAccess domain local group.

5.

Domain Local Group	Membership	Where Deployed
Lima\AppMgrAccess	■ Lima\AppManagers ■ Seattle\AppManagers ■ London\AppManagers	■ HRLima
Lima\HRMgrAccess	■ Lima\HRManagers ■ Seattle\HRManagers ■ London\HRManagers	■ HRLima
Lima\HRAccess	■ Lima\HRDept ■ Seattle\HRDept ■ London\HRDept	■ HRLima
Lima\HRAppEEAccess	■ Lima\Domain Users* ■ Seattle\Domain Users* ■ London\Domain Users*	■ HRLima

* If custom global groups were created to represent employees, these global groups would be a member of the HRAppEEAccess domain local group.

6.

Domain Local Group	Membership	Where Deployed
Seattle\AppMgrAccess	■ Lima\AppManagers ■ Seattle\AppManagers ■ London\AppManagers	■ HRSeattle
Seattle\HRMgrAccess	■ Lima\HRManagers ■ Seattle\HRManagers ■ London\HRManagers	■ HRSeattle
Seattle\HRAccess	■ Lima\HRDept ■ Seattle\HRDept ■ London\HRDept	■ HRSeattle
Seattle\HRAppEEAccess	■ Lima\Domain Users* ■ Seattle\Domain Users* ■ London\Domain Users*	■ HRSeattle

* If custom global groups were created to represent employees, these global groups would be a member of the HRAppEEAccess domain local group.

7. For each collection of three global groups, you must define a universal group that would contain the three global groups as members. The universal group would then be made a member of the domain local group associated with the universal group.

8. WAN traffic related to changes in universal group memberships can be minimized by limiting membership in universal groups to global groups. This way the changes to the global groups won't affect the membership of the universal groups. Doing this will prevent changes to the storage of universal group membership in the global catalog.

Page 170

Answers to Exercise 2 Questions

1. The name of the account should not in any way reflect the service account's function. Just looking at the name of the account shouldn't reveal what access it may have on the network.

2. You could create the service account in either the london.contoso.tld or contoso.tld domains (because the head office is in London).

3. No. With the Windows 2000 transitive trust model, the account could be located in any of the four domains for usage in all domains.

4. In each of the three domains, you must collect the Human Resources application servers into a single OU. Creating a custom OU ensures that Group Policy can be applied uniformly only to the Human Resources application servers for the application of user rights at that OU.

5. You must assign the service account the Log On As A Service and Act As Part Of The Operating System user rights.

Page 171

Answers to Review Questions

1. Universal groups are stored in the global catalog. Changes in membership of a universal group will cause WAN replication traffic as the modifications are replicated to all global catalog servers in the forest.

2. If the universal group contains members who aren't from the same domain, this will prevent the conversion to a global group. By definition, global groups can only contain members from the same domain where the global group is defined.

3. Eva didn't assign the user rights to allow her account to log on locally at the correct location. Local policy is always overwritten if Group Policy is defined at the site, domain, or OU. Because Eva can log on locally at all other servers, there must be an OU Group Policy that assigns the Log On Locally user right at the Marketing OU. Using another account, Eva must grant her account the Log On Locally user right at the Marketing OU.

4. The Add Workstations To A Domain user right allows the assigned user to add only up to 10 computers within the domain. Since the contractor will be adding more computers than that to the domain, you must delegate the Create Computer Objects permission to the domain so that the contractor can continue to add newly created computers to the domain.

Chapter 6

Page 190

Answers to Activity Questions

1. Megan's effective permissions would be as follows:

   - Marketing: No access. Megan isn't a member of the Marketing project, the Marketing department, or management.

   - E-commerce: While based on NTFS permissions, Megan would have Modify permissions based on her membership in the E-commerce group, her effective permissions would only be Read permissions as the Share permissions would be the more restrictive permissions.

   - PKI Deployment: Although based on NTFS permissions, Megan would have Modify permissions because of her membership in the PKI Project group, her effective permissions would only be Read permissions, as the Share permissions would be the more restrictive permissions.

   - Windows 2000 Migration: Both NTFS permissions and share permissions offer Megan Read permissions for the Windows 2000 Migration folder. The IT Department is assigned the Read NTFS permission and the share permissions allow the Users group Read permissions.

2. You must change the share permissions to allow Change permissions. You could do this in a number of ways. One way would be to grant the Users group change permissions for the Projects share. Alternatively, you could assign the four project teams (Marketing Project, E-commerce Project, PKI Project, and Migration Project) Change permission to the projects share.

3. This wouldn't affect Megan's effective permissions because the Modify permissions assigned to the PKI Project and E-commerce Project teams are closer to the folder where the permissions are applied. These permissions would take precedence over the inherited permissions from the Projects folder.

Answers to Exercise 1 Questions

Page 206

Planning Share Security

1. The Users domain local group must be assigned the Change permission. This permission allows users to read, create, modify, and delete documents in their personal folders. It also allows them to create, modify, and delete personal documents in the transfer folder. In addition, the Administrators group requires Full Control permissions to the shared folder to allow them to manage permissions and documents in the hierarchy.

2. You should set the share permissions for the each username share so that there is only a single entry. You should set the share permissions so that only the user who the folder is named for has Change permissions. This ensures that only that user can connect to the share.

3. You don't have to create individual user folders if all client computers are running Windows 2000. If they are, the users could connect to \\server\users\username and this would be established as an artificial root directory. Previous versions of Windows didn't provide this functionality.

Page 207

Planning NTFS Security

1. Contoso requires that only the creator of a document should be allowed to modify the file; all other users of that file are restricted to Read permissions. This circumstance requires that you define special permissions for the Transfer folder.

2.

Folder	Permissions
D:\Users	▪ Administrators: Full Control ▪ Users: List Folder Contents
D:\Users\User1	▪ User1: Modify
D:\Users\User2	▪ User2: Modify
D:\Users\User3	▪ User3: Modify
D:\Users\Transfer	▪ Creator Owner: Modify ▪ TransferAdmins: Modify ▪ Users: Read ▪ Users: Create Files

The d:\users folder requires that only administrators have Full Control permission. This permission will be inherited by all other folders in the hierarchy by default and doesn't have to be assigned elsewhere. Likewise, users require only the List Folder Contents permission to see the folders that they have permission to access.

The individual user accounts are the only security principals that require access to their individual home directories. Modify permissions will meet security requirements. If you assign Full Control permissions, this could result in the user changing the permissions to allow other users access to the home folder.

The transfer folder requires the use of special permissions. Assigning Read and Create Files permissions to the Users group allows users to create new files and read existing files. By making use of the special group Creator Owner, you can allow the creator of the document to have Modify permissions. You do this by examining the document to determine who owns it. Finally, the Transfer Admins domain local group also requires Modify permissions to manage documents in the Transfer folder.

3. In Active Directory Users And Computers, the home directory attribute is defined in the Account tab of the individual user's Properties dialog box.

Page 207

Answers to Exercise 2 Questions

1. By changing the printer permissions for the Legal printer, you can create a domain local group that will have Print permissions to the legal department. The Everyone group should be removed from the DACL so that the Everyone group no longer has Print permissions.

2.

Group	Permissions
Administrators	Print, Manage Printers, Manage Documents
Print Operators	Print, Manage Printers, Manage Documents
Legal Department	Print
Creator Owner	Manage Documents

3. The Legal printer must be physically placed in a location that's accessible only by authorized users. This could be as simple as putting the printer in a room that requires a card key, a PIN code, or another method of identification to enter the room.

4. You can define IPSec to protect all print jobs submitted to the Legal printer. To provide total end-to-end protection, the Legal printer must be directly attached to the print server hosting the Legal printer. At this time IPSec aware network cards for printers aren't available. If the printer is a network-attached printer, the print job would be vulnerable to inspection by a network sniffer as it's sent from the print server to the network printer. Network sniffers are able to view the contents of unencrypted data packets as they're transmitted across the network.

Page 208

Answers to Exercise 3 Questions

1. In Active Directory you must create a separate OU in each domain for laptop computers. The OU might or might not have additional child OUs defined to separate the laptop computers by department. The separate OU is required so that a Group Policy object can be defined that will implement an EFS recovery agent.

2. The Group Policy object must be linked to OU=Laptops, OU=Corporate Computers, DC=london, DC=contoso, DC=tld. You don't need to apply it at the two child OUs because Group Policy inheritance results in the Group Policy being applied to both child OUs.

3. In the Default Domain policy, the existing EFS recovery agent must be deleted from Computer Configuration\Windows Settings\Security Settings\Public Key Policies\Encrypted Data Recovery Agents. Be sure to save this as an empty set, and don't delete the entire policy. Only an empty set prevents EFS encryption from being performed.

4. The EFS recovery private key can be stored in a PKCS#12 file on a removable medium such as a Jaz drive, a floppy disk, or a CD-ROM. Then it can be stored in a safe that requires two-factor authentication. For example, each administrator might know only half of the safe's combination so neither can open the safe without the other's cooperation.

5. During the export process you can protect the private key with a password. Unless you know the password, you can't extract the private key from the PKCS #12 file.

Page 210

Answers to Review Questions

1. Yes. If Scott's computer dual boots with Windows 98, the C drive must be either FAT or FAT32. This means that Scott can't define NTFS permissions to further secure the data. If anyone were to log on locally at Scott's computer, that person could access the contacts database and either delete it or modify entries.

2. The default Share permissions allow the Everyone group the Full Control permission. If Bob hasn't configured NTFS permissions to allow only his and Brian's accounts access, then anyone on the network can access documents in the newly shared folder. Leaving the default Share permissions forces you to have exact NTFS permissions.

3. Network print devices currently don't have IPSec capabilities. While IPSec protects data transmissions from the client computers to the print server, it can't be used to protect the data transmission to the network print device. To provide the required level of security, the print device must be locally attached to the print server.

4. The administrator of the domain can open all encrypted files on the network. Many people consider this counterproductive to security. To better secure EFS recovery, you must define a separate EFS recovery agent and you must export the private EFS recovery key to removable storage for use in the future.

5. This proposal won't work because EFS is based on a single user's private key to decrypt the file encryption key. The only way to share the document securely is to store the document on an NTFS partition and configure NTFS permissions to allow the two users only Modify access to the document. No other accounts should have access to the document.

Chapter 7

Page 229

Answers to Activity Questions

1. The application of software can be either a computer or a user setting in Group Policy. This makes troubleshooting this problem more complicated.

2. If the software is assigned in user configuration, Don's user account probably wasn't moved to the Accounting OU from the Human Resources OU. This results in the Group Policy still being applied to his user account. If the software is assigned in computer configuration, Don's computer account probably wasn't moved to the Accounting OU and the Human Resources Group Policy is still being applied to his computer.

3. Don's user account must still be a member of the Human Resources domain local group. Group membership deletions are commonly missed when a user is transferred from one department to another.

Page 233

Answers to Exercise 1 Questions

1. Assuming that you don't want to implement the Block Policy Inheritance or No Override attributes, you could apply the Hide Entire Network Group Policy object at one of two locations: either at the domain (seattle.contoso.tld) or at the Seattle Users OU (OU=Seattle Users, DC=seattle, DC=contoso, DC=tld). Either location would affect all users in the domain.

2. Within the Active Directory hierarchy, client computers could include both portable and desktop computers. Because of default inheritance, you'd have to apply the Group Policy object named "Rename Default Accounts" at both the Desktops OU (OU=Desktops, OU=Seattle Computers, DC=seattle, DC=contoso, DC=tld) and the Portables OU (OU=Portables, OU=Seattle Computers, DC=seattle, DC=Contoso, DC=tld).

3. You could apply the Disable Control Panel Group Policy object at either the domain (seattle.contoso.tld) or at the Seattle Users OU (OU=Seattle Users, DC=seattle, DC=contoso, DC=tld). Either location would affect all users in the domain.

4. You would apply the Accounting Logon Script Group Policy object at the Desktops OU to meet design requirements. There isn't a separate OU that contains only computers for the Accounting department.

5. Yes. The Hide Entire Network, Disable Control Panel, and Accounting Logon Script Group Policy objects all require security group filtering to fully meet design requirements.

Page 233

Answers to Exercise 2 Questions

1. You must configure security group filtering so that the Administrators group and a custom Domain Local group that contains the members of the IT department would have the Deny permission for Apply Group Policy. The Users or Authenticated Users group would have the Read and Apply Group Policy permissions. The Deny permission would take precedence over the Allow permissions.

2. You must configure security group filtering so that the Administrators group and the Server Operators group would have the Deny permission for Apply Group Policy. The Users or Authenticated Users group would have the Read and Apply Group Policy permissions. The Deny permission would take precedence over the Allow permissions.

3. You can't combine the two Group Policy objects into a single Group Policy object because the settings are applied to different sets of users. You can combine them into a single Group Policy object only if the Group Policy settings are to be applied to the same security groups.

4. If you apply the Rename Default Accounts Group Policy object at the Seattle Computers OU, you have to apply security group filtering so that the Group Policy object was applied only to desktop and portable computers. This would require you to create two custom domain local groups that contained the computer accounts for all desktop and laptop computers in the domain. These Domain Local groups would require Read and Apply Group Policy permissions for the Group Policy object.

5. Create another OU named Accounting below the Desktops OU and apply the Accounting Logon Script to the new OU.

Answers to Exercise 3 Questions

Page 234

Determining Effective Group Policy Settings

1. No. The Disable Control Panel policy is applied at the Seattle Users OU and by inheritance, Julie would be unable to access the Control Panel.

2. No. The Hide Entire Network Group Policy is applied to the Sales OU and as a member of the Sales group, Julie wouldn't be able to access the Entire Network icon in My Network Places.

3. Yes. The Enable Control Panel Group Policy is applied to the IT OU. This setting would have precedence over the Disable Control Panel Group Policy applied to the Seattle Users OU.

Page 235

Determining the Effect of Blocking Policy Inheritance and No Override

1. Yes. The Block Policy Inheritance setting would prevent the application of the Disable Control Panel Group Policy applied at the Seattle Users OU. This is true even though the Group Policy object applied at the Sales OU has nothing to do with the Disable Control Panel setting.

2. No. The Hide Entire Network Group Policy is applied to the Sales OU and as a member of the Sales group, Julie wouldn't be able to access the Entire Network icon in My Network Places.

3. The administrator could enable the No Override attribute for the Disable Control Panel at the Seattle Users OU to ensure that Block Policy Inheritance would have no effect on the child OUs.

4. You must change the discretionary access control list (DACL) for the Disable Control Panel Group Policy object at the Seattle Users OU so that the IT Department is assigned the Deny permission for Apply Group Policy. This ensures that the Disable Control Panel Group Policy isn't applied to members of the IT Department.

Page 237

Answers to Review Questions

1. The Group Policy settings take precedence if the default inheritance model ensues. Group Policy settings at the OU where the object is located take precedence over settings applied at the domain.

2. Yes. The Deny Apply Group Policy permission would supersede the Allow Apply Group Policy setting assigned to the Users group.

3. No. You must apply account policy settings at the domain to affect all domain users. In this scenario the two domains would require you to configure account policy settings at the domain.

4. You could apply Group Policy to the computer from the following locations:

   - The Corporate Site

   - The DC=abc, DC=com domain

   - The OU=Europe, DC=abc, DC=com OU

   - The OU=Lisbon, OU=Europe, DC=abc, DC=com

   - The OU=Accounting, OU=Lisbon, OU=Europe, DC=abc, DC=com

   - The OU=Computers, OU=Accounting, OU=Lisbon, OU=Europe, DC=abc, DC=com

   - The computer's local GPO

5. The Gpresult utility shows which Group Policy objects were applied to a user or computer. If you used **GPRESULT /C /S**, you'd receive a super verbose listing of all Group Policy objects applied to the computer.

Chapter 8

Page 261

Answers to Activity Questions

1. At first glance, the security template appears to prevent users from reusing passwords within 2 years. Passwords have a two-month maximum password age and password history is enforced at 12 passwords being remembered. Unfortunately, with the minimum password age set to be 2 days, a user can reuse a previous password within 24 days.

2. You must increase the minimum password age to 60 days. In reality, a minimum password age of 30 days is probably all that's required, because after 30 days the user will probably be used to the new password and unwilling to change it. You would set the minimum password age at 60 days only if you require strict enforcement of the password reuse policy.

3. The security template actually exceeds the minimum password length requirement.

4. No. The security template stores passwords with reversible encryption, which weakens the security of passwords in Active Directory. You should use this setting only if you use Challenge Handshake Authentication Protocol (CHAP) for remote access or implement digest authentication for Web services.

5. Yes. The proposed security template enables the use of complexity requirements for passwords. The enabling of complexity requirements ensures that passwords must contain three of the four components: uppercase letters, lowercase letters, numbers, and symbols. The complexity requirements also prevent users from using their account names as their passwords.

6. Password policies are part of account policies within Group Policy. You must import the security template into the Default Domain Policy to ensure that all domain controllers enforce the password policy settings.

Page 279

Answers to Exercise 1 Questions

1.

Server Classification	Total # of Computers
Domain controllers	13 computers (2 in the contoso.tld domain, 2 in the london.contoso.tld domain, 5 in the seattle.contoso.tld domain, and 4 in the lima.contoso.tld domain)
File and print servers	6 computers (2 in the london.contoso.tld domain, 2 in the seattle.contoso.tld domain, and 2 in the lima.contoso.tld domain)
Mail servers	4 computers (1 in the contoso.tld domain, 1 in the london.contoso.tld domain, 1 in the seattle.contoso.tld domain, and 1 in the lima.contoso.tld domain)
Terminal servers	3 computers (1 in the london.contoso.tld domain, 1 in the seattle.contoso.tld domain, and 1 in the lima.contoso.tld domain)
Web servers	Two Web servers in a workgroup
Sales force operations	Two servers in the contoso.tld domain servers

2.

Computer Type	Template	Installation Method
DCs (Windows NT 4.0 upgrades)	Basicdc.inf	Manual
DCs (new installations)	Defltdc.inf	Automatic
Mail servers (new installations)	Defltsv.inf	Automatic
Client computers (new installations)	Defltwk.inf	Automatic
Client computers (upgrades from Windows NT 4.0)	Basicwk.inf	Manual
Client computers (upgrades from Windows 98)	Defltwk.inf	Automatic

Answers to Exercise 2 Questions

Page 280

Determining Incremental Template Requirements

1. No. Applying the High Security security template prevents down-level clients from participating in the network. When you apply the High Security security templates, only Windows 2000 computers can participate in the network.

2. You could deploy the Secure security template to increase the security over the default level.

3. The Nottssid.inf security template will remove the Terminal Services Users group from all DACLs. Removing this group from all DACLs will require users to have explicit permissions to resources on the terminal server.

Page 281   ## Designing Custom Templates for Server Classifications

1. Two. The account policy settings for password requirements must be applied at the domain, and the audit settings for the domain controllers must be applied at the Domain Controllers OU.

2. The domain controller must configure Password Policy to require a minimum password length of eight characters and to enable password complexity requirements.

3. Password policies are a subset of account policies, and to enforce them you must apply them at the domain by importing the security template into the Default Domain Policy.

4. The domain controller must configure auditing for success and failure for account management and account logon events.

5. You must import audit configuration to the Domain Controllers OU.

6. Yes. You can define NTFS permissions in the security template and import them into each domain—as long as the NTFS permissions are consistent across the domains and use default security groups.

Page 281   ## Extending the Security Configuration Tool Set to Support the Sales Force Operations Application

1. No. You must extend the Security Configuration Tool Set to include additional registry settings.

2. You must edit the Sceregvl.inf file to include the additional registry entries.

3. ```
[Register Registry Values]
MACHINE\Software\Contoso\SFO\Parameters\EnableSSL,3,%SFOSSL%,0
MACHINE\Software\Contoso\SFO\Parameters\SSLPort,4,%SFOPort%,1
```

4. ```
[Strings]
SFOSSL = Enable SSL Encryption for Sales Force Operations
SFOPort = Configure the SSL Listening Port for the Sales Force
Operations Application
```

5. You must reregister Scecli.dll by running the command REGSVR32 SCECLI.DLL.

Page 282   # Answers to Exercise 3 Questions

1. You can import all the security templates into Group Policy, with the exception of the Web Server security template because the Web servers aren't members of the Windows 2000 domain structure. The Web servers are members of a workgroup.

2.

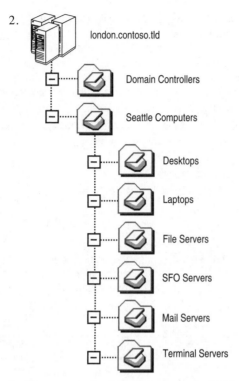

london.contoso.tld

Domain Controllers

Seattle Computers

Desktops

Laptops

File Servers

SFO Servers

Mail Servers

Terminal Servers

3. You can use the Secedit command with the /CONFIGURE parameter to ensure that the Web server security template is always applied to the Web servers. By using the Scheduled Tasks program in Control Panel, you can run the Secedit command at regular intervals.

Page 283

Answers to Review Questions

1. The Default security templates are applied automatically during a new installation of Windows 2000. You can apply Basic templates to Windows 2000 installations that are upgraded from Windows NT 4.0. The Basic template applies the default security of Windows 2000 to an upgraded computer. The main difference between the two templates is that the Basic template doesn't modify any existing user rights assignments.

2. An upgrade from Windows 95 to Windows 2000 automatically uses the Defltwk.inf security template. This upgrade requires the file system to be upgraded to NTFS to ensure the highest level of security. In addition, any user accounts that were created in Windows 95 (if multiple profiles are enabled), are made members of the Administrators local group.

3. By default, DACLs on the terminal server include the Terminal Server Users domain local group. This group includes all users who are connected to the terminal server. If you apply the Notssid.inf security template, the Terminal Server Users domain local group is removed from all DACLs and user access is based on the individual user accounts and their group memberships.

4. You have three alternatives for configuring the application to run in a Windows 2000 environment. First, you can apply the Compatws.inf security template to the Windows

2000–based computers to downgrade security to emulate the default Windows NT 4.0 environment. Second, you can make the Domain Users global group a member of the local Power Users group. This group is security equivalent to the Users group in Windows NT 4.0. Finally, you can determine which areas of the disk and registry the application requires elevated access to. Once you determine these areas, you can modify permissions to allow the application to execute correctly.

5. Because Novell NetWare 4.11 is your default network, you won't be able to use Group Policy to deploy the security template. In this case the easiest way to apply the security template would be to create a logon script that runs the Secedit command with the /CONFIGURE parameter.

6.

Setting	Rating (Below, Meets, Exceeds)	Rationale
Enforce password history	Exceeds	The current settings will remember the last 18 passwords, while the template recommends 0 passwords.
Maximum password age	Below	The security template recommends changing passwords every 42 days, while the current settings require changing passwords every 70 days.
Minimum password age	Meets	Both settings are 0 days.
Minimum password length	Exceeds	The current settings require a minimum pass word length of seven characters, while while the template allows NULL passwords.
Passwords must meet complexity requirements	Exceeds	The current settings require complex passwords, while the security template doesn't.
Store passwords using reversible encryption	Below	The current settings enable this option. Unless digest authentication or Challenge Handshake Authentication Protocol (CHAP) authentication is required, don't use this setting.

7. You should design Active Directory so that an OU exists for each computer classification. By doing this, you can import the associated security template into the Group Policy object for the OU so that the template is applied to all computer accounts in the OU or within any sub-OUs.

Chapter 9

Page 296

Answers to Activity Questions

1. The external DNS server must host only the organization.tld domain.

2.

Host	IP Address or Contents
mail.organization.tld	131.107.2.45
www.organization.tld	131.107.2.25
ftp.organization.tld	131.107.2.24
dns.organization.tld	131.107.2.20

3. You must create a Mail Exchanger (MX) resource record that sets mail.organization.tld as the mail exchanger for the organization.tld domain. This action allows incoming e-mail to reach the organization.

4. The internal DNS server must host only the ad.organization.tld domain.

5. No. You could simply configure a forwarder so that unresolved DNS requests at the internal DNS server are forwarded to the external DNS server. This would be the case for any DNS queries for the organization.tld DNS domain because the internal DNS server wouldn't be authoritative for that zone.

6.

DNS Resource Record	IP Address or Contents
mail.organization.tld	192.168.2.10
MX record for organization.tld	mail.organization.tld

Page 325

Answers to Exercise 1 Questions

1. Yes. The DNS zone is configured to allow dynamic updates, rather than enforcing secure dynamic updates. This configuration doesn't meet the security requirement to allow only authenticated computers to register DNS resource records in the zone. Change the Allow Dynamic Updates option to Only Secure Updates to enforce security on DNS dynamic updates.

2. The DNS servers for contoso.tld are currently available to requests from both internal and external DNS clients. Because contoso.tld is also the Active Directory forest root, this exposes their internal network addressing scheme.

3. You must establish a separate DNS server for external queries to contoso.tld. The external DNS server requires that only the specified resource records are included in the zone data. All address information for the DNS zone must be external IP addresses, not internal IP addresses.

4. Domain controllers in the London, Seattle, and Lima domains must configure secondary DNS zones for the contoso.tld DNS domain. Active Directory–integrated zones are stored in the domain naming context and can't be replicated outside of the domain. Only by using zone transfers can the data be made available in the child domains.

5. You must restrict the properties for zone transfers of the contoso.tld domain so that zone transfers can be requested only by the following IP addresses: 172.28.5.2, 172.28.5.3, 172.28.9.2, 172.28.9.3, 172.28.13.2, and 172.28.13.3. You don't have to include the two DNS servers in the contoso.tld domain, because the zone information is replicated by using Active Directory replication.

6. You must configure all DNS zones stored on the DNS servers in the London, Seattle, and Lima domains to prevent zone transfers.

Page 326

Answers to Exercise 2 Questions

1. The DHCP Service at the Lima office is installed on a domain controller and is also a member of the DNSUpdateProxy group. Membership in this group prevents the DHCP server from taking ownership of the resource records it registers in DNS.

2. The domain controller won't take ownership of the SRV resource records or any resource records that it registers in DNS. The resource records could be "hijacked" and replaced with incorrect address information.

3. Move the DHCP Service to a member server, rather than hosting the DHCP Service on a domain controller.

4. Only Windows 2000–based DHCP services can be registered in Active Directory. Previous versions of Windows DHCP services don't verify if they are authorized in Active Directory before activating their scopes. The same holds true for third-party DHCP services.

5. Contoso must watch for symptoms of an unauthorized DHCP server. You can identify the unauthorized DHCP server by inspecting the IP configuration of a client that has received incorrect DHCP configuration information. You can't prevent unauthorized DHCP servers from issuing IP configuration information if they aren't Windows 2000–based.

Page 326

Answers to Exercise 3 Questions

1. The DACLs for the Templates subfolder within each RIS Image folder structure must be modified to allow read permissions to only members of the department who are associated with the RIS image. If the client can't read the Templates subfolder, the RIS image won't be presented to the client.

2. Create a Windows 2000 security group that contains all user accounts that are members of the department. Create domain local groups for the Sales, Marketing, IT, and Accounting departments. For the specific image, only the domain local group allowed to install the image must be assigned Read permissions to the Template subfolder.

3. No. Separate RIS servers must be deployed with each RIS server hosting only a single image. Configure each RIS server to create the computer account in the OU related to the RIS image hosted on that RIS server.

4. Configure the RIS Server so that it doesn't respond to unknown client computers. Only client computers that have been prestaged with a computer account in Active Directory should be allowed to download RIS images.

5. The Lima and Seattle domains must delegate the ability to modify the attributes of the prestaged computer accounts in the OU structure. If the user doesn't have this permission, the RIS client installation will fail.

Page 327

Answers to Exercise 4 Questions

1. No. You can assign only a single right for an SNMP community. The Public community covers the entire organization, but you can assign it only a single user right. You must add two additional communities, NetworkDevices and Windows2000, to assign permissions to the WAN management team and the Windows 2000 deployment team. The WAN management team requires Read-Write or Read-Create permissions for the community while the Windows 2000 deployment team requires Read-Only permissions.

2. Public is the default community name deployed with SNMP. You should never use the Public community name on your network because this is the first community that SNMP attacks will use. To limit risk, you could assign this community the None permission.

3.

Community	Permissions
Public	None
NorthAmerica	Read-Only
SouthAmerica	Read-Only
Europe	Read-Only
Windows2000	Read-Only
NetworkDevices	Read-Write

4. Configure each SNMP agent to accept SNMP requests only from approved SNMP management stations for the community. Configure the SNMP agent to send SNMP authentication traps to the designated SNMP management station for the community.

5. Configure the Windows 2000 SNMP agents at the London office to be members of both the Windows 2000 and Europe communities. Because they're members of two communities, SNMP authentication traps must be sent to both the SNMP management stations for the Windows 2000 deployment team (172.16.3.254) and the London office (172.28.6.254).

6. The Windows 2000 community is the only community that could use IPSec protection because it contains Windows 2000–based computers that all support IPSec. You must configure the IPSec security associations to encrypt only SNMP status messages and SNMP trap messages sent to the Windows 2000 deployment team SNMP management station. This action ensures that encryption isn't used for SNMP messages sent to other SNMP management stations.

Page 328

Answers to Exercise 5 Questions

1. Terminal Services must be installed in Remote Administration Mode. Only administrators of the network can use Terminal Services when it's configured in Remote Administration Mode.

2. No. If you centrally enforce that the Winterm clients use the Time Billing application as their Terminal Services shell, then you will require a separate terminal server for the Windows for Workgroups clients.

3. The Winterm clients can change the Winterm settings so that they don't use the Time Billing application as their shell. By configuring the setting at the terminal server, you can prevent the client from overriding the desired shell application.

4. Apply the Notssid.inf security template to the terminal server that hosts the Windows for Workgroups clients to ensure that the Terminal Server Users group is removed from all DACLs.

5. Configure the terminal server to use either medium or high security to ensure that traffic both to and from the terminal server is encrypted. Low encryption encrypts only data sent from the client to the terminal server.

Page 329

Answers to Review Questions

1. There are two possibilities. If the domain controller is hosting the DHCP Service and is a member of the DNSUpdateProxy group, the domain controller won't take ownership of its DNS resource records. Not taking ownership allows an unauthorized server

to overwrite the resource records. The second possibility is that the DNS zone is not Active Directory–integrated or the zone isn't configured to allow Only Secure Updates. In either case, security isn't applied to the dynamic update process.

2. This can happen if the Windows 2000 server is a stand-alone server that isn't a member of the domain and no DHCP servers that are already authorized in Active Directory are on the local network. In this situation the DHCP Service continues to run. The DHCP server still issues DHCPInform packets every five minutes to find an Enterprise directory service.

3. In the NTFS partition where the images exist on the RIS server, you can change the DACLs on the Templates subfolder to allow only the authorized group to read the contents of the folder. By default, the Users domain local group has the necessary permissions.

4. You must configure the RIS Server so that it doesn't install the computer accounts in the default location. Configure the RIS server to create the computer accounts in a specific folder location.

5. Configure the SNMP agents to respond only to authorized SNMP management stations and enable SNMP authentication traps. When the unauthorized computer attempts an SNMP query, the SNMP agent sends an authentication trap to the configured SNMP management station.

6. Configure Terminal Services to use Remote Administration Mode, which restricts access to members of the Administrators group while allowing a maximum of two simultaneous connections.

7. This is expected behavior. Any network connections (including VPNs and dial-up connections) are shared by all Terminal Service clients (local and remote). The only way to prevent this would be to remove the modem from the server or have the manager use a different computer.

Chapter 10

Page 372

Answers to Activity Questions

1. Certificates issued by the Root CA can have a validity period of only up to two years. A CA cannot issue certificates that have a longer validity period than the certificate issued to the CA.

2. Certificates issued by the Division CA can have a validity period of only up to two years. The certificate issued to the Division CA can only have a maximum validity period of two years. A CA cannot issue certificates with a validity period longer than the certificate issued to the CA.

3. Certificates issued by the Department CA can have a validity period of only up to two years. The certificate issued to the Department CA can only have a maximum validity period of two years. This is because the Division CA can only issue CA certificates that have a validity period less than or equal to the validity period of its CA certificate. A CA cannot issue a certificate with a validity period longer than the certificate issued to the CA.

4. The Root CA must have a validity period that is longer than the five-year validity period required by the Division CA.

Page 383

Answers to Exercise 1 Questions

1. A single CA structure can be defined to meet all Contoso Ltd. PKI requirements.

2. You should remove the root CA from the network so that an administrator can only manage the root CA from the console of the root CA.

3. Once all necessary certificates are issued by the root CA, you can protect the root CA from natural disaster by creating a system image of the root CA and storing the system image off-site.

4. You should base the second level of the CA hierarchy on geography. Each office requires its own CA. Each CA could be named after the office where the CA is located.

5. You should base the third level of the CA hierarchy on usage. This arrangement meets the design requirement to have a separate CA for each project.

6. You should configure the top two levels of CAs as offline CAs. Offline CAs are always Standalone CAs.

7. You should install the root CA using a Capolicy.inf configuration file. This configuration file ensures that the CRL publication point is set to a location that's available on the network when the root CA is removed from the network.

8.

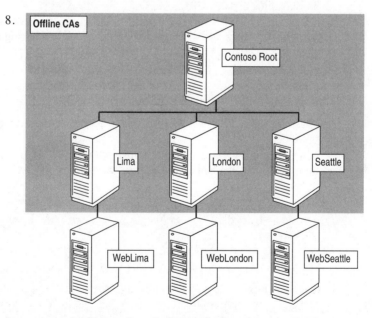

Page 384

Answers to Exercise 2 Questions

1. Contoso should obtain the certificate for the Web servers hosting the subscription Web site from public CAs such as Verisign or Entrust. The private key and public key associated with the public CA certificate will be used to encrypt the session key that encrypts traffic between a Web client and the Web server.

2. You should configure IIS to accept client certificates. This configuration allows the user to choose between certificate-based or user-entered authentication. When you configure IIS to require client certificates, only certificate-based authentication is supported.

3. The issuing CA for the Web CAs should be a Standalone CA. Only a Standalone CA allows a certificate administrator to review certificate requests and either issue or deny the request based on the information provided by the customer in the Web-based form.

4. The certificate mappings should be defined in IIS. This is the only server the certificates will use for authentication. There's no need to define the mappings in Active Directory.

5. One-to-one mappings are required for the subscription Web site. Each user will have a unique subscription. Because of this, all users must have their own certificates and user accounts.

6. You should define the CRL publication schedule as a value less than 24 hours. This setting ensures that certificate revocations are effective within a day.

7. Every hour, clients and the subscription Web server would have to download an updated version of the CRL. If an average of 10 certificates are revoked in a single day, the size of the CRL would grow rapidly and require lots of network traffic to download the updated CRL.

Page 385

Answers to Exercise 3 Questions

1. A cross-certification hierarchy can be defined between the root CAs of the Northwind Traders and Contoso Ltd. CA hierarchies.

2. The Contoso CA should trust only certificates issued by the Cooperation CA in the Northwind Traders CA hierarchy. The proposed solution will result in any certificates issued by any CA in the Northwind Traders CA hierarchy being trusted by clients in the Contoso forest.

3. You can define a CTL that allows only certificates for the purpose of user authentication issued by the Cooperation CA to be trusted from the Northwind Traders CA hierarchy.

4. You can configure a many-to-one mapping to allow any users who've received a certificate from the Cooperation CA to be mapped to an account created at the Web server.

5. You could define the account mapping in IIS because the Web server is located in the extranet and may not have access to Active Directory to determine the account mapping.

6. You must trust that the CA administrator in the other organization maintains the CA and that only approved users for the project have acquired Web authentication certificates from the partner's CA.

Page 386

Answers to Review Questions

1. You can restore the root CA from backup if the system state is included in the backup set. If the root CA also uses the Web enrollment pages, you also must include the IIS metabase in the backup set. Alternatively, you can back up the Certificate Services database from the Certification Authority console.

2. You can remove Certificate Services from the root CA and then reinstall it. When the reinstallation takes place, you should reuse the previous private and public key of the

root CA so that issued certificates aren't invalidated by the root CA's having a different private key.

3. Amy's computer or the server hosting the Human Resources Web site has cached the previous version of the CRL. Even though the CRL has been updated, the Web server and the client computer won't download the updated CRL until the existing CRL expires in the local cache.

4. The defined permissions allow any authenticated user on the network to request an enrollment agent certificate. An Enrollment Agent certificate allows a user to request certificates on behalf of other users. The DACL should be changed to only grant Authenticated Users the Read permission and to grant the SmartCardDeployment group Enroll permissions.

5. The certificate mapping must be defined at the IIS server because the Web server isn't a member of the client's domain. Only domain members can take advantage of Active Directory mappings.

6. The certificate mapping can be defined in Active Directory because the Web servers are located on the internal network and are probably members of the domain. Active Directory mapping allows the mappings to be defined only once and used throughout the domain. Only domain members can take advantage of Active Directory mappings.

Chapter 11

Page 417

Answers to Activity Questions

1. a. Eva's private key is used to encrypt the message digest that's used to determine authenticity and integrity of the digitally signed message. Eva's use of her own private key proves that the message can have originated only from her.

2. b. Don must use Eva's public key to decrypt the message digest. Any time a private/public key pair is used, the other key in the key pair must be used to decrypt the encrypted payload.

3. b. Don must use Eva's public key to encrypt the contents of an e-mail message sent to Eva. Using Eva's public key ensures that only Eva can decrypt the message.

4. a. Eva must use her private key to decrypt the message content that was encrypted by using her public key. Only the matching key in a public/private key pair can be used to decrypt a message.

5. a and d. Eva must use both her private key and Don's public key for this task. Eva's private key is used to encrypt the message digest that protects the message's contents for authenticity and integrity. Don's public key is then used to encrypt the message contents to protect the message from observation during transmission.

6. b and c. Don must first use his private key to decrypt the message content. Once the message content is decrypted, he uses Eva's public key to decrypt the message digest that protects the message content from being altered during transmission.

Page 421

Answers to Exercise 1 Questions

1. SMB signing ensures that mutual authentication takes place between a client and a server.

2. Yes. Currently, two Windows 95–based computers require access to the PHOENIX server. Windows 95–based computers don't support SMB signing.

3. The Group Policy object applied to the PHOENIX server must be configured to Digitally Sign Server Communication (When Possible). It can't be configured to always require digitally signed server communications, because that would prevent the Windows 95 clients from connecting to the server.

4. The Windows 2000–based computers must have the Digitally Sign Client Communication (When Possible) security option enabled to allow SMB signing to be used when requested.

5. Place the PHOENIX server in an OU that's assigned a GPO that has the Digitally Sign Server Communication (When Possible) security option enabled. All computers involved in the new magazine project should be placed in a separate OU that is assigned a GPO that has the Digitally Sign Client Communication (When Possible) security option enabled.

6. You can change the GPO applied to the PHOENIX server to enable the Digitally Sign Server Communication (Always) security option. In addition, you must modify the registry on the Windows 98 computers to enable SMB signing. Since there are only two computers, you can perform this registry change manually.

7. You must configure NTFS permissions to allow only project team members access to all data stored on the PHOENIX server.

Page 422

Answers to Exercise 2 Questions

1. You must determine which e-mail applications are being used by the lawyers and Contoso to ensure that a common e-mail protection protocol can be used. The choice is between PGP and S/MIME.

2. The CA certificates and CA certificate revocation lists must be published to an external location so the lawyers can verify the CA certificates and the certificate revocation status of the certificate used to sign and encrypt messages.

3. The Contoso employees can send a digitally signed message to the lawyers. The digitally signed message will include the certificate with the message. One of the attributes of the certificate is the public key associated with the certificate.

4. Each lawyer must send a digitally signed message to each Contoso employee instructing that employee to distribute the lawyer's public key. Because the lawyers and the Contoso employees don't share a common directory, public keys must be manually exchanged.

5. Exchange stores public key information in either the Exchange directory (for Microsoft Exchange Server 5.5) or in Active Directory (for Exchange 2000 Server). Clients can acquire another user's public key by querying the directory.

6. The message must be both digitally signed and encrypted when sent to the lawyers. The digital signature protects the message from modification and the encryption protects the message from inspection.

Page 422

Answers to Exercise 3 Questions

1. No. Only the subscription and back-issue ordering Web pages require SSL encryption. You could leave the rest of the site unprotected.

2. You can configure the Web server to require 128-bit encryption when using SSL.

3. Because the Contoso Web site will be involved in an e-commerce project, you should acquire the Web server certificate from a third-party CA or public CA such as Verisign or Entrust. Using a public CA increases consumer confidence in the Web site.

4. The digital certificates for customers should be issued by a privately managed CA within the Contoso organization. By using a private CA, Contoso can reduce the time it takes to revoke an issued certificate.

5. You must make the CRL for the issuing CA and the CRLs for any other CAs in the CA hierarchy publicly available on the Internet to ensure availability to customers. In addition, you need to adjust the CRL publication period so that cached versions of the CRLs don't create a long period between the certificate revocation and its recognition by all PKI participants.

Page 424

Answers to Review Questions

1. To use e-mail balloting, you must address several issues. You have to establish a registration system to acquire certificates for the voters. The voters require a private key to digitally sign their vote. You could do this by creating an SSL-protected Web site where voters register for a certificate. The voting system requires both digital signatures and mail encryption. The digital signature would provide authenticity for the voter. The mail encryption protects the vote from being read as it's transmitted to the voting committee. The voter also requires the public certificate from the voting station so that the message can be encrypted.

2. You can configure the PROJECT1 server to Digitally Sign Server Communications (Always) because Windows 98, Windows NT 4.0, and Windows 2000 all support SMB signing. You must also enable the client operating systems for SMB signing or the connection attempts will fail.

3. You must configure the PROJECT1 server to Digitally Sign Server Communications (When Possible) because Windows 95 clients don't support SMB signing. This setting allows Windows NT 4.0– and Windows 2000–based computers to use SMB signing but still allows Windows 95 clients to connect without using SMB signing.

4. The e-mail applications may not support the same protocol for mail signing and encryption. If one e-mail application supports only PGP and the other supports only S/MIME, secure e-mail exchange isn't possible.

5. The CRLs and certificates for your certificate's certificate chain aren't available to the business associate over the Internet. If the CRL isn't available for the issuing CA (or any other CAs up to the root of the CA hierarchy) certificate revocation checking will fail and invalidate the certificate.

6. The gas company has enabled the requirement for browsers to support 128-bit encryption. The clients who can't connect don't have the high encryption packs installed. For Windows 98 and Windows NT 4.0, the clients must install the strong encryption patch for their browsers. For Windows 2000, this involves the installation of the High Encryption Pack for Windows 2000. The gas company can make the installation easier by creating a Web page with links to the browser's download sites for the encryption packs.

Chapter 12

Page 455

Answers to Activity Questions

1. You can't use IPSec in this case because Windows NT 4.0 server doesn't support it. You can use IPSec only between operating systems that support it. In this scenario you could use SMB signing to provide the same functionality provided by IPSec AH.

2. No. The IP addresses shown in Figure 12.17 indicated that the firewall in this scenario is performing NAT, and IPSec can't pass through firewalls that perform NAT. You can tell the firewall is performing NAT because the server is using an external IP address and the client computer is assigned an RFC 1918 address in the 192.168.0.0/16 network.

3. Yes. In this scenario, although both the client and server are using RFC 1918 addressing, the firewall isn't performing NAT services. NAT services are performed only when one interface of the firewall uses private network addressing as defined in RFC 1918 and the other interface uses public network addressing.

4. No. The dual-homed computers connecting to the Internet are performing NAT, and IPSec can't pass through the NAT servers.

5. You could configure IPSec tunnel mode between the perimeter servers at each office. Even though the two perimeter servers are performing NAT, the IPSec tunnel would terminate before the NAT process is performed against the incoming data packets.

Exercise 1 Questions

Page 470

Designing IPSec Policies for the Web Server

1. You can apply IPSec to the Web server and protect data streams between the internal network and the DMZ. Although RFC 1918 addressing is being used, both the internal network and the DMZ are using RFC 1918 addressing. This indicates that the internal firewall isn't performing NAT. Likewise, it's a good idea to protect ports exposed to the Internet by using IPSec to ensure that protection is provided in the event an attack is launched from within the DMZ.

2. No. The external firewall is performing NAT. IPSec is unable to pass through a firewall or perimeter server that performs NAT.

3. The protected data streams require both AH and ESP protocol protection. To prevent source routing attacks, the entire packet must be signed. Only AH applies the digital signature to all fields in a packet (excluding mutable fields). ESP is required to encrypt the data that's transmitted between the internal administrator computers and the Web server.

4. The Web server requires that all IPSec filters require IPSec transport mode. You don't need to implement IPSec tunnel mode for the solution.

5.

Protocol	Source IP	Destination IP	Protocol	Source Port	Destination Port	Action
HTTP	Any	My IP address	TCP	Any	80	Permit
HTTPS	Any	My IP address	TCP	Any	443	Permit
SQL-Data	My IP address	172.30.10.10	TCP	Any	1433	Negotiate
Any	172.30.0.0/16	My IP address	Any	Any	Any	Negotiate
Any	Any	My IP address	Any	Any	Any	Block

6. You must enable the option to mirror the listed rules. Mirroring ensures that response packets are also secured based on the action defined for the protocol.

7. The administrator computers must authenticate with the Web server by using public key authentication. Kerberos can't be used in this scenario because the Web server isn't a member of the contoso.tld forest. Only members within the same forest can use Kerberos authentication. Using a preshared key isn't considered a highly secure authentication method.

8. Both the connections to the SQL server and connections from administrators require the use of 3DES encryption. The IPSec encryption algorithms should be edited to accept only connections that support 3DES. This ensures that DES encryption isn't supported.

9. All participating computers require the installation of the Windows 2000 High Encryption Pack. Windows 2000–based computers support 3DES and 128-bit encryption with the High Encryption Pack installed.

Page 472

Designing IPSec Policies for the Sales Order Server

1. You can apply IPSec to protect all data transmitted to the sales Application server. The secured segment and the public segments all use RFC 1918 addressing, so the firewall isn't performing any NAT services.

2. The protected data streams require both AH and ESP protocol protection. The requirement to prevent replay attacks requires AH protection and the requirement to encrypt all data requires ESP protection.

3. The sales Application server requires that all IPSec filters require IPSec transport mode. You don't need to implement IPSec tunnel mode for the solution.

4.

Protocol	Source IP	Destination IP	Protocol	Source Port	Destination Port	Action
Sales Updates	Any	My IP address	TCP	Any	77889	Negotiate
Sales Queries	Any	My IP address	TCP	Any	77890	Negotiate
Any	Any	Any	Any	Any	Any	Block

5. The administrator computers must authenticate with the sales Application server by using Kerberos authentication. Kerberos is the default authentication protocol and all computers will have accounts in the domain that will allow Kerberos authentication to be implemented.

6. The firewall must be configured to pass ISAKMP packets (UDP port 500), IPSec AH packets (Protocol ID 51), IPSec ESP packets (Protocol ID 50), and Kerberos packets (UDP port 88 and TCP port 88).

7. The firewall loses the ability to determine which protocols are encrypted by IPSec. The firewall will only recognize the packets as ESP-encrypted packets and won't know what protocol is being passed through the firewall.

Page 473

Answers to Exercise 2 Questions

1. You can place the administrator computers that will connect to the Web server from the London site in an OU that has the Client (Respond Only) default IPSec policy assigned. This policy allows the computers to use IPSec when requested.

2. Certificates must be deployed to both the Web server and to the administrator computers at the London office. All involved computers will require a computer certificate or an IPSec certificate for authentication purposes.

3. You can define a custom Group Policy object that both configures an automatic certificate request for an IPSec certificate and assigns the Client (Respond Only) IPSec policy. You can then modify the permissions for the Group Policy object to allow only the Web Server Administrators group the Read and Apply Group Policy permissions. This limits access to only the designated computers.

4. You must modify the permissions on the IPSec certificate template to grant the Web Server Administrators group Read and Enroll permissions. Additionally, you must configure an Enterprise CA on the network to include the IPSec certificate template in its Policy Settings so that the CA can issue IPSec certificates.

5. Since the SA isn't being established, you must determine what's causing the SA to fail. You can test authentication by applying a filter different than the one for the Web server. This ensures that authentication isn't causing the problem. For this problem, you may have to look at the Oakley logs to determine why the negotiation fails. The most likely cause of failure is that the Windows 2000 High Encryption Pack may not be applied to the newly installed computer. The SA for the IPsec filter requires that 3DES encryption is applied. Only computers with the Windows 2000 High Encryption Pack can use 3DES for encryption purposes.

Page 475

Answers to Review Questions

1. Yes. ESP packets can be enabled to prevent replay attacks. ESP does this by using a combination of the SPI and sequence number fields. If the server receives a packet with a previously used sequence number for the SPI, the packet will be discarded.

2. AH will prevent manipulation of the data during transmission, but AH doesn't offer any encryption services to the transmitted data. To fully meet the requirements, you must apply ESP.

3. No. The solution prevents inspection of the files only as they are transmitted through the IPSec tunnel. The data can still be inspected on the Payroll LAN and on the external accounting company's LAN. To provide total encryption, the two companies

could implement IPSec transport mode through the IPSec tunnel. This action allows end-to-end protection of the file against inspection as it's transmitted across the network.

4. There are two solutions. The easiest one would be to stop or disable the Telnet service on the FTP server. Alternatively, you could assign an IPSec policy to the FTP server that blocks all connections to the Telnet port (TCP port 23). This action prevents all connections to the Telnet port, no matter where the attack is launched.

5. Preshared key authentication data is often stored in plaintext at the host performing IPSec. While preshared keys offer the most flexibility for implementing IPSec, the risk that someone could copy the preshared key from the IPSec configuration and use it at another computer or network device is usually unacceptable in high security networks.

6. When an IP packet is protected from modification, AH applies a digital signature to all fields in the IP packet except mutable fields. Mutable fields are fields that have values that must change as the data is transmitted across the network. For example, the Time To Live (TTL) field isn't included in the protected fields as the field decrements by one every time the IP packet crosses a router. If the TTL field were included in the protected fields, the packet would be invalidated if it were sent to any other network segments.

Chapter 13

Page 520

Answers to Activity Questions

1. The connection is failing because the connection attempt is using L2TP as the tunneling protocol and the remote access policy is configured to accept only PPTP connections. The automatic setting always attempts to use L2TP before using PPTP. Because both the VPN server and the VPN clients have computer certificates installed, the connection attempts to use L2TP as the VPN protocol.

2. You could configure the VPN client's connection object to use PPTP rather than automatically determining the tunnel type. The automatic setting attempts to use L2TP because both computers have computer certificates installed.

3. You could modify the conditions for the VPN Client Access remote access policy to allow both PPTP and L2TP connections or to allow only L2TP connections.

4. Removing the computer certificate from either the VPN server or the VPN client results in the use of PPTP as the tunneling protocol. L2TP requires computer certificates to be used for authenticating the machine accounts involved in the L2TP connection attempt.

Answers to Exercise 1 Questions

Page 531

Determining a Solution

1. Contoso can enter into an agreement with an ISP, such as UUNet or America Online (AOL), that provides worldwide connectivity. The ISP can be used to provide local access phone numbers. Once connected to the Internet, remote clients can connect to their corporate office using a VPN connection.

2. PPTP must be deployed to support both the Windows NT 4.0 and Windows 2000 Professional–based laptops.

3. No. The VPN server is located behind a firewall that isn't performing NAT. The IP address of the VPN server doesn't fall into any of the RFC 1918 pools of IP addresses.

4. You can configure RADIUS authentication at the ISP so that authentication requests are forwarded to an IAS server running at Contoso's London office.

5. Separate remote access policies can be defined for each operating system. By placing the laptops into operating system-specific groups, you can define conditions that determine which remote access policy to apply to a remote access connection.

Page 533

Designing the Firewall

1. You must configure the firewall to allow traffic destined to the VPN server to pass through the firewall. For PPTP, this requires allowing data that's destined to TCP port 1723 on the tunnel server and uses protocol ID 47. For L2TP, data destined to UDP port 500 on the tunnel server using protocol ID 50 must be passed.

2. No. The traffic will be encrypted within the VPN tunnel as it passes through the external firewall.

3. Yes. Once the data reaches the tunnel server, it's unencrypted and transferred to internal servers through the internal firewall. Normal firewall processing can be performed to inspect all network traffic.

Page 533

Designing Remote Access for Laptops Running Windows 2000 Professional

1. You can create a group that contains only the sales force users that are running Windows 2000 Professional. You can then create a condition to allow access only if the users are members of the security group. You can apply an additional condition that requires the use of L2TP as the tunneling protocol. You can then configure the profile to match the requirements for connections using Windows 2000 Professional.

2. You can configure the remote access policy profile to only accept EAP authentication using a smart card. This action ensures that smart cards are required.

3. Smart card logon requires that each user has a certificate assigned to their smart card for user authentication. This can be done with either a smart card logon or a smart card user certificate. The VPN server must also have a computer certificate so that mutual authentication of the server can take place.

4. Yes. Each laptop must be assigned a computer certificate to allow the machine accounts to be authenticated for the IPSec association.

5. You can configure the remote access policy profile for Windows 2000 Professional clients to enforce the desired settings.

6. You must configure the remote access policy profile to require EAP authentication using smart cards, to accept connections only if the strongest form of encryption is used, and to disconnect connections if they are idle for more than 30 minutes. Requiring the strongest form of encryption forces all connections to use 3DES encryption when using L2TP. The use of 3DES requires that the Windows 2000 High Encryption Pack is installed on the VPN server and on the remote access clients.

7. You can configure a CMAK package that defines the required defaults for a remote access connection. By preventing user access to the tabs in the connection object where the defaults are defined, you can prevent the user from modifying the connection object.

Page 534

Designing Remote Access for Laptops Running Windows NT 4.0 Workstation

1. You can create a group that contains only the sales force users who are running Windows NT 4.0. You can then create a condition that allows access only if the users are members of the security group. You can apply an additional condition that requires the use of PPTP as the tunneling protocol. You can then configure the profile to match the requirements for connections using Windows 2000 Professional.

Page 534

Identifying RADIUS Design Decisions

1. A RADIUS proxy must be used at the ISP to forward RADIUS requests to an IAS server at the corporate network.

2. The RADIUS proxy requires the sales force users to provide either a prefix or suffix that identifies the RADIUS server to which the authentication requests should be passed. You can define the RADIUS prefix or suffix in the CMAK package installed at the clients.

3. You could place the RADIUS server on the internal network. This reduces the number of ports that must be opened on the internal firewall to allow RADIUS authentication requests to pass through the firewall.

4. You would configure the VPN servers located at the London, Seattle, and Lima offices as RADIUS clients.

5. Remote access policy is now defined at the IAS server on the corporate network, rather than at each of the VPN servers. This centralizes remote access policy definition and application.

Page 535

Answers to Exercise 2 Questions

1. You must use L2TP/IPSec for the VPN between the London and Barcelona offices. Only L2TP/IPSec meets the requirement to authenticate both the computer accounts and the user accounts associated with the VPN. PPTP only authenticates user accounts and IPSec tunnel mode only authenticates computer accounts.

2. Yes. If you configure a separate remote access policy that defines the connection from the Barcelona VPN server, you can define specific connection requirements for the VPN.

3. You can configure the conditions for the remote access policy to identify the Barcelona server. By setting the Client IP address to the IP address of the Barcelona server and setting the tunnel type to L2TP, you will identify all connection attempts from the Barcelona VPN server.

4. The tunnel servers must acquire computer certificates so that the IPSec agreements can be authenticated. L2TP requires that the machine authentication take place using certificates.

5. You must configure the external interface of the Barcelona VPN server to only accept packets to and from the IP address of the London VPN server using UDP port 500. Additionally, the packet filters should allow packets using ESP packets to be exchanged between the two VPN servers. You do this by configuring a filter that allows protocol ID 50. ESP packets provide the encryption of the L2TP tunnel.

Page 537

Answers to Review Questions

1. EAP provides support for two-factor forms of authentication. Retinal scans are considered two-factor because no two retinas are identical and each approved retina pattern is associated with a user account in the domain.

2. At first glance, you may want to deny remote access to the former employee's user account. This won't work if the former employee knows the account and password for other accounts with dial-in permissions. The best action in this case would be to revoke the machine certificate issued to the former employee's computer. Without a machine certificate, the connection will fail machine authentication and prevent L2TP connections.

3. Configure Group Policy to disable RRAS on all Windows 2000–based computers in the domain. You can enable RRAS for authorized servers by placing the servers in the same OU or in a common OU structure and applying a Group Policy object that enables RRAS.

4. If you suspect the local phone company of inspecting data transmitted on your WAN links, the only solution is to enable encryption of confidential data as it's transmitted over the WAN link. You can use either IPSec or a tunnel solution to encrypt the transmitted data.

5. Use the Connection Manager Administration Kit to create a connection profile that doesn't permit users to save their passwords for remote access connections. This precaution would prevent a thief from connecting to the corporate network using a stolen laptop.

6. If the firewall protecting the firewall implements NAT, you can use only PPTP as the VPN protocol. L2TP/IPSec and IPSec tunnel mode packets can't cross a firewall that performs NAT.

Chapter 14

Page 557

Answers to Activity Questions

1. Content scanning allows the content of an e-mail message to be scanned to determine if an attachment includes a virus. You could configure the firewall to strip any infected attachments from incoming messages and inform an administrator that an infected e-mail has entered the system.

2. Configure static address mapping to translate any packets addressed to the external IP address of the Web server to the private network address of the Web server.

3. Configure packet filtering at the firewall to only allow connections using authorized protocols. Any attempts to scan the external IP address at the firewall will identify only ports that are permitted by the packet filters.

4. Use stateful inspection to track UDP protocol connections. Both SNMP (UDP port 161) and SNMP traps (UDP port 162) are connectionless protocols. Stateful inspection will track the host IP address and host port for any connections using SNMP and SNMP traps to ensure that the exchange is occurring only between two hosts and that the session isn't hijacked.

5. Configuring acceptable time-outs at the firewall for nonestablished sessions will prevent a SYN flood attack by dropping half-open session establishment exchanges. If the session isn't established within the defined interval, the session will be dropped so that other sessions can be established.

6. NAT will protect the private network addressing scheme by replacing all private network IP addresses with a public network IP address configured in the NAT protocol. After the NAT process is completed, all outbound packets will have the same IP address.

Page 596

Answers to Exercise 1 Questions

1. Yes. Two different subnets are exposed on the DMZ. The VPN server has an address from the 131.107.100.0/24 network, while the other computers in the DMZ have addresses from the 172.29.100.0/24 network. You can't combine two sets of IP addresses on the same subnet.

2. No. The VPN server must accept both PPTP and L2TP/IPSec connections. 172.29.100.206 is a private network address that requires NAT at the server for outgoing packets. IPSec can't pass through a NAT service.

3. You must define an additional zone that uses public network addressing. You must place the VPN server in this zone so that NAT isn't applied to data entering and exiting this new zone. For this configuration to be possible with only two firewalls, the external firewall must support three NICS.

4.

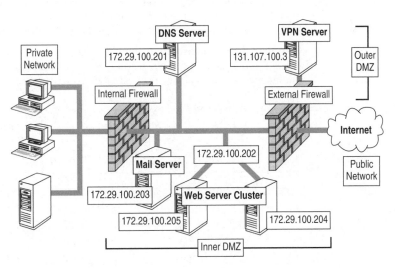

Answers to Exercise 2 Questions

Page 598

Securing DNS Access

1.

Protocol	Source IP	Source Port	Target IP	Target Port	Transport Protocol	Action
DNS	172.30.1.2	Any	172.29.100.201	53	TCP	Allow
DNS	172.30.1.2	Any	172.29.100.201	53	UDP	Allow
DNS	172.30.1.3	Any	172.29.100.201	53	TCP	Allow
DNS	172.30.1.3	Any	172.29.100.201	53	UDP	Allow
DNS	172.30.0.0/24	Any	Any	53	TCP	Deny
DNS	172.30.0.0/24	Any	Any	53	UDP	Deny

The first two packet filters allow the ns2.contoso.tld server (172.30.1.2) to forward DNS queries to the ns.contoso.tld server (172.29.100.201). The third and fourth packet filters allow the ns1.contoso.tld server (172.30.1.3) to also forward DNS requests to the ns.contoso.tld DNS server. The last two packet filters prevent any other computers in the private network (172.30.0.0/24) from sending DNS queries through the internal firewall. This packet filter restricts DNS clients to using DNS servers on the private network.

2.

Protocol	Source IP	Source Port	Target IP	Target Port	Transport Protocol	Action
DNS	172.29.100.201	Any	Any	53	TCP	Allow
DNS	172.29.100.201	Any	Any	53	UDP	Allow
DNS	Any	Any	172.29.100.201	53	TCP	Allow
DNS	Any	Any	172.29.100.201	53	UDP	Allow

The first two packet filters allow the ns.contoso.tld server (172.29.100.201) to send DNS requests to any DNS service on the Internet as required for DNS servers configured to use root hints. The last two packet filters allow DNS client and servers on the Internet to send DNS queries to the ns.contoso.tld DNS server.

3. Configure the ns.contoso.tld to allow only DNS zone transfers to recognized preconfigured secondary DNS servers. This configuration prevents an attacker from forcing a zone transfer to acquire all DNS resource records in the contoso.tld zone.

Page 600

Securing Web Access

1.

Protocol	Source IP	Source Port	Target IP	Target Port	Transport Protocol	Action
IKE	172.29.100.204	500	172.30.10.10	500	UDP	Allow
ESP	172.29.100.204		172.30.10.10		ID 50	Allow
IKE	172.29.100.205	500	172.30.10.10	500	UDP	Allow
ESP	172.29.100.205		172.30.10.10		ID 50	Allow
IKE	172.30.10.200	500	172.29.100.204	500	UDP	Allow
ESP	172.29.10.200		172.29.100.204		ID 50	Allow
IKE	172.30.10.200	500	172.29.100.205	500	UDP	Allow
ESP	172.29.10.200		172.29.100.205		ID 50	Allow
HTTP	172.30.0.0/24	Any	172.29.100.202	80	TCP	Allow
HTTPS	172.30.0.0/24	Any	172.29.100.202	443	TCP	Allow

The first two packet filters allow the first node in the NLBS Web cluster (172.29.100.204) to establish an IPSec SA using ESP encryption with the SQL Server on the private network (172.30.10.10). The third and fourth packet filters allow the second node in the NLBS Web cluster (172.29.100.205) to do the same thing. The fifth, sixth, seventh, and eighth packet filters allow the Web administrator's computer (172.30.10.200) to establish IPSec SAs using ESP encryption with the two nodes in the NLBS Web cluster. The last two packet filters limit access from the private network (172.30.0.0/24) to the NLBS cluster address (172.29.100.202) to only using HTTP and HTTPS.

2. IPSec SAs must be established between computers. The Web administrator will be connecting to one of the two nodes in the NLBS cluster, not to the cluster itself, for management functions.

3.

Protocol	Source IP	Source Port	Target IP	Target Port	Transport Protocol	Action
HTTP	Any	Any	172.29.100.202	80	TCP	Allow
HTTPS	Any	Any	172.29.100.202	443	TCP	Allow

The two packet filters limit public network computers to accessing the NLBS Web cluster (172.29.100.202) only by using HTTP or HTTPS protocols.

4. The IIS 5.0 security checklist includes a secure Web server security template that you can apply to the Web server nodes. This security template ensures that the recommended security configuration is applied to the Web servers.

5.

Host Name	External IP Address	Internal IP Address
ns.contoso.tld	131.107.99.2	172.29.100.201
mail.contoso.tld	131.107.99.3	172.29.100.203
www.contoso.tld	131.107.99.4	172.29.100.202

Page 602

Securing VPN Server Access

1.

Protocol	Source IP	Source Port	Target IP	Target Port	Transport Protocol	Action
RADIUS-Auth	131.107.100.3	Any	172.30.10.50	1812	UDP	Allow
Any	131.107.100.128/25	Any	172.30.10.0/24	Any	Any	Allow

The first packet filter allows the VPN server (131.107.100.3) to forward RADIUS authentication packets to the IAS server (172.30.10.50) located on the private network. The second packet filter allows the IP addresses assigned to VPN client computers (131.107.100.128/25) to access any computers on the private network (172.30.10.0/24) using any protocol. Because no RADIUS accounting packets are required no packet filter is included for RADIUS accounting packets (UDP 1813).

2.

Protocol	Source IP	Source Port	Target IP	Target Port	Transport Protocol	Action
PPTP	Any	Any	131.107.100.3	1723	TCP	Allow
GRE	Any		131.107.100.3		ID 47	Allow
IKE	Any	500	131.107.100.3	500	UDP	Allow
ESP	Any		131.107.100.3		ID 50	Allow
RADIUS-Accting	131.107.100.3	Any	172.30.10.50	1812	UDP	Allow
Any	131.107.100.128/25	Any	172.30.10.0/24	Any	Any	Allow

The first two packet filters allow VPN clients on the public network to connect to the VPN server (131.107.100.3) using PPTP connections. The third and fourth packet filters allow VPN clients on the public network to connect to the VPN server using L2TP/IPSec connections. The fifth packet filter allows the VPN server to forward RADIUS authentication requests to the IAS server (172.30.10.50) on the private network, and the final packet filter allows the pool of IP addresses assigned by the VPN server to remote access clients (131.107.100.128/25) to access any resources on the private network (131.107.30.0/24) using any protocol.

3. The VPN server is located in a DMZ that's attached to the external firewall. For the traffic to enter the mid-ground DMZ between the external and internal firewalls, the external firewall must first evaluate the traffic.

Page 604

Securing Mail Access

1.

Protocol	Source IP	Source Port	Target IP	Target Port	Transport Protocol	Action
Any	172.30.0.0/16	Any	172.29.100.203	Any	Any	Allow

This packet filter allows private network users (172.30.0.0/16) to access the mail server (172.29.100.203) in the DMZ using any protocol.

2. No. The current packet filter allows any client computer in the London network to connect to the mail server using any protocol.

3.

Protocol	Source IP	Source Port	Target IP	Target Port	Transport Protocol	Action
SMTP	Any	Any	172.29.100.203	25	TCP	Allow
SMTP	172.29.100.203	Any	Any	25	TCP	Allow
Any	131.107.100.128/25	Any	172.29.100.203	Any	Any	Allow

The first packet filter allows the mail server (172.29.100.203) to accept incoming SMTP messages from any computer on the Internet. The second packet filter allows the mail server to send SMPT messages to any SMTP servers on the Internet. The final packet filters allows remote access clients (131.107.100.128/25) to connect to the mail server using any protocol.

4.

Protocol	Source IP	Source Port	Target IP	Target Port	Transport Protocol	Action
HTTPS	Any	Any	172.29.100.203	443	TCP	Allow

This packet filter allows public network computers to connect the mail.contoso.tld server only by using HTTPS protocol. If a connection is attempted using HTTP, the connection attempt would be denied.

Page 605

Answers to Review Questions

1. The Web interface that external hospitals and emergency response organizations use to view information shouldn't access these fields from the SQL server. You could also restrict the data within these fields by using views in the SQL server that are limited to specific groups for access. The account that the Web server uses to query the SQL server must not be a member of groups that have access to the disease screening and donor identity fields.

2. The protocol filters are incorrectly entered. The HTTP protocol listens on TCP port 80 for connections. The client uses a random port above 1024 when establishing the HTTP connection. Likewise, the HTTPS protocol listens on TCP port 443 for connections.

3.

Protocol	Source IP	Source Port	Target IP	Target Port	Transport Protocol	Action
HTTP	Any	Any	10.10.10.10	80	TCP	Allow
HTTPS	Any	Any	10.10.10.10	443	TCP	Allow

4. The Web server and the FTP server are both members of the contoso domain. Servers in a DMZ should be members of a different forest to protect the account information in the contoso domain. If you configure a trust relationship between the domain in the DMZ and the contoso.tld domain, account information can still be acquired from the contoso domain.

5. You can take a few measures to protect your Web site. The first is to configure your firewall to drop connections that don't complete session initialization within a specified time period. If the time period expires, the session is dropped. Second, you can identify which ports the "zombie" computers are using and block the ports at the firewall. This assumes that the "zombie" computers aren't connecting to the HTTP or HTTPS ports on the Web server.

6. You must verify the firewall to ensure that only authorized protocols are allowed to reach the server in your DMZ. If a public network user was able to install the software application, the Web server's local security must be weak. By applying the IIS 5.0 Security Checklist to the Web server, you apply stronger local security that prevents unauthorized software from being loaded to the Web server. Because passwords may be compromised, all users on the network should be forced to change their passwords immediately to prevent the attacker from gaining access to the network.

Chapter 15

Answers to Activity Questions

Page 631

Locating the Proxy on the Private Network

1.

Protocol	Source IP	Source Port	Target IP	Target Port	Transport Protocol	Action
HTTP	192.168.10.0/24	Any	192.168.20.8	80	TCP	Allow
HTTPS	192.168.10.0/24	Any	192.168.20.8	443	UDP	Allow
DNS	192.168.10.10	Any	192.168.20.7	53	TCP	Allow
DNS	192.168.10.10	Any	192.168.20.7	53	UDP	Allow
Any	192.168.10.2	Any	Any	Any	Any	Allow
Any	192.168.10.0/24	Any	Any	Any	Any	Deny

You don't need to configure a packet filter to allow private network clients to connect to the Proxy Server because the Proxy Server is located on the private network segment. The internal firewall requires packet filters to allow computers in the private network (192.168.10.0/24) to access the Web server (192.168.20.8), as shown in the first two packet filters. The third and fourth packet filters restrict the DNS server located on the private network (192.168.10.10) to connecting only to the DNS server in the DMZ (192.168.20.7). The fifth packet filter allows the Proxy Server (192.168.10.2) to connect to any resources on the Internet, and the final packet filter prevents client computers on the private network from connecting to the Internet and any other computers in the DMZ that aren't defined in the internal firewall packet filters.

2.

Protocol	Source IP	Source Port	Target IP	Target Port	Transport Protocol	Action
DNS	192.168.20.7	Any	131.107.1.1	53	TCP	Allow
DNS	192.168.20.7	Any	131.107.1.1	53	UDP	Allow
Any	192.168.10.2	Any	Any	Any	Any	Allow

The first two packet filters allow the DNS server in the DMZ (192.168.20.7) to forward DNS requests to the DNS server at the ISP (131.107.1.1). The final packet filter allows packets originating at the Proxy Server (192.168.10.2) to be sent to any resources on the Internet.

3. No. If configured correctly, the internal firewall would drop any packets sent to the Internet from the private network clients. However, there would be nothing wrong with blocking the private network clients just to ensure that they're blocked if the packet filters were configured incorrectly at the internal firewall.

Page 632

Locating the Proxy in the DMZ

1.

Protocol	Source IP	Source Port	Target IP	Target Port	Transport Protocol	Action
HTTP	192.168.10.0/24	Any	192.168.20.8	80	TCP	Allow
HTTPS	192.168.10.0/24	Any	192.168.20.8	443	UDP	Allow
DNS	192.168.10.10	Any	192.168.20.7	53	TCP	Allow

Protocol	Source IP	Source Port	Target IP	Target Port	Transport Protocol	Action
DNS	192.168.10.10	Any	192.168.20.7	53	UDP	Allow
Any	192.168.10.0/24	Any	192.168.20.2	Any	Any	Allow
Any	192.168.10.0/24	Any	Any	Any	Any	Deny

The first two packet filters allow the client computers on the private network (192.168.10.0/24) to connect to the Web server in the DMZ (192.168.20.8) using HTTP and HTTPS. The third and fourth packet filters allow the DNS server on the private network (192.168.10.10) to forward DNS requests to the external DNS server (192.168.20.7). The fifth packet filter allows private network client computers (192.168.10.0/24) to forward DNS requests to the Proxy Server located in the DMZ (192.168.20.2), and the final packet filter prevents the private network client computers from connecting to the Internet and any other computers in the DMZ that aren't defined in the internal firewall packet filters.

2. No. The Proxy Server is located in the DMZ. Any packets that have the source IP address as the Proxy Server will be response packets sent back to Proxy Server client computers.

3.

Protocol	Source IP	Source Port	Target IP	Target Port	Transport Protocol	Action
DNS	192.168.20.7	Any	131.107.1.1	53	TCP	Allow
DNS	192.168.20.7	Any	131.107.1.1	53	UDP	Allow
Any	192.168.20.2	Any	Any	Any	Any	Allow

The first two packet filters allow the DNS server in the DMZ (192.168.20.7) to forward DNS requests to the DNS server at the ISP (131.107.1.1). The final packet filter allows packets originating at the Proxy Server (192.168.20.2) to be sent to any resources on the Internet.

Page 647

Answers to Exercise 1 Questions

1. Yes. The IT department must determine the authorized protocols in discussions with the technology specialists from each department.

2. Yes. The guidelines propose termination for employees if they knowingly access unauthorized sites on the Internet.

3. The guidelines don't define the private network user's responsibilities. Without a definition of responsibilities, it will be very difficult to enforce disciplinary action. For example, if you don't define that protection of the user's password is the user's responsibility, users could provide their credentials to an attacker without any disciplinary action. It doesn't matter whether the private network user provides the password intentionally or unintentionally.

Page 648

Answers to Exercise 2 Questions

1.

Protocol	Source IP	Source Port	Target IP	Target Port	Transport Protocol	Action
Any	172.30.0.0/24	Any	172.29.100.203	Any	Any	Allow
HTTP	172.30.0.0/24	Any	172.29.100.202	80	TCP	Allow
HTTPS	172.30.0.0/24	Any	172.29.100.202	443	TCP	Allow
Any	172.30.40.40	Any	Any	Any	Any	Allow
Any	172.30.0.0/24	Any	Any	Any	Any	Deny

The first packet filter allows all computers on the private network (172.30.0.0/24) to connect to the mail server (172.29.100.203) using any protocol. The second and third packet filters allow the private network computers to connect to the Web server cluster (172.29.100.202) using HTTP and HTTPS only. The fourth packet filter allows the Proxy Server (172.30.0.0/24) to connect to any resources in the DMZ or the Internet using any protocol, and the last packet filter prevents computers on the private network from connecting to any other resources in the DMZ or on the Internet.

2. You must configure the client computers to bypass the Proxy Server for local network addresses and include the Web cluster Fully Qualified Domain Name (FQDN) in the list of local network servers.

3. You can populate this listing by using the IEAK Profile Manager to create a .ins file with default settings. If the client computer is configured to detect proxy settings automatically, the .ins file will be read at startup and apply the configuration changes. In addition, you can use Group Policy to prevent changes to the Connections tab by hiding the Connections tab.

4.

Protocol	Source IP	Source Port	Target IP	Target Port	Transport Protocol	Action
Any	172.30.40.40	Any	Any	Any	Any	Allow
SMTP	172.29.100.203	Any	Any	25	TCP	Allow
DNS	172.29.100.201	Any	Any	53	TCP	Allow
DNS	172.29.100.201	Any	Any	53	UDP	Allow

The first packet filter allows the Proxy Server (172.30.40.40) requests sent from the private network to connect to resources on the Internet using any protocol. The second packet filter allows the mail server (172.29.100.203) to connect to other mail servers on the Internet using SMTP. The final two packet filters allow the DNS server in the DMZ (172.29.100.201) to connect to any DNS server on the Internet using connection-oriented and connectionless DNS queries.

Page 649

Answers to Exercise 3 Questions

1. You must add the adatum.tld domain to the listing of domains in the domain filter properties. This prevents connections to any computers in the adatum.tld Internet domain.

2. You must configure the Local Intranet zone and the Trusted Site zone to a security setting of Medium. Medium allows the download of signed ActiveX controls and doesn't prompt the user when the download of an ActiveX control is attempted.

3. The Web Proxy service allows access to the HTTP and HTTPS protocols. Permissions must be configured so that they are granted only to the members of the Marketing, Human Resources, Accounting, IT, and Training departments.

4. Create separate global groups for each department. For example, create global groups named Marketing Internet Users, HR Internet Users, Accounting Internet Users, IT Internet Users, and Training Internet Users. Add these global groups to a Web Users domain local group that's assigned the permissions to the Web and Secure protocols in the Web Proxy service.

5. The Telnet, NNTP, POP3, SMTP, and NetMeeting protocols all require the use of the WinSock Proxy service. One group strategy would be to create separate domain local groups for each of the protocols. For example, you could create a Telnet Protocol domain local group. Into each of these groups you could then place the departmental global group that requires the use of the associated protocol.

6. Each computer that requires access to protocols secured by the WinSock Proxy service will require the installation of the WinSock Proxy client software.

7. Enable the Content Advisor and set restrictions on nudity and sex to prevent access to pornographic Web sites. In addition, you should probably prevent access to unrated sites to ensure that unrated pornographic sites can't be loaded at a Web browser.

8. For Windows 2000–based clients you can use a mix of the IEAK and Group Policy to lock down the configuration of Internet Explorer. You can use the IEAK to define the required configuration and to apply updates to the configuration. Group Policy allows you to restrict access to the Internet Options configuration. By restricting access, you prevent the required settings from being modified.

9. You can protect non-Windows 2000–based clients only by using the IEAK to define the required configuration settings and to restrict access to specific options in the Internet Explorer configuration.

Page 651

Answers to Review Questions

1. You must control the firewall at the Vancouver branch office to prevent access to the Internet by any computer located in the Vancouver subnet (172.16.8.0/22). This packet filter must prevent Internet access from any computer in the 172.16.8.0/22 subnet using any protocol.

2. You could use the IEAK to create a more restrictive configuration for Internet Explorer to deploy at the Mexico City office. In addition, you could create a global group that contains only Mexico City Internet users. Lastly, you would make the global group a member of the local groups that allow the use of protocols required by the Mexico City office.

3. The downloading of pirated DVD movies could lead to a raid of your organization's network by government authorities looking to crack down on pirated media downloaded to computers from the Internet. A raid could lead to the public humiliation of your organization.

4. When designing packet filters for the Proxy Server, you could have created specific filters that allow the Proxy Server to use only authorized protocols when connecting to the Internet. A packet filter strategy such as this would prevent the Proxy Server from using undefined protocols to access the Internet.

5. Ensure that your virus scanning software enforces the update of virus signatures for all installations of the software. In addition, you must create logon scripts that inspect the disks of client computers to verify the installation of the software. If the software isn't installed, the connection attempt should be terminated.

6. NNTP requires the WinSock Proxy client to be installed on all computers that requires access to the WinSock Proxy service. The new computers don't have the WinSock Proxy client installed.

7. The WinSock proxy and Web Proxy on the client computer need to be modified to not use the Proxy Server when the user connects to the Internet using her personal ISP. The Proxy Server is unavailable when she connects by using the ISP, and therefore all Internet connections fail.

Chapter 16

Page 668

Answers to Activity Questions

1. System 7 File Sharing uses clear text authentication. Configure the Macintosh client to use Apple Standard Encryption or install the MS-UAM to provide Microsoft encryption for authentication.

2. Samba version 2.0.5 uses clear text authentication, which increases the risk of password interception. You should use Samba version 2.0.6 or above to enable NTLM authentication for Samba clients.

3. Telnet uses clear text authentication, which can result in credentials being viewed as they are transmitted to the Telnet server from the Telnet client. To protect authentication credentials, you must configure an IPSec security association between the UNIX computer and the Windows 2000 Server hosting the Telnet service to encrypt all Telnet transmissions.

4. FPNW provides secure authentication for NetWare clients. Installing FPNW on the Windows 2000 Server ensures that there are no risks when a Novell client authenticates directly with an FPNW server.

5. The use of the Attach command stores the Active Directory password in the NetWare login script. This could allow another user or supervisor in the NetWare network to view the Active Directory password. You should modify trustee rights on the NetWare 3.12 server to prevent the user from modifying her NetWare login script.

6. AH protects the FTP messages only from being modified during transit. Because the data isn't encrypted, the user account and password entered in the FTP client are observable as they are transmitted across the network. To protect the user credentials, the security association should use IPSEC Encapsulating Security Payloads, which encrypt the transmitted data.

7. There are no risks when the FTP transmissions are encrypted using IPSec ESP. All authentication data is encrypted during network transmission.

Page 695

Answers to Exercise 1 Questions

1. The Macintosh clients require that the MS-UAM be installed. Security requirements require that all authentication be encrypted, and only the MS-UAM supports passwords greater than eight characters.

2. You must define two separate Mac-accessible volumes in the Computer Management console, one for the Data folder and one for the Graphics folder.

3. You can configure security in two ways. First, you must create global groups for access to the Data and to the Graphics folders. You must place users in one of the two groups. Additionally, you could create volume passwords for each of the Mac-accessible volumes. By providing only the volume password to authorized users, you can control access.

4. File Services for Macintosh requires that Mac-accessible volumes be located on NTFS partitions.

5. You must assign the global group for the Data folder the Change permission and assign the global group associated with the D:\Graphics folder the Change permission.

6. Because the employees have the same account name, they should always authenticate by indicating their domain and account name. For example, the Director of Marketing should always authenticate as London\FRamirez to ensure that authentication requests are passed to a domain controller in the london.contoso.tld domain.

Page 696 ## Answers to Exercise 2 Questions

1. CSNW can be used only at the London office where the BIGRED NetWare server exists. The WAN uses only TCP/IP, and the CSNW client requires NWLink IPX/SPX to be used.

2. No. The solution won't work because the GSNW server must connect to the BIGRED server using IPX/SPX and the WAN supports only TCP/IP. Only London office clients will have access to the BIGRED server through the LondonGate GSNW server. The GSMW servers must either be moved to the London network segment or IPX/SPX must be enabled on the WAN.

3. Yes. The accounting clients from the Lima and Seattle offices will be able to connect to the LondonGate GSNW server using TCP/IP. Being on the same network segment, the LondonGate GSNW server will be able to connect to the BIGRED server using IPX/SPX.

4. No. NetWare administration requires the installation of the Novell Client for Windows 2000. The Novell Client for Windows 2000 must be installed on her computer to grant her administrative access to the NetWare server.

5. You must configure the GSNW share to only allow members of the accounting department access. You can place the members into global groups at each of the three domains. You can then make the three global groups members of a domain local group in the London domain that's granted Read permissions to the data.

6. OU=accounting.OU=london.O=contoso

7. You must make the service account used by the LondonGate GSNW server a member of the Ntgateway group. In addition, you should configure trustee rights for the directory containing the historical accounting data to grant the gateway account only Read and File Scan trustee rights.

Page 698 ## Answers to Exercise 3 Questions

1. FTP uses clear text authentication, which could result in Active Directory User accounts and passwords being compromised on the network.

2. The GRAPHICS server must load Server for NFS to allow the UNIX users to use NFS to transfer data to the GRAPHICS server.

3. You must configure User Name Mapping to associate the UIDs and GIDs of the UNIX users to Active Directory user accounts. The associated Active Directory accounts will be assigned permissions in the DACL associated with the FromUNIX folder.

4. A domain local group that contains the Active Directory accounts for the UNIX users must be assigned the Change permissions for the FromUNIX folder.

5. You must configure Two-Way Password Synchronization to ensure that the passwords stored on the NISCONTOSO.contoso.tld NIS server are synchronized with the associated user accounts in Active Directory.

Page 699
Answers to Review Questions

1. You must install File Services for Macintosh on the source code server to allow the Macintosh users to access the source code. To ensure secure access, the Macintosh clients must install the MS-UAM to enforce encrypted passwords up to a maximum of 14 characters. To enforce this, configure File Services for Macintosh to require Microsoft authentication.

2. The accounting department will require the same level of access to the LINDATA server. Rather than installing NetWare client software on each computer, you can install GSNW on a single Windows 2000 server. You must make the service account associated with GSNW a member of the Ntgateway group in NDS, and you should assign the account only the necessary trustee rights to access the payroll data. At the GSNW server, you can further restrict access by allowing only the accounting department users access to the GSNW share.

3. You must implement MSDSS to ensure that passwords are synchronized between Active Directory and NDS. The Windows 2000 server that hosts MSDSS must have the Novell Client for Windows 2000 installed to ensure that the service has sufficient access to NDS to synchronize passwords.

4. You must deploy MMS. With MMS you must configure a management agent for each directory service to support a single integrated metadirectory. Within each management agent, you can configure which attributes the directory service is authoritative for. This process ensures that only modifications at the authoritative directory service cause modification of the metadirectory.

5. The users who have lost the ability to log on to the network must not be using the MS-UAM for authentication. Apple Standard Encryption only supports eight character passwords. To enable the users to log on to the network from the Macintosh computers, the organization must deploy the MS-UAM to all Macintosh computers and configure Files Services for Macintosh to accept only Microsoft authentication.

Chapter 17

Page 716
Answers to Review Questions

1. An organization's security policy provides the guiding framework for all security plans. Without such a policy, an organization can't establish the appropriate level of security to deploy.

2. The implementation of increased security can result in a loss of functionality or a loss in user convenience. Security can cause some business practices to be removed due to the vulnerabilities that they expose.

3. The security manager can keep abreast of the latest security issues by subscribing to security bulletins and reviewing industry publications (both paper and electronic) to be aware of the latest security issues facing the network.

4. Service packs include the latest Windows 2000 hot fixes in a single package but do become out of date in a short time. In addition to installing the latest service pack, you should also consult windowsupdate.microsoft.com/ to determine if any further updates related to security are required.

5. When the new management is in place, the larger organization's security policy may not be the same as yours. The plans should eventually be modified to reflect the acquiring organization's security policy.

Index

Note to the reader   Italicized page numbers refer to tables and illustrations.

S

Get a **Free**
e-mail newsletter, updates,
special offers, links to related books,
and more when you
register on line!

Register your Microsoft Press® title on our Web site and you'll get
a FREE subscription to our e-mail newsletter, *Microsoft Press Book
Connections.* You'll find out about newly released and upcoming books
and learning tools, online events, software downloads, special offers
and coupons for Microsoft Press customers, and information about
major Microsoft® product releases. You can also read useful additional
information about all the titles we publish, such as detailed book
descriptions, tables of contents and indexes, sample chapters, links to
related books and book series, author biographies, and reviews by other
customers.

Registration is easy. Just visit this Web page and fill in your information:

http://www.microsoft.com/mspress/register

Microsoft®

Proof of Purchase

Use this page as proof of purchase if participating in a promotion or rebate offer on
this title. Proof of purchase must be used in conjunction with other proof(s) of
payment such as your dated sales receipt—see offer details.

MCSE Training Kit: Designing Microsoft® Windows® 2000 Network Security
0-7356-1134-3

CUSTOMER NAME

Microsoft Press, PO Box 97017, Redmond, WA 98073-9830

Comprehensive **technical** *information* and *tools* for deploying and supporting the **Windows 2000 Server** operating system in your organization.

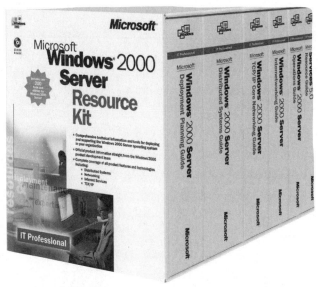

This RESOURCE KIT is packed with official product information—straight from the Microsoft® Windows® 2000 product development team. It contains complete coverage of all product features and technologies, plus more than 200 tools to help you deploy, manage, and support the Windows 2000 operating system, including tools for distributed systems, networking, Internet services, and TCP/IP.

U.S.A.   **$299.99**
U.K.   £189.99
Canada $460.99 [V.A.T. included]
ISBN: 1-57231-805-8

mspress.microsoft.com

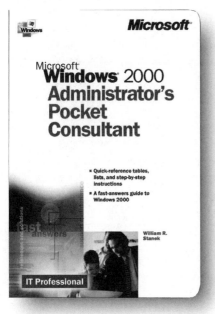

Test *your* readiness *for the* MCP exam

If you took a Microsoft Certified Professional (MCP) exam today, would you pass? With each READINESS REVIEW MCP exam simulation on CD-ROM, you get a low-risk, low-cost way to find out! The next-generation test engine delivers a set of randomly generated, 50-question practice exams covering real MCP objectives. You can test and retest with different question sets each time—and with automated scoring, you get immediate Pass/Fail feedback. Use these READINESS REVIEWS to evaluate your proficiency with the skills and knowledge that you'll be tested on in the real exams.

MICROSOFT LICENSE AGREEMENT
Book Companion CD

IMPORTANT—READ CAREFULLY: This Microsoft End-User License Agreement ("EULA") is a legal agreement between you (either an individual or an entity) and Microsoft Corporation for the Microsoft product identified above, which includes computer software and may include associated media, printed materials, and "online" or electronic documentation ("SOFTWARE PRODUCT"). Any component included within the SOFTWARE PRODUCT that is accompanied by a separate End-User License Agreement shall be governed by such agreement and not the terms set forth below. By installing, copying, or otherwise using the SOFTWARE PRODUCT, you agree to be bound by the terms of this EULA. If you do not agree to the terms of this EULA, you are not authorized to install, copy, or otherwise use the SOFTWARE PRODUCT; you may, however, return the SOFTWARE PRODUCT, along with all printed materials and other items that form a part of the Microsoft product that includes the SOFTWARE PRODUCT, to the place you obtained them for a full refund.

SOFTWARE PRODUCT LICENSE

The SOFTWARE PRODUCT is protected by United States copyright laws and international copyright treaties, as well as other intellectual property laws and treaties. The SOFTWARE PRODUCT is licensed, not sold.

1. **GRANT OF LICENSE.** This EULA grants you the following rights:

   a. **Software Product.** You may install and use one copy of the SOFTWARE PRODUCT on a single computer. The primary user of the computer on which the SOFTWARE PRODUCT is installed may make a second copy for his or her exclusive use on a portable computer.

   b. **Storage/Network Use.** You may also store or install a copy of the SOFTWARE PRODUCT on a storage device, such as a network server, used only to install or run the SOFTWARE PRODUCT on your other computers over an internal network; however, you must acquire and dedicate a license for each separate computer on which the SOFTWARE PRODUCT is installed or run from the storage device. A license for the SOFTWARE PRODUCT may not be shared or used concurrently on different computers.

   c. **License Pak.** If you have acquired this EULA in a Microsoft License Pak, you may make the number of additional copies of the computer software portion of the SOFTWARE PRODUCT authorized on the printed copy of this EULA, and you may use each copy in the manner specified above. You are also entitled to make a corresponding number of secondary copies for portable computer use as specified above.

   d. **Sample Code.** Solely with respect to portions, if any, of the SOFTWARE PRODUCT that are identified within the SOFTWARE PRODUCT as sample code (the "SAMPLE CODE"):

      i. **Use and Modification.** Microsoft grants you the right to use and modify the source code version of the SAMPLE CODE, *provided* you comply with subsection (d)(iii) below. You may not distribute the SAMPLE CODE, or any modified version of the SAMPLE CODE, in source code form.

      ii. **Redistributable Files.** Provided you comply with subsection (d)(iii) below, Microsoft grants you a nonexclusive, royalty-free right to reproduce and distribute the object code version of the SAMPLE CODE and of any modified SAMPLE CODE, other than SAMPLE CODE, or any modified version thereof, designated as not redistributable in the Readme file that forms a part of the SOFTWARE PRODUCT (the "Non-Redistributable Sample Code"). All SAMPLE CODE other than the Non-Redistributable Sample Code is collectively referred to as the "REDISTRIBUTABLES."

      iii. **Redistribution Requirements.** If you redistribute the REDISTRIBUTABLES, you agree to: (i) distribute the REDISTRIBUTABLES in object code form only in conjunction with and as a part of your software application product; (ii) not use Microsoft's name, logo, or trademarks to market your software application product; (iii) include a valid copyright notice on your software application product; (iv) indemnify, hold harmless, and defend Microsoft from and against any claims or lawsuits, including attorney's fees, that arise or result from the use or distribution of your software application product; and (v) not permit further distribution of the REDISTRIBUTABLES by your end user. Contact Microsoft for the applicable royalties due and other licensing terms for all other uses and/or distribution of the REDISTRIBUTABLES.

2. **DESCRIPTION OF OTHER RIGHTS AND LIMITATIONS.**

   - **Limitations on Reverse Engineering, Decompilation, and Disassembly.** You may not reverse engineer, decompile, or disassemble the SOFTWARE PRODUCT, except and only to the extent that such activity is expressly permitted by applicable law notwithstanding this limitation.

   - **Separation of Components.** The SOFTWARE PRODUCT is licensed as a single product. Its component parts may not be separated for use on more than one computer.

   - **Rental.** You may not rent, lease, or lend the SOFTWARE PRODUCT.

- **Support Services.** Microsoft may, but is not obligated to, provide you with support services related to the SOFTWARE PRODUCT ("Support Services"). Use of Support Services is governed by the Microsoft policies and programs described in the user manual, in "online" documentation, and/or in other Microsoft-provided materials. Any supplemental software code provided to you as part of the Support Services shall be considered part of the SOFTWARE PRODUCT and subject to the terms and conditions of this EULA. With respect to technical information you provide to Microsoft as part of the Support Services, Microsoft may use such information for its business purposes, including for product support and development. Microsoft will not utilize such technical information in a form that personally identifies you.

- **Software Transfer.** You may permanently transfer all of your rights under this EULA, provided you retain no copies, you transfer all of the SOFTWARE PRODUCT (including all component parts, the media and printed materials, any upgrades, this EULA, and, if applicable, the Certificate of Authenticity), **and** the recipient agrees to the terms of this EULA.

- **Termination.** Without prejudice to any other rights, Microsoft may terminate this EULA if you fail to comply with the terms and conditions of this EULA. In such event, you must destroy all copies of the SOFTWARE PRODUCT and all of its component parts.

3. **COPYRIGHT.** All title and copyrights in and to the SOFTWARE PRODUCT (including but not limited to any images, photographs, animations, video, audio, music, text, SAMPLE CODE, REDISTRIBUTABLES, and "applets" incorporated into the SOFTWARE PRODUCT) and any copies of the SOFTWARE PRODUCT are owned by Microsoft or its suppliers. The SOFT-WARE PRODUCT is protected by copyright laws and international treaty provisions. Therefore, you must treat the SOFTWARE PRODUCT like any other copyrighted material **except** that you may install the SOFTWARE PRODUCT on a single computer provided you keep the original solely for backup or archival purposes. You may not copy the printed materials accompanying the SOFTWARE PRODUCT.

4. **U.S. GOVERNMENT RESTRICTED RIGHTS.** The SOFTWARE PRODUCT and documentation are provided with RESTRICTED RIGHTS. Use, duplication, or disclosure by the Government is subject to restrictions as set forth in subparagraph (c)(1)(ii) of the Rights in Technical Data and Computer Software clause at DFARS 252.227-7013 or subparagraphs (c)(1) and (2) of the Commercial Computer Software—Restricted Rights at 48 CFR 52.227-19, as applicable. Manufacturer is Microsoft Corporation/One Microsoft Way/Redmond, WA 98052-6399.

5. **EXPORT RESTRICTIONS.** You agree that you will not export or re-export the SOFTWARE PRODUCT, any part thereof, or any process or service that is the direct product of the SOFTWARE PRODUCT (the foregoing collectively referred to as the "Restricted Components"), to any country, person, entity, or end user subject to U.S. export restrictions. You specifically agree not to export or re-export any of the Restricted Components (i) to any country to which the U.S. has embargoed or restricted the export of goods or services, which currently include, but are not necessarily limited to, Cuba, Iran, Iraq, Libya, North Korea, Sudan, and Syria, or to any national of any such country, wherever located, who intends to transmit or transport the Restricted Components back to such country; (ii) to any end user who you know or have reason to know will utilize the Restricted Components in the design, development, or production of nuclear, chemical, or biological weapons; or (iii) to any end user who has been prohibited from participating in U.S. export transactions by any federal agency of the U.S. government. You warrant and represent that neither the BXA nor any other U.S. federal agency has suspended, revoked, or denied your export privileges.

DISCLAIMER OF WARRANTY

NO WARRANTIES OR CONDITIONS. MICROSOFT EXPRESSLY DISCLAIMS ANY WARRANTY OR CONDITION FOR THE SOFTWARE PRODUCT. THE SOFTWARE PRODUCT AND ANY RELATED DOCUMENTATION ARE PROVIDED "AS IS" WITHOUT WARRANTY OR CONDITION OF ANY KIND, EITHER EXPRESS OR IMPLIED, INCLUDING, WITHOUT LIMITA-TION, THE IMPLIED WARRANTIES OF MERCHANTABILITY, FITNESS FOR A PARTICULAR PURPOSE, OR NONINFRINGEMENT. THE ENTIRE RISK ARISING OUT OF USE OR PERFORMANCE OF THE SOFTWARE PRODUCT REMAINS WITH YOU.

LIMITATION OF LIABILITY. TO THE MAXIMUM EXTENT PERMITTED BY APPLICABLE LAW, IN NO EVENT SHALL MICROSOFT OR ITS SUPPLIERS BE LIABLE FOR ANY SPECIAL, INCIDENTAL, INDIRECT, OR CONSEQUENTIAL DAM-AGES WHATSOEVER (INCLUDING, WITHOUT LIMITATION, DAMAGES FOR LOSS OF BUSINESS PROFITS, BUSINESS INTERRUPTION, LOSS OF BUSINESS INFORMATION, OR ANY OTHER PECUNIARY LOSS) ARISING OUT OF THE USE OF OR INABILITY TO USE THE SOFTWARE PRODUCT OR THE PROVISION OF OR FAILURE TO PROVIDE SUPPORT SERVICES, EVEN IF MICROSOFT HAS BEEN ADVISED OF THE POSSIBILITY OF SUCH DAMAGES. IN ANY CASE, MICROSOFT'S ENTIRE LIABILITY UNDER ANY PROVISION OF THIS EULA SHALL BE LIMITED TO THE GREATER OF THE AMOUNT ACTUALLY PAID BY YOU FOR THE SOFTWARE PRODUCT OR US$5.00; PROVIDED, HOWEVER, IF YOU HAVE ENTERED INTO A MICROSOFT SUPPORT SERVICES AGREEMENT, MICROSOFT'S ENTIRE LIABILITY REGARDING SUPPORT SERVICES SHALL BE GOVERNED BY THE TERMS OF THAT AGREEMENT. BECAUSE SOME STATES AND JURISDICTIONS DO NOT ALLOW THE EXCLUSION OR LIMITATION OF LIABILITY, THE ABOVE LIMITATION MAY NOT APPLY TO YOU.

MISCELLANEOUS

This EULA is governed by the laws of the State of Washington USA, except and only to the extent that applicable law mandates governing law of a different jurisdiction.

Should you have any questions concerning this EULA, or if you desire to contact Microsoft for any reason, please contact the Microsoft subsidiary serving your country, or write: Microsoft Sales Information Center/One Microsoft Way/Redmond, WA 98052-6399.

System Requirements

To use the Supplemental Course Materials CD-ROM, you need a computer equipped with the following minimum configuration:

- 133-MHz or higher Pentium-compatible CPU

- Microsoft Windows 95, Windows 98, or Microsoft Windows NT or later

- 16 MB of RAM

- 500 MB hard drive with 15 MB of available disk space

- 24x CD-ROM drive

- Microsoft mouse or compatible pointing device (recommended)

- Microsoft Internet Explorer 5, or later

- Microsoft Word or Microsoft Word Viewer (Word Viewer is included on this CD-ROM)

An Evaluation Edition of the Microsoft Windows 2000 Advanced Server is included with this book. This software is not necessary to do the activities or labs in this book, although it is helpful to have a system with which to practice. To install the Evaluation Edition of the Microsoft Windows 2000 Advanced Server, you need computer equipped with the following minimum configuration:

- 133-MHz or higher Pentium-compatible CPU

- 256 MB of RAM

- Hard disk with a minimum of 1.0 GB free space

- 12x CD-ROM drive